P9-ARV-520

Readings in American Archaeological Theory: Selections from *American Antiquity* 1962–2002

Compiled by Garth Bawden

SOCIETY FOR AMERICAN ARCHAEOLOGY

The Society for American Archaeology, Washington, D.C. 20002
Copyright © 2003 by the Society for American Archaeology
All rights reserved. Published 2003
Printed in the United States of America

Library of Congress Card Number: 2003100471

ISBN No. 0-932839-25-8

Table of Contents

READINGS IN AMERICAN ARCHAEOLOGICAL THEORY: SELECTIONS FROM *AMERICAN ANTIQUITY* 1962–2002

Compiled by Garth Bawden

The purpose of this book is to introduce the reader to the history and content of the theoretical debates that characterize current American archaeology using articles that have been published in the pages of *American Antiquity,* the flagship journal of the Society for American Archaeology. The volume is chiefly oriented toward upper-division undergraduate and introductory graduate-level education. It is intended to be used as a unit, brief enough to be assigned in its entirety, yet of sufficient breadth to convey the overall development of theory in our discipline during the past 40 years or so. While there is of course some overlap between the various theoretical themes, chapters are generally organized so as to sequentially cover recent theoretical developments and their related rebuttals and debates. Thus articles on the various branches of New Archaeology precede the more recent movements that reject its premises—Post-Processual, Critical, and Evolutionary archaeologies. Given the large number of works available, the volume is of necessity very selective. However, it does provide the reader with easy access to some of the more influential scholars of the past 20 years and to their ideas concerning the purpose, strategies, and methods of archaeology. The perspectives documented here are all inspired by the desire to understand the archaeological record and thereby to access the people who created it. The diversity of approaches underscores the challenges that accompany this goal as archaeologists use their available intellectual and academic tools to confront the ideas and behavior of people distant from them in time and space.

Over the decades American archaeology has engendered a variety of guiding concepts to bridge the divide between past and present, inspired variously by the natural sciences, the humanities, and the social sciences. Each of these theoretical approaches possesses its individual strengths. Equally, each has been critiqued for perceived weaknesses. However, there can be little disagreement that interplay between these ideas has led to debates that have enlivened and expanded the discipline of archaeology. While such debates are sometimes rather unkindly dismissed as being the arena of "armchair scholars," in fact they motivate their participants to evaluate and refine the conceptual foundation for all facets of archaeology. Theory permeates practice and guides its goals, methods, and strategies. This relationship is clearly demonstrated in the *American Antiquity* articles published in this volume. In many instances they include field applications that inform their theoretical discussion and vice versa. Theory, then, transcends dry philosophical polemic to ensure that archaeology as a vital discipline is grounded in ideas that are carefully and constantly examined, assessed, and challenged in the practice of material investigation.

While the articles in this volume unavoidably focus on developments central to American archaeology, it should be stressed that in varying degrees the related debates were paralleled elsewhere. Such correspondence applies most closely to British prehistorians who have significantly participated in the trends described in these chapters and who have contributed mightily to shaping the viewpoints documented here. Scholars like David Clarke and Colin Renfrew were major players in the advocacy of a new processual archaeology with emphasis on the study of cultural systems, while Ian Hodder is rightfully acknowledged as the principal inspirer of the Post-Processual movement in archaeology on both sides of the Atlantic. In most other countries archaeological theory and application have taken somewhat different paths that cannot be addressed in this book. However, it is important that readers recognize that other strong traditions exist in Europe and Latin America and that a more comprehensive understanding of the history of archaeological theory should include their study.

After a half-century or more of emphasis on archaeological description, classification, and chronology, the early 1960s marked the explicit re-emergence of explanation as the major goal of American archaeology (chapters 1 and 4). The "New Archaeology" self consciously attempted to separate the epistemological basis of archaeology as an anthropological science from its preceding culture historical phase and set in motion a period of strong and sometimes contentious debate about the theoretical basis of the discipline that continues to this day (chapters 1–9). New Archaeology, which granted eminence to anthropological and scientific emphases in equal measure, sought to explain the process of change in sociocultural systems by applying approaches based on the formulation and testing of archaeological hypotheses. A central interest involved the search for mechanisms that enabled these systems to adapt to their ecological environments so as to ensure structural equilibrium as they evolved through progressively more complex organizational stages (chapter 2). Another somewhat later development emphasized ethno-archaeological study of modern peoples in order to identify the formation mechanisms that produce the observed patterning of material residue in the sites created by earlier peoples—the essence of Middle-Range Theory (chapters 3, 8, 9). Critics of the processual approaches confronted their entire range of tenets, challenging adherence to the deductive approach to scientific testing and dependency on the covering law model (chapter 5), the utility of systems theory as a strategy for explaining change (chapter 6), the application of Middle-Range Theory (chapter 8), and the accuracy of the premise that New Archaeology constituted a paradigmatic change in the history of the discipline (chapter 9).

From the late 1970s, a number of archaeologists became increasingly dissatisfied with the flaws that they perceived in the scientific and methodological applications of New Archaeology and its neglect of the ideational aspects of human cultural creativity. The British archaeologist Ian Hodder and his associates played a central role in the crystallization of these reservations into a new set of complementary arguments that largely reject the scientific principles asserted by the New Archaeologists. These approaches collectively identify the Post-Processual position (chapters 10–13), which asserts that it is not generally possible to test archaeological hypotheses in the manner advocated by processual archaeologists; that there are no general laws governing human social formation; that vastly greater emphasis must be placed on the subjective, ideational component on human mentality and the role of the individual in addressing change; and that we are incorrect in assuming that there can ever be a truly objective archaeological science. Post-Processualists believe that irrespective of their theoretical stances archaeologists implement their programs according to their political, social, and ethnic experiences in a diverse dialogue that necessarily leads to different versions of the past rather than any single scenario. Thus the material record should be regarded as a number of overlapping contexts in which individual objects take on different meanings according to the intent of the makers and the biased experiential circumstance of the observer. The hermeneutic dialogue between the two comprises a conceptual negotiation that may bring a sense of past meaning but can never assure objective knowledge (Chapter 10).

Post-Processual interests converge with those of other areas of current critical archaeology that favor the subjective in their emphasis on the conceptual aspects of human social construction. Thus, Marxist, Gender, and Indigenous archaeologies, while possessing different aims and utilizing distinct strategies, all place similar emphasis on the influence of the ideological in patterning the past record and influencing its interpretation (chapters 10–12). It is understandable that such controversial viewpoints should provoke strong response. Critique of the Post-Processual and critical positions at its extreme accuses them of attacking the very foundations of a coherent intellectual archaeological discipline, substituting fanciful speculation for rational science, bringing an anti-intellectual relativity to social and cultural studies, and intruding a dangerous political dimension into otherwise objective research (Chapter 13).

While Post-Processualist archaeologists mounted the most dramatic confrontation to New Archaeology, theirs is not the only one. Beginning in the 1970s an expanding current of theory based in Darwinian evolutionary tenets represent a very different challenge to the processual school (chapters 14–17, 19). They assert that human culture is subject to the same evolutionary pressures as biological organisms and reject the concepts that advocate generality. The Selectionist branch of Evolutionary archaeologists (chapters 14, 15, 20) believe that the notion of universal cultural stage typology with its associated search for similarity diametrically opposes Darwinian acceptance of variation within and between organisms as directed by random mutation and natural selection. They argue that the notion of transformational evolution through progressive cultural evolutionary stages is an essentialist construct that bears no relation to the formulations of Darwinian theory. They maintain that an approach based on scientific evolution can generate better explanations of human behavior and change. From this perspective archaeological artifacts are components of the behavioral phenotype, incorporating material trait variability that is subject to the evolutionary mechanisms central to the Darwinian premise. Just as in the biological context, replication of selected traits reflects evolutionary fitness and provides the basis for explanatory study. An alternative theoretical approach grounded in Human Evolutionary Ecology emphasizes the Darwinian concept of selective adaptation to explain change. Chiefly utilizing optimal foraging theory these scholars identify and trace the strategies devised by human groups to adapt to their specific natural and social environments and examine the processes of selective cultural transmission that gives them evolutionary fitness (chapters 16 and 17). While these Darwinian approaches are becoming increasingly influential, questions remain as to their applicability to the explanation of archaeological data (chapter 17).

The tenets of one important branch of recent archaeological thought—Behavioral Archaeology

(chapters 19, 20)—encompass basic principles of both processual and evolutionary theory. While incorporating a number of interests and goals, notably thorough analysis of site formation processes (chapter 19), Behavioral Archaeology espouses such Darwinian positions as acceptance of material culture as human behavior, the need to study human variability and change, and acceptance of the differential persistence of discrete variants due to specific historical processes (chapter 20). These beliefs appear to bring it close to evolutionary perspectives. Recent debate on the actual degree of correspondence between the two approaches productively informs on both (chapters 19, 20). Finally the concluding chapter (chapter 21), while certainly controversial in its basic premise, challenges the reader to enquire whether the theoretical disagreements that have characterized recent North American archaeology are more apparent than real. The authors certainly believe that these controversies can lead to a more integrated discipline that draws productively on the intellectual streams presented here.

We hope that the articles replicated here will inform the reader of the variety of important concepts and strategies current in the discipline and the diversity that they demonstrate as to the goals and methods of archaeology. We believe that this awareness will better enable students to critically compare and assess the intellectual content of the various perspectives and thereby to develop their own ideas. After all, this process of formulation, appraisal and modification is the way in which any discipline develops. We believe that by presenting the intellectual journey of modern American archaeology as represented in the pages of our flagship journal we can encourage this positive educational process, while also providing a useful reference for teachers and students alike.

ARCHAEOLOGY AS ANTHROPOLOGY

Lewis R. Binford

Abstract

It is argued that archaeology has made few contributions to the general field of anthropology with regard to explaining cultural similarities and differences. One major factor contributing to this lack is asserted to be the tendency to treat artifacts as equal and comparable traits which can be explained within a single model of culture change and modification. It is suggested that "material culture" can and does represent the structure of the total cultural system, and that explanations of differences and similarities between certain classes of material culture are inappropriate and inadequate as explanations for such observations within other classes of items. Similarly, change in the total cultural system must be viewed in an adaptive context both social and environmental, not whimsically viewed as the result of "influences," "stimuli," or even "migrations" between and among geographically defined units.

Three major functional sub-classes of material culture are discussed: technomic, socio-technic, and ideo-technic, as well as stylistic formal properties which cross-cut these categories. In general terms these recognized classes of materials are discussed with regard to the processes of change within each class.

Using the above distinctions in what is termed a systemic approach, the problem of the appearance and changing utilization of native copper in eastern North America is discussed. Hypotheses resulting from the application of the systemic approach are: (1) the initial appearance of native copper implements is in the context of the production of socio-technic items; (2) the increased production of socio-technic items in the late Archaic period is related to an increase in population following the shift to the exploitation of aquatic resources roughly coincident with the Nipissing high water stage of the ancestral Great Lakes; (3) this correlation is explicable in the increased selective pressures favoring material means of status communication once populations had increased to the point that personal recognition was no longer a workable basis for differential role behavior; (4) the general shift in later periods from formally "utilitarian" items to the manufacture of formally "nonutilitarian" items of copper is explicable in the postulated shift from purely egalitarian to increasingly nonegalitarian means of status attainment.

IT HAS BEEN aptly stated that "American archaeology is anthropology or it is nothing" (Willey and Phillips 1958: 2). The purpose of this discussion is to evaluate the role which the archaeological discipline is playing in furthering the aims of anthropology and to offer certain suggestions as to how we, as archaeologists, may profitably shoulder more responsibility for furthering the aims of our field.

Initially, it must be asked, "What are the aims of anthropology?" Most will agree that the integrated field is striving to *explicate* and *explain* the total range of physical and cultural similarities and differences characteristic of the entire spatial-temporal span of man's existence (for discussion, see Kroeber 1953). Archaeology has certainly made major contributions as far as *explication* is concerned. Our current knowledge of the diversity which characterizes the range of extinct cultural systems is far superior to the limited knowledge available fifty years ago. Although this contribution is "admirable" and necessary, it has been noted that archaeology has made essentially no contribution in the realm of explanation: "So little work has been done in American archaeology on the explanatory level that it is difficult to find a name for it" (Willey and Phillips 1958: 5).

Before carrying this criticism further, some statement about what is meant by explanation must be offered. The meaning which explanation has within a scientific frame of reference is simply the *demonstration* of a constant articulation of variables within a system and the measurement of the concomitant variability among the variables within the system. Processual change in one variable can then be shown to relate in a predictable and quantifiable way to changes in other variables, the latter changing in turn relative to changes in the structure of the system as a whole. This approach to explanation presupposes concern with process, or the operation and structural modification of systems. It is suggested that archaeologists have not made major explanatory contributions to the field of anthropology because they do not conceive of archaeological data in a systemic frame of reference. Archaeological data are viewed particularistically and "explanation" is offered in terms of specific events rather than in terms of process (see Buettner-Janusch 1957 for discussion of particularism).

Archaeologists tacitly assume that artifacts, regardless of their functional context, can be treated as equal and comparable "traits." Once differences and similarities are "defined" in terms of these equal and comparable "traits," interpretation proceeds within something of a theoretical vacuum that conceives of differences and similarities as the result of "blending," "directional influences," and "stimulation" between and among "historical traditions" defined largely on the basis of postulated local or regional continuity in the human populations.

I suggest that this undifferentiated and unstructured view is inadequate, that artifacts having their primary functional context in different operational sub-systems of the total cultural system will exhibit differences and similarities differentially, in terms of the structure of the cultural system of which they were a part. Further, that the temporal and spatial spans within and between broad functional categories will vary with the structure of the systematic relationships between socio-cultural systems. Study of these differential distributions can potentially yield valuable information concerning the nature of social organization within, and changing relationships between, socio-cultural systems. In short, the explanation of differences and similarities between archaeological complexes must be offered in terms of our current knowledge of the structural and functional characteristics of cultural systems.

Specific "historical" explanations, if they can be demonstrated, simply explicate mechanisms of cultural process. They add nothing to the explanation of the processes of cultural change and evolution. If migrations can be shown to have taken place, then this explication presents an explanatory problem; what adaptive circumstances, evolutionary processes, induced the migration (Thompson 1958: 1)? We must seek explanation in systemic terms for classes of historical events such as migrations, establishment of "contact" between areas previously isolated, etc. Only then will we make major contributions in the area of explanation and provide a basis for the further advancement of anthropological theory.

As an exercise in explication of the methodological questions raised here, I will present a general discussion of a particular systemic approach in the evaluation of archaeological assemblages and utilize these distinctions in an attempted *explanation* of a particular set of archaeological observations.

Culture is viewed as the extra-somatic means of adaptation for the human organism (White 1959: 8). I am concerned with all those subsystems within the broader cultural system which are: (a) extra-somatic or not, dependent upon biological process for modification or structural definition (this is not to say that the form and process cannot be viewed as rooted in biological process, only that diversity and processes of diversification are not explicable in terms of biological process), and which (b) function to adapt the human organism, conceived generically, to its total environment both physical and social.

Within this framework it is consistent to view technology, those tools and social relationships which articulate the organism with the physical environment, as closely related to the nature of the environment. For example, we would not expect to find large quantities of fishhooks among the recent archaeological remains from the Kalahari desert! However, this view must not be thought of as "environmental determinism" for we assume a systematic relationship between the human organism and his environment in which culture is the intervening variable. In short, we are speaking of the ecological system (Steward 1955: 36). We can observe certain constant adaptive requirements on the part of the organism and similarly certain adaptive limitations, given specific kinds of environment. However, limitations as well as the potential of the environment must be viewed always in terms of the intervening variable in the human ecological system, that is, culture.

With such an approach we should not be surprised to note similarities in technology among groups of similar levels of social complexity inhabiting the boreal forest (Spaulding 1946) or any other broad environmental zone. The comparative study of cultural systems with variable technologies in a similar environmental range or similar technologies in differing environments is a major methodology of what Steward (1955: 36–42) has called "cultural ecology," and certainly is a valuable means of increasing our understanding of cultural processes. Such a methodology is also useful in elucidating the structural relationships between major cultural sub-systems such as the social and ideological sub-systems. Prior to the initiation of such studies by archaeologists we must be able to distinguish those relevant artifactual elements within the total artifact assemblage which have the primary functional context in the social, technological, and ideological sub-systems of the total cultural system. We should not equate "material culture" with technology. Similarly we should not seek explanations for observed differences and similarities in "material culture" within a single interpretative frame of reference. It has often been suggested that we cannot dig up a social system or ideology. Granted we cannot excavate a kinship terminology or a philosophy, but we can and do excavate the material items which functioned together with these more behavioral elements within the appropriate cultural sub-systems. The formal structure of artifact assemblages together with the between element contextual relationships should and do present a systematic and understandable picture of *the total extinct cultural system*. It is no more justifiable for archaeologists to attempt explanation of certain formal, temporal, and spatial similarities and differences within a single frame of reference than it would be for an ethnographer to attempt explanation of differences in cousin terminology, levels of socio-cultural integration, styles of dress, and modes of transportation all with the same variables or within the same frame of reference. These classes or items are articulated differently within an integrated cultural system, hence the pertinent variables with which each is articulated, and exhibit concomitant variation are different. This fact obviates the single explanatory frame of reference. The processes of change pertinent to each are different because of the different ways in which they function in contributing to the total adaptive system.

Consistent with this line of reasoning is the assertion that we as archaeologists must face the problem of identifying *technomic* artifacts from other artifactual forms. Technomic signifies those artifacts having their primary functional context in coping directly with the physical environment. Variability in the technomic components of archaeological assemblages is seen as primarily explicable in the ecological frame of reference. Here, we must concern ourselves with such phenomena as extractive efficiency, efficiency in performing bio-compensatory tasks such as heat retention, the nature of available resources, their distribution, density, and loci of availability, etc. In this area of research and explanation, the archaeologist is in a position to make a direct contribution to the field of anthropology. We can directly correlate technomic items with environmental variables since we can know the distribution of fossil flora and fauna from independent data — giving us the nature of extinct environments.

Another major class of artifacts which the archaeologists recover can be termed *socio-technic*. These artifacts were the material elements having their primary functional context in the social sub-systems of the total cultural system. This sub-system functions as the extra-somatic means of articulating individuals one with another into cohesive groups capable of efficiently maintaining themselves and of manipulating the technology. Artifacts such as a king's crown, a warrior's coup stick, a copper from the Northwest coast, etc., fall into this category. Changes in the relative complexity of the socio-technic component of an archaeological assemblage can be related to changes in the structure of the social system which they represent. Certainly the evolutionary processes, while correlated and related, are not the same for explaining structural changes in technological and social phenomena. Factors such as demography, presence or absence of between-group competition, etc., as well as the basic factors which affect technological change, must be considered when attempting to explain social change. Not only are the relevant variables different, there is a further difference when speaking of socio-technic artifacts. The explanation of the basic form and structure of the socio-technic component of an artifactual assemblage lies in the nature and structure of the social system which it represents. Observable differences and changes in the socio-technic components of archaeological assemblages must be explained with reference to structural changes in the social system and in terms of processes of social change and evolution.

Thus, archaeologists can initially only indirectly contribute to the investigation of social evolution. I would consider the study and establishment of correlations between types of social structure classified on the basis of behavioral attributes and structural types of material elements as one of the major areas of anthropological research yet to be developed. Once such correlations are established, archaeologists can attack the problems of evolutionary change in social systems. It is my opinion that only when we have the entire temporal span of cultural evolution as our "laboratory" can we make substantial gains in the critical area of social anthropological research.

The third major class of items which archaeologists frequently recover can be termed *ideo-technic artifacts*. Items of this class have their primary functional context in the ideological component of the social system. These are the items which signify and symbolize the ideological rationalizations for the social system and further provide the symbolic milieu in which individuals are enculturated, a necessity if they are to take their place as functional participants in the social system. Such items as figures of deities, clan symbols, symbols of natural agencies, etc., fall into this general category. Formal diversity in the structural complexity and in functional classes of this category of items must generally be related to changes in the structure of the society, hence explanations must be sought in the local adaptive situation rather than in the area of "historical explanations." As was the case with socio-technic items, we must seek to establish correlations between generic classes of the ideological system and the structure of the material symbolism. Only after such correlations have been established can archaeologists study in a systematic way this component of the social sub-system.

Cross-cutting all of these general classes of artifacts are formal characteristics which can be termed stylistic, formal qualities that are not directly explicable in terms of the nature of the raw materials, technology of production, or variability in the structure of the technological and social sub-systems of the total cultural system. These formal qualities are believed to have their primary functional context in providing a symbolically diverse yet pervasive artifactual environment promoting group solidarity and serving as a basis for group awareness and identity. This pan-systemic set of symbols is the milieu of enculturation and a basis for the recognition of social distinctiveness. "One of the main functions of the arts as communication is to reinforce belief, custom, and values" (Beals and Hoijer 1955: 548). The distribution of style types and traditions is believed to be largely correlated with areas of commonality in level of cultural complexity and in mode of adaptation. Changes in the temporal-spatial distribution of style types are believed to be related to changes in the structure of socio-cultural systems either brought about through processes of in situ evolution, or by changes in the cultural environment to which local socio-cultural systems are adapted, thereby initiating evolutionary change. It is believed that stylistic attributes are most fruitfully studied when questions of ethnic origin, migration, and interaction between groups is the subject of explication. However, when explanations are sought, the total adaptive context of the socio-cultural system in question must be investigated. In this field of research archaeologists are in an excellent position to make major contributions to the general field of anthropology, for we can work directly in terms of

correlations of the structure of artifact assemblages with rates of style change, directions of style-spread, and stability of style-continuity.

Having recognized three general functional classes of artifacts: technomic, socio-technic, and ideo-technic, as well as a category of formal stylistic attributes, each characterized by differing functions within the total cultural system and correspondingly different processes of change, it is suggested that our current theoretical orientation is insufficient and inadequate for attempting explanation. It is argued that explanations of differences and similarities between archaeological assemblages as a whole must first consider the nature of differences in each of these major categories and only after such evaluation can adequate explanatory hypotheses be offered.

Given this brief and oversimplified introduction, I will turn to a specific case, the Old Copper complex (Wittry and Ritzenthaler 1956). It has long been observed and frequently cited as a case of technological "devolution" that during the Archaic period fine and superior copper utilitarian tools were manufactured, whereas, during Early and Middle Woodland times copper was used primarily for the production of nonutilitarian items (Griffin 1952: 356). I will explore this interesting situation in terms of: (1) the frame of reference presented here, (2) generalizations which have previously been made concerning the nature of culture change, and (3) a set of hypotheses concerning the relationships between certain forms of socio-technic artifacts and the structure of the social systems that they represent.

The normal assumption when thinking about the copper artifacts typical of the Old Copper complex is that they are primarily technomic (manufactured for use in directly coping with the physical environment). It is generally assumed that these tools were superior to their functional equivalents in both stone and bone because of their durability and presumed superiority in accomplishing cutting and piercing tasks. It is a common generalization that within the realm of technology more efficient forms tend to replace less efficient forms. The Old Copper case seems to be an exception.

Absolute efficiency in performance is only one side of the coin when viewed in an adaptive context. Adaptive efficiency must also be viewed in terms of *economy*, that is, energy expenditure versus energy conservation (White

1959: 54). For one tool to be adaptively more efficient than another there must be either a lowering of energy expenditure per unit of energy of conservation in task performance, or an increase in energy conservation per unit of performance over a constant energy expenditure in tool production. Viewed this way, we may question the position that copper tools were technologically more efficient. The production of copper tools utilizing the techniques employed in the manufacture of Old Copper specimens certainly required tremendous expenditures of both time and labor. The sources of copper are not in the areas of most dense Old Copper implements (Wittry 1951), hence travel to the sources, or at least the establishment of logistics networks based on kin ties extending over large areas, was a prerequisite for the procurement of the raw material. Extraction of the copper, using the primitive mining techniques exemplified by the aboriginal mining pits on Isle Royale and the Keewenaw Peninsula (Holmes 1901), required further expenditure of time and labor. Raw materials for the production of the functional equivalents of the copper tools was normally available locally or at least available at some point within the bounds of the normal exploitative cycle. Extraction was essentially a gathering process requiring no specialized techniques, and could be accomplished incidental to the performance of other tasks. Certainly in terms of expenditures of time and energy, as regards the distribution of sources of raw materials and techniques of extraction, copper required a tremendous expenditure as opposed to raw materials of stone and bone.

The processing phase of tool production appears to present an equally puzzling ratio with regard to expenditure of energy. The processing of copper into a finished artifact normally requires the separation of crystalline impurities from the copper. Following this processing phase, normal procedure seems to have been to pound and partially flatten small bits of copper which were then pounded together to "build" an artifact (Cushing 1894). Once the essential shape had been achieved, further hammering, grinding, and polishing were required. I suggest that this process is more time consuming than shaping and finishing an artifact by chipping flint, or even the pecking and grinding technique employed in the production of ground stone tools. It follows that there was a much greater expenditure of time and energy in the production of copper tools than in the production of their functional equivalents in either bone or stone.

Turning now to the problem of energy conservation in task performance, we may ask what differentials existed. It seems fairly certain that copper was probably more durable and could have been utilized for a longer period of time. As far as what differentials existed between copper and stone, as regards cutting and piercing functions, only experiments can determine. Considering all of the evidence, the quality of durability appears to have been the only possible realm which could compensate for the differentials in expenditure of energy between stone and bone as opposed to copper in the area of procurement and processing of the raw material. What evidence exists that would suggest that durability was in fact the compensatory quality which made copper tools technologically more efficient?

All the available evidence suggests the contrary interpretation. First, we do not have evidence that the raw material was re-used to any great extent once an artifact was broken or "worn out." If this had been the case, we would expect to have a general lack of battered and "worn out" pieces and some examples of reworked pieces, whereas evidence of use is a common characteristic of recovered specimens, and to my knowledge reworked pieces are uncommon if not unknown.

Second, when found in a primary archaeological context, copper tools are almost invariably part of burial goods. If durability was the compensatory factor in the efficiency equation, certainly some social mechanism for retaining the copper tools as functioning parts of the technology would have been established. This does not appear to have been the case. Since durability can be ruled out as the compensatory factor, we must conclude that copper tools were not technologically more efficient than their functional equivalents in both stone and bone. Having reached this "conclusion," it remains to explore the problem of the initial appearance of copper tools and to examine the observation that there was a shift from the use of copper for the production of utilitarian tools to nonutilitarian items.

It is proposed that the observed shift and the initial appearance of copper tools can best be explained under the hypothesis that they did not function primarily as *technomic items*. I suggest that in both the Old Copper and later cultural systems to the south, copper was utilized primarily for the production of *socio-technic items*.

Fried (1960) discusses certain pertinent distinctions between societies with regard to systems of status grading. Societies on a low general level of cultural complexity, measured in terms of functional specialization and structural differentiation, normally have an "egalitarian" system of status grading. The term "egalitarian" signifies that status positions are open to all persons within the limits of certain sex and age classes, who through their individual physical and mental characteristics are capable of greater achievement in coping with the environment. Among societies of greater complexity, status grading may be less egalitarian. Where ranking is the primary mechanism of status grading, status positions are closed. There are qualifications for attainment that are not simply a function of one's personal physical and mental capabilities.

A classic example of ranking is found among societies with a ramage form of social organization (Sahlins 1958: 139–180). In such societies status is determined by one's proximity in descent from a common ancestor. High status is accorded those in the direct line of descent, calculated in terms of primogeniture, while cadet lines of descent occupy positions of lower status depending on their proximity to the direct line.

Another form of internally ranked system is one in which attainment of a particular status position is closed to all except those members of a particular kin group who may occupy a differentiated status position, but open to all members of that kin group on an egalitarian basis.

Other forms of status grading are recognized, but for the purposes of this discussion the major distinction between egalitarian and ranked systems is sufficient. I propose that there is a direct relationship between the nature of the system of status grading within a society and the quantity, form, and structure of socio-technic components of its archaeological assemblage.

It is proposed that among egalitarian societies status symbols are symbolic of the technological activities for which outstanding performance is rewarded by increased status. In many cases they will be formally technomic items manufactured of "exotic" material or elaborately decorated and/or painstakingly manufactured. I do not imply that the items could not or were not used technomically, simply that their presence in the assemblage is explicable only in reference to the social system.

Within such a system the structure of the socio-technic component as regards "contextual" relationships should be simple. Various status symbols will be possessed by nearly all individuals within the limits of age and sex classes, differentiation within such a class being largely quantitative and qualitative rather than by formal exclusion of particular forms to particular status grades. The degree to which socio-technic symbols of status will be utilized within an egalitarian group should largely be a function of group size and the intensity and constancy of personal acquaintance among all individuals composing the society. Where small group size and general lack of interaction with nearby groups is the normal pattern, then the abundance of status symbols should be low. Where group size is large and/or where between-group interactions are widespread, lowering the intimacy and familiarity between interacting individuals, then there should be a greater and more general use of material means of status communication.

Another characteristic of the manipulation of status symbols among societies with essentially egalitarian systems of status grading would be the destruction at death of an individual's symbols of status. Status attainment being egalitarian, status symbols would be personalities and could not be inherited as such. Inclusion as grave accompaniments or outright destruction would be the suggested mode of disposal for status items among such groups.

Among societies where status grading tends to be of a nonegalitarian type, the status symbols should be more esoteric in form. Their form would normally be dictated by the ideological symbolism which rationalizes and emphasizes the particular internal ranking system or the means of partitioning the society. The structure of the socio-technic component of the assemblage should be more complex, with the complexity increasing directly as the complexity of the internal ranking system. Possession of certain forms may become exclusively restricted to certain status positions. As the degree of complexity in ranking increases there should be a similar increase in the differentiation of contextual associations in the form of differential treatment at death, differential access to goods and services evidenced in the formal and spatial differentiation in habitations and storage areas, etc. We would also expect to observe differentiation among the class of status symbols themselves as regards those which were utilized on a custodial basis as opposed to those that were personalities. Similarly, we would expect to see status symbols more frequently inherited at death as inheritance increases as the mechanism of status ascription.

Certainly these are suggestions which must be phrased as hypotheses and tested against ethnographic data. Nevertheless it is hoped that this discussion is sufficient to serve as a background against which an explanatory hypothesis concerning the Old Copper materials can be offered as an example of the potential utility of this type of *systemic* approach to archaeological data.

I suggest that the Old Copper copper tools had their primary functional context as symbols of achieved status in cultural systems with an egalitarian system of status grading. The settlement patterns and general level of cultural development suggested by the archaeological remains is commensurate with a band level of socio-cultural integration (Martin, Quimby, and Collier 1947: 299), that level within which egalitarian systems of status grading are dominant (Fried 1960). The technomic form, apparent lack of technomic efficiency, relative scarcity, and frequent occurrence in burials of copper artifacts all suggest that their primary function was as socio-technic items. Having reached this "conclusion," we are then in a position to ask, in systemic terms, questions concerning their period of appearance, disappearance, and the shift to nonutilitarian forms of copper items among later prehistoric socio-cultural systems of eastern North America.

I propose that the initial appearance of formally "utilitarian" copper tools in the Great Lakes region is explicable in terms of a major population expansion in the region following the Nipissing stage of the ancestral Great Lakes. The increase in population density was the result of increases in gross productivity following an exploitative shift to aquatic resources during the Nipissing stage. The increased populations are generally demonstrable in terms of the increased number of archaeological sites ascribable to the post-Nipissing period. The shift to

aquatic resources is demonstrable in the initial appearance of quantities of fish remains in the sites of this period and in the sites of election for occupation, adjacent to prominent loci of availability for exploiting aquatic resources. It is proposed that with the increasing population density, the selective pressures fostering the symbolic communication of status, as opposed to the dependence on personal recognition as the bases for differential role behavior, were sufficient to result in the initial appearance of a new class of socio-technic items, formally technomic status symbols.

The failure to perpetuate the practice of the manufacture of copper tools on any extensive basis in the Great Lakes region should be explicable in terms of the changing structure of the social systems in that area during Woodland times. The exact type of social structure characteristic of Early Woodland period is at present poorly understood. I would suggest that there was a major structural change between the Late Archaic and Early Woodland periods, probably in the direction of a simple clan and moiety basis for social integration with a corresponding shift in the systems of status grading and the obsolescence of the older material means of status communication.

The presence of copper tools of essentially nonutilitarian form within such complexes as Adena, Hopewell, and Mississippian are most certainly explicable in terms of their socio-technic functions within much more complex social systems. Within the latter societies status grading was not purely on an egalitarian basis, and the nonutilitarian copper forms of status symbols would be formally commensurate with the ideological rationalizations for the various ascriptive status systems.

This explanatory "theory" has the advantage of "explaining": (1) the period of appearance of copper and probably other "exotic" materials in the Late Archaic period; (2) the form of the copper items; (3) their frequently noted contextual relations, for example, placement in burials; (4) their disappearance, which would be an "enigma" if they functioned primarily as technomic items; and (5) the use of copper for the almost exclusive production of "nonutilitarian" items in later and certainly more complex cultures of the eastern United States. This explanatory theory is advanced on the basis of currently available information, and regardless of whether or not it can stand as the correct explanation of the "Old Copper Problem" when more data are available, I suggest that only within a systemic frame of reference could such an inclusive explanation be offered. Here lies the advantage of the systemic approach.

Archaeology must accept a greater responsibility in the furtherance of the aims of anthropology. Until the tremendous quantities of data which the archaeologist controls are used in the solution of problems dealing with cultural evolution or systemic change, we are not only failing to contribute to the furtherance of the aims of anthropology but retarding the accomplishment of these aims. We as archaeologists have available a wide range of variability and a large sample of cultural systems. Ethnographers are restricted to the small and formally limited extant cultural systems.

Archaeologists should be among the best qualified to study and directly test hypotheses concerning the process of evolutionary change, particularly processes of change that are relatively slow, or hypotheses that postulate temporal-processual priorities as regards total cultural systems. The lack of theoretical concern and rather naïve attempts at explanation which archaeologists currently advance must be modified.

I have suggested certain ways that could be a beginning in this necessary transition to a systemic view of culture, and have set forth a specific argument which hopefully demonstrates the utility of such an approach. The explanatory potential which even this limited and highly specific interpretative approach holds should be clear when problems such as "the spread of an Early Woodland burial cult in the Northeast" (Ritchie 1955), the appearance of the "Buzzard cult" (Waring and Holder 1945) in the Southeast, or the "Hopewell decline" (Griffin 1960) are recalled. It is my opinion that until we as archaeologists begin thinking of our data in terms of total cultural systems, many such prehistoric "enigmas" will remain unexplained. As archaeologists, with the entire span of culture history as our "laboratory," we cannot afford to keep our theoretical heads buried in the sand. We must shoulder our full share of responsibility within anthropology. Such a change could go far in advancing the field of archaeology specifically, and would certainly advance the general field of anthropology.

BEALS, RALPH L. AND HARRY HOIJER
    1953 *An Introduction to Anthropology*. The Macmillan Company, New York.

BUETTNER-JANUSCH, JOHN
    1957 Boas and Mason: Particularism versus Generalization. *American Anthropologist*, Vol. 59, No. 2, pp. 318–24. Menasha.

CUSHING, F. H.
    1894 Primitive Copper Working: An Experimental Study. *American Anthropologist*, Vol. 7, No. 1, pp. 93–117. Washington.

FRIED, MORTON H.
    1960 On the Evolution of Social Stratification and the State. In *"Culture in History: Essays in Honor of Paul Radin,* edited by Stanley Diamond, pp. 713–31. Columbia University Press, New York.

GRIFFIN, JAMES B.
    1952 Culture Periods in Eastern United States Archaeology. In *Archaeology of Eastern United States,* edited by James B. Griffin, pp. 352–64. University of Chicago Press, Chicago.
    1960 Climatic Change: A Contributory Cause of the Growth and Decline of Northern Hopewellian Culture. *Wisconsin Archeologist*, Vol. 41, No. 2, pp. 21–33. Milwaukee.

HOLMES, WILLIAM H.
    1901 Aboriginal Copper Mines of Isle Royale, Lake Superior. *American Anthropologist*, Vol. 3, No. 4, pp. 684–96. New York.

KROEBER, A. L.
    1953 Introduction. In: *Anthropology Today,* edited by A. L. Kroeber, pp. xiii–xv. University of Chicago Press, Chicago.

MARTIN, PAUL S., GEORGE I. QUIMBY AND DONALD COLLIER
    1947 *Indians Before Columbus*. University of Chicago Press, Chicago.

RITCHIE, WILLIAM A.
    1955 Recent Suggestions Suggesting an Early Woodland Burial Cult in the Northeast. *New York State Museum and Science Service, Circular* No. 40. Rochester.

SAHLINS, MARSHALL D.
    1958 *Social Stratification in Polynesia*. University of Washington Press, Seattle.

SPAULDING, ALBERT C.
    1946 Northeastern Archaeology and General Trends in the Northern Forest Zone. In *"Man in Northeastern North America,"* edited by Frederick Johnson. *Papers of the Robert S. Peabody Foundation for Archaeology*, Vol. 3, pp. 143–67. Phillips Academy, Andover.

STEWARD, JULIAN H.
  1955 *Theory of Culture Change.* University of Illinois Press, Urbana.

THOMPSON, RAYMOND H.
  1958 Preface. In "Migrations in New World Culture History," edited by Raymond H. Thompson, pp. v–vii. *University of Arizona, Social Science Bulletin*, No. 27. Tucson.

WARING, ANTONIO J. AND PRESTON HOLDER
  1945 A Prehistoric Ceremonial Complex in the Southeastern United States. *American Anthropologist*, Vol. 47, No. 1, pp. 1–34. Menasha.

WHITE, LESLIE A.
  1959 *The Evolution of Culture.* McGraw-Hill Book Company, New York.

WILLEY, GORDON R. AND PHILIP PHILLIPS
  1958 *Method and Theory in Archaeology.* University of Chicago Press, Chicago.

WITTRY, WARREN L.
  1951 A Preliminary Study of the Old Copper Complex. *Wisconsin Archeologist*, Vol. 32, No. 1, pp. 1–18. Milwaukee.

WITTRY, WARREN L. AND ROBERT E. RITZENTHALER
  1956 The Old Copper Complex: An Archaic Manifestation in Wisconsin. *American Antiquity*, Vol. 21, No. 3, pp. 244–54. Salt Lake City.

UNIVERSITY OF CHICAGO

Chicago, Illinois

April, 1962

ARCHAEOLOGICAL SYSTEMATICS AND THE STUDY OF CULTURE PROCESS[1]

Lewis R. Binford

ABSTRACT

It is argued that the normative theory of culture, widely held among archaeologists, is inadequate for the generation of fruitful explanatory hypotheses of cultural process. One obvious shortcoming of this theoretical position has been the development of archaeological systematics that have obviated any possibility of measuring multivariate phenomena and permit only the measurement of unspecified "cultural differences and similarities," as if these were univariate phenomena. As an alternative to this approach, it is proposed that culture be viewed as a system composed of subsystems, and it is suggested that differences and similarities between different classes of archaeological remains reflect different subsystems and hence may be expected to vary independently of each other in the normal operation of the system or during change in the system. A general discussion of ceramic classification and the classification of differences and similarities between assemblages is presented as an example of the multivariate approach to the study of cultural variability. It is suggested that a multivariate approach in systematics will encourage the study of cultural variability and its causes and thereby enhance the study of culture process.

WILLEY and Phillips (1958: 50) have expressed doubts that current archaeological concepts such as "phase" have consistent meaning in terms of human social units. It is the purpose of this paper to explore some of the reasons for this lack of congruence and to offer a theoretical framework more consistent with social reality.

In any general theoretical framework there are at least two major components: (1) one that deals with criteria for isolating the phenomenon under study and with the underlying assumptions about the nature of the units or partitive occurrences within the recognized generic class of phenomenon, and (2) assumptions concerning the way in which these partitive units are articulated in the operation of a system or during change.

Most of the analytical means and conceptual tools of archaeological systematics have arisen in the context of a body of culture theory which is referred to here as the "normative school." Under this normative view the phenomenon being studied is variously defined, but there is

general agreement that culture with a capital C is the subject. In this the normative theorists are in agreement with others. It is in the definition of partitive concepts and the assumptions concerning the processes of between-unit dynamics that normative theorists differ markedly from the position taken here. A typical normative statement is given by Taylor (1948: 110):

> By culture as a partitive concept, I mean a historically derived system of culture traits which is a more or less separable and cohesive segment of the whole-that-is-culture and whose separate traits tend to be shared by all or by specially designated individuals of a group or society.

A similar view is expressed by Willey and Phillips (1958: 18) when speaking of spatial divisions of cultural phenomena:

> In strictly archaeological terms, the locality is a geographical space small enough to permit the working assumption of complete cultural homogeneity at any given time.

The emphasis in these two quotations and in the writings of other archaeologists (Ford 1954: 47; Rouse 1939: 15–18; Gifford 1960: 346) is on the shared characteristics of human behavior. Within this frame of thought, culture is defined as an abstraction from human behavior.

> According to the concept of culture being developed here, culture is a mental construct consisting of ideas (Taylor 1948: 101).

Or as Ford (1954: 47) has argued:

> First, it must be recalled that these buildings are cultural products — not the culture. These arrangements of wood, bamboo, and grass are of interest to the ethnologists solely because they illustrate the aborigine's ideas as to the proper ways to construct dwellings.

In summary, a normative theorist is one who sees as his field of study the ideational basis for varying ways of human life — culture. Information is obtained by studying cultural products or the objectifications of normative ideas about the proper ways of life executed by now extinct peoples. The archaeologist's task then lies in abstracting from cultural products the normative concepts extant in the minds of men now dead. (For criticism of this general view see White 1954: 461–8.)

In examining the problem of how we may observe and study cultural phenomena, a crucial

[1] This paper was presented at the 29th Annual Meeting of the Society for American Archaeology, Chapel Hill, North Carolina, 1964.

11

question arises: What types of units can be isolated for the meaningful study of culture? For adherents of the normative school, the assumptions about units or the natural "packages" in which culture occurs are dependent upon assumptions about the dynamics of ideational transmission. Learning is the recognized basis of cultural transmission between generations and diffusion the basis of transmission between social units not linked by regular breeding behavior. The corollary of this proposition is that culture is transmitted between generations and across breeding populations in inverse proportion to the degree of social distance maintained between the groups in question. Since culture is viewed as a great "whole" transmitted through time and across space, any attempt to break up this cultural "whole" is considered arbitrary and thought of as a methodological expedient (Ford 1954: 51; Brew 1946: 49). The partitioning of culture is often termed a heuristic device for measuring the degree of social distance between the groups whose cultural products are being observed. (An excellent criticism of this view is found in Spaulding 1957: 85–7). Spatial discontinuities in the distribution of similar formal characteristics are perceived as either the result of (1) natural barriers to social intercourse, or (2) the presence of a value system which provides a conservative psychological matrix that inhibits the acceptance of foreign traits, or (3) the migration or intrusion into the area of new peoples who disrupt the previous pattern of social intercourse. Formal changes in the temporal distribution of items are viewed as the result of innovations or the operation of a built-in dynamics sometimes designated as "drift" (Ford 1954: 51; Herskovits 1948: 581–2). (For criticism of this concept, see Binford 1963: 89–93.) Both innovation and drift are considered natural to culture and, as Caldwell (1958: 1) has said: "other things being equal, changes in material culture through time and space will tend to be regular." Discontinuities in rates of change or in formal continuity through time are viewed as the result of historical events which tend to change the configuration of social units through such mechanisms as extensions of trade, migration, and the diffusions of "core" ideas such as religious cults (Ritchie 1955).

Cultural differences and similarities are expressed by the normative school in terms of "cultural relationships" which, if treated rigorously, resolve into one general interpretative model. This model is based on the assumption of a "culture center" where, for unspecified reasons, rates of innovation exceed those in surrounding areas. The new culture spreads out from the center and blends with surrounding cultures until it is dissipated at the fringes, leaving marginal cultures. Cultural relationships are viewed as the degree of mutual or unilateral "influence" exerted between culture centers or subcenters.

This interpretative framework implies what I choose to call the aquatic view of culture. Interpretative literature abounds in phrases such as "cultural stream" and in references to the "flowing" of new cultural elements into a region. Culture is viewed as a vast flowing stream with minor variations in ideational norms concerning appropriate ways of making pots, getting married, treating one's mother-in-law, building houses, temples (or not building them, as the case may be), and even dying. These ideational variations are periodically "crystallized" at different points in time and space, resulting in distinctive and sometimes striking cultural climaxes which allow us to break up the continuum of culture into cultural phases.

One of the most elegant and complete criticisms of the normative theorists to appear in recent years is that of David Aberle (1960). He has pointed out that adherents of the normative position are forced to explain cultural differences and similarities in terms of two factors, historical and psychic. He summarizes the normative position as follows:

No culture can be understood solely by reference to its current situation. As a result of the accidents of history, it has had contacts with a variety of other cultures. These other cultures provide the pool of potential cultural material on which cultures can draw. Since there is no general basis for predicting what cultures will have contact with what others, the historical factor has an accidental and fortuitous character. With respect to the psychic factor, there are qualities of men's minds — whether general tendencies to imitate or specific attitudes held by a particular group — which determine whether or not any available cultural item will be borrowed. Although the contacts are unpredictable, the laws of psychology may account for acceptance and rejection. Hence the laws of culture are psychological laws (Aberle 1960: 3).

The normative view leaves the archaeologist in the position of considering himself a culture historian and/or a paleo-psychologist (for which most archaeologists are poorly trained). This leaves him competent to pursue the investigation of culture history, a situation which may partially account for failure to develop the explanatory level of archaeological theory noted by Willey and Phillips (1958: 5).

It is argued here that a new systematics, one based on a different concept of culture, is needed to deal adequately with the explanation of cultural process. If we define culture as man's extrasomatic means of adaptation (White 1959: 8), in the partitive sense culture is an extrasomatic adaptive system that is employed in the integration of a society with its environment and with other sociocultural systems. Culture in this sense is not necessarily shared; it is participated in by men. In cultural systems, people, things, and places are components in a field that consists of environmental and sociocultural subsystems, and the locus of cultural process is in the dynamic articulations of these subsystems. This complex set of interrelationships is not explicable by reduction to a single component — ideas — any more than the functioning of a motor is explainable in terms of a single component, such as gasoline, a battery, or lubricating oil.

It was stated above that in our definition culture is not necessarily shared; it is participated in. And it is participated in differentially. A basic characteristic of cultural systems is the integration of individuals and social units performing different tasks, frequently at different locations; these individuals and social units are articulated by means of various institutions into broader units that have different levels of corporate inclusiveness. Within any one cultural system, the degree to which the participants share the same ideational basis should vary with the degree of cultural complexity of the system as a whole. In fact, a measure of cultural complexity is generally considered to be the degree of internal structural differentiation and functional specificity of the participating subsystems (White 1959: 144-5). Within any given cultural system, the degree to which all the participants share common ideational preferences should vary inversely with the complexity of the system as a whole. The sharing of cultural elements by distinct systems will be a function of the nature of the cultural means of articulating distinct groups with each other.

At present our explicitly stated systematics is based on the degree to which cultural traits are shared. The Midwestern taxonomic system (McKern 1935: 70-82; and 1939: 301-13) is a hierarchical arrangement of archaeologically defined culture traits as they appear in spatially or temporally discrete manifestations. Similarly, such units as the phase (Willey and Phillips 1958: 50; Rouse 1955: 713-14) are groupings of archaeological complexes on the basis of shared traits.

This emphasis on shared traits in our system of classification results in masking differences and in lumping together phenomena which would be discrete under another taxonomic method. Culture is not a univariate phenomenon, nor is its functioning to be understood or measured in terms of a single variable — the spatial-temporal transmission of ideas. On the contrary, culture is multivariate, and its operation is to be understood in terms of many causally relevant variables which may function independently or in varying combinations. It is our task to isolate these causative factors and to seek regular, statable, and predictable relationships between them.

Our taxonomies should be framed with this end in mind. We should partition our observational fields so that we may emphasize the nature of variability in artifact populations and facilitate the isolation of causally relevant factors. Our categories should be justifiable in terms of possessing common structural or functional properties in the normal operation of cultural systems. These categories should then be analyzed in terms of their behavior in various systems and in situations of systematic change.

By such a method we may achieve our aim of expressing the laws of cultural process. Archaeological systematics should be an aid in accomplishing analytical tasks. As an example of the suggested method of partitioning our observational framework, two general problems will be discussed: ceramic classification and the classification of archaeological assemblages.

Formal variation in ceramics occurs because of differences in either the techniques of manufacture or in the general design of the finished product; both kinds of variation may occur independently of each other. (This distinction is analogous to Rouse's [1960: 314] distinction between procedural and conceptual modes). One example is the production of an abrupt shoulder as opposed to a gently sloping shoulder while continuing to execute the same basic set of manufacturing techniques. Such variation is termed *morphological variation*. In addition to morphological variation, there is *decorative variation* or modifications that are made as discrete steps in the terminal phases of the manufacturing process. Painted and incised designs are examples of decorative variation. We can therefore speak of two major classes of variation or analytic dimensions, in terms of which ceramic forms can be studied — *technical* and *design dimensions.* Morphological and decorative variation may be observed along either dimension.

With regard to the sociocultural context of formal variability, two broad classes of variation can be recognized which crosscut the categories mentioned above. *Primary functional variation* is that which is directly related to the specific use made of the vessel in question; for example, the difference between a plate and a storage jar. *Secondary functional variation* is a by-product of the social context of the manufacturers of the vessel or of the social context of the intended use of the item, or both. This variation may arise from a traditional way of doing things within a family or a larger social unit, or it may serve as a conscious expression of between-group solidarity. Certain design characteristics may become standardized as symbols appropriate to vessels used in specific social contexts. At this level of analysis we may recall Linton's (1936: 403–21) statement that any given cultural item may vary with regard to form, meaning, use, and function in variable cultural contexts. Such distinctions are particularly important if the social context of manufacture and use are not isomorphic, as in the case of items circulated widely through exchange systems, or are used primarily in the context of institutions functioning for intersocietal articulation.

Formal variation in artifacts need not and, in most cases, probably does not have a single meaning in the context of the functioning cultural system. The study of primary functional variation is essential to the understanding of the sociocultural systems represented by the artifacts, in this case ceramics. The nature and number of occurrences of functionally differentiated container types can yield valuable information about the size of social segments performing different tasks. Even in cases where specific functions cannot be determined for the recognized types, the spatial configuration of their occurrence tells something about the spatial structure of differentiated activities within or between sites.

Variables of primary function may remain stable, change abruptly, or change at rates different from variables of secondary function. The relative rates of change in these two classes of

variables can tell us much about the nature of the changes within the systems in question. An example of this can be seen by comparing the Havana tradition of Illinois with the Scioto tradition of Ohio.

Containers of the Havana tradition are predominantly large, open-mouthed cauldrons, but there are occasional flat-bottomed "flowerpot" forms. This suggests that food was prepared in these societies for relatively large groups of people — larger than nuclear families — and that food was stored corporately. This pattern of cooking and storing was common to essentially all the societies participating in the Havana tradition. Secondary functional variation, on the other hand, with respect to both decoration and design exhibits differences through space and time, suggesting that among the participants in the Havana tradition social contacts and generational continuity were changing.

Container forms of the Scioto tradition in Ohio, which is believed to be contemporaneous with the Havana tradition, were smaller vessels with rounded bottoms; the large cauldron is an infrequent form. Nevertheless, there are common design and technical attributes in the ceramics of both traditions. This suggests that, in the Ohio groups, the social units for which food was prepared were smaller and that modes of food storage were correspondingly different.

In the traditional view, the elements in common between the Havana and Scioto traditions would be interpreted as indicating "cultural relationships," and at present the two are grouped into the "Hopewell phase," with each group sharing different traits of the "Hopewell culture." It is suggested here that the sociocultural systems represented in the two traditions may be and probably are totally different, and that the common ceramic elements reflect patterns of common regional interaction facilitated through different institutions. This view differs markedly from one which pictures the flowing of "Hopewell culture" out of a "culture center."

The comparative study of secondary functional variation within one class of containers makes it possible to determine the degree of work specialization in discrete social segments as well as the degree of craft specialization in the manufacture of specific container classes. Empirical demonstration of the validity of the assumptions underlying sociological interpretation of variability in craft products is accumulating, and a number of recent studies show that

TABLE 1. CONTINGENCY OF FORMAL VARIATION

	Morphological variation	Decorative variation
Technical dimension		
Design dimension		

this kind of "meaning" is recoverable from ceramic data. For example, Cronin (1962: 109) has demonstrated greater similarity in the conventional use of decorative design elements between pottery types at a single site than between types of the same pottery from different sites. Comparable results are suggested by recent discussions of taxonomic problems encountered by others (Sears 1960: 327–8; Smith 1962). I have recently proposed a processual model for this type of phenomenon (Binford 1963). Several recent studies have utilized the measurement and spatial distributions of stylistic minutiae in the construction of sociological models for prehistoric communities (Deetz 1960; Longacre 1963; Freeman and Brown 1964).

If we expand our analytical perspective to include the problem of formal variability in contemporaneous sociocultural systems and sociocultural systems through time, then our analysis must be even more critical. What is ideosyncratic secondary functional variation in one group may symbolize political ties in another. Primary functional variation in one social system may be partially incorporated as secondary functional variation in another.

The complexities facing the archaeologist who attempts this kind of analysis necessitate the use of multiple taxonomies framed to express multivariate attributes. Such taxonomies should replace the conventional ones, which are either classes based on unspecified kinds of likeness or difference, or are hierarchically arranged traits presumed to reflect generic relationships (Willey and Phillips 1958: 31; Rouse 1960). We suggest that classification should proceed independently with regard to technical and design attributes and that crosscutting categories should be used to express morphological and decorative variation (Table 1).

The result of such an analysis would be the recognition of numbers of classes of variables, referable to one or more of the column-and-row contingency boxes in Table 1. Analysis would then proceed to the question of the cultural context of the observed classes or variables distinguished in the four categories above. This step is schematically diagrammed in Table 2. Each column and row contingency box would contain the formal classes of demonstrable variables derived from the initial classification.

The next step would be the definition of populations of artifacts in terms of recognizable and demonstrably different cultural factors. Discussions of differences and similarities would be based on independent and dependent variables and not on an undifferentiated conglomeration of multivariate phenomena.

The current systematics of archaeological assemblages also stresses the quantity of shared traits. Assemblages are referred to a phase or a focus without due allowances for either seasonal or functional variability. Although it is premature to attempt a final presentation of assemblage systematics since such a presentation should be based on more complete knowledge of the range of classes of variability, we feel that at least three major types of broad cultural alignments can be distinguished which may vary independently of one another.

TABLE 2. CONTINGENCY OF CULTURAL VARIATION

	Primary functional variation	Secondary functional variation	
		Context of use	Context of Production
Techno-morphological			
Morphological design			
Decorative techniques			
Decorative designs			

The first such category is the *tradition*, whose meaning we choose to make somewhat narrower than is conventional in archaeological literature. (For a discussion of the concept as generally used, see Willey and Phillips 1958: 34–40.) We define tradition as a demonstrable continuity through time in the formal properties of locally manufactured craft items, this continuity being seen in secondary functional variability only. There may or may not be such continuity with respect to primary functional variability. To put it another way, the tradition is seen in continuity in those formal attributes which vary with the social context of manufacture exclusive of the variability related to the use of the item. This is termed stylistic variability (Binford 1962: 220), and on a single time horizon such a tradition would be spatially defined as a style zone. Through time we may study the areal extent and stability of style zones and the comparative history of local traditions within the framework of the macrotradition. Historical continuity and social phylogeny are particularly amenable to analysis through the study of stylistic attributes. It should be noted that the concept of tradition as it is used here may refer to either a single class of artifactual materials, such as ceramics, or to several classes of artifacts of a single sociocultural system which exhibit continuity through time. It is assumed that formal variability in secondary function is directly related to the social matrix of production and use. In the case of stability through time in the social matrix of production, we would expect to observe temporal continuity and a regular rate of change. In the case of a changing social matrix of production, we would expect to find discontinuities in rates of change and in the spatial and temporal distribution of formal properties.

A second broad class of sociocultural relationships is reflected in items that are widely exchanged and which occur in a context of social distinctiveness, that is, sociotechnic items (Binford 1962). Such items would be analyzed in terms of their primary functional variability as inferred through correlation with other archaeological remains which define the context of social relations. Through the study of the spatial distributions of such items on a single time horizon we may define *interaction spheres* — the areal matrices of regular and institutionally maintained intersocietal articulation. This term is adopted from Caldwell (1962). It is my impression that I have seen the term used by other archaeologists, but I have not been able to find it in the literature. Caldwell (1962) has pointed to the essential characteristics of the interaction sphere:

> An interaction sphere is a kind of phenomenon which can be regarded as having properties different from a culture . . . the various regional traditions were present before there was a Hopewellian situation. The term culture would be better applied to each of these separately than to the overall situation with which they are interacting.

What is essential to the concept of an interaction sphere is that it denotes a situation in which there is a regular cultural means of institutionalizing and maintaining intersocietal interaction. The particular forms of the institutions and the secondary functions which may accrue to them will be found to vary widely in the spectrum of history. Interaction spheres may crosscut both traditions and culture areas. The sharing of symbols and the appearance of similar institutions are less a function of the traditional enculturative milieu of individual societies than of complex articulation of societies of different ethnic backgrounds, levels of cultural complexity, and social types.

The comparative structural and functional analysis of interaction spheres is suggested as an approach which allows us to define, quantify, and explain the observation of Redfield (1941: 344) that rates of cultural change may be directly related to rates of social interaction. The distinction between the "shared" culture of a stylistic nature and the "shared" culture of a sociopolitical nature is the basis for distinguishing the tradition from the interaction sphere.

Examples of the interaction sphere come readily to mind. The presence of Mississippian "traits" in local traditions on the Piedmont of the southeastern United States is one. Another is the common "Hopewellian" items in tombs of Illinois (the Havana tradition) and in the charnel houses of Ohio (the Scioto tradition). The nature of the cultural processes responsible for the widespread occurrences of similar cultural items in these two cases cannot be explained by the simplistic reference to sharing of similar ideas concerning the proper ways to manufacture items.

The third category we wish to discuss is that of the adaptive area. An adaptive area is one which exhibits the common occurrence of artifacts used primarily in coping directly with the physical environment. Such spatial distributions would be expected to coincide broadly with culture areas as they are conventionally defined; however, this concept differs from the culture-area concept in that stylistic attributes are excluded from the definition. The adaptive means of coping with changes in physical environment need not coincide with those which are designed to cope with changes in the social environment. Therefore, we need to study traditions (based on styles), interaction spheres (based on intersocietal relations), and adaptive spheres (based on common means of coping with the physical environment), and treat these three isolates as independent variables.

Summary. It has been argued that the normative theory of culture is inadequate for the generation of fruitful explanatory hypotheses of cultural process. An approach is offered in which culture is not reduced to normative ideas about the proper ways of doing things but is viewed as the system of the total extrasomatic means of adaptation. Such a system involves a complex sets of relationships among people, places, and things whose matrix may be understood in multivariate terms.

The steps in such an analysis proceed by means of the partitioning of demonstrable variability into a multidimensional framework. Use of such a framework will facilitate isolation of the causes of various kinds of changes and differences and provide the basis for studying comparatively the rates and patterns of change in different classes of cultural phenomena. Such an approach would, it is argued, facilitate and increase our understanding of cultural processes.

Acknowledgments. I would like to acknowledge the intellectual stimulation of many of my colleagues in the formulation of the ideas presented in this paper. Stuart Struever, Joseph Caldwell, Howard Winters, James Brown, Melvin Fowler, and the author have had frequent discussions over the past three years in an attempt to increase our understanding of the prehistory of the Midwest. Although individually all of the participants in our own "interaction sphere" have contributed to the formulation of the arguments presented here, I accept full responsibility for the particular form in which the ideas are presented. In addition, I would like to express my gratitude to Carl-Axel Moberg of the Göteburg Museum, Sweden, who participated in the joint teaching of a class along with Robert J. Braidwood and me. Moberg's arguments and rebuttals have aided appreciably in definition of the ideas presented. My students over the past three years — particularly William Longacre, James Hill, Leslie Freeman, and Robert Whallon — have been a constant source of stimulation and have initiated agonizing reappraisals of my own thinking. Of particular importance is the role played by my wife, Sally Binford. She has been a severe critic of my logic as well as of my syntax, and I gratefully acknowledge her editorship of this manuscript.

ABERLE, DAVID R.
1960 The Influence of Linguistics on Early Culture and Personality Theory. In *Essays in the Science of Culture: In Honor of Leslie A. White*, edited by Gertrude Dole and Robert Carneiro, pp. 1–49. Thomas Y. Crowell, New York.

BINFORD, LEWIS R.
1962 Archaeology as Anthropology. *American Antiquity*, Vol. 28, No. 2, pp. 217–25. Salt Lake City.

1963 Red Ocher Caches from the Michigan Area: A Possible Case of Cultural Drift. *Southwestern Journal of Anthropology*, Vol. 19, No. 1, pp. 89–108. Albuquerque.

BREW, JOHN OTIS
1946 Archaeology of Alkali Ridge: Southeastern Utah. *Papers of the Peabody Museum of American Archaeology and Ethnology, Harvard University*, Vol. 21. Cambridge.

CALDWELL, JOSEPH R.
1958 Trend and Tradition in the Prehistory of the Eastern United States. *Memoirs of the American Anthropological Association*, No. 88. Menasha.

1962 Interaction Spheres in Prehistory. Unpublished paper presented at the Annual Meeting of the American Association for the Advancement of Science, Philadelphia 1962.

CRONIN, CONSTANCE
1962 An Analysis of Pottery Design Elements Indicating Possible Relationships between Three Decorated Types. In "Chapters in the Prehistory of Eastern Arizona I," by Paul S. Martin and others. *Fieldiana: Anthropology*, Vol. 53, pp. 105–41. Chicago Natural History Museum, Chicago.

DEETZ, JAMES D. F.
1960 An Archaeological Approach to Kinship Change in Eighteenth Century Arikara Culture. Unpublished Ph.D. dissertation, Harvard University, Cambridge.

FORD, JAMES A.
1954 The Type Concept Revisited. *American Anthropologist*, Vol. 56, No. 1, pp. 42–57. Menasha.

FREEMAN, L. G., JR. AND JAMES A. BROWN
1964 Statistical Analysis of Carter Ranch Pottery. In "Carter Ranch Site" by Paul S. Martin and others. *Fieldiana: Anthropology* (in press). Natural History Museum, Chicago.

GIFFORD, JAMES C.
1960 The Type-Variety Method of Ceramic Classification as an Indicator of Cultural Phenomena." *American Antiquity*, Vol. 25, No. 3, pp. 341–7. Salt Lake City.

HERSKOVITS, MELVILLE J.
1948 *Man and His Works*. Alfred A. Knopf, New York.

LINTON, RALPH
1936 *The Study of Man*. Appleton-Century-Crofts, New York.

LONGACRE, WILLIAM A.

1963 Archaeology as Anthropology: A Case Study. Unpublished Ph.D. dissertation, University of Chicago, Chicago.

McKERN, W. C.

1935 Certain Culture Classification Problems in Middle Western Archaeology. In "The Indianapolis Archaeological Conference," pp. 70–82, issued by the Committee on State Archaeological Surveys. *National Research Council, Circular* No. 17. Washington.

1939 The Midwestern Taxonomic Method as an Aid to Archaeological Culture Study. *American Antiquity*, Vol. 4, No. 4, pp. 301–13. Menasha.

REDFIELD, ROBERT

1941 *The Folk Culture of Yucatan.* University of Chicago Press, Chicago.

RITCHIE, WILLIAM A.

1955 Recent Discoveries Suggesting an Early Woodland Burial Cult in the Northeast. *New York State Museum and Science Service, Circular* No. 40. Albany.

ROUSE, IRVING

1939 Prehistory in Haiti: A Study in Method. *Yale University Publications in Anthropology*, No. 21. New Haven.

1955 On the Correlation of Phases of Culture. *American Anthropologist*, Vol. 57, No. 4, pp. 713–22. Menasha.

1960 The Classification of Artifacts in Archaeology. *American Antiquity*, Vol. 25, No. 3, pp. 313–23. Salt Lake City.

SEARS, WILLIAM H.

1960 Ceramic Systems and Eastern Archaeology. *American Antiquity*, Vol. 25, No. 3, pp. 324–9. Salt Lake City.

SMITH, WATSON

1962 Schools, Pots and Pottery. *American Anthropologist*, Vol. 64, No. 6, pp. 1165–78. Menasha.

SPAULDING, ALBERT C.

1957 Review of *Method and Theory in American Archaeology*, by Gordon W. Willey and Philip Phillips. *American Antiquity*, Vol. 23, No. 1, pp. 85–7. Salt Lake City.

TAYLOR, WALTER W.

1948 A Study of Archeology. *Memoirs of the American Anthropological Association*, No. 69. Menasha.

WHITE, LESLIE A.

1954 Review of "Culture: A Critical Review of Concepts and Definition," by A. L. Kroeber and Clyde Kluckhohn. *American Anthropologist*, Vol. 56, No. 3, pp. 461–8. Menasha.

1959 *The Evolution of Culture.* McGraw-Hill, New York.

WILLEY, GORDON R. AND PHILIP PHILLIPS

1958 *Method and Theory in American Archaeology.* University of Chicago Press, Chicago.

UNIVERSITY OF CHICAGO
Chicago, Illinois
October, 1964

AMERICAN ANTIQUITY

Volume 32	January, 1967	Number 1

SMUDGE PITS AND HIDE SMOKING: THE USE OF ANALOGY IN ARCHAEOLOGICAL REASONING

Lewis R. Binford

ABSTRACT

It is argued that as a scientist one does not justifiably employ analogies to ethnographic observations for the "interpretation" of archaeological data. Instead, analogies should be documented and used as the basis for offering a postulate as to the relationship between archaeological forms and their behavioral context in the past. Such a postulate should then serve as the foundation of a series of deductively drawn hypotheses which, on testing, can refute or tend to confirm the postulate offered. Analogy should serve to provoke new questions about order in the archaeological record and should serve to prompt more searching investigations rather than being viewed as a means for offering "interpretations" which then serve as the "data" for synthesis. This argument is made demonstratively through the presentation of formal data on a class of archaeological features, "smudge pits," and the documentation of their positive analogy with pits as facilities used in smoking hides.

THE PURPOSE of this paper is two-fold: (1) to present a discussion of analogy and provide an example of the use of analogy in archaeological reasoning, and (2) to present a functional argument regarding a particular formal class of archaeological feature. The justification for this type of presentation is a conviction that (a) archaeologists have generally employed analogy to ethnographic data as a means of "interpreting" archaeologically observed phenomena, rather than as a means for provoking new types of investigation into the order observable in archaeological data. It is the latter role for analogy which is hopefully exemplified; (b) archaeologists have neglected the formal analysis and investigation of relationships between classes of archaeological features. That this situation should be corrected can best be defended by the demonstration of provocative results obtained through the analysis of features.

Analogy is the term used to designate a particular type of inferential argument. Thus, in discussing analogy we may profitably consider the criteria employed in judging the relative strength of such an argument regardless of subject matter. Having explored the general characteristics of such arguments, we may turn to a consideration of *anthropological* arguments from analogy, attempting to isolate more general characteristics. Finally, using the conclusions from these two kinds of discussions, we shall offer certain programmatic suggestions which we believe could be profitably followed.

The term *analogy* is defined in Webster's Unabridged Dictionary with the following discussion:

A relation of likeness, between two things or of one thing to or with another, consisting in the resemblance not of the things themselves, but of two or more attributes, circumstances or effects . . .

Analogy is frequently used to denote similarity or essential resemblance but its specific meaning is a similarity of relations and in this consists the difference between the argument from example and that from analogy. In the former we argue from the mere similarity of two things, in the latter we argue from the similarity of their relations . . .

Biology — correspondence in function between organs of parts of different structures with different origins — distinguishing from homology . . .

Logic — form of inference in which it is reasoned that if two or more things agree with one another in one or more respects they will probably agree in yet other respects. The degree of probability will depend upon the number and importance of their known agreements (Neilson 1956: 94).

The crucial or distinctive characteristic common to all the definitions is that an analogy is not strictly a demonstration of formal similarities between entities; rather it is an inferential argument based on implied relationships between demonstrably similar entities. All those arguments which exhibit this form can be studied, and we can ask what characteristics are shared by those arguments which on investigation were verified. Three such characteristics have often been found to characterize successful arguments by analogy (these are paraphrased from Stebbing 1961: 243–56):

19

(1) *If the initial resemblances are such that the inferred property would account for the resemblances, then the conclusion is more likely to be true.* A good example might be the following argument: (1) A distinctive pattern of wear is observable on the unmodified end of an end scraper recovered from a Magdalenian site in western Europe. (2) The same pattern of wear is observable on the unmodified end of an end scraper hafted in a wooden haft collected from the Plains Indians of North America. (3) One infers the presence of a functionally similar haft during the period when the archaeologically recovered (Magdalenian) end scraper was in use. The inferred property, the haft, would account for the resemblances in wear observed on both end scrapers. In this case, where it can be said that the inferred relationship or property accounts for the known positive analogy, the positive analogy is said to consist of "important" properties. The term "important" refers to properties which, on the basis of other knowledge or conviction (in this case knowledge regarding the properties resulting from mechanical friction under certain conditions), the posited relationship is said to be justified.

The obvious corollary of the above generalization is that *if the initial resemblances are not such that the inferred property would account for the resemblances, then the conclusion is more likely to be false.* For example, almost any case of attempting to infer specific meaning from an abstract design on an artifact by analogy to a design of known context when there is no demonstrable continuity between the symbolic contexts of the two designs in question would be more likely to be false.

(2) *The more comprehensive the positive analogy and the less comprehensive the inferred properties, the more likely the conclusion is true.*

This criterion simply recognizes a major distinction between an argument from example and one from simple enumeration, where a large number of cases sharing limited numbers of attributes are cited, as opposed to an argument from analogy in which a large number of common attributes are cited and the number of cases may be quite small. The more numerous the similarities between analogs, the greater the probability that inferred properties are similar. The corollary of this is: *the more comprehensive the inferred properties, the less likely is the*

conclusion to be true. This guide to judging the strength of an argument from analogy rests with the common-sense notion that the more detailed the inference, the more specific must be one's ability to cite the determinants of the positive analogy.

These criteria are derived as arguments from example, since they can be viewed as generalizations from a large sample of arguments by analogy. The incidences of confirmation, as opposed to the incidences of disproof, are tabulated and studied for common properties. In short, these "criteria" are simply a statement of probable outcome generalized from a large sample of cases of reasoning by analogy. They are believed to be independent of the content of particular arguments.

In the examination of anthropological arguments from analogy, we are not concerned with the criteria which will allow us to judge the *form* of a particular argument from analogy as in the previous discussion. Instead, we are concerned with the *content* of the argument. The only guide which I can discover for aiding in this evaluation rests with our previous mention of the citation in an argument of "important" properties. We mean by this properties which, on the basis of other knowledge or conviction, are posited as relevant to the relationship argued. A common situation in which argument from analogy is offered by archaeologists is that in which similarities in form of artifacts are cited between archaeologically and ethnographically observed data, with the proposition that behavior observed in the ethnographic situation (unobserved in the archaeological situation) was also present in the past when the artifacts were in use.

Several persons have addressed themselves to a consideration of the problem of citing "important" properties in argument from analogy and have offered the following suggestions for establishing the conditions of relevance for archaeological arguments from analogy.

(1) Relevance can be established by demonstrating, or accepting as demonstrated, that there is a historical continuity between the archaeologically observed unit and the ethnographically cited society or social unit.

(2) In the absence of the above demonstrated justification, relevance could be justified by seeking analogies in cultures

which manipulate similar environments in similar ways (Ascher 1961).

While certainly not subject to question as such, one wonders at the utility of attempting to specify in the form of suggestions for the "new analogy" all those conditions under which one would expect to find functional linkages between cultural elements. For only with such an exhaustive listing of contemporary anthropological theory and knowledge could one hope to enumerate all of the conditions of relevance which might arise in various anthropological arguments from analogy. Stating this point another way, the only means open to anthropologists attempting to evaluate by inspection any given argument by analogy is in terms of the degree to which the inferred property could be expected to vary concomitantly with the cited features in the positive analogy. Such an evaluation must therefore be made on the basis of our current understanding of the form, structure, and functioning of cultural systems. It is my hope that contemporary understanding goes far beyond the "canon for the selection of analogs" recently advanced (Ascher 1961).

We now turn to the crucial question of the function of arguments from analogy in the broader field of archaeological reasoning. I have chosen to offer one example of such an argument and to attempt an analysis of its form and structural position in a broader logical system of analytical method. Hopefully by such a procedure the formal, functional, and structural characteristics of arguments from analogy in archaeological analytical method will be made explicit.

Previous archaeological reports have occasionally cited the occurrence of small "caches" of carbonized corncobs (Cole 1951: 34, 40); yet the specific functions of these small pits have not been previously considered analytically nor has there been any formal analysis of the characteristics common to a number of samples of these "corncob caches." Recent archaeological investigations in the Carlyle Reservoir of south-central Illinois resulted in the excavation of a number of these caches (Binford, Schoenwetter, and Fowler 1964). The recognized formal homogeneity of these features prompted their analysis and systematic description and justification as a distinctive class of feature which, in all probability, had a single function in the activities of the extinct societies represented.

Our procedure here will be: (1) provide a summary of the formal characteristics of this class of cultural feature; (2) document and evaluate the analogy which is demonstrable between this class of feature and certain facilities described ethnographically; (3) offer a postulate as to the function of the archaeological features; (4) develop certain deductively drawn hypotheses that could be investigated to test the probability of the postulates; and (5) cite the procedure employed as an example of a role for analogy in archaeological reasoning which is not believed to be commonly employed among practicing archaeologists.

FORM OF THE FEATURES

The particular cultural features under discussion are best known from the Toothsome site, Clinton County, Illinois, where a total of 15 such features were excavated and detailed observations were made (Binford, Schoenwetter, and Fowler 1964). Since this sample constitutes the best available data, I will duplicate here the original description of this sample of 15 features.

The features exhibited so little internal formal variability that there is little doubt that they represent a single type of feature and a single activity. The contents of the pit are always primary and are unaltered by subsequent cultural activity. In addition, the size, shape, and contents of each feature are almost identical to all others included in this category.

Size. These pits are slightly oval, having a mean length of 30.27 cm. and a mean width of 27.40 cm. They extend below the present surface to a mean depth of 33.53 cm.

Shape. All are slightly oval and are generally straight-sided, with essentially flat bottoms.

ELEMENTS OF THE FEATURE

(a) Grayish loam soil.
(b) Charred and carbonized corncobs.
(c) Charred and carbonized twigs (possibly corn stalks).
(d) Charred and carbonized bark of an as yet unidentified tree.
(e) Charred vegetable material, possibly from other as yet unidentified plants.
(f) Occasionally a minor oxidation of soil near the mouth of the pit.

DISTRIBUTION OF THE ELEMENTS

The very bottom of the pit is filled with the charred material for a variable depth of from 7 cm. to within 8 cm. of the mouth of the feature. The charred twigs are generally curled around in the bottom of the pit with the cobs nested in the center. The upper part may be partially filled with the grayish loam soil which was the characteristic soil on the surface of the site. The latter would have *no* included charred material.

GENERAL OBSERVATIONS

The invariable presence of the grayish loam soil in the upper fill demonstrates intentional covering of the pit contents, rather than an accumulative filling with midden and surface debris.

Distribution of these features on the site. The pits are distributed peripherally around a small Mississippian farmstead composed of two house structures and one storage structure. In addition to these buildings, the site is internally differentiated into several activity areas, which include outdoor cooking areas and a dump. There is no obvious tendency for these features to cluster; they appear rather well dispersed in a peripheral fashion around the boundary of the site.

Discussion. In the original report on these features it was suggested that they were probably small "smudge pits," since the conditions of combustion which would have resulted in the carbonization of the recovered plant materials would certainly have produced vast quantities of smoke. It was further speculated whether these obvious sources of smoke might have been employed in the control of mosquitoes, which in the experience of the excavators, had constituted a real pest during the summer months.

Possible occurrence at other locations. In addition to the occurrence of these features at the Toothsome site, pits of identical form were observed at a slightly earlier Mississippian farmstead site at the Sandy Tip site in the Carlyle Reservoir (Binford 1964). Later investigations at the Texas #1 site, also in the Carlyle Reservoir, exposed nine additional features of this type (Morrell 1965). The small size of the feature led the investigator to interpret eight of them as postmolds.

Features 22, 23, 26, and 27; small pits or postmolds filled with charred corncobs. Average diameter .21

meters. A total of nine cob concentrations were located within Unit No. 3, 8 of which appear to have been postmolds. The cobs are arranged generally in a crescent on the outer edges of the molds, possibly indicating the use of cobs for post tamping and support (Morrell 1965: 24–7).

Cutler (1963) suggests that the cobs were broken before they were deposited and probably before they were carbonized. Cutler further suggests that the cobs do not represent a cache of cobs discarded after shelling. Radiocarbon dates were obtained from Features 22 and 23; these are A.D. 1030 ± 85 (GX-0364) and A.D. 1090 ± 100 (GX-0365) respectively (Morrell 1965: 24–7).

Small features characterized by the clustering of carbonized corncobs were recently reported from the Lloyd Village site in the American Bottoms near East Saint Louis, Illinois (Hall and Vogel 1963: 25–6), and similar features were noted on the nearby Cahokia site (Cutler 1963: 16).

The Kincaid site on the Ohio River in southern Illinois, extensively investigated during the 1930's, yielded features which appear to be identical to those described from the Toothsome site. It is interesting that, although they were observed at three different locations on the site (Mx^v1D Section I and East Section; Mx^v1c), all were in the village area, while none was reported from the mounds so intensively investigated on the site (Cole and others 1951: 34, 40, 53, Fig. 3).

Quimby (1957: 105) noted the occurrence of "a deposit of fragmentary corncobs that had been burned" in the village deposits under Mounds 1 and 2 at the Bayou Goula site, which is interpreted by Quimby as the remains of a historically known group, closely related to the Natchez, occupying the location between 1700 and 1739.

The archaeological feature of this type believed to be the earliest thus far known is reported from the Williams site, Gordon County, Georgia. This find is described as follows:

The most important find ... was Feature 7. This was a group of 30 to 40 burnt corn cobs in an area about eight inches in diameter and four inches in depth .... Also included mixed in with the cobs was ash, wood, cane and one half of a shelled acorn. No pit was discernible since the group was in the dark brown sand. The cobs were oriented in every conceivable direction and it appears as if the whole unit was thrown into a pit .... At 9-Wd-L ... a group of cobs were found which exhibited evidence of being deposited during a corn planting ceremony. These differed from the Williams Site specimens in being placed in four orderly rows in a specially prepared pit . . . . The Williams Site cache does not give evidence for or against a corn ceremony. However, the cobs were not badly broken up and some sort of a ceremony would be expected, whether at planting, harvesting, or in between, in a culture concerned with the success of a corn crop. There are many instances of corn ceremonialism in the eastern United States, but they are mainly found in a Mississippian or historical context (Morse and Morse 1960: 88).

The Williams site find has been radiocarbon dated at A.D. 470 ± 75 (M-1107, Crane and Griffin 1963: 239).

Carbonized corncobs were recovered in two general contexts at the George C. Davis site, Cherokee County, Texas (Newell and Krieger 1949: 248–9). Five cases of recovered corncobs are reported from "postmolds" of Structures 31, 8, and 6 respectively, all of which are buildings not constructed on mounds. Three finds were of "caches" of quantities of carbonized cobs similar to those features described from the Toothsome site. Recent radiocarbon dating suggests that these features date at A.D. 1307 ± 150 (M-1186), a period somewhat later than originally proposed (Griffin and Yarnell 1963).

Summarizing our findings, one point is strikingly clear: the geographical distribution of these features is spotty. On sites from the same general geographical provinces, where they are documented, and where one would expect them to have been reported had they been present, there is no suggestion that they were observed. For example, they are absent from sites in the Chickamauga Lake section of the Tennessee River (Lewis and Kneberg 1946); similarly they are unreported from the Norris Basin and the Pickwick Basins of the Tennessee drainage (Webb and DeJarnette 1942; Webb 1938). Moreover, they are not present at the Bessemer site in north-central Alabama (DeJarnette and Wimberly 1941), nor at the Rood's Landing site in Stewart County, Georgia (Caldwell 1955), nor at the Macon Group (Kelly 1938) at Macon Georgia. The Gordon site also appears to lack these features (Myre 1928). This list of eastern sites apparently lacking the "corncob" features could be greatly expanded. On the other hand, a search of the literature for the Upper Illinois valley and prairie fringe areas as well as for the Great Plains, the Eastern coastal region, the Upper Ohio valley, and the Great Lakes regions failed to yield a single incidence of the "corncob pit." This latter finding

is based on my investigation of the context of all the reported incidences of corn which were recently inventoried by Yarnell (1964). In all cases where the context of finds of corn could be determined, it was generally as charred kernels, and, when cobs were reported, they were generally single or in small numbers occurring in the midden fill of recognizable cooking or storage pits.

These investigations suggest that the smudge pits are a feature characteristic of the societies of the Middle and Lower Mississippi River area, with extensions into the Georgia-Creek area to the east and the Texas-Caddo area to the west. The spotty distribution and the lack of data from numbers of sites in this area, however, further suggest that this feature is probably restricted in use to certain limited kinds of activities. This inference is further supported by the documented cases being limited to associations with village house-remains and never with public buildings. Although the functional specificity of the feature may be a major contributor to the spotty distribution of documented examples, my search of the literature made it painfully obvious that archaeologists have neglected the analysis and systematic description of cultural features, which makes it impossible to assess the degree to which the spotty distribution is a function of events in the past or of the data-collecting techniques and analytical methods employed by archaeologists.

The earliest documented example is from the Williams site in northwest Georgia, A.D. 470 ± 75 (M-1107) where such an early date stands as a unique case. All of the other known examples (if one accepts the revised dating of the George C. Davis site corn) are relatively late, post-dating A.D. 1000. These data suggest that we could reasonably expect the activity in the context of which these features were used to have been practiced by the historically documented groups in the "agricultural east."

There is a variety of functional interpretation offered by investigators who observed these features. At Kincaid they were interpreted as "caches" (Cole and others 1951: 156) in spite of the fact that none of the corncobs had kernels attached. Morse and Morse (1960: 88) entertain the probability of a "ceremonial" function for the feature. At both the George C. Davis site (Newell and Krieger 1949: 248–9) and the Texas site (Morrell 1965) they were interpreted as postmolds, presumably because of their small size. The author (Binford, Schoen-wetter, and Fowler 1964) offered the interpretation of a smudge pit, but at that time he could only suggest that the smudge was produced as a means of controlling mosquitoes!

In summary, smudge pits are a class of archaeological features sharing (a) small size, (b) contents composed diagnostically of carbonized corncobs, lacking kernels, and (c) contents exhibiting a primary depositional context. These features are documented from a number of Mississippian sites in the southern Illinois area as well as from sites in the lower reaches of the Mississippi Valley, northern Georgia, and eastern Texas. The context in which the features occur at these sites is invariably that of house areas, as opposed to areas of public buildings, and, in the case of the known farmstead, they are distributed peripherally around the centers of activity within the site. These features are dated as early as A.D. 470; however, the majority are referable to a post-A.D. 1000 time period.

Previous attempts at "interpretation" have shown considerable originality, but all must be considered as conjecture.

RELEVANT ETHNOGRAPHIC OBSERVATIONS

The distinctive form of these features, together with their necessarily limited possible range of uses (all of which must have involved the production of quantities of smoke), made an optimistic search for relevant ethnographic descriptions and references realistic and potentially profitable. The following descriptions from ethnographic accounts were located.

I. *Descriptions of the process of smoking hides as observed among the Southeastern Indians.*

A. *The Natchez, 1700–1750*

According to Swanton (1911: 64), Dumont in 1753 said:

They first dig a hole in the earth about 2 feet deep, with a diameter of six inches at the top and a little less toward the bottom. They fill this hole with cow dung, rotted wood, and maize ears and place it over two rods in the shape of a cross, the four ends of which are slanted in the earth so as to form a kind of cradle on which they stretch the skin they wish to tan. They then set fire to the combustible substance in the hole and fasten the skin down all around by means of many little pegs driven into the ground. Then they cover it with earth over and along the edges, so as to keep in the smoke. The materials in the hole becoming consumed without throwing out the flame, the thick smoke that comes out of it, especially owing to the lack of any exit

... fastens itself to the skin which it smoke-dries and dyes a yellow color.

B. *The Creek, 1900–1950*

... next, they scooped a hole in the ground, built a fire in it, and put corncobs upon this so that a thick smoke was produced with little flame. The hide was fastened down over this pit with the other surface down and left until it was smoked yellow (Swanton 1946: 445).

C. *The Choctaw, 1900–1950*

If the skins are to be smoked, a process that renders them more durable, a hole a foot or more in depth is dug in which a fire is kept until a bed of hot ashes accumulates. On this are put pieces of rotten oak, no other wood being used for this purpose, these are not permitted to blaze, as the more smoke that arises the better is it for the skins. These already tanned soft and white and perfectly dry, are stretched over the hole and allowed to remain in the smoke an hour or more (Bushnell 1909: 11–12).

D. *The Seminole, 1900–1950*

Usually, however, the leather is finished by smoking. The skin is sewed up in a bag-like form and suspended, bottom up from an inclined stick. The edges are pegged down about a small hole in which a smouldering fire burns. The smoke and fumes are allowed to impregnate the hide thoroughly, and then the tanning is completed.... (Skinner 1913: 72–3).

II. *Description of the process of smoking hides as observed among the Plains Tribes.*

A. *The Omaha, 1850–1900*

Skins to be used in making moccasins were browned by smoke (Fletcher and La Flesche 1911: 345).

B. *The Dacotah (Sioux), 1800–1850*

If after all this working, the skin is hairy or stiff, it is drawn over a cord as large as a finger, for some time, as hard as they can pull, which softens it much: sometimes this is the last process, except smoking. This is done by digging a hole in the ground about a foot deep, putting in a little fire and some rotten wood, when the skin is sewed into a bag and hung over the smoke: in ten minutes the skin is ready for use (Schoolcraft 1856: 61).

C. *The Blackfoot, 1850–1900*

The color and finish were imparted by smoking. The skins were spread over a frame similar to that of a sweat house, a hole was dug underneath and a smouldering fire maintained with sage or rotten wood (Wissler 1910: 65).

D. *The Crow, 1800–1850*

The greater part of these skins, however, go through still another operation afterwards, which gives them a greater value and renders them much more serviceable — that is, the process of smoking. For this, a small hole is dug in the ground and a fire is built in it with rotten wood, which will produce a great quantity of smoke without much blaze; and several small poles of the proper length stuck in the ground around it and drawn and fastened together at the top, around which the skin is wrapped in form of a tent, and generally sewed together at the edges to secure the smoke within it, within this the skins to be smoked are placed, and in this condition the tent will stand a day or so, enclosing the heated smoke (Catlin 1880: 52).

E. *The Arapaho, 1900–1939*

... After it was as soft as she wanted it she dug a hole, about 20 inches deep and about 15 inches in diameter, and built a smudge in it, using either fine chips of wood or bark of cottonwood. She then sewed up the hide to make a sack of it with one end open. She placed this sack over a tipi-shaped framework made of saplings and set this over the smudge. She watched the smudge carefully so there would be no blaze, but only smoke. At the closed end of the sack she had sewed a strip of buckskin with which she tied the sack to the top of the saplings. This held the hide in place. When one side of the hide was sufficiently smoked, the sack was turned inside out and again smoked, thus giving both sides a tan (Hilger 1952: 184).

III. *Descriptions of the process of smoking hides as observed among the Indians of the Great Lakes region.*

A. *Iroquois — General, 1850–1860*

... a smoke is made, and the skin placed over it in such a manner as to inclose it entirely. Each side is smoked in this manner until the pores are closed, and the skin has become thoroughly toughened with its color changed from white to a kind of brown (Morgan 1901: 13).

B. *Iroquois — Specifically the Seneca, 1800–1890*

A hole 18 inches in diameter was then made in the ground and the skin suspended above it on upright sticks and smoked until the desired color is produced, by burning rotten wood beneath. The skin was then ready for use (Mason 1891: 573).

C. *Ojibwa, 1930–1940*

After the hide was dry the informant removed it from the stretcher, laid it on the ground folding it on head-to-tail line, turned both edges together, and beginning with head end fastened them together by means of clothespins. This made a nearly airtight compartment. In former days edges were sewed together tightly with basswood fiber. The head end of the hide was next fastened to the branch of a tree; the tail end placed so it encircled the rim of a pail of smudge. Two granddaughters ... prepared the smudge by placing bits of birchbark on burning embers fetched from the kitchen stove and packing the remainder of the pail with white pine and Norway cones. Punk was sometimes used in place of cones since it was less inflammable. Jack pine cones were not used. They give an unsatisfactory color.

The worker swung the pail back and forth several times to enhance the smudge and then placed it under the hide, holding it there carefully as to permit the hide to fill with smoke.... When it was sufficiently tanned, she loosened the clothespins, turned and folded the edges and again pinned them, she then tanned the reverse side. Smoking not only gave color to hides but preserved them from moths (Hilger 1951: 131–2).

D. *Menomini, 1900–1920*

A hole about a foot wide and six inches deep is dug in the earth in a locality sheltered from the wind, and a slow glowing, smoky fire is made in the bottom of the pit with dead branches, punk, or even dry corn cobs. Over this the inverted bag is suspended and pegged down about the base (Skinner 1921: 228).

It is readily observable that two of the documented incidences of the use of corncobs as fuel for smoking hides fall within the distribution as known archaeologically for corncob-filled smudge pits. The single exception, the Menominee, are described as making use of corncobs in the 1920's. It seems reasonable to suggest this might be a relatively recent practice, related to the reservation period rather than to the period of aboriginal adjustment to the northwestern Great Lakes region. This suggestion is further credited by the fact that in all the cases of ethnographic documentation which fall outside of the area of archaeologically known smudge pit distribution, with a single exception, the Choctaw, fuels other than corncobs are cited as being used. This supports the archaeological observations of the absence of corncob-filled smudge pits in the Plains, Great Lakes, and northern Ohio valley. In short, the ethnographic and archaeological distributions of the use of corncobs as fuel in smudge pits are strikingly similar, in spite of obvious lacks in the coverage from both sources.

The correspondence in *form* of smudge pits as known archaeologically and of hide-smoking smudge pits as described ethnographically is essentially perfect. Table 1 presents in summary the comparative information regarding the form of the facilities as known from archaeological and ethnographic sources.

On the basis of (a) the convincing correspondence between the formal attributes of smudge pits as known archaeologically and smudge pits used in smoking hides as known ethnographically, (b) the strong positive analogy between the distribution of smudge pits in which corncobs were used as fuel and the use of corncobs as fuel for smoking hides as docu-

TABLE 1. SMUDGE PIT ATTRIBUTES

Class of attributes	Archaeologically observed attributes		Ethnographically described attributes

1. *Size:* Relatively small, shallow excavations in the ground when the facility is a pit.

	Mean	Range	
Length	30.27 cm.	23.0–42.0 cm.	The cited sizes range from 15.24–30.48 cm.
Width	27.40 cm.	20.2–31.0 cm.	(6″–12″) in diameter and 15.24–60.96 cm.
Depth	33.53 cm.	25.0–37.1 cm.	in depth.

2. *Contents:* Soft, porous, poorly combustible organic materials. Corncobs, bark, twigs, and possibly cornstalks.

Corncobs, bark, twigs, (dead branches), rotten wood, dung, pine cones, and sage.

3. *Treatment of contents*

Contents burned in a reducing atmosphere resulting in the carbonization of the fuels.

Contents burned in a reducing atmosphere resulting in the production of quantities of smoke.

4. *Final condition of the facility*

The facility was abandoned with no disturbance of the carbonized fuels; nothing was removed from the pit, showing that it did not contain the fuels and the items being processed as in the case of roasting pits, fire pits, etc. The archaeological remains of the pit exhibit a primary fill, and secondary fill if present is superimposed.

All the descriptions cite the suspension of the hides over the smudge pit. The items being processed are not contained in the facility with the fuels. Completion of the smoking process and the removal of the hides for use does not result in a disturbance of the contents of the smudge pit.

---

mented ethnographically, and (c) the relatively late archaeological documentation for the use of smudge pits, which would make continuity between the archaeological and ethnographic periods reasonable, we postulate that the archaeologically-known features described were in fact facilities employed in the task of smoking hides by the former occupants of the archaeological sites on which they were found.

The procedure which should be followed in refuting or increasing the probability of the validity of the proposition would be as follows:

(1) Determine if there are any spatial correlates of the activity of smoking hides; in other words, determine if the activity was regularly conducted in any particular location. If so, determine whether or not the smudge pits exhibit such a distribution.

(2) Determine if there are any temporal correlates of the activity of smoking hides; was the activity regularly conducted at any particular period of the annual cycle? If so, determine whether or not the smudge pits exhibit such an association with respect to relevant seasonally variable phenomena.

(3) Determine if there are any formal correlates of the activity with respect to other imple-

ments or facilities which were employed as parts of a set which also included hide-smoking pits. Was hide smoking normally conducted at the same place and at approximately the same time as the manufacture of clothing from the hides? If so, then there should be demonstrable concomitant variation between the incidence of smudge pits and implements used in clothing manufacture, such as needles.

(4) Determine if there are any other activities which employed facilities which shared the same formal attributes as observed in hide-smoking pits. If so, then the specific postulate could be refuted, but a more general one could be stated which could then be tested along the dimensions of time, space, and form.

The following observations are made in the hope that they are pertinent to the formulation of systematic hypotheses:

(a) In all the ethnographic cases cited the smoking of hides was women's work; therefore, we would expect stylistic variation in smudge pits to vary directly with stylistic variation in other female-produced items such as ceramics.

(b) In all the ethnographic cases cited, when temporal data were given, hide smoking was a spring and summer activity conducted in the "base camp" after the major hunting season was concluded and before the winter hunts were begun. We therefore offer the following hypothesis: Smudge pits should occur almost exclusively in "base camps" occupied during the period of the year when hunting activity was at a minimum.

(c) In many cases there were indications in the ethnographic literature that hide smoking and the related manufacture of clothing from smoked hides were activities which would be more frequently performed by individuals possessing recognized skills in these tasks. Therefore, the incidence of smudge pits might be expected to vary independently of the number of persons occupying the appropriate site for any given unit of time. In short, they would be expected to vary independently of such direct measures of the number and duration of occupants as cooking-fires and sleeping facilities.

Aside from these interesting and potentially informative avenues for future research, I think it is necessary to point out another and as yet unmentioned potential source of additional understanding; namely, that the survey of ethnographic literature demonstrated that the practice of smoking hides, particularly deer hides, for use in the manufacture of moccasins, shirts, and leggings, was a practice common to most, if not all, of North America. The major characteristic which appeared to vary from region to region was the fuel used in the smudge pits, as well as the idiosyncracies of construction for suspension of hides over the smudge pit. Our investigations have been limited to the citation of archaeological remains in which corncobs were the fuel. An acquaintance with the general range of size of the feature and with the depth of it can be extremely beneficial. The size appears to be limited by the circumference of a deer skin when sewn into a "bag"; the depth seems to be limited by two general considerations: (a) deep enough to provide an oxygen-starved environment; (b) shallow enough to contain only a limited amount of fuel. This knowledge, along with an acquaintance with the generic class of fuel, and the probability that the contents would not be disturbed (resulting in the archaeological recovery of fairly complete carbonized fragments of soft spongy fuels), enables the recall of numerous examples of features observed on sites from the east coast, the Great Lakes, and the pre-Mississippian occupa-

tions in central Illinois which were almost certainly smudge pits in which fuels other than corncobs had been burned.

Our investigations have resulted in the recognition of a generic class of facility which can be expected to vary regionally with respect to the specifics of its contents. This recognition could aid in the documentation of seasonally variable activities in the areas of less aboriginal sedentism, such as the Great Lakes.

The final consideration to be taken up is the degree to which this study can be cited as an example of the use of analogy in archaeological argument and its pertinence to general statements regarding the role of analogy in archaeological reasoning.

The logical steps followed in this argument were as follows:

A. *The Analogy*

(1) The recognition and demonstration of a positive formal analogy between a class of archaeologically observed phenomena and a class of ethnographically observed phenomena.

(2) A consideration of the positive analogy between the spatial distribution of the facility as documented archaeologically and ethnographically, and the observation that, although poorly documented, the known distributions show a strong positive analogy.

(3) A consideration of the degree to which it would be reasonable to expect a continuity between the archaeologically and ethnographically known cases; for example, the dating of the archaeologically known materials as reasonably viewed as cases of historical priority to the ethnographic data.

B. *The Postulate*

(1) The behavioral context of the use of the archaeologically known features was the same as that described ethnographically for the analogous facilities.

C. *The development of testable hypotheses in a deductive framework given the postulate offered*

(1) An examination of the ethnographic "context" of the activity for correlated formal characteristics which could be directly observed or studied archaeologically.

(2) Given the postulate set forth in B (1) above and the knowledge of the formal, spatial, and temporal correlates of the activity designated in the postulate, the specification of a number of hypotheses as to the predicted mode of variation expected between the archaeologically observed analog and other archaeologically observable phenomena as specified by the studies of C (1) above.

(3) The testing of the stated hypotheses and the refutation, refinement, or verification in probabilistic terms of the truth of the stated postulate.

D. Finally this particular procedure should lead the investigator into the recognition of previously unrecognized relationships as suggested in C (1): the explanation of previously unexplained variation in archaeological data as the outcome of (C) and, as in the case of this particular example, the recognition of a generic class of phenomena definable by certain general formal characteristics where previously only a restricted class was recognized, isolated by the common occurrence of specific formal similarities (for example, charred corncobs).

CONCLUSIONS

The procedure discussed here is appropriate in the context of a positivistic philosophy of anthropology and archaeology. It denies categorically the assertion of antipositivists that the final judgment of archaeological reconstruction must be based on an appraisal of the professional competence of the archaeologist (Thompson 1956: 331). The final judgment of the archaeological reconstruction presented here must rest with testing through subsidiary hypotheses drawn deductively. Questions were also raised concerning the argument made by Robert Ascher (1961) that by following certain of his suggestions for "placing analogy on a firmer foundation" we could in any way directly increase our knowledge of archaeologically documented societies. The arguments presented by Ascher (1961), if followed, could at best serve to increase our understanding of archaeological observations in terms of ethnographically described situations. The archaeologist would be performing a role analogous to that of a historical critic who attempts to translate data of

the past into the context of relatively contemporary or culturally prescribed experience. It is maintained here that as anthropologists we have a task quite different; we seek to explain cultural differences and similarities. We approach our task by developing methods and procedures that will permit us to demonstrate order in our data. It is assumed that the demonstration of order implies a set of systematic relationships among cultural phenomena that existed in the past. The understanding of the operation of systems rests in the measurement of concomitant variation between various classes of ordered phenomena and the eventual statement of general laws of cultural variability.

The role of analogy in this process has hopefully been demonstrated in this particular example. Analogy serves to provoke certain types of questions which can, on investigation, lead to the recognition of more comprehensive ranges of order in the archaeological data. In short, we ask questions about the relationships between types of archaeologically observable phenomena that had possibly not been placed in juxtaposition or viewed as orderly. In doing so we can develop a common "explanation" for observed variability in a number of formally independent classes of archaeological data, and thereby we can approach more closely the isolation of systematic variables which operated in the past. It should be pointed out that these gains may obtain regardless of whether the original analogy led to a correct postulate. In short, I do not view interpretations, or syntheses of interpretations as an end product of our investigations; on the contrary, we should be seeking generalizations regarding the operation of cultural systems and their evolution — something which has not been described ethnographically nor thus far achieved through the observation and analysis of contemporary events.

This paper was presented at the 31st Annual Meeting of the Society for American Archaeology, Reno, Nevada, 1966.

ASCHER, ROBERT
    1961 Analogy in Archaeological Interpretation. *Southwestern Journal of Anthropology*, Vol. 17, pp. 317–25. Albuquerque.

BINFORD, LEWIS R.
    1964 The Sandy Tip Site; Carlyle Reservoir. Manuscript at University of California, Los Angeles.

Binford, Lewis R., James Schoenwetter, and
M. L. Fowler
    1964 Archaeological Investigations in the Carlyle
    Reservoir. *Southern Illinois University Museum,
    Archaeological Salvage Report* No. 17, pp. 1–117.
    Carbondale.

Bushnell, David I., Jr.
    1909 The Choctaw of Bayou Lacomb, St. Tammany
    Parish, Louisiana. *Bureau of American Ethnology, Bulletin* 48. Washington.

Caldwell, Joseph R.
    1955 Investigations at Rood's Landing, Stewart Co.,
    Georgia. *Early Georgia*, Vol. 2, No. 1, pp. 22–49.
    Calhoun.

Catlin, George
    1880 *North American Indians*, Vol. 1, p. 52. Egyptian Hall, Piccadilly, London.

Cole, Fay-Cooper and others
    1951 *Kincaid, A Prehistoric Illinois Metropolis*. University of Chicago Press, Chicago.

Crane, H. R. and J. B. Griffin
    1963 University of Michigan Radiocarbon Dates
    VIII. *Radiocarbon*, Vol. 5, pp. 228–53. New
    Haven.

Cutler, Hugh C.
    1963 Identification of Plant Remains. In *Second
    Annual Report: American Bottoms Archaeology*,
    edited by Melvin L. Fowler, pp. 16–18. Illinois
    Archaeological Survey, Urbana.

DeJarnette, David L. and Steve B. Wimberly
    1941 The Bessemer Site. Excavation of Three
    Mounds and Surrounding Village Areas near
    Bessemer, Alabama. *Geological Survey of Alabama, Museum Paper* 17. University of Alabama, University.

Fletcher, Alice C. and Francis LaFlesche
    1911 The Omaha Tribe. *Twenty-seventh Annual
    Report of the Bureau of American Ethnology*,
    pp. 15–655. Washington.

Griffin, James B. and Richard A. Yarnell
    1963 A New Radiocarbon Date on Corn from the
    Davis Site, Cherokee County, Texas. *American
    Antiquity*, Vol. 28, No. 3, pp. 396–7. Salt Lake
    City.

Hall, Robert L. and Joseph O. Vogel
    1963 Illinois State Museum Projects. In *Second
    Annual Report: American Bottoms Archaeology*, edited by Melvin L. Fowler, pp. 24–31.
    Illinois Archaeological Survey, Urbana.

Hilger, Sister M. Inez
    1951 Chippewa Child Life and its Cultural Background. *Bureau of American Ethnology, Bulletin* 146. Washington.
    1952 Arapaho Child Life and Its Cultural Background. *Bureau of American Ethnology, Bulletin* 148. Washington.

Kelly, A. R.
    1938 A Preliminary Report on Archaeological Explorations at Macon, Georgia. *Bureau of American Ethnology, Bulletin* 119, pp. 1–68. Washington.

Lewis, Thomas M. N. and Madeline Kneberg
    1946 *Hiwassee Island, an Archaeological Account of
    Four Tennessee Indian Peoples*. University of
    Tennessee Press, Knoxville.

Mason, Otis T.
    1891 Aboriginal Skin Dressing; A Study Based on
    Material in the U.S. National Museum. *Report
    of the National Museum*, 1888–1889, pp. 553–89. Smithsonian Institution, Washington.

Morgan, Lewis H.
    1901 *League of the Ho-De-No-Sau-Nee or Iroquois*,
    Vol. 2, p. 13. Dodd, Mead and Company, New
    York.

Morrell, L. Ross
    1965 The Texas Site, Carlyle Reservoir. *Southern
    Illinois University Museum, Archaeological Salvage Report* No. 23. Carbondale.

Morse, Dan and Phyllis Morse
    1960 A Preliminary Report on 9-Go-507: The Williams Site, Gordon County, Georgia. *The Florida Anthropologist*, Vol. 8, No. 4, pp. 81–91.
    Gainesville.

Myre, William Edward
    1928 Two Prehistoric Villages in Middle Tennessee.
    *Forty-first Annual Report of the Bureau of
    American Ethnology*, pp. 485–626. Washington.

Neilson, W. A. (editor)
    1956 *Websters New International Dictionary of the
    English Language* (Second Edition, Unabridged).
    G. C. Merriam Co., Springfield.

Newell, H. Perry and Alex D. Krieger
    1949 The George C. Davis Site, Cherokee County,
    Texas. *Memoirs of the Society for American
    Archaeology*, No. 5. Menasha.

Quimby, George I.
    1957 The Bayou Goula Site, Iberville Parish, Louisiana. *Fieldiana: Anthropology*, Vol. 47, No. 2,
    pp. 91–170. Chicago Natural History Museum,
    Chicago.

Schoolcraft, H. R.
    1856 *Indian Tribes of the United States*, Pt. IV, p.
    61. J. B. Lippincott and Company, Philadelphia.

Skinner, Alanson
    1913 Notes on the Florida Seminole. *American Anthropologist*, n.s., Vol. 15, pp. 63–77. New York.
    1921 Material Culture of the Menomini. *Indian
    Notes and Monographs, Miscellaneous* No. 20,
    edited by F. W. Hodge, p. 228. Museum of the
    American Indian, Heye Foundation, New York.

Stebbing, L. Susan
    1961 *A Modern Introduction to Logic*. Harper
    Torchbooks Edition, Harper and Brothers, New
    York.

Swanton, John R.
    1911 Indian Tribes of the Lower Mississippi Valley
    and Adjacent Coast of the Gulf of Mexico.
    Bureau of American Ethnology, Bulletin 43.
    Washington.
    1946 The Indians of the Southeastern United States.
    Bureau of American Ethnology, Bulletin 137.
    Washington.

THOMPSON, RAYMOND H.
    1956 The Subjective Element in Archaeological In-
        ference. *Southwestern Journal of Anthropology*,
        Vol. 12, No. 3, pp. 327–32. Albuquerque.

WEBB, WILLIAM
    1938 An Archaeological Survey of the Norris Basin
        in Eastern Tennessee. *Bureau of American
        Ethnology, Bulletin* 118. Washington.

WEBB, WILLIAM AND DAVID DEJARNETTE
    1942 An Archaeological Survey of Pickwick Basin
        in the Adjacent Portions of the States of Ala-
        bama, Mississippi and Tennessee. *Bureau of
        American Ethnology, Bulletin* 129. Washington.

WISSLER, CLARK
    1910 Material Culture of the Blackfoot Indians. *An-
        thropological Papers of the American Museum
        of Natural History*, Vol. V., Pt. 1. New York.

YARNELL, RICHARD ASA
    1964 Aboriginal Relationships between Culture and
        Plant Life in the Upper Great Lakes Region.
        *Anthropological Papers, Museum of Anthro-
        pology*, No. 23. University of Michigan, Ann
        Arbor.

UNIVERSITY OF CALIFORNIA
Santa Barbara, California
July, 1966

THE NATURE OF ARCHAEOLOGICAL EXPLANATION

JOHN M. FRITZ
FRED T. PLOG

ABSTRACT

We argue that the development and use of law-like statements by archaeologists to explain characteristics of the archaeological record has been and should continue to be one of the most important goals of archaeological research. Using a model for explanation developed by the philosophers of science, Carl Hempel and Paul Oppenheim, we indicate the role of such statements in archaeological classification. However, in archaeology such statements are found to be implicit, untested, and extremely general in referent.

We further argue that the testing of potential laws requires a shift from an inductive procedure, or from one in which undirected data collection forms the first and the "abstraction" of laws from data forms the last research step, to a deductive procedure in which the explicit formulation of potential laws and their empirical consequences precedes and directs the collection of data.

Department of Anthropology
University of California, Santa Cruz

Department of Anthropology
University of California, Los Angeles
December, 1969

ALL ARCHAEOLOGISTS employ laws in their research. Those of us who are interested in processual analysis have made the formulation and testing of laws our goal. Other archaeologists, those more interested in explicating prehistory or in reconstructing past lifeways, employ laws whenever inferences about the past are used in interpreting data excavated in the present. One measure of the attainment of a science is the degree to which laws are *explicitly* formulated, *explicitly* tested, and *explicitly* used.

We argue that the acquisition and employment of laws necessitates two distinct but related scientific methods. These have been described and defined by the philosophers of science belonging to the logical positivist school (Hempel and Oppenheim 1948; Nagel 1961; Hempel 1966). Our positivist view contrasts with the empiricist view held implicitly by many archaeologists. In one of the rare discussions of the logic of archaeological inquiry, Raymond H. Thompson explicitly formulated this position. He asserts, for example, that "deductive methods of formal logic are not appropriate to the interpretation of empirical data of a discipline like archaeology" (1958:1). We argue that deduction and deductive methods are not only appropriate to but also necessary conditions for valid archaeological explanations.

We will first describe a model for the use of knowledge in scientific explanation which has been proposed by Carl Hempel and Paul Oppenheim (1948:135-175), and will show that it characterizes certain kinds of archaeological explanations. We then describe a method for acquiring laws and contrast it with the empiricist method proposed by B. K. Swartz (1967).

Explicit definitions of the terms to be used in the following discussion are given below:

LAW: A statement of relationship between two or more variables which is true for all times and places.

HYPOTHESIS: A testable statement of relation between two or more variables which is plausible but not confirmed.

EXPLANATION: The subsumption of the relation between two or more phenomena under a general law; the demonstration that the relation was predictable given the law.

CONFIRMATION: (1) A law is confirmed when the researcher demonstrates that a relationship between variables postulated in a hypothesis is true. This definition refers to the outcome of a given piece of research. Clearly, the more independent cases of confirmation of a law, the more confidence one may have in its validity. (2) An explanatory proposition is confirmed when the researcher demonstrates that the relation of phenomena is predicted by a law.

THE HEMPEL-OPPENHEIM MODEL

We argue that the Hempel-Oppenheim model for scientific explanation is, at worst, an important heuristic device which provides insight into the structure of archaeological knowledge. At best it points the way archaeologists must travel if they are to contribute to the corpus of laws of human behavior. The form of this model, that is also known as the Deductive-Nomological (D-N) model (Hempel 1966:51), is given in Fig. 1.

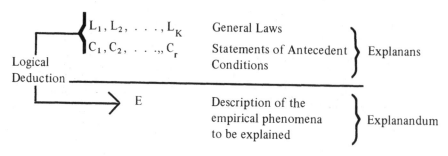

Fig. 1. The Hempel-Oppenheim model for scientific explanation. Adapted from Hempel and Oppenheim, 1948:138.

In this model, explanation is divided into two sections: the explanans and the explanandum; and each section is a division of a deductive argument. The explanans contains the premises or the statements from which the conclusion, or explanandum, can be deduced. In fact, one logical condition of adequacy for an explanation is that "the explanandum must be a logical consequence of the explanans" (Hempel and Oppenheim 1948:137). Unless this requirement is fulfilled the logical connection between the premises and the conclusion is not sufficient and the conclusion does not follow.

The conclusion or explanandum is defined as "the sentence describing the phenomenon (not that phenomenon itself). . ." (Hempel and Oppenheim 1948:137). Anything that can be observed and described is a potential explanandum phenomenon. The forms of stars, glaciers, cells, or artifacts are one kind of example. The distributions of galaxies, land forms, trees, or sites are another kind. Descriptions of diachronic processes or events such as the evolution of the solar system, the drifting of the continents, the adaptation of *Homo sapiens,* or the French Revolution are also potential conclusions.

It is important to recognize that an explanandum sentence does not describe the whole or entirety of an object, pattern, or event. All events, for example, are unique in the sense that they do not share all characteristics with other events, but events are similar in the sense that some characteristics are held in common (Hempel and Oppenheim 1948:142). It is the *recurrent* characteristics of phenomena which are described and explained, not the unique. Thus, the conclusion—and, for that matter, the premises—of an explanatory argument refer to specified characteristics of phenomena rather than to the phenomena themselves.

The explanans is defined as "the class of those sentences which are adduced to account for the phenomenon. . .[It is divisible] into two subclasses: one of these contains certain sentences C_1, C_2,. . .C_r which state specific antecedent conditions; the other is a set of sentences L_1, L_2,. . .L_k which represent general laws" (Hempel and Oppenheim 1948:137). These laws have several characteristics. First, they must be true. This means not only that they are plausible or believed to be true, but also that they have been tested. Second, they must be universal in form. That is, they assert that "In *all* cases when conditions of kind F are realized, conditions of kind G are realized as well" (Hempel 1966:55). These are termed deterministic or causal laws because they "assert general and unexceptional connections between specified characteristics of events. . ." (Hempel 1966:55). In this, these laws differ from laws which state that "In the long run, an explicitly stated percentage of all cases satisfying a given set of conditions are accompanied by an event of a certain specified kind" (Hempel and Oppenheim 1948:139). These latter are termed statistical laws and the logic employed when they are used in explanation is quite different from that of this model.

Third, these deterministic laws are generally conditional in form; that is, they relate two or more phenomena in a statement which says that *if* one occurs, *then* the other occurs (or will occur) as well. Thus, the variable occurring in the "if" half of the statement is a sufficient condition for the variable in the "then" half. This "if...then" form is characteristic of most scientific laws and, as we shall see, necessary for the derivation of explananda. Finally, a law used in this type of explanation cannot be an "accidental generalization" (Hempel 1966:54-58). Accidental generalizations are true, universal, and conditional in form, yet we would not want to call them laws. An example would be, "All houses in this site are semi-subterranean." This is not the kind of statement we would cite to explain why a given house in this site was semi-subterranean. Rather, we would refer to certain socio-cultural laws.

Laws refer to phenomena abstractly and universally, but explanations refer to phenomena concretely and particularly. According to this model, one moves from generals to particulars by means of statements of antecedent conditions, C; these state that in a particular instance the phenomena referred to in the "if" half of the law (or laws) occurred. Because its occurrence is sufficient to produce the occurrence of the phenomena referred to in the "then" half of the law, it must follow that a particular instance of the latter phenomena also occurred (occurs or will occur). The latter phenomena are, in fact, the phenomena which we are explaining.

In short, according to this model, we explain a particular phenomenon by citing another particular phenomenon. The latter is an explanation for the former; and the former occurred because the latter occurred. Our citation of this relationship between cause and effect is not arbitrary; rather, we cite this because we recognize that the relationship between the particular phenomena is an example or special case of the relationship between all such phenomena. The characteristics of and the relationship between the phenomena are defined by laws. The laws are, in effect, the explanation for the particular explanation we have made. Without a law we would be unable to choose *the* causal phenomenon out of all possible phenomena. With it, we are able to select the cause and deduce the effect.

CLASSIFICATION AS EXPLANATION

So much for the model. Does it accurately describe explanations made by archaeologists? We submit that classifications of archaeological data often share many features with this model. In the first place, such classifications have dual referents; that is, they refer not only to certain empirically observable formal and contextual properties of the phenomena classified, but also to the functions of such phenomena. To classify a feature as a "pit house," for example, is to refer both to the fact that it was a large, enclosed space partially sunken into the ground, *and* to the uses to which this space was put. A "hearth" is not simply a pit with burned walls or with charcoal in its fill, but it once contained fuel which produced heat and light energy, and various by-products. Similarly, a "chopper" is both a cobble with an edge unifacially or bifacially flaked, and an instrument for chopping things.

The functional referent of a classification refers not only to the kind of use that a particular artifact or feature had in the past, but also to the behavior of constructing and using it. Thus, to say that a "house" "houses" people is to imply that people constructed and used the house in order to obtain "housing." A "hearth" both "hearthed" (that is, did whatever a hearth should do) and was used for "hearthing" (that is, for whatever a hearth would be used). A "chopper" not only "chopped," but also was used for "chopping."

The second characteristic that such classifications share with the Hempel-Oppenheim model for explanation is that the phenomena are related in a causal or deterministic sense. That classifications refer to *form* on the one hand and to *function and behavior* on the other is not arbitrary. They imply that one set of phenomena (past behavior) was 'sufficient to produce the second set (the characteristics of the artifact or feature). They further imply that if the latter did not occur, then the former also did not occur. Thus, a hearth, a chopper, or a house did not simply spring from the earth but occurred because it was made and used.

33

Thirdly, such classifications appear to be certain. When one reads through a site report, he finds that the majority of features are unequivocally assigned to one functional class or another. Archaeologists apparently feel confident in their ability to distinguish "metates," "floor polishers," "beads," and "projectile points," for example. The unequivocal nature of particular explanations derives, in the Hempel-Oppenheim model, from the use of formal reasoning or deductive logic. In fact, such logic is the *only* form of reasoning that can produce a necessary or certain conclusion. It is reasonable, therefore, to expect that the certainty of classificatory explanations also derives from the use of deductive reasoning. To determine this a final parallel must be shown—that of the subsumption of particular explanations under universal laws.

There are sound reasons for believing that such universal laws exist in archaeological theory. First, in order to relate one particular phenomenon to another, it is necessary to have certain ideas about the relation of such phenomena *in general*. This is particularly true when such relating is done by many people in many parts of the world and in many particular cases. Thus there would seem to be agreement among Old and New World archaeologists that a feature with certain characteristics would have these characteristics because they were once "hearths." We can see no way of explaining this regularity except by assuming that they hold general ideas in common which they consistently apply in particular cases.

Secondly, such general ideas are necessary when the rationales for the relation of phenomena are not self-evident. We all know that archaeologists can directly observe the formal and contextual properties of their data, while we cannot directly observe the functions of these data. Yet we are quite willing to assign particular objects to particular uses. This is not done arbitrarily, but with the belief that *such* objects had *such* uses. Without such beliefs there can be no rationale for selecting certain characteristics out of the potentially infinite number that an object possesses, and for stating that these occur because of the "function" of the object. But there must be a *reason* for this belief. We suggest that archaeologists state that such relation exists in a *particular* case because we believe that it exists in *all* such cases. These beliefs, thus, have the form of universal conditional statements. They state, in essence, that if a particular activity has occurred, then a certain set of characteristics will be found in the archaeological record. For example, when we classify an object as an "axe," we do so because we believe that all objects used as axes share certain characteristics which this object has as well.

In short, we suggest that many classifications are explanatory and conform to the Hempel-Oppenheim model. Prior to the classification of particular archaeological data, certain beliefs or laws exist in the form of general classificatory concepts. These relate the function of data to certain formal and contextual properties. We observe a *particular* object or feature and note that it has a certain set of characteristics. We explain these characteristics by classifying it; that is, by stating that it had a certain function in the past. The classification is certain or logically necessary because the reasoning is deductive; that is, it proceeds from a general premise through a particular premise to a particular conclusion.

We feel sure that many other kinds of archaeological reasoning could be shown to conform to the Hempel-Oppenheim model. Classifications of "cultures," or other, more general taxa, for example, require certain assumptions or laws about the nature of "cultures" in general, and about their empirical manifestations. Interpretations of generic relations between specific cultures or of cultural processes within a given cultural sequence are also derived from laws about such phenomena in general.

THE FORM AND VALIDITY OF ARCHAEOLOGICAL THEORY

Several implications follow from the applicability of the Hempel-Oppenheim model. In the first place, deductive logic is not only appropriate to archaeological interpretation, but also actually employed by archaeologists. Thus, Thompson's position is misleading at best. Assuming that some archaeologists reason less well than others, we argue that objective criteria exist for the evaluation of the logical validity of explanatory arguments and the elimination of false arguments.

In the second place, there is a set of ideas or beliefs which function as laws. They relate various behavioral and cultural phenomena to various characteristics of the archaeological record. These assumptions, which jointly might be said to constitute archaeological theory, have the further characteristic of referring to extremely general phenomena. To say that something is a house, a hearth, or a projectile point is saying something about it, but it is also leaving many things unsaid. Was the hearth used for cooking, heating, lighting, or smudging? The term "hearth" does not tell us. Thus, present archaeological theory contributes less to our understanding of specific human phenomena than many of us would like.

This archaeological theory is also usually implicit rather than explicit. We have noted that classifications rarely give the empirical properties of data and the past behavior which explain them. They are simply implied by the classificatory term. When they *are* discussed, it most commonly occurs when the proper classification of a particular feature is uncertain. Thus, is a feature a "hearth" or a "heating pit"? Is a biface a "projectile point" or a "knife"? The characteristics of each *kind* of feature or artifact may be presented and an explicit judgment made based upon the characteristics of the specific artifact or feature.

Allusions to laws which subsume particular explanations are even more infrequent. In other disciplines, such laws are commonly found in textbooks (Kuhn 1964:10). But it would be quite difficult to find an archaeological textbook which describes the relationships of human behavior and archaeological data. Laws also do not occur explicitly in explanations because the use of such laws is hidden by the implicit nature of explanations.

Finally, these laws do not occur as conclusions to works which establish their validity. It would be difficult—if not impossible—to find in the archaeological literature any argument, demonstration, or proof of the empirical truth of any of these laws. This is a most important characteristic, for it implies that archaeological theory consists of statements which have not been subjected to the same evaluative procedures as have the theories of many other scientific disciplines.

Thus far we have discussed a technique for *using* laws in archaeological research, the largely implicit use of laws to date, and the need for a research design which makes explicit a technique for validating hypotheses giving them the status of laws so that their explicit use is possible. We will now discuss a traditional design for validating hypotheses, present our alternative which we found more suitable, and compare the two approaches. To repeat, the discussion to this point has focused on the use of laws. What we will now discuss is how we obtain these laws in the first place.

A TRADITIONAL RESEARCH DESIGN

The research design which archaeologists have claimed to have used corresponds in essentials to what philosophers of science have termed the empiricist or narrow inductivist approach. Carl Hempel describes this design as follows: ". . .(1) observation and recording of all facts, (2) analysis and classification of these facts, (3) inductive derivations of generalizations from them and (4) further testing of the generalizations" (1966:11).

A recent statement of this approach in archaeological terms was made by B. K. Swartz (1967). According to Swartz, the following would constitute an ideal model for research:

1. Preparation—"Preparation is the acquainting of oneself with the nature of the archaeological problem or basic objective to be resolved. . . .There are two aspects of preparation: (1) survey of work already done, and (2) preparation for the technical problems of field work" (pp. 487-488).
2. Acquisition—"Acquisition is the mechanical process of deriving data from the field for later study and analysis" (p. 488).
3. Analysis—"Analysis is the procedure whereby archaeological data are placed in a framework of time and space. . ." (p. 489).
4. Interpretation—"The goal of interpretation is to discover how an assemblage of artifacts was manufactured and used at a certain place at a specific time. . ." (p. 489).
5. Integration—"There are two aspects of integration: reconstruction and synthesis. The objective of the first is to reconstruct, as completely as possible from inferential data, how a group of people lived in a certain place and at a certain time. . . .Synthesis is the procedure by which larger culture-content units of a taxonomic nature are formulated and described" (p. 493).

6. Comparison—". . .Comparison is not a step developing out of integration, but it is an alternative approach to interpretative data" (p. 494).
7. Abstraction—"The ultimate goal of integration and comparison is the abstraction of general laws or principles, from persisting uniformities and regularities" (p. 494).

The goal of archaeological research according to Swartz is abstraction (1967:494). Swartz maintains, as we have, that archaeologists should seek laws. However, we believe that while empiricists claim that the discovery of laws is their goal, the method which they employ is in direct conflict with this goal. There are two reasons why this is the case.

First, the empiricist approach assumes that all archaeologists collect all the data relevant to any explanatory proposition which might propose itself later in the research. In fact, no archaeologist does this. No archaeologist could do it. In the absence of some specific problem, archaeologists collect those data which they have been taught to perceive. But, there is no guarantee that these data will be sufficient for solving more than a limited number of problems which might occur to the researcher after he has collected his data.

This same objection is extended to the level of analysis and classification by Hempel when he states that ". . .if a particular way of analyzing and classifying empirical findings is to lead to an explanation of the phenomena concerned, then it must be based on hypotheses about how those phenomena are connected: without such hypotheses, analysis and classification are blind" (1966:13). If explanation is to be the product of our research, it must also be the organizing principle. Relevant data, analysis, and classification must be defined before research is actually begun.

Second, the empiricist approach assumes that facts will speak for themselves and that explanations or laws are summaries of facts. If one collects sufficient data, analyzes, classifies, and otherwise juggles it sufficiently, explanations or laws are supposed to begin to propose themselves.

Most philosophers of science would instead argue that trial formulations derive from the creative capacity of the scientist. Abduction—reasoning in which the scientist perceives patterns—is the term which Aristotle applied to the use of this capacity (see Hanson 1965). If discovery is a function not of the time spent in looking at data, but of a conscious attempt on the part of a researcher to perceive patterns, then this fact should be reflected in any model of an ideal research process. By the same argument generalizations, laws, or explanations cannot be regarded as simple statistical or non-statistical summaries of data.

THE EXPLANATORY RESEARCH DESIGN

These criticisms of the empiricist research design are overcome by what we call the explanatory research design. In discussing this research design, we will be considering the case where the researcher wishes to evaluate the validity of a proposed law.

Research would proceed as follows:

1. Acquisition of a hypothesis—research begins at the point when, in the course of his research, the archaeologist acquires a hypothesis to be tested. This would include the antecedent conditions which are offered as the particular explanation for a phenomenon as well as the law or laws which make this explanation predictable. The hypothesis might be an original abduction or might be taken from the literature of any social science.
2. Formulation of test implications—given a hypothesis, the next step is to deduce test implications: statements of relationship between variables which predict these relationships within the data to be collected which should exist if the hypothesis is a valid one. The data to be collected are specified and tests to be used in evaluating postulated relationships are formulated.
3. Formulation of a research strategy—the primary task undertaken at this point in the research is the design of a statistically random or other rigorous sampling plan for collecting the appropriate data. Technical problems of data collection should also be solved.
4. Acquisition of data.
5. Analysis of data—analysis is the process whereby data derived from the field are put into the form in which they will be used in testing.

6. Testing of hypotheses—here the specified tests of the degree of association between variables are carried out.
7. Evaluation of the research—this step involves evaluating the explanatory proposition from which test implications were deduced by referring to the tests. If the relationship between variables, which should have been discovered if the explanation were a valid one, is discovered, then the explanatory proposition is confirmed and an explanation is obtained. If the predictions do not hold, then the explanation must be rejected in terms of the current research.

The employment of this research design would overcome the weakness of the empiricist model. First, data, analysis, and classification relevant to the explanation under consideration are defined at the outset of the research. (Data not vital to the research which is disturbed in the process of acquiring data should, of course, be recorded and preserved. The archaeologist should, however, feel obligated to analyze only those data which are relevant to his research.)

Second, the research design does not assume that facts will speak for themselves. It assumes that valid explanations result from research designed to test the validity of explanations. If explanation is our goal, research must be based upon a model which sets out to test the validity of explanations. If laws are our goal, then research must be based upon a model which sets out to test the validity of hypotheses. Neither laws nor explanations can be an afterthought. They must be the purpose of research and must be allowed to define the appropriateness of research design.

CONCLUSIONS

Two further points should be made. One relates to the present nature of archaeological theory, and the second to the relevance of any archaeological theory. If scientific knowledge can be defined as a set of tested statements describing reality, prescientific knowledge might be defined as a set of statements which are plausible and accepted, but which have not been tested. In this sense current archaeological theory is prescientific. It has not been tested.

Current explanations in archaeology must be considered prescientific in the same sense. One of the conditions of adequacy for the Hempel-Oppenheim model is the empirical truth of the statements employed. Because that condition has not been met, archaeological explanations cannot be considered true in the same sense as explanations using proven laws. To the degree that it is possible that archaeological theory will be proved to be false by testing, explanations using this theory are also potentially false. Since it is impossible to evaluate this possibility without performing the necessary tests, it is also impossible to evaluate the truth or falsity of archaeological explanations. Thus it is impossible to evaluate the validity of classifications or of any other current archaeological explanations.

We believe that this characteristic of archaeological theory is recognized by many archaeologists. We are often reluctant, for example, to assign past function to our data. When we do, we may prefer to use the word "possible," for example "possible water container," or more often, we assign such a general function that we feel the odds for being found incorrect are small. We are more likely to be correct if we classify a feature as a hearth than if we classify it as a cooking pit, for example.

But we all want our discipline to contribute to the knowledge of laws of human behavior. One of the easiest ways that this is can be done is to demonstrate the empirical validity of the regularities we think exist. We have described a research design by means of which this can be accomplished. It entails (1) the explicit definition of the form and relation of specific variables, (2) the argument that specific instances of these variables are predicted by specified laws, and (3) the confirmation (or disconfirmation) that the variables occur (or do not occur) in the predicted form and relation in observed cases.

Another problem deserving of primary attention is the kind of explanations we should set out to test. In the past, archaeologists have felt bound by the explanations which their data "suggested." The explanatory approach removes this restriction, but it forces the anthropologist to justify the explanations which he chooses to test as being valuable uses of research time. In the long run, this obligation can be met only by taking as explanations to be tested problems which are relevant not only to archaeologists but to social science as a whole. Archaeologists claim to have a set of data which is of unique value in studying processes of long-term change and development. Yet, we have rarely used our data to do this. Given the freedom to choose explanations for testing, we have incurred the obligation to strive to be relevant. We suspect that unless archaeologists find ways to make their research increasingly relevant to the modern world, the modern world will find itself increasingly capable of getting along without archaeologists.

Acknowledgments. Presented at the Thirty-third Annual Meeting of the Society for American Archaeology, Santa Fe, New Mexico, May, 1968, as two separate papers. We wish to be considered joint authors of this paper.

We wish to thank the following who have read and offered comments on all or part of this paper: Pedro Armillas, Robert M. Adams, Sally R. and Lewis R. Binford, Leslie G. Freeman, Paul S. Martin, Milton Singer, and Nathalie F. S. and Richard B. Woodbury. The responsibility for our views is, of course, our own. We also acknowledge the support of the National Science Foundation, and of the Southwestern Expedition of the Field Museum of Natural History, Paul S. Martin, Director. Our personal debt and gratitude for the support given by Martin in our efforts to understand scientific method is greatest of all.

HANSON, NORWOOD RUSSELL
    1965 *Patterns of discovery. An inquiry into the conceptual foundations of science.* Cambridge University Press.

HEMPEL, CARL G.
    1966 *Philosophy of natural science.* Prentice-Hall (Foundations of Philosophy Series).

HEMPEL, CARL G., and PAUL OPPENHEIM
    1948 Studies in the logic of explanation. *Philosophy of Science* 15:135-175.

KUHN, THOMAS S.
    1964 *The structure of scientific revolutions.* University of Chicago Press (Phoenix Books).

NAGEL, ERNST
    1961 *The structure of science. Problems in the logic of scientific explanation.* Harcourt, Brace, and World.

SWARTZ, B. K.
    1967 A logical sequence of archaeological objectives. *American Antiquity* 32:487-497.

THOMPSON, RAYMOND H.
    1958 Modern Yucatecan Maya pottery making. *Memoirs of the Society for American Archaeology*, No. 15.

COMMENT

CONFIRMATION AND EXPLANATION IN ARCHAEOLOGY

MERRILEE H. SALMON

In recent discussions by archaeologists who are committed to the scientific nature of archaeology, philosophic commitment to an excessively narrow view of "the scientific method" is common. These narrow conceptions can be broadened, clarified, and made more adequate without diminishing a commitment to scientific archaeology.

The hypothetico-deductive method of confirmation is an oversimplified account of scientific reasoning. There are severe limitations for its application, particularly in archaeology. The deductive-nomological model of scientific explanation likewise has serious drawbacks for explaining the sorts of phenomena which interest archaeologists. Understanding of the problems with this model is hampered by trying to force systems models of explanation into the deductive-nomological mold. Worse still, the separate issues of confirmation and explanation are not kept distinct.

In "Two Points of Logic," Steven A. LeBlanc (1974:199-214) argues that it is permissible to use data which were responsible for suggesting a hypothesis to test that hypothesis, and that the use of the hypothetico-deductive method is appropriate to test some of the statements used in explanations in systems theory as well as the statements which serve as covering laws in the deductive-nomological model of explanation. Both of these claims seem correct. I also agree with his claim that it is important to describe correctly the reasoning involved in the confirmation of hypotheses, and because I believe that his account is misleading in several important respects, I would like to discuss some of his remarks.

Hypotheses, or statements to be tested, may be of various logical types. They may be universal generalizations, such as "All hunters and gatherers are patrilocal," particular statements, such as "This is a chert projectile point," statistical generalizations, such as "90% of all potters are women," or mixed statements, such as "70% of the lithic material in a particular site is chert."

At the outset, it should be noted that the hypothetico-deductive method (H-D) is fundamentally inappropriate for testing statistical statements since no statement concerning the composition of any sample can be *deduced* from the statistical statement. Many of the hypotheses which archaeologists are interested in testing are statistical. Moreover, many of LeBlanc's examples of universal hypotheses, such as "The amount of resources used by a group for social purposes increases faster than the population growth of that group," are qualitatively stated hypotheses which might be more scientifically acceptable, i.e., informative and precise, if they were stated quantitatively. When such statements are translated into quantitative statements they are apt to become statistical. Statistical statements are most appropriately tested by various familiar statistical sampling techniques. The theory of confirmation of statistical hypotheses is well developed, though, like any lively scientific theory, it is not without its controversies.

The hypothetico-deductive method of testing universal generalizations and particular statements is the same for each type: deduce other statements, called implications, from the hypothesis, and check the implications against empirical data to determine whether the implications are true. Because the logical relation of deductive implication is truth-preserving, all implications of a true statement are true. A true hypothesis cannot have any false implications. However, since false statements may also have true implications, we may not say that a hypothesis is *true* simply because it has some true implications.

While we may not be able to determine the truth of a given hypothesis (H), we are sometimes entitled to accept it because it is strongly confirmed. LeBlanc proposes three criteria for strength of confirmation: (1) the number of I's (implications that can be shown to be empirically true); (2) the independence of the true I's (the greater their independence from one another, the stronger the confirmation of **H**); and (3) the logical completeness of the **I**'s (the greater the probability that all possible **I**'s have been deduced and found to be true the stronger the confirmation of **H**).

I shall argue that the third criterion is incorrect, and that the other two are inadequate. The third is incorrect because the probability that all possible **I**'s have been deduced and found to be true is *zero* for almost any hypothesis a scientist would be interested in testing. This is perhaps obvious for LeBlanc's example, "All hunters and gatherers are patrilocal." Such a statement refers not only to all past and present groups of hunters but also to any possible future group of hunters. Any universal generalization has an infinite number of possible implications, so no matter how many are tested, the probability that all have been tested remains zero. It is not merely practically difficult, as LeBlanc suggests, but logically impossible to test all the implications. Even a particular statement, such as "This is a chert projectile point," may have an infinite number of implications. If we consider possible tests which might be made of this hypothesis we have to consider such things as what experiences anyone could have with that particular piece of stone at any future time as well as what is happening to it now and what happened to it in the past. C. I. Lewis (1962:171-178) presents a clear discussion of these issues.

The problem of the adequacy of (1) and (2) remains. (1) and (2) are tests of the strength of a hypothesis, but only with important qualifications which LeBlanc fails to discuss. In the first place (1) and (2) contribute to the confirmation of a hypothesis only in the absence of disconfirming evidence. LeBlanc says that he does not wish to discuss disconfirmation of hypotheses. He does, however, admit that *logically* if one **I** deduced from an **H** is shown to be false, then **H** is disconfirmed and must be rejected. Then he makes the surprising claim that one need not adhere to the logical requirements in practice because no scientist claims that any logical model fits the world exactly (LeBlanc 1974:202). If this is so one might wonder why LeBlanc puts so much emphasis on understanding the logic of confirmation. The difficulty here is not that there is a conflict between logic and the world, but that LeBlanc

has neither represented the logical features of confirmation adequately, nor has he recognized that there are problems connected with confirmation which are not logical problems—hence, it is not surprising that the use of deductive logic cannot solve them.

One problem is that hypotheses can rarely, if ever, be isolated for independent testing. This is true not only for high level generalizations and for interconnected sets of hypotheses, such as those with which systems theorists are concerned, but also for rather simple hypotheses. Consider the hypothesis that a particular society, known only archaeologically, was a patrilocal society of hunters and gatherers. At the very least, there are auxiliary hypotheses (**A**'s) involved regarding the reliability of our procedures for analyzing archaeological remains, and regarding whether the initial conditions are in fact correctly specified. A particular **I** then follows not from **H** alone, but from **H** together with a number of **A**'s. If an **I** is shown to be false this does not logically imply that **H** is false, but only that either **H** or at least one of the **A**'s must be false.

Because of the difficulty of isolating **H**'s, we do not count every false implication from **H** together with its auxiliary hypotheses as disconfirming evidence for **H** itself. If, however, we are reasonably sure that all the **A**'s we are using are explicitly recognized and that they are themselves well-confirmed, then a false **I** deduced from **H** and the **A**'s would tend to disconfirm **H**. We could not just overlook this disconfirming evidence no matter how many true implications had been found.

Another difficulty with LeBlanc's criteria is that they tend to present a view of confirmation which is misleadingly quantitative. LeBlanc's second criterion attempts to avoid this by requiring variety in the data used to confirm **H**. Although he makes this clear in his examples, his wording of the requirement in terms of "independence of true **I**'s" is unfortunate. Implications are statements, and independence is a logical relation between statements. But statements are independent just so long as there are no relations of entailment between the statements or their denials. Thus, the statement "Group A of hunters and gatherers is patrilocal" and the statement "Group B of hunters and gatherers is patrilocal" are deductively independent statements even though Group A and Group B may both be Australian tribes in the same linguistic group.

Variety in the data is what is important, not the mere absence of logical implication between statements describing the data. A mere listing of points of difference and similarity between various data does not answer the crucial question of which differences are *relevant*. When we want to confirm a hypothesis we try to divide the domain of its applicability (for our example this is the class of all groups of hunters and gatherers) into partitions such that it would be plausible to suppose that the hypothesis might hold in one part of the domain but not another. Since our general background knowledge indicates that members of the same linguistic group who live in close geographical proximity to one another and who have similar life-support systems are apt to have similar patterns of post-marital residence, we want to partition the class of all groups of hunters and gatherers into subgroups of hunters and gatherers from different geographical areas and different linguistic groups.

Suppose we know that Group A is patrilocal; then the prior probability that Group B, from the same linguistic and geographic subclass as Group A, is also patrilocal is already very high. Discovering that Group B is also patrilocal does not do much to increase our confidence that *all* groups of hunters and gatherers are patrilocal. However, the prior probability that a Group C of hunters and gatherers, from prehistoric North America, for example, are also patrilocal will be significantly lower since this group is from a different part of the domain. Ascertaining that Group C was also patrilocal has much more bearing on the confirmation of our hypothesis. The structure of hypothesis testing here is a *supplemented* **H-D** method, a method which is taken from inductive logic, and which might assume the form of Bayes theorem (Salmon 1967:129-131). Virtually every contemporary inductive logician who has dealt with this problem recognizes that the **H-D** method is an oversimplification, and must be supplemented in some appropriate way.

Whether a hypothesis is confirmed depends not only on the number of true I's and the variety of the confirming data, but also on the significance of the I's, or the importance of the data represented by the true I's. A hypothesis such as "All hunters and gatherers are patri-

local," has an infinite number of implications. Some of these are significant while others are genuinely trivial. In this case trained anthropologists, not logicians, are those best qualified to determine which are which. Only a limited number of implications can be tested. The important implications will be most useful for the confirmation of the hypothesis, and a large number of trivially true implications will not go far toward confirmation. Like the question of relevant variety, the question of significance is a deep and difficult one, essential to the problem of confirmation, and not answered by use of the **H-D** method.

LeBlanc gives the impression that hypothesis confirmation is purely a matter of deductive logic, that all one needs to know to decide whether a hypothesis is confirmed is the list of true, independent I's (LeBlanc 1974:202). However, a philosopher, even one with superb logical ability, who was presented with a hypothesis in archaeology along with such a list would be hard-pressed to say whether the hypothesis was confirmed because, assuming he knew little about archaeology, he would be in no position to judge the significance of the implications or whether the variety represented in them was of the relevant sort.

Explicit formulation and testing of hypotheses is an important part of the scientific method. For this reason, the "new archaeologists," given their desire to establish archaeology as a science, are correct in urging the formulation and testing of archaeological hypotheses as a way to achieve this goal. At the same time, those engaged in such an enterprise should be very clear about the limitations of the **H-D** method. Aside from the limitations which have already been discussed, several others are worth noting.

First, the method is a method for *testing* hypotheses. It is not a method for *deriving* hypotheses. LeBlanc at times seems very unclear about this point (1974:208). Hypotheses may be suggested by data (LeBlanc's use of "derive" indicates that he believes that hypotheses are sometimes implied by the data) or they may be merely wild guesses. There is no *logical* method for formulating hypotheses. Insight, imagination, training in a field, etc., are the factors operating in the formulation of hypotheses. Furthermore, although one can use logic to check whether a given statement is implied by a hypothesis, there is no logical method for generating implications from hypotheses. Finding implications, like finding hypotheses, is a problem located in the context of discovery rather than the context of justification. For the past half-century logicians have shown a lively interest in the problem of whether there are mechanical ways (decision procedures) for answering such questions as whether a given sentence can be deduced from a given set of premises. In almost all cases where the answer to this question is "yes," however, the answer to whether there is a decision procedure for generating the validly deducible sentences from a set of premises is negative. A recent issue of *Scientific American* contains an interesting, informal discussion of decision procedures (Davis and Hersh 1973:84-91).

Second, the method is employed as an aid to confirm or disconfirm hypotheses, not to establish conclusively their truth or falsehood. LeBlanc seems to misunderstand this point when he says such things as, "The crucial point is that *all* I's must be considered in testing H, and none may be disregarded; this is true because H is confirmed logically. If an I can be validly deduced from H, it must be shown to be empirically true if H is to be confirmed" (1974:203). If, however, it were possible to deduce all the I's from a particular H, and to show them all to be true, this would establish the *truth* of the hypothesis.

Third, the H-D method is a method for confirming universal generalizations and particular statements. It is not a method for confirming *laws*. Even well confirmed universal generalizations may be "accidental" generalizations rather than genuine laws. The acceptance of the H-D method by archaeologists in no way commits them to the view that there are any universal laws of archaeology which can be established by the H-D (or any other) method.

LeBlanc tends to conflate three separate issues: (1) the problem of hypothesis confirmation; (2) the problem of whether there are any universal laws in archaeology; and (3) the problem of providing a correct theory of archaeological explanation. The use of the H-D method does not guarantee the establishment of any laws, nor does the acceptance of the H-D method of confirmation commit one to the acceptance of the deductive-nomological model of explanation.

Many accounts of explanation require that explanations include laws. However, the nature of explanation is much less well understood than that of confirmation, and the type of laws required in explanations as well as the exact role which laws play in explanations is controversial. Various models for scientific explanation have been proposed; arguments and counter-arguments regarding their plausibility have been given. But, as things stand now, one cannot be criticized as being "unscientific" for not adopting a particular model of explanation, nor could a particular field of knowledge be denied the title of "science" because its explanations do not all conform to that model.

LeBlanc, in the last section of his article, argues that there is no basic logical difference between systemic explanations and deductive-nomological explanations. In support of this conclusion he says that laws play a role in both types of explanations, and that systemic generalizations are merely more complex sets of covering laws than the ordinary covering laws used in D-N explanations.

Even if both these claims were correct LeBlanc's conclusion would not follow. The D-N model of explanation is not distinguished from other models merely by its use of laws. Even Hempel, who first formulated the D-N model, recognizes other models of explanation (deductive-statistical and inductive-statistical) which also employ laws (Hempel 1962:7-33). A distinguishing feature of all of Hempel's models is that explanations are *arguments* which show that the event (or law) to be explained *is to be expected* in view of the laws and initial conditions cited in the premises of the arguments. In the D-N model the phenomenon to be explained must follow deductively from the explanatory statements, and the laws occurring in the explanatory statements must be universal laws.

LeBlanc quotes Meehan's definition of a system: "A system consists of a set of variables $(V_1, V_2, V_3, \ldots V_n)$ and a set of rules that define the interactions among these variables $(R_1, R_2, R_3, \ldots R_n)$." Then LeBlanc goes on to say, "Clearly these R's are nothing more than an expression of a covering law, whether it be a formula such as $F = ma$ or the statement that 'The amount of resources used for social purposes by a group increases faster than the population of that group'" (1974:211). Here, I merely wish to point out that the laws expressed in the "R's" may be statistical laws rather than universal laws, and if they are statistical then they are not logically similar to the laws used in the **D-N** model.

It is difficult to understand why LeBlanc is so reluctant to countenance statistical laws in explanations. "Hard" sciences, such as physics, certainly recognize the importance of such laws in explanations. For example, the physical law governing the decay of C-14 is a statistical law, and is one with great significance for archaeologists.

LeBlanc admits that systemic explanations may be more adequate than **D-N** explanations, but he maintains that adequacy is an "external" characteristic of explanations rather than an "internal" (one which affects the logical structure) characteristic (1974:210). He distinguishes two sorts of adequacy:

(1) A **D-N** explanation may fail to be adequate because, while the explanatory argument is logically correct, it may not employ the sort of law which is of interest to a particular researcher. For example, the explanation that a particular swan is white because it is a European swan and all European swans are white, will not satisfy a scientist who is interested in the evolutionary processes which determined whiteness in European swans. Here, the researcher really wants an answer to the question "Why are European swans white?" and requires evolutionary laws in a satisfactory explanation. In such a case a different **D-N** explanation might be perfectly adequate.

(2) Another sense of "adequacy" in explanations is "completeness." Here, LeBlanc admits that systemic explanations may be superior to simple **D-N** explanations which use only a single universal law rather than a set of interrelated laws, but maintains that these systemic explanations are really just complex **D-N** explanations. There is, after all, no restriction in the **D-N** model on the number of laws used in an explanation.

Without trying to assess the relative merits of the **D-N** and the systems approach, I want to discuss another type of adequacy which, I believe, is an internal criterion of explanation and which is the real problem bothering systemic theorists and other critics of Hempel's models. In any explanation we want the laws occurring in the explanans to be *relevant* to the phenomenon to be explained. Since the **D-N** model says that explanations are arguments and

requires only that the explanandum be deducible from the explanans, and since the proper kind of relevance cannot be guaranteed by logical entailment, the **D-N** model is inadequate in this respect.

To demonstrate this point I borrow an example from *Statistical Explanation and Statistical Relevance* (W. C. Salmon 1971:29-88): John Jones avoided becoming pregnant during the past year, for he has taken his wife's birth control pills regularly, and every man who regularly takes birth control pills avoids pregnancy.

This "explanation" fits the **D-N** model, but no one would be willing to accept it as an explanation of why John Jones avoided pregnancy. This is not merely because the explanation is "externally" inadequate. The law occurring in the "explanation" is simply not causally or statistically relevant to the fact to be explained, even though the fact can be deduced from the law and the initial conditions.

The statistical relevance (**SR**) model of explanation, which is proposed by Salmon, like Hempel's models and like the systemic model, requires laws for explanations. Briefly, the **SR** model says that to explain an event is to assemble the total set of conditions relevant to its occurrence and to assess the probability of the event's occurrence, given those conditions. The total set of relevant conditions must include at least one law-like generalization.

Besides attempting to account for relevance, this model differs from the **D-N** model in several other important respects. There is no requirement that the laws employed in explanations be universal rather than statistical. Since we do not know whether universal laws govern every event (a belief that they do involves a metaphysical commitment to *determinism* and is not required by scientific knowledge), this is an advantage.

Although Hempel's other models of explanation (**I-S** and **D-S**) allow statistical laws, they, like the **D-N** model, require that explanations be *arguments* which show that the explained event was to be expected or was likely to occur. The **SR** model does not require that explanations be arguments of this sort. This too, is an advantage, because, so far as we know, improbable or unlikely events *do* occur, and on Hempel's accounts these must be unexplainable, since even on Hempel's weakest model

(I-S) to explain an event is to show that it was to be expected, i.e., that it was highly probable.

It is not appropriate here to give a detailed presentation of the **SR** model. I have used it as an example to show the deep *logical* differences between different models of explanations in spite of their agreement as to the requirement for laws in explanations, as well as to point out some serious shortcomings of the **D-N** model. The systems theorists' objections to the **D-N** model seem to be well-taken, and are dismissed too easily by LeBlanc. The type of explanation which systems theorists propose seems to me to represent an attempt to come to grips with the problem of *relevance*. Moreover, since systems theorists do not require explanations to be arguments, they avoid the difficulties surrounding this view.

I share the "new archaeologists'" commitment to the scientific nature of archaeology, to the use of archaeology for studying past cultures, and to the relevance of archaeology for understanding contemporary cultural processes. I also share LeBlanc's belief that hypothesis testing is necessary for the development of scientific archaeology. In actual practice, scientific archaeologists use much more sophisticated methods of hypothesis testing than that characterized by the simple **H-D** method. My point in criticizing the **H-D** method is not to discourage hypothesis testing, but to prevent misunderstanding and unfavorable criticism of the techniques and methods actually employed by the "new archaeologists."

LeBlanc's chief concern with explanation is his insistence that *laws* are required in explanations. And with this point I am in complete agreement. But to identify the insistence on the importance of laws with acceptance of the **D-N** model (or even with the acceptance of **D-N** and **I-S** models) is seriously misleading. It leaves archaeologists open to attack (such as that by Morgan 1973) on the deficiencies of these models, when a more careful statement of the archaeologists' requirements could have avoided this.

It is my hope in presenting some of these issues and suggesting alternative models, that fruitful discussions of confirmation and explanation in archaeology will ensue. The task of the new archaeology is an important and exciting one, but a misleading impression of commitment to a narrow philosophical view which equates "scientific method" with acceptance of **H-D** confirmation and **D-N** explanation is detrimental to the cause.

Acknowledgments. I am deeply grateful to William A. Longacre, Wesley C. Salmon, and the editor of *American Antiquity* for advice, instruction, and encouragement in connection with this paper.

Davis, Martin, and Reuben Hersh
    1973   Hilbert's 10th problem. *Scientific American* 229(5):84-91.
Hempel, Carl
    1962   Explanation in science and in history. In *Frontiers of science and philosophy*, edited by R. C. Colodny, pp. 7-33. University of Pittsburgh Press, Pittsburgh.
LeBlanc, Steven A.
    1974   Two points of logic. In *Research and theory in current archaeology*, edited by Charles L. Redman, pp. 199-214. John L. Wiley, New York.
Lewis, C. I.
    1962   *An analysis of knowledge and valuation.* Open Court, La Salle.
Morgan, Charles G.
    1973   Archaeology and explanation. *World Archaeology* 4:259-276.
Salmon, Wesley C.
    1967   *The foundations of scientific inference.* University of Pittsburgh Press, Pittsburgh.
    1971   *Statistical explanation and statistical relevance.* University of Pittsburgh Press, Pittsburgh.

WHAT CAN SYSTEMS THEORY DO FOR ARCHAEOLOGY?

MERRILEE H. SALMON

This paper examines the relevance of systems theory to archaeology. General Systems Theory and Mathematical Systems Theory are considered. Although it is important for archaeologists to look at the materials they study as components of a larger cultural and ecological context, neither version of systems theory can offer archaeologists much help in constructing archaeological theories or in providing models of archaeological explanation.

In fact, the world is full of hopeful analogies and handsome dubious eggs called possibilities [G. Eliot].

MANY ARCHAEOLOGISTS who have a strong interest in developing the theoretical structure of their discipline have turned to systems theory for assistance. In a recent review article, Fred Plog (1975) presents a comprehensive summary of the various types of influence that systems theory has had on current archaeological thinking, ranging from the whole-hearted commitment of David Clarke (1968) to the more selective approaches of Watson, LeBlanc, and Redman (1971), Kent Flannery (1968), and others. As archaeology emerges as a full-fledged social science, its students and practitioners are urged to equip themselves with the tools, such as a working knowledge of statistics, appropriate for such a science. It is easy to get the impression from references in the current literature (Flannery 1973; Tuggle, Townsend, and Riley 1972) that knowledge of systems theory also is an indispensable addition to the archaeologists' tool kit.

In this paper I want to challenge the relevance of systems theory for archaeology. Although a number of archaeologists have claimed that systems theory provides them with a novel, exciting, and useful theoretical approach to their discipline, I believe that these claims are somewhat exaggerated. Some archaeologists have found a number of systems theory concepts such as negative feedback, positive feedback, and dynamic equilibrium useful for characterizing archaeologically interesting phenomena. I do not wish to quarrel with the use of such terminology. However, it is important to recognize the limits of its utility for archaeology. In the absence of any general theory concerning such concepts they have only descriptive and no explanatory force. At best they can only direct archaeologists to seek certain types of explanatory principles rather than others, and even here the choices are rather broad. At worst, they amount to the importation of a pseudo-scientific jargon which tends to obscure rather than to clarify the issues.

The term "systems theory" is often indiscriminately applied to two distinct fields of study: General Systems Theory and Mathematical Systems Theory. In this paper I shall try to show that, for different reasons, neither has much to offer archaeology.

General Systems Theory is not a genuine theory. It has established no general principles that are applicable to all systems. General Systems Theory is a program to develop such a theory, but the program has become enmeshed in difficulties at such a basic level that it has never really gotten off the ground.

Mathematical Systems Theory is a genuine theory, but it is a theory of pure mathematics. It has limitations that make it applicable to few, and only very simple, real systems. It is not complex enough to handle the sorts of situations that interest archaeologists.

I shall try to support these claims in what follows, with particular attention to the attempts of some archaeologists to use systems theory in their work. My purpose is not to show that all such attempts are totally misguided, but only to show that archaeological theory cannot be extracted from either version of systems theory. I'm not sure why appeals to systems theory have been so popular in archaeology, but I think this stems in part from a failure to keep the two versions of systems theory distinct from one another, and thus to overestimate the accomplishments of General Systems Theory and the usefulness of Mathematical Systems Theory.

SYSTEMS

We are all familiar with many types of systems, or organized wholes, which are in some sense more than the sum of their parts. There are physical systems, both living, e.g. human beings, and non-living, e.g. automobiles, and also non-physical systems such as linguistic systems and sociocultural systems. In spite of our intuitive understanding of what systems are, as we shall see later, it is not easy to formulate a precise definition of "system" which can capture these intuitions.

It is clear that if we are to have any adequate understanding of the world we live in, our knowledge must include knowledge of the organized wholes which we call systems, as well as knowledge of component parts of these systems. Knowledge of systems may be divided into two basic categories:

1. Our knowledge may be of the structure, or interrelationships among components, of the system. Such structural knowledge is possible even when we may know little about the nature of the components that make up the system. We may know, for example, that the key that starts an automobile turns on a switch that is connected by wires to the starter and battery. This is an example of structural knowledge of the starter system of an automobile.

2. Our knowledge may consist of an account of a complex entity in terms of its behavior. That is, we may be able to say what a system does (describe its output) when it is acted on in various ways (its input). Such behavioral knowledge is sometimes possible even when nothing is known about the structure of the system. For example, many people who have no knowledge of the mechanical structure of an auto can describe it in terms of what happens when keys are inserted, pedals depressed, and steering wheels turned. If we have only behavioral knowledge but no structural knowledge of some system, that system may be referred to as a "black box." A great deal may be learned about such systems from the study of inputs and their corresponding outputs.

Of course, there are some systems that are so well understood that we have both structural and behavioral knowledge of them. In anthropological terms, knowledge of the first type is synchronic, and knowledge of the second type is diachronic knowledge. It should be clear that recognition of the importance of systemic knowledge is nothing new. Anthropologists were engaged in analyzing social and cultural systems long before the advent of modern systems theory.

GENERAL SYSTEMS THEORY

General Systems Theory began as a research program under the auspices of the Society for the Advancement of General Systems Theory in 1954 (Boulding 1972). The participants in the program, inspired by the work of L. von Bertalanffy, recognized the important role that the study of various kinds of systems played in many different disciplines, and they envisioned an abstract empirical theory whose results would apply to *any* system, whether physical, biological, symbolic, or social.

In view of all the interest in systems in otherwise unrelated fields of study, it seemed that the time was ripe for the development of a general systems theory. One would only need to look at various systems in different disciplines to discover their common features. By a process of abstraction general principles could be formulated, and they could be tested by seeing whether they applied to still other systems. In this way it was hoped to construct a theory of great generality, which was at the same time capable of precise expression. This project has involved the careful attention of many serious thinkers since the 1950s, but while there have been some interesting results, the originally stated goal is not even in sight. Consider this report by Rapaport, one of the originators of General Systems Theory, in a work published in honor of von Bertalanffy:

> General systems theory, in generalizing the notion of a system, has instigated speculations of this sort [attempts to characterize in a precise way analogies between linguistic and biological evolution, and between the evolutions of organisms and artifacts]. To the extent that the speculations are not yet amenable to validation in the scientific sense of the word, this aspect of general systems theory should not, I suppose, be subsumed under "theory." If a theory is a collection of theorems, as it is in any exact science, then *general systems theory is not a theory*. I cannot think of a single thing to say that applies to all systems, except tautologically. That is, properties of systems that apply to all systems are those that are consequences of the definition of a system, hence devoid of empirical content [1972:29, emphasis mine].

The failure of General Systems Theory to provide any principles applicable to all systems might not destroy its utility for archaeology if work done under its auspices provided some principles applicable to archaeological data. Even when principles are offered for limited types of systems, for example, principles for living systems, General Systems theory has not been successful in providing non-tautologous principles.

Many beautiful examples of vacuous systems principles can be found in one of the sources cited by Plog (Miller 1965). Miller does not intend his propositions to be tautological. He requires of each that "it must be possible to specify practical operations, at two levels at least, whereby it can be confirmed or disconfirmed" (Miller 1965: 382). But consider: "Hypothesis 3.3.7 2-17. A system cannot survive unless it makes decisions that maintain the functions of all its subsystems at a sufficiently high efficiency and their costs at a sufficiently low level that there are more than enough resources to keep it operating satisfactorily" (Miller 1965: 397).

This claim is typical of the sort of systems principles offered by Miller. It retains the semblance of a genuine empirical claim only because of its vagueness. Although it employs a "technical" terminology, none of the terms is precisely defined. There are no criteria offered for "sufficiently high efficiency" or "sufficiently low costs" except survival or failure to survive. No hint is offered as to how the notion of "decision" is to apply in general to living systems. We have some understanding of what it is for a human to make a decision, but it is not clear how this can be transferred to other living systems. If we eliminate the jargon this hypothesis makes only the empty claim that a system cannot survive unless it can keep operating satisfactorily.

If someone objects that this is an inadequate paraphrase, then one can look at Miller's own "evidence" for his claim. He does not specify any practical operations for testing the claim, but rather offers some examples of "systems" that have not survived. I shall discuss only the first example, because none of the others avoids the difficulties inherent in the first one. His example is "Dinosaurs became extinct when they grew too large to function in their environments. Their moving was probably too slow for them to survive in the presence of faster antagonists and their skeletons may have been too weak to support their bulk" (Miller 1965: 397).

Presumably the "system" that fails to survive is the "system of dinosaurs," although this is not spelled out by Miller. It is difficult to understand in what sense a pair of closely related biological orders constitutes a system, or to see what the subsystems of such a system could be. Perhaps the most generous interpretation would be that each order constitutes a system, and the individual members of the order are the subsystems. But even if we allow this, what sense can we make of the failure of such a system to make a "decision" to maintain the function of all its subsystems at a sufficiently high efficiency and their costs at a sufficiently low level that there are more than enough resources to keep it operating satisfactorily? The whole notion of a biological order "deciding" not to let its members get "too large" is hopelessly obscure.

Clearly, dinosaurs did not survive, at least not in their prehistoric form. Clearly, also, they were large. (Recent evidence, however, indicates, that they were not slow.) But whether they failed to survive *because* they were too large is not known. The only evidence for the claim that they grew too large to function is that they did not survive. Even if their size caused their demise we cannot regard this as a result of some decision of the system.

If one still insists that Miller's hypothesis is an empirical one even though his evidence was poorly chosen, then we challenge him to produce a possible counterexample to Miller's hypothesis. All genuine empirical hypotheses have such counterexamples. Such an exercise should make obvious the vacuous character of such notions as "sufficiently high efficiency."

DEFINITION OF "SYSTEM"

From what Rapaport says (above), one might think that at least systems theorists have provided an unproblematic definition of "system." However, this is not the case. The failure to provide a satisfactory definition has been regarded by some as the chief obstacle to the development of General Systems Theory. Some writers believe that such a definition is impossible because either the variety of uses of "system" shows that there is no one sense of "system" that can be captured by a single definition, or because any definition broad enough to cover all the legitimate uses of "system" would be so vague that anything at all would count as a system.

J. D. Marchal (1975) tries to meet this two-fold challenge. He cites a number of proposed definitions of "system," taken from widely varied sources, and extracts a common core meaning from them. Differences in the use of "system," he argues, are a result of a focus on different kinds of systems, not a result of many different senses of the word "system." Analogously, to use an archaeologist's example, the existence of many different kinds of projectile points does not preclude a single sense of "projectile point" that is applicable to the different kinds.

Marchal's own proposed definition uses the language of set theory to make this core meaning more precise: S is a system only if S is a set of elements and relations between the elements (Marchal 1975:460).

This definition is broad enough to cover definitions of "system" offered by archaeologists. Consider, for example: "SYSTEM. An intercommunicating network of attributes or entities forming a complex whole. An ensemble of attributes" (Clarke 1968:669). Clarke's definition emphasizes the transfer of information among components of a system, an important relation for systems that interest social scientists. Other definitions offered by archaeologists are "A system is understood to mean a series of groups (families, communities, lineages, etc.) exchanging goods, services, and information with each other in such a way that a change in one component is likely to produce changes in the other" (Plog 1973:196), and "Human ecosystems are characterized by exchanges of *matter, energy,* and *information* among their components" (Flannery and Marcus 1976:374-5). These are accounts that impose further restrictions, both as to the nature of components of systems, and to the type of relations that may hold among these components.

Marchal is not successful in defending his definition against charges of vacuity. He insists that a system is not merely a set of components that might be related in various ways. The sorts of relations important for systems are a special kind. Yet he admits (1975:446) that no general account of systemic relations that could distinguish them from other relations is available, and that this is an area where further research is required. In the absence of such a general account, however, his definition is not very helpful. For although it may be true that not everything is a system, this definition does not enable us to distinguish those sets that are systems from those that are not. In spite of Marchal's analysis it should be clear that a completely satisfactory definition of "system" is not available.

Given the goals of General Systems Theory, absence of such a definition is a serious problem. That is regarded as such is attested by the amount of effort general systems theorists have expended on the issue. Failure to solve this problem is one of the chief reasons why General Systems Theory is still more a program than a solid body of work.

While the absence of such a definition need not be of particular concern to the archaeologists, who after all are interested only in particular types of systems, archaeologists who want to use General Systems Theory in their research are indirectly affected. Since General Systems Theory regards the definition problem as fundamental, a major part of its research effort has been directed to its solution. Some work has been done on limited types of systems, but the goal of this work is construction of a General Systems Theory, not the complete analysis of these systems. Little work has been done to develop systems principles that are of specific interest to archaeologists. General Systems Theory provides no answer to such questions as "What are the components of archaeologically interesting systems?" "What are the important relations among these components?"

THE RELEVANCE OF GENERAL SYSTEMS THEORY TO ARCHAEOLOGY

All the archaeologist can pick up from the General Systems Theory literature are a few key concepts such as "feedback" and "equilibrium." Furthermore, these concepts did not originate in General Systems Theory; they were borrowed from physics and engineering. I am aware of claims that modern systems theory has greatly refined and elaborated these concepts (Buckley 1967), but I am not convinced of the value of such "refinements," which consist mainly of elaborate jargon. Moreover, to their credit, archaeologists have not been enthusiastic about adopting the jargon.

Consider Flannery (1968). In this work Flannery, following Maruyama (1963), claims to use "first" and "second" cybernetics as a model for explaining prehistoric culture change. "The first cybernetics involves the study of regulatory mechanisms and 'negative feedback' processes which promote equilibrium, and counteract deviation from stable situations . . . . The second cybernetics is the study of 'positive feedback' processes which amplify deviation, causing systems to expand and eventually reach stability at higher levels" (Flannery 1968:68).

Flannery describes early Mesoamerican procurement systems and points out some regulatory mechanisms, i.e. seasonality and scheduling, which were instrumental in maintaining stability of the ecosystem. This is an interesting piece of work, but General Systems Theory deserves no credit for it. As we have said before, the recognition of the importance of systems long antedates General Systems Theory. If stability of a system is to be explained, then it makes sense to look for stabilizing mechanisms. This again is no original insight of General Systems Theory. General Systems Theory provides no help as to the nature of regulatory mechanisms. No esoteric elaboration of the "negative feedback" concept is required for Flannery's analysis. In fact, Flannery's use of the concept is closer to what Buckley (1967:52) calls the "vulgarized" use rather than its use as a "principle underlying the goal-seeking behavior of complex systems." Flannery does not say, or even imply, that the ecosystem was a purposive system, nor does he use the concept of feedback to account for such purposiveness.

After a long period of stability the ecosystem did change, and Flannery invokes positive feedback processes to account (at least partially) for the changes that occurred. Minor and accidental genetic changes in maize and beans were exploited and reinforced in various ways. It is not clear, however, what additional explanatory value labeling these processes as "positive feedback" has. The real value of Flannery's analysis lies in his rejection of a search for a single first cause that could account for the establishment of an agricultural subsistence pattern. But the recognition of multiple causal factors, and their ability to modify minor events to effect significant change, is a common feature of scientific study that does not depend on any contribution of General Systems Theory. See, for example, the interesting study of White (1962).

No one would take issue with the claim that archaeologists who look at the units they study, artifacts and so forth, not as isolated individual entities, but as parts of a larger system with social, cultural, ecological, technological, and other components, will find their understanding enhanced. Such a general outlook might be described as taking a "systemic approach" to archaeological data. Such an approach is not a result of General Systems Theory however. Rather, it is the sort of insight that motivated work on General Systems Theory. Taking the systemic approach, moreover, is such vague advice that it accomodates almost *any* more specific theoretical approach. For example, Watson, LeBlanc, and Redman, according to Plog (1975:208) see the "systemic perspective" as a cure for the normative view of culture that "sought to identify the norms or mental templates that lay behind artifacts." In contrast, David Clarke, whose *Analytical Archaeology* (1968) Plog describes as "by far the most complex and thorough effort to apply general systems theory to archaeology," (1975:210) sees such mental templates as an integral part of the systems with which archaeologists should be concerned. There are many different kinds of systems, and admitting systems that have mentalistic components such as templates is perfectly compatible with a systems approach.

Watson, LeBlanc and Redman regard the "systemic perspective" as conducive to behaviorism, but other writers such as Powers (1973), and those in Buckley (1968) find systems theory an *antidote* to behaviorism. Even Buckley (1967:163-4) warns of the danger of applying inappropriate systems concepts, taken from the study of machines, to human behavior. Attention generated by the program of the general systems theorists has been instrumental in expanding our conception of systems and their importance, but we cannot look to General Systems Theory for an explicit methodology.

MATHEMATICAL SYSTEMS THEORY

Mathematical Systems Theory, unlike General Systems Theory, is a genuine theory with a well-developed body of theorems. It is pure mathematical theory that was developed, as the differential calculus was, with an intended interpretation in mind. Furthermore, as with the calculus, Mathematical Systems Theory has turned out to have broader applications than the original work suggested. Whether it is applicable to archaeology at this time is a serious question to which I will turn shortly.

The original intended application of Mathematical Systems Theory was the construction of electronic computers. The first computers were designed to solve computational problems that were excessively time-consuming for a human computer. They were designed (and here I am talking about mathematical systems design or "software" not the actual physical realization of the machines) to behave like humans when they are following a routine, or step-by-step process, as one would who reads a pair of single digit numbers, receives an instruction to multiply them, looks up the answer in a multiplication table, and writes the answer on a sheet of paper. A system designed to function this way is said to *model* human behavior with respect to this kind of rote performance. Formal characterization, or modeling, of other features of biological systems, such as goal seeking and reproductive behavior, has been an important part of the development of Mathematical Systems Theory. A brief, excellent, and non-technical account of the relationships between biology and Mathematical Systems Theory is in Burks (1975a).

Various types of mathematical systems have been defined in precise ways, and theorems have been proved about the systems that are so defined. Even though some of these results were suggested by analyzing the behavior of biological systems, the results are theorems in pure mathematics. For example, theorems about deterministic systems and about Markov systems depend only on definitions and the principles of logic, not on whether there are any biological systems that meet the conditions of the definitions. As Burks (1975a: 306) points out, up to now the "fit" of such formalisms or models to biological phenomena has been rough. Furthermore, he argues that before such fitting can be improved, biology itself must become broader and better developed. Much more must be known about crucial components of biological systems and their important relationships before they can be modeled successfully. And biologists, not systems theorists, are the ones who are equipped to do this sort of work.

I believe that archaeology is in a position similar to that of biology in this respect. Archaeology, even more than biology, studies extremely complex systems whose boundaries are not well defined. Modeling always ignores some, often fundamental, aspects of a system in order to focus on others. No one model should or does model every feature of a system. Whether a model is good or bad depends partly on our purposes in constructing the model. Unless the components of a system and their systemic relationships are well understood it is difficult to decide which features may be ignored in constructing useful models.

"Hard" sciences, such as physics, are often contrasted with social sciences because of what appears to be their greater simplicity. But in the early stages of the development of modern physics things did not seem so simple. Only after such properties as color, taste, odor, tactile qualities, and heard sounds came to be regarded as "secondary" qualities, irrelevant to physics, did physical systems seem to possess the sort of simplicity that we now attribute to them. Physics deals with extremely complex phenomena. But it has succeeded in reducing the number of variables needed to account for these phenomena by explaining some in terms of others, and by treating still others as irrelevant. Social sciences have not been successful in reducing the number of variables that account for the phenomena that interest them. However, it is still to early to know whether this is possible in principle. Biology has been more successful in this enterprise than the social sciences, but it has not yet achieved the simplicity of physics and chemistry.

THE RELEVANCE OF MATHEMATICAL SYSTEMS THEORY TO ARCHAEOLOGY

Archaeologists have regarded assistance with the construction of models as one of the chief benefits of looking at work done in Mathematical Systems Theory. Mathematical models may be distinguished from physical models, such as topographical maps. In mathematical models the components of the real system and the relations among them are represented by mathematical relations among variables. For example, a given sample of helium gas at moderate temperature and pressure is modeled with respect to changes in pressure, volume, and tempterature by the ideal gas law: $PV = kT$. In a mathematical model the real system is modeled by a mathematical system. The classification and analysis of such models is thus an important part of Mathematical Systems Theory.

A distinguishing feature of the advanced physical sciences is their success in developing mathematical models. In their desire to make their own disciplines more scientific many social scientists have taken the development of such models as a task of primary importance. Some have tried to borrow and modify the mathematical models that are found in Mathematical Systems Theory in order to achieve this goal.

Among archaeologists, David Clarke's attempts along these lines are the most ambitious. Clarke, like many other anthropologists, regards cultures as systems whose chief function is the transmission of information. Like other anthropological archaeologists, Clarke believes that archaeology is a behavioral science that has as its goal the understanding of past cultures, and that this goal can be achieved through the study of the material remains of those cultures.

> Artefacts, according to our view, embody information—congealed information about the actions integrated in their fabrication, information about their intent, and information about the 'sensory' level of the culture's technology. It is part of the case maintained here that artefacts represent coded information of great variety and capable of direct interpretation or misinterpretation by individuals [Clarke 1968:120].

At some points in his work Clarke suggests that past cultures might be regarded as "black boxes" whose outputs, or fragments of outputs, are studied by archaeologists. But a system can be treated as a black box only when we have access to an unlimited number of inputs as well as their correlated outputs. Obviously this is impossible in the case of an extinct cultural system (Steiger 1971).

The passage quoted from Clarke suggests another approach though, one which he tries to implement. Complex systems can sometimes be analyzed into sets of subsystems that are distributed throughout the underlying system. For example, the system of rational numbers is such a subsystem of the system of real numbers, which includes the irrationals as well as the rationals. A physical example is provided by considering the sample of a gas mentioned earlier. This can be regarded as a system of molecules that are traveling at various speeds (the underlying microscopic system), with a macroscopic subsystem described by such gross quantities as pressure, volume, and temperature. A study of the subsystem can be an aid to understanding the underlying system because some of the same rules may govern both the subsystem and the underlying system. For example, both the system of rational numbers and the underlying real number system are dense systems—i.e., between every two members of each system there is another member.

Clarke claims that cultural systems are made up of various subsystems: religious, economic, social, psychological, and the material culture subsystem, which in its partially preserved form is the primary concern to the archaeologist. He believes that a study of relations between members of the material culture subsystem will yield knowledge of the underlying cultural system relations.

There are a number of serious difficulties with this approach. In the first place Clarke does not present sufficient evidence to show that the material culture constitutes a *subsystem* of the culture system of which is is a part, let alone a subsystem whose function, like that of the underlying cultural system, is the transmission of information. To show that something is a subsystem, one must exhibit its systemic relations. Not every collection of parts of a system constitutes a subsystem. For example, all the plastic parts of a heating system do not constitute a system in any obvious sense of the term, let alone a subsystem whose function is that of heating the house. The supposed systemic relations in the material culture cannot simply be derived from relationships that form the basis for regarding cultures as systems. The fact that *we* can gain information from artifacts does not show that artifacts transmit information among themselves. To suppose that they do comprise such an information transmission system would involve ignoring important causal relations rather than focusing on them.

Further, even if it could be shown that a given material culture was a system of a certain sort, we could not use this information to infer that the culture system of which it was a subsystem was governed by the same principles as the subsystem. The subsystem of rational numbers has many features that are not properties of its underlying real number system. The macroscopic subsystem modeled by the ideal gas law is a deterministic system, whereas the underlying microscopic system of molecules that is modeled by the kinetic theory of gases is not deterministic. Thus, even when systems and their subsystems are precisely characterized, trying to infer properties of the system from known properties of a subsystem is a risky business.

In the case of material cultures, it is true that one often finds patterns in the interrelationships between elements of the material culture, such as design elements becoming more ornate through time, which indicate some sort of changes in the culture that produced them. These relations are important and worth investigating. But the principle that underlies the utility of this procedure is that which says that different effects proceed from different causes. This principle is not a special feature of systems theory; it is common to many scientific investigations. And it should be used with some caution

51

because it applies strictly only when deterministic laws are operating. Even when cultures are regarded as systems they are rarely considered deterministic systems. Archaeologists are properly interested in the causal relations between material cultures and the cultures that produced them, but it does not seem that viewing material cultures as *subsystems* is the best way to gain knowledge of these cultures.

We can agree with Clarke's claims that archaeologists can extract information about past cultures from the variety in the material remains of these cultures. I am certainly not opposed to much of what Clarke suggests, such as the use of statistical methods in archaeology, the use of computers to handle data more efficiently, computer simulation experiments, and the attempt to quantify concepts that have been dealt with up to now only in a qualitative manner. However, all of this can be done without any particular knowledge of Mathematical Systems Theory.

As Clarke admits, the culture systems that interest archaeologists are highly complex systems. Even if we had more information about such systems, that is, if archaeology itself were better developed, there would still remain another serious difficulty in applying the results of Mathematical Systems Theory to archaeology. The mathematical models developed in Mathematical Systems Theory are, at this stage, far too simple to be applied with much success to the complex systems that interest archaeologists. Mathematical Systems Theory is limited by its own lack of mathematical richness to applicability to only rather simple real systems. The mathematics used is, for the most part, discrete, non-continuous, and deterministic rather than statistical. In order to achieve a good fit between mathematical models and archaeology, the mathematical theory as well as the archaeological theory must be better developed (Burks 1975a:306). This does not preclude archaeologists from doing mathematical modeling, but successful models are more apt to come from mathematically sophisticated archaeologists than from the literature of Mathematical Systems Theory.

SYSTEMS EXPLANATIONS

Another area in which some archaeologists (Tuggle, Townsend, and Riley 1972) have claimed usefulness for systems theory is in "the systems approach" to explanation. Finding an alternative approach to explanation has not been a strong motivating factor in most work on systems theory. On the contrary, systems theorists such as Wiener (1948) have tried to use systems concepts to *reduce* functional explanation to standard deductive-nomological (Hempel 1965) explanation. But Meehan (1968) claims that Hempel's account does not do justice to the multiplicity of causes since it presupposes a simple cause-effect relationship. As LeBlanc (1973:208) correctly points out, Hempel's account of explanation has no restrictions as to the number of laws, or the number of variables in the laws, which may be used in an explanation, so this accusation of oversimplification is ungrounded.

However, in spite of this, Hempel does fail to do justice to the causal nature of explanation, not for Meehan's reasons, but because the laws required by the D-N model need not be *causal* laws. Hempel (1965:352) himself is explicit in admitting this. Archaeologists have a legitimate complaint when they criticize models of explanation that ignore the importance of causal factors. When an archaeologist asks why a particular event occurred—why a pueblo was abandoned or how corn became the most important crop—he is asking for an explanation that involves causes. A deductive-nomological explanation of the event might not mention any causal factors at all.

Examination of Meehan's systems model of explanation, however, shows that it is no better in this respect than Hempel's model. Meehan says that phenomena are explained when a mathematical model (or "deductive system") that fits the phenomena is constructed. But one can produce a mathematical model that fits the real system very well, and still fail to provide a causal explanation for the phenomena. Most scientists, for example, recognize that the ideal gas law does not *explain* the behavior of gases under changes of temperature and pressure, though it can certainly *predict* such behavior. The correct explanation of this phenomena is given in terms of the statistical laws governing motions of molecules that make up the gases.

One feature of Meehan's account is that the mathematical model may come from any source at all— if it fits then it explains. An amusing example of the inadequacy of a mathematical model to the task of explanation was reported to me recently by an historian who was the outside examiner in a sociology doctoral defense. The candidate attempted to explain the decline in birthrate in the U.S. in recent years by showing that the birthrate curve fitted an equation that had been developed from the studies of fruit-fly populations. The "explanation" did not involve any acknowledgement of such factors of the availability of various contraceptives, the widespread publicity about the dangers of overpopulation, or the existence of family planning agencies. I think most of us could agree that the historian was not being "unscientific" or "showing a humanistic bias" in objecting to the student's thesis.

In criticizing the systems account of explanation in this way, I am not saying that the explanations that attempt to conform to such an account never mention causal factors. But in spite of this, the *model* of explanation itself does not require attention to causality, and it is theoretically deficient on this ground. Mathematical models, even when they fit, do not in and of themselves constitute satisfactory explanations.

CONCLUSION

In view of what has been shown, I think it would be unreasonable for archaeologists to expect either General Systems Theory or Mathematical Systems Theory to provide them with a developed theory that could be adapted to archaeology, or even with much specific help in constructing an archaeological theory. Even Flannery's work, often cited as a model of work done under systems theory guidelines, makes no real use of concepts that are unavailable outside of systems theory, let alone any general principles or laws unique to systems theory.

How then do we account for the impact that systems theory has had on archaeology? If not a theory, what does it offer to the archaeologist? Well, some flashy vocabulary for one thing: "feedback," "kickers," "dynamic equilibrium," and "homeostasis." A new language does sometimes enable us to look at things in new ways. And if it can do that it is not merely jargon. Nor is it jargon if it can clarify our thinking by reducing imprecision. But we should be wary of trying to apply precisely defined terms outside their restricted limits. "Isomorphism" has been much abused in this way. An isomorphism is a mathematically defined relation: an order preserving one to one correspondence between two sets. The concept of isomorphism is simply not applicable to two sets or systems that do not have exactly the same number of members or components. It should be apparent that it is almost never applicable to any two systems that interest archaeologists. "Analogy" is more vague than "isomorphism," but it is more useful because of its vagueness. It would be more productive for archaeologists to investigate what sorts of analogies provide good bases for inferences of various sorts than to try to set up "isomorphisms" between systems that have only a rough structural similarity. Archaeology will not become scientifically respectable by merely adopting systems theory jargon.

The holistic approach of systems theory has also the healthy effect of reducing tendencies to excessive narrowness in research efforts. For this purpose, however, a brief dose is sufficient and will enable one to avoid the unpleasant side effects of prolonged treatment.

Systems theory has been an inspiration to many. And doubtless, in a very general way, the systemic approach, adopted as a supplement to diffusionist or evolutionary accounts of archaeological phenomena, can help with new insights for organizing and explaining the data. But adopting the systemic approach, as has been shown, is compatible with different and conflicting archaeological theories. And the literature of General Systems Theory and Mathematical Systems Theory is not particularly useful even to the archaeologist who decides to organize research along systemic lines.

Nothing that has been said here is intended to preclude the possibility of some form of systems theory that is applicable to archaeology. But at this time there is only the possibility.*

* After this paper was written, Berlinski's (1976) attack on systems theory was published. Readers who are unconvinced by my arguments may be persuaded by this book.

Acknowledgments. I am grateful for help received from M. B. Schiffer and the anonymous reviewers for *American Antiquity,* J. J. Reid, Director of Grasshopper Field School in 1976, and his students, W. A. Longacre and members of his seminar in Fall, 1976, W. C. Salmon, and the National Science Foundation.

Berlinski, David
1976　*On systems analysis.* The MIT Press, Cambridge, Mass.

Boulding, Kenneth
   1972   Economics and general systems. Lazlo 1972:77-92.
Buckley, Walter F.
   1967   *Sociology and modern systems theory.* Prentice-Hall, Englewood Cliffs.
   1968   *Modern systems research for the behavioral scientist.* Aldine, Chicago.
Burks, A. W.
   1975a   Logic, biology and automata—some historical reflections. *International Journal of Man-Machine Studies* 7:297-312.
1975b   Models of deterministic systems. *Mathematical Systems Theory* 8:295-308.
Clarke, David L.
   1968   *Analytical archaeology.* Methuen, London.
Flannery, Kent
   1968   Archeological systems theory and early Mesoamerica. *Anthropological Archeology in the Americas.* B. J. Meggers, Anthropological Society of Washington, Washington, D.C.
   1973   Archeology with a capital S. In Redman 1973:47-53.
Flannery K. and Marcus, J.
   1976   Formative Oazaca and the Zapotec cosmos. *American Scientist* 64:374-83.
Hempel, Carl G.
   1965   *Aspects of scientific explanation.* The Free Press, New York.
Lazlo, Ervin
   1972   *The relevance of general systems theory.* Geo. Braziller, New York.
LeBlanc, S.
   1973   Two points of logic concerning data, hypotheses, general laws, and systems. In Redman 1973:199-214.
Marchal, J. H.
   1975   The concept of a system. *Philosophy of Science* 42:448-68.
Maruyama, Magorah
   1963   The second cybernetics. *American Scientist* 51:164-179.
Meeham, Eugene
   1968   *Explanation in social science—a system paradigm.* The Dorsey Press, Homewood, Illinois.
Miller, James G.
   1965   Living systems: cross-level hypothesis. *Behavioral Science* 10:380-411.
Plog, Fred T.
   1973   Diachronic anthropology. Redman 1973:181-98.
   1975   Systems theory in archeological research. *Annual Review of Anthropology.* B. J. Siegel, Ed. Annual Reviews, Inc. 4:207-224, Palo Alto, California.
Powers, William T.
   1973   Feedback: beyond behaviorism. *Science* 179:351-356.
Rapaport, Anatol
   1968   Foreword. In Buckley 1968:xiii-xxii.
   1972   The search for simplicity. In Lazlo 1972:13-20.
Redman, C. L.
   1973   *Research and theory in current archeology.* John Wiley & Sons, Inc., New York.
Steiger, W. L.
   1971   Analytical archaeology? *Mankind* 8:67-70.
Tuggle, H. D., Townsend, A. H., Riley, T. J.
   1972   Laws, systems, and research designs. *American Antiquity* 37:3-12.
Watson, P. J., Leblanc, S., and Redman, C. L.
   1971   *Explanation in archeology: an explicitly scientific approach.* Columbia University Press, New York.
White, Lynn Jr.
   1962   *Medieval technology and social change.* Oxford University Press, Oxford.
Wiener, Norbert
   1948   *Cybernetics.* John Wiley and Sons, New York.

"BRAND X" VERSUS THE RECOMMENDED PRODUCT

Lewis R. Binford

Richard Gould has built a substantial literature treating the subject of archaeological method with an emphasis on ethnoarchaeology. His writings have been received with mixed feelings by the field and have recently sparked an interesting "debate." Much of Gould's criticism of the recent literature stems from his misunderstanding of that material. In similar fashion, I suspect that much misdirection in the current "debate" stems from Gould's naivete regarding his own philosophy. Therefore, I have attempted an analysis of Gould's works that will, I hope, clarify his position as well as the character of the points he raises that are in need of debate.

Gould's Comment on Binford appears in this issue. Editor.

THE ANALOGY PROBLEM

In a recent series of publications Richard Gould (1971, 1974, 1977, 1978a, 1978b, 1980a) has presented his views on what he considers the major problems of contemporary archaeology. He has offered suggestions as to how these might be solved. His efforts have received mixed responses within the field.

Gould crafts a persuasive alternative to explanation by direct analogy. In so doing, *he renounces several propositions fundamental to modern archaeology. . . . Serious doubt is cast upon the pervasive assumption that archaeological sites represent fossilized human behavior. . . .* He cautions against uncritical applications of the principle of *uniformitarianism, which is more appropriate to the physical sciences than to archaeology* but which is a central assumption in the use of argument by direct analogy. . . . *Living archaeology is among the more profound statements on archaeological theory and practice to appear in recent years* [McIntosh 1980: 117–118]. [The emphases are all mine.]

Quite clearly the reviewer considers Gould's work to be a major, even classic, contribution to our field. On the other hand, the same book was reviewed by Patty Jo Watson (1982), who obviously found it difficult and somewhat obscure.

The book is entertaining, but it is not easy to extract from it precisely what Gould believes ethnoarchaeology is and should be, and thus to compare his position with previous views [Watson 1982:455].

After discussing Gould's positions, Watson seems to come to the conclusion that far from being one of the more profound statements on archaeological theory and practice to date, nothing very new or profound was to be found. Watson's position has been summarized by Wylie (1982:385) as follows:

. . . Watson draws the critical conclusion . . . arguing that Gould is only able to differentiate his position from its forebears as sharply as he does by rhetorical sleight of hand and that, in doing this, a considerable amount of confusion has been introduced into the ethnoarchaeological literature. . . . This is a serious charge when directed, as it is, against a position intended to clear away confusion and provide ethnoarchaeology with a comprehensive and unifying conceptual framework.

I (Binford 1980) reviewed Gould's book and reached negative conclusions as regards his contribution. On my recent rereading of Gould, I found as Watson did, that his writing is opaque and

Lewis R. Binford, Department of Anthropology, University of New Mexico, Albuquerque, NM 87131

American Antiquity, 50(3), 1985, pp. 580–590.
Copyright © 1985 by the Society for American Archaeology

hard to follow. More serious, however, was my impression that his presentation was frequently illogical and philosophically "innocent."

Paradoxically, however, I found myself in general agreement with Gould's (1980b) comments and criticism of Carol Kramer's (1979) book and particularly Watson's contribution:

> The theoretical basis for ethnoarchaeology is the use of analogies derived from present observation to aid interpretation of past events and processes [Watson 1979:277].

If Watson is correct, then I would have to side with Gould in pointing out that analogies are reasoned inferences from observed similarities. The simple faith that similar forms had similar causes seems to be a very naive position, particularly when it is realized that the judgment of similarity is at least partially dependent upon how we choose to conceptualize our observations. Viewed in this context, Gould's objections seemed to be germane and to echo objections that I raised long ago (Binford 1967). Watson would reply with the claim that analogies are only trial "interpretative hypothesis" floated by the investigator as ideas to be tested (Gould and Watson 1982:359). We are also instructed that the major way to increase the "plausibility" of our arguments from analogy is to increase the scope of the similarities between the cases being compared (see Gould and Watson 1982:362–363). I need not point out that this is not a test of an inductive argument, it is simply an extension of it. Watson does not offer any suggestion as to how such arguments are to be "tested" regardless of how limited or extensive the positive analogies among compared cases might be. Her suggestion is what I consider to be a simple expansion of an operational definition for the properties to be inferred (see Binford 1977:3–7, 1983a:7–13). I consider the term definition appropriate here since most inferential arguments that appeal to analogies use the analogy as a justification for adopting a definition for the properties to be inferred. Under normal conditions the argument from analogy serves as a warrant for adopting a definitional equation between dynamic conditions and some static properties of the archaeological record. This situation exists because the archaeological record is static and hypotheses regarding the relationships between statics and dynamics *cannot* be tested by an exclusive appeal to the static properties of the archaeological record (see Binford 1983a:14–17). Watson does not recognize this problem and in fact suggests that testing is possible using the archaeological record.

> Gould stresses alertness to anomalies in the process of checking the fit of interpretive models to archaeological data. . . . I stress use of a procedure that centers on testing to confirm or disconfirm the fit between hypothesized relationships (based ultimately on analogy with living systems) and the empirical reality of the archaeological record [Watson in Gould and Watson 1982:363].

On the issue of analogies Gould seems to have put his finger on a major problem for archaeologists and Watson seems oblivious to the problem, as I see it. At least on the issue of problem recognition Gould has taken up an important issue. In fact, on this issue I am more comfortable with Gould's position than with that of Watson. Why then have I been critical of Gould? Why do I find it difficult to understand his arguments and views? Why have I largely been negative toward his works? These were questions that I asked myself as I read the Gould-Watson (1982) dialogue and the additional comments by Alison Wylie (1982).

GOULD, NEW ARCHAEOLOGY, AND PARADIGM CONFLICT

I suppose my reactions to much of Gould's work were conditioned by a hostile and misleading review by Gould (1979) of my (1978) Nunamiut book. A negative approach was common to most of Gould's statements about the "new archaeology." For instance, speaking of what he is clearly setting up as the popular position represented by the "new archaeology," Gould likens the situation to a commercial on television in which the popular "Brand X" is compared to the "real thing" sponsored in the commercial. As everyone knows, "Brand X" is *always set up as the inferior product relative to the one named in the commercial.* Gould's choice of metaphor is perhaps more appropriate than he realized, since he has either misunderstood the major thrusts of Americanist archaeology over the past 20 years or has, as in many of the commercials to which he alludes, quite literally "set up" the new archaeology as a straw man for showing off his own commercial product.

One could analyze Gould's works using traditional tactics, as he has done to others, so that ad hominem questioning of his professional competence (see Binford 1981:239–240; Thompson 1956) would be considered the appropriate procedure for evaluating his arguments. Following this approach we might ask, is he well educated, is he a nice guy, is he honest, is he fair, etc. with the quality of the answers serving as the basis for accepting or rejecting his arguments and ideas. Rejection of this approach was, however, at the very root of what I hoped would develop into a truly "new" archaeology (Binford 1983a:8). I suppose it was the widespread character of this type of personal attack and evaluative innuendo that originally prompted me to advocate a more "scientific" approach to archaeology where we sought to analytically use our experiences in the external world as arbiters of our ideas instead of the traditional procedure where we evaluated the worth of a person as the basis for accepting or rejecting his or her ideas about the external world.

Basic to my position was recognition of the need for exploring our own ideas as conditioners for how we approach experience. It seemed clear to me that the archaic idea that objectivity was a state of mind that "honest" people could achieve was most certainly incorrect (see Binford 1983b). Our ideas and assumptions condition quite fundamentally what we see and what we accept as fact. We need to explore new ways of achieving objectivity. We need to gain new perspectives on the arguments we mount (see Binford 1982) and we desperately need to "lose our innocence" (see Clarke 1973) regarding the role of our paradigm—the culture that we bring to experience, as a conditioner of what we see, how we judge significance, and how we use our observations.

Much of the argument in contemporary archaeology stems from paradigmatic incompatibility among the disputants. Unfortunately, most of the time the paradigmatic issues are not discussed and argument proceeds as if it were the "objective" empirical world or the personal characteristics of the disputants at issue. We need to become much more skilled at paradigmatic criticism because paradigmatic self-awareness is basic to the growth of knowledge and understanding. I have insisted on this point numerous times but most commonly it is not understood, or it is ignored (see Binford 1978b:357–358, 1983b, 1983c, 1984; Binford and Sabloff 1982). Becoming self-aware regarding the intellectual role of our paradigms and increasing our ability to specify their contents so that they can be subjected to evaluation should be a major goal of practitioners within a maturing field.

Gould advocates a particular world view regarding the nature of humankind and the world of archaeology. As part of this paradigm he adopts a particular philosophical position as regards the way we should proceed in our search for knowledge and understanding. I suggest that it is Gould's uncritical adoption of both a paradigm and a particular epistemological theory that guides his behavior and his thought as an archaeologist. These "ethnocentric" views lead him to criticize the works of others, who do not subscribe to his views, as if their work were misguided, poorly conceived, or motivated out of "churlishness" (Gould 1979:738). *I will try to demonstrate that Gould's behavior does not necessarily derive from character flaws or "bad" motives on his part,* instead it is considered here to be a consequence of his paradigm. I hope to show in this critique that, given his viewpoint, his arguments and his treatment of others' ideas possess a legitimate internal logic. I hope further to illustrate that the inadequacies in his argument and views reflect negatively on his paradigm and therefore that one should not "innocently" adopt it, as some of the positive reviewers cited earlier seem to have done.

GOULD'S GOALS

As anthropologists we are interested in questions of symbolism and meaning, but as archaeologists we are inclined to examine such questions from a materialist point of view [Gould 1980:160].

Only in living human societies . . . could one expect to understand the operation of the *really important and interesting aspects of human behavior, namely those having to do with the human use of symbols.* Since these are mainly non-material in nature, it seemed reasonable to conclude that archaeologists with their reliance on material remains . . . could never hope to do more than deal *with a limited and rather unimportant part of the story of the human species* [Gould 1980:3]. [Emphasis mine.]

I think it should be clear that Gould's position assumes that we should be studying symbolism and ideology, yet acknowledges that unfortunately all we have are material things. His assumption seems clear; it is ideas that guide human history. This position is not up for evaluation by Gould, it is simply assumed to be self-evident and, of course, "true." For him, the paradox is clear, archaeology provides the only direct source for potential information about the non-literate history of the human species. This must be understood in terms of the symbols and ideology used by ancient people, yet the *archaeological record is a material record.* The challenge for the archaeologist is to find ways of studying the material record as a means to illuminate the symbolic and ideological domain considered basic or "causal" in human history.

Gould as a Strict Empiricist

It is in dealing with the apparent paradox—idealist's goals and material remains—that Gould, to my mind, makes his first big mistake: he accepts as accurate the traditional arguments regarding the limitations of the archaeological record (see Gould 1980:2). Gould notes, ". . . the problem is basically the same as it has always been since the beginning of archaeology . . . finding and improving ways to overcome the limitations posed by the nature of archaeological evidence" (Gould 1980:2). The limitations to which Gould alludes are, of course, the material character of the archaeological record. The magnitude of this perceived limitation is made clear when it is realized that Gould operates as a *strict empiricist.* That is, he views the scientific approach as one that considers the source of knowledge to be derived directly from one's sense perceptions. Reason, in turn, supplies only analytical tools, that is, conventions and statements true by definition. Furthermore, all important synthetic knowledge is observational in character. For the strict empiricist, theory is conceived of as being synthesized from observational or empirical "laws" and these are simply confirmed empirical generalizations. That is, we offer hypotheses from our experience, and if these trial laws tend to be confirmed by future observations then the hypothesis may be raised to the status of law. Theory is knowledge synthesized or built up step by step. For the strict empiricist, laws are things we *discover* about the world.

> Patterned regularities in our evidence would . . . lead us to discover laws of human behavior [Gould 1980a: 40]. . . . on the basis of this single case we can posit a general principle . . . assuming, for the sake of argument, that cross-cultural testing proves that such a principle exists, we can then apply this principle as an explanatory prediction . . . in the archaeological record [Gould 1981:280].

More surprising than Gould's adherence to the traditional archaeologist's view of science is his belief that I and other "new archaeologists" also adhered to such a position! When Gould comments on the new archaeology's criticism of particularism he states:

> Underlying the overall attack on archaeological particularism was the notion that *it is the regularities in the archaeological data that will provide the basis for laws or lawlike propositions about human behavior* [Gould 1981:40]. [Emphasis mine.]

Gould's belief that everyone subscribes to the strict empiricist view of science leads to his distortion of my work and that of others. I do not think Gould consciously assumes this posture from sophistic motives—I believe that Gould really thinks all persons are empiricists like himself.

The position I adopted regarding the traditional archaeologists' views on the limitations of the archaeological record was stated in 1968:

> The practical limitations on our knowledge of the past are not inherent in the nature of the archaeological record: the limitations lie in our methodological naivete, in our lack of development for principles determining the relevance of archaeological remains to propositions regarding processes and events of the past [Binford 1968:23].

Standing behind this statement was the philosophy that theory represents *inventions* of the human mind, that we cannot observe cause, that we mold "thought experiments" as to the dynamics of causation. In short, we invent, rather than discover, theories or parts of theories. Theories are arguments as to how the world works, not what it is like.

> The transition from data to theory requires creative imagination. Scientific hypotheses and theories are not derived from . . . facts but invented . . . to account for them [Hempel 1966:15].

58

I have said many times that empirical generalizations, the building blocks of theory for the strict empiricist, are only statements about how the world appears to be (see Binford 1978b:358). Theories are arguments or causal models regarding dynamics that seek to deal with the question of why the world appears as it does (see Binford 1981:25). In short, empirical generalizations are the things we seek to explain, they do not themselves explain. "At each juncture of explaining observations from the archaeological record, we must question anew to what variables operative in the past our observations refer" (Binford 1968:25).

His misunderstanding of this issue plus his commitment to empiricism serves to rationalize Gould's recent interest in defining a domain to which we should limit our generalizations. He has called archaeology the "anthropology of human residue formation" (Gould 1978c:815). That is, we cannot properly study or discuss most or even many of the aspects of human behavior that social and cultural anthropologists discuss because we do not have direct access to the relevant empirical domains. We cannot generalize about phenomena to which we do not have access. We do have access to the archaeological record, and following Schiffer, Gould (1978a:2) sees the archaeological record as essentially "rubbish."

> Thus the empirical attitude of the ethnoarchaeologist in studying anthropological processes leading to human residues enables him to move from his discovery of "rules" of behavior as they occur in particular human societies to the possibility of discovering in residue formation "laws" of behavior that are universal to mankind [Gould 1978a:8].

This statement makes explicit Gould's belief that we generate empirical generalizations. For him, it is perfectly clear that we cannot generate generalizations about domains of phenomena that we do not have *empirically* available. Gould's failure to understand that the issues and arguments of the 1960s were aimed at *rejecting* the principles of strict empiricism leads him to assume that I and others must also operate from the same perspective that he adopts—the traditional perspective. Given his viewpoint, my attempts, as well as those of others, to talk about features of the past not "recoverable" archaeologically, such as social organization, were viewed by Gould as misguided attempts to "enliven" our discipline.

> The more archaeologists tried to enliven their interpretations of the past by applying ideas about the past derived from social and cultural anthropology, the more they exposed themselves to the criticism of social and cultural anthropologists whose studies encompassed a wider and presumably more satisfying range of human behavior [Gould 1980a:3].

This statement illustrates Gould's empiricism. Properties of social organization, ideas of how cultural systems work, etc., could be studied only by social and cultural anthropologists. Only they observed the appropriate empirical domain about which only they could offer generalizations. Archaeologists did not study a domain of social phenomena, they studied material things. Gould seems to see the discussions of social organization during the early 1960s as misguided attempts to "make a silk purse out of a sow's ear."

> Not all anthropology is appropriate to the aims of archaeology, and what is perhaps even more important we cannot allow archaeology to be presented as a kind of imperfect anthropology of the past. Archaeology sailed perilously close to this particular intellectual iceberg during the 1960s when it set out to discover matrilineal pottery and other "signatures" of prehistoric social organization. I concur with Roland Fletcher's recent arguments (personal communication) that such efforts created false expectations for archaeologists while at the same time demeaned the discipline of archaeology [Gould 1980a:250].

Gould's beliefs have not only led him to advocate very outdated positions, but he has also assumed that everyone else is or should be a strict empiricist. Given such an assumption he has great difficulty with the writings of those of us who had rejected such positions. He sees our actions as illegitimate, stemming from questionable motives, or perhaps chauvinistic. For him, any thinking person can see that many interpretations offered by some of us have not been based on empirical generalizations from the data!

GOULD'S DESCRIPTIONS OF MY WORK

> In seeking uniformitarian linkages between past and present day human behavior, Binford has invoked the biological concept of adaptation as a potential source of uniformities, and he goes on to construct a detailed model of human behavioral adaptations in relation to immediate circumstantial facts (seasonality, terrain

and distances, modes of transport, movement of game species, and so on). Whatever variability in Nunamiut meat use and faunal residues occurs is seen by Binford as arising from human adaptive behavior in relation to differences in situational and circumstantial factors under which animal products were procured, transported, stored, consumed and ultimately discarded, rather than being due to mental templates or any other kind of normative cultural category shared by these Eskimos. For Binford, it is circumstance rather than culture that determines human behavior in relation to meat procurement and faunal remains [Gould and Watson 1982:366].

This is a distortion of both my work as well as the implications of the Nunamiut studies for anthropology. I will begin my critique of Gould's distortions with a comment I made many years ago, which Edmond Leach seemed to have enjoyed greatly, namely: "Behavior is the by-product of the interaction of a cultural repertoire with the environment" (Leach 1973:762). Given this viewpoint, I designed my Nunamiut studies to demonstrate that when we hold *culture* constant, that is, the repertoire of convention and knowledge, we nevertheless see variable behavior. This variability must be seen as responsive, flexible behavior that the repertoire facilitates in the face of variable environmental conditions. The sites and contexts that I studied among the Nunamiut were largely occupied at different times *by the same individuals*. One could hardly argue that there was a cultural change or ethnic difference between a fall site occupied by Frank Rulland in 1948 and a winter site occupied by Frank Rulland in the same year! Nevertheless, it was demonstrable that there were significant differences between the faunal assemblages at two such sites. These differences were referable to differential transport, dependence upon storage, phase of consumption from stores, etc., characteristic of each occupation. The purpose of my studies was to demonstrate that sites generated by the same men, carrying the same culture, were nevertheless formally different in archaeological content. The point of contention between myself and F. Bordes had been over the degree that cultures were internally homogeneous, that is, recognizable by their consistent similarities, as noted among assemblages, or whether assemblages could be formally different and still referable to a single socio-cultural system. In no place was the argument made that some behavior was ecologically determined and other behavior culturally determined. My research was about how culture works and the character of the behavior that culture facilitates and organizes. The statement by Gould (Gould and Watson 1982:366) that "for Binford, it is circumstance rather than culture that determines human behavior" is a misrepresentation of just about everything I have ever done.

This pattern of misrepresentation is continued when Gould suggests that my ecological arguments were warrants for making uniformitarian assumptions. Gould clearly suggests that my uniformitarian assumptions were about the way humans would respond to such environmental conditions as seasonality, terrain, and distance. This is simply not correct. I made uniformitarian assumptions about the economic anatomy of caribou and sheep. I used these assumptions to evaluate the character of behavioral biases manifest in the differential distribution of anatomical parts on sites.

> To use the principle of uniformitarianism effectively in ethnoarchaeology we must not only ask the right questions but also ask them in the right order. What about hunter-gatherer societies which procure, transport, consume, and discard meat products in a manner patterned altogether differently from the Nunamiut? [Gould and Watson 1982:366]

My uniformitarian assumptions made possible an evaluation of the degree that past peoples responded differently to constant conditions, not, as Gould suggests, an assumption that all people must behave like the Nunamiut. After his telling criticism of my work, Gould goes on to note that he has observed episodes of kangaroo butchering and that, regardless of circumstantial variability, the Australians always butchered the animals into the same nine anatomical units. He notes that he looked for variability in "eco-utilitarian" terms, but found none, at least with respect to butchering.

> The strict adherence to a fixed pattern of initial divisions of meat was explained more parsimoniously with reference to social relations based upon kin-based sharing of food and access to resources . . . than to direct influence of the immediate circumstances under which hunting occurs. While the "extra step" involved in this initial butchering and sharing of meat is ultimately adaptive, it would be hard to explain if one adhered to a simple deterministic notion of how human behavior relates to circumstances. In other words, one must look first at the eco-utilitarian relationships that occur in the situation one observes and see to what extent variation in the observed behavior can be accounted for by these immediate circumstances. If one has exhausted this level of explanation without totally satisfactory results, then one is entitled to go on to the

next higher level of explanation, namely the ideational realm of shared traditions [Gould and Watson 1982: 367].

We see in these statements the confusion wrought by Gould when he translates the works of those who are not his kind of empiricists into his paradigm. Gould saw my discussions of Nunamiut behavior, not as directed toward the understanding of the archaeological record and its variability, but instead as a search for empirical patterns that through ethnographic analogy could be projected as universally relevant to all people. His experiences in Australia seemed a "spoiler" (Yellen 1977: 133) for what he thought I was projecting as potential laws of human behavior. As I have pointed out, I was not making the argument that Gould attributes to me, hence his counterpoint is misdirected.

GOULD'S POSITION: A PHILOSOPHICAL PARADOX

When I discussed Gould's goals I cited him to the effect that symbolism and ideology were the "aspects" of the human experience that we needed to study if we were to understand human history in human terms. This is a common component of most idealist philosophical positions, of which historicism is one expression.

> Historicism in extreme form is the view that human behavior has a special character which precludes explanation by scientific methods because it is not governed by scientific laws; understanding is attained not through scientific explanation but rather through our peculiarly human ability to empathize, to enter into passions, fears, calculations, and aspirations of past humans [Bamforth and Spaulding 1982:179].

True to the above characterization of historicism, Gould argues for the "special character" of human behavior and against the position that scientific explanations could be developed for human phenomena. Gould acknowledges that for "natural phenomena" other than human behavior the methods of science are perhaps sometimes applicable. He also acknowledges that human beings live in a naturalistic matrix, hence the findings of the natural sciences are relevant as a framework in terms of which to view human behavior, but not to explain it (see Gould 1980a:112, where nature is viewed as a limiting factor). This is just another way of stating the ancient folk wisdom expressed in the Mother Goose rhyme "Wear you a hat or wear you a crown, all that goes up must surely come down."

Gould sees human behavior as a strictly human product variable from place to place and time to time. This human "expression" could not be understood in terms of the naturalistic matrix, but instead must be understood in terms of the local characteristics of ideology, philosophy, and symbolism, which presumably vary among societies "historically." Culture conceived in these terms becomes the explanation for variable human behavior and it is considered to be particularistically distributed and variable, both temporally and spatially, in form and content.

It is from this perspective that Gould argues against the search for "laws" of human behavior (see Gould 1980a:36–39). If one believes that laws are discovered and that they are "successful" empirical generalizations, then empirical material—which for Gould appears to be unique, idiosyncratic, or not subject to generalization—would of "necessity" be inappropriate. It appears self-evident that cultural "data" could not serve the goals of generalization as viewed from his perspective. Gould's idealistic philosophy leads him to believe that the results of important human behavior, conditioned by symbolism, philosophy, ideas, values, etc., are not subject to understanding by scientific methods. As an empiricist he expects science to proceed by generating empirical generalizations, then raising such generalizations to law-like status through arguments from enumeration. He suggests that the use of such procedures would overlook the unique and particular, for him the human characteristics, and hence the important aspects of the archaeological record. Gould abhors this "waste" of the particular and unique. It is in this context of reasoning that Gould suggests that the search for "laws" is a shortsighted and wasteful use of archaeological data.

> To this might be added the further recognition that it may be precisely those aspects of human behavior that prove least susceptible to measurement and scientific analysis that could prove, in the end, to be the most decisive. Could it be that the more restrictively quantitative archaeology tries to become, the more trivial it becomes, too? [Gould 1980a:38].

61

Here we see Gould's dilemma. On the one hand, he is an idealist committed to the study of uniquely human characteristics that are thought to require a special kind of explanation. In the latter we use our own human capacities to empathize with those of the past by virtue of our ability to recognize our own humanity in others. At the same time, he is committed to an outdated idea of science, which proposed that knowledge was obtained, not as a result of intellectual activity, but directly through sense perceptions. In this view, scientists clear their minds of bias and observe the world in good faith. They seek to generalize their observations, and over time these generalizations may be raised to the status of laws by the accumulation of an increasing number of confirmed cases.

All statements of regularity are provisional to a degree, since they are always being tested . . . [Gould 1980a: 161].

. . . like anomalies, laws and lawlike statements are relative and must be understood in relation to the process of testing in which they are constantly subjected in science [Gould 1980a:161].

Given this view, Gould sees science as inappropriate to his humanistic, particularizing goals for understanding human behavior. The logic is clear; culture is a human expression otherwise called ideology, philosophy, symbolism, or tradition, which does not vary with respect to "natural laws" and, therefore, represents a domain not amenable to study by the basic procedures of science. Since archaeological remains are presented to us in confused units, one of the ways we may recognize the role of past culture as a conditioner of pattern in archaeological remains is by the very fact that "natural laws" appear to be broken—an anomaly appears.

Gould's objections to ethnographic analogy as cited in the beginning of this paper derive neither from an understanding of its logic nor from philosophical insights into inferential argument. They derive from his strict empiricist views coupled with his belief that human behavior is guided by an "inner" logic derived from local philosophy, ideology, and symbolism. The latter relativistic position leads Gould to view arguments from ethnographic analogy as misguided attempts to offer one's ethnographic experiences as if they were governed by uniform tendencies of human nature. This viewpoint makes it appear to him that we assume "the very things we should be trying to find out" (Gould 1980a:29).

If we view Gould's reading of my (1978) Nunamiut report as an attempt by me to describe "human behavior" and then project this experience, suggesting that all humans would in turn behave in analogous ways, then his distortion of my work makes some sense as does his insistence that there were other peoples who do not behave like the Nunamiut. Given such a view of analogy, the argument that Gould offers regarding anomaly also makes some sense. That is, an anomaly is an ethnographic or archaeological experience that differs empirically from the "standard" that had been presented from some prior ethnographic experiences and by analogy projected as if it applied to all peoples. In short, an anomaly is an example of Yellen's "spoiler" tactics relative to analogical arguments.

Gould views archaeologists, misguided by scientific models, as seeking out experiences and then attempting to generalize these experiences as trial "laws" of human nature. In turn, when we meet an empirical case to the contrary, relative to such generalizations, we then know we are not dealing with universalistic phenomena and must, in his view, shift perspectives from the universalistic to the particular—the particular ideological and symbolic context of the peoples involved.

Anomalies discovered by means of ethnographic studies *compel* archaeologists to expand their explanations in many cases to aspects of the socio-ideational realm of human residue behavior [Gould 1980a:229]. [Emphasis mine.]

"Spoiling" arguments from ethnographic analogy, as he sought to do with my Nunamiut writings (see Gould and Watson 1982:365–368), is one route to discovering "anomalies"; however, the recommended way is to use the findings of natural science to enlighten the historicist's domain.

Instead of trying to discover laws of human behavior, the living archaeologist is concerned with using relationships that have already achieved the status of law in other fields as frameworks for making discoveries about human behavior . . . [Gould 1980a:140].

. . . one must look first at the eco-utilitarian relationships that occur in the situation one observes and see to what extent variation in the observed behavior can be accounted for by these immediate circumstances. If one has exhausted this level of explanation without satisfactory results, then one is entitled to go on to the next higher level of explanation, namely the ideational realm of shared tradition [Gould and Watson 1982: 367].

Patterns, characteristics, and properties of the archaeological record that do not "fit" the natural science laws as conceived by Gould are anomalies and as such betray the role of unique, idiosyncratic, and idealistically based human behavior. This paradigmatic belief renders it possible for Gould to pursue his goal:

If we can put aside analogies and laws, with their uniformitarianist assumptions about how humans *ought to behave*, and instead explore methods that will help us find out how they really do behave, perhaps we will develop wider and more satisfying explanations [Gould 1980:39].

Statements such as this are perhaps the most ironic of Gould's writings because they suggest that his procedures will lead us to "objective" truths and "accurate" insights into human behavior!

Gould's writings are not unique in strangely combining philosophies. What renders Gould's writings most interesting and unique is his naivete regarding the role played by his own beliefs and philosophy in conditioning how he sees the world and particularly how he sees the works of others. As an empiricist, he believes he sees nature clearly, not distorted or filtered by his own thoughts— his paradigm (see Sabloff and Binford 1982). As an empiricist, he believes that his philosophy is given by nature and therefore must be shared by any other honest observer. His empiricism blinds him to the reality that there are others who do not share his empiricist views. Consequently, when he reads my writings he re-creates me in his image. He imparts to me his own strong convictions. As pointed out, he discusses the Nunamiut study as if I were seeking to project the particular behaviors observed among the Nunamiut as universalistic expressions of human nature and hence expectable in the behavior of others. He criticizes the search for laws as if the only meaning of the word was empirical generalization. In his view, the single-minded search for such general phenomena would overlook the unique and, for him, the interesting. He is unaware that laws need not be conceived as successful empirical generalizations (see Binford 1978b). He must be puzzled by statements such as: "The relevance of theory is . . . this, a statement of universal form, whether empirically confirmed or as yet untested, will qualify as a law if it is implied by an accepted theory" (Hempel 1966:58).

Gould's work is perhaps the best demonstration I know of the bankruptcy of the traditionalist's position. His view of "reality" is not given by nature, but through its interaction with the assumptions and intellectual biases he holds. Ironically, his own insistence on the general utility of the empiricist view of science contradicts his alleged commitment to the cultural relativist's position, where the symbols, ideas, and values of different cultures dictate that their practitioners see the world differently, evaluate rationality differently, and behave differently in similar environments or "limiting situations." Why shouldn't this also be true among archaeologists coming from different "traditions"?

I do not adhere to either of the positions advocated by Gould. I am fully convinced that our paradigms condition in awesome ways how we conceive of experience. On the other hand, I am not committed to the sterile skepticism of cultural relativism. I think we can learn how paradigms constrain our thought and conceptualizations of experience. I think we can learn how to use different conceptual approaches to nature. "Science is a method or procedure that directly addresses itself to the evaluation of cultural forms. That is, if we view culture as at least referring to the particularly human ability to give meaning expediently to experience, to symbol, and, in turn, view experience through this conceptual idiom, science is then concerned with evaluating the utility of the cultural tools produced" (Binford 1977:3).

I consider the "new archaeology" as a move toward achieving a more sophisticated self-consciousness regarding the problems inherent in trying to infer a past from contemporary observations. Phrasing the problem this way emphasizes the creative role that the archaeologist plays in constructing a past. This creative role is always in terms of ideas concerning the meanings that contemporary artifacts and other archaeological traces hold for the events and dynamics of the past. The new archaeology advocated a move toward the difficult task of evaluating the cultural tools that we use to aid in our task of constructing a past.

The paradigmatic dependence illustrated in the writings of Gould should emphasize the utility of this position. The critique presented here should also illustrate some of the concerns that were recognized years ago and that prompted many of my suggestions favoring a "new archaeology."

Traditional archaeology was largely an approach that assumed a strict empiricist view of science. Traditional archaeology in its "theoretical" posture assumed an idealistic historicist's perspective for viewing humankind and its works. I have tried to show that these postures are also representative of Gould's views. Gould is trying very hard to reject "Brand X"—the new archaeology—as a laxative for purging intellectual particularism from archaeology. He suggests that he has developed a "recommended brand." As I have studied the recommended product, I have come to realize that, strangely enough, it has all the properties of the disease!

REFERENCES CITED

Bamforth, D. B., and A. C. Spaulding
  1982   Human Behavior, Explanation, Archaeology, History, and Science. *Journal of Anthropological Archaeology* 1(2):179–195.
Binford, L. R.
  1967   Smudge Pits and Hide Smoking: The Use of Analogy in Archeological Reasoning. *American Antiquity* 32:1–12.
  1968   Archaeological Perspective. In *New Perspectives in Archeology,* edited by S. R. Binford and L. R. Binford, pp. 5–32. Aldine Publishing, Chicago.
  1977   General Introduction. In *For Theory Building in Archaeology,* edited by L. R. Binford, pp. 1–10. Academic Press, New York.
  1978a   *Nunamiut Ethnoarchaeology.* Academic Press, New York.
  1978b   Dimensional Analysis of Behavior and Site Structure: Learning from an Eskimo Hunting Stand. *American Antiquity* 43:330–361.
  1980   Review of *Living Archaeology* by R. Gould. *American Scientist* 68(6):704–705.
  1981   *Bones: Ancient Men and Modern Myths.* Academic Press, New York and London.
  1982   Objectivity-Explanation-Archaeology—1981. In *Theory and Explanation in Archaeology,* edited by C. Renfrew, M. J. Rowlands, and B. A. Seagraves, pp. 125–138. Academic Press, New York and London.
  1983a   *Working at Archaeology.* Academic Press, New York and London.
  1983b   Reply to 'More on the Mousterian: Flaked Bone from Cueva Morin' by L. G. Freeman. *Current Anthropology* 24(3):372–377.
  1984a   Bones of Contention: A Reply to Glynn Isaac. *American Antiquity* 49:164–167.
  1984b   An Alyawara Day: Flour, Spinifex Gum, and Shifting Perspectives. *Journal of Anthropological Research* 40(1):157–182.
Binford, L. R., and J. Sabloff
  1982   Paradigms, Systematics, and Archaeology. *Journal of Anthropological Research* 3(2):137–153.
Clarke, D. L.
  1973   Archaeology: The Loss of Innocence. *Antiquity* 47(1):6–18.
Gould, R. A.
  1971   The Archaeologist as Ethnographer: A Case from the Western Desert Aborigines of Australia. *World Archaeology* 3(2):143–177.
  1974   Some Current Problems in Ethnoarchaeology. In *Ethnoarchaeology,* edited by C. B. Donnan and C. W. Clewlow, pp. 29–48. Monograph IV, Institute of Archaeology, University of California, Los Angeles.
  1977   Ethno-archaeology: Or Where Do Models Come from? In *Stone Tools as Cultural Markers,* edited by R. V. S. Wright, pp. 162–168. Australian Institute of Aboriginal Studies, Canberra.
  1978a   From Tasmania to Tucson. In *New Directions in Ethnoarchaeology,* edited by R. A. Gould, pp. 1–10. University of New Mexico Press, Albuquerque.
  1978b   Beyond Analogy in Ethnoarchaeology. In *Explorations in Ethnoarchaeology,* edited by R. A. Gould, pp. 249–293. University of New Mexico Press, Albuquerque.
  1978c   The Anthropology of Human Residues. *American Anthropologist* 80(4):815–835.
  1979   Caribou Hunters—Review of *Nunamiut Ethnoarchaeology,* by L. R. Binford. *Science* 20(4394):737–739.
  1980a   *Living Archaeology.* Cambridge University Press, New York.
  1980b   Review of *Ethnoarchaeology* edited by C. Kramer. *Archaeology* 33(4):737–739.
  1981   Brandon Revisited: A New Look at an Old Technology. In *Modern Material Culture: The Archaeology of Us,* edited by R. A. Gould and M. B. Schiffer, pp. 269–281. Academic Press, New York and London.

Gould, R. A., and P. J. Watson
  1982   A Dialogue on the Meaning and Use of Analogy in Ethnoarchaeological Reasoning. *Journal of An-thropological Archaeology* 1(4):355–381.
Hempel, C. G.
  1966   *The Philosophy of Natural Science.* Prentice-Hall, Englewood.
Kramer, C. (editor)
  1979   *Ethnoarchaeology: Implications of Ethnography for Archaeology.* Columbia University Press, New York.
Leach, E.
  1973   Concluding Address. In *The Explanation of Culture Change: Models in Prehistory,* edited by C. Renfrew, pp. 761–771. Duckworth, London.
McIntosh, R. J.
  1980   Review of *Living Archaeology* by R. A. Gould. *Science* 210(4474):1117–1118.
Thompson, R. H.
  1956   The Subjective Element in Archaeological Inference. *Southwestern Journal of Anthropology* 12(3):327–332.
Watson, P. J.
  1979   The Idea of Ethnoarchaeology: Notes and Comments. In *Ethnoarchaeology: Implications of Ethnography for Archaeology,* edited by C. Kramer, pp. 227–287. Columbia University Press, New York.
  1982   Review of *Living Archaeology* by R. A. Gould. *American Antiquity* 47:445–448.
Wylie, A.
  1982   An Analogy by Any Other Name is Just as Analogical: A Commentary on the Gould-Watson Dialogue. *Journal of Anthropological Archaeology* 1(4):382–401.
Yellen, J. E.
  1977   *Archaeological Approaches to the Present: Models for Reconstructing the Past.* Academic Press, New York.

comments

THE EMPIRICIST STRIKES BACK: REPLY TO BINFORD

Richard A. Gould

A reply to Lewis Binford's criticism concerning my views on archaeological inference and the relationships of such inferences to various kinds of ethnoarchaeology, with special reference to the Australian data included in Binford's critique.

I am glad Lewis Binford regards me as a "strict empiricist" and attempts to evaluate my work accordingly, since this indicates that he has understood the direction I am taking in my ethnoarchaeological research and the relationship of that work to the rest of archaeology. For years, Binford has been telling colleagues and students that the evidence of the archaeological record does not speak for itself but requires the self-conscious application of particular paradigms in order to explain the behavior that produced it, and he repeats this view here. In the 1960s this was a position that promoted refreshing changes in the nature of archaeology and led to stimulating debates. Today Binford's assertions of this position have begun to sound increasingly doctrinaire, because they place too much emphasis on a mentalist view of archaeology that confuses the role of ideas in the history of the discipline with the realities of what it is that archaeologists seek to discover. Perhaps now is a good time to consider the alternative to Binford's view; namely that there is a real world out there, and ask to what extent it is knowable to us through our observations. To accept such a view would mean, of course, that the evidence does speak for itself if we will allow ourselves to be guided by it.

As anyone who has read *Living Archaeology* knows, I have found the field of astronomy to be a valuable source of illustrations and models for the empirical science of archaeology. This is no accident, since astronomy, like archaeology, is a science based upon inference. To a large extent, too, astronomy is a historical science, in which the explanation of past events must be based upon uniformitarian principles observed to be operating in the present. My position here is that discoveries are possible in archaeology just as they are in astronomy, geology, paleontology, or any other historical science. Discoveries take place in astronomy for the blindingly obvious reason that there really are phenomena in the universe that can be perceived, measured, and predicted. But it is also true that this process of discovery can occur only when observations are organized according to the expectations of the observers, and ideas about the universe and the place of humankind in it have changed—thus, so have these expectations. Binford is not wrong when he stresses the importance of ideas with respect to their role in organizing the observations one makes of the world or the universe, as such "paradigm shifts" as the Copernican Revolution demonstrate. Yet these same shifts can also be interpreted as the result of a willingness by the observers to be *guided by the evidence* of their observations. This is the position I would like to argue for in archaeology generally and in ethnoarchaeology in particular. The views expressed by Binford in this paper and elsewhere can be regarded as part of an extreme mentalist position that, while advocated by social-cultural anthropologists in some quarters, is not necessarily the most appropriate for archaeologists today. Indeed, I have always admired many of the empirical aspects of Binford's research (especially in

Richard A. Gould, Department of Anthropology, Brown University, Providence, RI 02912

67

his ethnoarchaeological studies of the Nunamiut) and have singled out these discoveries, based as they are upon the recognition and measurement of relationships between circumstantial and behavioral factors, as among the most convincing results he has achieved. Ironically, Binford appears to regard such recognition as a negative treatment of his work, perhaps because I do not praise his mentalistic attitudes with equal enthusiasm. My argument here is that, as far as ethnoarchaeology is concerned, Binford's best results lie in precisely those situations where he has been able to observe the interactions of various components of the material culture and the circumstances that structure those situations. These circumstances obviously include biogeographical factors such as terrain, seasonality, and vegetation, as well as such aspects of learned behavior as available technology, information about weather, habits of game animals, and social expectations in relation to the other people in the situation. Many of the accounts in *Nunamiut Ethnoarchaeology* that describe and analyze the effects of these circumstantial factors on the outcomes of situations involving butchering, consumption, and discard of caribou products are among the best of their kind in the ethnoarchaeological literature today. Binford is also on firm empirical footing when he extends these observations to larger generalizations about the nature of "logistical" organization among certain kinds of hunter-gatherers (Binford 1978:88–90). If one were looking at only this kind of result, I would suggest that there was little real difference between our philosophies and that we are interested in very much the same kinds of ethnoarchaeology. That is, the empirical approach in ethnoarchaeology should include not only a detailed, firsthand knowledge of the behavior in the particular society one is studying closely but also a good knowledge of comparative ethnology and archaeology — something Binford has also demonstrated.

Although his name was never mentioned in this connection, Binford has evidently identified himself and the "new archaeology" as the target of the critique I offered of "Brand X." Since he has now risen (see his article in this issue) to defend "Brand X" against all real or imagined opponents, I would like to use this opportunity to clarify the differences between our positions and make it easier for our archaeological colleagues to do what I hope they were going to do anyway, which is to compare the alternative products available and choose the one that suits their goals best. I shall, of course, argue strictly for the empiricist position. At no time, however, did I ever claim that Binford adheres to such a view, and I am at a loss to understand where Binford got this idea. What I have done, as suggested earlier, is sift for empirical "nuggets" in his research results as well as in the backdirt of Binfordian rhetoric and then try to relate my own results to these solid finds. Such efforts, however, are complicated by Binford's failure to distinguish between the role of mental constructs in the history of ideas, as exemplified by his characterization of Hempel's views about the invention of theories, and the empirical realities of a world of behavioral phenomena that exists independently of those theories and that can be discovered through controlled observation and measurement.

THE OATH OF MEASUREMENT

Binford's 1968 statement about the practical limitations of our knowledge of the past being due to inadequacies of method and theory rather than anything inherent in the nature of the archaeological record is only partly true. In fact, the archaeological record does impose insurmountable limitations to the scope of archaeological inference, although I do recognize that the history of archaeology has been one of overcoming apparent limitations imposed by the material record. On the one hand we can look back over the history of archaeology and agree that methodological improvements have led to tangible gains in reconstructing prehistoric diets, technologies, and other key elements such as relevant chronologies and ecology. Yet if we look again we can see important domains of human behavior that are not likely to yield themselves to archaeological explanations, no matter how theoretically sophisticated we become. This was the point of the first chapter in *Living Archaeology*. Is Binford seriously implying, for example, that we will ever be sure of the specific phonological or grammatical characteristics of prehistoric languages through archaeological research? Although Binford takes a more optimistic view on this point, I would ask the same about the details of prehistoric social organization that several of the "new archaeologists" of the late

1960s were then claiming to have reliably inferred from archaeological evidence, especially in the Southwestern Pueblos. What we have here is an extreme position—stimulating and partly true, but not necessarily in touch with the realities of preservation and deposition in the archaeological record. Like Binford, I support the testing of new ideas that will lead archaeologists to overcome these limitations, but I seriously doubt that they will ever be overcome entirely.

In fact I would go further and argue that application of inappropriate theories in this way can, at times, be counterproductive. So many basic relationships between human behavior and material residues still require explanations that we need to assign priorities in our choices of theory and the levels to which we apply them. Two brief examples from the corpus of Binford's research illustrate this; the failure by Binford and Binford (1969) to demonstrate the relationship between different tasks and the factors produced in their factor analysis of Mousterian stone artifacts, and the lingering doubts about the utility indices developed by Binford (1978) in his caribou butchering and meat-use study. In the case of the former, we lack any behavioral basis for connecting the different clusters of attributes generated by a sophisticated analytical technique to the behaviors that produced them. We cannot even be certain to what extent these attributes and their clustering was due to human behavior or physical factors in the natural environment. In the latter case, the utility indices used rigorously throughout this analysis were based on the anatomical study of a single animal (a bull approximately three to five years old; Binford 1978:15). While the dissection of this animal was done with care and described in detail, it does not control for differences in age, sex, and general condition due to variations in diet or disease, within the larger caribou population. Binford does not exaggerate concern about his statistical procedures when he says, "I realize that the sample size is quite small" (1978:18). In fact, there is detailed information of this kind available in published form (often in English, or with English summaries) from Scandinavia related to the large-scale modern reindeer ranching industries of Fennoscandia. Neither of these studies satisfies the requirements of empiricist science, which asserts that there is a real caribou population out there, or that there are real-world factors of both human and non-human origin that structure stone-artifact morphology. From a strictly empirical point of view what is needed is better measurement of the actual variations that exist in these populations before attempting to construct generally applicable categories or indices. In short, I agree with Binford's idea of organizing his observations along these lines, but I am critical of the assumed relationships between those ideas and the realities they are supposed to represent.

All empirical social scientists take a kind of "oath of measurement" and attempt to observe human behavior accordingly. But certain kinds of measurements are essential before others can be of use. It is as important to be guided by the evidence as by one's ideas in deciding about what to measure first and the order in which other measurements should follow. In the two examples cited above, overconcern for the integrity of the hypotheses being tested appears to have led to a lack of recognition of variables that are potentially important factors in the material domain being studied. If, according to Binford's assertions, I am to be regarded as a strict empiricist, we may now regard Binford as an idealist who has taken to an extreme his conception of Hempelian doctrine concerning ideas as prime determinants in the history of science and applied it directly to his own research. Actually, I do not regard Binford as a pure idealist, any more than I regard myself as a pure empiricist (whatever that may be!), but there are real differences in our research priorities.

In a previous paper (Gould and Saggers, 1985), also criticized by Binford and Stone, Sherry Saggers and I pointed out another example of this difference in priorities. The Binford-Stone critique presents a good example of how inappropriate theory can be when it does not adhere to the empirical facts it purports to explain. Binford and Stone have what sounds like a good idea when they propose that the relative frequencies of local versus exotic lithic material for stone adzes from the excavated sites at Puntutjarpa and James Range East are best explained as being due to curation from use as personal gear. Perhaps these adzes qualify as "personal gear," in Binfordian terms, but that whole idea remains a mentalist construct until some measurements that are external to the cultural system of either the producers (in this case, the Nunamiut) or the observer are available to connect this argument to the material world. The "anticipated future needs" claimed by Binford must be evaluated against measurement of the actual performance of those materials in relation to those needs.

In order to measure that kind of performance, Saggers and I undertook the experiments described in our paper, and Saggers (1984) has gone on to develop a further series of by-product experiments that afford even better control over variations within as well as between different classes of lithic raw materials. Binford's position would not adequately measure or control for the physical and material properties that relate to the anticipated future needs of the desert Aborigines of Australia with respect to their lithic technology. We cannot simply assume that people always "decide" to behave in the most efficient or optimal manner. Observed behavior of this sort must always be tested against real-world measurements, and when dissonances appear, as they often do, other kinds of explanations may be required. Anyone reading our paper will note that Saggers and I had already backed away from the "righteous rocks" explanation (Binford and Stone are beating a dead horse here) in favor of a lower-order materialist explanation for the Puntutjarpa and James Range data. I would say now that Binford's "personal gear" explanation may fit the data from Puntutjarpa and James Range East, but only after the controls provided by our measurements of the relative efficiency of procurement and edge-holding properties of different lithic raw materials occurring at those sites have been applied. Moreover, Binford's argument adds little to ours, which was that utility must be measured before inferences concerning "decisions" or choices in prehistoric technologies are attempted. Binford's idea of "personal gear" lacks an empirical basis outside the observed behavior and attitudes of the Nunamiut.

The nature of this problem is apparent when Binford and Stone go on to argue that:

> At Puntutjarpa the best material was local and that was the dominant material used for adzes. At James Range East the best material was exotic to the area and much more exotic material, relative to Puntutjarpa, was in fact used for adzes. It would be interesting to know if at James Range East there was also a more exhaustive use of the adzes of exotic material than was observed at Puntutjarpa; we would expect such a pattern [1985:153].

Indeed, it would be interesting. This same idea was considered by Saggers and me early in our research program. But it was quickly put aside because an empirical consideration of desert Aborigine adze-making, use, and discard showed that this test is unworkable. In order to apply it, one would have to know the size of the original stone-adze flake before it was progressively worn down by use and resharpening. The worn out remnants of these adze flakes (termed slugs) provide no reliable clues as to the original size of the flake from which each one was derived, so a measurement of the end-product, namely the slug, cannot inform us accurately about the relative exhaustion of the flake, which is what we would have to know in order to compare relative degrees of exhaustive use at these two sites and in relation to different raw materials. In other words, Binford and Stone's hypothesis lacks a useful test implication, which is one of the requirements of empirical science. This problem should not come as a surprise to anyone working in the field of lithic technology, since it has been long recognized that lithic manufacture and use are essentially subtractive processes, involving progressive removal of material (hence the widely used term, lithic reduction sequence) to achieve the final shape and size of the object. The problem referred to here is actually a corollary of an idea proposed by Don Crabtree (1972:3) in which the final finishing or use to which a stone artifact was subjected obscures or erases the preceding stages in the lithic reduction sequence. So another stimulating Binfordian idea bites the proverbial dust for want of a reliable empirical basis.

In fact, the empirical basis and accuracy of measurement are at least as important as theory in establishing the usefulness of a piece of archaeology or ethnoarchaeology. Binford's insistence on his conception of the Hempelian view of science accords inadequate recognition to the way improvements in measurement within the material and chronological domains of archaeology have transformed the discipline. One can, I believe, argue that the development of radiometric dating measurements has done at least as much, if not more, to change the direction of modern archaeology as the "new archaeology," and the same can be said for many other equally scientific approaches to measurement in areas like paleoecology, diet, materials analysis, and others. I am not seriously questioning Binford's point of view that the use of these methods must be guided by relevant theory, but I think it is appropriate here to assert that archaeological theories that do not adequately apply such measurements or control for the material variables that affect human behavior will be suspect on empirical grounds. It is a truism in science that major discoveries follow from improvements in measurement as much as they do from paradigmatic shifts. Astronomy today amply demonstrates this proposition, as new techniques of measurement like radio and infra-red astronomy completely change our concept of the universe (Burbidge 1983; Rubin 1983). Binford is categorically wrong when he claims that empirical science is ". . . derived directly from one's sense perceptions" (this issue, p. 583). Anyone who practices empirical science knows only too well that one's sense perceptions may be just as misleading as one's reasoning, which is why the "oath of measurement" is so important. Unless, of course, Binford is equating the measuring abilities of such methods as radio or infra-red astronomy with "sense perceptions." My argument, quite simply, is that we need more, not less empirical science based upon better measurements of the material world as it relates to human behavior, with due regard for a continuous need to review our theoretical assumptions about the relationship between the material world and human behavior as we do so. This is, I believe, exactly what archaeological theorists like Schiffer are proposing when they talk about "site-formation processes."

IS THIS "THAT OLD-TIME ARCHAEOLOGY"?

Binford regards empirical science of the sort I am advocating as "outdated" and claims to have replaced it with something better for archaeologists. What I have done, in fact, is to argue for a disaggregation of cognition and behavior in our research, and in this respect much of Binford's actual research in ethnoarchaeology and mine are remarkably similar. When Binford states that his examination of the variations in Frank Rulland's behavior in different locations in 1948 provides a control for differences in ethnicity or culture change among the Nunamiut, he is using the identical approach that I applied in 1966 when I observed the variations in stone toolmaking, use, and discard by a single Ngatatjara Aborigine (Tjungurayi) as he went from a kind of "block-on-block" mode of lithic reduction on one occasion to a more economical "prepared core" technique on another (Gould 1980:125–127). Controlled observations of this kind that monitor variations in human behavior in different situational contexts without the interference that could result from differences in human cognition or culture change are exactly the kind of empirical science that works best for ethnoarchaeology, and they are the sort of "nuggets" in Binford's work that I referred to earlier. Despite his rhetoric to the contrary, Binford and I are both adhering to David Clarke's (1972) dictum here of treating human thought as a cognitive "black box" and using this idea to control our observations of variability of human behavior in relation to materials. I consider this to be a good application of empirical science to the study of human behavior, however much Binford may wish to disavow it as such. It certainly has nothing to do with the state of American archaeology in the late 1950s and early 1960s, which was uneven and generally lacking in the application of these sorts of controls.

Of course, there are good reasons for studying human cognition and its effects upon behavior, both with respect to the observer and the observed, and I would argue that ethnoarchaeology can encompass such studies. But this calls for a different kind of ethnoarchaeology from the one I advocated in *Living Archaeology* and to which I have been referring here as empirical science. By applying uniformitarian assumptions we can use empirical science to infer accurately when non-material, cognitive, or ideational factors are affecting outcomes (the argument by anomaly) that differ from our predictions. But for attempts at explanation in such cases we would have to turn to other, essentially qualitative or even non-scientific, approaches that address the cultural and historical particularities of the observed behavior. I will not dwell on this point in detail here except to say that it is important to recognize that there is more than one kind of ethnoarchaeology. I find it easier to deal with the problem Binford has raised by considering so-called "emic"[1] approaches to account for the cognitive dimension in human behavior. For example, stimulating efforts of this kind are at present being tried by Leone (1973, 1982) and Hodder (1982), but these efforts should not necessarily be regarded as scientific, because they do not attempt to generalize cross-culturally on the basis of uniformitarian principles of any kind. They are, however, empirical, and I would not wish to see them excluded from the domain of ethnoarchaeology. The point is that their methods, which partake of a linguistically-derived approach to the study of human culture that has been a mainstream component of anthropology ever since Boas, are consistent with their goals that have to do with explaining the transformations of particular cultural systems.

71

There are also many ethnoarchaeologists whose interests have to do with accounting for changes in particular prehistoric cultural traditions, especially in areas like the Southwest and Great Basin of the United States and the Iranian Plateau. This, indeed, has been the dominant theme in ethnoarchaeology so far, with the emphasis on direct application of ethnoarchaeological observations to archaeological sequences within the same region. This approach, which I refer to as "dirt ethnoarchaeology," is as particularistic as the more "emic" variety but deals explicitly with excavated archaeological sequences. This last-mentioned approach to ethnoarchaeology has been beset with difficulties arising from the use of unsubstantiated or improbable analogies, but its basically culture-historical goals remain intact even after many years of assault by the "new archaeology." Rather than interpreting the persistence of this approach as a perverse unwillingness to examine basic theoretical positions, I credit this to a desire by its practitioners to adhere to the continuing mainstream effort by stratigraphic archaeologists to establish empirically satisfying culture-historical sequences by using the best available controls and measurements. As anyone who has read *Living Archaeology* or the Gould-Watson dialogue (1982) knows, I have some serious questions about the ethnographic analogies that are often used when attempts are made to account for the characteristics of these culture-historical sequences. But I do not despise the culture-historical goals of these efforts, and I would argue that the validity of their results needs to be assessed on the same empirical grounds as the other approaches to ethnoarchaeology.

Each of these different kinds of ethnoarchaeology presents us with a different set of priorities, according to the realities that are the primary goals of the researchers involved. The "etic" approach focuses on observation and inference to discover uniformitarian relationships between human behavior and material remains that are potentially generalizable. The "emic" approach concentrates on cognitive realities within the context of particular cultural systems. The "dirt" approach attempts to account for the specific features of particular culture-historical sequences with references to ethnographic analogues. These are differences in priorities and do not constitute separate types of ethnoarchaeology. My earlier argument by anomaly should be viewed as nothing more than an empirically-satisfying way of moving from one kind of archaeological reality to another, just as, in astronomy, perturbations occurring in the observed behavior of phenomena in space occurring in relation to accepted laws of mass and motion lead one to infer the measurable effects of other, less well understood but equally discoverable, phenomena that may operate according to different principles. Anomalous behavior in the material domain of human residue-formation may require a different kind of explanation—that is, particularistic and more cognitive or more historical explanations. Thus it is perfectly possible for ethnoarchaeologists to use more than one kind of approach, as long as they retain an awareness of the appropriateness of the goals of the research relative to the approaches used. By accusing me of advocating that "old-time archaeology" Binford appears to repudiate the established traditions of empirical scholarship that have always been among archaeology's most positive features. There will always be a place for the critical review of theories and assumptions in archaeology, but not at the expense of the empirically-based understanding that archaeologists share in their ability to discover a knowable past. I hope anyone who chooses "Brand X" will keep this in mind.

AD HOMINEM AD NAUSEUM

The tone of Binford's recent responses to my work is reminiscent of the robber barons of recent American business history who vigorously argued for unrestrained free enterprise and competition but who did their utmost to build monopolies. On the one hand, he reiterates the position that constant critical evaluation of theories and assumptions is needed—a point with which I agree entirely—and that paradigmatic differences exist between his position and mine—again true, as this short essay affirms. He even disavows the appropriateness of personal attacks on the competence or personal characteristics of the disputants. Yet, when one is critical, even indirectly, of Binford's position, the response is that one is being "hostile," "self-serving," or "misleading," that one is creating "misguided debates" and "distortions," to mention but a few of the pejorative terms applied whenever there is disagreement over our paradigms.

It would be unfortunate for an emerging subdiscipline like ethnoarchaeology, which is now hitting its stride, to embrace this as a role-model for the conduct of such debates. I urge that my colleagues read *Living Archaeology* and the other items Binford has referred to in this campaign of his in order to satisfy themselves about whether or not these pejorative assertions of his need to be taken seriously. As indicated earlier, I regard Binford as one of the most stimulating scholars in archaeology today. So I do not wish to say anything that would detract from his contribution. At the same time, we are entitled to ask if this stimulation of ideas is matched by lasting results in the domain of empirical scholarship, whether Binford consents to see his work evaluated in that way or not.

Acknowledgments. This paper has benefited from advice and criticism by several colleagues, especially Douglas Anderson, Sherry Saggers, and Stephen Mrozowski. However, I take full responsibility for the views expressed here.

NOTE

[1] I am aware of the difficulties this term raises for social anthropologists and do not wish to evoke them here.

REFERENCES CITED

Binford, Lewis R.
 1968 Archaeological Perspective. In *New Perspectives in Archaeology,* edited by Sally R. and Lewis R. Binford, pp. 5–32. Aldine Publishing, Chicago.
 1978 *Nunamiut Ethnoarchaeology.* Academic Press, New York.
Binford, Lewis R., and Nancy M. Stone
 1985 "Righteous Rocks" and Richard Gould: Some Observations on Misguided "Debate." *American Antiquity* 50:151–153.
Binford, Sally R., and Lewis R. Binford
 1969 Stone Tools and Human Behavior. *Scientific American* 220:70–82.
Burbidge, E. Margaret
 1983 Adventure into Space. *Science* 221(4609):421–427.
Clarke, David L.
 1972 Models and Paradigms in Contemporary Archaeology. In *Models in Archaeology,* edited by David L. Clarke, pp. 1–60. Methuen, London.
Crabtree, Don E.
 1972 An Introduction to Flintworking. *Occasional Papers of the Idaho State University Museum,* 28, Pocatello.
Gould, Richard A.
 1980 *Living Archaeology.* Cambridge University Press, Cambridge.
Gould, Richard A., and Sherry Saggers
 1985 Lithic Procurement in Central Australia: A Closer Look at Binford's Idea of Embeddedness in Archaeology. *American Antiquity* 50:117–136.
Gould, Richard A., and Patty Jo Watson
 1982 A Dialogue on the Meaning and Use of Analogy in Ethnoarchaeological Reasoning. *Journal of Anthropological Archaeology* 1:355–381.
Hodder, Ian
 1982 *Symbols in Action.* Cambridge University Press, Cambridge.
Leone, Mark P.
 1973 Archaeology as the Science of Technology: Mormon Town Plans and Fences. In *Research and Theory in Current Archaeology,* edited by Charles L. Redman, pp. 125–150. Wiley, New York.
 1982 Some Opinions about Recovering Mind. *American Antiquity* 47:742–760.
Rubin, Vera C.
 1983 The Rotation of Spiral Galaxies. *Science* 220(4604):1339–1344.
Saggers, Sherry
 1984 Materialism and Archaeological Experimentation: Testing the Exotic Stone Hypothesis in the Central Desert of Australia. Ph.D. dissertation, Department of Anthroplogy, Boston University, Boston.

PARADIGMS AND THE NATURE OF CHANGE IN AMERICAN ARCHAEOLOGY

David J. Meltzer

Aspects of Kuhn's The Structure of Scientific Revolutions *are discussed and criticized. Problems are pointed out in three general areas: the latitude Kuhn allows in the concept paradigm, his views on the nature of scientific change, and his notion of incommensurability and the accompanying problems of relativism. The utilization of Kuhn's model by archaeologists is then critiqued, with a focus on the varying interpretations of the paradigmatic state of the discipline. Finally, consideration is given to the recent changes in archaeology that have led to the claim that there has been a scientific revolution in the field. It is argued that those ostensibly fundamental changes are neither revolutionary nor particulary beneficial to a scientific archaeology.*

More than one social scientist has pointed out to me that now at last he had learned to turn his field into a 'science'—by which of course he meant that he had learned how to improve it. This recipe, according to these people, is to restrict criticism, to reduce the number of comprehensive theories to one, and to create a normal science that has this one theory as its paradigm.

Feyerabend (1970:198)

In the absence of progress toward usable theory, there is no new archaeology, only an antitraditional archaeology at best.

Binford (1977:9)

AS A WHOLE, ARCHAEOLOGISTS AGREE that some fundamental changes have occurred in the discipline since the early 1960s. Many have called the changes revolutionary. Yet simultaneously there has been disagreement regarding the nature or definition of the various historical stages (e.g., Wilmsen 1965; Willey and Sabloff 1974); moreover, there is disagreement regarding the causal factors of the supposed revolution (Martin 1971; Leone 1972).

These interpretive differences are a function of the manner in which the history of the discipline is approached. Like much of the substantive work in archaeology, the more traditional schemes treat the discipline's history as the accumulation of various periods and stages (Strong 1952; Belmont and Williams 1965; Willey 1968; Willey and Sabloff 1974). This sort of history requires the construction of static chronological divisions, those constructions often being largely arbitrary and consequently rarely agreed upon. Such schemes assume a linear accretion of knowledge, which presupposes some historical inevitability. As Schuyler has pointed out in some detail (1971), this approach suffers from the malaise of presentism; to this we might also add historicism (Popper 1957:3).

Scholars in the history and philosophy of science have attempted, since the turn of the century, to develop a method of history that steers a course away from this form of static historical determinism. This has been achieved, but it was only after the individuals in that discipline "became aware of the fact that mythologies encrusting the traditional view of the progress of scientific knowledge could be overthrown only by uncovering the motivations and philosophical presuppositions of each scientific epoch" (Colodny 1966:xiii). Studies beginning with Duhem (1954, original 1906) and conducted as recently as Kuhn (1970a) and Shapere (1974) illustrate this approach.

In the last decade or so, archaeologists have begun to discover some of these notions, especially as they were formulated in the work of Kuhn (1970a). His model of scientific change by revolution was applied, often wholesale, to explain the history and most especially the rise of contemporary archaeology. In a sense, the acceptance of Kuhn's model reflects a tacit recognition that the history of archaeology should be seen as nonlinear, complex, and (in some fashion) irregular. In and of itself this change in perspective is a significant step. It is still, however, unclear what the

David J. Meltzer, Department of Anthropology, University of Washington, Seattle, WA 98195

causal factors were, and what kinds of features serve to distinguish pre- and postrevolutionary programs. This problem is compounded by the "ideological programs" that arose in the midst of the revolutionary fervor (e.g., Watson, et al. 1971). They are remarkable for internal inconsistencies between their goals (processual or evolutionary archaeology) and their methods (static functionalism as manifest in General Systems Theory and cultural reconstructions).

These debates on the nature of the archaeological revolution and the ambiguities of its product appear to be the result of difficulties at two levels. At one level, use of the Kuhn model is characterized by a lack of understanding of its theoretical basis, which is a necessary, but often misunderstood, part of the model. Indeed, Kuhn himself has pointed out that the model "can be too nearly all things to all people" (1974:459). Nonetheless, archaeologists use the model as support for their revolution. As a consequence, its inherent ambiguities, coupled with a superficial understanding on the part of those using it, result in some widely varying interpretations.

At another level, it seems that problems arise because the supposed revolution in archaeology may be more of a polemic than a reality. To be sure, some kind of change has occurred. Yet the question must be asked, Have there been any structural changes in the discipline that might represent change in metaphysical or ontological realm? Have there been changes, for example, in the manner in which we view the archaeological record? It is this variety of change that is clearly felt to be "revolutionary" (Leone 1972). It will be argued here that there have been no structural changes and, as a result, no revolution in archaeology, and that this is why there have been so many problems in defining the revolution and, indeed, the new archaeology.

This essay, then, has a dual purpose. First, Kuhn's *The Structure of Scientific Revolutions* (1970a) will be examined critically in terms of the presented model's inherent problems and its presumed utility as both a descriptive and a prescriptive model of scientific change. Second, those changes that have occurred in the discipline, and which are ostensibly revolutionary, will be assessed in terms of both the Kuhn model and the discipline's internal structure. The juxtaposition of the discussion of the Kuhn model with the discussion of changes in archaeology is of obvious value since, by and large, this reflects the manner in which these subjects are treated in the literature. On the other hand, though the connection in the literature is rather superficial, I will also argue that it is indicative of a deeper structural interdependence. Indeed, it comes as no surprise that the Kuhn model, essentially a heuristic device, is used as corroborative evidence to somehow (perhaps by appeal to authority) lend credence to the revolutionary polemic.

THE STRUCTURE OF SCIENTIFIC REVOLUTIONS

Kuhn's *The Structure of Scientific Revolutions* is, above all, a "sustained attack on the prevailing image of scientific change as a linear process of ever increasing knowledge" (Shapere 1964:383). As such, it occupies a prominent, though often criticized, position in the literature of the history and philosophy of science (e.g., Lakatos and Musgrave 1970; Shapere 1964, 1966, 1971; Suppe 1974, 1975, 1977).

Central to Kuhn's model is the assumption that scientific communities are structured, and that this structure is created, sustained, and ultimately defeated by what Kuhn terms a "paradigm." Paradigms are "universally recognized scientific achievements that for a time provide model problems and solutions to a community of practitioners" (Kuhn 1970a:viii). In fact, Kuhn would argue that in the absence of a paradigm, "all the facts that could possibly pertain to the development of a given science are likely to seem equally relevant" (Kuhn 1970a:15).

Prior to the formulation of the discipline as a science, however, there are any number of contrasting and competing "schools of thought." This "pre-paradigm stage" is characterized by the absence of a common body of belief. Each practitioner "built [his] field anew from its foundations" (Kuhn 1970a:13). Fact gathering is restricted to data that are readily available; borrowing from established crafts and technological innovation facilitates this.

With the emergence of a particular scientific achievement, an achievement that is "sufficiently unprecedented to attract an enduring group of adherents away from competing modes of scientific activity" and is "sufficiently open-ended to leave all sorts of problems for the redefined group of practitioners to resolve" (Kuhn 1970a:10), a paradigm is created. Works that fit this description of unprecedented achievement, and which (according to Kuhn) create new paradigms, include Ptolemy's *Almagest*, Newton's *Principia* and *Opticks*, Franklin's *Electricity*, and Lyell's *Geology*. At first, however, the paradigm is "largely a promise of success . . . an object for further articulation and specification under new or more stringent conditions" (Kuhn 1970a:23); "to be accepted as a paradigm, a theory must seem better than its competitors, but it need not . . . explain all the facts with which it can be confronted" (Kuhn 1970a:17–18). Regardless, there are created from these works particular coherent traditions of scientific research, which Kuhn terms "normal science."

> Normal science consists of extending the knowledge of those facts that the paradigm displays as particularly revealing, by increasing the extent of the match between those facts and the paradigm's predictions, and by further articulation of the paradigm itself (Kuhn 1970a:24).

It is, so Kuhn claims, a *mopping up* operation. The paradigm formulates the fundamental rules and standards of scientific research; it suggests research problems, the means to solve the problems, and the criteria for judging the adequacy of the solutions. These restrictions are seen to benefit rather than hinder scientific progress. The paradigm gives the scientist the confidence to ignore, or at least take for granted, the basic issues and go on to more esoteric problems, which he can investigate "in detail and depth that would otherwise be unimaginable" (Kuhn 1970a:24). Interestingly, this research does not aim to produce novelties; rather, it attempts to solve problems whose outcome is easily anticipated. In fact, one of the reasons why normal science seems to progress so rapidly, according to Kuhn, is that "its practitioners concentrate on problems that only their lack of ingenuity should keep them from solving" (Kuhn 1970a:37). The obvious question to ask is, Why call this scientific progress at all? Kuhn's answer would be that the challenge and the progress lie in solving the puzzle better than it has ever been done previously. Since the paradigm sets the problem, and determines the adequacy of the solution, the puzzles provide a measure of skill and thereby a challenge.

In the end, however, nature is neither so predictable nor so "knowable" as the paradigm supposes. Therefore, even though normal science does not aim at anomalies and, when it is successful, finds none, "new and unsuspected phenomena are repeatedly recovered" (Kuhn 1970a:53). Depending, of course, on the degree of articulation of the paradigm, the failure to achieve a solution to an anomaly may initially discredit only the scientist involved, and not the paradigm. In fact, only after the anomaly has defied solution over an extended period of time, or perhaps when its solution is an immediate practical necessity, does it become more than just another puzzle of normal science and begin a crisis in the paradigm.

The crisis is manifest in the "growing sense . . . that an existing paradigm has ceased to function adequately, the proliferation of competing versions of a theory, the willingness to try anything, the expression of explicit discontent, and the recourse to philosophy and to debate over fundamentals" (Kuhn 1970a:92). In short, a scientific revolution occurs. The revolutions are noncumulative developmental episodes in which an older paradigm is replaced in whole or in part by an incommensurable or incompatible new one. Kuhn attributes this incommensurability between paradigms to several factors. First, the proponents of competing paradigms will often disagree about the list of problems that any candidate for a paradigm must resolve (1970a:148). Second, communication across the revolutionary divide is inevitably partial (1970a:149). Third, the individuals practice their trades in different worlds (1970a:150). In essence, Kuhn is arguing that the competition between paradigms is not the sort of battle that can be resolved by proofs (1970a:158). Acceptance of the new paradigm is advanced when (1) the new paradigm can claim to solve the problems that led the old one to a crisis (Kuhn feels this claim is especially successful if the new paradigm displays a quantitative precision better than that of its older competitor), (2) the new paradigm permits the prediction of phenomena that had been entirely unsuspected while the old one prevailed, or (3) the new paradigm has an aesthetic appeal (1970a:153–154).

77

THE CRITICISM

Criticisms of the model, though related, fall into three separable categories: those that criticize (1) the basic definition and concept of a paradigm, (2) Kuhn's notion of scientific change, or (3) the incommensurability and relativism entailed by Kuhn's model. Kuhn has published responses to most of the critiques leveled against him (Kuhn 1970a:174–210, 1970b, 1970c, 1974). These responses will not be addressed here for two reasons. The first is the desire to avoid an infinite regress of point-counterpoint; the interested reader can view the debate in Lakatos and Musgrave (1970) and Suppe's edited volume (1977:459–517). The second reason is that this essay is admittedly more concerned with presenting the issues than discoursing on the sometimes complex attempts at their resolution. There are, not surprisingly, no simple solutions to the problems that will be outlined below. The debate that began in 1962 with the publication of *The Structure of Scientific Revolutions* continues.

The Concept Paradigm

In a review published shortly after the first edition of *The Structure of Scientific Revolutions*, Shapere points out that Kuhn's interpretation of scientific development "places a heavy burden indeed on the notion of a paradigm" (1964:384). He then proceeds to note that, by Kuhn's own usage, the term paradigm:

> covers a range of factors in scientific development including or somehow involving laws and theories, models, standards and methods (both theoretical and instrumental), vague intuitions, explicit or implicit metaphysical beliefs. . . . In short, anything that allows science to accomplish anything can be a part of (or somehow involved in) a paradigm (1964:385).

Masterman advanced a similar, though more systematic, critique. After a careful reading of *The Structure of Scientific Revolution*, she was able to outline 21 different uses of the concept paradigm. She then classified these into three main groups: metaphysical paradigms, sociological paradigms, and artifact or construct paradigms (1970:65).

Viewing paradigms in Masterman's first (metaphysical) sense suggests that the scientific community shares a whole *Weltanschauung* or ontology. In contrast, a sociological paradigm is a set of scientific habits. It is an accepted method of practicing science prior to the development of a theory. The final (construct) paradigm supplies the tools and techniques for solving particular puzzles.

It thus seems intuitively obvious that a metaphysical paradigm may incorporate one or more artifact and sociological paradigms. In fact, given this range of definition that both Masterman and Shapere point out, there would seem to be little chance of distinguishing different paradigms (in Kuhn's sense) or different articulations of the same paradigm (again in Kuhn's sense). This is clearly illustrated in the history of physics, which exhibits as few as one "paradigm" and as many as eight operating simultaneously during the seventeenth and eighteenth centuries (Shapere 1974:150–151; personal communication). At the time of Isaac Newton, there was the general paradigm (Paradigm 00) of the mechanical philosophy of nature. This view assumed that nature could be explicated in terms of matter and motion-forces, and encompassed at least two sub-paradigms. The first (Paradigm 000) had two variants, manifest in the debate between Newton and the followers of Descartes as to the exact nature of those forces (Shapere 1974:150–151). On the one hand there were the "Deists-Cartesians" who believed God was omnipotent and therefore could create a perfect world which would always function on the basis of knowable laws. One could understand the laws of nature, which did not require the active interference of God for their operation. This view did not fare well with the Church. On the other hand there were the "Theists-Newtonians" who, after accusing the Cartesians of atheism, advanced the argument that God was good and created a universe which required his ever watchful eye. Science could not know all and, ultimately, left final explanations to God (interestingly, this view also faired poorly with the Church since it suggested God had faults, i.e., He created an imperfect world). Opposed to both of these views in many respects was that of Leibniz.

The second subparadigm (Paradigm 0000), also with variants, emerged in the writings of Newton. His *Opticks* was based almost explicitly and entirely on the experimental method of science; it was heavily empirical. However, his *Principia* included gravity and the action of forces at a distance, and as a consequence it was based on a mathematical foundation and thus seemed to some to be compatible with rationalism.

My model is expanded if one considers the rise of the electromagnetic-field philosophy in the nineteenth century and, later, the unified field theory, and how they opposed the mechanical philosophy. Indeed, though they were drastically different viewpoints, each was a part of the same metaphysical paradigm at the Paradigm 0 level. All incorporated the notion of scientific determinism—the view that one can predict or determine the laws of nature.

The point of this example is that in Masterman's terms, Paradigms 0 and 00 are metaphysical paradigms, Paradigm 000 is a sociological paradigm, and Paradigm 0000 is a construct paradigm. Which paradigm would, or could, Kuhn choose to signify the paradigm in seventeenth and eighteenth century physics? Which should be used to monitor scientific change? Beyond that, Kuhn (1970a:10) noted that Newton's *Opticks* and *Principia* created paradigms. What were the paradigms created by these obviously different works? were they really paradigms? and if so, in what sense?

Normal Science and the Nature of Scientific Change

This issue lies at the heart of the debate between Kuhn and Popper. Popper claims there is no "normal science" in Kuhn's sense. He agrees that scientists are prisoners caught in the framework of their theories, expectations, and experiences. However, he feels they are prisoners only in a "Pickwickian" sense (1970:56): they can break out of the framework at any time. He argues that critical discussion and comparison between frameworks is always possible, that, in fact, Kuhn's notion of normal science is more representative of what he would call "applied" science (Popper 1972). Popper feels this notion of science as a "mopping-up" operation suffers from, and is an excuse for, dogma in scientific research. This is a view shared by Watkins (1970) and Feyerabend (1970) who, along with Popper, feel it is detrimental to scientific progress.

The implications of these arguments on normal science are reflected in the differing views on the nature of scientific change. Whereas in Kuhn's view changes in normal science are revolutionary, in Popper's view they are not. The "Pickwickian" frameworks are easily erected and easily destroyed through the use of bold conjectures and subsequent criticism and falsification (Popper 1963:36–67). Science does not undergo revolution, but rather a logical progression, a view shared by Toulmin (1970). It progresses in the direction of an "absolute truth" (Popper 1970:56).

Incommensurability and Relativism

These same authors have also taken issue with Kuhn's notion of an absolute (incommensurable) transition from one paradigm to the next. Toulmin, for example, argues that change should be measured in terms of units of variation, since the change was being brought about by scientists operating under common selection procedures and rules. Though there is no common body of scientific principles and axioms, both groups are utilizing common "principles constitutive of science" (1970:44). By suggesting that change is a sequence of greater or lesser conceptual modifications, Toulmin is also suggesting there is no absolute (incommensurable) change between paradigms, and that science progresses gradually rather than revolutionarily.

Popper and Shapere also address the issue, but take differing views. Popper argues that there is a logic to scientific discovery, and that change is progressive and moving toward a particular goal. His logical progression rules out incommensurable change. As might be expected, Shapere argues that the vague definition of the notion paradigm precludes any discussion of incommensurability.

In the absence of a clear idea of the extent of the [paradigm's] determination [of meaning and views of nature] it is impossible to be clear about the extent to which meanings determined by one paradigm can be [or not be] expressed in the language of another (Shapere 1971:708).

Interestingly, it is the very vagueness of definition that Shapere and Masterman point out that causes variation within the criticism. In Kuhn, Toulmin was reading a definition of a paradigm as a set of scientific habits. He denied incommensurability in a sociological paradigm. Feyerabend, on the other hand, defended the notion of incommensurability at least when dealing with *metaphysical* paradigms. He argues (1970) that if an explanation were valid with regards to its *own* respective kinds of experience, then incommensurability was simultaneously present and justified. He feels explanation does not necessarily presuppose a continuity of concepts: "the one task we can legitimately demand of a theory is that it should give us a correct account of [our] world" (1970:227).

Kuhn is accused of relativism because of his acceptance of incommensurability. Relativism is the notion that there is no "truthful" or independent order to meaning, which is related to one's ontology and epistemology and is thus arbitrary and internal. If a world is "seen" through a paradigm, and if that paradigm is by definition incommensurable with its predecessors, then one cannot speak of the two paradigms in relation to each other but only in relation to themselves.

This view has been criticized from a number of perspectives (e.g., Suppe 1975), but perhaps most importantly, it falls down empirically: "such a view of relativism is no more implied by *historical facts* than by opposing views . . . of purely incremental advances towards final truth" (Shapere 1964:393, emphasis added).

It would thus be simply false to say that the transition from Newton's theory of gravity to Einstein's is an irrational leap, and that the two are not rationally comparable . . . there are many points of contact (such as the role of Poisson's equation) and points of comparison: it follows from Einstein's theory that Newton's theory is an excellent approximation. Thus in science, as distinct from theology, a critical comparison of competing theories, of competing framework, is always possible. In science (and only in science) can we say that we have made genuine progress: that we know more than we did before (Popper 1970:57).

There is more to Kuhn's model than a simple scheme of change. There are many constraints and conditions that accompany the approach, not the least of which is the latitude he allows with the concept paradigm. It is, nonetheless, an important model. It recognizes the theory-laden character of "independent facts and observations" and illuminates the often cyclic, non-cumulative, and drastic nature of scientific change.

ARCHAEOLOGY: PARADIGMS AND CHANGE

Paradigms

It might seem incongruous at this point to speak of such things as paradigms and paradigm change. Moreover, since there are many difficulties with the Kuhn model, what is the use in pointing out problems in the archaeologist's utilization of it? There are three considerations here. First, the use of Kuhn's model in this context will illustrate what little there is to gain in the casual adoption of theories or models without simultaneously attempting to understand them in their entirety. Second, there are important elements in Kuhn's approach which do serve to illuminate certain areas in the history of American archaeology. When the use of the Kuhn model is appropriately restricted, it will show where significant disciplinary change can occur. Finally, it is significant that archaeologists have attempted to manufacture a Kuhnian revolution; it is indicative of their much broader attempt to become a different kind of discipline.

I will define a scientific revolution as a change in the metaphysical paradigm (Masterman 1970). The reason behind this usage is self-evident: "Change of theory [theory and method] is almost routine ('normal') . . . change in metaphysics or Weltanschauung is an earthquake" (Jarvie 1975:261). With a change in the discipline's ontological structure—its metaphysic—a new and revolutionary view is introduced. One thinks the hitherto unthinkable (Wittgenstein 1974:3). Ultimately I suspect this is the main thesis of Kuhn, though problems with his paradigm concept and his earlier insistence on incommensurability between competing paradigms prevent this thesis from being explicit. Indeed, a revolution need not be incommensurable and may be evolutionary (Kuhn 1974) in the sense that sections of one paradigm may have utility in the next paradigm (Kuhn 1970a:130). Nonetheless, in the absence of basic structural changes (much like, for instance, the introduction of the Copernican view of the solar system), most variety of change is predictable, expectable, and normal.

Many, of course, have seen the changes that took place in archaeology in the 1960s as revolutionary. Indeed, many have utilized the Kuhn model to validate that revolution; see, for instance Adams (1968), Martin (1971), Hill (1972), Leone (1972), Zubrow (1972), Fitting (1973), and Sterud (1973). An examination of these arguments shows the following: (1) all agree at some level that there has been a change in the discipline since the early 1960s, (2) many see that change as revolutionary, (3) there is little agreement as to where archaeology or the archaeological change should be placed in the Kuhn model, (4) there is disagreement on the nature of the anomaly or anomalies that caused the changes, and (5) most of the cited change is *methodological* or within the construct paradigm (Masterman 1970).

Evidence for the first four points is readily available. For example:

1. On the change in archaeology:

... profound changes can be discerned not only in immediate research strategies but also in the underlying structures of thought (Adams 1968:1187).

2. On the nature of those changes:

The structure of a scientific revolution has a haunting familiarity to anyone who has followed the course of American archaeology over the past ten years. There can be no question about the occurrence of a revolution (Fitting 1973:11).

3. Disagreement regarding the position of archaeology within the Kuhn model:

... archaeology is in the preparadigm stage but there are indications that the first explicit paradigm is already in the process of being developed (Zubrow 1972:180).
The new paradigm that has emerged was a direct response to the crisis that had arisen because the traditional archaeological paradigm was askew (Martin 1971:5).

4. Disagreement regarding the nature of the anomaly in the traditionalist archaeology:

If there is a crisis in archaeology, it is because one of our goals, an outline of prehistory, is largely at hand (Leone 1972:21).
The reason for this [state of flux] is that traditional theories and methods have failed to solve many of the problems for which they were intended (Hill 1972:61).

Archaeology is variously placed in the preparadigm stage (Zubrow 1972:180), in the midst of a revolution (Hill 1972), or in a post revolution paradigm (Martin 1971). The causal factors that brought about the changes are attributed to either the *failure* of the traditional goals (Martin 1971; Hill 1972) or the *fulfillment* of the traditional goals (Leone 1972). Only a desire to show change is common to all the arguments.

Yet what is the manner of that change? It was suggested (point five) above that the changes are largely methodological; if this is the case, then arguments about a revolution in archaeology are severely weakened. To demonstrate this point, we might examine in more detail some aspects of the discussion of Zubrow (1972) and Martin (1971). These articles are useful examples because they explicitly focus on the changes in archaeology.

Zubrow (1972) feels that a paradigm of "scientific archaeology" is assembling; it is a paradigm based on a change of goals, the use of formal explanation, a methodology for comparison and testing of hypotheses, and a systematic definition of cultures and their environments. He structures his argument as a test by examining the literature on the general topics of environment, subsistence, and society for evidence of change.

81

Of interest to this discussion is neither his manner of testing nor, necessarily, his results. What must concern us instead is the type of paradigm concept Zubrow utilizes. Although he is not explicit, and certainly makes no distinction among the types of paradigms, it is readily apparent that he views a paradigm as a puzzle-solving device. His concern with environment, subsistence, and society, to the exclusion of other equally important topics, such as archaeological theory, explanation, seriation, and so on, belies his view of scientific archaeology as a *program*. These concerns simply reflect particular approaches to a problem; the studies of environment, subsistence, and society are all part of a larger *theoretical* whole—cultural reconstruction. To be sure, Zubrow demonstrates variance in the literature he examines, yet it is variance among or within his construct paradigm; it is not revolutionary change. It is noteworthy that of the eight parameters he monitored, only the *methodological* one exhibits a steady increase in the recent years (Zubrow 1972:194).

Martin (1971) argues for a revolutionary change within the discipline by pointing to fundamental shifts in its nature (from a history to a science), goals (trait lists to general laws), concept of culture (normative to systemic), and methods (inductive to deductive). Two considerations, however, prevent us from accepting Martin's argument. First, it is not entirely clear that the changes he has outlined are anything more than methodological, and second, it is not clear whether the changes cited have actually occurred. As Martin himself points out, one should be able to specify and demonstrate the shifts in order to verify the paradigm change (Martin 1971:5).

Examine, for instance, his argument that the new archaeology is explicitly deductive. As has been pointed out many times (Levin 1973; Morgan 1973, 1974; Sabloff et al. 1973; Salmon 1976; Smith 1977), this notion of a purely deductive research methodology does not characterize archaeology, nor is it necessarily the essential element of "good" science. As both Morgan (1973) and Salmon (1976) note, there is an equation being made between deductive and deterministic (and thus causal) reasoning. This leads to the false and unnecessary assumption that the derivation of causality must lie in deductive reasoning. Of course, no manner of scientific knowledge is purely deductive. Moreover, to be concerned with the manner in which a science is practiced belies methodological (and thereby nonrevolutionary) concerns.

To take another example, Martin argues that the concept of culture as a "participatory system" is an innovation of the New Archaeology, whereas the view of culture as "shared behavior" (the so-called Normative view) is indigenous to the Old Archaeology. Clearly, this is simply a polemical distinction (Aberle 1970; Dunnell 1973) and is not supported by a critical reading of the nonpolemical period literature. In fact, the very phrase "culture as a participatory system" was used in the early 1950s by an "Old Archaeologist" (Rouse 1953:72).

The difference between the two views of culture, as originally defined by Binford (1965), is important not so much because it is an attempt to replace one concept with another, but rather because it introduces, for the first time in an explicit fashion, the concept of culture into archaeological strategy (Dunnell 1973). That is, the systemic view of culture allowed inferences about the elements of the cultural system (e.g., social organization) not immediately apparent in the archaeological record. Regardless, the concern is again clearly with method, the manner in which the archaeological record is addressed.

As will be discussed below, this concern with methodological matters is wholly expectable in the context of the suggested change. Of course, the various paradigm models have neither recognized nor addressed the real (methodological) nature of those changes. The shifts were simply *assumed a priori* to be revolutionary, and thus within the metaphysical realm. This ignorance of the methodological nature of the changes in the discipline is especially interesting in light of the fact that many individuals were quite explicit about the necessity of improving archaeology within just this parameter (Binford 1968a; Watson et al. 1971; Hill 1972). In sum, the change was assumed to be metaphysical, but only methodological differences were apparent and asserted.

Change

In the previous examples, change is equated with revolution. However, there is disagreement on the anomaly or anomalies in the old paradigm and on the definition of the new paradigm. It is thus not surprising that there is no agreement on the position of archaeology within the Kuhn model. In fact, the only theme common to all these articles is the desire to demonstrate a revolution.

Three hypotheses can be offered to explain the wide variety found among the interpretations. The differences could be the result of (1) poor use of the Kuhn model, (2) historical proximity to the revolution, or (3) the absence of a scientific revolution.

The first hypothesis, that the problems arise through the misuse of Kuhn, is quite satisfying, especially given the multitude of difficulties inherent in the model. On the other hand, the satisfaction is only superficial: borrowing and abusing models, even those that are ambiguous to begin with, should not prevent the recognition of a change that is alleged to be self-evident. The problem must lie elsewhere.

The second explanation, historical proximity, is not altogether unlikely. To many of these authors, the revolution may be ongoing and for this reason difficult to define. If this is the case, some form of empirical evidence should substantiate a change even when those looking at the change cannot. For example, we might examine the data presented in a recent citations analysis of *American Antiquity* (Sterud 1978). The study analyzed citations in five-year periods, noting the frequency and nature of the top 10 works cited for each period. Examining just the frequencies seems to evince that a change of some sort did occur in the discipline, though at the same time it seems to have left no coherent product. That is, it is quite significant that over the past 50 years the total frequency with which the top 10 works have been cited has declined. Prior to 1960, it seemed to be apparent to those writing in *American Antiquity* just what the top 10 articles were. These articles were cited in the following frequencies:

Before 1931	1931–1935	1936–1940	1941–1945	1946–1950	1951–1955	1956–1960
140	155	205	256	220	240	207

On the other hand, in the post-1960 era (the alleged revolutionary era) the total number of citations for the top 10 decreased as follows:

1961–1965	1966–1970	1971–1975
127	101	11

Of course, these figures are not statistically definitive because (1) Sterud only included those works cited five or more times in his top 10 category; (2) the decrease may be reflecting sample-size changes since the quantity of articles, as well as the number of individuals contributing articles, may have been changing; (3) it is unclear how representative *American Antiquity* is of American archaeology; and (4) it is not clear whether that representativeness has changed. Nonetheless, it is not unreasonable to interpret the relative decrease in the frequency of citations as being reflective of an increase in the heterogeneity of the discipline since 1960. In the years prior to 1960 almost everyone was doing essentially similar things, and duly cited the same works. After 1960, heterogeneity increased, and thus the nature and number of the citations changed.

In a way Sterud's data seem to support "historical proximity" as a possible explanation for the ambiguities on the revolution issue. That is, some changes obviously did occur around the time that the Kuhn-related articles were published; thus, many of the authors may not have been able to view the proceedings in their proper perspective. Regardless, I would suggest that although historical proximity may be a valid explanation, the explanation seems exceedingly difficult to test at the current time.

In any event, a more powerful and readily testable explanation can be offered: there has simply been no archaeological revolution in a Kuhnian sense. It is this lack of revolutionary change that causes the confusion.

I have noted that revolutionary change is one of structure, not method. It is neither simply the manner in which the discipline approaches its data nor the goals of the discipline itself that must change. It is, instead, change in the underlying metaphysic that is required to produce a revolution. To be sure, changes of the methodological sort can cause changes in the metaphysical structure of a discipline; witness, for example, the impact of Lyell's arguments for a fully uniformitarian method in geology (Rudwick 1972; Hooykaas 1963, 1970). It is, therefore, important to examine the relationship of the methodological changes that did occur to the underlying archaeological structure, the archaeological metaphysic. Continuity in that structure would evince the absence of a revolution; a change in that structure, even if caused by methodological change, would demonstrate a revolution.

I see the basic components of the archaeological metaphysic to be as follows. The archaeological record was, and is, viewed as a special case anthropological phenomenon. Artifacts, pottery distributions, and the like are treated as if they were systems of fossilized behavior, capable of reconstruction in anthropological terms. The presence of this structure is apparent in the literature of both the New and Old Archaeology. For example:

> ... identifying distinct patterns of behavior ... which can be acquired by one human being from another ... [can] serve as the tools for the retracting of cultural development and interactions .... It is therefore the task of the analysis ... to recover ... the mental patterns which lay behind these manifold works (Krieger 1944:272);

> ... the archaeologist is faced with the responsibility of finding ... forms and systems of forms that are not only comparable to each other but also comparable to, or at least compatible with, the forms and systems of forms of cultural and social anthropology (Willey and Phillips 1958:2-3);

> ... we have put processual interpretation and ethnology ... side by side ... to suggest a further convergence of aims ... at this point, that [an] archaeologist is in effect a cultural anthropologist (Willey and Phillips 1958:6);

> Artifacts are man made objects; they are also fossilized ideas (Deetz 1967:45);

> ... archaeology tries to describe culture history ... and to reconstruct extinct cultural systems ....Both objectives involve the reconstruction of past behavioral patterns (Deetz 1967:105);

> ... the archaeologist ... has direct access to immense quantities of behavioral data (Watson et al. 1971:25).

It is clear in all these examples that the metaphysic assumes an underlying ethnological reality, the discovery of which, in archaeological data, is the discipline's goal. Thus, the only significant difference between the New and the Old has to be in the manner in which those behavioral-anthropological reconstructions are brought about. The Old Archaeology accomplished this in a largely intuitive and implicit fashion; the New Archaeology operates in an explicit and more clearly anthropological manner. This alone accounts for many of the differences that Martin, among others, saw between the approaches.

The methodological change is an explicit result of the desire to work more convincingly and efficiently within the *traditional* metaphysic. From the start it was argued that this type of change was the real need and goal of the New Archaeology (Binford 1968a). It was fully recognized that:

> Whether we admit it or not, most archaeologists are trying to describe and explain various aspects of prehistoric human behavior; the literature amply supports this assertion. The difficulty is that our commonly accepted methods have not been conducive to achieving our goals (Hill 1972:101);

and that:

> ... much of the work of scientific archaeologists ... has been directed toward the development of archaeological methods designed to elicit information concerning significant cultural events and processes from the archaeological record .... These methods and the resulting information are necessary prerequisites to the contributions archaeology can make to anthropology and the whole of social science (Watson et al. 1971:25).

Yet, with rare exceptions, methodological change is unrevolutionary and essentially precludes any scientific revolution. Even within the context of the methodological changes in archaeology, there was no attempt made to reject the traditional "archaeology as anthropology" view (Willey and Phillips 1958). The shifts that occurred in the 1960s were wholly *commensurate* with the metaphysic of the previous "paradigm."

In short, the changes that took place in the discipline were incremental, not revolutionary. In fact, to deal with these differences of *degree* one must ignore the Kuhn model altogether, since that model only addresses changes of *kind*. An alternative, for model-minded archaeologists, would be the linear-continuum model of Thompson (1972). The model applies to change within a finite system, bounded, it could be argued, by a metaphysic. The most common sort of change (whether in technique, method, or theory) is incremental and consists of variation on a specific theme (metaphysic).

Ultimately, there is very little of the New Archaeology that cannot fit on the same linear continuum with the Old Archaeology. The limits of the continuum are defined by its metaphysic; the contents of the continuum are characterized by theoretical, methodological, and technological variability. It is only when a new metaphysic is introduced, one which by definition cannot fit on the same continuum, that a revolution results.

There has been no revolution in archaeology.

EPILOGUE

Before closing, I would like to point out that the archaeological literature evinces a growing discomfort with the "archaeology as anthropology" metaphysic (Clarke 1968; Binford 1977; Dunnell 1978a, 1978b). The discomfort is due, in large part, to the influence of the metaphysic on what was to be a processual account of the past. The influence is manifest most obviously by the lack of any purely archaeological theory (Binford 1977). Archaeological explanation is seen as necessarily couched in anthropological terms.

Yet the theories of anthropology were created to deal with static phenomena, and are thus a poor fit when imposed on the archaeological record (Harris 1968). The result is an attempt to address culture change within a mechanistic and "functional" framework (Schuyler 1973; Athens 1977).

It is, of course, the gap between anthropological theory and the archaeological record that created the presumed need to develop our methods. After 15 years, it should now be apparent that no amount of methodological virtuosity will reduce the void between archaeological data and anthropological theory. Nor is it really necessary. We need, instead, to develop an archaeological theory and then, within that frame, pose questions that can be answered given archaeological data. In the absence of an archaeological theory, a concern with method alone seems strangely misguided (Binford 1977:7).

In retrospect, the goal of archaeology in the 1960s was to become a different discipline. A new "paradigm" was to be created, and it was to be explicitly scientific and evolutionary in character (Binford 1968b). The scientific aspect was asserted, but only through the recitation of the "scientific method" (e.g., Fritz and Plog 1970; Watson et al. 1971). Unfortunately, the source of the method was the philosophy of science rather than science per se. In the former, the method as outlined is necessarily post hoc; it is a description concerned with ideal scientific behavior, not a prescription for that behavior (Hempel 1965; Masterman 1970).

The evolutionary aspect of the paradigm has been largely nonexistent, with some important exceptions. Much of the New Archaeology is cultural reconstruction commonly aimed at prehistoric social organization (Leone 1968; Hill 1970; Longacre 1970). In fact, many of the studies that are ostensibly evolutionary (Flannery 1972) have been shown to be noncausal descriptions (Leone 1975; Athens 1977). What was to be evolutionary archaeology ended up, as a result of the metaphysic, being a variant of anthropological functionalism (Leach 1973; Schuyler 1973).

The presence of the anthropological metaphysic *coupled with* the absence of an explicit archaeological theory has prevented a scientific and evolutionary archaeology. It is, of course, the scientific and evolutionary aspects that were used as the vehicles by which the traditionalist "paradigm" was critiqued. As expected, ambiguities regarding science and evolution resulted in a critique that was polemical and ad hoc. It was polemical in the sense that a variety of straw men were created (e.g., the inductive-deductive contrast); it was ad hoc in that it was not founded on a coherent theory or metaphysic, such that a new "paradigm" could be readily implemented upon the demise of the old "paradigm."

The ambiguity evident in the use of the Kuhn model demonstrates the ad hoc nature of the New Archaeology. Apparently no one knows what it is.

Acknowledgments. Many of the issues raised in this essay have been discussed with Robert C. Dunnell, Donald K. Grayson, Russell G. Handsman, Mark P. Leone, and Suzanne L. Siegel. I thank them for their help and, more important, for their criticisms. I am especially grateful to professors Dunnell and Grayson and my wife, Suzanne Siegel, for their collective editing of the many versions of this paper. Their fortitude is noteworthy. Jeremy Sabloff and my two anonymous reviewers made constructive comments on an earlier draft.

A course at the University of Maryland with Professor Dudley Shapere (of the Committee on History and Philosophy of Science) significantly influenced my thinking on many Kuhn-related matters. I would also like to thank Dr. Shapere for his comments on a portion of the manuscript and for permission to utilize his unpublished material on seventeenth and eighteenth century science.

Of course, the conclusions reached here are the sole responsibility of the author.

REFERENCES CITED

Aberle, David F.
 1970 Comments. In *Reconstructing prehistoric Pueblo societies,* edited by W. A. Longacre, pp. 214–223. University of New Mexico Press, Albuquerque.
Adams, Robert McC.
 1968 Archaeological research strategies: past and present. *Science* 160:1187–1192.
Athens, J. Stephen
 1977 Theory building and the study of evolutionary process in complex societies. In *For theory building in archaeology,* edited by L. R. Binford, pp. 353–384. Academic Press, New York.
Belmont, John S., and Stephen Williams
 1965 The foundations of American archaeology. Ms. on file, Peabody Museum, Harvard University.
Binford, Lewis R.
 1965 Archaeological systematics and the study of cultural process. *American Antiquity* 31:203–210.
 1968a Archaeological perspectives. In *New perspectives in archaeology,* edited by S. R. Binford and L. R. Binford, pp. 5–32. Aldine, Chicago.
 1968b Post-Pleistocene adaptations. In *New perspectives in archaeology,* edited by S. R. Binford and L. R. Binford, pp. 313–341. Aldine, Chicago.
 1977 General introduction. In *For theory building in archaeology,* edited by L. R. Binford, pp. 1–10. Academic Press, New York.
Clarke, David L.
 1968 *Analytical archaeology.* Methuen, London.
Colodny, Robert G.
 1966 Introduction. In *Mind and cosmos,* edited by R. Colodny, pp. xi–xvii. University of Pittsburgh Press, Pittsburgh.
Deetz, James
 1967 *Invitation to archaeology.* Natural History Press, Garden City, New York.
Duhem, Pierre
 1954 *The aim and structure of physical theory.* Princeton University Press, Princeton (originally published, 1906).
Dunnell, Robert C.
 1973 *The normative straw man: an oblique defense.* Paper presented at the 38th Annual Meeting of the Society for American Archaeology, San Francisco.
 1978a Style and function: a fundamental dichotomy. *American Antiquity* 43:192–202.
 1978b *Natural selection, scale and cultural evolution: some preliminary considerations.* Paper presented at the Current Issues in Primate and Human Evolution Colloquium, University of Washington, Seattle.
Feyerabend, Paul K.
 1970 Consolations for the specialist. In *Criticism and the growth of knowledge,* edited by I. Lakatos and A. Musgrave, pp. 197–230. Cambridge University Press, London.
Fitting, James E.
 1973 History and crisis in archaeology. In *The development of North American archaeology,* edited by J. Fitting, pp. 1–13. Doubleday, New York.
Flannery, Kent V.
 1972 The cultural evolution of civilizations. *Annual Review of Ecology and Systematics* 3:399–426.
Fritz, John M., and Fred T. Plog
 1970 The nature of archaeological explanation. *American Antiquity* 35:405–412.
Harris, Marvin
 1968 Comments. In *New perspectives in archaeology,* edited by S. R. Binford and L. R. Binford, pp. 359–361. Aldine, Chicago.

Hempel, Carl G.
    1965   *Aspects of scientific explanation, and other essays in the philosophy of science*. The Free Press, New York.

Hill, James N.
    1970   Broken K Pueblo: prehistoric social organization in the American Southwest. *Anthropological Papers of the University of Arizona* 18.
    1972   The methodological debate in contemporary archaeology: a model. In *Models in archaeology*, edited by D. L. Clarke, pp. 61-107. Methuen, London.

Hooykaas, Reijer
    1963   *Natural law and divine miracle; the principle of uniformity in geology, biology and theology*. E. J. Brill, Leiden.
    1970   *Catastrophism in geology; its scientific character in relation to actualism and uniformitarianism*. North-Holland, Amsterdam.

Jarvie, I. C.
    1975   Epistle to the anthropologists. *American Anthropologist* 77:253-266.

Krieger, Alex D.
    1944   The typological concept. *American Antiquity* 9:271-288.

Kuhn, Thomas S.
    1970a   *The Structure of scientific revolutions*. [Second ed.] University of Chicago Press, Chicago (originally published in 1962).
    1970b   Logic of discovery or psychology of research? In *Criticism and the growth of knowledge*, edited by I. Lakatos and A. Musgrave, pp. 1-23. Cambridge University Press, London.
    1970c   Reflections on my critics. In *Criticism and the growth of knowledge*, edited by I. Lakatos and A. Musgrave, pp. 231-278. Cambridge University Press, London.
    1974   Second thoughts on paradigms. In *The structure of scientific theories*, edited by F. Suppe, pp. 459-482. University of Illinois Press, Urbana.

Lakatos, Imre, and Alan Musgrave (editors)
    1970   *Criticism and the growth of knowledge*. Cambridge University Press, London.

Leach, Edmund R.
    1973   Concluding address. In *The explanation of culture change: models in prehistory*, edited by C. Renfrew, pp. 761-771. University of Pittsburgh Press, Pittsburgh.

Leone, Mark P.
    1968   Neolithic economic autonomy and social distance. *Science* 162:1150-1151.
    1972   Issues in anthropological archaeology. In *Contemporary archaeology: a guide to theory and contributions*, edited by M. P. Leone, pp. 14-27. Southern Illinois University Press, Carbondale.
    1975   Views of traditional archaeology. *Reviews in Anthropology* 2:191-199.

Levin, Michael E.
    1973   On explanation in archaeology: a rebuttal to Fritz and Plog. *American Antiquity* 38:387-395.

Longacre, William A.
    1970   Archaeology as anthropology: a case study. *Anthropological Papers of the University of Arizona* 17.

Martin, Paul S.
    1971   The revolution in archaeology. *American Antiquity* 36:1-8.

Masterman, Margaret
    1970   The nature of a paradigm. In *Criticism and the growth of knowledge*, edited by I. Lakatos and A. Musgrave, pp. 59-90. Cambridge University Press, London.

Morgan, Charles G.
    1973   Archaeology and explanation. *World Archaeology* 4:259-276.
    1974   Explanation and scientific archaeology. *World Archaeology* 6:125-137.

Popper, Karl R.
    1957   *The poverty of historicism*. Basic Books, New York.
    1963   *Conjectures and refutations: the growth of scientific knowledge*. Harper & Row, New York.
    1970   Normal science and its dangers. In *Criticism and the growth of scientific knowledge*, edited by I. Lakatos and A. Musgrave, pp. 51-58. Cambridge University Press, London.
    1972   *Objective knowledge: an evolutionary approach*. Oxford University Press, Oxford.

Rouse, Irving B.
    1953   The strategy of culture history. In *Anthropology today*, edited by A. Kroeber, pp. 57-76. University of Chicago Press, Chicago.

Rudwick, Martin J.
    1972   *The meaning of fossils: episodes in the history of paleontology*. MacDonald and Co., London.

Sabloff, Jeremy A., Thomas W. Beale, and Anthony M. Kurland, Jr.
    1973   Recent developments in archaeology. *Annals of the American Academy of Political and Social Science* 408:103-118.

Salmon, Merrilee H.
    1976   "Deductive" versus "inductive" archaeology. *American Antiquity* 41:376-381.

Schuyler, Robert L.
  1971   The history of American archaeology: an examination of procedure. *American Antiquity* 36:383–409.
  1973   Review of "Explanation in archaeology: an explicitly scientific approach." *American Antiquity* 38:372–374.
Shapere, Dudley
  1964   The structure of scientific revolutions. *The Philosophical Review* 73:383–394.
  1966   Meaning and scientific change. In *Mind and cosmos*, edited by R. Colodny, pp. 41–85. University of Pittsburgh Press, Pittsburgh.
  1971   The paradigm concept. *Science* 172:706–709.
  1974   *Galileo: a philosophical study.* University of Chicago Press, Chicago.
Smith, Bruce D.
  1977   Archaeological inference and inductive confirmation. *American Anthropologist* 79:598–617.
Sterud, Eugene L.
  1973   A paradigmatic view of prehistory. In *The explanation of culture change: models in prehistory*, edited by C. Renfrew, pp. 3–17. University of Pittsburgh Press, Pittsburgh.
  1978   Changing aims of Americanist archaeology: a citations analysis of American Antiquity—1946–1975. *American Antiquity* 43:294–302.
Strong, William D.
  1952   The value of archaeology in the training of professional anthropologists. *American Antiquity* 54:318–321.
Suppe, Frederick
  1974   Exemplars, theories and disciplinary matrixes. In *The structure of scientific theories*, edited by F. Suppe, pp. 483–499. University of Illinois Press, Urbana.
  1975   Kuhn's and Feyerabend's relativisms. Paper presented at the Committee on History and Philosophy of Science Colloquia Series, University of Maryland, College Park.
  1977   Afterword—1977. In *The structure of scientific theories*, [Second ed.] edited by F. Suppe, pp. 617– University of Illinois Press, Urbana.
Suppe, Frederick (editor)
  1977   *The structure of scientific theories.* University of Illinois Press, Urbana.
Thompson, Raymond H.
  1972   Interpretive trends and linear models in American archaeology. In *Contemporary archaeology: a guide to theory and contributions*, edited by M. P. Leone, pp. 34–38. Southern Illinois University Press, Carbondale.
Toulmin, Stephen E.
  1970   Does the distinction between normal science and revolutionary science hold water? In *Criticism and the growth of knowledge*, edited by I. Lakatos and A. Musgrave, pp. 39–47. Cambridge University Press, London.
Watkins, John W. N.
  1970   Against normal science. In *Criticism and the growth of knowledge*, edited by I. Lakatos and A. Musgrave, pp. 25–37. Cambridge University Press, London.
Watson, Patty Jo, Steven A. LeBlanc, and Charles L. Redman
  1971   *Explanation in archaeology: an explicitly scientific approach.* Columbia University Press, New York.
Willey, Gordon R.
  1968   One hundred years of American archaeology. In *One hundred years of anthropology*, edited by J. O. Brew, pp. 29–53. Harvard University Press, Cambridge.
Willey, Gordon R., and Philip Phillips
  1958   *Method and theory in American archaeology.* University of Chicago Press, Chicago.
Willey, Gordon R., and Jeremy A. Sabloff
  1974   *A history of American archaeology.* W. H. Freeman, San Francisco.
Wilmsen, Edwin N.
  1965   An outline of Early Man studies in the United States. *American Antiquity* 31:172–192.
Wittgenstein, Ludwig
  1974   *Tractatus logico-philosophicus.* Humanities Press, New Jersey (originally published 1921).
Zubrow, Ezra B. W.
  1972   Environment, subsistence and society: the changing archaeological perspective. *Annual Review of Anthropology* 1:179–206.

INTERPRETIVE ARCHAEOLOGY AND ITS ROLE

Ian Hodder

This paper seeks further to define the processes of the interpretation of meaning in archaeology and to explore the public role such interpretation might play. In contrast to postmodern and poststructuralist perspectives, a hermeneutic debate is described that takes account of a critical perspective. An interpretive postprocessual archaeology needs to incorporate three components: a guarded objectivity of the data, hermeneutic procedures for inferring internal meanings, and reflexivity. The call for an interpretive position is related closely to new, more active roles that the archaeological past is filling in a multicultural world.

Este artículo intenta definir los procesos de la interpretación de significación en arqueología y explorar el papel público que esta interpretación podría ῑ⁓ner. En contraste con la perspectiva postmodernista y postestructuralista, el debate hermenéutico incluye una perspectiva crítica. Una arqueología interpretativa postprocessual necesita incorporar tres componentes: una estricta objetividad de los datos, procedimientos hermenéuticos para inferir significados internos, y reflexividad. El interés en una posición interpretativa está relacionado a papeles nuevos y más activos que el pasado arqueológico cumple en un mundo multicultural.

What is interpretation and why does it seem an appropriate term to use in the archaeology of the 1990s? In this paper I hope to answer both these questions. While I have elsewhere discussed interpretation in terms of a contextual approach (Hodder 1986), I have not situated the latter in relation to wider traditions except the rather outdated views of Collingwood (1946). I intend in this paper to provide a wider definition of contextual archaeology within an interpretive framework.

This article will discuss hermeneutics as an important component in an interpretive or contextual archaeology. For many writers, hermeneutics is more than an epistemology for the human sciences in that it accounts for being. I recently came across a good example of the everyday working of hermeneutic principles while listening to the radio in the United States. I heard the phrase, or thought I did, "it was necessary to indoor suffering." Inspecting these "data" I first thought the phrase was an example of the liberty that North Americans often take with the English language. After all, North Americans often make nouns and adjectives into verbs (as in "to deplane"), so it seemed entirely possible that "to indoor suffering" meant "to take suffering indoors." I did not see why it should be necessary to suffer indoors, but then I know that North Americans, especially if they live in California from where the program came, are willing to try anything. So initially I understood the term as it sounded to me and assumed that the same word had the same meaning. I then corroborated and adjusted this meaning by placing it in the peculiar and particular rules of North American culture. This was the first stage of my hermeneutic interpretation.

Gradually, however, this process of internal evaluation made less and less sense as I continued to listen to the radio program. My interpretation of the sound "indoor" no longer made what was being said coherent. The program was about suffering in general, not just about suffering indoors. Sentences such as "to indoor the suffering I took a pain killer" made little sense. I could only make sense of these examples when I hit upon the idea of another component of my understanding of the North American context: North Americans often pronounce words "wrongly." Coming back from this contextual knowledge to my own general knowledge about English words and their meanings I searched and found "endure." Now everything made coherent sense and the whole had been reestablished. The hermeneutic circle had been closed.

Of course, all this happened in a few seconds. But the speed and trivial nature of the process cannot but emphasize the wide dependence of human communication and understanding on the

Ian Hodder, Department of Archaeology, University of Cambridge, Downing Street, Cambridge CB2 3DZ, England

American Antiquity, 56(1), 1991, pp. 7–18.
Copyright © 1991 by the Society for American Archaeology

procedures of hermeneutic interpretation. We evaluate many arguments not so much by testing universal, general knowledge against data using universal, independent instruments of measurement but by interpreting general understanding or foreknowledge in relation to our understanding of particular contexts. We place the thing to be understood (in this case the sound "indoor") more and more fully into its context, moving back and forth between "their" and "our" context until coherence is achieved. The emphasis is on part–whole relations. We try to fit the pieces into an interpretive whole at the same time as constructing the whole out of the pieces. We measure our success in this enmeshing of theory and data (our context and their context) in terms of how much of the data is accounted for by our hypothesis in comparison to other hypotheses. This working back and forth between theory and data, this absorption in context and texture tends to be more concerned with understanding the data in their own terms and in using internal, as well as external, criteria for judgement.

It has for some time been argued (Hodder 1986; Trigger 1989) that processual archaeology placed little emphasis on interpreting general knowledge in relation to internal understanding. But it is also appropriate to ask whether postprocessual archaeology has sufficiently engaged in interpretation of the general in relation to the particular. I would claim that, so far, much postprocessual archaeology has avoided an interpretive position, except superficially. On the whole, postprocessual archaeology has concerned power, negotiation, text, intertext, structure, ideology, agency, and so on. Many of these concerns may move us in an interpretive direction but they remain general and theoretical interests that dominate our present thoughts. They represent the interests of a predominantly Western, white, male discourse. There have been very few postprocessual studies that have said "I will put the theory in second place, treat it simply as baggage, and set off to tell a story about, for example, the development of Bronze Age society in Bavaria." On the whole, postprocessual archaeologists, including the author of this article, have been more concerned with showing the validity of our universal theoretical apparatus. The data have been only examples manipulated to demonstrate, often inadequately, some theoretical point. There has been insufficient interpretation.

The tendency to develop a universal theoretical discourse and impose it on the past is common to both processual and postprocessual archaeology. In both cases there is insufficient sensitivity to the independent difference of past contexts and to contextual meanings. This insensitivity derives from two different directions. Processual archaeology put many of its eggs in the basket of methods. A universal method was supposed to allow us to read off dynamics from statics, and so there was little attempt to construct interpretive procedures that were sensitive to internal meanings. Conversely, to a large extent, postprocessual archaeology has been weak on method (Watson 1986). Indeed, it might be claimed that so much emphasis has been placed on theoretical discussion and theoretical criteria that the method of postprocessual archaeology is theory. The rigors of theoretical criteria have replaced those of method but have detracted equally from the interpretation of specific, internal historical meanings.

The scarcity of interest in internal meanings in both processual and postprocessual archaeology also relates to an inadequate concern with the context of archaeologists. The lack of reflexivity in processual archaeology is accepted widely, but the claim in relation to postprocessual archaeology is perhaps surprising. My suggestion derives from the observation made above that in practice, postprocessual archaeological writings largely have concerned theory rather than method. It was mainly at the theoretical level that processual archaeology was shown wanting. The practical result of a purely theoretical debate tends to be posturing. Theoretical debate involves defining terms, defining boundaries, and setting up oppositions. Theoretical meaning is always referential (to other theories) and tends to be confrontational by nature. Argument is over the top of, rather than through the data that become relevant only as examples. The argument is entirely about the present, not about the past. It manipulates the data for presentist concerns, and while postprocessual archaeology successfully has opened up the area of critique it has scrutinized insufficiently its own preconceptions.

I would argue that as a result, as radical as postprocessual archaeology would claim to be, it merely reestablishes older structures of archaeological research. It tends towards doing the same thing in a different way. Perhaps a good example of continuity in structures of power within academic discourse, despite claims for radical change in the content of ideas, is the fact that Grahame Clark, David

Clarke, Ian Hodder, Christopher Tilley, and Michael Shanks, covering a range of different theoretical positions through time, were or are all associated with Peterhouse—one small, reactionary, exclusive college in Cambridge.

Much of what postprocessual archaeology has argued for has not been evaluated critically and the effects of its actions have not been reflexively probed. For example, the new theories and the new ways of writing them often serve to make archaeological texts more obscure and difficult for anyone but the highly trained theorist to decipher. How can alternative groups have access to a past that is locked up both intellectually and institutionally? Subordinate groups who wish to be involved in archaeological interpretation need to be provided with the means and mechanisms for interacting with the archaeological past in different ways. This is not a matter of popularizing the past but of transforming the relations of production of archaeological knowledge into more democratic structures.

One danger of this view, as has been argued by Renfrew (1989) for example, is that if we accept that the past is constructed partly in the present (in the dialectic between past and present, object and subject), and that we must listen to and incorporate other voices and historical meanings constructed by, for example, women and ethnic minorities, where can we draw the lines around legitimate archaeological research? Should we also welcome the voices of creationists, looters, metal-detector users and other "fringe" archaeologists within a tower of babbling? On what grounds is it possible to claim a legitimacy and primacy for the different but universal projects of, for example, processual or postprocessual archaeology?

One alternative to hermeneutic approaches within the humanities and social sciences emanates from writers—precursors and champions of postmodern and poststructuralist thought—who raise similar questions about the boundaries of legitimate research by seeking multivocality, fragmentation, and dispersal. These writers, including Nietzsche, Foucault (Tilley 1990b), Kristeva, Barthes (Olsen 1990), and Derrida (Yates 1990) suspend meaning within chains of signifiers, and emphasise the openness of interpretations within our dependence on language. Poststructuralist work is having an increasing influence in archaeology (Bapty and Yates 1990; Tilley 1990a; see also Hodder 1989b) and is important because it opens up a central issue. What is the boundary between an open multivocality where any interpretation is as good as another and legitimate dialogue between "scientific" and American Indian, black, feminist, etc. interests?

In my view, the nonhermeneutic, noninterpretive strands in postprocessual archaeology and in all postmodern social science, serve further to reestablish positions of dominance that are threatened by the same openness to alternative, nonscientific perspectives as is feared by processual archaeologists (e.g., Renfrew 1989). The influence of poststructuralism (Bapty and Yates 1990; Hodder 1989b; Tilley 1990a) is towards multivocality and the dispersal of meaning. Truth and knowledge are claimed as contingent and multiple, and relativism is to some extent entertained. At first sight, this development toward a nonhermeneutic, poststructuralist position seems benign. It opens up the past to other voices and deconstructs the universality of truth claims. But the feminist critique of postmodernism (e.g., Mascie-Lees et al. 1989) is particularly revealing here. Dominant theorists and specialists have, since the excited certainties of the 1960s, increasingly lost the monopoly to define archaeological truths as alternative positions have been argued by women, ethnic minorities, and by all the different perspectives in archaeological theory, never mind all the fringe archaeologies. As identified by Mascia-Lees et al. (1989; see also Eagleton 1983), the poststructuralist response to this loss of authority is subtle. The notion that truth and knowledge are contingent and multiple undermines the claims of subordinate groups. It *disempowers them* by alienating them from the reality they experience. Irony and relativism appear as intellectual possibilities for dominating groups at the point where the hegemony and universality of their views is being challenged (Mascie-Lees et al. 1989). In effect, a new, more subtle universal claim to truth is produced out of the critique of truth. The poststructuralist emphasis on multivocality, metaphor, and fragmentation may be constructed to capture the complex and contradictory nature of social life. But in fact what is provided is a resolution of conflict into a pleasing whole in which the author is scarcely present. He or she also is fragmented, distanced, uncommitted, disengaged; powerful but always absent and therefore not answerable to criticism.

The postmodern theoretical discourse, then, subtly disempowers critique and establishes a new distanced authority. Its radical political claims are undermined by the insecurity and multivocality of knowledge claims. Poststructuralist archaeology becomes a movement without a cause. As a result of its links with poststructuralism and postmodernism (Hodder 1989b), postprocessual archaeology has not always been concerned with opening dialogue with "other groups." There has been little incorporation of alternative claims on the past in a multiethnic Britain or United States. There has been little dialogue with feminist archaeology in for example the writing of Shanks and Tilley (1987a, 1987b), despite the fact that it can be claimed plausibly that the growth of postprocessual archaeology depended on the growth of feminism and feminist archaeology. But this "other voice" often has been appropriated and dominated within postprocessual archaeology (M. Conkey, personal communication 1990).

Rather than embracing poststructuralism, postprocessual archaeology should grasp an interpretive position in order to avoid the above problems and to break from established relations of dominance in the production of the archaeological past. In this initial discussion I have begun to identify three essential aspects of an interpretive approach in archaeology.

First, a guarded objectivity of the past needs to be retained so that subordinate groups can use the archaeological past to empower their knowledge claims in the present and to differentiate their claims from fringe, ungrounded archaeologies. By "guarded" objectivity I mean that the "data" are formed within a dialectical relation. In the example I gave of the radio program, I heard, *or thought I did*, the phrase "to indoor suffering". The sound I picked up from the radio only became sound data through my interpretation of voice from crackling background and through my (incorrect) recognition of certain words. My interpretation was based on objective sound waves but it also penetrated into their definition as data. The data are produced dialectically. Second, an internal, hermeneutic component needs to be retained in interpretation. We need to be sensitive to the other. The attempt to understand the past in terms of the experiences of social actors allows the past to be released from abstract specialist theory into the realms of everyday human understanding and simultaneously provides a basis for the critique of universal propositions in the present. It allows for a relevant human story to be told. There is a need to move away from theory and get on with interpreting data, by which I mean move away from an assumption of the primacy of theory towards relating theory to data as part of a learning process. Third, a reflexive consideration of the production of archaeological knowledge will lead to a critical engagement with the voicing of other interests, by identifying the causes for which the past is constructed, and by locating the mechanisms that make it exclusive.

The search, then, within postprocessual archaeology is for an adequate integration of these three aims with clearly defined methodological procedures. There is a need to give science a context in archaeology as methodology, not as a final goal or as the only relevant body of theory. I have already argued that this scientific component of archaeological work is necessary to avoid ungrounded undermining of knowledge claims by interested groups and in order to avoid a subsuming of the past within a homogenised theoretical present. But how are we to integrate such scientific concerns for a guardedly objective past within a nonpositivist archaeology? How are we to accept the commitment to process that is broader than ecological and adaptive relations and that incorporates human action? In my view, answers to these questions can be gained from developments in the debate surrounding hermeneutic studies.

HERMENEUTIC PROCEDURES

Beyond the trivial example given at the beginning of this paper, what does a hermeneutic, contextual approach involve and how might the inferential methods be employed in archaeology? Does the approach allow us to get at internal meanings while maintaining a guarded commitment to objectivity and independence and while remaining reflexive?

It may be helpful to outline the main ideas and problems of a hermeneutic archaeology by discussing briefly the history and development of hermeneutic ideas since the founding work of Friedrich Schleiermacher and Wilhelm Dilthey (Ormiston and Schrift 1990). Their starting point was the principle that understanding and knowledge depend on the dialectical relation between part and whole—the hermeneutic circle. Dilthey extended Schleiermacher's concern with the intentions of the author in producing texts to include a wider hermeneutic circle such as historical background, social customs, cultural and political institutions, and so on. Martin Heidegger (1958) dealt with some of the problems of this approach. In particular, he emphasized that our understanding of the past "other" is dependent on prejudice and tradition. In other words, the past hermeneutic we are trying to interpret is dependent on, and may be enclosed by, the hermeneutic circles within which we work as archaeologists and members of society. Shanks and Tilley (1987a) identify four hermeneutic circles within which the contemporary archaeologist works when trying to understand past material culture "texts." Although Heidegger claimed that the enclosing hermeneutic circles are not vicious, in that they do not involve hermetically sealed "circular arguments," it is difficult to see how, within his version of hermeneutic procedures, it is possible to do more than interpret the past in our own terms. The same criticisms have been made of contextual archaeology (Binford 1987).

Although I have argued (Hodder 1991a) that Hans-Georg Gadamer (1975) tried to deal effectively with these problems of circularity of argument it can nevertheless be claimed that he retained a subjectivist position. Indeed, this is the criticism of Emilio Betti (1955, translated 1984), who argued for a hermeneutic methodology that would safeguard the objective standards of interpretation. Betti's approach is of interest to the current debate in archaeology in view of the call that is made frequently, particularly by North American archaeologists, for postprocessual archaeologists to define their methods (e.g., Earle and Preucel 1987; Watson 1986). Betti's methodological guide involved the following principles: (a) the autonomy of the object—the idea that a past context should be judged in its own terms; (b) the notion of coherence (see also Collingwood 1946) or the principle of totality—the idea of part–whole relations and the notion that the "best" hypothesis is the one that makes sense of most of the data; and (c) the fact that the past "other" has to be appropriated and translated in the present so that (d) the aim of the analyst should be to control prejudice while bringing his or her subjectivity into harmony with the data.

The latter parts of this proposal remain ambiguous so that Gadamer was able to respond by questioning the validity of the subjective–objective opposition and showing that understanding is not a matter of a subject confronting an alien object (Ormiston and Schrift 1990). Rather it is a dialectical process of question and answer. Thus the past object and the present subject constitute each other in the hermeneutic process of interpretation. Thus, in my analysis of Neolithic Çatal Hüyük I interpreted the site in my own terms, but in the experience of trying to understand the "other" of Çatal Hüyük "my own terms" changed (Hodder 1990). For example, my assumptions about the roles of women were contradicted by the evidence for the roles of men. I had assumed that the dominance of representations of women in the earlier Neolithic could be read as a subordination of women and as a misrepresentation of their roles. In the later Neolithic, however, I found I was using the evidence for dominant representations of men as a straightforward indication of male power. I was using a double standard in relation to the evidence for women and men. As a result I changed my views on the nature of female powers (Hodder 1991b). I had in the end both changed my own position and changed the past so that a new hermeneutic circle was produced that made more complete sense of both past and present.

Nevertheless it can be argued, following Jurgen Habermas (1990), that Gadamer did not sufficently critique the tradition within which preconceptions and prejudices about the data are formed. The tradition needs to be subject to the critique of ideology and needs to be examined as distorted communication within certain historical conditions. It is Ricoeur (1971; 1990; see also Moore 1990; Thompson 1981) who has dealt most effectively with the linking of hermeneutics and Marxist critical theory. In archaeology, the relevance of various forms of critical theory has been brought increasingly into postprocessual discussion (e.g., Leone 1982; Leone et al. 1987; Shanks and Tilley 1987a). Ricoeur points out that the Marxist critique of ideology is itself founded on a hermeneutic (see also Hodder 1986:168) in the sense that any critical reflection makes claims for a privileged understanding and makes claims for universality which appear dogmatic. In other words, the Marxist critique is locked into its own hermeneutic circle. Indeed, Ricoeur sees hermeneutics and the critique of ideology as necessarily complementary.

According to Ricoeur, not only are critical approaches dependent on hermeneutic circles, but hermeneutics retains within itself the basis of critique and a way out of the circularity of interpretation. In this, in my view, he emphasizes the partially objective nature of other contexts as suggested by Betti. Ricoeur argues that rather than only emphasizing prejudice in the process of going to the past with questions, we can place emphasis on the return from the past with answers. He shows that any "text" (written or material culture) is distanced from its "author." It is the product of meaningfully organized activity, and it is itself patterned by those activities. This patterned organization, distant from its original meanings, has an independence that can therefore confront our interpretations. In attempting to understand the past "other" it is possible to suggest hypotheses (about past cultural rules and meanings) that make more or less coherent sense of the objectively patterned remains by moving back and forth between whole and part. The answers we return with can be unexpected. As a result no horizon (viewpoint or perspective) is universal because the tension between self and other is not surmountable. Only by placing myself in relation to the independent (objectively organized and different) other can I confront myself and my society with its taken for granteds. There is a need for the "creative renewal of cultural heritage" (Ricoeur 1990:332) as the basis for the critique of contemporary ideologies.

The moment of critique in the hermeneutic process is the interaction with data to produce "possible worlds" (Bruner 1986) or stories that open up possibilities beyond the conventional. Always the distance of the "text" defines and critiques my subjectivities and opens my closed "false consciousness." Material culture as excavated by archaeologists is different from our assumptions because it is organized partly at least according to other cultural rules (from social organization to refuse deposition). But past material culture also confronts our interpretations and assumptions in so far as it is not only meaningfully but also pragmatically organized (Hodder 1989a). In other words, *we are not just interpreting interpretations*, but dealing with objects that had practical effects in a noncultural world—an ecological world organized by exchanges of matter and energy. These universal, necessary relations confront the tendency of our interpretations to "run free" as has been shown, for example, in Binford's (1983) reappraisal of hypotheses of early hominid behavior through a consideration of the universal nature of scavenging animals and their "signatures."

So we need to retain from positivist and processual archaeology a guarded "objectivity" of the material "other" that provides the basis of critique through the reality of difference. The supposed viciousness or closure of the hermeneutic circle resides in the view that in "fitting theory to data" in the search for coherence we enclose the data entirely within our prejudices. But the organized material remains have an independence that can confront our taken for granteds. The notion that the data are partly objective is an old one in archaeology, and it was the basis for processual and positivist archaeology. But the trouble with positivist and processual archaeologists was that they did not incorporate hermeneutic and critical insights. From a hermeneutic point of view, the failure of the processual archaeology of the 1970s and early 1980s was that it too often took a cavalier, externally based approach where the data were simply examples for the testing of universal schemes, with too little attention paid to context and to understanding the data in their own terms (Hodder 1986; Trigger 1989:348–357). The possibility that radically different processes might be encountered was thus difficult to entertain. From the point of view of critique, the failure of processual archaeology was its blindness to its own ideologies (e.g., Conkey and Spector 1984; Patterson 1986; Trigger 1980).

Both processual and hermeneutic approaches accept that every assertion can be understood only in relation to a question. But in hermeneutic archaeology, prejudice and tradition are not opposed to reason without supposition. Rather they are components of understanding linked to the historical nature of being human. We need a perspective to understand the world. Archaeology poses meaningful questions, does meaningful research, and gets meaningful results only in terms of a perspective or a set of questions. Processual and hermeneutic approaches of course differ in their approach to the validation of hypotheses, emphasizing external and internal criteria of judgment respectively, but both have suffered from the same blindness to the conditions that make their different perspectives possible. Both fail to explore the way in which the asking of questions and the expectation of certain answers are situated in historical processes. There is thus a need to retain the Marxist emphasis on critical reflection. We can only understand the past in its own terms if we understand our own context in the dialectic between past and present. The past can only inform the present through the dual endeavors of understanding present and past as different but dependent. Objectivity may help us to define the past as different, and hermeneutics may help us to understand what it meant through the part–whole, question-and-answer method, but it is critical reflection that shows most fully what it means to us.

So far I have identified three directions within archaeology that also are found throughout the social sciences. These correspond to the spheres of interest identified by Habermas (1971) (see Preucel 1991). The first is technical or instrumental interest and corresponds with what most North American archaeologists identify as the "science" of processual, ecological, evolutionary, behavioral, and positivist archaeology. The second concerns the historical or hermeneutic sciences dealing with communication, understanding, meaning and action (cf. Patrik 1985). The third concerns emancipation, critical social science and self-reflection (e.g., Leone et al. 1987).

These three directions each have roles to play in archaeology, but modified in relation to the others. Thus processual archaeology needs to be subsumed within a relation to critique and hermeneutics, and postprocessual archaeology needs to react to the charge of methodological naiveté. An integrated but diversified approach needs to incorporate three perspectives. (1) The past is objectively organized in contexts that differ from our own. It is in the experience of this objective and independent difference that we can distinguish among competing hypotheses to see which fits best. (2) However, if the present is not simply to be imposed on the past we need not impose external criteria but must accommodate our external knowledge to internal relations. We need to understand the past partly in its own terms by using the criterion of coherence in part–whole relations. This internal understanding includes symbolism, meaning, the conceptual, history, action as opposed to behavior, people as well as systems. This is not a cognitive archaeology (Renfrew 1989) because the latter does not deal with the central question of meaning, and it does not involve getting into peoples' minds. Rather, the hermeneutic approach involves getting at the public and social structures of meaning through which people make sense of the world. It is recognized that these secondary, conceptual realms of meaning are historical and arbitrary, but it is argued that they nevertheless can be interpreted, using the part–whole hermeneutic approach, because the secondary, abstract meanings were used in social action and thus produced repeated patterned effects in material culture and the organization of spatial and temporal relations. Returning to point (1), these objective patternings allow us to distinguish between hypotheses about which secondary conceptual meanings were operative in producing the archaeological remains.

(3) The third component of interpretive archaeology is the self-reflexive aspect of new ethnographic and some emerging archaeological writing (Clifford and Marcus 1986; Hodder 1989c; Tilley 1989). This perspective involves being aware that writing has an audience to which it needs to be critically responsible, and a rhetoric that acts to persuade. It involves introducing the "I" into archaeological accounts, dialogue between co-workers or between researchers and indigenous "owners" of the past, and it involves telling the story of the contingent context of work in which hypotheses were formulated.

We might gloss these three points by saying that interpretive archaeology is about constructing narratives, or telling stories. Of course, all archaeology always has told stories about evolution, diffusion, maximization, adaptation, survival, and so on. But in these stories the rhetoric of the story line was not acknowledged or criticized as contributing to the construction of the message or hidden agenda. The stories were often not told at the human scale, and were not inclusive of the viewpoints of the actors. The accounts were validated through external science rather than internal meaning, and they lacked the narrator, who was mysteriously absent. In all these ways, the stories were not interpretations.

INTERPRETIVE ARCHAEOLOGY AND CULTURAL HERITAGE

In many ways, the calls for an interpretive archaeology mirror contemporary concerns for heritage and the environment. It is no accident that more interpretive or heritage "centers" rather than museums are appearing on the landscape in both Britain and North America as interpretive approaches are discussed increasingly within the discipline. These new centers often are more concerned with telling a story and may contain few artifacts. They often involve a narrator, whether it be a recorded voice at the Yorvik Centre, York, England, or cardboard cut-out Asterix and Obelix figures in the reconstructed Iron Age huts in the Bois de Boulogne, Paris. Increasingly emphasis is placed on showing sequences of activities and involving the public in experiencing the past.

In order to understand these relations and the need for an active interpretive archaeology within environmental and heritage management it may be helpful to return to the traditional goals of anthropology. The latter may be described as the salvage of distinct forms of life from the processes of global Westernization, the recognition of the non-Western as an element of the human just as crucial as the Western, and skepticism concerning Western claims to knowledge and understanding.

These traditional anthropological concerns have been reasserted in postmodern anthropology (e.g., Clifford and Marcus 1986), and they imply that anthropology has a countercultural potential. It can be argued that the current increases in student enrollment and job openings in sociocultural anthropology in the United States relate to a switch from the "me" generation to one more concerned with green issues (Roy Rappaport, personal communication 1990).

The rise in the centrality of global environmental issues has a double effect on anthropology. On the one hand, many of these global effects are ecological and involve a world of universal measurements, energetics, causes, and effects. On the other hand, the realization that we are destroying each other on a global scale leads to a greater concern with other cultures. In order to arrest the environmental impact of oil spillage, pipe lines, the use of fossil fuels among the growing populations of the developing world, and rain-forest depletion we are forced to understand the needs and practices of other cultures and to enter into dialogue with them. The cost of destruction of societies by the agents of development cannot simply be *counted* numerically. It is not only a question of numbers and of survival but also of values and morality. In such a context, the call is for a qualitative anthropology that can inform on and assist dialogue with other cultures that we might destroy or that might destroy us.

Archaeology readily fits in here, as several of the "One World Archaeology" volumes have shown (e.g., Gathercole and Lowenthal 1989; Layton 1989a, 1989b). A concern for the archaeology of a region is a concern for the environment of that region—not just a physical environment but a *peopled* environment—given cultural values and meanings. Peoples around the world use archaeology to help maintain their pasts in the face of the universalizing and dominating processes of Westernization and Western science. The physical archaeological remains help people to maintain, reform, or even form a new identity or culture in the face of multinational encroachment, outside powers, or centralized governments. Related arguments concern the use of the past by ethnic minorities, women, and other groups to define and reform their social positions within national boundaries in relation to the dominant culture.

The past that is used by subordinate voices in this way is not just a resource, and here is the link to the need for an interpretive archaeology. Subordinate groups do not necessarily want to fit their archaeologies into universal schemes in Western academic institutions. Rather, subordinate groups may wish to explore, perhaps archaeologically, the meaning that their monuments have for them. The past is not a resource that can simply be quantified, tabulated, or otherwise manipulated at arm's length within our theoretical frameworks. Rather than that terrible term "cultural-resource management," what is needed is a qualitative archaeology, sensitive to context and meaning, open not to multivocality for its own sake but to dialogue that leads to change. Many peoples do not want a past defined as a scientific resource by us but a past that is a story to be interpreted. In these ways the public debates about the contemporary role of archaeology and the dissemination of archaeological knowledge run parallel to the call for an interpretive archaeology.

In North America the confrontation between desires to tell different stories, as in the reburial debate, has a particular form. In Britain archaeology plays a role in a different context of great public interest and nationalist concerns for, for example, an "English Heritage." But even here, in this cocoon that denies the multiethnic nature of "our" past, archaeology may be playing a countercultural, interpretive role. The heritage boom that we have witnessed in Britain over recent years

(Merriman 1989) has included a massive increase in numbers of so-called museums. In fact, as already noted, these often contain few objects and are devoted more to interpreting the landscape or the past and/or telling a story about a local area, giving it a meaning to local inhabitants and visitors. In England, archaeologists increasingly are employed by environmental and planning consultants. Developers need to take account of local desires and senses of place if planning authority is to be achieved. Archaeology is literally the price that often has to be paid for development. In some cases developers are keen to provide means not only for archaeology to be conducted but also for the results to be displayed permanently. Thus the past is being used to give a sense of local identity and place in the face of universalizing large-scale development and destruction of the environment. The heritage or interpretive centers tell a story that links people into communities that increasingly are being threatened and fragmented.

Clearly there is a danger that I present a romanticized view. Archaeology in Britain is being manipulated by big business to make money, to buy development, and to excuse its activities. Many of the interpretations are commercialized, fragmented, and unconcerned with local or any social issues (Shanks and Tilley 1987a). Nevertheless, in the negotiation that occurs between developers, planning authorities, and local inhabitants, the archaeology can play an active role. The past can sometimes be used by people to tell a story about themselves in the face of external pressures. In my own involvement with excavating and displaying information from prehistoric sites near Cambridge, I was impressed by the attempts of a local village community to retain access to its own past. I also had to confront the fact that the community did not want an abstract past defined by me. Rather, the local people wanted me to engage with them in working out a set of stories, told at the human level, which they could enter. In a regional Fenland context of community fragmentation, high residential mobility, and destruction of traditional farming employment, the archaeological remains helped in practice to form a local community.

CONCLUSION

This experience of mine is just a small example of the way the archaeological past is being used by social groups—including ethnic minorities, women, and non-Western peoples—to find a voice. My claim is that an interpretive approach in archaeology is more able to articulate this voice than are processual or poststructuralist archaeologies. This is because, to answer directly the first question posed at the beginning of this paper, interpretation is translation. It involves the archaeologist acting as interpreter between past and present, between different perspectives on the past, and between the specific and the general. Interpretation therefore involves listening, understanding, and accommodation among different voices rather than solely the application of universal instruments of measurement. This response leads directly to the answer to my second question posed at the beginning. The role of interpretive archaeology is to facilitate the involvement of the past in a multicultural present. This function is integral to the three aspects of the definition of interpretive archaeology that I have given in this paper.

(1) The partially objective, grounded, and material nature of the past allows subordinate groups to empower themselves through the evidential aspect of archaeology. For example, it is possible to show unambiguously that indigenous communities inhabited South Africa before the arrival of white settlers. Equally, the objective component of archaeological data means that the analyst can be confronted with the otherness of the past. Since argument is through, rather than over, the data, we have to shift our positions in the experience of the data. The data and I bring each other into existence dialectically. The past then allows the possibility for a sense of other that is increasingly being eroded in an expanding, homogenized Western ethic.

(2) Interpretive approaches at least try to understand the other in its own terms in that they look for internal rather than external criteria of plausibility in order to support their arguments. They thus encourage other groups to develop their own senses of past. In addition, interpretive approaches incorporate the conceptual, i.e., the way people made sense of the world. They therefore bring the past to the human scale rather than locking it up in distant, abstract science or theory. To interpret is therefore to act because the interpretation releases the past into public debate. It forces us to

translate the past into a story we can understand. Interpretation forces us to *say something*, and therefore to engage with others who would tell different stories. It forces us to unlock the abstract ivory-tower theory and show what it means in practice, in relation to the data.

(3) Interpretive approaches encourage self-reflexivity and dialogue. The past always is "owned" by someone in some sense. But ownership is always an interpretation. Archaeologists need to retain the authority to be able to say that a particular interpretation does not fit the data (point 1 above), but they also need to be open to dialogue and conflicts with vested interests other than their own and to understand the social implications of the knowledge they construct. And they need to realize that subordinate groups can be provided with the mechanisms (the material and educational possibilities) for engaging with the past in their own ways. A critical position recognizes that the telling of stories grounded in the data depends on the relations of production of archaeological knowledge.

As indigenous, different interpretations of ownership increasingly develop, there is a real concern, both in the United States and in other parts of the world, about whether archaeology as it has been defined scientifically will be able to continue to exist (Kintigh 1990; Lovis 1990). Archaeology must change if it is to exist in the contemporary multicultural world. The issue is not just one of getting American Indians to change or of teaching them "our" archaeology. Rather, it is one of involving them as we change ourselves and our concepts of science. There is a need to break the mold in archaeology, discussing not from within a closed science, but opening up that science to dialogue, narrative, rhetorical analysis, and meaning. These are the topics now being debated in sociocultural anthropology. But there is also a need to build interpretations of the archaeological past informed by these issues. We cannot continue to cling to a narrow science.

Interpretive archaeology can be an active, "doing" archaeology. We need to see postprocessual archaeologists launching into coherent and sustained interpretations of the past, involving themselves in whatever contemporary issues those interpretations raise. In my case the relevant interpretations may involve the nature of Neolithic burial near Cambridge, or the nature and origins of the concept of prehistoric Europe after the events of 1989 and as the unification of 1992 approaches. In the United States the relevant debates may concern interpretations of slave quarters on a South Carolina plantation or the interpretation of American Indian remains. There is a direct link between these calls for interpretations in archaeology and reburial issues, land claims, public archaeology, the presentation of the past, and so on. Postprocessual archaeology should not involve going into an ivory tower of abstract theory and slamming the door. The way postprocessual, in fact all archaeology, will endure is by not remaining indoors.

Acknowledgment.   I am grateful to Bob Preucel for discussions on some of the key points in this paper.

REFERENCES CITED

Bapty, I., and T. Yates
  1990   *Archaeology after Structuralism.* Routledge, London.
Binford, L.
  1983   *In Pursuit of the Past.* Thames and Hudson, London.
  1987   Data, Relativism and Archaeological Science. *Man* 22:391–404.
Betti, E.
  1984   The Epistemological Problem of Understanding as an Aspect of the General Problem of Knowing. In *Hermeneutics: Questions and Prospects,* edited by G. Shapiro and A. Sica, pp. 25–53. University of Massachusetts Press, Amherst.
Bruner, J.
  1986   *Actual Minds, Possible Worlds.* Harvard, University Press, Cambridge.
Clifford, J., and G. Marcus
  1986   *Writing Culture.* University of California Press.
Collingwood, R.
  1946   *The Idea of History.* Oxford University Press, Oxford.
Conkey, M., and J. Spector
  1984   Archaeology and the Study of Gender. In *Advances in Archaeological Theory and Method,* vol. 7, edited by M. B. Schiffer, pp. 1–38. Academic Press, New York.

Eagleton, T.
  1983   *Literary Theory.* Blackwell, Oxford.
Earle, T., and R. Preucel
  1987   Processual Archaeology and the Radical Critique. *Current Anthropology* 28:501–538.
Gadamer, H. G.
  1975   *Truth and Method.* Seabury, New York.
Gathercole, P., and D. Lowenthal.
  1989   *The Politics of the Past.* Unwin Hyman, London.
Habermas, J.
  1971   *Knowledge and Human Interests.* Beacon Press, Boston.
  1990   The Hermeneutic Claim to Universality. In *The Hermeneutic Tradition,* edited by G. L. Ormiston and A. D. Schrift, pp. 245–272. State University of New York Press, Albany.
Heiddeger, M.
  1958   *The Question of Being.* University Press, New Haven.
Hodder, I.
  1986   *Reading the Past.* Cambridge University Press.
  1989a   This is Not an Article About Material Culture as Text. *Journal of Anthropological Archaeology* 8: 250–269.
  1989b   *The Meanings of Things.* Unwin Hyman, London
  1989c   Writing Archaeology: Site Reports in Context. *Antiquity* 63:268–274.
  1990   *The Domestication of Europe.* Blackwell, Oxford.
  1991a   The Postprocessual Debate. In *Processual and Postprocessual Archaeologies,* edited by R. Preucel. Southern Illinois University Press, Carbondale, in press.
  1991b   Gender Representation and Social Reality. In *Proceedings of the 1989 Chacmool Conference,* edited by University of Calgary Press, in press.
Kintigh, K. W.
  1990   A Perspective on Reburial and Repatriation. *SAA Bulletin* 8(2):6–7. Society for American Archaeology, Washington, D.C.
Layton, R.
  1989a   *Conflict in the Archaeology of Living Traditions.* Unwin Hyman, London.
  1989b   *Who Needs the Past? Indigenous Values and Archaeology.* Unwin Hyman, London.
Leone, M.
  1982   Some Opinions About Recovering Mind. *American Antiquity* 47:742–760.
Leone, M., P. Potter, Jr., and P. Shackel
  1987   Toward a Critical Archaeology. *Current Anthropology* 28:283–302.
Lovis, W. A.
  1990   How Far Will It Go?: A Look at S.1980 and other Repatriation Legislation. *SAA Bulletin* 8(2):8–10. Society for American Archaeology, Washington, D.C.
Mascia-Lees, F., P. Sharpe, and C. B. Cohen
  1989   The Postmodernist Turn in Anthropology. *Signs* 15:7–33.
Merriman, N.
  1989   Museum Visiting as a Cultural Phenomenon. In *The New Museology,* edited by P. Vergo, pp. 38–61. Reaktion Books, London.
Moore, H.
  1990   Paul Ricoeur: Action, Meaning and Text. In *Reading Material Culture,* edited by C. Tilley, pp. 85–120. Blackwell, Oxford.
Olsen, B.
  1990   Roland Barthes: From Sign to Text. In *Reading Material Culture,* edited by C. Tilley, pp. 163–205. Blackwell, Oxford.
Ormiston, G. L., and A. D. Schrift
  1990   *The Hermeneutic Tradition.* State University of New York Press, Albany.
Patterson, T.
  1986   The Last Sixty Years: Toward a Social History of Americanist Archaeology in the United States. *American Anthropologist* 88:7–26.
Patrik, L. E.
  1985   Is There an Archaeological Record? In *Advances in Archaeological Theory and Method,* vol. 8, edited by M. B. Schiffer, pp. 27–62. Academic Press, New York.
Preucel, R. (editor)
  1991   *Processual and Postprocessual Archaeologies.* Southern Illinois University, Carbondale, in press.
Renfrew, C.
  1989   Comments on Archaeology into the 1990s. *Norwegian Archaeological Review* 22:33–41.
Ricoeur, P.
  1971   The Model of the Text: Meaningful Action Considered as Text. *Social Research* 38:529–562.
  1990   Hermeneutics and the Critique of Ideology. In *The Hermeneutic Tradition,* edited by G. L. Ormiston and A. D. Schrift, pp. 298–334. State University of New York Press, Albany.

Shanks, M., and C. Tilley
   1987a   *Re-constructing Archaeology.* Cambridge University Press.
   1987b   *Social Theory and Archaeology.* Polity Press, Oxford.
Thompson, J.
   1981   *Critical Hermeneutics.* Cambridge University Press.
Tilley, C.
   1989   Discourse and Power: The Genre of the Cambridge Inaugural Lecture. In *Domination, Power and Resistance,* edited by D. Miller, M. Rowlands, and C. Tilley, pp. 45–62. Unwin Hyman, London.
   1990a   *Reading Material Culture.* Blackwell, Oxford.
   1990b   Michel Foucault: Towards an Archaeology of Archaeology. In *Reading Material Culture,* edited by C. Tilley, pp. 281–347. Blackwell, Oxford.
Trigger, B.
   1980   Archaeology and the Image of the American Indian. *American Antiquity* 45:662–676.
   1989   *A History of Archaeological Thought.* Cambridge University Press.
Watson, P. J.
   1986   Archaeological Interpretation, 1985. In *American Archaeology Past and Future,* edited by D. Meltzer, D. Fowler, and J. Sabloff, pp. 439–458. Smithsonian Institution Press, Washington, D.C.
Yates, T.
   1990   Jacques Derrida: "There is Nothing Outside the Text." In *Reading Material Culture,* edited by C. Tilley, pp. 206–280. Blackwell, Oxford.

Received July 17, 1990; accepted November 12, 1990

SOME OPINIONS ABOUT RECOVERING MIND

Mark P. Leone

Archaeologists have tried to reconstruct patterns of thought, meaning, and ideas, using theories of struc-
turalism, cognition, and ideology. Case studies involving each of the theories are described, and the strengths
and weakness of their application to archaeological data are presented. Structuralism is found to yield
substantial examples with well-worked treatments of archaeological data. These examples tend to ignore
economic context, however. Materialism, especially neo-Marxism, contains thorough definitions of ideology
that may be useful to archaeology because they preserve economic context. However, such definitions are new
to the field and presently offer few well-worked examples of how to handle archaeological data.

I WOULD LIKE to try to sort out some of the recent intellectual crosscurrents in archaeology that have led to renewed interest in structuralism, cognition, and ideology. Structuralism, as I would like to use it here, is the set of ideas put forward by Lévi-Strauss (1963, 1968). I recognize, but do not want to deal with, the many variants of it in the British and American usages, variants meant to deal with the theory's shortcomings (Leach 1967; Pettit 1977). Recent interest in cognition stems from the experiments in ethnoscience (Tyler 1969), themselves deeply formed by the work of Chomsky and Jacobsen in structural linguistics. Ideology, in the sense employed here, is a term from materialist scholarship—ecological, evolutionist, and Marxist—and refers either to notions about explicit belief in the sacred or secular sense, or the givens of life held unawares (Althusser 1971:127–186; Gurevich 1976:229–245). These theories are currently having an impact on archaeology and, rather than summarize the cases in which they are found, I would like to examine only a few to see the strengths and weaknesses in their treatments of archaeological data. My intention is to highlight trends, not to make recommendations for the future.

STRUCTURALISM AND COGNITIVE THEORY

Structuralism is the theoretical foundation of the most important innovation in archaeology since the new archaeology was introduced in the early 1960s. Structuralism is opposed to most of the basic assumptions made by the evolutionary and ecological materialists, but I doubt that its advent can be explained by reference to either the shortcomings or the incompleteness of that very productive school of thought. Structuralism has been used in prehistory by Leroi–Gourhan (1968) and Hodder (1982; Hodder, ed. 1982) but has received wider and more noticeable use in historical archaeology in the work of Glassie (1975), Deetz (1977), Schmidt (1978), and Leone (1978). The theory is used in different ways by most of these authors and others as well; few use the whole theory; some use it to justify a position; and some, maybe most, use it to try to analyze data in a new way without intending to borrow more than a theoretical insight for puzzling material. But all authors employing structuralism either maintain or are subject to the theory's basic assumptions. Those assumptions presume that the mind works in orderly ways that are not self-evident, using, it is sometimes said, a logic like arithmetic or a grammar. The basic assumption is that the human mind categorizes and divides; creates contrasts and opposition; that it reverses, displaces, and distinguishes between inside and outside, culture and nature, male and female; furthermore, that the mind uses a limited repertoire of contrastive categories like these to think about virtually all reality. This is the fundamental ability of the mind to "spawn logical and

---

Mark P. Leone, Department of Anthropology, University of Maryland, College Park, MD 20742

Copyright © 1982 by the Society for American Archaeology
0002-7316/82/040742-19$2.40/1

analogical oppositions, forever replacing binary opposition already installed with new ones in a round . . . (that) cannot transcend the matrix of nature that had given rise to it" (Wolf 1980).

Few structuralists aside from Lévi-Strauss are concerned with the origins of this quality of the mind. But they all perceive the productivity of assuming a fairly basic and simple ordering ability of the mind because of all the data and observations that can be linked or understood if the same mental operations are assumed to affect everything that the mind deals with. For an archaeologist, or any cultural anthropologist, the promise held out by structuralist analysis is that it is no longer necessary to assume that levels of culture like technology, social organization, and myth are separate, nor do either efficiency or function have to be found within these phenomena or their artifacts. The benefit for an archaeologist is that from this point of view all artifacts can be treated as having equivalent significance regardless of their function. Another benefit is that prehistoric thought patterns, long assumed to be irretrievable, can now be approached since no class of artifacts, whether of subsistence or of religion, is any further from the root of the culture than any other: the human mind ordered them all.

Although structuralism has been used by archaeologists in remarkably different ways, all who employ this approach share common assumptions. Just as the new archaeologists held mind to be unreconstructable and condemned paleopsychology (Binford 1965:203–210), structuralists took for their basic proposition that mind was primary and its primary role a proper object of study. Just as social organization and myth were structures articulated by mind through action, it followed for archaeologists that all three-dimensional objects were things shaped by this fundamentally mental structural, as well as by primary use. Structuralism could thus be used to interrelate all concrete artifacts produced by a society, because each was assumed to have been stamped by the same structure regardless of any particular use to which it might be put, that is, with the same structure as social and mythological life. A secondary assumption, not much used by archaeologists, is that there exist a limited number of rules that serve to specify how the basic sets of oppositions can be played out; or what can go with what, live with what, or be found together. So, in addition to categories of inside/outside and male/female, it should be possible to discover the rules for how these categories are applied to the world. Such a set of rules is usually referred to as a grammar.

Just as the new archaeology took, unexamined, an older view that the past was difficult to know because it could not be observed directly and tried to overcome that basic assumption, structuralism assumed the past to be knowable because the structure of the human mind has been constitutive of that past since reaching its modern condition tens of millennia ago. Thus, even though the order of a particular set of oppositions is worked out differently from culture to culture, the appearance of antinomies is universal. Therefore, while the details of a culture may be lost, the components of the underlying logical organization cannot be.

The two most basic assumptions of a structuralist archaeology as it has been practiced are: first, that all objects in a particular culture are equal with respect to the overall organization and coherence of the total structure of that culture. And second, while the details and particulars of a past culture may be lost, the principles of that organization, or structure, may be suggested through what remains. These assumptions have been used differently by different archaeologists, and important modifications have followed depending on the approach of a particular user. Some implications of the first assumption, which interrelates all artifacts of a culture in space, can be seen in some broad dimensions in Leroi–Gourhan's (1967a, 1967b, 1968:58–68, 70) structuralist understanding of Upper Paleolithic cave art.

Leroi–Gourhan took the whole corpus of cave art in space and suggested a universality of organization that had not been conceived before. He suggested that regardless of date, place, or variants in items painted, the art was ultimately a unity. He took only one class of artifacts, cave paintings, and created a coherence among his data by showing the fundamental organizational principles that were used to arrange the paintings in a given cave: inside/outside; nature/culture; male/female; life/death.

Instead of categorizing the materials by date, place, and material considerations such as food sources available in a locale, or artifacts from a cave site, Leroi-Gourhan arranged the primary data a different way. He excluded time, place, ecology, and all artifacts other than the paintings; he ignored all daily context and substituted instead the context of the paintings' relationship to each other. This definition of context would have been impossible had he not ignored chronology, location, and subsistence. Again, his method rested on the assumption that mind was primary and that it ordered all artifacts regardless of material considerations. He argued that paintings were painted where they were and depicted what they did because of other paintings, and that all caves were painted with the same "grammar" because the same set of principles guided thought; mind came first and structured everything.

To perform such an analysis Leroi-Gourhan had to take much of Western Europe over a 10,000-year period and analyze its art as a potentially unified entity. Such an analysis could not attempt to account for, and probably could not even have recognized, differences in place or time. Hence, we can see that in the structuralist approach, what counts is not so much that structuralism assumes no change in culture, but rather that if a structuralist analysis can account for details in place or time, then such analysis presumes that the basic organization, or structure, of a culture is continuous.

Leroi-Gourhan found that the standard Upper Paleolithic cave contained set statements that life and death depend on each other: that males, weapons, and death-dealing animals are opposed to females, animals traditionally hunted by paleolithic peoples, and wounded and dying people or animals. The two fundamental oppositions, one *inflicting* pain and death and the other *suffering* pain and death, are essential to each other in providing life. Thus, Magdalenian logic linked women and wounded bison, horses, and ibex, and counterposed them to men, lions, and bears, while seeing all within a single paradigm, not as scattered unrelated items of sympathetic magic.

Leroi-Gourhan thus took a single artifact category as it had appeared across time and space and showed its unity by positing a single structure that had great geographical breadth and temporal duration. A similar experiment has been tried by James Deetz (1977) who took very diverse categories of artifacts and posited the same kind of structural unity among them. Deetz took house floor plans and facades, tableware, and gravestones and presumed that they must all illustrate the cognitive pattern of colonial New England. Deetz has worked more with cognitive or ethnoscientific analysis than with structuralism, as we can see from his effort to establish a grammar of baskets and projectile points in *Invitation to Archaeology* (1967). But his major effort to recover mental patterns occurs in *In Small Things Forgotten* (1977), where no grammar is attempted but rather a series of symmetrical relations is discovered.

Earlier, in *Invitation to Archaeology* (1967) Deetz had tried to compose a grammar of artifacts through an explicit use of transformational analysis. He derived his ideas from componential analysis, a form of cognitive anthropology. Even though such analysis presupposed that a deep structure existed, Deetz was concerned at that time with a grammar that would yield an efficient description of artifacts. He was not concerned with a possible deep structure behind Chumash baskets. But the principle that a deep structure must exist behind such a grammar, which is a principle found within cognitive analysis, does appear in *In Small Things Forgotten* and is the cognitive pattern he calls bilateral symmetry. Deetz argues that a notion of bilateral symmetry, held unawares by almost everyone in New England after 1680, is evident in classes of artifacts and would probably be found in other categories of contemporary artifacts because all were created by the same people thinking through the same structure. He thereby unified Georgian architecture, concepts of individuality, privacy, and the afterlife by showing them to be simultaneous expressions of a conceptual whole. The plausibility of such homogeneity of outlook reveals the strength of an approach that sees all cultural artifacts as being equally the product of mind.

The strength of Deetz's analysis comes from its applicability to diverse ranges of artifacts like gravestones, pottery, and window placement. This orderliness or grammaticality might be a demonstration of a deeper order. Deetz certainly claims such an order but does not then suggest that if other kinds of artifacts were examined, the order would also be found in them. Further, Deetz never takes up the issue of the source of bilateral symmetry, which is presumably equiva-

103

lent to a deep structure. As a consequence, we do not know whether he holds that bilaterality is universal and common to all minds or whether it is grounded in context.

And when we compare Deetz with Leroi-Gourhan, we see that Leroi-Gourhan attempted to unify 10,000 years of cave art from the Atlantic to the Urals and forsook context, while Deetz took a very small area for a short period of time but tried to unify utterly different classes of artifacts. Both ultimately forsook context when employing structuralist principles.

The most complete structuralist analysis of artifacts to date is Glassie's *Folk Housing of Middle Virginia* (1975). In it Glassie tried to correct for the two classic weaknesses attributed to structuralism. He attempted to show that structural analysis did not have to deny history in the sense that Leroi-Gourhan had amalgamated time, or in the sense of ignoring contemporary material context as Deetz had done. There is little doubt that one can be awed by reading Leroi-Gourhan on cave art, but one learns nothing about its age, duration, extent, or function. Similarly, when one finishes *In Small Things Forgotten*, colonial New England is shown to have had a cultural coherence which makes a kind of sense not available before. But one still has no firm idea of why bilateral symmetry existed, why it was different from what went before, or how it varied from what was happening simultaneously in Virginia, or in England. Further, one cannot determine these things because the analysis is not tied to the history of the region before, during, or after the pending question. These are examples of weaknesses in structuralism which Glassie has tried to overcome. He has used the written record to overcome structuralism's tendency to ignore context, and he has used transformational analysis to preserve the cultural details of his data.

Glassie began by describing a "grammar" of houses in an area of Virginia and Maryland, writing the rules, in Chomskian fashion, for an architectural competence. Only standing houses were taken—no other classes of artifacts were admitted and no archaeology was undertaken. But all *parts* of houses were scrutinized: internal partitions, window and door placement, fireplace and chimney placement, stairway location, stories, depth, roof alignment, even door latches. Using descriptions and measurements of well over a hundred houses, Glassie inductively evolved the rules that predicted how the basic elements composing a house would be combined to produce a building. He wrote a grammar, which he referred to as an architectural competence. Middle Virginia's architectural competence produced two different kinds of houses with a few subtypes for each. The grammar was rather narrow in the kinds of results it could produce, which accords with the relatively insignificant variation in the region's architectural styles.

Architectural competence, which is governed by a grammar, locates room size, stairway, fireplace, and governs choices over logs, clapboards, shingles, and bricks. The binary sets that lie behind such choices in architecture are intellect/emotion, private/public, and artificial substance/natural substance. These oppositions in thinking mediate relations between man and man, with Middle Virginians preferring intellect, privacy, and artificial substance versus emotion, openness, and natural substance in building houses, which of course are one major way of dealing with fellow human beings. These oppositions transferred to other aspects of Virginian culture because they are categories of thought. Further, Glassie uses the oppositions artificial/natural and internal/external to show that in the relationship between man and nature Middle Virginians chose the artificial and internal. The population chose a practical, closed, repetitive, and scattered way of life, not just in housing but in all ways of life, and did so to express control over chaos, which is the basic opposition Glassie sees governing their way of life (Glassie 1975:135, 161).

Glassie used methods borrowed from Chomsky to write an architectural grammar applied to buildings in a clearly bounded locale. Then he used sets of structural oppositions, like artificial/natural and internal/external, which are analogous to Deetz's principle of bilateral symmetry, to tie houses to other aspects of Middle Virginian culture, such as attitudes toward kinsmen, neighbors and strangers; toward wilderness, social mobility, and hierarchy. Finally, in order to tie such attitudes to changing material circumstances, he used a convincing set of documentary citations which showed that eighteenth-century Virginian culture was "a culture under rigid control" (Glassie 1975:188) by its own people who were poor, fearful, and conservative. And thus, the architectural competence for houses existed within the context of a broad range of cultural values.

104

Once Glassie had written the grammar, its rules defined a universe that existed in a particular space and time and did not—or should not be expected to—apply outside of that specific time and space. He thus made replicability possible in the following way. Since Glassie had stipulated a clear geographical boundary and precise description of the organizational rules he found within it, buildings that were exceptions to structures so defined should become immediately noticeable as anomalous. If it happened that ruined outbuildings or burned houses were excavated, they would have to conform to Glassie's rules or his analysis would be void, or at least revealingly incomplete. Thus, he created the possibility of a test.

The boundary of the culture Glassie tried to preserve also included its particular history, in the sense that it incorporated both the events that occurred there, and their local meaning. It was not enough to isolate a culture by place, saying where it was not found; it was also necessary for Glassie to try to preserve the history of the area and to use the local context, as preserved in the area's documents (Glassie 1975:176–193), in his analysis. Whereas Lévi-Strauss tended to deal with the relationship between forms as Leroi-Gourhan showed, Glassie, on the other hand, used the local meaning of the forms studied to define a difference between Middle Virginia and everywhere else. Had he not done this, he would have run the risk of discovering, in the worst possibility for a structuralist, that Middle Virginians used the same sets of oppositions, even if they might not have applied them in the same way to daily life, as the Magdalenians. To avoid such homogenization at the level of categories of thought, Glassie sought the meaning of the houses that had been built with a particular architectural competence. For his answer Glassie used contemporaneous documents to reveal a Virginian mind preoccupied with isolating neighbors, strangers, life's functions, and wilderness.

Glassie's treatment considers an aspect of Virginian life not usually considered by historians. The mental life of the eighteenth century, which he describes, is not merely rural, anonymous, or folk. It predominated in Virginia while the elite were scribbling about toleration of plurality and acceptance of changeability. We come away from his analysis knowing much more about eighteenth-century forms and the life that went along with them for the great majority of Virginians. Nonetheless, while Glassie makes a plausible and fascinating case, we still do not understand what the "grammar" of Middle Virginia has to do with the rest of Virginia, like the Tidewater, or why the grammar finally disappeared. Like Leroi-Gourhan's treatment of cave art, we come away knowing much more about the forms, in this case architecture, but not as much as we would like to know about their historical context.

Glassie's work is of great importance to archaeology, and particularly to historical archaeology. None of the material described in the rest of this essay is as comprehensive as his, although some of its possesses different strengths. Glassie has offered a complete description of a class of artifacts and has offered a cultural reconstruction built on that description which, given other archaeological reconstructions, is more comprehensive and evocative. Even though I tend to side more with a materialist strategy in archaeology, none of its achievements yet matches those of Glassie, and to a lesser degree, of Deetz. It is the shortcomings of a structuralist and cognitive approach that invite turning now to an exploration of how materialism has attempted the reconstruction of mental life.

NEOEVOLUTIONISTS' SELF-CRITIQUE AND USE OF COSMOLOGY

From Leslie White (1949:363–393) and Lewis Binford (1962:217–225) onward, archaeologists operating within a materialist framework have been familiar with the concept of "ideology," usually taken broadly to mean a system of sacred or secular beliefs that rationalize an economic or political order. Primary causality has not been assigned to these rationalizing beliefs or thoughts. They are normally considered epiphenomenal, and materialist theory in archaeology has never developed a comprehensive idea like structure, cognitive pattern, or theory of the unconscious, to describe and recover these patterns.

Within archaeology lately, however, a number of scholars have called attention to the need for systematic attention to religion, ritual, and ideology. These, of course, comprise the data that

Leroi-Gourhan, Deetz, and Glassie have been struggling with, albeit using different definitions of these terms and employing arguments grounded in material referents. For example, Flannery and Marcus (1973:374–383) outlined the likely importance of cosmology in early Oaxaca and recommended examining its function through the calendar, including the ritual cycle. They suggest that Rappaport's (1971:57–76) ideas on the ritual regulation of subsistence variables would complement and extend a systems analysis to cover religion, ritual, and world view. A similar call for attention to symbolic systems has been made by Robert Hall (1977:499–518) who criticized "econo-think" among archaeologists and borrowed from cognitive psychology to analyze a range of North American aboriginal pipe forms, using these to reconstruct Hopewellian ideology. Hall sees an analysis of Hopewellian symbolism as a way to explain how that tradition maintained effective interaction between large numbers of communities over a wide area by reducing regional differences through a shared ideology. Use of "ceremonial staffs, fetishes, society emblems," by "societies, bands, clans, or some other corporate group," maintained unifying ideas about water which in turn meant life, or continuity. Thus, the emblems came to symbolize universals beyond a locale (Hall 1977:514–515). Margaret Conkey (1978:61–85, 1980:225–248) has used Upper Paleolithic art to deal with the same issue but has chosen to combine an analysis of style (Wobst 1977: 317–342) with cognitive and information theory (Margalef 1968). She sees engraved art and, to a lesser extent, wall art as encoding "patterns or structures . . . employed in the process of group boundary-maintenance" (Conkey 1980:233). The assumption behind such reasoning is that a design or style provides specific information about territorial boundaries through repeated patterns that are recognizable because they are redundant. Style in art is therefore analogous to information in a genetic code and is one of the aspects of culture that replaces biology in human evolution. All four authors—Flannery, Marcus, Hall, and Conkey—depart very little from a functionalist viewpoint which argues that recognizable information passed via religion or art assists in communication, which is basically practical. Working along these lines, but with subtleties introduced from symbolic anthropology, John Fritz (1978:37–59) described directional symmetry at eleventh-century Chaco Canyon in New Mexico and argued that adaptation involved information communicated through architecture that "encoded in stone and space the organizing principles of secular and sacred existence" (1978:55–56). Using ideas from the works of Geertz (1957), Colby (1975), and Ortiz (1969) as justifications, Fritz sees architectural and village placement as a series of symmetries and asymmetries expressing "the articulation of the sacred and the everyday for the region" (1978:54). "Architectural asymmetry expressed the organizational basis for theocratic control, yet it also expressed the necessary role of the provision for those who were controlled" (1978:54).

David Freidel has begun to work out "the symbols of cosmic and world order that make up a state religion and ideology" within hierarchical societies (1981:188–227). He surveys a wide range of archaeological materials from the highland and lowland Maya from the Preclassic through the Postclassic in an effort to illustrate how hieroglyphic writings, astronomy, astrology, ritual, art, and architecture were combined to create a uniform, widespread set of symbols that empowered Maya states. These elements worked because they were tied to routine cyclical events that allowed prognostication.

> Routine cyclical events, such as the flow of the seasons relative to agriculture, played a minor role in such prognostication. Of primary interest were disasters, both natural and man-made, and great events in the history of society. Wars, conquest, plague, drought, the advent of great leaderships, economic depression, and prosperity are the kinds of events that figured prominently in public foretelling. Moreover, such prognostication was a matter of central concern to Maya governments. Beyond the functions of historical record keeping and the transmission of information, hieroglyphic writing as used by the highland Maya and subsequently by the lowland Maya was the central instrument of a predictive science of astrology. It was a source of legal and historical precedent and a guide to the future. Government by historical precedent that is accumulated, recorded, and codified is government by law. Such government is one of the key ingredients in the establishment of state society [Freidel 1981:199].

Freidel casts his argument within an evolutionary context and sees social relations, such as hierarchy, as symbolically constituted, not ecologically determined. Thus, a universalizing religion employed its rituals to promote the standardization of economic encounters. "The result was a regional social stratum of chiefly nobles and merchant priests whose joint control of the mode of distribution provided a solid economic alternative to kinship sanction as a source of permanent power" (Freidel 1981:225).

Freidel's arguments are important even though they are not yet conclusive. They build on those of Marcus (1973:911–916), who suggested that religious symbols, when related to space, marked out political relationships. Freidel's work also bears uncanny similarity to that of Ian Thorpe, discussed below, who has been using structural Marxism to understand the relationship between Bronze Age political organization in Britain and the well known predictive capacity of the henge monuments.

From even such a limited survey of the available literature it is possible to conclude that a number of prominent evolutionists and materialists have recognized the need for archaeological analyses of ideology. Hence they have produced analytic attempts of sufficient maturity and ingenuity to make it possible for us to consider the effort begun. These preliminary and provocative efforts at understanding the ideational attributes of culture make it clear that no thorough, tested reconstruction of an archaeological ideology has been produced within the materialist tradition. Nothing approximating Leroi–Gourhan's work or Glassie's can be cited, despite the recognition of the need and its importance. This is the same conclusion reached by Kohl (1981:89–118) in an important review of materialist contributions to prehistory.

MARXISM AND IDEOLOGY

A number of scholars in archaeology has begun to explore various traditions within historical materialism to discover whether its ideas on mind may be useful. Some archaeologists have tried structural Marxism and some neo-Marxism. The exploration is obviously new in archaeology and the results largely unevaluated.

The term used within the various materialist traditions to deal with mind is "ideology." Within historical materialism the term means the mental "givens," or "taken-for-granteds" held unawares by members of a society; things that are taken as being "obvious" and "naturally so," not the explicit beliefs of a group. Since the social relations of production, which are the relations between classes or groups within a society, may be in conflict or may contradict each other, ideology hides or masks this reality by positing quite another reality as "true." Note that if ideology plays such a role, it is a very powerful social force and not an epiphenomenon, for it is said to be rooted in inevitable social conflict, not in smooth adaptive functioning. Thus, "ideology" is a structure of misrecognition, where the members of different classes share the same notions of truth, notions that hide the actual antagonistic or exploitative relationships between those classes. Shared viewpoints are expressed through the "natural" or "inevitable" and have as their function the masking of conflict. None of the neoevolutionists just discussed shares this definition of ideology.

Suppression of conflict is the key to the operation of ideology, and both suppressed class conflict and internal contradiction are part of structural Marxist and neo-Marxist analyses. A society with a changing technology or means of production, or a society with a shifting mode of production—which means shifting distribution of ownership and wealth between its segments—will experience conflict and contradiction because of the change. It will not experience ongoing homeostasis or adaptation.

Maurizio Tosi (1976:173–180), a Marxist-oriented archaeologist, analyzes the place of contradiction in the process of state formation in the ancient Near East. He notes the appropriation of labor and its products by the temple economy, the resulting social stratification, and the use of religion to misrepresent sectional interests as universal. He describes the dialectics of state formation as resident in latent conflict, itself stemming from the continual shift of power to an urban elite for which religion ultimately becomes the mask that hides exploitation.

Tosi's work and Kohl's (1975) are much more geared to the analysis of materialist dynamics than to ideology, but each fully understands the role played by ideology and its evolution within

Mesopotamian society. They see that as the more relations between classes or sections emerged as contradictory, the more ideology masked the removal of the elite from any direct contribution to production.

Christopher Tilley (1981a:363–386), and some of his colleagues who are students of Ian Hodder at Cambridge, are shifting from structural Marxism to neo-Marxism and use the idea of internal contradiction to analyze the changing mode of production in western neolithic Europe, 4700–3800 B.C. Tilley has suggested that some megalithic monuments and associated rituals served to sustain the forces and means of production in the face of social fissioning and fragmentation by acting to define levels of people within a society and their interrelationships in such a way that the older but now strained relations of production were maintained (1981a:382). Tilley is thus concerned with "ideology," which he calls "mind, meaning, and intention" (1981a:382), and tries, in his initial effort which is structural Marxist, to be empirical by showing how economic and environmental constraints can be overcome by ritual and thought. He takes as axiomatic inevitable contradiction or disharmony between people at different levels of power within a social system. Tilley's approach, as it uses ideology, sees meaning as not merely a map or guide to reinforce the social order but a mask hiding economic reality from some people while guaranteeing their participation, productive activity, and social rank at the same time.

The key to such an archaeological analysis is found in the arguments of relevance which link to the archaeological record conflict or contradiction between emerging groups based on differential wealth. How does one find archaeological evidence of contradiction? Lévi-Strauss assumes the existence of contradiction in most ranked societies and the Cambridge school is adapting Marx to find conflict and potential conflict between groups within neolithic societies. Since contradiction is normally hidden or masked to prevent conflict, if we use the Marxist definition of ideology, and since such masking is achieved by cultural assumptions grounded in nature or in the "obvious," the artifacts of such masks should be the artifacts of ideology. The extension of this argument is that all neolithic and more advanced societies, that is, all societies having unequal distribution of resources and thus subject to potential conflict, will postulate a world in nature, supernature, or the inevitable that underlies the way humans are related to each other. In this deeper or second world are grounded the "inevitabilities" of daily life. This world beyond human control, which guarantees the givenness of everyday life, may be expressed through astronomy, as, for example, the European henge and megalithic monuments and Maya astronomy/astrology; through geometry and imitation of nature, as, for example, mounds, hills, or pyramids that are artificial mountains; or through polysemous human forms that manifest multiple characteristics and thus evince plural relationships: the surface and the deeper or hidden. Examples would be doubleheaded figurines, masked heads, heads or bodies showing dual characteristics, and mirrors of all sorts. All such artifacts including those enabling prognostication like those Freidel cites, may be indices of the establishment by a given culture of its relations of production in a reality beyond human perception or agency, i.e., beyond culture itself. This grounding is the "ideology," which serves to mask the actual relations of production. Such artifacts are taken to be artifacts of ideology, or misrepresentation and misperception, because they serve to ground exploitative relations and definitions in a sphere that seems beyond question.

Using Marxist notions, I. J. Thorpe (1981) has suggested that the development of neolithic societies in northwest Europe demonstrates that the evolution of ideology proceeds along with economic changes in the relations between social strata within those societies. Thorpe uses Jonathan Freidman's concept of the tribal mode of production, that postulates rival lineages which may become ranked. Such a mode operates through a chief, with his control over prestige goods as well as a considerable portion of production. The tribal mode crosscuts the old band, tribe, chiefdom series because it is defined by the determining nature of the economy, i.e., material production and social reproduction, not sociocultural level of integration. Thorpe has tried to illustrate the evolution of this mode of production in the Bronze and Iron Ages in Britain and postulates an increasing degree of social rigidity, but not the appearance of class. Social rigidity brings with it the divorce of the hierarchy from the means of production and the tension or contradiction attendant upon such a divorce.

108

This means that contradiction must be mastered in order to keep it from becoming conflict, and the means by which contradiction is mastered is astronomy. Thorpe argues that hierarchy legitimizes itself by reference to ancestors who may actually have held authority because they produced more, or at least gave greater feasts. Thus, the tombs of ancestors are significant. Those ancestors, now deified and seen as heavenly bodies, can thus have predictable relations to possible current success. This may explain why some tombs mark the passage of some astronomical events. Later, as ancestors no longer serve as masks, and the divorce of hierarchy from production progresses, astronomy combined with rituals marking heavenly events serves to mystify completely the otherwise empty basis for authority of a hierarchy. Thorpe thus relates tombs, henge monuments, and hierarchy. He shows their evolving relationship using the idea of contradiction and offers an argument remarkably similar to Freidel's on the Maya.

Both Thorpe and Freidel have broken away from functional models as well as from ecological models. Neither sees symbols, religion, or ritual as regulatory. Both know heaven-gazing is astrology, not primitive astronomy; both know writing is mostly mystification, not primitive accounting. Both understand that reproducing social relations in stratified societies involves ideas so powerful that they disguise the perpetuation of asymmetrical relationships, which may be neither efficient nor adaptive.

Structural Marxism and neo-Marxism, two different approaches which include the work of archaeologists like Kohl, Gilman (1975), Tosi, Thorpe, and Tilley (1981b) agree on the importance of social reproduction and contradiction. Social reproduction, i.e., stability, is achieved in the presence of contradictions that would normally lead to transformations by (1) the mystification of the contradictions, (2) "representing sectional interests as universal," (3) grounding the social order in nature or the "objectively real," i.e., reification.

Relations of dominance are sustained at various levels: (i) the relation of structuring principles (sources of action) to the lived experience (ii) the relationship between structural principles to the asymmetry of resources . . . (iii) the reflexivity of the indivudal—the individual's practical . . . consciousness of activity and object [Tilley 1981b].

MARXISM AND CONSCIOUSNESS

Marx created the idea of ideology, not to reconstruct any part of the past, but to understand why workers failed to see their true economic and political condition. He felt that once this condition was brought to their awareness or consciousness, they would then have a vision of their unity and therefore of their power. He knew such glimpses were always revolutionary but very rare, and thus Marx defined the power of ideology but felt he had to link it with the idea of consciousness in order to tie it to the possibility of workers creating change. His point was that if ideology were analyzed and the true conditions of existence seen, then the resulting consciousness would provoke change. Once the Marxist idea of ideology has been introduced into archaeology, we incur some obligation to look at the implications of using the associated idea of consciousness. Archaeologists can do this by asking two questions, neither of which necessarily involves reconstructing a past society's consciousness. The first is: since we are members of a capitalist society with an ideology of its own, and since we know that one way ideology operates is to make the present look inevitable by making the past look like precedent for modern conditions, then to what degree does our modern archaeology create the past in its own image? This is not a new question, but it does raise the possibility that archaeology may serve modern economic or political functions. The second question is: since the aim of archaeology is to explore the relationships between past and present, can archaeology adduce the origins or early stages of any ideology? Both questions are argued to be indicative of a self-critical or self-reflexive process (Barnett and Silverman 1979:41–81).

Once an archaeologist understands that history and archaeology are not neutral or culture-free pursuits, but part of the ideological process of his or her own society, then the categories that generate a particular reconstruction of the past may be examined for their role in generating interpretation of it. Three different archaeologists have recently been concerned with self-reflection and have pointed out that the discipline might become conscious that interpretations are influenced by what can be called ideology. Although Trigger (1980:662–673) does not use the concept of self-reflection per se, he elaborates the history of American impositions on the history and archaeology of North American Indians. Trigger has a forerunner in Keen (1971), who exhaustively traced the imposition of European ideas that systematically misrepresented Aztec culture over nearly 500 years. Trigger describes for the archaeological discipline how the "culture" of archaeology has inevitably misunderstood the archaeological record because of biases it held unawares. He then goes on to say that such biases can be made visible and, once that is done, a different understanding of the past, more credible and responsible to its descendants, can be created. Trigger does not follow Keen in treating his observations as neutral intellectual history, but rather he calls for awareness of the culture-centered basis of all observations and then he calls for change in the direction of how interpretations are established and defended. Trigger understands the power of history when told, written, and believed, to establish national or tribal identity, including its influence on political and economic conditions. Implicitly, but not so well articulated, Trigger also shows that a truer or more faithful interpretation is not the only aim, but that we must also take note that the activity of shaping the past is an inevitable, ongoing process.

Kohl, too, is aware of the political tie between current uses of history, general conditions within our own culture, and interpretations of the past which rest on archaeological evidence. He cites three examples: first, the tie in the 1920s between the theory of hyperdiffusionism and fascism; second, the current tie between archaeological hypotheses of environmental management/mismanagement and contemporary concern with overpopulation; and third, archaeology's use of scientific positivism during the last 15 years and current popular reliance on science to solve technical problems. Kohl points to these parallel events to show "the reflection of broader concerns of late twentieth-century Western society within the dominant materialist models in archaeology" (Kohl 1981:92). Kohl is able to make this analysis through his understanding of the ideas of self-reflection and consciousness in Marxist theory.

The consistent method needed to extend Trigger's and Kohl's argument about the imposition of bias through any archaeologically based interpretation is supplied by Meltzer (1981:113–125) who uses Althusser and a number of other scholars who were influenced directly by Marx. The method identifies with precision that process through which ideology is imposed on data. Meltzer analyzes a contemporary history museum in the United States and shows that its exhibits use developmental sequences that make it appear that progressive or evolutionary change guides the relationship between past, present, and future. He argues that such sequences appear to make the epistemologically different equally knowable. Insofar as the segments isolated by the museum help us to identify the future with space (outer), the museum ultimately equates time with space. He identifies this not as myth, physics, history, cognition, or bias, but the museum communicating our "own ideology of time and space" (1981:124). Meltzer, an archaeologist, has analyzed the National Air and Space Museum in Washington in order to identify the contemporary ideology of time and change, which are of course central concepts in archaeology. Once identified, and seen as arbitrary projections or impositions on historical data, the ideology of technological progress enables him to differentiate between the modern ideas, which are imposed by archaeologists onto materials to which they may be foreign, and the ideas native to cultures studied by archaeologists that, in contrast with our own, do not necessarily organize concepts of time or of change as we do.

The works of the authors cited above have made it possible to think that we may improve our access to some part of mind and meaning as they have existed in the past through self-reflection or a self-critical attitude. The ideas of self-consciousness or of critical examination, when applied to modern ideology, enable us to distinguish between different ideologies and those we ourselves may be imposing, and may make us aware that our own activities are also part of a process that itself is embedded in the living-out of an ideology. In contradistinction to structuralists and non-Marxist materialists, those who advocate the reconstruction of mind or of cognition require critical self-awareness, and the positioning of oneself in the present as an essential step in the process of attempting to understand the thought of another time. Both Trigger and Meltzer demonstrate the need for this step as crucial for helping us distinguish between past and present. Hence, it should be possible to recover a past society and its ideology as distinguished from a contemporary imposition.

Authors like Meltzer who deal with cultural concepts of time and space and the relationship between the two, or like Glassie who deal with oppositions like order/chaos, invite us to face the bigger problem of the locus of such ideas. Are ways of perceiving reality context-dependent or are they the product of an innate ordering ability of the mind? Marxists and most materialists would argue the first, and Lévi-Strauss and Chomsky, the second. Marxists argue that there is great power in ideology in stratified societies but place the nature of ideology in material conditions. Material means natural and empirical, not just economic or political. Marx refuses analyses of mind based on spirit, genius, or God. Structuralists posit an innate ordering ability of the mind, which is what makes cultures comparable across time and which is the key ability at the core of human being. These then are the basic positions within the two theories dealing with mind, and any archaeologist who takes up these difficulties ultimately comes to rest in one framework or the other.

The power of the Marxist, as opposed to a neoevolutionist position on mind, is that the method of critical self-reflection recognizes the need for situating science within its own context. If all knowledge is context-dependent, one can at least explore that dependence with a method more powerful than logical positivism.

The crucial distinction used by Trigger, Kohl, and Meltzer is between archaeological interpretation created with a critical awareness of the categories used for the reconstruction of the past on the one hand, and vulgar history, which can be called modern ideology, on the other. Trigger and Meltzer have caught the distinction; Schrire (1980:890–891) has also joined in this opening effort to distinguish between vulgar history and a history created after criticism of contemporary impositions. She has shown how anthropological interpretations grounded in archaeology are publicized by the Australian government to keep Australian Aborigines "natural," primitive, and isolated, with the consequence that they are denied another identity and therefore access to concepts of disease and health, legal information, and power—all of which would be useful to their survival. The process of subordinating Aborigines in Australia involves everyday discourse in the argot of anthropology and archaeology, and so appropriates the discipline for a political purpose of which its practitioners are for the most part unaware. In other words, public discussion of Aboriginal origins in terms of their being hunter-gatherers, Stone Age peoples, or paleolithic remnants, when such discussions occur inthe context of land claims, acts to keep the Aborigines primitive and, therefore, subordinate. The archaeologists, Schrire concludes, are not normally guilty of this leap but they might be able to do more than merely lament it. Her suggestion does not involve a practice of archaeology different from that already current in Australian prehistory; it involves an understanding that "prehistory" occurs in an active and sometimes appropriating context.

Within the American context Yentsch et al. (1980) are now in the process of showing how Plimoth Plantation's portrayal of Indian/white relations from the 1600s mirrors modern visitor and town expectations not only for Indians but for blacks. Such mirroring within an "accurate" archaeological museum reproduces contemporary expectations by placing them in history, thus eliminating history as a commentary on alternative ways of life for the viewer. In order to correct this circularity, evident through self-reflection and an alternative sense of past custom, it is necessary to reconstruct both Indian and Pilgrim ideology. Such a reconstruction would highlight the differences between past and modern ideological assumptions about Indian-white relations and would show that within the Puritan ideology may be found the roots of the modern. We presume the two, Puritan and modern, are similar to some degree, but the presumption, when explored through documents and archaeology, can be specified, thus giving a history to ideology, whose categories are normally so unexamined they appear to have no beginning.

An exploration of Pilgrim or any other early American ideology will deal inevitably with discontinuity as well as with continuity, factuality as well as fictional imposition. The likelihood is that the seventeenth century in New England or in the Chesapeake would be very difficult to comprehend if we saw it as it was. Ideas of person, time, and order would have been very different, and if we could understand them, they would likely highlight extraordinary differences with our own ideology. Nonetheless, that century and culture is antecedent to our own insofar as they are a form and function of early capitalism and saw the start of many modern assumptions common to that economic form. An exploration of ideology would attempt to sort out this complex succession of attitudes.

Most scholars who are aware of the impact of their own culture on their reconstructions of the past have felt that awareness is difficult enough to establish, but, that once established, it is sufficient and agree with Schrire's position that one does not proceed differently as a scholar. Instead, one becomes aware of the meaning self and society may impose on the products of scholarship. This position leads inevitably to seeing self-reflection as having two parts. The first explores how the culture of the archaeologist shapes the culture under archaeological study. The second explores how the personal history, personality, or social status of an individual archaeologist may have the same effects. The publication of Malinowski's diary (1967) is part of a long tradition in the field, a tradition based on the assumed need to explore systematically the relations between a person and the object studied. This may be done to distinguish more scientifically between observer and observed. Within archaeology such an explicit approach to self-reflection has not been strongly developed, but both Binford (1962:1-13, 17-19, 125-134, 187-194, 329-342, 450-456) and Flannery (1976:1-11, 13-16, 49-51, 161-162, 251-253, 283-286, 329-333, 369-373) have used autobiography, parable, and parody to point out that the person and his or her own unseen propensities play a role in archaeological research. Sometimes humorous, sometimes graceless, these early efforts at self-reflection admit and explore the role of personal factors in science. That role is inevitable, and these authors, whatever else they may have intended, have introduced the personal level of self-reflection into the discipline. Personal awareness can control for bias just as awareness of one's culture can help control the imposition of modern categories. Again, the point of introducing the need that we become aware of this process is to achieve a different and more accurate view of the past.

While Schrire's position and Binford's and Flannery's are valid, they provide no link to changing the archaeology. Not even Trigger, or Meltzer or Yentsch suggest how archaeology can or should proceed any differently, once the self-reflective exploration has been done. Self-reflection offers no real link to the past and, even though it may impose constraints upon the archaeologist, it has not offered a different interpretation of prehistory, nor is it likely to.

The concept of "consciousness" involves two ideas which are not interchangeable. Self-reflection acts to make conscious the position of oneself and of one's work in the context of one's own society. It stems from phenomenology and has been explored in the works of scholars like Frye (1964), Ricoeur (1970), and Sartre (1968). A phenomenologist position has been most recently articulated in anthropology by Clifford Geertz who stresses translation and understanding of another culture as the task of the anthropologist. A second kind of "consciousness" is critical theory, or critical self-reflection. This places the cultural position of the scholar in his or her own political context to create awareness or consciousness, often called self-positioning. This method is part of neo-Marxist theory and is the method used to explore the imposition of modern cultural notions like efficiency, adaptative functioning, progression, modern kinship, or modern temporal organization on the past (Barnett and Silverman 1979:41-81).

"VULGAR HISTORY" AND HISTORY AS CONSCIOUSNESS

Still remaining, then, is the tie between consciousness and archaeology. Can there be any such thing beyond self-reflection? The following argument, now emerging in the literature, may create such a tie. One of the characteristics of ideology is that it appears to have neither a history nor origins. Hence, ideology appears "inevitable" or "natural." Because Marxists assume that ideology stabilizes and reproduces economic and political conditions, a materialist definition suggests the exploration of those conditions, called the infrastructure, and of the advent and change of ideology along with them. Because our own ideology is made visible through a critical analysis, and because that ideology's actual history can be discovered in its tie to material variables, and because those variables are the subject matter of historical archaeology, then there exists the possibility for an important extension of materialist archaeology into historical archaeology. This could be useful because historical archaeology under South (1977a, 1977b) among others has already oriented itself to the new archaeology and because historical archaeology deals with more complex societies, including capitalist ones, which contain ideologies more powerful and complex than any earlier. There is, then, the possibility that archaeological practice could build upon the link between consciousness and ideology as both have been defined within neo-Marxism.

A few archaeologists have suggested that such a link could exist between the two within historical archaeology since consciousness is by definition "awareness" of the ideology, or the discovery that the ideology governs one's interpretation of all data. Our own very hidden assumptions are thus shown to have their origins and histories in the data of historical archaeology. It follows that since historical archaeology often explores the origins of modern society, it may also explore the origins and early phases of modern ideology and its infrastructure. This would create a strong direct link between self-reflection and archaeology. Because there is no clean break between the present and the subject matter of historical archaeology, as there is for prehistory, there is an opportunity to ground modern ideology using archaeology.

There are two twentieth-century historical materialists whose work attempts to provide such a method for giving ideology a history in a way that might be useful to historical archaeologists. Louis Althusser's ideas (1971:127-186) have been used by Meltzer (1981) to define ideology as the givens and taken-for-granteds of everyday life; ideology is to be found in peoples' notions of person, time, object, or wealth, among others. Althusser's proposition can be used to reconstruct ideology in past complex societies, as well as to identify our own ideology, and he allows us to infer that there is a relationship between how our ideology works and its impact on our discoveries about the past.

Georg Lukacs (1971:83-222) specifies the relationship between past and present more fully than does Althusser. He argues that it is the task of the historian, and by my extension of his argument, of the archaeologist, to write the history of ideology. This is a particularly useful suggestion for a historical archaeologist. The inference is that instead of isolating evolving kinship, bilateral symmetry, and Virginian insularity, the archaeologist or historian should concentrate on these as expressions of notions of, say, gender and how they are tied to the family and work; or as ideas about time and how these are tied to personal development and individualism; or as the manipulation of the past as precedent and how that does or does not influence relations between competing classes in a society. Historical archaeologists, following Lukacs, would first discover their own culture's ideology through the kind of self-reflection illustrated by Trigger and Meltzer, and then write the history of bias, a history discovered through documentation and archaeology. This approach may be particularly appropriate for historical archaeologists since they dig virtually nothing but material from the dawn of the modern age to its present.

A fully articulated archaeological method using ideology and consciousness depends on three assumptions: (1) the past can and must be known with some integrity, including past ideologies; (2) when the past is interpreted and thus made history, it tends to become ideology; and (3) consciousness of that process (in historical archaeology at least) may help those who write or dig the history to become aware of the ideological notions that generate modern everyday life. Central among these issues for the archaeologist is the impossibility of ever permanently separating history from ideology. This impossibility suggests that an archaeologist must have an active involvement with the ideological process in order to distinguish between that knowledge of the past that is needed to understand the present accurately, and that knowledge of the past that present society would emphasize in order to reproduce itself as it is now constituted.

Marx called those histories written without awareness of how knowledge is related to the context of its creation and use "vulgar history," which is a form of ideology and a function of modern economic and political processes. He also argued that there will always be a struggle to separate the distinctiveness of the past from its vulgarization. Trigger and Meltzer have both made this same distinction.

Handsman (1980b:255–286, 1981:1–21), working within historical archaeology, has also used the distinction between vulgar history and self-critical or self-reflexive history in order to actually improve the archaeology. He has shown in detail (1980a:2–9) how New England social historians who have reconstructed kinship have also populated the colonial era with a bourgeois family centered on the idea of individuality. He has taken several locales in modern Connecticut and shown how the remains of early industrialization, which was neither capitalist nor urban, were eliminated in Victorian times by tearing down the factories, by building a colonial veneer on early Victorian houses and churches, and by celebrating an agrarian heritage in popular history books. Since industrialism precedes capitalism in New England, and since the tie between the two is not historically essential but has only been made to appear so, he has shown how the evidence of the earlier conditions has been disguised by a vulgar history.

Vulgar history has as its centerpiece the idea of the individual. The individual is characterized by voluntary choice, freedom to act, personal responsibility, rationality, and economic motivation. Handsman shows this definition to be an attribute of industrial capitalism, shows when it emerged in Connecticut, and contrasts these developments with the earlier world portrayed by Deetz (1977), which was communal, diffuse in its social relations, and medieval in not segregating life's activities or people into discrete parts. Handsman argues that the idea of the individual was propagated by giving it historical depth, and this in turn wiped out an earlier history. Of course, Deetz has more to say than has Handsman about how to analyze artifacts in order to achieve a reconstructed ideology of the earlier time, but Handsman has shown the origins of a central element in the modern complex of ideological notions, i.e., the individual. He could do this by being conscious of the imposition of present constructs on the past. Whereas Deetz is not concerned with linking past and present, Handsman has found a way, via self-reflection, to link the two. A neo-Marxist definition of ideology is essential to his effort. So, by self-reflection, Handsman has isolated a modern ideological imposition; he then pointed to a contrasting time when this imposition could be shown to have misidentified reality. Then he spotted the roots of the modern notion that had hitherto appeared to be grounded in "self-evidence" and timelessness. He thus gave the "obvious" a history, whereas Deetz, who had pointed out the arrival of the idea of the individual in the archaeological record, had neglected both an explanation of why the concept appeared, as well as how it was tied to the present.

My point in describing Handsman's work and its complementarity to that of Deetz is not to judge its accuracy, but to describe the method, newly emergent in archaeology, which is behind it. Of course, any new research is valuable if something novel and enlightening is achieved, and Handsman's work and my own, to be described below, are still at the stage of hypothesis formation. Further, as Deetz and Glassie have found when dealing with an era so thoroughly and competently covered by historians, the only sound way to ground the importance of research is to know the history of the area and to array one's hypotheses against the documents and work of established historians. So, when Handsman deals with colonial and Victorian Connecticut or with the idea of the individual there, he will ultimately have to deal with the plurality of viewpoints within an era that in turn may depend on what class one was in. Ultimately, too, he will have to deal with precedents to the idea in Roman times and in Christian theology, as well as with how these harmonize with his own critical analysis which makes the individual a function of the emergence of capitalism in the late Middle Ages.

During ethnographic and archival work at Colonial Williamsburg, Virginia, and at St. Mary's City, Maryland, I came to realize (Leone 1978, 1981) that outdoor, living history museums and farms were an ideal setting for a historical archaeology informed by the notion of ideology. The first discovery was that Colonial Williamsburg sometimes unintentionally reproduces modern relations between blacks and whites, men and women, and adults and children by placing them in the past. In this sense, Colonial Williamsburg, despite its premium on accuracy and research, was animated in part by vulgar history or ideology. This happened by giving modern notions of person,

114

precedent, and change a seemingly independent existence at an important time before our own. Thus, it seemed inevitable or natural that we express similar ideas and patterns at present. These givens are perpetuated through archaeology when discoveries are placed in museums where archaeology is used to naturalize the present by extending it onto the past, thus duplicating the present while obliterating the integrity of a past culture. While Trigger found American Indian history misappropriated, I realized that our own was no safer. A radical Marxist analysis of Williamsburg, which was parallel to and independent of my own, came to similar conclusions (Wallace 1981:63-96).

Once the process of mystifying history was recognized, Williamsburg as an archaeological presentation could become two things. Such a living history museum could be a place to see early capitalism and its ideology founded and worked out before both became linked to industrialism and took on their present form. Thus, Williamsburg would be a museum of eighteenth-century ideology, as well as of our society's use of the past. This suggestion is based on the fact that virtually all sites investigated by historical archaeology were created during the emergence of capitalism. They can be made to demonstrate that, and thus they can also serve to illustrate the growth of capitalism, that main cultural process that led to our present, instead of herb gardens, plantations, and silversmiths.

For example, our notion of vectorial or universal time has two characteristics that had not emerged in the Chesapeake prior to the mid-eighteenth century. We presume, conventionally, that time is a function of the revolution of heavenly bodies and is therefore not under human control and, second, that everything is subject to it (Gurevich 1976). This makes work, reading, child-rearing, dancing, holidays, thinking, writing, changes in the seasons, and changes in people all appear commensurable insofar as they are subject to time. This is how we think now, which is a process begun in the late Middle Ages (LeGoff 1980:29, 43), and a trip through Williamsburg at present shows implicitly that there had been no fundamental change from then to now in this regard, just gradual progress. But in fact, before the 1740s and before the era when mercantile capitalism became rigidly established in Tidewater Virginia (Isaac 1982), diaries show many events not tied to a calendar, agrarian time tied to the seasons instead of the clock; the seasonal birth of animals dated in one year and not in another; no consistent placement of all events in an absolute scale, and no commensurability between urban, which is to say merchant's time, and rural or farmer's time. Yet, changes from then to now have occurred and have had profound impact on money, wages, capital, and work; they could be shown at Williamsburg (Isaac 1982:318-319). Such changes could be shown to have been a function of the beginning of wage labor by the second quarter of the eighteenth century: mass production, the removal of wealth from work, and the removal of the worker from the definition of a whole person with many needs. All these are processes attendant upon capitalism, its arrival and health, and all are invisible in the history as now presented at Williamsburg. All things became subject to our conceptions of time only with use of wages, which had begun to remove the laborer from his product, and the emergence of capital (Braudel 1979:436-478). Since capital emerges at different times in the colonies, so does the appearance of universal time. Thus, uniformly measured time actually appeared in Williamsburg in the early 1700s and not at all on the Virginia frontier of the same time. The origins of the modern notions of time make their appearance in the Tidewater at a particular time, amid specific economic conditions, which a visitor could be shown at Williamsburg. This would not only create a contrast with the present but would also show the origins of a part of the present. It would put a different aspect of history on display.

A second major historical event that could be illustrated at Williamsburg is the imposition of the present through the components of ideology like time, person, cause, or object. Visitors could be made aware of their own ideology of time as well as of their own culture's appropriation of the past. Precapitalist and early capitalist societies were built on different notions, producing different lives. Seeing the differences between the two ideologies and recognizing the fact that we eliminate the earlier and impose our own in order to make ours appear inevitable, enables us to see how museums, using archaeology, act to reproduce modern everyday life and therefore how they serve as ideology. If Williamsburg could show people the roots of modern ideology (and there is no question it could), as well as the imposition of the present on the past, it would contribute to both the history of ideology and consciousness. It does do this from time to time, and audiences have reacted with fascination at being told that history is a creation of the moment and with even more rapt attention when it is explained that various ideas of the present, sometimes thought to be exploitative, had an origin in past processes that operated at Williamsburg. Even though such occasions are rare, they are sufficient to demonstrate the possibility of a materialist archaeology that encompasses an expanded definition of ideology. Such an archaeology aims at understanding mental phenomena through the concept of ideology; it would recommend that archaeologists attend to how their artifacts are placed in public displays and given an interpretation. After noticing how the present begins to confer meaning upon artifacts, thus incorporating them into ideology, a historical archaeologist might display the process of meaning-conferral as well as the roots of the particular ideological notion conferred.

CONCLUSIONS

My intent here has been to summarize the strengths of recent archaeological works by structuralists and materialists concerned with reconstructing patterns of thought. At best it has been an incomplete survey of a fast-changing and often confusing scene. I have not addressed all the issues, nor have I taken note of the place of positivism and objectivity in structuralism and materialism, nor have I attempted to link the new archaeology and Marxism, which at this point seems a needed step.

I do feel it essential to emphasize a few points. Reconstructing mind, no matter what it is called, has begun, appears possible, and has made greatest progress so far by proceeding from the basis laid by structuralism. The weakness of the structuralist approach is that no effective explanation or relation to economic or political context is offered. The materialist approach to reconstructing mind has not made as much progress, but it offers important potential because of the viability of methodological definitions, including an examination of the culture-centered relationship between subject and object. All this makes mind measurable and material, through analysis of the constituent parts of the concept of ideology. It is better to label such ideas as materialist and leave the political involvement associated with Marxism behind, as all the archaeologists cited above have done. The ideas can then be regarded most usefully as extensions of the successful materialist approach of the new archaeology, a move which will abandon the cumbersome and emotion-laden parts of Marxism.

The call for thinking about nonecological issues in archaeology is clear enough. The call comes at a time when archaeology is more and more concerned with more complex societies, including our own, and is potentially in the position to provide the theoretical extensions that would take archaeology beyond those societies so successfully treated by the new archaeology into those areas so in need of a more complex and appropriate theory.

Acknowledgments.   I am indebted to Garry Wheeler Stone for a conversation and an article (1976) clarifying Glassie; to Ann M. Palkovich for insisting on a specific tie between archaeology and self-reflection, and for essential help with an overview of much of the material presented. JoAnn Magdoff gave a careful reading concerning critical theory. R. Joseph Dent helped organize much of the material in this paper. M. Alison Wylie (1981) and Russell G. Handsman caused me to rethink completely the logic of my position in an earlier version of this paper. Russell Handsman's work has been crucial in forming my position. David J. Meltzer, William T. Stuart, and William Y. Adams offered important suggestions in organization and information. I. J. (Nick) Thorpe has given permission to use his material. Wendy Ashmore and Christopher Fennell called my attention to the work of David Freidel. Christopher Tilley has given permission to quote from his Introduction.

REFERENCES CITED

Althusser, Louis
   1971   Ideology and ideological state apparatuses. In *Lenin and philosophy,* pp. 127–186. Monthly Review Press, New York.
Barnett, Steve, and Martin G. Silverman
   1979   *Ideology and everyday life.* University of Michigan Press, Ann Arbor.

Binford, Lewis R.
    1962   Archaeology as anthropology. *American Antiquity* 28:217–225.
    1965   Archaeological systematics and the study of culture process. *American Antiquity* 31:203–210.
Braudel, Fernand
    1979   *The structures of everyday life: civilization and capitalism, 15th–18th century* (vol. 1). Harper & Row, New York.
Colby, Benjamin
    1975   Culture grammars. *Science* 187:913–919.
Conkey, Margaret W.
    1978   Style and information in cultural evolution: toward a predictive model for the Paleolithic. In *Social archeology: beyond subsistence and dating*, edited by Charles L. Redman, Mary Jane Berman, Edward V. Curtin, William T. Langhorne, Jr., Nina M. Versaggi, and Jeffery C. Wanser, pp. 61–85. Academic Press, New York.
    1980   Context, structure, and efficacy in Paleolithic art and design. In *Symbol as sense*, edited by M. L. Foster and S. Brandes, pp. 225–248. Academic Press, New York.
Deetz, James F.
    1967   *Invitation to archaeology*. Natural History Press, New York.
    1977   *In small things forgotten*. Doubleday, Garden City.
Flannery, Kent V. (editor)
    1976   *The early Mesoamerican village*. Academic Press, New York.
Flannery, Kent V., and Joyce Marcus
    1973   Formative Oaxaca and the Zapotec cosmos. *American Scientist* 64:374–383.
Freidel, David A.
    1981   Civilization as a state of mind. In *Transformations to statehood*, edited by Gordon Jones and Robert Kautz, pp. 188–227. Cambridge University Press.
Fritz, John M.
    1978   Paleopsychology today: ideational systems and human adaptation in prehistory. *In Social archeology, beyond subsistence and dating*, edited by Charles L. Redman, Mary Jane Berman, Edward V. Curtin, William T. Langhorne, Jr., Nina M. Versaggi, and Jeffery C. Wanser, pp. 37–59. Academic Press, New York.
Frye, Northrop
    1964   *The educated imagination*. University of Indiana Press, Bloomington.
Geertz, Clifford
    1957   Ethos, world view and the analysis of sacred symbols. *Antioch Review* 17:421–437.
Gilman, Antonio
    1975   Bronze age dynamics in southeast Spain. *Dialectical Anthropology* 1:307–319.
Glassie, Henry
    1975   *Folk housing of middle Virginia*. University of Tennessee Press, Knoxville.
Gurevich, A. J.
    1976   Time as a problem of cultural history. In *Cultures and time*, edited by Paul Ricoeur, pp. 229–245. The UNESCO Press, Paris.
Hall, Robert L.
    1977   An anthropocentric perspective for eastern United States prehistory. *American Antiquity* 42:499–518.
Handsman, Russell G.
    1980a   The domains of kinship and settlement in historic Goshen: signs of a past order. *Artifacts* IX:1:2–9. American Indian Archaeological Institute, Washington, Connecticut.
    1980b   Studying myth and history in modern America: perspectives for the past from the Continent. *Reviews in Anthropology* 7:2:255–268.
    1981   Early capitalism and the center village of Canaan, Connecticut, a study of transformations and separations. *Artifacts* IX:3:1–21. American Indian Archaeological Institute, Washington, Connecticut.
Hodder, Ian
    1982   *The archaeology of mind*. Cambridge University Press, in press.
Hodder, Ian (editor)
    1982   *The past in its context*. Cambridge University Press, in press.
Isaac, Rhys
    1982   *The transformation of Virginia, 1740–1790*. University of North Carolina Press, Chapel Hill.
Keen, Benjamin
    1971   *The Aztec image*. Rutgers University Press, New Brunswick.
Kohl, Philip L.
    1975   The archaeology of trade. *Dialectical Anthropology* 1:43–50.
    1981   Materialist approaches in prehistory. *Annual Review of Anthropology* 10:89–118.
Leach, Edmund R. (editor)
    1967   *The structural study of myth and totemism*. Association of Social Anthropologists, Monograph 5. Tavistock Publishers, London.

117

LeGoff, Jacques
  1980   *Time, work, and culture in the Middle Ages.* University of Chicago Press.
Leone, Mark P.
  1978   Time in American archeology. In *Social archaeology, beyond subsistence and dating,* edited by
         Charles L. Redman, Mary Jane Berman, Edward V. Curtin, William T. Langhorne, Jr., Nina M. Versaggi,
         and Jeffery C. Wanser, pp. 25–36. Academic Press, New York.
  1981   Archaeology's relationship to the present and the past. In *Modern material culture, the archaeology
         of US,* edited by Richard A. Gould and Michael B. Schiffer, pp. 2–14. Academic Press, New York.
Leroi-Gourhan, André
  1967a *The art of prehistoric man in western Europe.* Thames and Hudson, London.
  1967b *Treasures of prehistoric art.* H. N. Abrams, New York.
  1968   The evolution of Paleolithic art. *Scientific American* 218(2):58–68, 70.
Lévi-Strauss, Claude
  1963   *Structural anthropology.* Basic Books, New York.
  1968   *The savage mind.* University of Chicago Press.
Lukacs, Georg
  1971   Reification and the consciousness of the proletariat. In *History and class consciousness,* pp. 82–222.
         MIT Press, Cambridge, Mass.
Malinowski, Bronislaw
  1967   *A diary in the strict sense of the term.* Harcourt, Brace & World, New York.
Marcus, Joyce
  1973   Territorial organization of the lowland Maya. *Science* 180:911–916.
Margalef, Ramon
  1968   *Perspectives in ecological theory.* University of Chicago Press.
Meltzer, David J.
  1981   Ideology and material culture. In *Modern material culture, the archaeology of US,* edited by Richard
         A. Gould and Michael B Schiffer, pp. 113–125. Academic Press, New York.
Ortiz, Alfonso
  1969   *The Tewa world.* University of Chicago Press.
Pettit, Philip
  1977   *The concept of structuralism.* University of California Press, Berkeley.
Rappaport, Roy A.
  1971   Ritual, sanctity, and cybernetics. *American Anthropologist* 73:59–76.
Ricoeur, Paul
  1970   *Freud and philosophy.* Yale University Press, New Haven.
Sartre, Jean-Paul
  1968   *Search for a method.* Vintage Books, New York.
Schmidt, Peter R.
  1978   *Historical archaeology: a structural approach to an African culture.* Greenwood Press, Westport,
         Conn.
Schrire, Carmel
  1980   Hunter-gatherers in Africa. *Science* 210:890–891.
South, Stanley
  1977a *Method and theory in historical archaeology.* Academic Press, New York.
  1977b *Research strategies in historical archaeology.* Academic Press, New York.
Stone, Garry Wheeler
  1976   Artifacts are not enough. *The Conference on Historic Site Archaeology Papers* II:43–63. Institute of
         Archaeology and Anthropology, University of South Carolina, Columbia.
Thorpe, I. J.
  1981   *Anthropological orientations on astronomy in complex societies.* Paper read at the Third Theoretical
         Archaeology Group Conference, Reading, U.K.
Tilley, Christopher
  1981a Conceptual frameworks for the explanation of sociocultural change. In *Pattern of the past: studies
         in honour of David Clarke,* edited by I. Hodder, G. Isaac and N. Hammond, pp. 363–386. Cambridge
         University Press.
  1981b *Ideology and the archaeological record.* Introduction to Session, paper presented at the Third
         Theoretical Archaeology Group Conference, Reading, U.K.
Tosi, Maurizio
  1976   The dialectics of state formation in Mesopotamia, Iran, and Central Asia. *Dialectical Anthropology*
         1:173–180.
Trigger, Bruce G.
  1980   Archaeology and the image of the American Indian. *American Antiquity* 45:662–676.
Tyler, Stephen A. (editor)
  1969   *Cognitive anthropology.* Holt, Rinehart & Winston, New York.

Wallace, Michael
    1981   Visiting the past: history museums in the United States. *Radical History Review* 25:63–96.
White, Leslie A.
    1949   Energy and the evolution of culture. In *The science of culture,* pp. 363–393. Grove Press, New York.
Wobst, Martin H.
    1977   Stylistic behavior and information exchange. In *For the Director, research essays in honor of James
        B. Griffin,* edited by Charles E. Cleland. *Anthropology Papers* 61:317–342. Museum of Anthropology,
        University of Michigan, Ann Arbor.
Wolf, Eric
    1980   They divide and subdivide, and call it anthropology. *The New York Times,* Sunday, November 30,
        p. E3.
Wylie, M. Alison
    1981   *Positivism and the new archaeology.* Ph.D. dissertation, State University of New York, Binghamton.
        University Microfilms, Ann Arbor.
Yentsch, Anne, June MacDonald, and Richard Ehrlich
    1980   *"What species of Indian are you?"* Encounters between the museum public and museum interpre-
        ters. Paper presented at the 79th annual meetings of the American Anthropological Association, Wash-
        ington, D.C.

THE INTERPLAY OF EVIDENTIAL CONSTRAINTS AND POLITICAL INTERESTS: RECENT ARCHAEOLOGICAL RESEARCH ON GENDER

Alison Wylie

In the last few years, conference programs and publications have begun to appear that reflect a growing interest, among North American archaeologists, in research initiatives that focus on women and gender as subjects of investigation. One of the central questions raised by these developments has to do with their "objectivity" and that of archaeology as a whole. To the extent that they are inspired by or aligned with explicitly political (feminist) commitments, the question arises of whether they do not themselves represent an inherently partial and interest-specific standpoint, and whether their acceptance does not undermine the commitment to value neutrality and empirical rigor associated with scientific approaches to archaeology. I will argue that, in fact, a feminist perspective, among other critical, explicitly political perspectives, may well enhance the conceptual integrity and empirical adequacy of archaeological knowledge claims, where this is centrally a matter of deploying evidential constraints.

Durante los últimos años han comenzado a aparecer programas de conferencias y publicaciones que reflejan un creciente interés entre arqueólogos norteamericanos en iniciativas de investigación centradas en la mujer y el rol de los sexos como temas de estudio. Uno de los principales interrogantes planteados por estos desarrollos se refiere a la objetividad de estas investigaciones y de la arqueología en general. En la medida en que tales estudios están inspirados por, o comprometidos con programas políticos feministas explícitos, surge la pregunta de si no representan un punto de vista intrínsecamente parcial relacionado a intereses específicos, y de si su aceptación no socava el compromiso con la neutralidad y el rigor empírico asociados con enfoques científicos en arqueología. Sostengo que una perspectiva feminista, entre otras perspectivas críticas políticamente explícitas, bien puede fortalecer la integridad conceptual y la pertinencia empírica del conocimiento arqueológico, cuando se trata principalmente de expandir los límites de la evidencia.

It is a striking feature of North American archaeology that there is very little in print advocating or exemplifying a feminist approach to archaeology; certainly there is nothing comparable to the thriving traditions of feminist research on women and gender that have emerged, in the last twenty years, in such closely aligned fields as sociocultural anthropology, history, various areas in the life sciences (including evolutionary theory), classics, and art history. The first paper to explore systematically the relevance of feminist insights and approaches for archaeology was published in 1984 by Conkey and Spector, and the first collection of essays dedicated to reporting original work in the area has just appeared (Gero and Conkey, *Engendering Archaeology: Women and Prehistory*, 1991).[1] This collection is the outcome of a small working conference convened in South Carolina in April 1988 specifically for the purpose of mobilizing interest in the questions about women and gender that had been raised by Conkey and Spector in 1984. Its organizers, Gero and Conkey, were concerned that, in the four years since the appearance of this paper, very little work had appeared, or seemed imminent, that took up the challenges it posed (see Gero and Conkey 1991:xi–xiii). They approached colleagues who represented a wide range of research interests in prehistoric archaeology and asked if they would be willing to explore the implications of taking gender seriously as a focus for analysis in their fields; most had never considered such an approach and had no special interest in feminist initiatives, but agreed to see what they could do. In effect, Gero and Conkey commissioned a series of pilot projects on gender that they hoped might demonstrate the potential of research along the lines proposed by Conkey and Spector in 1984.[2]

Alison Wylie, Department of Philosophy, University of Western Ontario, London, Ontario, Canada N6A 3K7

American Antiquity, 57(1), 1992, pp. 15–35.
Copyright © 1992 by the Society for American Archaeology

Between the time of this initial conference and the appearance of *Engendering Archaeology*, many of the papers prepared for discussion in South Carolina were presented in a session on gender and archaeology at the annual meeting of the Society for American Archaeology in April 1989; they drew a substantial and enthusiastic audience, to the surprise of many of the participants. But most significant, one much more public conference, the 1989 Chacmool conference held the following November at the University of Calgary, took "The Archaeology of Gender" as its focal theme. It drew *over 100* contributions on a very wide range of topics, all but four of which (the invited keynote addresses) were submitted, directly or indirectly, in response to an open call for papers (most will appear in Walde and Willows [1991]).[3] So despite the fact that little more than Conkey and Spector's 1984 paper was in print at the time the Chacmool conference was being organized and the SAA session presented, an awareness of the issues they raised and an enthusiasm about the prospects for archaeological work on gender seem to have had taken hold across the length and breadth of the field.[4]

This precipitous emergence of broadly feminist initiatives raises a number of questions. First are questions about the development itself: Why has there been no sustained interest before now in women and gender as subjects of archaeological inquiry and/or in scrutinizing the interpretive assumptions routinely made about women and gender in extant practice?; and, Why is such an interest emerging at this juncture? These are questions I have addressed elsewhere (Wylie 1991a, 1991b), but which bear brief discussion here as a basis for considering a second set of issues to do with the implications of embracing, or tolerating, feminist approaches. For many I believe the real question raised by these developments is not why research on gender is emerging (only) now, but why it should ever emerge. The genre of question posed in this connection is, "why do we need it?"; "what does it have to offer?" or, more defensively, "why should we take any of this seriously?" (after Wylie 1991b). Often the most dismissive responses reflect, not just uneasiness about feminist initiatives, but a general wariness about intellectual fads and fashions. Given the rapid emergence of the scientific new archaeology, displacing so-called "traditional" modes of practice, and now the equally dramatic reaction against the new archaeology and the emergence of a plethora of warring anti- or postprocessualist and critical alternatives, many are deeply weary of debate. Renfrew's review of "isms" of our time (Renfrew 1982:8) and the challenge Watson (in Watson and Fotiadis 1990) issue to the advocates of some of these "isms" to deliver the goods, as it were, convey a sense of alarm at the instability of this succession of research programs. Viewed in this light, the call to study women and gender may seem especially tenuous, even self-destructive.

I want to argue that a feminist perspective, which questions entrenched assumptions about women and gender and directs attention to them as subjects of inquiry, promises to substantially enhance the conceptual and empirical integrity—the "objectivity," properly construed—of archaeological inquiry. To this end, I consider how feminist initiatives have arisen and how the debate over "isms" has unfolded such that they might be viewed with particular scepticism. I offer general arguments against this scepticism, questioning the terms of abstract debate from which it derives, and then turn, in the final section, to an analysis of several examples of the new research on gender, drawn from *Engendering Archaeology* (Gero and Conkey 1991), which illustrates how evidential considerations can challenge and constrain political and theoretical presuppositions, even where these constitute the encompassing framework of inquiry.

WHY NOW? WHY EVER?

Why is the Archaeology of Gender Emerging Only Now?

Where the preliminary questions—"why not before now?" and, "why now?"—are concerned, my thesis is that a number of factors have been relevant both in forestalling and in precipitating these developments in archaeology, similar to the situation described by Longino (1987) and by Longino and Doell (1983) for the life sciences.[5] The conceptual and methodological commitments of scientific, processual archaeology have tended to direct attention away from what Binford (1983, 1986a, 1989: 3–23, 27–39) has vilified, in his most uncompromising defenses of processual approaches, as "ethnographic," internal variables; gender dynamics, which would be included among such variables in most analyses, are just one example of the sort factor he considers explanatorily irrelevant and scientifically inaccessible (for a more detailed analysis, see Wylie [1991a:35–38]). While anti- and postprocessual challenges to this general orientation have certainly been crucial in opening a space for the development of an interest in gender, among other symbolic, ideational, social, and broadly "ethnographic" dimensions of the cultural past, it is striking that none of the chief exponents of postprocessualism have done a great deal to develop a feminist analysis of archaeological method or theory (see Note 1). Indeed, as Ericka Engelstad (1991) argues, they have largely avoided any sustained reflexive critique of their own proposals and practice, with the result that these remain resolutely androcentric. Moreover, postprocessualists had established the need for work on variables like gender fully a decade ago, and yet there was no sustained archaeological work on gender, per se, and no serious consideration of the implications for archaeology of feminist research in other fields, until the last few years. Given this, I suggest that social and political (i.e., "external," non-cognitive) factors must play a central role in the emergence of an interest in gender at this juncture.

To be more specific, it would seem implausible, given the experience reported in other disciplinary contexts, if the preparedness to consider questions about gender, and in some cases, the willingness to champion research that addresses them, did not have to do with the influence of explicitly political, feminist thinking on practitioners in the field (Wylie 1991b).[6] In most cases I expect this influence will be only indirect; whether many practitioners identify as feminists or are in any sense sympathetic to feminism, a great many will have been affected by a growing if still liminal appreciation of women's issues, starting with equity issues, that grows out of second-wave feminist activism and has become evident, in recent years, in the discourse and practice of archaeologists.[7] No doubt this is closely tied to the demands for equity they face as members of academic institutions, consulting businesses, and government agencies, and to resulting changes in the representation, roles, and status of women in these larger institutional contexts. But however they arise, and however welcome or unwelcome they may be, as these changes enforce some level of awareness of gender politics in contemporary contexts they also produce (in some) a growing awareness that gender is not a "natural," immutable given, an insight which is seen by many as the pivotal discovery of feminist theory (Flax 1987; Harding 1983). And (in some) this has influenced, in turn, scholarly thinking about the subjects of archaeological study. Whatever their political commitments, they may begin to question entrenched assumptions about sexual divisions of labor and the status of women in prehistory, and to consider previously unexplored questions about the diversity of gender structures in prehistoric contexts, about the significance of gender dynamics in shaping past cultural systems, and about the origins and emergence of contemporary and/or ethnohistorically documented sex/gender systems.

In some cases the influence of feminist thinking has been direct. For example, both organizers of the South Carolina conference have long been active on issues to do with the status of women in archaeology. Gero has published a number of groundbreaking articles on these issues and been actively involved in promoting research on the political dynamics, including the gender dynamics, of the discipline (Gero 1983, 1985, 1988). And Conkey was a member of the American Anthropological Association (AAA) Committee on the Status of Women from 1974 (chair in 1975–1976) in which capacity she was drawn into the organization of a panel for the 1977 AAA meetings on gender research in the various subfields of anthropology. Charged with presenting a section on archaeological research on gender, Conkey confronted the dearth of literature in the area; for the most part she found that "women [and gender] were considered by chance rather than by design," if they were considered at all (M. Conkey, personal communication 1991). In these connections both organizers were drawn into contact with feminists working in other fields, especially sociocultural anthropology, and were aware of the insights, both critical and constructive, that had resulted from the systematic investigation of questions about the status, experience, and roles of women in their various research fields. It was quite explicitly this exposure to, and engagement in, feminist discourse outside archaeology that led them to question the assumptions about gender underlying archaeological theorizing and to see both the need and the potential for a focused program of feminist research in archaeology. As they came to question the assumptions about gender that underpin *contemporary* sex roles, they came to see that these same assumptions infuse the theories about other people's lives they were engaged in constructing as archaeologists. In organizing events and publications that they hoped would generate wider interest among archaeologists in questions about gender they, and, specifically, the feminist commitments that had come to inform their own work, have been instrumental in mobilizing the latent grass-roots interest in these questions that now seems widespread, even among archaeologists who would never identify as feminists and have had no contact with feminist research in other contexts. On this account it is, most simply, the experience of women and, more important, the emerging feminist analysis of this experience, which figures as a key catalyst (both directly and indirectly) for skepticism about entrenched conceptions of women and gender and for research in this area as it is now emerging in archaeology.

Relativist Implications

But if this is the case—if the new research on gender is motivated and shaped, at least in part, by explicitly feminist commitments—does it not follow that it is to be identified and, for many, dismissed, with the extreme anti-objectivist positions defended by postprocessualists? Does it not exemplify precisely the sort of partisan approach to inquiry that they endorse, and that Binford (1989:32), for example, has condemned as conceptual "posturing"? To be more specific, if political interests are allowed to set the agenda of archaeology, do they not irrevocably compromise the commitments to objectivity and value neutrality—most broadly, the commitment to settle empirical questions by appeal to the "world of experience" (Binford 1989:27; see also Binford 1982:136), rather than to prejudgements or sociopolitical interests—that stand as a hallmark of science? And in this case, what credibility can such inquiry claim on its own behalf; are its results not as limited and biased as those they are meant to displace? Perhaps more disturbing, if an explicitly partisan feminist standpoint reveals the partiality (the unacknowledged standpoint specificity) of our best existing accounts of the past and brings into view a different past, or new ways of understanding the past, does it not follow that any number of other standpoints might do the same? And in this case, what is to stop the proliferation of conflicting views of prehistory and, with this, a slide into extreme standpoint relativism according to which the credibility of each of these "versions" is strictly context or perspective and interest specific?

Such conclusions only follow, I argue, if you accept the sharply polarized terms in which much current debate about the aims and status of archaeology has been cast, and assume that any critique of objectivist ideals, any break with the scientific canons of processual archaeology (originally construed in rigidly positivist terms), leads irrevocably to what Trigger (1989:777) calls "hyperrelativism." This oppositional response to questions about the standards and goals of inquiry is not unique to archaeology; on Trigger's account the social sciences as a whole are marked by

> an increasingly vociferous confrontation . . . between, on the one hand, an old-fashioned positivist certainty that, given enough data and an adherence to "scientific" canons of interpretation, something approximating an objective understanding of human behavior can be achieved . . ., and on the other hand, a growing relativist scepticism that the understanding of human behavior can ever be disentangled from the interests, prejudices, and stereotypes of the researcher [Trigger 1989:777; see also Bernstein (1983); Wylie 1989b].

On the former view, the aim of producing "objective" knowledge—knowledge which is credible, "true," transhistorically and cross-contextually, not just given a particular standpoint (Bernstein 1983:8–25)—can only be realized if researchers scrupulously exclude all "external," potentially biasing (idiosyncratic or contextually specific) factors from the practice of science, so that judgments about the adequacy of particular knowledge claims are made solely on the basis of "internal" considerations of evidence, and of coherence and consistency. Positivist/empiricist theories of science, including those that influenced North American archaeology in the 1960s and 1970s and are still evident in archaeological thinking, made much of a distinction between the context of discovery, in which such "external" factors might be given free reign, and the context of verification or confirmation in which the fruits of creative speculation, however inspired or shaped, would be subjected to rigorously impartial testing against (independent) evidence; the body of empirical "facts" deployed as evidence was presumed to be the stable foundation of all (legitimate, nonanalytic) knowledge, and was, in this capacity, the final arbiter of epistemic adequacy.[8]

It is by now commonly held that this view of knowledge production (specifically scientific-knowledge production) is deeply problematic. The sharp distinction between the contexts of discovery and verification, and "foundationalist" faith in facts as the source and ground of legitimate knowledge, has broken down in face of a number of challenges. Even the proponents of a robust (empiricist/positivist) objectivism had, themselves, long acknowledged that all available evidence (sometimes even all imaginable evidence) routinely "underdetermines" interesting knowledge claims about the world, that is, evidence rarely entails or supports a unique explanatory or interpretive conclusion and eliminates all potential rivals (for a summary, see Laudan and Leplin [1991]; Newton-Smith [1981]; Suppe [1977]). Furthermore, the analyses of "contextualist" theorists (e.g., Hanson 1958; Kuhn 1970) suggest that the facts, data, or evidence against which theoretical constructs are to be tested are all too intimately connected with these constructs to stand as a secure and autonomous "foundation" of knowledge; data are, famously, "theory laden." This opens up considerable space for the insinuation of "external" interests and values into the processes of both formulating and evaluating empirical knowledge claims. Indeed, sociologists of science have argued, on the basis of innumerable detailed studies of the practice (rather than just the products) of science, that "facts" are as much made as found and that judgments about their evidential significance are radically open.[9] The most thoroughgoing "social constructivists" among them maintain that facts, and the theoretical claims they are used to support, are equally a product of the local, irreducibly social and political, interests that inform the actions and interactions of scientific practitioners in particular contexts; in their most radical moments, they seem to suggest that scientists quite literally create the world they purport to know (see Woolgar's [1983:244] discussion of the range of positions at issue here). It seems a short step from the original contextualist and constructivist arguments against naive objectivism and foundationalism to the conclusion that cognitive anarchy is unavoidable; "anything goes" in the sense (not intended by Feyerabend [1988:vii, 1–3]) that virtually any knowledge claim one can imagine could, in principle, find some perspective or context in which it is compelling, and that there are no overarching grounds for assessing or challenging these context-specific judgments.

In an archaeological context, the outlines of this reaction emerge in some anti- or postprocessual literature. The point of departure is typically a "contextualist" argument to the effect that, where archaeological data must be theory laden to stand as evidence, it is unavoidable that archaeologists have always, of necessity, actively *constructed* (not reconstructed, recaptured, or represented) the past, no matter how deeply committed they may have been to objectivist ideals. In some of his early critical discussions, Hodder insists, in this connection, that any use of archaeological data as test evidence is mediated by "an edifice of auxiliary theories and assumptions which *archaeologists have simply agreed not to question*" (Hodder 1984a:27, emphasis added); evidential claims thus have nothing but conventional credibility. In short, archaeologists literally "create 'facts' "(Hodder 1984a:27). From this it follows that archaeologists are "without any ability to test their reconstructions of the past" (Hodder 1984a:26); as Shanks and Tilley put the point four years later, "there is literally nothing independent of theory or propositions to test against. . . . any test could only result in tautology" (Shanks and Tilley 1987b:44, 111). As a consequence, archaeological data, test evidence, and interpretive claims about the past must be regarded as all *equally* constructs: "knowledge consists of little more than the description of what has already been theoretically constituted" (Shanks and Tilley 1987a:43; see also 1987a:66). "Truth is," they declare, "a [mobile] army of metaphors" (Shanks and Tilley 1987b:22). More specifically, Shanks and Tilley argue that what counts as true or plausible, indeed, what counts as a "fact" in any relevant sense, is determined by contextually specific interests: individual, micropolitical interests, as well as class interests, broadly construed. It is thus unavoidable that archaeology is a thoroughly and irredeemably political enterprise, one which is engaged in creating a past thought expedient for, or dictated by, present interests (Shanks and Tilley 1987b:209–212, but see also 192–193). And where there are no independent factual resources with which to counter the influence of "external" factors—where pretensions to objectivity can only be, on their account, a masking of the effects of these influences—Shanks and Tilley advocate self-consciously political reconstruction of the past(s) thought necessary for "active intervention in the present" (Shanks and Tilley 1987b:103). In this vein, Hodder (1983:7) once enjoined archaeologists to avoid "writ[ing] the past" for others, or for societies in which they are not themselves prepared to live.

The process of polarization described by Trigger (1989:777) is complete when objectivists, reacting against what they consider the manifestly untenable implications of "hyperrelativism," insist that there *must* be "objective foundations for philosophy, knowledge, [and] language" (Bernstein 1983: 12); they reject out of hand the critical insights that arose, originally, from the failure of objectivist programs cast in a positivist/empiricist mold, and renew the quest for some new Archimedean point, some "stable rock upon which we can secure our lives," and our knowledge, against the insupportable threat of "madness and chaos where nothing is fixed" (Bernstein 1983:4; see also Wylie 1989b:2–4). Just such a turn is evident, in the context of archaeological debate, in the exceedingly hostile counterreaction of (some) loyal processualists: in the caricatures in terms of which the positions of anti- and postprocessualists are assessed and rejected (e.g., in Binford's [1989: 3–11] "field guide" and discussion of "yippie" archaeology; and in R. Watson's [1990] treatment of Shanks and Tilley); in uncompromising restatements of the central doctrines of processualism (e.g., by Binford 1983:137, 222–223; and by Renfrew 1989:39; for fuller analysis of Binford's position, see Wylie [1989a:103–105]); and in the frequent accusations, on both sides, that the opposition has simply missed the point, that they indulge in "wafting . . . [red herrings] in front of our noses" (Shanks and Tilley 1989:43; Binford 1989:35; see discussion in Wylie [1992]).

It is clear where feminist research initiatives will be placed in the context of debates such as these. In the past two decades, feminist-inspired research across the social and life sciences has provided strong substantive grounds for questioning the "self-cleansing" capacity of scientific method—they have identified myriad instances of gender bias that have persisted, not just in instances of "bad science," but in "good" science, "science as usual"—and frequently they have done this by bringing to bear the distinctive "angle of vision" afforded by various feminist and, more generally, women's perspectives (for a summary see Wylie [1991a:38–44]). In this, feminist researchers have made clear (sometimes unintentionally) the theory- and interest-laden, contextual, and constructed nature of scientific knowledge. Where debate is polarized in the manner described by Trigger (1989), some argue that the move to embrace a radically deconstructive, postmodern standpoint is irresistible; it is the logical outcome of their critiques (see Harding 1986).

But are the polarized options defined in the context of these debates the only ones open to archaeologists or other social scientists who have been grappling with an acute awareness "of how fragile is the basis on which we can claim to know anything definite about the past or about human behavior" (Trigger 1989:777)? More specifically, is the radically anti-objectivist stance endorsed, most strongly, by Shanks and Tilley the only alternative to uncompromising faith in the foundational nature of "facts" and the capacity of the "world of experience" to adjudicate all "responsible" claims to knowledge? In fact, as has been noted by virtually every commentator on their work, both sympathetic and critical (e.g., see comments published with Shanks and Tilley [1989]; Wylie 1992), Shanks and Tilley are not consistent, themselves, in maintaining a radically deconstructive position. Indeed, this ambivalence is a consistent feature of anti- or postprocessual literature. As early as 1986, Hodder had substantially qualified his earlier position (1983), insisting that, although "facts" are all constructs, they derive from a "real world," which "does constrain what we can say about it" (Hodder 1986:16). He has recently urged what seems a rapprochement with processualism, and endorsed a "guarded commitment to objectivity" (Hodder 1991:10). Although Shanks and Tilley (1987a:192) indicate distaste for this attempt to "neutralize and depoliticize" archaeological inquiry, they themselves hasten to add, in the same context, that they "do not mean to suggest that all pasts are equal" (Shanks and Tilley 1987a:245); there is a "real" past (Shanks and Tilley 1987a: 110), moreover, archaeological constructs are to be differentiated from purely fictional accounts of the past by the fact that they are constrained by evidential considerations ("data represents a network of resistances") that can "challenge what we say as being inadequate in one manner or another" (Shanks and Tilley 1987a:104). The turn away from an uncompromising constructivism seems to come, in every case, at the point where anti- or postprocessualists confront the problem that radical constructivism (or, its "hyperrelativist" implications) threatens to undermine their own political and intellectual agendas as much as it does those they repudiate.

It is striking, in this connection, that many *feminists* working in the developed traditions of feminist research outside archaeology are likewise deeply "ambivalent" about the relativist implications that are sometimes seen to follow from their own wide-ranging critiques of objectivism (see Lather 1986, 1990; Fraser and Nicholson 1988). For example, despite endorsing postmodern approaches, the feminist philosopher of science, Sandra Harding, argues that we cannot afford to give up either the strategic advantages that accrue to more conventional modes of scientific practice—in effect, feminist uses of the tools of science—or the emancipatory vision embodied in postmodern transgressions of these "successor science" projects (Harding 1986:195; see Wylie 1987). Others (like biologist Fausto-Sterling [1985]) quite clearly want to preserve the option of defending feminist insights as *better* science in quite conventional terms, and a great many social scientists routinely privilege "facts" of some description—often as the grounds for conclusions about the gender-biased nature of the theories they criticize—even when they insist that facts cannot be treated as a stable, given "foundation" of knowledge (for a more detailed account, see Wylie [1991c]). One commentator from political science, Mary Hawkesworth (1989:538), takes the even stronger position that "the feminist postmodernists' plea for tolerance of multiple perspectives is altogether at odds with feminists' desire to develop a successor science that can refute once and for all the distortions of androcentrism" (Hawkesworth 1989:538). She clearly hopes that feminism has not reached "such an impasse that its best hope with respect to epistemological issues is to embrace incompatible positions and embed a contradiction at the heart of its theory of knowledge" (Hawkesworth 1989: 538).

I myself find inescapable the suspicion that strong constructivist and relativist positions embody what seems patently an ideology of the powerful. Only the most powerful, the most successful in achieving control over their world, could imagine that the world can be constructed as they choose, either as participants or as observers. Any who lack such power, or who lack an investment in believing they have such power, are painfully aware that they negotiate an intransigent reality that impinges on their lives at every turn. Certainly, any serious attempt to change inequitable conditions of life requires a sound understanding of the forces we oppose; self-delusion is rarely an effective basis for political action. It is, then, precisely their political commitment to the emancipatory potential of feminism—their commitment to learn about how gender structures operate so that they can act effectively against the inequities that these structures perpetuate—that enforces, for many feminist practitioners and theorists, as much scepticism about extreme relativisms as about the (untenable) objectivism that has so long masked androcentric bias in the social and life sciences (this point is acknowledged in Hodder [1991]). They are persistently forced back from either of the extremes that emerge in abstract debate by a clear appreciation of how intransigent are the practical, empirical constraints binding on both inquiry and activism. A similar turn is evident in postpositivist philosophy of science; the critical insights of "contextualists" and "constructivists" are by now incontrovertible, where directed against "received view" positivism and empiricism (Suppe 1977), but the positions that have carried these critiques to an extreme have proven as untenable as those they displace. Consequently, there has been considerable interest in making sense of how, exactly, data come to be "laden" with theory, such that it acquires evidential significance through rich interpretive construction, and yet still has a capacity to surprise, to challenge settled expectations (see, e.g., Shapere [1985] on the constitution of "observations" in physics, and Kosso [1989] on observation in science generally; see also the recent work on experimental practice, e.g., Galison [1987]; Hacking [1983, 1988]; for further discussion of how this bears on archaeology, see Wylie [1990]).

Where feminist initiatives in *archaeology* are concerned, the encompassing philosophical problem at issue is precisely that which has attracted attention in recent postpositivist history and philosophy of science, and of feminist theorists in many contexts, viz., that of how we can conceptualize scientific inquiry so that we recognize, without contradiction, *both* that knowledge is constructed and bears the marks of its makers, *and* that it is constrained, to a greater or lesser degree, by conditions that we confront as external "realities" not of our own making. I want to argue that just this sort of mediating position is emerging in and through the new archaeological work on gender. It is political and should be aligned with antiprocessualist approaches insofar as it repudiates narrow objectivism of a positivist/scientistic cast. But it is not altogether assimilable to, indeed, it embodies a serious, politically and epistemically principled critique of, the more extreme claims associated with post-processualism. That is to say, social and political factors are crucial in directing attention to questions about gender but, at least in the case of the South Carolina conference, which I will take as the focus of my analysis here, these do not account for the successes of the research they inspire or inform. It is the substantive results of this research that make it a serious challenge to extant practice, and these results are to a large degree autonomous of the political motivations and other circumstances responsible for the research that produced them.

"ENGENDERED" ARCHAEOLOGY

The results of the preliminary investigations reported at the South Carolina conference are remarkable in a number of respects. Most of the contributors reported that they began with serious reservations about the efficacy of the approach urged on them by Gero and Conkey; they did not see how questions about gender could bear on research in their fields or subfields, given that they had never arisen before.[10] But even the most sceptical conceded that attention to such questions did result in quite striking "discoveries" of gender bias in existing theory and in clear evidence of gender-related variability in familiar data bases that had been completely overlooked.

One especially compelling critical analysis, due to Watson and Kennedy (1991), exposes pervasive androcentrism in explanations of the emergence of agriculture in the eastern United States. Whatever the specific mechanisms or processes postulated, the main contenders—Smith (1987) and the proponents of coevolutionary models that postulate a local, independent domestication, and Prentice (1986), among those who support a diffusionist model—all read women out of any active, innovative role in developing cultigens, even though it is commonly assumed that women are primarily responsible for gathering plants (as well as small game) under earlier foraging adaptations, and for the cultivation of domesticates once a horticultural way of life was established. Prentice does attribute some degree of initiative to members of Archaic period societies in adopting imported cultigens, but he identifies this firmly with the authority and magical/religious knowledge of shamans, who are consistently referred to as male (Prentice 1986, as cited in Watson and Kennedy 1991:263). It was their role as "high-status" (commerce-oriented) culture brokers that would have ensured the success of an agricultural innovation, once introduced, and it was they, Prentice maintains, who "would have had the greatest knowledge of plants" (Prentice 1986, as cited in Watson and Kennedy 1991:263), and the motivation to cultivate and domesticate them. To be more specific, it was the knowledge they would have developed of plants for ritual purposes, and their interest in securing a source of rattles and exotic medicine, that led to the introduction of tropical gourds (*Cucurbita*) and, subsequently, to the development of indigenous cultigens in the Eastern Woodlands. In effect, women passively "followed plants around" when foraging, and then passively tended them when introduced as cultigens by men.

The dominant alternative, as articulated by Smith (1987), postulates a process whereby horticultural practices emerged as an adaptive response to a transformation of the plant resources that occurred without the benefit of any deliberate human intervention. At most, human patterns of refuse disposal in "domestilocalities," and the associated disturbance of the environment around base camps and resource-exploitation camps, would have unintentionally introduced artificial selection pressures that generated the varieties of indigenous plants that became domesticates. On this account "the plants virtually domesticate themselves" (Watson and Kennedy 1991:262), and women are, once again, assumed to have passively adapted to imposed change.

Watson and Kennedy make much of the artificiality of both models. Why assume that dabbling for ritual purposes would be more likely to produce the knowledge and transformations of the resource base necessary for horticulture than the systematic exploitation of these resources (through foraging) as a primary means of subsistence (Watson and Kennedy 1991:268)?[11] And why deny human agency altogether when it seems that the most plausible ascription of agency (if any is to be made) must be to women (Watson and Kennedy 1991:262–264)? Watson and Kennedy make a strong case against the presumption, central to the coevolution model, that cultural change as extensive as adopting or developing domesticates could plausibly have been an "automatic process" (Watson and Kennedy 1991:266–267), and observe that they are "leary of explanations that remove women from the one realm that is traditionally granted them, as soon as innovation or invention enters the picture" (Watson and Kennedy 1991:264). Their assessment is that both theories share a set of underlying assumptions, uncritically appropriated from popular culture and traditional anthropology, to the effect that women could not have been responsible for any major culture-transforming exercise of human agency (Watson and Kennedy 1991:263–264).

In a constructive vein, a second contributor who works on Prehispanic sites in the central Andes, Hastorf, drew on several lines of evidence to establish that gendered divisions of labor and participation in the public, political life of Prehispanic Sausa communities were profoundly altered through the period when the Inka extended their control in the region; that is, the household structure and gender roles encountered in historic periods cannot be treated as a stable, "traditional" feature of Andean life that predates state formation (Hastorf 1991:139). In a comparison of the density and distribution of plant remains recovered from household compounds dating to the periods before and after the advent of Inka control, Hastorf found evidence of both an intensification of maize production and processing, and of an increase in the degree to which female-associated processing activities were restricted to specific locations within the sites over time. In addition, she reports the results of stable-isotope analysis of skeletal remains recovered from these sites,[12] comparing male and female patterns of consumption of meats, and various plant groups (mainly tubers and quinoa, and maize). Although the lifetime dietary profiles of males and females are undifferentiated through the period preceding the advent of Inka control in the valley, she finds evidence, consistent with the results of the paleobotanical analysis, that the consumption of maize increased much more dramatically for (some) men than for any of the women, at the point when evidence of Inka presence appears in the valley (Hastorf 1991:150). Given ethnohistoric records that document Inka practices of treating men as the heads of households and communities, drawing them into ritualized negotiations based on the consumption of maize beer (*chicha*) and requiring them to serve out a labor tax that was compensated with maize and *chicha*, she concludes that, through this transitional period, the newly imposed political structures of the Inka empire had forced a realignment of gender roles. Women "became the focus of [internal, social and economic] tensions as they produced more beer [and other maize foodstuffs] while at the same time they were more restricted in their participation in the society" (Hastorf 1991:152); indeed, their increased production was an essential basis for the political order imposed by the Inka, an order that drew male labor and political functions out of the household.

Similar results are reported by Brumfiel (1991) in an analysis of changes in household production patterns in the Valley of Mexico through the period when the Aztec state was establishing a tribute system in the region. She argues, through analysis of the frequencies of spindle whorls, that fabric production, largely the responsibility of women (on ethnohistoric and documentary evidence), increased dramatically in outlying areas but, surprisingly enough, decreased in the vicinity of the urban centers as the practice of extracting tribute payments in cloth developed. On further analysis, she found evidence of an inverse pattern of distribution and density in artifacts associated with the production of labor-intensive and transportable (cooked) food based on the use of tortillas; the changing proportion of griddles to pots suggests that the preparation of griddle-cooked foods increased near the urban centers and decreased in outlying areas, where less-demanding (and preferred) pot-cooked foods continued to predominate. She postulates, on this basis, that cloth may have been exacted directly as tribute in the hinterland, while populations living closer to the city center intensified their production of transportable food so that they could take advantage of "extra-domestic institutions" in the Valley of Mexico (Brumfiel 1991:243)—markets and forms of production that "drew labor away from the household context" (Brumfiel 1991:241)—that required a mobile labor force. In either case, Brumfiel points out, the primary burden of (directly or indirectly) meeting the tribute demands for cotton and maguey cloth imposed by Aztec rule was shouldered by women and was met by strategic realignments of their household labor. Where the Aztec state depended on such tribute to maintain its political and economic hegemony, its emergence, like the spread of the Inka state, as studied by Hastorf, must be understood to have transformed, and to have been dependent on a transformation of, the way predominantly female domestic labor was organized and deployed.

Finally, several contributors considered assemblages of "artistic" material, some of them rich in images of women, and explored the implications of broadening the range of conceptions of gender relations that inform their interpretation. Handsman undertook a critical rethinking of the ideology of gender difference, specifically, the "male gaze" (Handsman 1991:360), that infused a British exhibition of "The Art of Lepenski Vir" (Southampton, 1986), a Mesolithic site along the Danube River dating to the sixth millennium B.C. Where this "art" is represented as the product of men who "were not ordinary hunter–gatherers" (Handsman 1991:332), while the women of Lepenski Vir are treated exclusively as their subjects (Handsman 1991:335), Handsman objects to the ways in which this exhibit, and archaeological discourse generally, is "productive and protective of [hierarchical relations between men and women] inside and outside the discipline" (Handsman 1991:334), especially where it represents these hierarchies as timeless and natural, as "a priori, as a constant and universal fact of life" (Handsman 1991:338). In short, he challenges the notion that gender (or "art") can be treated in essentialist terms in this or in any context. In countering the uncritical standpoint of the exhibit, Handsman explores several interpretive strategies by which "relational histories of inequality, power, ideology and control, and resistance and counter-discourse" might be explored, where gender dynamics are concerned (Handsman 1991:338–339). And in the process, he points to a wide range of evidence—features of the "artistic" images themselves, differences between them and other lines of evidence, and associations with architectural and artifactual material that (could) provide them context—that constitute "clear signs" (Handsman 1991: 340) of complexities, contradictions, "plurality and conflict" (Handsman 1991:343), which undermine the simple story of natural opposition and complementarity told by the exhibit.

In a similar vein, Conkey has developed an analysis of interpretations of paleolithic "art," especially the images of females or purported female body parts, in which she shows how "the presentist gender paradigm" (Conkey with Williams 1991:13)—the contemporary ideology of gender difference that represents current definitions and relations of men and women as "a matter of bipolar, essential, exclusive categories" (Handsman 1991:335), locked in stable and predetermined relations of inequality—has infused most reconstructions of Upper Paleolithic 'artistic' life," yielding accounts in which "sexist 20th century notions of gender and sexuality are read into the cultural traces of 'our ancestors' " with remarkable disingenuity (Conkey with Williams 1991:13).[13] She concludes that whatever the importance of these images and objects, it is most unlikely that they were instances of either commodified pornography or "high art," as produced in contemporary contexts, which is indeed how many treatises on such images consider them (see also Mack 1990). Moreover she, like Handsman, urges that we scrutinize the ideological agenda that lie behind the quest for closure in such cases, viz., the compulsion to naturalize those features of contemporary life most crucial to our identity as human and cultural beings, by tracing them back to our "origins" (as human and cultural).

None of these researchers, not even Handsman who moves furthest in the direction of a deconstructive (postprocessual) stance, considers their results merely *optional*, standpoint-specific alternatives to the androcentric models and paradigms they challenge. They purport to *expose error*, to demonstrate that formerly plausible interpretive options are simply false (empirically) or untenable (conceptually), and to improve on previous accounts. Watson and Kennedy (1991:267–268) draw attention to a straightforward contradiction implicit in much current theorizing about the emergence of horticulture in the Eastern Woodlands: Women are persistently identified as the tenders of plants, whether wild or under cultivation, and yet are systematically denied any role in the transition from foraging to horticulture, whatever the cost in terms of theoretical elegance, plausibility, or explanatory power. Hastorf, and Brumfiel, bring into view new facts about the structure of otherwise well-understood data bases that call into question, not just the conceptual integrity but also the empirical adequacy of otherwise credible models of the political and economic infrastructure of states in Mesoamerica and the Andes. Brumfiel advances, on this basis, an alternative model that effectively fills (some of) the gaps and solves (some of) the puzzles she exposes as problematic for extant theories. And Handsman, and Conkey, argue that, although the artistic traditions they deal with are enormously rich and enigmatic, some interpretive options, including many that accord with the assumptions about gender taken for granted in our own contemporary societies, are simply unsustainable. Although the quest for closure, for one right answer, may be misguided when dealing with this sort of material, it does not follow that "anything goes."

EVIDENTIAL CONSTRAINTS

In all of these cases, the results—both critical and constructive—turn on the appraisal of constraints imposed by, or elicited from, various kinds of relevant evidence. This is significant inasmuch as it suggests that however thoroughly mediated, or "laden," by theory archaeological evidence may be, it routinely turns out differently than expected; it generates puzzles, poses challenges, forces revisions, and canalizes theoretical thinking in ways that lend a certain credibility to the insights that sustain objectivist convictions. Consequently, while we cannot treat archaeological data or evidence as a given—a stable foundation—it is by no means infinitely plastic. It does, or can, function as a highly recalcitrant, closely constraining, "network of resistances," to use the terms of Shanks and Tilley's (1987a:104) discussion. What we need now is a nuanced account of *how* data are interpretively laden such that, to varying degrees, they can stand as evidence for or against a given knowledge claim. Such an account has not been developed by Shanks and Tilley, or by Hodder, even though they are themselves manifestly ambivalent about their strongest constructivist claims. Their response has been to juxtapose with claims about the radical instability of all evidence and the vicious circularity of all empirical testing, counterclaims to the effect that archaeological data can (and sometimes do) decisively resist theoretical appropriation. But, with the exception of Hodder's (1991) most recent discussion, they do not then reassess their original constructivist assertions. The result is incoherence.

The point of departure for an account that could make sense of these contradictory insights must be the now-familiar thesis that the empirical evaluation of knowledge claims, including claims about the past, is never a "lonely encounter of hypothesis with evidence" (Miller 1987:173). Evidential relevance is constructed as a three-place relation (Glymour 1980); archaeologists inevitably constitute data as evidence or, ascribe it "meaning" (Binford 1983) as evidence of specific events or conditions in the past, by means of linking hypotheses and interpretive principles. The key to understanding how evidence (as an interpretive construct) can constrain is to recognize, first, that the content and use of these linking principles is, itself, subject to empirical constraint and, second, that a great diversity of such principles figure in any given evidential argument. The credibility of these principles is by no means necessarily a matter of convention, but can often be established empirically and quite independently of any of the theories or assumptions that inform archaeological theorizing (i.e., the theories that might be tested against interpretively constituted evidence). Their independence from one another further ensures that error in any one line of interpretation may be exposed by incongruity with others that bear on the same (past) subject. Archaeologists thus exploit a great variety of evidence when they evaluate knowledge claims about the past; not just different kinds of archaeological evidence, but evidence from a wide range of sources, which enters interpretation at different points, and which can be mutually constraining when it converges, or fails to converge, on a test hypothesis.

In the cases considered here and, indeed, in most archaeological interpretation, claims about the past are invariably shaped by an encompassing theory, or at least by some set of precepts about the nature of the cultural subject, which can also inform the interpretation of archaeological data as evidence for or against these claims. When the theoretical framework is closely specified, a structurally circular interdependence between test evidence and test hypotheses can emerge, i.e., where the test hypothesis in question derives from a theory about cultural dynamics that also supplies the linking principles used to interpret the data as evidence for or against this hypothesis. It is presumably circularity of this sort that led postprocessualists to declare that archaeologists quite simply "create facts" (Hodder 1984a:27), and that testing is inevitably futile, being viciously circular.

When practice is examined more closely, however, I suggest that any examples of full-fledged circularity that antiprocessualists might cite fall at one end of a continuum of types of interpretive inference, most of which do not sustain radically pessimistic judgments about the indeterminacy of archaeological inference and hypothesis evaluation. Even when the threat of self-validating circularity is realized, which is, in part, what Watson and Kennedy (1991) object to in explanations for the emergence of horticulture in the eastern United States, it is often possible, as they demonstrate, to establish evidential grounds for questioning the assumptions that frame both the favored hypothesis and the constitution of data as supporting evidence. Sometimes even data used to support the hypothesis can play this role. A traditional model of gender relations, underpinned by sexist assumptions about the nature and capabilities of women, infuses the interpretations of archaeological data that Watson and Kennedy consider, ensuring that, inevitably, these data will be seen as evidence of a "natural" division of labor in which women are consistently passive and associated with plants. Nevertheless, this does not (also) ensure that the record will obligingly provide evidence that activities identified as male in the terms of this model mediated the transition from a foraging to a horticultural way of life, however strong the expectation (on this model) that they must have. Where Smith's coevolution hypothesis is concerned, Watson and Kennedy point out that a very large proportion of the activities around "domestilocalities," which he cites as causes of the disturbances that would have transformed the weedy plant species into indigenous domesticates, were the activities of women, given (for the sake of argument) the traditional model they find presupposed by his account (Watson and Kennedy 1991:262).

But even if the interpretation of archaeological data as evidence is so "overdetermined" by orienting presuppositions that tensions and contradictions such as these never arise, critiques of these presuppositions—including critiques of the linking principles used to establish the evidential significance of specific data, as well as of the central tenets of the encompassing conceptual framework—may be based on independent evidence, that is, evidence generated outside the (archaeological) context to which these presuppositions are applied, evidence established in the "source" contexts from which interpretive linking principles are drawn. Watson and Kennedy make effective use, in this connection, of background (botanical) knowledge about the range and environmental requirements of the relevant varieties of maize to argue that many of the contexts in which they appear prehistorically are far from optimal (indeed, "inhospitable," "adverse"; Watson and Kennedy [1991:266]). Hence, it is not altogether plausible that they could have arisen under conditions of neglect; it is "more plausible" that humans knowledgeable about these plants (e.g., women foragers) must have taken a role in their cultivation and development. When Watson and Kennedy call into question the proposal that male shamans must have played this role (due to Prentice [1986]), they indicate some appreciation that the traditional model of sexual divisions of labor, which they find implicit in all the hypotheses they consider and accept for the sake of argument, is itself profoundly problematic given ethnographic evidence of foraging practices and the (gendered) distribution of botanical information among members of foraging societies (Watson and Kennedy 1991:256–257, 268). Over the past three decades, feminist anthropologists have documented enormous variability in the roles played by women, in the degrees to which they are active rather than passive, mobile rather than bound to a "home base," and powerful rather than stereotypically dispossessed and victimized.[14] All of this decisively challenges any presupposition that women are inherently less capable of self-determination and strategic manipulation of resources than their male counterparts. Where independent botanical and ecological information provides a basis for calling into question specific interpretive principles (i.e., concerning the import of data bearing on the spatiotemporal distribution of early maize varieties in the eastern United States), these ethnographic data challenge the credibility of the interpretive framework itself, rendering suspect any interpretation that depends on such an assumption, quite independently of archaeological results.

Straightforward circularity is generally not the central problem in archaeological interpretation, however. Given the state of knowledge in the relevant fields, explanatory hypotheses about particular past contexts, and the linking principles deployed to interpret the record of these contexts, are rarely integrated into a single, unified, encompassing culture theory; indeed, given the complexity of most archaeological subjects, it is almost unimaginable that a single unified theory (e.g., of cultural systems) would have the resources to provide both the necessary explanatory hypotheses and the grounds for testing them (i.e., the relevant linking principles) in a given archaeological context. Despite disclaimers, analogical inference is generally the basis for ascribing evidential significance to archaeological data, and here the worry is usually underdetermination, not overdetermination. Nevertheless, as in the case just described, analogical inference is subject to two sets of evidential constraints that can significantly limit the range of evidentially viable options: those determining what can be claimed about the analog based on knowledge of source contexts and those deriving from the archaeological record that determine its applicability to a specific subject context (Wylie 1985). In linking women with the use of spindle whorls in weaving, and with the use of pots and griddles in food preparation, Brumfiel (1991) relies on a direct historic analogy that postulates that the same sorts of food and cloth production were involved in archaeological as in ethnohistoric contexts (given a judicious reading of codices dating to the sixteenth century; Brumfiel [1991:224–230, 237–239, 243–245]); this is, in turn, the basis for postulating further limited similarities in the relations of production where gender is concerned. Similarly, archaeologists dealing with evidence of horticultural lifeways routinely postulate a division of labor in which women are primarily responsible for agricultural activities, but they base this not on an appeal to the completeness of mapping between source and subject, which Brumfiel's case illustrates, but on the persistence of this association across historically and ethnographically documented contexts, however different they may be in other respects (see, for example, Ehrenberg's discussion of the ethnographic bases for assuming these correlates; Ehrenberg [1989:50–54, 63–66, 81–83, 90–105]).

In these cases, evidence of extensive similarity (the completeness of mapping) between source and subject contexts, and of reliable correlation between clusters of attributes in source contexts, suggests that the linkage postulated between archaeologically observed material and its inferred functional, social, ideational, or other significance is not entirely arbitrary. To be specific, this kind of source-derived information constitutes evidence that the general association of women with the foraging of plant resources and with horticulture, and their local association with cooking and weaving in Aztec contexts, is to some (specifiable) degree nonaccidental; it is at least preliminary evidence that an underlying "determining structure" links the artifactual material in question to specific functions, gender associations, or activity structures securely enough to support an ascription of the latter attributes to the archaeological subject (for the details of this analysis, see Wylie [1985, 1988]).[15] A change in background knowledge about the sources, as much as in what archaeologists find in the record, can decisively challenge these interpretive claims. Where the feminist research on foraging societies (mentioned above) calls into question all aspects of the assumption that women passively "followed plants around" (as Watson and Kennedy characterize the traditional model), indeed, where it provides evidence that the "gathering" activities of women often include the hunting of small game, it becomes necessary to reconsider simplistic interpretive assumptions to the effect that "hunting" artifacts are indicative of the presence or activities of men. But most important, when the linking principles used to "ascribe meaning" to archaeological data as evidence are uncontested—when their credibility is well established and independent of any of the hypotheses that archaeologists might want to evaluate—archaeological evidence can very effectively stabilize the assessment of comprehensively different claims about the cultural past.[16] The power of the challenge posed by Brumfiel to extant models of the economic base of the Aztec empire depends on precisely this. Her identification of spindle whorls, and pots and griddles, with cloth and food production by women is unproblematic for any she might engage in debate and wholly independent of both the hypotheses she challenges and those she promotes. Hence, when she shows that variability inheres in these data that cannot be accounted for on standard models *when interpreted in these shared terms*, she establishes a challenge that is by no means an artifact of the feminist standpoint that led (directly or indirectly) to her analysis, or that is compelling only for those who share a feminist understanding of gender relations.

Insofar as analogical inferences often allow considerable scope for (independent) empirical assessment, they fall into the middle ranges of a continuum of types of inference, where degrees of insecurity and the potential to be systematically insulated from critique (as in the case of vicious circularity) are concerned. The limiting case on this continuum of theory-ladening inferences—the ideal of security in the ascription of evidential significance to data—are instances where archaeologists can draw on completely independent, nonethnographic sources for biconditional linking principles (laws or law-like principles) that specify unique causal antecedents for specific components of the surviving record.[17] Among the cases considered here, Hastorf's use of the analysis of bone composition comes closest to the ideal. If the background knowledge deployed in stable-isotope analysis is reliable (and this is always open to critical reassessment) it can establish, in chemical terms, what dietary intake would have been necessary to produce the reported composition of the bone marrow recovered from archaeological contexts. And where this can be linked, through paleobotanical analysis, to the consumption of specific plant and animal resources, it can underwrite the inference of dietary profiles that is very substantially independent of, and can seriously challenge (can provide a genuine test of), any interpretive or explanatory presuppositions about subsistence patterns and/ or social practices affecting the distribution of food that archaeologists might be interested in testing. The independence and security of linking arguments based on background knowledge of this physical, chemical, bioecological sort is exploited in many other areas: in morphological analyses of skeletal remains that provide evidence of pathologies and physical stress; in radiocarbon, archeomagnetic, and related methods of dating; and in some reconstructions of prehistoric technology and paleoecology, to name a few such examples. As the degree of independence between linking principles and test hypotheses or framework assumptions evident in these cases is approximated, archaeologists secure a body of evidence that establishes provisionally stable parameters for all other interpretation and a stable basis for piecemeal comparison between contending claims about the cultural past (a further analysis of independence is developed in Wylie [1990]). Something along the lines of these limiting cases constitute the ideal on which Binford bases his arguments for middle-range theory (e.g., Binford 1983:135, 1986b:472).

It is important to note, however, that the import of evidence of this sort (i.e., evidence that is constituted on the basis of extremely reliable, deterministic, and independent linking principles) is often very limited, taken on its own. As indicated, Hastorf must rely on a number of collateral lines of evidence to establish that the anomalous shift in diet evident in male skeletons was likely due to increased consumption of maize beer, to link this to the advent of Inka-imposed systems of political control in the valley, and to draw out the implication that this political transformation depended on a profound restructuring of gender relations at the level of the household. Indeed, this reliance on multiple lines of evidence is an important and general feature of archaeological reasoning; archaeologists rarely ascribe evidential significance to items taken in isolation. But this is not necessarily cause for despair. In such cases the security of archaeological evidence depends not just on the credibility of particular linking principles, taken in isolation, or on their independence from the test claims they are used to support or refute, but also, and crucially, on the independence *from one another* of the various linking principles used to establish diverse lines of evidence bearing on these claims. That is to say, where the constraints inherent in the relation between evidence and hypothesis operate on *a number of different vertical axes* (i.e., running from different elements of the data base, via a range of linking hypotheses, to the claims in question), a network of "horizontal" constraints comes into play between the lines of inference by which various kinds of data, bearing on a particular past context, are interpreted as evidence of this context. If diverse evidential strands all converge on a given hypothesis—if you can use different means to triangulate on the same postulated set of conditions or events—then you may be able to provide it decisive, if never irreversible, support simply because it is so implausible that the convergence should be the result of compensatory error in all the inferences establishing its evidential support (for philosophical discussion of these considerations, see Kosso [1988:456]; Hacking [1983:183–185]).

Like Hastorf, Brumfiel operates under this sort of constraint when she shows that independently constituted lines of evidence concerning both cloth and food production converge on the counterhypothesis that change in the organization of domestic labor was a key component in establishing the economic basis for the Aztec empire. This convergence is a strong argument for her account precisely because it cannot be counted on. Even when, taken separately, each line of evidence relevant to a particular model of past events or conditions of life enjoys strong collateral support (i.e., from the sources that secure the linking principles on which they depend), undetected error or weakness may become evident when one line of evidence persistently runs counter to the others, when dissonance emerges among lines of interpretation; the failure to converge on a coherent account makes it clear that error lies somewhere in the system of auxiliary assumptions and linking principles, however well entrenched they may be. In the extreme, which might be represented by the sorts of cases Handsman and Conkey consider (i.e., interpretations of "artistic" images and traditions), persistent dissonance may call into question the efficacy of *any* interpretive constitution of the data as evidence. Ultimately, there may be no determinate fact of the matter where the symbolic import of gender imagery is concerned or, as Conkey suggests, we may have to conclude that we simply are not (and may never be) in a position to determine what the fact of the matter is in such cases. It is, paradoxically, the fragmentary nature of the archaeological record that is its strength in setting up evidential constraints of these sorts, even in establishing the limits of inquiry.

The key point to be taken from reflection on these examples of gender research in archaeology is that although archaeological data stand as evidence only under (rich) interpretation, the process of interpretation—of ladening data with theory so that it has evidential import—is by no means radically open ended. The linking principles and background knowledge that mediate the constitution of data as evidence are by no means necessarily or inherently arbitrary conventions, as Hodder (1984a:27) once suggested. Values and interests of various kinds do play a crucial role not just in setting the agenda of archaeological inquiry—determining what questions will be asked—but in determining what range of interpretive and explanatory options will be considered fruitful or plausible; in this they shape not just the direction, but also the content and outcome of archaeological research. But this does not mean that such "external" influences determine the shape of inquiry seamlessly, or irrevocably; they can be very effectively challenged on conceptual and empirical grounds, as has been demonstrated repeatedly by feminist social scientists over the past two decades, and by the critical analyses described here. It is significant, however, that the impetus for reassessing a discipline's "taken-for-granteds," at all levels (i.e., at the level of specific interpretations and linking principles, as well as at that of broad framework assumptions), very often comes from those who bring to bear a standpoint, a socially and politically defined "angle of vision," that differs from that typical of the established status quo in a field (whatever form this takes). It is precisely a shift in the values and interests informing the work of these critics that directs their attention to new questions, which throws into relief gaps and incongruities in established theories, and which leads to a questioning of settled judgements of plausibility that have otherwise never been challenged (see Longino 1990). And while the insights that result from such a turn, for example, from the work of those who bring to bear a feminist perspective, are always themselves open to further critique—as feminist discussions of class and ethnic, cultural, and racial difference have made clear, they have their own limitations—it is not the case that they are on the same footing, in this respect, as the (partial) perspectives they critique and sometimes displace. Once our understanding is expanded (indeed, many argue, transformed) so that it takes women and gender fully into account, there is no return to the traditional androcentric models described by Watson and Kennedy; the process of inquiry is, in this sense, open-ended, but it is not anarchic.

CONCLUSION

Although it can no longer be assumed that there is one set of standards or reference points to which all models, hypotheses, and claims can be referred—there is no "transcendental grid" (Bernstein 1983; Wylie 1989b)—at any given time, there will be a number of stable, shared evidential reference points that can be exploited piecemeal in the comparison and evaluation of contending claims, and these can sometimes yield "rationally decisive" (Bernstein 1983), if never final, conclusions. This means that, at least sometimes, it is plausible to say that we have quite literally "discovered" a fact about the world, or that we have shown a formerly plausible claim to be "just false." Such claims are established by a good deal of politically motivated, explicitly feminist research, including that which has begun to emerge in archaeology; the critical analysis by Watson and Kennedy, and the constructive proposals of Hastorf, and of Brumfiel, are cases in point. In other cases the outcome of inquiry is more equivocal. As Handsman, and Conkey, illustrate, sustained investigation may lead us to question basic assumptions about the existence and the accessibility of certain "facts" about a given subject domain. In short, there is a whole continuum of inferences, ranging from the viciously circular, through analogical and other forms of ampliative inference, to the nearly deductive naturalistic inferences favored by Binford, that manifest enormously different degrees of security and open-endedness; none of these parts should be read for the whole.

I suggest, then, that the question of what epistemic stance is appropriate—whether we must be relativists or objectivists, processualists, or postprocessualists—should be settled locally, in light of what we have come to know about the nature of specific subject matters and about the resources we have for their investigation. We should resist the pressure to adopt a general epistemic stance appropriate to all knowledge claims. The ambivalence expressed by Harding (1986) and inherent in the contradictory impulses evident in postprocessualism is well founded, but need not lead us to build inconsistencies into the core of our epistemology and practice.

If these general points are accepted, it follows that feminist research, including feminist research in archaeology, is not "political" in any especially distinctive or worrisome sense (Wylie 1991b). Sociopolitical factors are key in explaining how and why it has arisen at this point, but the results of inquiry are not the "overdetermined" products of (viciously) circular inference that takes, as both point of departure and conclusion, the political convictions from which it draws inspiration. In fact, if any general lesson is to be drawn from reflection on feminist practice, it is that politically engaged science is often much more rigorous, self-critical, and responsive to the facts than allegedly neutral science, for which nothing much is at stake.

Acknowledgments. The research resulting in this paper has been supported by a three-year research grant from the Social Sciences and Humanities Research Council of Canada and was undertaken while on sabbatical leave from the University of Western Ontario, as a "visiting scholar" in the Department of Anthropology at the University of California at Berkeley. I am deeply indebted to my colleagues at Berkeley, who have provided an enormously stimulating and supportive environment in which to work, as well as to a large number of others who commented on earlier drafts of this paper when I read it in the various contexts that sabbatical leave allowed me to visit during the academic year 1990–1991. I particularly appreciated the spirited discussions in which I was engaged by participants in the Australian conference, "Women in Archaeology," by members of the Departments of Archaeology at Cambridge University and at the University of Southampton, by Norwegian archaeologists affiliated with the University of Tromsø and with Tromsø Museum, and with the Universities of Bergen and Oslo, by Fellows of the Boston University Humanities Foundation, and by the anthropologists, philosophers, and women's studies students and faculty to whom I spoke at Arizona State University, the University of California at Berkeley, and the University of Calgary. Finally, this paper would not have been possible without generous input from those who have been centrally involved in the developments I have taken as my subject. It is with gratitude and admiration that I dedicate this paper to all of those who have pioneered the exploration of feminist initiatives in archaeology. Although I know many of them take very different positions than I do on various of the issues I have raised, I hope they can, nonetheless, find something of value in the foregoing discussion.

REFERENCES CITED

Arnold, K., R. Gilchrist, P. Graves, and S. Taylor (editors)
    1988   Women in Archaeology. *Archaeological Reviews from Cambridge* 7(1):2–8.
Barstow, A.
    1978   The Uses of Archeology for Women's History: James Mellaart's Work on The Neolithic Goddess at Çatal Hüyuk. *Feminist Studies* 4(3):7–17.
Bernstein, R. J.
    1983   *Beyond Objectivism and Relativism: Science, Hermeneutics, and Praxis.* University of Pennsylvania Press, Philadelphia.
Bertelsen, R., A. Lillehammer, and J. Naess (editors)
    1987   *Were They All Men?: An Examination of Sex Roles in Prehistoric Society.* Arkeologist museum i Stavanger, Stavanger, Norway.
Binford, L. R.
    1982   Objectivity - Explanation - Archaeology 1981. In *Theory and Explanation in Archaeology*, edited by C. Renfrew, M. J. Rowlands, and B. A. Segraves, pp. 125–138. Academic Press, New York.
    1983   *Working at Archaeology.* Academic Press, New York.
    1986a   Data, Relativism, and Archaeological Science. *Man* 22:391–404.
    1986b   In Pursuit of the Future. In *American Archaeology Past and Future*, edited by D. J. Meltzer, D. D. Fowler, and J. A. Sabloff, pp. 459–479. Smithsonian Institution Press, Washington, D.C.
    1989   *Debating Archaeology.* Academic Press, New York.

Braithwaite, M.
  1984   Ritual and Prestige in the Prehistory of Wessex c. 2200–1400 BC: A New Dimension to the Archae-
         ological Evidence. In *Ideology, Power, and Prehistory*, edited by D. Miller and C. Tilley, pp. 93–110.
         Cambridge University Press, Cambridge.
Brumfiel, E. M.
  1991   Weaving and Cooking: Women's Production in Aztec Mexico. In *Engendering Archaeology: Women
         and Prehistory*, edited by J. M. Gero and M. W. Conkey, pp. 224–251. Basil Blackwell, Oxford.
Conkey, M. W., and J. D. Spector
  1984   Archaeology and the Study of Gender. In *Advances in Archaeological Method and Theory*, vol. 7, edited
         by M. B. Schiffer, pp. 1–38. Academic Press, New York.
Conkey, M. W., with S. H. Williams
  1991   Original Narratives: The Political Economy of Gender in Archaeology. In *Gender at the Cross-roads
         of Knowledge: Feminist Anthropology in the Post-Modern Era*, edited by M. di Leonardo. University of
         California Press, Berkeley, in press.
Ehrenberg, M.
  1989   *Women in Prehistory*. University of Oklahoma Press, Norman.
Engelstad, E.
  1991   Images of Power and Contradiction: Feminist Theory and Post-Processual Archaeology. *Antiquity* 65:
         502–514.
Fausto-Sterling, A.
  1985   *Myths of Gender: Biological Theories About Men and Women*. Basic Books, New York.
Feyerabend. P.
  1988   *Against Method*. 2nd ed. Verso, London.
Flax, J.
  1987   Postmodernism and Gender: Relativism in Feminist Theory. *Signs* 12:621–643.
Frazer, N., and L. J. Nicholson
  1988   Social Criticism without Philosophy: An Encounter Between Feminism and Postmodernism. *Com-
         munications* 10:345–366.
Galison, P.
  1987   *How Experiments End*. University of Chicago Press, Chicago.
Gathercole, P., and D. Lowenthal
  1989   *The Politics of the Past*. Unwin Hyman, London.
Gero, J. M.
  1983   Gender Bias in Archaeology: A Cross-Cultural Perspective. In *The Socio-Politics of Archaeology*, edited
         by J. M. Gero, D. M. Lacy, and M. L. Blakey, pp. 51–58. Research Report No. 23. Department of
         Anthropology, University of Massachusetts, Amherst.
  1985   Socio-Politics and the Woman-at-Home Ideology. *American Antiquity* 50:342–350.
  1988   Gender Bias in Archaeology: Here, Then and Now. In *Feminism Within the Science and Health Care
         Professions: Overcoming Resistance*, edited by S. V. Rosser, pp. 33–43. Pergamon Press, New York.
Gero, J. M., and M. W. Conkey (editors)
  1991   *Engendering Archaeology: Women and Prehistory*. Basil Blackwell, Oxford.
Gibbon, G.
  1989   *Explanation in Archaeology*. Basil Blackwell, New York.
Glymour, C.
  1980   *Theory and Evidence*. Princeton University Press, Princeton, New Jersey.
Hacking, I.
  1983   *Representing and Intervening*. Cambridge University Press, Cambridge.
  1988   Philosophers of Experiment. *PSA 1988*, vol. 2, edited by A. Fine and J. Leplin, pp. 147–156. Philosophy
         of Science Association, East Lansing, Michigan.
Handsman, R.
  1991   Whose Art Was Found at Lepenski Vir?: Gender Relations and Power in Archaeology. In *Engendering
         Archaeology: Women and Prehistory*, edited by J. M. Gero and M. W. Conkey, pp. 329–365. Basil Blackwell,
         Oxford.
Hanson, N. R.
  1958   *Patterns of Discovery*. Cambridge University Press, Cambridge.
Harding, S.
  1983   Why Has the Sex/Gender System Become Visible Only Now? In *Discovering Reality: Feminist Per-
         spectives on Epistemology, Metaphysics, Methodology and Philosophy of Science*, edited by S. Harding and
         M. B. Hintikka, pp. 311–325. D. Reidel, Dordrecht, Holland.
  1986   *The Science Question in Feminism*. Cornell University Press, Ithaca.
Hastorf, C. A.
  1991   Gender, Space, and Food in Prehistory. In *Engendering Archaeology: Women and Prehistory*, edited
         by J. M. Gero and M. W. Conkey, pp. 132–159. Basil Blackwell, Oxford.
Hawkesworth, M. E.
  1989   Knowers, Knowing, Known: Feminist Theory and Claims of Truth. *Signs* 14:533–557.

Hodder, I.
    1982   *Symbols in Action.* Cambridge University Press, Cambridge.
    1983   Archaeology, Ideology and Contemporary Society. *Royal Anthropological Institute News* 56:6–7.
    1984a   Archaeology in 1984. *Antiquity* 58:25–32.
    1984b   Burials, Houses, Women and Men in the European Neolithic. In *Ideology, Power, and Prehistory,* edited by D. Miller and C. Tilley, pp. 51–68. Cambridge University Press, Cambridge.
    1985   Post-processual Archaeology. In *Advances in Archaeological Method and Theory,* vol. 8, edited by M. B. Schiffer, pp. 1–25. Academic Press, New York.
    1986   *Reading The Past: Current Approaches to Interpretation in Archaeology.* Cambridge University Press, Cambridge.
    1991   Interpretive Archaeology and Its Role. *American Antiquity* 56:7–18.
Kehoe, A.
    1983   The Shackles of Tradition. In *The Hidden Half: Studies of Plains Indian Women,* edited by P. Albers and B. Medicine, pp. 53–73. University Press of America, Washington, D.C.
Kelley, J., and M. Hanen
    1992   Gender and Archaeological Knowledge. In *Metaarchaeology,* edited by L. Embree. Boston Studies in Philosophy of Science. Reidel, Holland, in press. Ms. 1991.
Knorr, K., and M. Mulkay (editors)
    1983   *Science Observed: Perspectives on the Social Study of Science.* Sage Publications, London.
Kosso, P.
    1988   Dimensions of Observability. *British Journal of Philosophy of Science* 39:449–467.
    1989   Science and Objectivity. *Journal of Philosophy* 86:245–257.
Kramer, C., and M. Stark
    1988   The Status of Women in Archaeology. *American Anthropological Association Newsletter* 29(9):1, 11–12.
Kuhn, T. S.
    1970   *The Structure of Scientific Revolutions.* 2nd ed. University of Chicago Press, Chicago.
Lather, P.
    1986   Issues of Validity in Openly Ideological Research: Between a Rock and a Soft Place. *Interchange* 17(4): 63–84.
    1990   Postmodernism and the Human Sciences. *The Humanist Psychologist* 18:64–83.
Latour, B.
    1987   *Science in Action.* Harvard University Press, Cambridge.
Latour, B., and S. Woolgar
    1986   *Laboratory Life: The Construction of Scientific Facts.* Princeton University Press, Princeton, New Jersey.
Laudan, L., and J. Leplin
    1991   Empirical Equivalence and Underdetermination. *Journal of Philosophy* 88:449–472.
Longino, H. E.
    1987   Can There Be a Feminist Science? *Hypatia* 2:51–65.
    1990   *Science as Social Knowledge.* Princeton University Press, Princeton, New Jersey.
Longino, H. E., and R. Doell
    1983   Body, Bias, and Behavior: A Comparative Analysis of Reasoning in Two Areas of Biological Science. *Signs* 9:206–227.
Mack, R.
    1990   Reading the Archaeology of the Female Body. *Qui Parle* 4:79–97.
Miller, D., and C. Tilley (editors)
    1984   *Ideology, Power, and Prehistory.* Cambridge University Press, Cambridge.
Miller, R.
    1987   *Fact and Method: Explanation, Confirmation and Reality in the Natural and Social Sciences.* Princeton University Press, Princeton, New Jersey.
Moore, H. L.
    1988   *Feminism and Anthropology.* Polity Press, Cambridge.
Mukhopadhyay, C. C., and P. J. Higgins
    1988   Anthropological Studies of Women's Status Revisited: 1977–1987. *Annual Review of Anthropology* 17:461–495.
Newton-Smith, W. H.
    1981   *The Rationality of Science.* Cambridge University Press, Cambridge.
Pickering, A.
    1984   *Constructing Quarks: A Sociological History of Particle Physics.* Edinburgh University Press, Edinburgh.
    1987   Essay Review: Forms of Life: Science, Contingency and Harry Collins. *British Journal for the History of Science* 20:213–221.
    1989   Living in the Material World: On Realism and Experimental Practice. In *The Uses of Experiment: Studies in the Natural Sciences,* edited by D. Gooding, T. Pinch, and S. Schaffer, pp. 275–297. Cambridge University Press, Cambridge.

Prentice, G.
  1986   Origins of Plant Domestication in the Eastern United States: Promoting the Individual in Archaeological
    Theory. *Southeastern Archaeology* 5:103–119.
Renfrew, C.
  1982   Explanation Revisited. In *Theory and Explanation in Archaeology*, edited by C. Renfrew, M. J. Row-
    lands, and B. A. Segraves, pp. 5–23. Academic Press, New York.
  1989   Comments on Archaeology Into the 1990s. *Norwegian Archaeological Review* 22(1):33–41.
Rosaldo, M. Z., and L. Lamphere (editors)
  1974   *Women, Culture, and Society*. Stanford University Press, Stanford.
Rudner, R.
  1966   *Philosophy of the Social Sciences*. Prentice Hall, Englewood Cliffs, New Jersey.
Shanks, M., and C. Tilley
  1987a   *Re-constructing Archaeology*. Cambridge University Press, Cambridge.
  1987b   *Social Theory and Archaeology*. Polity Press, Cambridge.
  1989   Archaeology Into the 1990s; Questions Rather Than Answers. Reply to Comments on Archaeology
    Into the 1990s. *Norwegian Archaeological Review* 22(1):1–14, 42–54. (With comments, pp. 15–41.)
Shapere, D.
  1985   The Concept of Observation in Science and Philosophy. *Philosophy of Science* 49:485–525.
Smith, B. D.
  1987   The Independent Domestication of the Indigenous Seed-Bearing Plants in Eastern North America. In
    Emergent Horticultural Economies of the Eastern Woodlands, edited by W. Keegan, pp. 3–47. Occasional
    Paper No. 7. Center for Archaeological Investigations, Southern Illinois University, Carbondale.
Spector, J. D.
  1983   Male/Female Task Differentiation Among the Hidatsa: Toward the Development of an Archeological
    Approach to the Study of Gender. In *The Hidden Half: Studies of Plains Indian Women*, edited by P.
    Albers and B. Medicine, pp. 77–99. University Press of America, Washington, D.C.
Suppe, F.
  1977   *The Structure of Scientific Theories*. 2nd ed. University of Illinois Press, Urbana.
Trigger, B. G.
  1989   Hyperrelativism, Responsibility, and the Social Sciences. *Canadian Review of Sociology and Anthro-
    pology* 26:776–797.
Tringham, R. E.
  1991   Households with Faces: The Challenge of Gender in Prehistoric Architectural Remains. In *Engendering
    Archaeology: Women and Prehistory*, edited by J. M. Gero and M. W. Conkey, pp. 93–131. Basil Blackwell,
    Oxford.
Walde, D., and N. Willows (editors)
  1991   *The Archaeology of Gender*, Proceedings of the 22nd Annual Chacmool Conference. The Archaeological
    Association of the University of Calgary, Calgary, in press.
Watson, P. J., and M. Fotiadis
  1990   The Razor's Edge: Symbolic-Structuralist Archeology and the Expansion of Archeological Inference.
    American Anthropologist 92:613–629.
Watson P. J., and M. C. Kennedy
  1991   The Development of Horticulture in the Eastern Woodlands of North America: Women's Role. In
    Engendering Archaeology: Women and Prehistory, edited by J. M. Gero and M. W. Conkey, pp. 255–275.
    Basil Blackwell, Oxford.
Watson, R. A.
  1990   Ozymandias, King of Kings: Postprocessual Radical Archaeology as Critique. *American Antiquity* 55:
    673–689.
Weitzenfeld, J. S.
  1984   Valid Reasoning by Analogy. *Philosophy of Science* 51:137–149.
Wildeson, L. E.
  1980   The Status of Women in Archaeology: Results of a Preliminary Survey. *American Anthropological
    Association Newsletter* 21(5):5–8.
Woolgar, S.
  1983   Irony in the Social Study of Science. In *Science Observed: Perspectives on the Social Study of Science*,
    pp. 239–266. Sage Publications, London.
Wylie, A.
  1985   The Reaction Against Analogy. In *Advances in Archaeological Method and Theory*, vol. 8, edited by
    M. B. Schiffer, pp. 63–111. Academic Press, New York.
  1987   The Philosophy of Ambivalence: Sandra Harding on *The Science Question in Feminism*. *Canadian
    Journal of Philosophy* (supplementary volume) 13:59–73.
  1988   "Simple" Analogy and the Role of Relevance Assumptions: Implications of Archaeological Practice.
    International Studies in the Philosophy of Science 2(2):134–150.
  1989a   Matters of Fact and Matters of Interest. In *Archaeological Approaches to Cultural Identity*, edited by
    S. Shennan, pp. 94–109. Unwin Hyman, London.

1989b Archaeological Cables and Tacking: The Implications of Practice for Bernstein's "Options Beyond Objectivism and Relativism." *Philosophy of the Social Sciences* 19:1–18.
1990 The Philosophy of Archaeology: Varieties of Evidence. Paper presented at the Annual Meeting of the American Philosophical Association Meetings, Eastern Division, Boston.
1991a Gender Theory and the Archaeological Record: Why Is There No Archaeology of Gender?. In *Engendering Archaeology: Women and Prehistory*, edited by J. M. Gero and M. W. Conkey, pp. 31–54. Basil Blackwell, Oxford.
1991b Beyond Objectivism and Relativism: Feminist Critiques and Archaeological Challenges. In *The Archaeology of Gender*, Proceedings of the 22nd Annual Chacmool Conference, edited by D. Walde and N. Willows. The Archaeological Association of the University of Calgary, Calgary, in press.
1991c Reasoning About Ourselves: Feminist Methodology in the Social Sciences. In *Women and Reason*, edited by E. Harvey and K. Okruhlik. University of Michigan Press, Ann Arbor, Michigan, in press.
1992 On "Heavily Decomposing Red Herrings": Scientific Method in Archaeology and the Ladening of Evidence with Theory. In *Metaarchaeology*, edited by L. Embree. Boston Studies in the Philosophy of Science. Reidel, Holland, in press. Ms. 1991.

NOTES

[1] There has been some important exploration of feminist themes in other connections, for example, in problem- or region-specific literatures where a developed anthropological and historical interest in the status and roles of women is extended to archaeology (see, for example, Barstow 1978; Kehoe 1983; Spector 1983). This is especially evident in historical archaeology where individual studies of women and gender in various historical contexts have appeared on Society for Historical Archaeology meeting programs since at least the mid-1980s, giving rise, in the last several years, to at least one session a year dedicated to research in this area. In addition, some postprocessual critics of the new archaeology have advocated feminist initiatives as an example of the sort of politically engaged approach they endorse (e.g., Hodder 1982, 1985, 1986:159–161; Shanks and Tilley 1987a: 246), although not many of them have undertaken sustained work in the area. Important exceptions are some of the contributions to Miller and Tilley's (1984) collection, *Ideology, Power and Prehistory* (for example, Hodder 1984b, and Braithwaite 1984) and to Gathercole and Loenthal's (1989) World Archaeology Congress collection, *The Politics of the Past*.

[2] By way of comparison, I was intrigued to learn that a group of Norwegian archaeologists had organized a conference called, "Were They All Men?", in November 1979—the proceedings were not published until 1987 (Bertelsen et al. 1987)—and that a group called "Norwegian Women in Archaeology" (the acronym is KAN in Norwegian) has been meeting and producing a journal, *KAN*, since 1985. In the same year as the Gero/Conkey conference, a special issue of *Archaeological Review from Cambridge* was produced on "Women and Archaeology" (Spring 1988), based in part on the "Cambridge Feminist Archaeology Workshops" in 1987–1988 and on presentations made at the annual Theoretical Archaeology Group Conferences held in the United Kingdom in 1987 (with antecedents in 1982 and 1985; see Arnold et al. 1988:1). In addition, a synthetic overview of the evidence pertaining to women and gender in European prehistory appeared in 1989, *Women in Prehistory* (Ehrenberg 1989).

[3] I say direct and indirect because some of those who participated undertook to organize special-topic sessions in response to the call for papers and solicited contributions from others who may not have seen the call for papers or planned to attend on their own. The number of contributions ultimately included in the program represents a substantial increase over the level of participation seen in previous years on more mainstream topics, e.g., long-distance trade, ethnicity, lithics and faunal analysis, and ecological models. However, in a paper that provides a content analysis of the abstracts contributed to "The Archaeology of Gender," Kelley and Hanen (1992) argue that the response to the 1989 call for papers is within the range expected given a general pattern of increase in the size of Chacmool conferences over the years. It is striking, nonetheless, that, given the dearth of published material in the area, a gender-focused conference would have maintained the rate of increase seen in previous years; several of the organizers indicated, in discussions about the genesis of the conference, that the momentum of the Chacmool institution itself had not always assured an increase in attendance (i.e., they could cite at least one previous topic that was specialized enough that participation had dropped relative to past years), and that the enthusiasm generated by their topic was quite unexpected, by both its supporters and its critics.

[4] In fact, as Kelley and Hanen (1992) argue, some subfields and specialties were more heavily represented than others at the Chacmool conference; for example, they note that papers tended to cluster in time periods closer to the historic (Kelley and Hanen 1992). Nonetheless, they note that the geographical distribution of archaeological subjects was very broad, with no evident clustering by field area, and with a representation of topics ranging from evolutionary theory and research on early hominids, through various problem areas and periods in prehistory, to ethnoarchaeology and ethnohistory, as well as historical archaeology. In addition, there was a full-day session on the status of women in archaeology.

[5] Longino argues persuasively that, although androcentrism pervades the social and life sciences, the form it takes, and the sources from which it derives in any given field of research, will be diverse and often quite specific to the intellectual agenda and history of the field; single-factor and widely generalized accounts of the nature or

roots of androcentrism across the sciences are inherently implausible (Longino 1987:61). She argues, more specifically, that it will be necessary to understand the "unstated and fundamental assumptions [of a particular field or research tradition] and how they influence the course of inquiry" (Longino 1987:62) in order to respond effectively to androcentric bias.

[6] What follows is a sketch of processes that I believe may underly the recent emergence of a visible interest in questions about women and gender, and in feminist initiatives, among North American archaeologists. The sketch itself is developed in more detail elsewhere (Wylie 1991b), but it remains to be filled in; I have recently undertaken a survey and a series of interviews that I hope will make it possible to give a fuller account of how those who organized and contributed to the groundbreaking archaeological conferences on gender in North America came to be involved in research in this area.

[7] As indicated, these concerns were well represented on the program of the Chacmool conference, which included a full-day session on the status of women in the discipline (see contributions to Walde and Willows [1991]), and have been articulated in a number of analyses of women's status in archaeology that have appeared in the last decade (e.g., Gero 1983, 1985, 1988; Kramer and Stark 1988; Wildeson 1980).

[8] For a summary of the main tenets of this position see Suppe (1977), and for a classic example of their application to the social sciences, see Rudner (1966). Gibbon (1989) provides an excellent account of their incorporation into archaeology.

[9] For a classic case study that was widely influential in supporting this position, see Latour and Woolgar (1986), and for further discussion, see Knorr and Mulkay (1983) and Latour (1987). One of the most uncompromising advocates of a strong constructivist view has been Pickering (1984, 1989), although he sometimes distances himself from some even more radical constructivists (Pickering 1987).

[10] Indeed, Tringham reports considerable resistance to the idea of the conference: "I was taken kicking and screaming to the conference 'Women and Production in Prehistory' in the marshes of South Carolina, convinced that gender differences were not visible in the archaeological record, least of all in the architectural remains of deep prehistory, with which I was most concerned" (Tringham 1991:93).

[11] Indeed, why assume that shamans were men?

[12] These were analyses undertaken by DeNiro at the University of California–Los Angeles (Hastorf 1991:153).

[13] This paper was not Conkey's contribution to the South Carolina conference, but several of its main points were discussed in this context.

[14] For an early series of arguments to this effect, see the contributions to *Women, Culture, and Society* (Rosaldo and Lamphere 1974), and for contemporary reviews and assessments see *Feminism and Anthropology* (Moore 1988) and Mukhopadhyay and Higgins (1988).

[15] The notion of "determining structures" derives from an analysis of analogical inference due to Weitzenfeld (1984) and refers to any systematic relation of dependence (functional, rule related, as well as causal); it does not imply a commitment to uniformitarianism or any strong or specifically causal sort.

[16] This argument is developed in more detail, with reference to proposals for the development and use of middle-range theory, in Wylie (1992).

[17] Biconditional laws take the form, "if and only if," specifying antecedent conditions that are both necessary and sufficient to produce the effects or outcome in question. In an archaeological context, a linking principle of this sort would specify past activities or events that had to have occurred for a particular archaeological record to have resulted, and it would exclude any other possible antecedents. Something along the lines of these limiting cases constitute the ideal on which Binford bases his arguments for middle-range theory (e.g., Binford 1983: 135, 1986b:472).

Received February 5, 1991; accepted September 18, 1991

OZYMANDIAS, KING OF KINGS: POSTPROCESSUAL RADICAL ARCHAEOLOGY AS CRITIQUE

Richard A. Watson

If it is true that there are but two kinds of people in the world—the logical positivists and the god-damned English professors—then I suppose I am a logical positivist.

Glymour 1980:ix

In Re-Constructing Archaeology *(1987a) and* Social Theory and Archaeology *(1987b), Michael Shanks and Christopher Tilley argue for an antiscience radical archaeology as critique. They use deconstructionist sceptical arguments to conclude that there is no objective past and that our representations of the past are only texts that we produce on the basis of our sociopolitical standpoints. In effect, they contend that there is no objective world, that the world itself is a text that human beings write. This is a form of subjective idealism. Their critique is a nihilistic attack on all objective knowledge.*

En Re-Constructing Archaeology *(1987a) y en* Social Theory and Archaeology *(1987b), Michael Shanks y Christopher Tilley proponen, como crítica, una arqueología radical y anticientífica. Usando argumentos escépticos "de-construccionistas," Shanks y Tilley concluyen que no existe un pasado objetivo y que nuestras representaciones del pasado son sólo textos que producimos en base a nuestra posición sociopolítica. De hecho, ellos afirman que no existe un mundo objetivo y que el mundo mismo es un texto escrito por los seres humanos. Este es un tipo de idealismo subjetivista. La crítica de Shanks y Tilley es un ataque nihilista a todo conocimiento objetivo.*

Literary texts often are ambiguous and open to multiple interpretation. Literary criticism trades on these possibilities. Usually, however, there is a standard—but not exclusionary—interpretation for each literary work. Standard interpretations change over the generations and obviously are influenced by contemporary culture. Despite changes, however, *Othello* is still thought to be about jealousy, and *Macbeth* about ambition.

Derrida (1976, 1978) uses traditional sceptical arguments to challenge the notion that there are privileged interpretations of any literary text or of any writing at all. Like the ancient sceptics, deconstructionists expose the flaws in all interpretations. The techniques of deconstructionist literary criticism recently have been introduced into the social sciences. In this paper, I examine a deconstructivist position in archaeology presented by Michael Shanks and Christopher Tilley in *Re-Constructing Archaeology* (1987a) and *Social Theory and Archaeology* (1987b). They represent the extreme view that the past did not exist, but is merely a text that we write, a position that is a form of subjective idealism. In effect, deconstruction in the social sciences is a nihilist attack on all science and objective knowledge.

DECONSTRUCTION

The deconstructionist attack on the social sciences appears to have initial plausibility for the following reason. The social sciences are the truly hard sciences. Technically, the hard sciences are those to which quantitative techniques are most applicable, and their hardness is in the extent and rigor of their mathematical representations. But a science also can be hard to the degree that it is difficult to make empirical tests of its hypotheses and theories. The harder it is to confirm or disconfirm hypotheses about a subject matter, the more interpretations can be given of it. Scientific

Richard A. Watson, Department of Philosophy, Washington University, St. Louis, MO 63130

American Antiquity, 55(4), 1990, pp. 673–689.
Copyright © 1990 by the Society for American Archaeology

143

texts are meant to represent an objective subject matter. In the social sciences, the complexity of the subject matter and the difficulty of collecting significant data sometimes make it hard to support one representation over others. In this sense, physics is soft or easy, sociology is hard.

In fact, any subject matter can be accounted for by many different scientific theories. The reason is that the scope of scientific theories extends beyond our empirical observations to all possible cases. Thus all theories are underdetermined by available data because the same data can be used to support radically different theories. We choose among theories by picking those that best explain and predict our future observations.

But Shanks and Tilley argue that all theories are biased irrevocably by sociopolitical interests, and that all language is theory laden in the sense that the meanings of concepts necessarily are determined by the theory or language to which they belong. Because we must use theory-laden language, they say that we impose a structure on the world. Thus they argue that scientists cannot construct better and better representations of the objective world because theory-laden concepts and sociopolitical bias cannot be avoided. They then deploy sceptical arguments to assert an egalitarian relativism among theories, raise the question of whether or not an objective world exists at all, and finally conclude that the world is our own sociocultural construction.

Deconstructive techniques are largely rhetorical. In *Re-Constructing Archaeology,* for example, Shanks and Tilley (1987a) use the word "data" as singular in four places before page 116, so the locution "data are" on that page strikes the reader. Shanks teaches classics, so this use is deliberate. The eventual occurrence of "data are" is meant to be provocative. The singular use of "data" is symbolic of the authors' iconoclastic intent toward tradition and conventional standards.

Shanks and Tilley intend to deconstruct the archaeological establishment. To this end, by using deliberate misinterpretations, fallacious and inconsistent arguments, and rhetorical tricks, they verge on exuberant intellectual dishonesty. Their general defense of this procedure is that concepts such as honesty and dishonesty belong to insupportable totalizing categorial schemes. But traditional questions of honesty and truth do apply to their work, and the implication that profession of integrity is itself a trick is just part of their game.

AGAINST SCIENCE

The postmodern, poststructural, postpositivist, deconstructive ideas and techniques that Shanks and Tilley import into postprocessual archaeology—and others (e.g., Barnes [1984] and Bloor [1983]) into the historical and social sciences as a whole—constitute dogmatic scepticism. Mitigated scepticism is part of the method of science in the sense that scientists make no claims to certainty. Scientific statements always are open to doubt. Science is thus not dogmatic, and scepticism in science is used to advance knowledge. But the absolute scepticism of those like Shanks and Tilley who attack empiricism, functionalism, positivism, objectivism, and systems theory in the social sciences impedes the advance of knowledge. They argue that there are only local, politically motivated, nonobjective conceptions of truth and falsehood. On this view, all social interactions, including the practice of archaeology, are motivated by desire for prestige and political power, and all societal activities either support or attack the status quo. "True" propositions support the power structure, "false" propositions do not. Positivist science, with its goal of universal understanding and its techniques of manipulating nature from elementary particles to human beings, should be rejected because it grew out of and supports oppressive capitalism. And there is no way out. To do science is to support oppression.

Such simplistic misrepresentation is Shanks and Tilley's primary rhetorical technique. In another example, they declare that contemporary science is "the world of physicalism, of extension, of geometric form, of number, which has been declared as real, while everything else has been condemned as fictional magic. This is the world in which people do not matter. It is the world of capitalism" (Shanks and Tilley 1987a:66).

This is a good gambit, for the opposition looks silly and pedantic when replying soberly that scientists do not say the nonquantifiable is fictional magic, or that people do not matter. Psychologists, after all, study both qualitative phenomena and people.

The quotation illustrates another rhetorical technique, the enormous inferential leap. Shanks and Tilley argue simplistically that alienation in capitalist society derives from the use of quantitative methods, and then leap to the conclusion that positivist science necessarily leads to oppressive political practices. But then—and this illustrates their methodic disdain for consistency—they also stress the primacy of human action over the influence of the material world, and thus, as so often in radical critique, try to have it both ways. Technology is, for them, both something we establish by the use of categorial schemes (so is not objective), but also (contradictorily) appears to be oppressive in itself.

Oddly enough, Shanks and Tilley overlook the fact that noncapitalist governments often use scientific techniques to oppress people, and that capitalist societies often use them to benefit people, which suggests that science is neutral with respect to its sociopolitical application.

The advent of postmodernism, poststructuralism, postpositivism, and deconstruction in archaeology is a continuation of an antiscience, anti-analysis movement among a number of historians, sociologists, and anthropologists who argue that human beings and culture are not part of nature and thus that human behavior cannot be understood, explained, or predicted with reference to general laws. This attack on the human sciences, the Enlightenment, and the primacy of reason over the emotions traditionally was mounted in defense of religion. It is an attack on secular humanism, now cast as a defense of free will in opposition to determinist, dehumanizing positivist science.

The basic source of Shanks and Tilley's rejection of a scientific approach to humans derives from Hegel and the nineteenth-century British idealists who opposed the analytic philosophy and science championed by G. E. Moore and Bertrand Russell. Idealists hold that the world is an organic whole in which everything necessarily is related to everything else so that analyzing into parts falsifies the whole. To say anything true about a part, one must say everything about the whole, so generalization that isolates some and sets aside other aspects of anything is falsification. Another route to idealist antiscience is from Heiddeger to Derrida.

Shanks and Tilley (1987a:34) claim that "People are not natural entities if we accept the primacy of sentience, intentionality, linguistic and symbolic communication." They argue that because humans have free will and are self-conscious, have intentions and beliefs, make decisions and undertake actions, there is no way to comprehend them even with probabilist, statistical, nonuniversal lawlike generalizations, explanation sketches, or models that are usual in the social sciences. In short, they claim that human behavior is in no way lawlike. Human beings are more than animals. Animals *move* in ways that can be explained and predicted with reference to general laws; humans *act* freely in ways that cannot be explained and predicted with reference to general laws:

> Even if human beings are indeed animals and subject to processes of natural selection in an equivalent manner to badgers, hedgehogs, or guinea-fowl, this by no means implies that any adequate explanation or understanding of social totalities, institutions or material cultural patterning can be achieved by reference either to natural selection or adaptation. Most social and material practices have no demonstrable physical survival value for human populations whatsoever [Shanks and Tilley 1987a, 1987b:154–155].

The authors know the last sentence is outrageously false. One result of their confrontational style is that shockingly false statements force on the reader their view that there are none but polemical grounds for the "truth" of any statement.

Postprocessualists claim it is a mistake to try to understand human activity and sociocultural institutions in terms of functionalism, systems theory, ecological integration, or environmental interactions between biological organisms and the physical world. They argue that because human society is constructed solely by intentional action, natural physical and biological (particularly evolutionary) processes play no role in its organization. Sociocultural reality is a free conceptual, linguistic production.

Thus only meaning is important, and meaning is imposed only by human beings. Material things and movements in themselves have no meaning. Meanings, Shanks and Tilley (1987a:35) say, are not natural:

AMERICAN ANTIQUITY

Natural phenomena, unlike social phenomena, have no inherent meaning or cognitive structure which needs to be taken account of in explanation. . . . Meanings are necessarily and not contingently connected to human actions and their projects. . . . Intentionality is a crucial concept which distinguishes mental from physical phenomena. . . . People possess the ability to act in and on the natural world and to systematically transform it and create their own world or social constructon of reality. . . . Human culture is not a part of nature but a transformation of it.

In other words, the social is mental and derives solely from the interpretive procedures of individual human beings. This is to deny not only that humans have any species-specific form of social interaction, but also that from our knowledge of climate, geography, and biological constraints (needs for food, protection, and reproduction), we can say anything generally true about human social institutions.

Certainly, contemporary ethnic groups show that a very large number of different myths, rituals, religious beliefs, conceptual systems, categorial schemes, and political ideologies are held by very different groups of people who are still alike in using hand axes and pots, tractors and nuclear reactors. A great variety of sociocultural institutions are based on the same material culture and environmental conditions, similar to the way that Chomsky theorizes that a multitude of different actual languages are based on one deep grammar.

Some configurations of artifacts we might interpret as individualistic and indicative of isolated families, others as signifying a communal way of life. We have seen such relations in our own experience, and have read about them in historical records. It is reasonable to use ethnographic analogy to interpret prehistoric remains. But there is no way to check our interpretations by observing, questioning, or reading the records of nonliterate prehistoric peoples. Perhaps they meant their material goods, drawings, and paintings to be signs, but the inference gap between these remains and any meanings we take them to have is large. On the other hand, Shanks and Tilley's theory that archaeological interpretations are signs of *our own* beliefs and intentions is at least as difficult to support as any interpretation of what they meant to prehistoric peoples themselves.

Even if we knew what prehistoric people thought, however, Shanks and Tilley say we cannot describe *any* aspect of the world neutrally, neither the sizes and shapes of things (exact measurements are tricks of capitalist exploitation), nor the colors of things (people with different concepts do not even see things the same way). This claim that language cannot be neutral is based on their general denial that any activity can be apolitical. Taking archaeology as an example, they say

any attempt to artificially separate archaeology from politics only serves to benefit existing power structures. A 'neutral' archaeology serves to sustain the existing social order by its failure to engage actively with it and criticize it. Thus any advocacy of an apolitical archaeology remains itself a form of political action [Shanks and Tilley 1987b:198–199].

There is no possibility of a neutral and autonomous 'middle way'. The effect of archaeology in socio-political terms depends on the place that it chooses to occupy within a wider socio-cultural field. A value-committed archaeology is one rejecting any position which would suggest that research merely mirrors the past. Instead it insists that research forms part of a process in which the archaeologist *actively decides* upon one past rather than another. Interpretation in archaeology constructs a *socio-political position* in the process of engagement with the artefactual traces of the past. Anything 'discovered' about the past is not a passive reflection of what the 'facts' may or may not tell us. Archaeological texts which re-present the past have an expressive, rhetorical and persuasive purpose. They are not, and cannot be, neutral expositions of facticity of the past [Shanks and Tilley 1987b:205].

Shanks and Tilley and other radical critics assert that you can never avoid being a pawn in someone's political game. If this is true—and probably it is not because political game players get away with ignoring lots of people—it is not obvious that you must accept any role imposed upon you, nor that you must strive to be a knight on either side.

Shanks and Tilley themselves warn against getting caught in a capitalist bag:

It is quite evident that the past may be used for expressing a wide variety of supportive ideas and values for capitalist society, naturalized and legitimized through an emphasis on tradition and long-term time scales: myths of genius; individuality; patriarchy; humanity's essential economic nature; the universality and inevitability of technological development as progressive; the naturalness of social stability as opposed to contradiction; the inferiority or superiority of certain forms of social organization, etc. Such views may be strongly supported by archaeological texts (they usually are), or they may be challenged [Shanks and Tilley 1987b: 204–205].

Obviously, however, myths of genius and patriarchy, for example, can be used to support other than capitalist societies. Certainly political views can be supported or challenged by archaeological texts. But who says that is the purpose of archaeology? Shanks and Tilley do. They say "archaeology is nothing if it is not cultural critique" (Shanks and Tilley 1987b:199). But while archaeology can be cultural critique, it is not necessarily cultural critique, nor is it necessarily nothing but cultural critique.

To support their extreme view, Shanks and Tilley argue that all knowledge is designed to support political power. "Archaeological discourse [for example] is a *form* of power while at the same time being the study of power" (Shanks and Tilley 1987b:viii). They also deny that there is any sense of truth that is not necessarily political:

The position we are taking involves the inscription of a fresh politics of truth, itself a form of power. This is a struggle waged in terms of the production of alternative regimes of truth. Truth is to be conceived as a series of coded rules which permit divisions to be drawn between various types of discourses in terms of a polar truth/falsity opposition. We should not do battle 'in favor of truth' but, rather, situate truths in relation to the social, economic and political roles they play in society. Our aim is not so much to change people's consciousness as to change the manner in which truth is produced and becomes accepted. Power can never be detached from truth; but we can work to subvert the power of truth being attached to the existing social order and instead link truth to a political future [Shanks and Tilley 1987b:199].

Even if we accept this sociopolitical view of truth, why should we detach ourselves from the existing social order? How do we know the future is better? And which future? Shanks and Tilley do not say. They only advocate change.

Shanks and Tilley claim to be Marxists, but this is difficult, for they deny material influences on culture. Thus, they oppose Marxism as science, saying that "Most Marxist approaches in archaeology . . . have a strong tendency to scientism." On the other hand, they continue, "We consider [the] critical [Frankfurt School] tradition of Marxism as one of the most important and essential sources for reconstructing archaeological theory and practice" (Shanks and Tilley 1987b:194). Thus they accept "Marxism as cultural critique."

They also owe a great deal to what is known as the strong program in social science (Barnes [1984]; critiqued by Roth [1987]):

The point of archaeology is not merely to interpret the past but to change the manner in which the past is interpreted in the service of social reconstruction in the present. There is no way of choosing between alternative pasts except on essentially political grounds, in terms of a definite value system, a morality. So, criteria for truth and falsity are not to be understood purely in terms of the logic and rationality, or otherwise, of discourses, but require judgements in terms of practical consequences of archaeological theory and practice for contemporary social change [Shanks and Tilley 1987b:195].

This view of truth seems obvious to Shanks and Tilley because they hold the position that language is a theory, so all concepts, categorial schemes, scientific theories, language games, and technical vocabularies are theory laden. This means that the sense of every concept derives from the theory or categorial scheme of which it is a part. That all concepts are theory laden in this sense generally is accepted.

Shanks and Tilley, however, take "theory laden" to mean "theory corrupted." They claim that because language itself is a theory, there is no neutral way of talking about anything. The model for this view is Kant's notion that the way we know the world depends on categories we provide, and since we cannot know the world except by categorizing it, we may not know the world as it really is. Kant leaves open the possibility that the world in itself is the way we categorize it. Shanks and Tilley, on the contrary, believe that without neutral concepts, there is no way we can know things as they are. Instead, categories—and language itself—impose a transformational sense and structure on the world. The forms of things as we necessarily know them are said to be imposed by the concepts we use to describe them.

Kant says the phenomenal world must be viewed as real because we know nothing of a noumenal world of things in themselves. Berkeley says what exists are merely sensory perceptions that *are* the world, though we mistakenly think they are *of* the world. Shanks and Tilley say that because we cannot have uncorrupted knowledge of the world beyond our texts, the world just *is* a text, a construct out of concepts and language. This is the position of nineteenth-century British idealists such as Bradley, McTaggart, and Green who say the world is constructed of ideas.

Their view of the world as idea or as text derives from the belief that God created the world and that the world is the word of God. Berkeley says that the world is a text of sensible ideas that God set for us to read. Shanks and Tilley and other contemporary idealists believe that we are the gods who write the texts.

Why, then, is the world not more to our liking? A secular answer is that all humans are writers competing for control. Or one could say with Berkeley that God imposes the meanings, or with Hegel that the World Spirit does. Of course, one can *say* anything at all.

Nevertheless, Shanks and Tilley, with only negative arguments and no solid position of their own, make a sobering point: Despite the immense amount of scientific knowledge that has falsified spiritualism, theories that the world is the product of human thought abound.

There are always theories of the world. Scientific theories compete as to which best represents the world. As texts, theories themselves are viable worlds. Shanks and Tilley use political power as the criterion for choosing among textual worlds. That world is "real," i.e., dominant, that is imposed by whomever is in power. Theories change when one sociopolitical power base is replaced by another. This is not, however, the reason scientific theories are replaced, as their persistence through change of sociopolitical power structures shows.

Shanks and Tilley attack positivism by using the phrase "subjective idealism" to characterize it. They say that subjective idealists believe that a subjectively generated ideal categorial scheme perfectly represents things as they really are. This is not in fact subjective idealism, but representative realism. Does Shanks and Tilley's use of "subjective idealism" stem from ignorance or guile? I don't know. Whatever. Most positivists are representative realists, but do not believe that our ideas represent things perfectly.

Shanks and Tilley raise the standard objection against the empirical verification and meaning principles of positivist philosophy and science—that no concepts are meaningful and no statements verifiable unless the things they describe can be observed empirically. Critics early pointed out that these principles themselves cannot be verified empirically, and thus logical positivism—meant to rule out metaphysics—itself rests on a foundation of metaphysical principles. But as Bergmann (1954) says in *The Metaphysics of Logical Positivism,* when we test these principles by applying them, we find that they facilitate the clarification of the language of science and contribute to the advancement of empirical knowledge.

Shanks and Tilley's position is similarly vulnerable to their own obiter dicta. One can ask how they know that all language is theory laden. This is just their theory, and on their theory no theory can have global application. Throughout their texts, they use stereotyped concepts of positivism, capitalism, and science uncritically as though they apply universally, as they cannot according to their own theory. Their own principles undercut their own position, just as the antimetaphysical conclusion of logical positivism undercuts the principles on which it rests. Shanks and Tilley's position that truth derives from imposition of systems is not so far vindicated by practical use.

Practice overrides theory. Never mind that the foundations of science are uncertain, that its hypotheses can never be confirmed absolutely, that its theories always are being replaced—knowledge continues to increase. Such mitigated scepticism—always a sceptical attitude, always willingness to doubt, to test, to revise, to replace—is a basic principle of modern science. Shanks and Tilley instead promote dogmatic scepticism, an attempted demonstration that because all concepts are theory laden and all meanings come from human beings, there is no real knowledge, only "truths" that fluctuate relative to conflicting categorial schemes, and there is no objective world at all.

Throughout their texts, Shanks and Tilley assume that stability and homeostasis are bad. They urge their readers to work for change, to oppose all established systems functioning to maintain themselves, because all establishments are oppressive. Their own text describes change as good, but if continuous revolution were established, would change itself become oppressive? By such paradoxes, Shanks and Tilley set up the dialectic of change. But the notion that contradiction is better than consistency is itself part of their text, which, like all texts, cannot validate itself, except that when your calculus contains contradictions, anything goes.

Shanks and Tilley (1987a:130) offer as an example of dialectic the case of social structures: "Contradiction between structures results in antagonistic beliefs and meanings regarding practice and clearly relates to social relations of inequality. Contradiction translated into antagonistic interests and open social conflict generates social change." Because social change is good, we should bring out the contradictions in things and society, and we should refuse to look for lawlike generalizations for they conceal contradictions and facilitate oppression. Shanks and Tilley (1987a:38) ask: "Why must the business of doing science necessarily be equated with the ability, or the will to generalize? This appears to be a procedural rule founded on the basis that generalizing, rather than considering all the particularity of the individual case, is a superior kind of activity. There seems to be no compelling reason why we should accept this."

Of course the compelling reason is because generalizing science works. It is spectacular how, throughout their texts, Shanks and Tilley avoid discussing the fact that science works. They admit it only backhandedly, by attacking scientific techniques because they are used by capitalists to oppress people.

Instead of examining the effectiveness of science, in their stress on the particular and attack on the general, Shanks and Tilley set up the straw-man positivist who always posits universal laws of the type "All X are Y." But statistical and probabilist laws, lawlike generalizations, explanation sketches, and models—all of which give generalizing pictures—are, in science, quite adequate, and by far more common than universal laws in the social sciences.

That science does not take account of particulars is false. Generalizations are used to explain and predict the behavior of particulars. We learn how particulars behave, not by concentrating on this or that particular, describing it in Baconian terms, seeking to know its unique individual essence or nature, but by generalizing over many particulars and testing our hypotheses in particular situations. Shanks and Tilley thus accuse positivists of seeking essences, but they themselves argue against generalization by championing the unique essence of particularity.

Shanks and Tilley stand against generalization on the particularist side of an old debate in the social sciences. They ask: "Where is the individual in the archaeological past?" (Shanks and Tilley 1987b:61). They conceive of the social construction of reality as depending solely on individual human intentions and actions. And they say these are factored out by generalizing positivist science. In the search for lawlike generalizations, "the human 'components' fall irrevocably out of view" (Shanks and Tilley 1987a:35).

Few would deny that if you want to know in detail about someone's life, immersion in the particular contributes to such knowledge. The same goes for ethnographic detail about living communities and societies. We live our lives in an ocean of human interaction, experiencing joy and despair, pride and humility, love and hate, triumph and failure, life and death, as particular individuals. It is terribly important—this lived life of individual intentions, actions, and passions. And sometimes an individual—Gandhi, Gorbachev, Golda Meir—makes a big difference by his or her actions. But the lives of most of us count only as they add up over space and time to contribute to the group character and behavior of human beings in general.

But *does* the particular, unique individual drop out in generalizing science? Yes. The beliefs and actions of Ozymandias, King of Kings, are not merely buried in the sand, they are obliterated entirely by the sands of time. The inspiration for Shelley's poem is the lawlike generalization that human intentions and actions are ephemeral, evanescent; none are preserved; most are unrecorded. Usually they are not just eliminable, they are eliminated.

Shanks and Tilley want to introduce the individual into archaeology. Archaeologists should account for individual intentions and actions of people of the past. Obviously we cannot reexperience the past as recommended by Dilthey (1954 [1907]) and Collingwood (1946). And archaeological remains are open to many interpretations. So in fact it is quite impossible to attain what Shanks and Tilley propose as the goal of archaeology—knowledge of the social construction of reality as individuals in the past knew it.

AGAINST ARCHAEOLOGY

Shanks and Tilley doubt the professed intentions of new archaeologists:

We would suggest that perhaps a more plausible reason for the development of the new archaeology is fundamentally to do with a drive for prestige and power, but on a disciplinary basis rather than in terms of individuals *per se*. During the last two decades archaeologists have distanced their work from history, conceived as being particularist and ideographic in character, and have characterized it as a nomothetic generalizing 'hard' science. Science, with a capital S, is the key word for understanding recent developments in archaeology. Why did the majority of archaeologists want to don the antiseptic white coat? This would seem to involve the acceptance of the myth of the supremacy of science as the ultimate mode of human understanding, the scientist as an heroic figure dispelling myths with incisive rationality. Given the increasing dominance of science and technology in contemporary society, to be cast in this image was to gain intellectual respectability and power, the power to be gained by producing or purporting to produce objective knowledge relevant to the modern world (Fritz and Plog, 1970, p. 412), relevance being conceived in terms of both ethical and political neutrality and thus inherently conservative [Shanks and Tilley 1987a:31].

Shanks and Tilley equate science with "empiricism" and "positivism." They characterize "empiricism" as the belief that things in the world are open to neutral observation and can be seen and known objectively just as they are. They characterize "positivism" as the belief that there is one stable world of objective things. They say that positivists dogmatically believe in the absolute certainty and comprehensiveness of scientific theories and categories from which they deduce truths about the world, and that such deduction is the only way to establish truths.

Shanks and Tilley (1987b:9) deplore that archaeologists follow this objectivist line: "Few archaeologists believe in induction any more. . . . Most realize that facts are selected and that research must be problem oriented; facts only answer the questions the archaeologist asks of them . . . and there is a growing realization that data are theory-laden. However, this has made very little difference to archaeology. There is still a wide consensus in the belief in 'objective reality' of the archaeological record."

Shanks and Tilley (1987a:32) say archaeologists have fallen into erroneous ways through blind worship of positivist science: "Positivist doctrines were transferred to archaeology at a time when many philosophers were rejecting virtually every major tenet on which positivism was based. The unfortunate spectacle is one of archaeology embracing thoroughly discredited and outmoded ideas as the framework for its own advance."

But so what if many philosophers reject positivism? All scientists and most philosophers of science are empiricist in the sense that they depend on empirical data and experiment to test their hypotheses, and they are positivist in the sense that they search for general laws, lawlike generalizations, or models with which to explain and predict particular events.

The brio, the chutzpah, the rhetoric is spectacular here. Shanks and Tilley defy response by casting their attack in the same form of non sequitur argument they accuse archaeologists of falling err to. Shanks and Tilley say that archaeologists make the dumb choice to be positivists because they think scientists are positivists, then, in turn, Shanks and Tilley propose the dumb argument that because philosophers reject positivism, archaeologists should too.

Shanks and Tilley avoid examining what scientists really are, to attack positivist philosophers, ad hominem:

Curiously enough this trend has continued and the papers presented at the recent Southampton conference (Renfrew, Rowlands, and Segraves (eds.) 1982) by those professional philosophers called in to 'advise' archaeologists, with the exception of Gellner's paper (Gellner 1982), all took a positivist, if diluted positivist line. Similarly the only semi-professional philosopher to have written a book with relation to archaeology (Salmon 1982) has retained a positivist position [Shanks and Tilley 1987a:32–33].

Who is this semiprofessional philosopher? She is a full professor at the University of Pittsburgh in one of the best philosophy departments in the United States, known for its preeminence in philosophy of science, and she is the editor of *Philosophy of Science,* the top journal in its field.

Shanks and Tilley really know how to get a guy. They quote from Morgan's (1973:273) attack on *Explanation in Archeology* by Watson et al. (1971): "In short, EA seems in places reminiscent of a religious revivalist, appealing to scripture to establish his points, while surrounding this doctrine with flowery phrases and redefinitions to make that doctrine more palatable" (Shanks and Tilley 1987a:33).

So, of all people, it devolves on *me* to point out that Shanks and Tilley do not cite Watson et al.'s (1974) reply that they are practicing archaeologists proposing heuristic use of the hypothetico-deductive method, not logicians defending a logical point. Nor do Shanks and Tilley cite Watson et al.'s (1984) *Archeological Explanation,* which shows that they never professed the rigid positivism antiscientists set up to caricature the new archaeology. How embarrassing!

Shanks and Tilley know Morgan is off base, so they next stand their complaint on its head to chide new archaeologists for *not* being undiluted positivists: "The failure of archaeologists to discover laws reduces the explanations archaeologists make, in the positivist dogma, to mere 'explanation sketches' (Hempel 1959)" (Shanks and Tilley 1987a:44).

Explanation sketches constitute a lot of scientific knowledge, but in fact, scientists can settle for even less. Shanks and Tilley, like Morgan, insist that new archaeologists and positivist scientists conceive of laws as absolutely universal and certain, but Hempel (1965, 1966) discounts such an extreme formulation. Even to say "That is a dog" is to appeal to the general concept dog, which implies that one has before one an animal with teeth, four legs, and a tail, and that if its tail is wagging, it probably won't bite. But be cautious. There are exceptions to all such lawlike generalizations.

Shanks and Tilley (1987b:8) assert that "the archaeologist is supposedly able to determine how the past was for once and all," that

> Traditional and new archaeology represent a desire for the past in itself and for itself . . . [but] . . . The past cannot be exactly reproduced. Exact reproduction is repetition, tautology, silence. The archaeological past is not re-created as it was or in whatever approximation. It is, of course, excavated away. As such, the archaeological past must be *written* [Shanks and Tilley 1987b:13].

The rhetorical gambit here is to take terms literally. So *who* would ever claim to *recreate* or *reproduce* the past, let alone exactly as it was? And the *past* is surely not excavated away, though evidence of it sometimes is. Shanks and Tilley's own literal inference from the fact that descriptions of the past are *in writing* to the conclusion that the past itself is *only writing* is quite breathtaking.

Shanks and Tilley insist that theories are not hypothetical descriptions of the world, but rather are dogmatic schemata deceptively imposed on people to control them. Their claim, finally, that the division between theory and practice is like that between capital and labor, and that organized methodology is ominous verges on hysterical paranoia:

> [T]he real practice of archaeology always tends to be separated from theory. This split is one homologous with that between mental and manual labour, decision and execution, ends and means. It is a split running throughout the capitalist division of labour. An emphasis on methodology is one on logistics, administration, management, surveillance: defining that which is 'reasonable', asserting realistic limits and goals to archaeological practice [Shanks and Tilley 1987b:11].

Shanks and Tilley (1987a:34) insist that "positivism is now more or less a term of abuse rather than a living philosophical tradition." Yet, a more moderate postprocessualist, Hodder (1987:516), says Earle and Preucel (1987) "are wrong to claim that I reject general laws":

> Earle and Preucel are also wrong to claim that "the radical critique rejects the scientific method." I for my part certainly do not reject and never have rejected all scientific method. I do reject a rigid positivism (although at times Earle and Preucel define positivism in such general terms that I find it difficult to disagree with it), the linking of explanation with prediction, and the belief that objective data can in some way be separated from subjective theory to allow independent testing. But the notion that I reject methodology or quantification is unfounded [Hodder 1987:517].

Shanks and Tilley give no references to positivist philosophers of science except Hempel (1959) and Salmon (1982). I suggest that the reader look at Glymour's (1980) *Theory and Evidence* and Roth's (1987) *Meaning and Method in the Social Sciences.* Then pick a dozen other recent books in the philosophy of science at random. They will contain a lot of argument about whether or not theoretical terms refer to real entities, but few denials that hypotheses are to be subjected to empirical tests, or that a general covering-law model is heuristically useful in the social sciences. For specific

151

responses to postprocessualism in archaeology, see Binford (1986, 1987, 1989), Chippendale (1988), Earle and Preucel (1987), Shanks and Tilley (1989), Watson (1990a, 1990b), Wylie (1989, 1990), and Schiffer (1988).

Shanks and Tilley attack not only general laws, but also representation itself, the description of the world by any categorial or conceptual scheme, all of which, they say, are ineradicably totalizing and biased. They maintain that if you describe the world, you necessarily impose a parochial structure. On the usual use of the terms, however, scientific categories, hypotheses, and theories are proposed only tentatively. They are tested by a method of multiple working hypotheses: *multiple* because hypotheses are a dime a dozen, *working* because if their predictions and explanations are wrong, others have to be tried, and *hypotheses* because they are not dogmatic knowledge claims. In this sense all laws of science are hypotheses. Even that there is an objective world is an hypothesis, so far confirmed by empirical evidence.

As quoted above, Shanks and Tilley (1987a:35) correctly say that no thing has meaning in itself. We always bring to things an interpretation or a theory. Even to identify something as a sign is to go beyond what it is and shows in itself. As the Stoics point out, ideas and even apparently iconic images do not come with tags saying they are signs, let alone saying what they mean or represent.

So what do archaeological remains in themselves suggest? Nothing. But on the basis of our experience and conceptual systems, we humans suggest the uses of material culture, of pots and hand axes. Our first hypotheses are that tools were used the way people use them now, houses were lived in as we do, people worked to satisfy needs as we must. But these hypotheses are subject to revision, for we cannot impose them on things if they do not fit. It can be shown, for example, that some chipped stones are not artifacts because natural collisions caused their angles of flake removal, which are different from those caused by human production.

Shanks and Tilley attack such applications of ordinary categories to archaeological remains:

> All the categories he [Gibson 1982] adopts—fabric, fine, coarse, burial, ritual, domestic—are categories of common sense, assumed as meaningful and self-evident. They remain unexamined, their definition regarded as essentially transparent. That there are variations in the meanings attached to different linguistic expressions of the same phenomena and differences in the meanings attached to the same words or phrases, according to who interprets them and according to their context of appearance, according that is to their inscription in textual and social practices, is forgotten. Nor are the categories of material culture, the social, ceramic production, critically theorized.... Nowhere has Gibson considered the concept of interaction (of pottery styles?), style, the 'natural', the individual, work, goods, or the aesthetic. All are taken from common sense, all remain untheorized [Shanks and Tilley 1987b:19].

When they are theorized, categories of common sense, according to Shanks and Tilley, do not describe the world, but impose a structure on it. But a thing is not made a pot by being called a pot; rather, if it corresponds to the description "pot," then that concept can be used to discuss that thing. If the thing is not described by "pot," then use of "pot" to discuss it will fail. An apt example is "potsherd." Broken pieces of clay or rock often look like potsherds. How do we tell they are not? Lithologic and chemical analyses show the difference.

Shanks and Tilley continue their attack on ordinary categories by pointing out that no concept is comprehensive:

> There are, then, flaws in every concept and these make it necessary to refer to other concepts. Each category, apparently self-referring and inside itself, is in reality defined by what it excludes, by its chronic relation of difference to other categories. The result is a texture of webs of meaning. Meaning is never fully present, never fully disclosed, never final or conclusive; it is always deferred, in some ways absent, subject to redefinition and negotiation.... The past, then, is gone; it can't be recaptured in itself, relived as object. It only exists now in its connection with the present, in the present's practice of interpretation.... according to our contention of the mediation of the past and present, subjectivity and objectivity, theory and data, the past like an oracle *requires* interpretation [Shanks and Tilley 1987b:26–27].

But of course categories are not meant to be complete and comprehensive. The point of categorization is to specify. The Hegelian holist objection to analytic science, that it is falsifying to describe parts of a whole separately because they cannot or do not exist separately, is thus wholly off the mark. Obviously meaning holism (see Feyerabend [1975] and Rorty [1979])—the position that if the meaning of every word and sentence is a function of the meanings of all other words and sentences, then changing the meaning of one changes the meaning of all—is in some sense true. But it does not follow that analysis is falsifying or that limited science is not knowledge.

But scientists cannot win. If they err on the one hand by analyzing, they err on the other by totalizing:

> Polemically, . . . politically and rhetorically . . . reason present[s] itself as a total reality. Hence a total system is a political project of fixing everything in place, a legal system of control. In this sense we need to convict totality of non-identity with itself, to deny a totalizing systematics, the final solution to all archaeological ills. But at the same time material culture can only be understood through teasing out its relations with other entities, setting it within a relational whole, tracing its dispersal, its meaning within social practice [Shanks and Tilley 1987b:59–60].

This passage contains a complex rhetorical movement, in which Shanks and Tilley flaunt contradiction within contradiction. They depend on a totalizing holism to attack analysis, while at the same time they accuse scientists of imposing just such a holism. Again at the same time, they attack holistic scientists on the ground that analysis is necessary for understanding material culture in an ambiguous sentence that also can be read as accusing scientists of contradictorily professing holism and analysis at the same time. This is very compound. To understand such a conjury of contradictions, the reader must contemplate not content, but logical form. The implication is that consistency does not count, and the culminating attack is on the principle of noncontradiction, the basis of science, knowledge, and reason.

Shanks and Tilley talk of imposition of conceptual models on the world, as though the world is infinitely malleable. But as model failure shows, the world rejects imposition of many models. Shanks and Tilley do to science what they claim scientists do to the world, impose a model on it. But their model of science as rigidly positivist is a bad fit. Scientists are not metaphysicians.

Shanks and Tilley's organic, holist idealism is inconsistent with their Derridian (1976, 1978, 1981) scepticism. But on the Hegelian ground that all limited statements are both false and pregnant with contradiction, Shanks and Tilley claim the *right* to be inconsistent.

They present archaeologists as trying to close the distance between present and past, which past inconsistently both does not exist and is discovered by interpretation. They resolve this contradiction by saying that our present interpretation *is* the past. So it is not just that we cannot better and better describe the past. We cannot describe the past at all because there is (was) no real (objective) past.

What, then, about Shanks and Tilley's statement that

> In an investigation of the past we are necessarily involved in making the elementary *presupposition that there is an objective reality* which exists beyond the realm of experience of any individual human subject. A real past exists but the pure essence of the objectivity of that past, i.e., how it really was, eludes us in that to begin to deal with the past involves us in *decisions* or *choices* as to how we might conceive of it. This is simply an extension of saying that we are inevitably involved in a process of *selection* and *subsumption* under some description. There are real past '*facts*' but the *facts* that the archaeologist deals in are not these. The *facts* employed in any study of the past are *not independent* of their theorization. They are *in no sense given* to us but *a product* of the process of knowledge acquisition. *Ideas*, or *the means for the factual constitution of the past*, do not fall from heaven, but like all cultural *products of human activity* are *formed* in given circumstances. The facts of the archaeological case are '*real*' as opposed to 'ideal' *constructions* in that they involve a transformation of aspects of data. *The facts are thus theory-laden constructions* constrained by resistances in the data [Shanks and Tilley 1987a:110–111; italics mine].

This passage could be taken to mean that Shanks and Tilley are realists who believe in the existence of the objective world and the past after all, in which case, one could say that this is another flaunted contradiction. But careful reading with concentration on the words I have stressed and those Shanks and Tilley put in "scare quotes" supports the view that even here they are contending that the past is our construction in the present. This interpretation is supported a few lines farther along where they specify that the constraining data are those "available in sense-perception" (Shanks and Tilley 1987a:111), which puts them in the camp of Berkeleyan idealism, if not Carnapian constructivism.

In starkest terms, Shanks and Tilley's view of the past as written, as language, implies that the world is a mental creation of a human or divine mind. They try to mitigate this result by saying that

To argue that the past is chronically subject to interpretation and reinterpretation does not imply that all pasts are equally valid. Nor can it be accommodated in a shrug of the shoulders or a scepticism which would doubt the ultimate validity of any archaeology. It means the past forms an expansive space for intellectual struggle in the present and that we must accept the necessity for self-reflection and critique, situating archaeology in the present. Critique involves evaluation and makes taking sides a necessity, accepting responsibility for a decision as to why and how to write the past, and for whom. This responsibility belongs to us however much we might try to privilege the objectivity of the artefact or the neutrality of academic discourse [Shanks and Tilley 1987b:27].

But Shanks and Tilley cannot have it both ways. Their notion of "expansive space" as an arena for "intellectual struggle in the present" does not cancel their nihilation of the past. There is no past for them, but only present, politically inspired texts, descriptions of what people call "the past" to further their own political ambitions.

Shanks and Tilley (1987b:28) say that "theory as a social practice which cannot be separated from the object of archaeology [is] itself indelibly social." They slide from the fact that all theories are social products to the implication that their content always has a social bias. In a way reminiscent of Kuhn (1970), Shanks and Tilley conflate the process of social development with the study of social process. Obviously science is cultural, but cultural biases can be noticed and controlled, a rectification that Shanks and Tilley deny is possible, but that the increase of knowledge since Bacon — who outlined the main sources of bias — proves is done.

Shanks and Tilley claim that practice, in turn, cannot be separated from theory. But the radical critics' passion for critique arises just from the fact that workers manage this separation all the time. Marxists say workers have false consciousness, and want to disillusion them. But this predicament itself shows that practice need not in fact be linked to theory.

The point in actual practice is to construct society, but the point in the study of society is to understand it. Shanks and Tilley do not say merely that their goal is not to understand the world, but to change it. They deny that there is a difference. In other words, despite insisting that there are contradictions in all concepts, Shanks and Tilley ignore overlapping. Scientific descriptions are both political products and knowledge. Shanks and Tilley claim there is no difference between them. But what of Lysenko, whose politically inspired biology was disconfirmed by empirical experiment, and mass graves in Poland that confute official histories?

[W]e write archaeology now. Discourse is not identical with [does not represent] the past; concepts are not identical with [do not represent] the past. . . . archaeological discourse is a contemporary event. . . . Knowledge is not a recognition of the eternal (as implied in a logic of necessity) but is fundamentally part of contemporary social practice, rooted therefore in political relations of power [Shanks and Tilley 1987b:58–59].

Here, on duty again, is their faithful scarecrow, the dogmatic scientist who uses "a logic of necessity" to claim "recognition of the eternal," which is their way of asserting that scientists dogmatically impose totalizing models on the world that they claim represent reality exactly.

Shanks and Tilley would do well to give up logical positivism as their stalking-horse, to look instead into the potential of attacking objectivism behind books critical of scientific realism such as Churchland's (1979) *Scientific Realism and the Plasticity of Mind,* Cartwright's (1989) *Nature's Capacities and their Measurement,* and van Fraassen's *Laws and Symmetry* (1989), though none of these philosophers believe the world is the way it is just because we impose categorial schemes on it.

Shanks and Tilley continue that all interpretations are local power plays:

We conceive interpretation as an act renouncing finality, as a denial of universal history, the idea of coherent unity and completed development. Interpretation is associated with a strategic knowledge (Shanks and Tilley, 1987[a], ch. 5), not abstracted from its social conditions of production, but polemically responding to specific conditions, attending to historical and political circumstances, a knowledge rooted in contemporary structures of power [Shanks and Tilley 1987b:60].

Among techniques especially congenial to maintenance of power, Shanks and Tilley single out systems theory:

Systems theory, as pre-defined method based on immediate objective appearance, is a theory of conservative politics, conservative in that it will lend support to anything that is, the immediate 'reality' of any social form. In this sense, systems theory is not only conservative, it is immoral in its acceptance of any empirical state as a state for the good. For the sake of an abstract value of equilibrium, systems theory implicitly justifies oppression. In identifying what is with what should be, it creates a tidy, ordered and timeless world. The message of systems theory is that 'goodness' is to be found in social stability while social unrest is an unfortunate 'pathology' [Shanks and Tilley 1987a:52–53].

It is pertinent here to quote Hume (1955 [1734]:469) who says he often has observed that an "author proceeds for some time in the ordinary way of reasoning, and ... makes observations concerning human affairs; when of a sudden I am surpriz'd to find, that instead of the usual copulations of propositions, *is,* and *is not,* I meet with no proposition that is not connected with an *ought, or ought not."*

It is not systems theorists who mistake what is for what ought to be. Shanks and Tilley deny the distinction between fact and value by committing the genetic fallacy—that origin determines nature. They argue that because human beings are reared in sociopolitical circumstances, all their categorial schemes, theories, language games, and activities contain ineradicable sociopolitical agendas that are imposed whenever they are used. Shanks and Tilley deny that one can be interested in knowledge for knowledge's sake (if you are, you are on the side of political conservatism), or that you can undertake objective research in science (because whether you want to think about it or not, the military–industrial–academic complex is paying you to help maintain power and oppress people, so you are immoral), or that any human activity at all is value free (because interests infect all facts, so all facts are value laden).

When Shanks and Tilley (1987a:55) say "Humans must be conceived as sentient social beings living in a symbolically structured reality which is, essentially, of their own creation," they are insisting on *must be,* when they have evidence at most for *can be.* Pascal argued fallaciously that there is only one choice, either you believe in the Christian God or not, and if not you will go to hell; so because agnosticism is as bad as atheism, you'd better believe, for there is no harm in believing if God does not exist, but plenty even in sitting on the fence if He does. Similarly, critical theorists say we have only one choice. Either we no not believe that all our activities are necessarily political, in which case we are on the side of the status quo, or else we believe it, and thus are morally obliged to oppose the (always bad) status quo.

Shanks and Tilley (1987a:66–67) say "archaeology is a rhetorical practice, historically situated, part of contemporary society and inherently political." If we do not believe this, the capitalists have us in their bag. If we do believe it, the only moral thing to do is to abolish scientific archaeology to write archaeology as propaganda against established political power.

AGAINST SHANKS AND TILLEY

How can Shanks and Tilley make such overriding pronouncements? They do it as we all do, by rising above a given vernacular and talking about it in another. Socrates, Augustine, Descartes, and recently Leiber (1988) and Lehrer (1990) show that self-consciousness is a standing above one's thoughts and actions to observe and criticize them from a metalevel. The biases that Shanks and Tilley say cannot be overcome are corrected for by using ordinary language as a metalanguage to critique the technical language of science. If this metalanguage approach were impossible, one could speak neither of contradictions in concepts, nor of their resolutions, which are not apparent within language games, theories, and categorial schemes, but are detected only in metalanguage discussion of them. Shanks and Tilley say that one cannot get outside a given language system, but they do it all the time.

But can you get outside language itself? What about the metalanguage? You can talk about it with another metalanguage. And does this lead to an infinite regress? Not for human beings, because we don't have the ability to mount an infinite ladder, nor the need, given that ordinary language is good enough for discussing most language games, and the language of science can be used to criticize ordinary language. And is this not a circle? No, it's a spiral. The one is used to improve the other, and the result is better representations by each.

So! You assume there is an objective world. Not assume, just hypothesize. All the sceptical reasons remain for doubting that our concepts represent the real world, that there is a real world. But sceptical arguments apply only against dogmatists who claim to have certain knowledge. Scientists claim to have neither the correct theory of the world nor certain knowledge. As a scientist, I don't have to have absolute certainty. All I need is assurance that my understanding and knowledge of the world is supported empirically. I have more evidence of this than I do that conceptual schemes are imposed on the world to gain power and prestige, or that the world itself is only a text.

Shanks and Tilley represent the social construction of reality as epiphenomenally unconnected either logically or causally with material culture. They insist that archaeology should be about this product of thinking, but they paradoxically also show that it is quite impossible ever to find out what ancient people thought. One cannot derive social structure from material structure because material structure in itself means nothing and is not a set of signs (although sometimes they say contradictorily that it is), and because a large number of sociocultural manifestations are consistent with any given material culture. So what do Shanks and Tilley propose? They propose that we make it up, not out of whole cloth, but out of the sociopolitical power matrix we favor.

One possible interpretation of these two books is that they are a put-on. Such high shenanigans are not unknown among deconstructionists (Evans 1990). Another is that Shanks and Tilley really intend the nihilist deconstruction of archaeology. But they are too earnest for a put-on, and it does not seem likely that total deconstruction is their intent, given how insistently they present their own sociopolitical preference. Disengagement is not evident in a plea like the following: "A radical value-committed archaeology involves a way of living that requires that intellectual struggle be carried into the heart of the discipline, on a daily basis as a willed personal act, and irrespective of the possible personal consequences of the reactions of those in authority" (Shanks and Tilley 1987b:206).

So they construct archaeology. They write it from the standpoint of their present interests in prestige and power. "Archaeology's appropriation of the past," Shanks and Tilley (1987b:136) testify, "is a moral and political act": "Choosing a past, that is, constituting a past, is choosing a future; the ideology of contemporary archaeology's temporality is that it is imposing a Western [capitalist] valuation of measured abstract [commodified] time on a multitude of pasts which cannot answer for themselves—even the dead aren't safe."

But do Shanks and Tilley think the honorable dead *really* ever were? And can we be sure Shanks and Tilley will save them? Just as the logical positivists have no grounds on which to validate their principles, neither do Shanks and Tilley have any grounds for talking about imposing present ideologies on the past, and certainly none for talking about the dead, about whom, if you take Shanks and Tilley seriously, you can say or know nothing at all, not even that they ever existed:

> Now the archaeological event does not exist: the event has no existential reality. There is no stable 'event', singular objective occurrence, 'this happened then'. . . . An event is an abstraction, but an abstraction from a configuration of which it is a component; an event only makes sense in terms of a meaningful whole, a historical plot. . . . So the practice of archaeology is a construction of pasts. It establishes event as event, artefact as artefact. The event emerges from archaeology; the event, time, duration is inscription. . . . metaphor and allegory are central to archaeology; archaeology is unavoidably historio-*graphesis*. It is a system of regimes for production of the 'past' [Shanks and Tilley 1987b:135].

Shanks and Tilley say oracularly that there are other ways of knowing, but they do not reveal them, and their own examples—the beaker and beer-can studies (Shanks and Tilley 1987a:135–240)—are within conventional science. In these studies, Shanks and Tilley (1987a:173–175) attack science by collecting beer cans with a genially casual sampling strategy calculated to drive purists up the wall. Then they analyze and generalize with graphs and calculations, just like real scientists.

In their two studies, Shanks and Tilley derive numerous lawlike generalizations about the spatial relations of material goods to graves, state policy to beer advertising, and so on. They say these generalizations are not meant to apply beyond the material being studied. But whether or not they have wide application remains to be checked by empirical tests. Shanks and Tilley are wrong in what they say about science, but if you watch what they do (which they deny is meant to support their thesis or to be examples of the method they would propose to replace science [Shanks and Tilley 1987a:3]), you see that what they do as archaeologists is science.

Another contradiction in Shanks and Tilley's practice is their combination of extreme particularlism with their holist attack on analysis and contemporary science. Thus they claim that to say anything about anything, one must say everything about everything. Any attempt to say less is falsifying. On the other hand, they want archaeologists to concentrate on knowledge of particular individual human beings.

So how does one read a text full of such contradictions? You cannot take it literally, you have to read for what it says overall. Shanks and Tilley make a mockery of science, reason, and archaeology. They sincerely care about individuals, but somewhere along the line they have missed the point that technology does not kill people, people kill people. Archaeology can be, but is neither necessarily, nor nothing but, the handmaid of capitalism. Nor should it be, as Shanks and Tilley urge, purposefully politicized. As they themselves make clear, it is hard enough already to control for unintended sociopolitical bias.

In particular, Shanks and Tilley attack functionalism because, they say, it implies that the status quo is good and thus can be used to support any established system. Thus they present Talcot Parsons as a conservative functionalist who supports capitalism. They claim that Parsons says that

capitalist America happens, conveniently, to embody all those evolutionary universals which, according to Parsons, have ever been invented. Furthermore, the communist nations are structurally unsound, inherently unstable, an evolutionary dead end:

I must maintain that communist totalitarian organization will probably not fully match 'democracy' in political and integrative capacity in the long run. I do indeed predict that it will prove to be unstable and will either make adjustments in the general direction of electoral democracy or . . . 'regress' into . . . less advanced and politically less effective forms of organization [Shanks and Tilley's deletions] (Parsons, 1964, p. 356).

In part, this is because 'those that restrict [the markets and money system] too drastically are likely to suffer from severe adaptive disadvantages in the long run' (ibid., p. 350). Had Parsons not assigned technology to the status of an evolutionary prerequisite but to an evolutionary universal, the sociopolitical conclusions that he draws regarding the relative merits of American and Soviet society might not have been so readily forthcoming [Shanks and Tilley 1987b:162–163].

Now note that Parsons describes totalitarian communism as disfunctional after that system had been the status quo in the Soviet Union for some forty years. We can test his grand societal theory that the system will collapse by using Hume's method of observing current events. In 1989/1990, seventy years after its establishment, the Soviet system is collapsing. On this test, Parsons seems so far vindicated.

Again note that Parsons says only that functionalism shows which systems work and why. Does Parsons then mean that disfunctional systems are bad and functional systems good? Not at all. Shanks and Tilley make that equation of fact and value, not Parsons.

Is totalitarian communism failing because capitalist ideology is now being imposed, or because it is disfunctional? Some of both, you say? Perhaps. But the Soviet experience seems most strongly to disconfirm Shanks and Tilley's thesis that sociopolitical systems do not grow out of objective circumstances but are imposed on people, for even with all the power Stalin commanded, a system cannot be permanently imposed if it does not fit actual conditions.

In the end, what is one to make of all this? Not much. Practicing archaeologists adopt scientific techniques not because of arguments about theory, but because their use leads to knowledge and understanding. Shanks and Tilley's rallying cry to make archaeology into culture critique, to write archaeology not to understand the past but to change the future, will not be heeded by many working archaeologists. Stalinism has demonstrated that writing history to support politics does not work. People do not like to be oppressed, which is a lawlike generalization about human beings assumed in Shanks and Tilley's texts. People remember, people are not stupid, and walls come tumbling down.

That people are not stupid is the main thing Shanks and Tilley forget. Scientists are not dupes. Archaeologists are not morons. But Shanks and Tilley think archaeologists are slow, subject to fads, and none too bright. Archaeologists have been bamboozled. They yearn for "the antiseptic white coat" of the scientist, have been co-opted by capitalism, and must be rescued by our heroes.

Archaeology is in fact a derivative science. It depends on all the other sciences (Watson 1972, 1976). But scientific results are so impressive that Shanks and Tilley's claim that science is just a categorial scheme imposed by capitalists will cause little alarm among practicing archaeologists. Their books, however, make a fun read, recommended to positivists not prone to high blood pressure.

So is it worth spelling these things out? I suppose so. One presumes that Shanks and Tilley's books will enjoy a certain success among antiscience archaeologists and anthropologists. It is as well, probably, to provide a critique that is measured (they would say commodifying), reasonable (they would say falsely generalizing), and careful (they would say conservative, and American to boot [Shanks and Tilley 1989:52]) by someone who appreciates practical scientific knowledge and archaeology, and who is not hung up on sceptical word games parading in the guise of the latest and best thing in philosophy.

Acknowledgments. For critical readings of various versions of this paper I thank Marc Ereshefsky, Roger Gibson, Patty Jo Watson, Alison Wylie, the members of the 1990 Washington University Faculty Seminar, and most especially Paul Roth.

REFERENCES CITED

Barnes, B.
1984   *T. S. Kuhn and Social Science.* Columbia University Press, New York.
Bergmann, G.
1954   *The Metaphysics of Logical Positivism.* Longmans, Green, London.
Binford, L. R.
1986   In Pursuit of the Future. In *American Archaeology Past and Future: A Celebration of the Society for American Archaeology, 1935–1985,* edited by D. J. Meltzer, D. D. Fowler, and J. A. Sabloff, pp. 459–479. Smithsonian Institution Press, Washington, D.C.
1987   Data, Relativism, and Archaeological Science. *Man* (n.s.) 22:391–404.
1989   *Debating Archaeology.* Academic Press, New York.
Bloor, D.
1983   *Wittgenstein and Social Theory.* Columbia University Press, New York.
Cartwright, N.
1989   *Nature's Capacities and their Measurements.* Oxford University Press, Oxford.
Chippendale, C.
1988   Ambition, Deference and Discrepancy: The Intellectual Place of Post-processual Archaeology. Paper presented at the 10th Annual Meeting of the Theoretical Archaeology Group, Sheffield, England.
Churchland, P. M.
1979   *Scientific Realism and the Plasticity of Mind.* Cambridge University Press, Cambridge.
Collingwood, R. G.
1946   *The Idea of History.* Oxford University Press, Oxford.
Derrida, J.
1976   *Of Grammatology.* Johns Hopkins Press, Baltimore.
1978   Structure, Sign, and Play in the Discourses of the Human Sciences. In *Writing and Difference,* by J. Derrida, pp. 278–293. Routledge and Kegan Paul, London.
1981   Plato's Pharmacy. In *Dissemination,* by J. Derrida, pp. 61–172. Athlone Press, London.
Dilthey, W.
1954 [1907]   *The Essence of Philosophy.* University of North Carolina Press, Chapel Hill.
Earle, T. K., and R. W. Preucel
1987   Processual Archaeology and the Radical Critique. *Current Anthropology* 28:501–513, 525–538.
Evans, C. C.
1990   *Strategies of Deconstruction: Derrida and The Myth of the Voice.* University of Minnesota Press, Minneapolis.
Feyerabend, P.
1975   *Against Method.* New Left Books, London.
Fritz, J., and F. Plog
1970   The Nature of Archaeological Explanation. *American Antiquity* 35:405–412.
Gellner, E.
1982   What is Structuralisme? In *Theory and Explanation in Archaeology: The Southampton Conference,* edited by C. Renfrew, M. J. Rowlands, and B. A. Segraves, pp. 97–123. Academic Press, New York.
Gibson, A. M.
1982   *Beaker Domestic Sites: A Study of the Domestic Pottery of the Late Third and Early Second Millenia B.C. in the British Isles.* BAR International Series 186. British Archaeological Reports, Oxford.

Glymour, C.
  1980   *Theory and Evidence.* Princeton University Press, Princeton.
Hempel, C. G.
  1959   The Function of General Laws in History. In *Theories of History,* edited by P. Gardner, pp. 344–356. Free Press, New York.
  1965   *Aspects of Scientific Explanation and Other Essays in the Philosophy of Science.* Free Press, New York.
  1966   *Philosophy of Natural Science.* Prentice-Hall, Englewood Cliffs.
Hodder, I.
  1984   Archaeology in 1984. *Antiquity* 58:25–32.
  1987   Comments on Earle and Preucel. *Current Anthropology* 28:516–517.
Hume, D.
  1955 [1734] *A Treatise of Human Nature: Being an Attempt to Introduce the Experimental Method of Reasoning into Moral Subjects.* Clarendon Press, Oxford.
Kuhn, T. S.
  1970   *The Structure of Scientific Revolutions.* 2nd ed. University of Chicago Press, Chicago.
Lehrer, K.
  1990   *Metamind.* Clarendon Press, Oxford.
Leiber, J.
  1988   "Cartesian" Linguistics? *Philosophia* 18:309–346.
Morgan, C. G.
  1973   Archaeology and Explanation. *World Archaeology* 4:259–276.
Parsons, T.
  1964   Evolutionary Universals in Society. *American Sociological Journal* 29:329–357.
Renfrew, C., M. J. Rowlands, and B. A. Segraves (editors)
  1982   *Theory and Explanation in Archaeology: The Southampton Conference.* Academic Press, New York.
Rorty, R.
  1979   *Philosophy and the Mirror of Nature.* Princeton University Press, Princeton.
Roth, P.
  1987   *Meaning and Method in the Social Sciences: A Case for Methodological Pluralism.* Cornell University Press, Ithaca.
Salmon, M.
  1982   *Philosophy and Archaeology.* Academic Press, New York.
Schiffer, M. B.
  1988   The Structure of Archaeological Theory. *American Antiquity* 33:461–485.
Shanks, M., and C. Tilley
  1987a *Re-Constructing Archaeology.* Cambridge University Press, Cambridge.
  1987b *Social Theory and Archaeology.* Polity Press, London.
  1989   Archaeology into the 1990s. *Norwegian Archaeological Review* 22:1–54.
Van Fraassen, B. C.
  1989   *Laws and Symmetry.* Clarendon Press, Oxford.
Watson, P. J.
  1990a The Razor's Edge: Symbolic-Structuralist Archeology and the Expansion of Archeological Inference. *American Anthropologist* 92:613–629.
  1990b A Parochial Primer: The New Dissonance as Seen from the Midcontinental U. S. A. In *Processualist vs. Post-Processualist Archaeology,* edited by R. Preucel. Southern Illinois University Press, Carbondale, in press.
Watson, P. J., S. A. LeBlanc, and C. L. Redman
  1971   *Explanation in Archeology: An Explicitly Scientific Approach.* Columbia University Press, New York.
  1974   The Covering Law Model in Archaeology: Practical Uses and Formal Interpretations. *World Archaeology* 6:125–132.
  1984   *Archeological Explanation: The Scientific Method in Archeology.* Columbia University Press, New York.
Watson, R. A.
  1972   The "New Archeology" of the 1960s. *Antiquity* 46:210–215.
  1976   Inference in Archaeology. *American Antiquity* 41:58–66.
Wylie, A.
  1989   Archaeological Cables and Tacking: The Implications of Practices for Bernstein's "Options Beyond Objectivism and Relativism." *Philosophy of the Social Sciences* 19:1–18.
  1990   A Proliferation of New Archaeologies: Scepticism, Processualism, and Post-Processualism. Ms. in possession of author.

Received March 1, 1990; accepted June 4, 1990

STYLE AND FUNCTION: A FUNDAMENTAL DICHOTOMY

Robert C. Dunnell

Our understanding of the archaeological record has been developed under the culture history paradigm. Its fundamental structure is shown to be stylistic; this characteristic, coupled with historical factors, is seen as the major reason why evolutionary processes have not been extensively employed in explaining cultural change. Consideration of an evolutionary approach suggests that such processes as natural selection have considerable explanatory potential, but it is also suggested that a substantial segment of the archaeological record is not best understood in terms of adaptation. The potential of an evolutionary approach cannot be realized without making a fundamental distinction between functions, accountable in terms of evolutionary processes, and style, accountable in terms of stochastic processes.

AN INCREASINGLY LARGE NUMBER of archaeologists are committed to a scientific approach that is linked at some level with both ecological and evolutionary concepts. In the last two decades, archaeology has moved decisively in the direction of more sophisticated analysis and procedural rigor. In particular, quantitative analysis, recognition of the relevance of probability sampling, and multidisciplinary efforts have made lasting contributions. Methodologically, archaeology has become more scientific.

Far less success is evident if our explanation and understanding of the archaeological record are considered. There have been changes to be sure. New discoveries have extended our knowledge of the archaeological record. New dating methods have revolutionized chronology. The application of specific ecological concepts has enriched our appreciation of space and population. But the character of our understanding of the past has not changed appreciably. And evolution, an important ingredient in the initial formulation of the processual approach, has yet to assume a major role in constructing either specific explanations or a more comprehensive understanding of the past.

I am inclined to attribute this failure to some high level deficiencies: (1) the absence and/or inappropriate formulation of disciplinary goals; (2) the failure to *invent* any specifically archaeological theory of universal scope; and (3) the persistent use of concepts developed under older paradigms that did not espouse scientific or evolutionary goals. Certainly there are more mundane reasons for a lack of progress, not the least of which is the necessity of acquiring new, better controlled data for many critical problems.

The issue that I want to address is whether the archaeological record can be effectively explained within an evolutionary framework that is also scientific, and if so, precisely what aspects of the record lend themselves to this treatment. At the same time, it is important to outline why we have not made substantial progress in this direction, to identify the problem areas, and to suggest at least the general direction in which solutions might be sought.

SOME PARAMETERS OF THE GENERAL PROBLEM

Archaeology is still largely atheoretical. Most of the discussion labelled theoretical is either concerned with the application of non-archaeological theory and method to archaeological problems or is limited to a small segment of the total archaeological endeavor.

Progress has been impeded by ambiguities introduced in the discussions themselves. Identical terms are given different meanings by different authors; different authors use different terms to mean the same thing. There is no evident agreement as to what archaeological laws are, if there are any, or how they should be developed if they are both possible and desirable. Programmatic statements may draw their rationale from one frame of reference while applications draw theirs from another.

Becoming scientific has been an explicit goal of many archaeologists (Watson, LeBlanc, and Redman 1971) and some real progress has been made; however, this transition is still incomplete. Scientific explanations employ both induction and deduction in important definable roles. Discovery and invention are both part of the process. Although we have developed an awareness of these aspects of explanation during the past decade, we have yet to resolve most of the ambiguities that surround making assessments of the value of particular explanations or answers. It is important to recognize that two *kinds* of judgments are employed in a scientific framework. The truth of an answer to an equation is assessed by examining *how* the answer was obtained by establishing that all of the mathematical conventions involved have been properly employed. This kind of standard I will term a *ritualistic judgment*. To decide whether the equation was the appropriate one to relate the variables it includes is established by ascertaining if the use of the equation predicts the observed values in one or more cases involving its variables. To this kind of standard, I will apply the term *performance judgment*. The unquestioned success of the sciences is linked to their ultimate recourse to the performance standard and the use of this standard to select their ritualistic ones. Ritualistic standards, by themselves, are not adequate in a scientific frame; all scholarship, scientific or not, employs ritualistic standards.

By and large, archaeology has tried to become scientific by adopting the ritualistic judgments of science without the commensurate performance criteria. This has led to some curious contributions in which new methods and techniques are proposed and asserted to be good because they produce results identical or compatible with those of approaches rejected by the authors (e.g., Sackett 1966; Whallon 1972). The emphasis of ritualistic standards is evident in such comprehensive treatments as *Analytical Archaeology* (Clarke 1968) and *Explanation in Archeology* (Watson, LeBlanc, and Redman 1971). Procedural rigor is, of course, absolutely essential to the transition to a scientific archaeology, but it is only part of the process. Before analytical methods can be adopted as standards, it is important to show that their use leads to solutions that are acceptable in performance terms. In my view, this is where we fall down. How can we tell that a rigorously derived answer is also "correct" in some sense? This is a difficult task in the absence of clearcut disciplinary goals that are cast in concrete terms. Our explanations are not really expected to "do" anything or have performance consequences; we hide this by calling them interpretations. To resolve this will require some agreement on the purpose of archaeology. Whether "becoming scientific" is virtuous depends heavily upon the answer. The latent evolutionary goals of processual archaeologists, it seems to me, provide both this potential and a means of linking past and present in a manner conducive to making performance judgments.

Symptoms of this incomplete transition to science are apparent in many areas of archaeological endeavor. A common one is borrowing techniques from other, more scientific disciplines and then rummaging around in the archaeological record to find some data to which they can be applied (Service 1969). The current flurry of interest in the philosophy of science is another. Placed in perspective, the philosophy of science attempts to account for the structure of scientific inquiry. To have a philosophy of science implies that you have a science. The appeal to this discipline is quite consonant with the emphasis on the ritualistic aspects of science and the apparent view that archaeology need only assume scientific rigor to become a science. Unfortunately, there are different accounts of how science works or ought to work (c.f., Hempel 1965; Morgan 1973; Meehan 1968). While a thorough acquaintance with the philosophy of science is valuable, it is not by itself an adequate game plan for becoming a science.

THREE ARCHAEOLOGICAL PARADIGMS

To identify the reasons why archaeology has failed to make more extensive use of evolutionary premises and complete the transition to a scientific approach requires a brief historical review. Three distinct and internally coherent approaches can be distinguished: culture history, cultural reconstructionism, and processual archaeology (Dunnell 1971a; see also Binford 1968; Deetz 1970).

Culture History

The earliest paradigm, and the one that still guides a substantial segment of archaeological research, is culture history. Retrospectively, when archaeology emerged as a distinct intellectual tradition in the mid-nineteenth century, its major accomplishment was the documentation of a human past that was qualitatively different from contemporary and historically documented human conditions. Demonstration of the antiquity of a human presence through bones and artifacts created the time-depth that made a qualitatively different past both possible and necessary. The character of the record, the Darwinian revolution, and the variability of living populations acted to make change a reasonable assumption. Having established a niche for archaeology, subsequent activity within this paradigm has largely been concerned with more detailed description of the archaeological record in an increasingly finer and more reliable time-space framework.

To a great degree, culture historical understanding relies on "common sense," i.e., it employs explanatory conventions that are implicit in our own cultural background. This is why culture historians generally display so little interest in theory. The role that explicit theoretical formulations play in the sciences are preempted by the "common sense" of western culture. As a result, conclusions seem self-evident once the requisite amount of data has been acquired. "Common sense," however, has little integrative power in the expanded temporal dimension of the archaeologist. Consequently, culture historians had to invent methods to deal with time and in this they followed Worsaae's dictum (Daniel 1950:47) on the utility of style in temporal discrimination. The reliance upon a common cultural background as a vehicle of understanding has many manifestations. One is evident in the ontological developmental organization of the archaeological record. Since we are the most "advanced" of contemporary cultures on a global scale, the archaeological record is often implicitly viewed as the development of culture from an initial non-cultural starting point to ourselves. The interest of culture historians in such global abstractions has varied over time, but when they have attempted it, it assumes this unilinear character.

In reality there is little of the culture history approach that can be characterized as evolutionary. In the early years of the paradigm, evolution was used as a justification for and a summary of the obvious tendency for temporal development of complexity and diversity in the archaeological record. Culture history did not use evolutionary processes to create the understanding, but employed a mixture of common sense and Worsaae's culture historical processes. One thing changes and blends into another, always more or less headed in the direction of complex, agricultural sedentary systems. Even today, there can be little doubt that all archaeologists tend to conceive of the past in these highly ethnocentric terms. Because the understanding is intrinsic to our own culture, this is a difficult obstacle to overcome. The widespread rejection of the scientific and even reconstructionist paradigms by culture historians is not so much a matter of specific objections as it is of a lack of interest because the newer paradigms are not perceived as relevant or necessary.

Cultural Reconstructionism

A second paradigm, cultural reconstructionism, began to emerge in the late 19th century but gained little notice until the late 1930s and 1940s. Cultural reconstructionism is a reaction to culture history that has its roots in the association of archaeology and anthropology in North America and in the observation that culture history is not very anthropological.

Adopting sociocultural anthropology as a model for the conduct of archaeological research had important consequences that contrasted markedly with culture history. Instead of treating the archaeological record as a set of traits that could vary independently, an anthropological view forced archaeologists to see the record as the material residue of functioning systems in which one element had entailments in others. The site, which for culture historians was a locus of traits representative of an area and period, became the principal investigatory universe and variability within this unit became a major focus of analysis. Measured against sociocultural data, the archaeological record is impoverished and incomplete. Thus, it became imperative to reconstruct the "behavioral correlates" of the record so that it could be integrated with anthropology and accounted for in anthropological terms. The end product is essentially where the ethnologist begins, a transactional description. If the archaeologist goes beyond this, he is acting as an anthropologist. Archaeological theory has little role in this approach since the theory required for explanation is anthropological, not archaeological.

The main strategy for reconstruction is one of uniformitarian analogy with contemporary behavioral settings, a process usually termed ethnographic analogy. Reconstruction, whether archaeological or not, places a heavy emphasis on proper procedure and ritualistic judgments because there is no unambiguous way to apply performance standards to its particularistic products. This structural problem with ethnographic analogy has been critiqued many times (e.g., Slotkin 1952; Mac-White 1956; Longacre 1970; Dunnell 1971b, 1978; Sabloff, Beale and Kurland 1973). Nonetheless, its use persists.

Because of the historical coincidence of this paradigm with the rise of scientific methods in archaeology, the two are often treated as the same thing. The "New Archaeology" (Caldwell 1959), for example, subsumes all of the approaches that contrast with culture history. Many of the scientific techniques, most especially inductive statistics, have found broad applications within the cultural reconstructionist paradigm. As a result, "anthropological" has been equated with scientific. This confusion has blunted critiques of reconstructionism because of the faith placed in scientific approaches.

Whereas culture history can be viewed in the main as ethnocentric and producing understandings that are intrinsic to western culture, the reconstructionists provide a relativistic framework with understandings that are intrinsic to the cultures that form its subject matter. The approach has contributed important notions of spatial variability and a serious interest in function, both of which were lacking in culture history. And it is largely responsible for the insistence on methodological rigor. In assuming a particularist stance, this paradigm has not made use of evolutionary premises; particularistic reconstruction must deny evolution if it is to be applied to the past. Because of its particularistic character, its major contributions have been methodological. It has had little impact on a substantive understanding of the human past on a global scale. That understanding is still culture historical in nature.

Processual or Scientific Archaeology

The processual paradigm is still more of a goal than a reality. In part this can be attributed to the short period of serious interest in the approach, but even more important are the limitations of the earlier paradigms on which it has had to draw and confusion with the reconstructionist position. Within this incipient paradigm, the purpose of archaeology is seen as generating laws that account for cultural change; the paradigm is frankly evolutionary in character (Leone 1972:26). This approach assumes that archaeological explanations must be extrinsic to both the culture of the investigator and that of the subject populations; in short, it assumes that an explicit archaeological theory will be developed.

Many scientific methods have been explored, but relatively few concepts have been developed. Certainly, no detailed archaeological framework has been invented to integrate our methodological advances. Typical of this situation is Binford's definition of culture as man's "extrasomatic adaptive system" (1965:205) and its subsequent use. Certainly this definition or a similar one is key to a scientific approach cast in evolutionary terms. In practice, the systemic aspects of the definition have been emphasized as a means of compensating for the incompleteness of the archaeological record in the reconstructionist framework. The adaptive aspects of the definition that potentially articulate with evolution in general and natural selection in particular have been largely ignored. When adaptation has been treated, the tendency has been to employ it in a synchronic ecological framework rather than an evolutionary one.

If the methodological sophistication that is really associated with the reconstructionists and the philosophical debate on how we should go about becoming a science are swept aside, we are left with little more than a statement of purpose. Two general notions that stem from our common sense approach have prevented further development: (1) a synchronic view of time (Plog 1974:43-45) carried over from both the culture historical and cultural reconstructionist paradigms that is incompatible with evolution and forces us to conceive of time as a sequence of homogeneous periods or systems rather than as continuous change; and (2) a belief that the appropriate subject matter is behavior rather than the hard phenomena of the archaeological record. This belief, inherited from the reconstructionists, forces us to manipulate inferences instead of phenomena and thereby deprives us of FULL USE of performance standards. As Leone (1972:25-26) implies, neither of these assumptions is necessary. This is not to say, however, that synchronic formulations of behavioral reconstructions are without ultimate value, only that they cannot be the foundation of an approach that professes to be both scientific and evolutionary.

ELEMENTS OF A SCIENTIFIC EVOLUTIONARY APPROACH

Any new paradigm must draw upon previous formulations. In the case of archaeology, serious deficiencies have been identified in both earlier paradigms measured against the goals set by the processual or scientific approach. The effects of these deficiencies in the earlier paradigms on the basic units that we use to describe and explain the archaeological record must be identified before specific suggestions for the development of an evolutionary paradigm can be suggested.

Archaeological Units

The terms we use to create archaeological data determine to a large degree the kind of subsequent operations that can be performed on these data (Binford 1968:23; Dunnell 1971a:59). Culture history employs two kinds of units. "Functional" units are intended to render sensible in ordinary terms the content of the past. These are drawn in an unstructured fashion from common experience. Thus we have axes, hoes, potsherds, and figurines. Because the process of unit definition is complex, wholly intuitive, and incidental to the main culture historical task, it is neither consistent nor easily reconstructed.

The units employed for chronological purposes are another matter. The process for their creation is certainly intuitive in most cases, but these units, usually called types, are the product of a distinctly archaeological analysis and are tested against a stylistic distributional model sometimes termed the "historical significance" criterion. Types are reformulated until they display the temporal-spatial contiguity required by this criterion (Krieger 1944; Ford 1954b). Because of the performance test employed, these types can be used to create chronologies using methods like seriation. Larger units defined by them retain the characteristic of temporal-spatial contiguity and produce phases and cultures that occur in spatially coherent areas over definite periods of time (e.g., Gifford 1960). In practice, because the process is intuitive and learned by imitative apprenticeship, any given application usually abounds with inconsistencies. Defining characteristics are dominantly stylistic but the test of historical significance does not exclude technological or functional attributes if they change over time in particular areas. Consequently, particular formulations often mix criteria (Jelinek 1976:26).

The reconstructionists pay more attention to functional units, largely by making the analogic process by which they are created more explicit and rigorous. Even with this improvement, functional units have not assumed an importance comparable to that of historical types. There are two reasons for this. First, functional units do not have distributional characteristics that allow them to structure the archaeological record in a time-space framework outside local areas. Second, the notion of function is not an archaeological concept comparable to "historical significance." It is an English word accompanied by all the behavioral connotations and denotations common to words from a natural language. The reconstructionists have simply made more explicit what the culture historians had been doing with function all along. The basic question still being asked is whether an object is an ax, or an adze, or an arrowhead. Deceptively, the "laws" (Fritz and Plog 1970) by which such naming takes place are not archaeological propositions but common cultural conventions of object naming enriched by an acquaintance with the ethnographic record. Thus, sense can be made of the archaeological record without recourse to explicit theory because once objects are named in English, they can be manipulated with common sense. Characteristically, for analogic constructions that employ uniformitarian principles, the products are not testable in performance terms (Sabloff, Beale, and Kurland 1973). Hence the concern with how the analogy is drawn (Ascher 1961; Binford 1967).

Types of a different sort were also developed on the basis of element configurations within particular collections of artifacts (e.g., Spaulding 1953). The rationale for the inductive statistical procedures employed did not come from the identification of a particular purpose they were intended to serve but lay instead in ritualistic judgments, namely that the procedures were explicit, rigorous, and repeatable. The resulting types are *real* because they can be shown to *exist* in the data. The procedures are attractive because of the methodological elegance, but the products, "statistical types," have not become a major force beyond the description of particular assemblages. The rationale for the approach is quite compatible with the reconstructionist paradigm because in a real way these procedures force the data to speak and the units are demonstrably intrinsic to the subject matter. The debate between Ford and Spaulding (Spaulding 1953, 1954; Ford 1954a, 1954b) centered on this issue. Ford, as a culture historian par excellence, understood intuitively that Spaulding's methods did not produce types that could be *used* for anything, and thus he felt compelled to reject the method. On the other hand, the characteristically intuitive rationale of culture history made Ford unable to cope with the methodological rigor of Spaulding's elegant argument. In the end, most archaeologists working with types cite Spaulding but follow Ford.

Recent years have seen considerable experimentation and elaboration of techniques for unit formation (see Doran and Hodson 1975 for a critical review of many techniques), basically all in the inductive reconstructionist mode established by Spaulding, even though many of the techniques are radically different in technical detail. These discussions are focused on the virtues of particular computational and statistical alternatives and omit discussion of archaeological theory, meaning, or utility of the products beyond assemblage description. The source of the initial variables remains intuitive and is not adequately addressed in any of these discussions. No particular procedure has produced a set of units that can replace the culture historical types.

In the last analysis, the reconstructionists contributed little to unit formation (although many of the techniques are powerful tools in other contexts). They have exposed the implicit, sloppy character of culture historical units but they have failed to improve the formulation of culture historical units or replace them with different units of equally broad scope. The fundamental structure of the archaeological record as we know it is a product of the culture history paradigm and its dominantly stylistic units: "our perception and use of the archaeological record" (Binford 1968:23) has not changed. The question that must be faced by processualists is a simple one: Can style be explained within a scientific and evolutionary framework with laws of cultural change? The answer, at least at a level that will address the evolutionary character of the record, is unfortunately, no. To explain this negative assessment and to suggest a new direction requires that we examine characteristics of stylistic formulations in the context of evolutionary theory.

Evolutionary Archaeology

Evolutionary archaeology should be understood as an explanatory framework that accounts for the structure and change evident in the archaeological record in terms of evolutionary processes (natural selection, flow, mutation, drift) either identical to or analogous with these processes as specified in neo-Darwinian evolutionary theory. This does not imply that cultural and genetic phenomena are identical. Obviously the processes themselves or the entities upon which they act must be redefined from the biological context unless one is prepared to assert that all cultural phenomena are genetically determined. Binford's "systemic" definition of culture provides a starting point, although the definition is better referred to as an "adaptive" one. The definition, however, may not be complete. For example, does the adaptive clause exclude a major segment of the phenomena that both archaeologists and anthropologists consider relevant and cultural? This question and similar questions cannot be addressed until both the implications of the definition and the implied evolutionary processes have been explored more thoroughly.

The first consequence we encounter in assuming an evolutionary point of view is that the specific origin or invention of new elements becomes a trivial inquiry. What is important is how and why a new element becomes fixed or accepted (Barnett 1953:291) and thus visable in the archaeological record. The overridingly important evolutionary mechanism in this process is natural selection. Invention is analogous to mutation in biological systems. On a global scale, it is probably a useful heuristic position to assume that invention is a random phenomenon, and, thus, that the total number of people is the major constraint on the raw material of culture change. Regional partitioning of this pool may be an effective account for more local rates of change. As the total human population increases geometrically, a similar logarithmic increase in the complexity of cultural elements is a natural consequence. It may well be that invention occurs at a nearly fixed rate (one new element every so many thousand or million man-years) as far back as the cultural record can be traced. If biological change or environmental circumstance exert any influence, our gross estimates of complexity and population size obscure these effects beyond a correlation of numbers of people and complexity. For our purposes here, however, the important consequence is that a given idea may appear spontaneously many different times in the same tradition or in different, widely separated traditions. What we will detect in the record is its acceptance or propagation in a cultural system. Both natural selection and stochastic processes may have a role in explaining cultural change in this context. Only in the case of natural selection will cultural systems have the adaptive character envisioned in the Binford definition of culture.

If it is possible to talk about cultural phenomena in evolutionary terms, we must address the matter of whether cultural laws in this framework will be distinct from biological ones. This question can be answered in the affirmative without appeal to the emotional distinction we maintain between ourselves and other creatures. S. J. Gould (1976) has summarized the importance of character transmission in understanding large scale evolutionary trends. In particular, he has concerned himself with the so-called "Cambrian Explosion." Briefly, although simple life forms had been around for a substantial period of time, almost all of the modern classes of living forms originated in the geologically brief period from the early Cambrian to the early Ordovician. Since then, "random" change has been characteristic. In seeking an explanation, Gould argues that the conditions which brought about the Cambrian explosion are not to be found in the Cambrian but in the preceding periods and that the explosion is simply the logarithmic phase of a normal growth curve that typifies the radiation of any organism with unlimited space and resources. Since the world was not lifeless before the Cambrian, this competition-free curve poses a problem. The answer to the paradox lies most likely in the observation that sexual reproduction appears as a new transmission mechanism and allows for much more rapid diversification, so much so that simple organisms persist only in those environments that are unoccupiable by the more complex forms. The ultimate limits on this explosion are set by the physical constraints of the planet.

Keeping in mind that our knowledge of the human record is more detailed and less objective, there is a striking parallel to the Cambrian explosion, one that would be expected if character transmission is of critical importance. If the production of artifacts is taken to mark the beginning of cultural transmission, the human record begins perhaps three million years ago. The "human explosion" measured either in number of people or cultural diversity does not begin until latest Pleistocene and early Holocene times. Cultural transmission has apparently had much the same impact as sexual reproduction in increasing diversity, shortening adaptive response time, and increasing the range of responses. If these two situations are at all analogous, there would appear to be ample room for cultural laws in an evolutionary model. Because cultural transmission appears to be a significant evolutionary factor, laws that cover its unique processes are clearly required. Cultural transmission does not replace and is not identical with sexual reproduction but it is a distinct, analogous process. Durham (1976) has reached a similar conclusion arguing from quite different premises. Failure to maintain this distinction would appear to be the source of Harris' critique of the Sahlins and Service evolutionary approach (Harris 1968:652).

Regardless of whether the analogy can be maintained after detailed examination, it would appear to be a valuable heuristic position until such a demonstration can be made. There are immediate practical consequences of this position. For example, it may be that we have been misled in seeking explanations for the development of civilization in the unique environmental conditions of the late Pleistocene and early Holocene and in the specific cultural forms extant during that period. This singularly important development in culture change may be simply the log phase of a natural growth curve initiated closer to the Plio-Pleistocene boundary than the Holocene. Observations of this order raise the question of whether an evolutionary model can assist us in accounting for particular forms or if it is limited to the grand structure of culture change. In an evolutionary framework, we would incline to explain the fixation of a particular form as a consequence of the increased Darwinian fitness that its presence confers on its transmitters. Traditional biological explanations argue that some elements are adaptive, that is, confer increased fitness, under a particular set of circumstances, and are thus fixed by natural selection while other elements are not adaptive and do not become fixed. In this sense, culture is truly "man's extrasomatic adaptive system." There is, however, an increasing awareness with other animal systems that not all elements can be assigned unambiguous positive or negative selective values (King and Jukes 1969; Lewontin 1974). Some, perhaps many, traits behave as if they are adaptively neutral (Gould and others 1977). This is not incompatible with an unreconstructed Darwinian view of natural selection. If the traits in question do not have large positive or negative selective values, and the environmental constraints that bring about selection are not fixed but vary randomly around gradually changing means, we should expect that a fair proportion of the total trait assemblage that makes up the description of an organism would behave on the whole in a rather random fashion even though no individual transmission could be said to be neutral. If anything, cultural transmission should act to increase the capacity for such neutral traits and increase the total diversity of cultural systems.

At first glance, the recognition of adaptively neutral elements forces the Binford definition of culture to exclude most of what we would like to think of as cultural. However, all traits have a cost in terms of energy, space, and matter and are thus an unavoidable part of the whole selective picture. In a cultural frame, many specific trait forms may lack adaptive value, but a reservoir of variability, some of which may ultimately acquire adaptive value with changing conditions, has a clear selective value. Analytically, this can be treated as a problem of scale. Specific, adaptively neutral forms may be functionally equivalent manifestations of larger entities that are accountable in terms of natural selection.

Style and Function in an Evolutionary Context

Having argued that an evolutionary approach does have applicability to the archaeological record, we must recognize that we have two effectively different kinds of elements involved in any system undergoing evolution. Traits that have discrete selective values over measurable amounts of time should be accountable by natural selection and a set of external conditions. Traits identified as adaptively neutral will display a very different kind of behavior because their frequencies in a population are not directly accountable in terms of selection and external contingencies. Their behavior should be more adequately accommodated by stochastic processes.

It is at this point that the distinction between style and function becomes critical. The dichotomy is an old one and has even been accorded evolutionary connotations (Service 1964; Binford 1968). In the context of evolutionary processes just outlined, these terms can be redefined. *Style* denotes those *forms that do not have detectable selective values. Function* is manifest as those *forms that directly affect the Darwinian fitness of the populations in which they occur.* In an archaeological context, the term *form* should be limited to artificial attributes without any specification of scale (e.g., attributes of object, objects, etc.). The dichotomy is mutually exclusive and exhaustive in principle. Because each kind of element has distinct behavioral expectations, the two can potentially be distinguished in practical terms. A profitable direction may lie in identifying stylistic elements by their random behavior (Gould and others 1977).

This definition of style is quite close to its usage in archaeology, particularly as employed by culture historians. Their chronological efforts provide a demonstration of the practicality of its identification in the archaeological record. Stylistic similarity is homologous similarity; it is the result of direct cultural transmission once chance similarity in a context of limited possibilities is excluded. This confers upon stylistic units the marvelous abstract statistical properties that have delighted archaeologists since the nineteenth century. These same properties made stylistic units indispensible to culture history. Only with variables independent of external conditions is it possible to obtain the purely historical, non-repetitive classes that are used to tell time. It is not surprising that some of the most "scientific" applications should have come about in chronology. The elegant simplicity of style behavior and the ability to distinguish a correct answer from one that is simply elegant have made style the archaeological forte. Because of the independence of style from its environment and its homologous character it can also be employed as a tool to delineate spatial interaction. But the very characteristics that make style such a useful archaeological tool prohibit its explanation in terms of natural selection. The explanation of specific styles will have to come from non-evolutionary, stochastic processes coupled with such devices as Markov chains to accommodate its mode of transmission.

The implicit use of style to define archaeological units at all scales is nowhere more evident than in the "explanations" offered by culture historians for similarity. Diffusion, acculturation, persistence, tradition, horizon, trade, migration are mechanisms to account for homologous similarities. As processes, they designate only the source of a particular form and identify temporal-spatial contact. Of the culture historical processes, only independent invention lies outside this framework and it has been used to explain such quasi-functional elements as pottery or agriculture. Even its application here is controversial, and strictly stylistic processes have been offered as explanations of grand scale phenomena (e.g., Meggers and Evans 1962; Ford 1969). All of the culture historical processes treat the source of particular forms; none addresses why those forms are fixed. An archaeological record structured by such stylistic concepts will be singularly difficult to explain in terms of evolutionary processes.

The definition of function, on the other hand, departs considerably from the traditional use of the word in archaeology where it is frequently a synonym of "use." The importance of distinguishing function from style has been realized (Jelinek 1976). In an evolutionary approach, the distinction is mandatory. Unfortunately, attempts to deal with function have almost exclusively been carried out with the reconstructionist framework. These attempts rely heavily upon analogy with contemporary functional forms like axes and hoes, a procedure that denies the evolution of functions. The contrastive behavior of functional elements should make them identifiable without recourse to behavioral correlates. Their necessary interaction with external conditions can provide the means of developing functional classifications at all scales comparable to the culture historical stylistic classifications. I have offered (1971b, 1978) a primitive scheme for the definition of functional classes at the scale of artifacts that is compatible with an evolutionary model. Refinements of this scheme or the development of others offer the potential of organizing the archaeological record in functional terms and provide entities that can be explained in terms of evolutionary processes.

CONCLUSIONS

The failure of processual archaeology to make extensive use of evolutionary principles in explanations of the archaeological record can be attributed to the history of archaeological development. The basic structure of the archaeological record has been provided by culture history. There is abundant evidence that this structure is dominantly stylistic. Cultural reconstructionism has been responsible for the introduction of scientific rigor into the discipline, but the particularistic nature of its formulations has prevented it from developing a global understanding of the archaeological record that can replace the culture historical structure. Its contribution remains methodological rather than substantive or theoretical.

The success of the culture historical structure is in large part attributable to use of performance standards in the important area of chronology. A more detailed examination of the nature of style shows that the behavior of style is fundamentally stochastic. This observation explains its success in chronological matters and illuminates the nature of culture historical "explanatory" processes like diffusion. At the same time, this observation explains why evolutionary processes such as natural selection have not been effectively employed.

I have attempted to sketch some elements of a scientific evolutionary approach. This attempt suggests that evolutionary processes do have considerable potential in explaining cultural phenomena and that laws unique to cultural phenomena are possible and necessary. It is also apparent that not all phenomena traditionally considered cultural can be explained with such processes. The development of the latent archaeological distinction between style and function will be required if an evolutionary approach is to produce a global understanding of the archaeological record comparable to that of culture history. Explanations of stylistic phenomena will be found in stochastic processes and devices such as Markov chains; styles will continue to be useful tools for chronology and defining spatial interaction. Functional elements can be explained with evolutionary processes.

Acknowledgments. Earlier drafts of this paper were read by Drs. D. K. Grayson, A. C. Spaulding, and R. J. Wenke; the present version has benefited from their comments. The whole has also benefited from the editorial suggestions of C. Benson, S. K. Campbell, J. C. Chatters, Dr. M. B. Schiffer, and most especially, M. D. Dunnell.

Ascher, Robert
    1961   Analogy in archaeological interpretation. *Southwestern Journal of Anthropology* 17:317-325.
Barnett, H. G.
    1953   *Innovation: the basis of cultural change.* McGraw-Hill, New York.

Binford, Lewis R.
  1965   Archaeological systematics and the study of cultural process. *American Antiquity* 31:203-210.
  1967   Smudge pits and hide smoking: the use of analogy in archaeological reasoning. *American Antiquity* 32:1-12.
  1968   Archeological perspectives. In *New Perspectives in Archeology*, edited by S. R. Binford and L. R. Binford, pp. 5-32. Aldine, Chicago.
Caldwell, Joseph R.
  1959   The new American archaeology. *Science* 129:303-307.
Clarke, David L.
  1968   *Analytical archaeology*. Methuen, London.
Daniel, Glyn E.
  1950   *A hundred years of archaeology*. Duckworth, London.
Deetz, James A.
  1970   Archaeology as a social science. *In* Current directions in anthropology, edited by Ann Fisher, pp. 115-125. *American Anthropological Association Bulletin* 3, Part 2.
Doran, J. E. and F. R. Hodson
  1975   *Mathematics and computers in archaeology*. Harvard University Press, Cambridge.
Dunnell, Robert C.
  1971a   *Systematics in Prehistory*. Free Press, New York.
  1971b   Anthropological and scientific models of function in archaeology. Paper presented at the 1971 meeting of the American Anthropological Association, New York.
  1978   Archaeological potential of anthropological and scientific models of function. In *Archaeological Essays in Honor of Irving B. Rouse*, edited by R. C. Dunnell and E. S. Hall, jr., pp. 41-73. Mouton, The Hague.
Durham, William H.
  1976   The adaptive significance of cultural behavior. *Human Ecology* 4(2):89-121.
Ford, James A.
  1954a   Comment on A. C. Spaulding: "Statistical techniques for the discovery of artifact types." *American Antiquity* 19:390-391.
  1954b   The type concept revisited. *American Anthropologist* 56:42-54.
  1969   A comparison of formative cultures in the Americas. *Smithsonian Contributions to Anthropology*, Vol. 11.
Fritz, John M. and Fred T. Plog
  1970   The nature of archaeological explanation. *American Antiquity* 45:405-412.
Gifford, James C.
  1960   Type-variety method. *American Antiquity* 25:341-347.
Gould, Stephan J.
  1976   The interpretation of diagrams. *Natural History* 85:18-28.
Gould, Stephan J., David M. Raup, J. John Sepkoski, Jr., Thomas J. M. Schopf, and Daniel S. Simberloff
  1977   The shape of evolution: a comparison of real and random clades. *Paleobiology* 3(1):23-40.
Harris, Marvin
  1968   *The rise of anthropological theory*. T. Y. Crowell, New York.
Hempel, Carl G.
  1965   *Aspects of scientific explanation, and other essays in the philosophy of science*. Free Press, New York.
Jelinek, Arthur J.
  1976   Form, function, and style in lithic analysis. In *Cultural Change and Continuity*, edited by C. E. Cleland, pp. 19-34. Academic Press, New York.
King, J. L. and T. H. Jukes
  1969   Non-Darwinian evolution: random fixation of selectively neutral mutations. *Science* 164:788-798.
Krieger, Alex D.
  1944   The typological concept. *American Antiquity* 9:271-88.
Leone, Mark P.
  1972   Issues in anthropological archaeology. In *Contemporary Archaeology*, edited by M. P. Leone, pp. 14-27. University of Southern Illinois Press, Carbondale.
Lewontin, R. C.
  1974   *The genetic basis of evolutionary change*. Columbia University Press, New York.
Longacre, William A.
  1970   Current thinking in American archaeology. *In* Current directions in anthropology, edited by Ann Fisher, pp. 126-138. *American Anthropological Association Bulletin* 3, Part 2.
MacWhite, Eoin
  1956   On the interpretation of archaeological evidence in historical and sociological terms. *American Anthropologist* 58:3-25.
Meehan, Eugene J.
  1968   *Explanation in social science*. Dorsey Press, Homewood.
Meggers, Betty J. and Clifford Evans
  1962   Machalilla culture: an early formative culture on the Ecuadorian coast. *American Antiquity* 28:186-192.

Morgan, Charles G.
1973   Archaeology and explanation. *World Archaeology* 4:259-276.
Plog, Fred T.
1974   *The study of prehistoric change.* Academic Press, New York.
Sabloff, Jeremy A., Thomas W. Beale, and Anthony M. Kurland, Jr.
1973   Recent developments in archaeology. *Annals of the American Academy of Political and Social Science* 408:103-118.
Sackett, James R.
1966   Quantitative analysis of Upper Paleolithic stone tools. *In* Recent studies in paleoanthropology, edited by J. D. Clark and F. C. Howell, pp. 356-394. *American Anthropologist* 68, Part 2.
Service, Elman R.
1964   Archaeological theory and ethnological fact. In *Process and Pattern in Culture*, edited by R. A. Manners, pp. 364-375. Aldine, Chicago.
1969   Models for the methodology of mouthtalk. *Southwestern Journal of Anthropology* 25:68-80.
Slotkin, J. S.
1952   Some basic methodological problems in prehistory. *Southwestern Journal of Anthropology* 8:442-443.
Spaulding, Albert C.
1953   Statistical techniques for the discovery of artifact types. *American Antiquity* 18:305-313.
1954   Reply to Ford. *American Antiquity* 19:391-393.
Watson, Patty Jo, Steven A. LeBlanc, and Charles L. Redman
1971   *Explanation in archeology.* Columbia University Press, New York.
Whallon, Robert, Jr.
1972   A new approach to pottery typology. *American Antiquity* 37:13-33.

THE ROLE OF ADAPTATION IN ARCHAEOLOGICAL EXPLANATION

Michael J. O'Brien and Thomas D. Holland

Adaptation, a venerable icon in archaeology, often is afforded the vacuous role of being an ex-post-facto argument used to "explain" the appearance and persistence of traits among prehistoric groups—a position that has seriously impeded development of a selectionist perspective in archaeology. Biological and philosophical definitions of adaptation—and by extension, definitions of adaptedness—vary considerably, but all are far removed from those usually employed in archaeology. The prevailing view in biology is that adaptations are features that were shaped by natural selection and that increase the adaptedness of an organism. Thus adaptations are separated from other features that may contribute to adaptedness but are products of other evolutionary processes. Analysis of adaptation comprises two stages: showing that a feature was under selection and how the feature functioned relative to the potential adaptedness of its bearers. The archaeological record contains a wealth of information pertinent to examining the adaptedness of prehistoric groups, but attempts to use it will prove successful only if a clear understanding exists of what adaptation is and is not.

La adaptación, un venerable ícono en arqueología, desempeña a menudo el papel huero de argumento ex post facto utilizado para "explicar" la aparición y persistencia de rasgos en grupos prehistóricos—una posición que ha obstaculizado seriamente el desarrollo de una perspectiva seleccionista en arqueología. Las definiciones biológicas y filosóficas de adaptación—y por extensión, las definiciones de lo adaptado—varían considerablemente, pero todas ellas difieren por completo de las habitualmente empleadas en arqueología. La concepción predominante en biología sostiene que las adaptaciones son características que fueron moldeadas por selección natural y que incrementan la adaptación de un organismo. De este modo las adaptaciones se distinguen de otras características que pueden contribuir a la adaptación pero son el resultado de diferentes procesos evolutivos. El análisis de la adaptación procede en dos etapas: la primera, demostrar que una característica se encontraba bajo selección; la segunda, demostrar cómo funcionaba la característica en relación con los estados adaptativos potenciales de sus portadores. El registro arqueológico contiene abundante información pertinente para examinar la adaptación de grupos prehistóricos, pero los intentos de utilizarla solo tendrán éxito si se comprende claramente qué es y qué no es adaptación.

In "The Archaeological Study of Adaptation: Theoretical and Methodological Issues," Kirch (1980:101) points out that of all the social sciences, archaeology, because of the kinds of data bases it can generate, should be in a position to develop a methodological basis for the examination of cultural adaptation. He highlights the adaptational rhetoric that has enjoyed widespread use by archaeologists, including such terms as "adaptive systems," "adaptive trajectories," and "preadaptation," noting that "Given such frequent appeal to an adaptational framework, one might expect that anthropologists and archaeologists would have expended considerable effort on defining fundamental principles of the adaptation process. Such is not the case" (Kirch 1980:101).

Our position is that anthropology in general, and archaeology in particular, are not even close to having a developed set of methods for the study of human adaptation. We also believe that not only are the methods lacking but that a critical lack of understanding exists on the part of anthropologists and archaeologists of what adaptation and its closely allied concept of adaptedness (fitness) are and are not. This misunderstanding not only cripples attempts to identify and understand specific human adaptations but also calls into question our understanding of principles that have received

Michael J. O'Brien and Thomas D. Holland, Department of Anthropology, University of Missouri–Columbia, Columbia, MO 65211

American Antiquity, 57(1), 1992, pp. 36–59.
Copyright © 1992 by the Society for American Archaeology

extraordinary treatment by evolutionary biologists and philosophers of biology, who themselves diverge sharply on the concepts of adaptation and adaptedness.

Most anthropologists would readily agree that the lack of congruence between biological and anthropological views of adaptation is epistemologically sound, since humans are such extraordinary organisms that as subjects they require a completely different philosophical and methodological approach. We argue, however, that human adaptedness and adaptation do not make us immune from natural selection and that despite historically based reasons for doing so, we cannot continue to equate the creative ability of humans with some bizarre, extraordinary means of escaping selective environments. Although adaptation is a consequence of selection acting on variation, it is only a limited consequence. Concerning humans, "It guarantees only that people who persist in less effective practices will not perpetuate their practices as well as will other people pursuing different practices. Adaptations, then, are sets of cultural practices that simply have allowed people to get by in the past, whose consequences have *so far* proved at least relatively less harmful to the perpetuation of their social groups than any others the people may have tried out" (Braun 1990:81, emphasis in original).

Lack of knowledge of the process of adaptation—and, by extension, of adaptedness—has led anthropologists to view the process as one by which groups of people add new and improved methods of coping with the environment to their cultural repertoire. Adaptation is, in one sense, a means of finding solutions to problems—of overcoming risk—but it in no sense is causal of future events, nor is it progressive. Where adaptation is invoked as an anthropological "explanation," it often is viewed as a product of vaguely referenced "selective agents"—elements of the natural or cultural environment—that force human groups to change or face decline or extinction. Unfortunately, the products of such exercises are vacuous, orthogenetic cause-and-effect statements that have the appearance and character of what Gould and Lewontin (1979) term "just so" stories.

Differences between how biologists and archaeologists view adaptation is an odd occurrence if (a) Alland (1975:63) is correct when he asserts, "In the early 1960s a group of anthropologists and archeologists took over adaptation from biology and ecology" and (b) Marks and Staski (1988:151) are correct in asserting that the "new archaeology" called for evolutionary thought. It may have made such a call, but apparently no one familiar with Darwinism answered. We argue that a Darwinian view of the archaeological record must be based on the premise that things contained in the record were parts of past human phenotypes (O'Brien and Holland 1990:35; see also Neff 1992). Importantly, the objects are not simply reflective of or related to phenotypes (Dunnell 1988: 23); they are parts of phenotypes in the same way beaver dams and bird nests are parts of phenotypes. As such, objects in the archaeological record potentially can contribute as much (and sometimes more) information regarding adaptedness and adaptation as can purely biological features. Because they are not units of reproduction, archaeological objects must be viewed in terms of replicative success (Leonard and Jones 1987), which can, through analysis, be tied back to the potential adaptedness of the humans responsible for the objects' replicative success or nonsuccess.

Importantly, this view does not place much emphasis on "culture." Although the concept has an important place in anthropological thought, without a clear understanding of what adaptation is and is not (and *cannot* be) little reason exists to discuss broader issues that rely on a solid understanding of adaptation. Whatever culture is, it includes more than "a set of behavior patterns that are learned by members of society from members of society and that are adaptations of their society to the environment" (Campbell 1966:288). We will show that (a) many cultural features, though they might contribute to *adaptedness*, are not adaptations and (b) other cultural features do not even contribute to adaptedness.

We emphasize repeatedly that the historical development of specific features, some of which will be adaptations, is critical to understanding the function of features. We strongly disagree with Alland's (1975:60) statement that "A processual theory of adaptation must account for continuity and change of evolutionary systems rather than the specific characteristics of the systems themselves. It must . . . generate transformational rules which can be used to explain and predict changes in behavioral systems with specific characteristics under stated sets of conditions." The only laws that interest us are laws of contingency. In other words, history matters. It is much easier to sit back and invoke an evolutionary model of change, with its attendant vague invocations of "selective pressure" and "adaptive response," than it is to begin to understand the "specific characteristics of the systems themselves." But the results of the two endeavors are incomparable.

When armed with a more-fundamental understanding of the concepts of adaptation and adaptedness, archaeologists can make solid contributions to the application of evolutionary theory to the study of previous cultures. Recent additions to the archaeological literature (e.g., Braun 1990; Dunnell 1978a, 1980, 1985; Leonard and Jones 1987; Marks and Staski 1988; Neff 1992; O'Brien and Holland 1990; Rindos 1989) suggest that archaeology is poised to make such contributions. But several critical misunderstandings—especially the mixing of traits that were and were not products of selection—have kept archaeologists from using the archaeological record to its fullest extent. Conceptual mixing of kinds of traits has seriously impeded any hope of using the archaeological record to understand human adaptedness and adaptation.

THE CONCEPTS OF ADAPTEDNESS AND ADAPTATION

"Adaptedness" ("fitness") and "adaptation," though related concepts, have distinct meanings. Conflation of the two stems in large part from the fact that the terms "adaptation," "adaptedness," and "adapting" sound like different words for the same thing. Sober (1984:211) notes whimsically that "In a simpler world, the process that produces adaptation would be certain to increase the level of adaptedness. In a simpler world, an organism's 'adapting' to its environment by modifying its behavior and physiology would be the same kind of process as a population's 'adapting' to its environment by modifying its genetic composition." This, as we discuss below, most decidedly is not the case.

Definitions of adaptation and adaptedness in the evolutionary-biology literature are so numerous that they would easily fill the space taken up by this paper (see Krimbas [1984] for several). For reasons explained in more detail later, we define adaptedness as the state an organism is in, relative to its conspecifics, as a result of its evolutionary history. We follow Futuyma's (1979:308) definition of adaptation—"a process whereby the members of a population become suited over the generations to survive and reproduce"—and Ayala's (in Dobzhansky et al. 1977:498) definition of adaptations— "features of organisms that have come about by natural selection because they serve certain functions and thus increase the reproductive success of their carriers." Because organisms relate to the environment on a constant—and constantly changing—basis, *adaptedness* must be viewed in an ahistorical sense; *adaptation* and *adaptations* must be viewed in a historical sense. Importantly, in the case of humans, because of their ability to transmit information intragenerationally, the historical development of adaptations may be short-lived. This is in clear contrast to other organisms.

Burian (1983:288) makes an excellent distinction between adaptedness and adaptation: "Fleetness contributes to the adaptedness of a deer (or makes the deer better adapted) if, and only if, other things being equal, it contributes to the solution of a problem posed to the deer—for example, escaping predation. Fleetness is an adaptation of the deer if, and only if, the deer's fleetness has been molded by an historical process in which relative fleetness of earlier deer helped shape the fleetness of current deer." This leads us to two critical points. First, adaptations were *not necessarily* evolved to solve a problem for which they later were well-suited to solve. In the above example, the mechanical equipment that led to fleetness was not *evolved* to make deer fleet, it simply led to fleeter deer. We return this point later. Second, *adaptedness is not necessarily a product only of adaptation*. Said a bit differently, because a trait increases the adaptedness of its possessor does not qualify it as an adaptation.

Surely such a distinction runs counter to the way in which the term "adaptation" is used in anthropology. How can we say that something that benefits an organism, i.e., something that contributes to its adaptedness, is *not* an adaptation? To be fair, some biologists and philosophers (e.g., Bock 1980; Ruse 1971) argue that *anything* that contributes to adaptedness is an adaptation. But not all traits have the requisite causal history to be adaptations (Brandon 1990:41). In other words, they were not shaped by natural selection. The interesting question becomes instead, Can we infer something about the evolutionary process by looking at those special effects of evolution that we term adaptations?

We should take heart in the fact that even Darwin wrestled extensively with adaptation, searching for a schema that took into account both (1) the perceived goodness of fit between organisms and their environments (the fact that organisms lived and reproduced in environments—and their offspring reproduced—was accepted as prima facie evidence that there was indeed a fit) and (2) the observation that organisms changed through time. Darwin based his early theory on the idea of *limited perfect adaptedness* (see Ospovat 1981; also Burian 1983), the basic tenet of which held that organisms are constrained by their structure and constitution, but within those limits organisms are perfectly adapted to their environment. That is, organisms are designed to meet and overcome specific environmentally induced hurdles. Selection was afforded the secondary role of urging populations to become perfect or face extinction.

By 1857 Darwin had developed the notion of *relative adaptedness* later used in *On the Origin of Species* (1859):

> Once Darwin came to realize that variation is ubiquitous and largely undirected with respect to the needs of the organism, he was forced to employ a relative concept of adaptedness. . . . All organisms face a multitude of problems bearing on survival and reproduction. If they all vary (at least slightly) in virtually all their features, then typical organisms are *not* perfectly adapted. Some, however, are at an advantage with respect to others—that is, they are better designed to meet the expected or expectable challenges of the environment [Burian 1983:292].

A key to understanding Darwin—and by extension adaptedness and adaptation—is keeping in mind that by 1859 the key to his theory of natural selection was *differential* (specifically *intraspecific*) reproductive success. In fact, Darwin's theory was designed to *explain* differential reproductive success, i.e., why different individuals leave different numbers of offspring in succeeding generations. In the process, it ultimately explains the origins and maintenance of adaptations in nature (Brandon 1990:9). Darwin explained differential reproductive success through reference to Thomas Malthus's (1798) notion of the "struggle for existence"[1] (or, in the terms of Herbert Spencer, whose words Darwin later adopted, "the survival of the fittest").

Malthus may have influenced Darwin, but the type of struggle postulated by Darwin was distinctly different from that described by Malthus (Sober 1984:17). The Malthusian struggle involves individuals competing for the same scarce resources. The Darwinian struggle, though it may on occasion involve intraspecific and interspecific competition for resources, is more of a competition between an individual and the environment. Sober compares the difference between the two conditions to the difference between golf and tennis. Both games have winners, but in tennis a point scored by one player means a point not scored by the other player. Not so in golf, where each player's score is independent of those of all other players. "In Darwin's 'large and metaphorical sense,' all that matters is that players end up with different scores—that they do unequally well in the 'struggle for existence' "(Sober 1984:17).

Adaptedness and the Problem of Tautology

Anyone with even a passing knowledge of evolutionary biology is familiar with the controversy over the perceived tautology implied in Darwin's "survival of the fittest" (e.g., Bethell 1976) and efforts to clear up misconceptions contained therein (Brandon 1978, 1990; Burian 1983; Ghiselin 1969; Gould 1976; Mills and Beatty 1979; Sober 1984; Williams 1986). Two red herrings have been slipped into these arguments. The first is that tautologies are inherently bad. But theory is full of tautologies. In fact, tautology is a characteristic of theory, but rarely have scientists worried so much about that point as they have about fitness. The second red herring is found in continued focus on the inadequacy of the term "survival of the fittest." It should be clear to anyone that the term does not do its intended job. If we somehow could rank all organisms within a group from the most fit to the least fit, only one of them would emerge as the fittest in the true, superlative sense of the word. Thus only one organism would survive. As Darwin himself figured out, there was no such thing as a perfectly adapted organism, and fitness had to be examined in a *relative* sense, organism against organism. Mayr (1982:589) wryly points out that "Selection cannot produce perfection, for in the competition for reproductive success among members of a population, it is sufficient to be superior and not at all necessary to be perfect." In other words, the hallowed phrase becomes "survival of the superior," with superiority determined by which organisms (actually their blood lines) persist and which do not.

The important issue is how to compare the relative fitness of organisms, namely does fitness apply to the *actual* reproductive success of organisms or does it apply to the *propensity* (see Mills and Beatty 1979) for organisms to be reproductively successful? In other words, at what point is fitness measured—before or after (and maybe long after) an organism reproduces? Clearly Darwin equated reproductive success with fitness—the ability to produce viable offspring (in current terminology either [1] the genetic contribution made by organisms to succeeding generations, measured in terms of the number of offspring, or [2] the average number of offspring left by members of a group of similar organisms). By Darwin's early account, organisms either were fit or unfit in an absolute sense—the features they contained either got the organism through environmental peril or they did not. Even a careful reading of Darwin yields some ambiguity as to what he later meant by the term "fitness," i.e., after he had abandoned the notion of "limited perfect adaptation." Did he mean the *actual* (*realized*) contribution made by organisms to succeeding generations, or did he mean the *potential* contribution that organisms *could* make? Differences between these two positions may appear to be subtle, but they most decidedly are not.

Realized fitness simply refers to the fact that organism a is more fit (better adapted) than organism b, if in fact organism a outreproduced organism b in a specific environment. The statement then becomes, If a is better adapted than b in environment E, then a will outproduce b in E. "Degree of adaptation, in this sense, is an empirical property of the organism (or of the class) in question, but one *which can only be known post hoc*" (Burian 1983:299, emphasis added). It is ironic that this concept has been labeled "Darwinian fitness," since as Burian (1983:299) points out, "Darwin almost certainly meant the phrase 'survival of the fittest' to stand for the *tendency* of organisms that are better engineered to be reproductively successful" (emphasis added). By adding the word "probably" to the above if–then statement, we overcome Burian's objection that what Darwin really meant was the tendency. Thus we have Brandon's (1990:11) view that the underlying tenet of Darwin's natural selection is simply, "If a is better adapted than b in environment E, then (probably) a will have greater reproductive success than b in E." This definition can be termed *expected fitness*.

We advocate focusing on potential (or "propensity for," to use Mills and Beatty's [1979] terminology) adaptedness instead of on realized adaptedness. This is exactly the position that Fisher (1985; see also Ghiselin 1966, 1969) takes when he argues that the "tautology problem" exists because, under some definitions of adaptedness, adaptedness and natural selection are viewed as dependent on one another instead of as related but separate constructs, each having its own theoretical and empirical basis.

Selection and Drift

Is adaptedness a product only of selection, or do other evolutionary processes, such as chance (drift), play a role? If drift does play a role, how significant is it? A related question is, Do selection and drift always produce better-adapted organisms? Selection, which we consider to be more of a process than a force,[2] is, at base level, *one* kind of "'biasing effect' in the composition of a population" (Sober 1984:29), i.e., it is but one "cause" of evolution. Simply put, selection is a "weeding-out" process that leads to the differential reproduction of transmissible (by whatever means) traits in a succeeding population. Selection is completely dependent on variation as a fuel—there can be no selection without variation among a group of organisms. Important as variation is, it is in no sense causal of anything: "variations may be compared with building materials, but the presence of an unlimited supply of materials does not in itself give assurance that a building is going to be constructed" (Dobzhansky 1982:119).

An important but all-too-often-overlooked point is that selection operates on individuals and not on traits. Various features allow organisms to persist and reproduce in a certain environment, but it is the organisms and not the features that are under selective control. This is not to say that there cannot be selection *for* properties, but a critical distinction must be made between selection *for* properties and selection *of* objects (organisms). The important point is that "selection of" does not imply "selection for." "Selection for" is, as Sober (1984:100) notes, "the causal concept *par excellence*"; "selection of" pertains to the effects of selection: "To say that there is selection for a given property means that having that property *causes* success in survival and reproduction. But to say that a given sort of object was selected is merely to say that the result of the selection process was to increase the representation of that kind of object" (Sober 1984:100, emphasis in original).

In evolutionary biology several distinct kinds, or more properly *modes*, of selection are recognized—among them stabilizing, directional, disruptive, and frequency dependent—and each produces different results in succeeding generations. Our guess is that among humans the effects of each of these are, theoretically, observable within a single generation. The one on which we will focus most attention is *directional* selection, where there is selection for a single formerly peripheral phenotype or phenotypic feature. The net result is to increase that phenotype or trait relative to its alternatives and thus to move the distribution curve in a specific direction. *Stabilizing* selection, on the other hand, acts to reduce the number of new variants that arise, in essence selecting phenotypes or features that are intermediate to the extreme variants. *Disruptive*, or *diversifying*, selection produces a coexistence of two or more phenotypes within a population. *Frequency-dependent* selection, in which the fitness of a phenotype is dependent on its frequency within a population, produces, in contrast to the other modes of selection, a complex, inconsistent relation between phenotype and adaptedness. Frequency-dependent selection probably plays a role in *all* selection (Futuyma 1986:166), but this mode must be operating constantly among humans, especially given that the frequency of humans within a group significantly alters the nature of the selective environment in which the individuals function.

Unlike selection, drift in its many guises is the random component (not to be confused with stochastic processes, as we note later) in evolution. For example, an allele for a trait not under selection can drift randomly in frequency across generations of a population until it becomes fixed or reaches zero and disappears. Drift also can refer to chance events among organisms in a population that affect the frequencies of different phenotypes and therefore of individual phenotypic traits. In theory, drift is an easy concept to understand, but in practice its effects often are difficult to distinguish from those of other evolutionary processes. Understanding drift is basic to understanding adaptedness and adaptation, since, as we discuss in more detail later, drift cannot produce adaptations but it can affect adaptedness. Since adaptations lead to adaptedness, we run the risk of misidentifying features as adaptations if we misread the processes responsible for the features. Although "adaptedness is a probabilistic disposition, so that greater relative adaptedness regularly leads to greater actualized [realized] fitness. . . . chance can intervene and break that regular connection" (Brandon 1990:45).

Adaptations and Nonadaptations

Features are adaptations only if they evolved because there was selection for organisms that carried the features. But what of the converse? Should every trait that has become prevalent because of selection be counted as an adaptation? Lewontin (1978; see also Gould and Lewontin 1979) says no, adding the proviso that features that arise by selection also must cause an increase in adaptedness. Part of his argument is sound and part is not. He argues, correctly, that features that arise in a population do not necessarily contribute to the adaptedness of constituent members. But his insistence that to be an adaptation a feature must contribute to the adaptedness of its possessors is linked to the erroneous view that adaptations are features that will, for all times, increase the adaptedness of possessors instead of as features that *once* were beneficial to possessors. In other words, "A trait can be an adaptation for performing some task, though performing that task in the present environment confers no benefit. The point is that it *was* beneficial" (Sober 1984:199). In other words, a trait evolved as a response to selection against organisms without the trait.

Note that the key word here is "evolved," which embodies the concept of cumulative change *over time*. We are not saying, obviously, that a trait began because an organism or group of organisms *needed* the trait. We simply are saying that selection, by means of differential reproduction, in essence "created" the trait. Organisms that had the characteristic did better *in a certain selective environment* than did organisms without the characteristic.

Brandon (1990:41) perhaps says it best:

> A trait may appear with one mutation. Such a trait is not an adaptation regardless of its effect on the adaptedness of its possessor. If the trait does increase the adaptedness of its possessors and thereby increases in frequency in the population it will then become an adaptation. But its initial appearance is explained by the chance mutation. Thus at that point it is not an adaptation. More interestingly, traits may actually evolve, that is, be the product of an evolutionary process, and still not be adaptations. The process is evolution by random drift.

Adaptive features, i.e., traits that increase an organism's adaptedness, take time to evolve (biologically) within a population, regardless of the mechanism(s) involved. Therein lies an interesting problem for biologists: How can organisms "predict" what will be "needed" in future environments, especially in light of the rapidity with which selective environments can change? The answer is, of course, they cannot predict anything. Given the extremely slow rate at which advantageous traits arise (and even then they may not be heritable), and the extreme unlikelihood that they will reach fixation (a rate of occurrence that is twice the selection coefficient, itself a small number), it seems miraculous that any trait ever reaches the point where it becomes characteristic. It seems that the same or similar mutation would have to be introduced repeatedly and that the environment would have to be stable enough for the trait to go to fixation.

Lewontin (1978) uses the term "tracking" to denote the relation between a population evolving under natural selection and its environment. In reality, there is no perfect fit between the two. Since selective environments rarely are stable, information available to the population is always slightly out of date so that in actuality a population is tracking a past environment. The faster the selective environment changes, the more out of sync the population will be with the environment. Under rapid environmental change, selection can hardly act to improve adaptedness (Sober 1984:174); evolution by natural selection requires periods of environmental stasis, not constant upheaval. Van Valen (1973), coining the term "Red Queen hypothesis," posits that the environment changes just fast enough to prevent organisms from gaining on it, while adaptation keeps organisms from lagging too far behind. This reminds us of Braidwood's (1967:80) observation that Paleolithic cultures of Europe after the Pleistocene "changed just enough so that they would not have to change."

The point we are making is that features that evolved in one selective environment (or in a series of consecutive environments) may once have been adaptations. When the environment changed, they may no longer have been adaptations, i.e., they may no longer better adapt an organism and may in actuality be detrimental to its survival. In other words, "In order to qualify as an adaptation, a feature does not have to be *currently* undergoing active directional or stabilizing selection. If variation for a feature is not present, there can be no selection for that feature, and it does not thereby cease being an adaptation. It is only necessary that the feature be a component of a causal interaction of which the average effect, over all the contexts in which the feature occurs, is an enhancement of reproductive potential" (Fisher 1985:126, emphasis in original). Timing, in essence, is everything. The bottom line is that adaptations lead to increased adaptedness *at specific times*. This point is critical. Adaptation and adaptedness are complementary concepts, but "The former looks to the past, reflecting the kind of history that a trait has had. The latter looks to the future, indicating the chances that organisms have for survival and reproductive success. These retrospective and prospective concepts are mutually independent" (Sober 1984:210).

Gould and Vrba (1982) coined the term "exaptations" to refer to features that, after some period, come under selective control (or "become functional," to use parlance that we will employ later). "Aptation," also coined by Gould and Vrba (1982), refers to a trait that increases the adaptedness of possessors but that did not evolve because of that use. "Aptation" and "exaptation" together form what biologists for decades have called "preadaptations," a term that Gould and Vrba note suggests planning and foresight. But the distinction among "adaptation," "aptation," and "exaptation" is not always cut and dried. Brandon (1990:172; see also Fisher 1985:123–124) makes a

179

point that is worth considering: Suppose a feature, because of some specific use, comes under selective control. Later in the lineage of the possessors, the trait, which no longer is under selective control, is co-opted for another use. It is then an exaptation. Suppose also that because of this new use the trait remains in the population for many generations, under the control of stabilizing selection. The trait has not changed, due in part to the role of stabilizing rather than directional selection. Since the trait is under selective control, Brandon views the trait as an adaptation.

Another class of features should be noted, though we are hard-pressed to devise a category for them. They usually are linked in the literature to discussions of pleiotropy, though they have more to do with architectural and engineering design. Gould and Lewontin (1979) point out two examples—the human chin and architectural spandrels—and show what the results would be if one decided that those indeed were adaptations. For example, the chin is simply the result of selection for other components of the jaw and not an adaptation. We recognize the chin as a facial landmark, but in actuality it hitchhiked its way to prominence through the force of selection working within certain architectural and engineering constraints on the mandibular portion of the phenotype. Similarly, architects did not build domed-roofed churches to create small triangular spaces (spandrels) in which to place paintings of the saints. Rather, spandrels are engineering by-products (that subsequently were filled with paintings) of mounting a dome on rounded arches. If there is another way to mount a dome on rounded arches *without* creating small, tapered spaces, we are unaware of it. The caveat here is that engineering studies—both of features and the organisms containing the features—are needed before we can recognize the features as more than simply tag-alongs.

This is precisely why Sober (1984:197) makes the following observation: "It follows that the concept of adaptation needs to be understood in terms of the idea of *selection for properties*; the idea of *selection of objects* will not suffice. . . . If a neutral trait is pleiotropically linked to an advantageous one, it may emerge because of a process of natural selection. It was selected, but this doesn't mean that it is an adaptation. The reason is that although it was selected, there was no selection *for* that trait" (emphasis in original). Sober is not suggesting that traits as opposed to organisms are the units of selection. He simply is attempting to highlight the causal emphasis that the phrase "selection for properties" connotes, i.e., that selection for and against properties produces evolution. "Selection of" has more to do with general adaptedness. Although we may be interested in differences in adaptedness among individuals, the presence of differences tells us nothing about the origin of those differences.

As a final consideration, we should point out that confusing the sequence of appearance of traits, i.e., what evolved from what (trait polarity), probably occurs as often in archaeology as in biology. If traits in question cannot be ordered chronologically, i.e., derived traits separated from primitive traits, we have little or no hope of ever knowing whether we have identified adaptations, let alone of ever knowing what the functions of the adaptations were.

Determining Traits To Be Adaptations

How do we determine that a trait *is* an adaptation? In other words, how do we know that a feature is the product of selection as opposed to the product of drift? Also, can we show that a certain trait, at a certain time, increased the adaptedness of the possessor(s)? These clearly are questions of cause and effect. If we accept that selection produces (causes) adaptations, which lead to increased adaptedness of the possessor(s) *at a particular* time, what can we infer about the selective process by examining adaptations? But doesn't this lead us back to the first question: How do we identify adaptations? In other words, without clear knowledge that a feature *is* an adaptation, how can we say anything about the process of selection, since drift may have created the trait? Is the whole exercise so difficult conceptually and methodologically that it is beyond our capabilities? Although we do not deny that the issues surrounding this problem merit considerable care and study, they do not pose insurmountable problems.

We might begin with the notion that adaptations were evolved for some purpose and that if we can (a) identify a function for a feature and (b) show how its possessors were more fit (relatively) than those organisms without it, then perhaps we can infer that we are looking at an adaptation—

a feature that came under selective control. But there are biologists who have rained extensive criticism on those who view adaptations as solutions to problems and who set about to discover the functions of traits. Perhaps the most vocal are Gould and Lewontin (1979), who in their often-quoted article "The Spandrels of San Marco and the Panglossian Paradigm: A Critique of the Adaptationist Programme" unmercifully attack studies that attempt to show the functions of organismic features (see also Lewontin 1986). They contend that organisms can be studied only as integrated wholes and that phylogenetic history, pathway development, and engineering constraint should be considered when attempting to identify adaptations and their functions. Their most-significant complaint is that many analyses result in adaptive stories that, while plausible, are untestable. Their view of the adaptationist program, however, is based on an erroneous belief that most studies of adaptation are reductionist in scope—traits are divided and subdivided into smaller and smaller increments and are continually searched to find a function for each unit.

But most adaptationist programs—including those in archaeology—do not operate this way (Mayr 1988:152–153). Properly conceived and carried out, a functional program is entirely appropriate. We hasten to point out, again, that function is at the heart of evolutionary change. Mayr (1988: 154) is right, of course: "the student of adaptation has to sail a perilous course between a pseudoexplanatory reductionist atomism and stultifying nonexplanatory holism." It would appear that to escape the criticism of Gould and Lewontin one not only must correctly identify adaptations as such but must then identify the *proper function* of the feature relative to the organism as a whole. If this were the case, however, few adaptations would have been identified and even fewer identified correctly. Contrary to their view, nothing is inherently wrong with the "try and try again" approach to analyzing features, whether they are adaptations or nonadaptations. What is needed is a method of falsification so that successive propositions can be constructed and their implications tested.

One method of analyzing features is through the examination of engineering design. It is clear from even a casual reading of *On the Origin of Species* that Darwin was fascinated with engineering design—both in terms of the features created and the process that created the design—to the point of referring to some features as "organs of extreme perfection and complication." Though he was ignorant of the mechanics of inheritance, Darwin saw no reason to treat even the most complex of features as anything more than cumulative modifications of earlier features—features that conferred some potential reproductive advantage on their bearers. These features, or adaptations, are the links between an organism and the environment in which the organism lives. To Darwin, the better engineered a feature was, the more potentially reproductively successful the organisms bearing that feature would be.

Any engineering-design study must keep several points in focus. First, as we have seen, not all features are adaptations, i.e., are the products of selection. Second, features that once were adaptations may not have been adaptations under different environmental regimes. Third, simply because a feature evolved as an adaptation does not imply that the feature was an end-all solution to a problem. The evolved feature may have "solved" one problem for the organism but in doing so may have created other problems. Still, as Sober (1984:81) notes, "a careful engineering analysis can in principle permit us to make reasonable judgments about fitness differences *in advance* of finding out who lives and who dies" (emphasis added).

Sober (1984:81–82) offers another strategy for analyzing features—a process he labels "bootstrapping": "One may begin by investigating fitness ex post facto—that is, by looking at differences in survival and reproductive success in one population and reasoning that these were a consequence of certain fitness differences. Then, when confronted with a second, similar population, one might be able to use one's previous experience to reason in the opposite direction. The hypothesis would be that the characteristics that determined fitness differences in the first population also do so in the second."

Both methods of determining whether features are (were) adaptations rest on inference. Engineering studies, for example, can show us how certain structures confer the ability to run fast, but *we* make the inference that the ability to run fast gave organisms a selective advantage over those that did not. Similarly, we can relate the presence of water-retention devices in vascular plants to their distribution in xeric environments. We base these inferences on our knowledge of how the world operates. Sometimes we might be wrong in our inference. Bootstrapping can be used to examine features in one group vis-à-vis survival and reproductive success, where our inferences are on solid footing, and then apply those results, inferentially, to another group. This appears to us to be the proper use of ethnographic data in attempting to solve select archaeological problems (O'Brien and Holland 1990:48).

ADAPTEDNESS, ADAPTATION, AND THE ARCHAEOLOGICAL RECORD

This brings us to the second theme of this paper. How do we use the ideas of potential adaptedness and adaptation, as defined here, to examine archaeological problems? At a more-general level, do these concepts apply to the study of humans? Our answer is emphatically yes, though we expect that not all anthropologists will agree. Few people familiar with Darwinian evolutionary theory have trouble accepting the premise that, except in a few technical ways (usually because of design constraints), selection is not directed toward some end. That is, selection is not what commonly is called "Lamarckian." To be precise, most people have no trouble with undirected selection when it applies to fruit flies, but when we start talking about humans, all bets are off. For when we speak of humans we are speaking of animals with intellect and will. Intention is, "if not the soul of Western man, a close approximation thereof" (O'Brien and Holland 1990:43). Humans are born actors and thinkers. As such, don't they have at their disposal the means to escape selection? On the other hand, under a "purely" biological perspective don't we completely discount the roles played by rationality and intent? The answer to both questions is, unequivocally, no. Steward (1956:72) sagely noted that "a specific invention is not explained by saying that man is creative." Instead of discounting human intention, selectionist theory assigns it the important role of introducing variation into a cultural system. Variation, not intent, is the significant component. In nonhuman biological evolution variation results largely from mutation and from the reshuffling of existing alleles during reproduction. In human evolution variation results in part from perception and intention. If it were the case that all outcomes of thought processes were those intended, then we have an excellent case of directed variation. But this is decidedly not so (see Reynolds 1984), since the simplest of "intended" actions can spawn an infinite number of outcomes and a dizzying array of variation.

At an intuitive level, no one would argue that a person who sits down to manufacture a stone tool does not have an intended outcome in mind. So in one sense—a trivial sense—we can speak of intent as a proximate "cause" of something. But of what analytical interest is such a statement? When we relate an evolved feature to the notion of intent, we close the book on further analysis. We argue elsewhere (O'Brien and Holland 1990:45) that some confusion surrounding the nature of selection relative to humans undoubtedly can be attributed to use of the term *cultural selection(ism)* (e.g., Rindos 1984, 1985, 1986), the basic tenet of which is that evolutionary processes can act independently on genes and on culturally transmitted behavior (the term "cultural selection[ism]" probably should be dropped from usage, despite its wide adoption [see Braun 1990:79]). Although we should never doubt Mayr's (1973:388) assertion that "Behavior is perhaps the strongest selection pressure operating in the animal kingdom" or Rindos's (1986:316) statement that learning is "one of the most important determinants of behavior," we should not assume that humans are governed by a different process than that which governs other organisms. If variation, whether by accident or design, confers increased adaptedness on an organism, and if the trait is inheritable or transmissible *by any means*, then all else being equal the trait will be represented differentially in the succeeding generation. What is important to the selectionist is that phenotypic (defined broadly) variation is available.

If we accept this position, then the question we asked earlier—How do we use the concepts of potential fitness and adaptation to solve archaeological problems?—should be inverted. The question now becomes, How can the archaeological record be used to analyze the fitness and adaptations of past groups of people? Further, what methods can we use to elicit such information? It seems reasonable to assume, given our premise that things in the archaeological record were parts of past human phenotypes, that the record contains fossilized traces both of features that bore directly on the potential adaptedness of their possessors as well as of features that did not. Additionally, some of those features were adaptations, and some were not. Step one in our analysis should be focused on separating features that affected adaptedness from those that did not. Step two should be focused on separating adaptations from nonadaptations.

Adaptations and Nonadaptations

Leonard and Jones (1987) make an interesting point about using traits to examine fitness. They distinguish between the success of the features (traits) themselves and the success of the trait possessors. Since features are not the units of selection (their possessors are), they must be viewed in terms of replicative, not reproductive, success. Leonard and Jones (1987:213–214) correctly note that "While the differential reproductive success of individuals may influence the expression of cultural variation, it does not determine it." Thus replicative success does not necessarily signal that a selective advantage has been passed to the possessors of the feature, nor does it imply that the feature was under selection.

Picking up on Leonard and Jones's notion of reproductive success, we note elsewhere (O'Brien and Holland 1990:50): "In terms of reproductive success, *possession* of a trait *may* make individuals more fit by giving them a selective advantage over individuals not possessing the trait. But if possession of that trait has no effect on the reproductive success of the possessor, then the trait is neutral" (emphasis in original). However, given our definition of adaptation and our emphasis on potential adaptedness rather than on realized adaptedness, we clearly no longer can subscribe to the point made in the last sentence. We would amend the sentence to read, "But if possession of that trait has no effect on the *adaptedness* of the possessor, then that trait is neutral; if the trait did not evolve because of selection, then it is not an adaptation."

Selective neutrality implies that an organism gains no selective advantage *by possessing one state of a trait over another state of that trait*, i.e., each state carries equivalent fitness values. Importantly, and we cannot emphasize this enough, neutrality of alternate states of a trait does *not* imply, as we discuss below, that possessing the *trait* carries no selective value. Also, neutrality is tied to a particular time, since, as we have seen, neutral traits can become nonneutral. Recall that not all traits that increase adaptedness are under selective control. Up to now we have ignored this subtle but important point. But this point, with the topic of neutrality, is so critical to archaeology that misinterpretation of them has led to massive confusion by archaeologists interested in developing and applying an evolutionary approach (e.g., Rindos 1989). The problem, in part, stems from misinterpretation of Dunnell's (1978a) dichotomization of function and style and his curious and perhaps counterintuitive linkage between style and neutrality. We elsewhere (O'Brien and Holland 1990) attempted to clear up the problem but were only partially successful.

The problem also stems from an implied equation, in the few instances where function and neutrality have been discussed in the archaeological literature (e.g., Dunnell 1978a, 1978b, 1980; Leonard and Jones 1987; Neff 1992; O'Brien and Holland 1990), of adaptations and "functional" traits and an equation of nonadaptations and neutral traits. Dunnell (1978a), for example, distinguishes between function and style both in terms of Darwinian fitness and of selective value. He uses *function* to refer to those forms that directly affect the Darwinian fitness of populations in which they occur and *style* to refer to those forms that have no detectable selective values. In other words, "style" refers to neutral traits. But what we have here is a shift in emphasis of criteria necessary for inclusion in the two categories. An increase in Darwinian fitness is used as the criterion for inclusion in the function category, while the absence of selective value is used as the criterion for inclusion in the neutral (style) category. But what do we do with features that increase the adaptedness of the possessor(s) but that are not products of selection? To bring the problem into focus and to avoid problems associated with the dichotomous terms "style" and "function," we create three categories of traits: (1) traits that are under selective control and that increase adaptedness; (2) traits that are not under selective control and that increase adaptedness; and (3) traits that are not under selective control and that do not increase adaptedness.

Clearly traits in category 1 are the products of selection. They are, by definition, adaptations. Traits in categories 2 and 3 are products of other processes, which we discuss below. Under Dunnell's use of the term "function"—as applied to traits that increase Darwinian fitness—traits in both categories 1 and 2 qualify, though it is clear from the contexts in which Dunnell uses the term that he is referring to traits in category 1, i.e., those that both contribute to adaptedness *and* are products of selection. Dunnell's use of "style" refers to traits in category 3—"traits" (in reality, states of traits) that do not contribute to adaptedness and therefore are neutral.

But can't "style" contribute to adaptedness, whether or not it comes under selective control? In one sense it can, and it is for this reason that confusion has reigned supreme over Dunnell's use of the term to imply neutrality. Style, as Dunnell (1978a) uses the term, is neutral only to the extent that at a given time any particular stylistic *feature* is as "fit" as any other stylistic feature. The critical point here is use of the word "feature" and the confusion it creates. It is precisely for this reason that we use the term "feature state" (or "trait state") instead of "feature" (or "trait"). What is important is that there may be several or many alternate states (attribute states of a specific dimension [see Dunnell 1971]) in which a trait can reside, with each state conferring equivalent (or, sometimes, nonequivalent) adaptedness to the possessor. Thus it is imperative to separate the concept of "style"—an ill-defined complex of traits and trait states—from the phenomena of "stylistic elements."

An example is the incision of circles, chevrons, or birds into moist exteriors of unfired pots. Two questions are relevant here. First, is it important that pots are decorated at all (the presence of decoration being a feature [trait])? Second, is it important that chevrons are used instead of birds or circles (the individual designs being states of traits)? It would make little sense to call a chevron an adaptation, but it might make sense to call pot decoration an adaptation *within a given setting*. We could construct several scenarios where loosely knit social groups spread across a landscape use decorative displays for social purposes—either for integration or information exchange (e.g., Braun and Plog 1982; Wobst 1977). By participating in the social-identification system of which the marked pots are a feature, a person might increase his/her adaptedness: Food can be shared in time of need, new mates are available, and so on. By not participating in the system, individuals (or a group of individuals) could be affecting their adaptedness relative to other individuals or groups in the region. But examining the role of pot decoration in this context is decidedly different from examining pot decoration abstractly. The mere fact that someone out of the blue decides to decorate a pot is, by itself, not a functional trait.

This raises a related point about selection and adaptedness. We might suggest that despite the wide range of decorative variants possible in the world, there are some that the groups using the pots find unacceptable. Or, more probable, there are variants that make no sense to the users. Thus there is an *acceptable range* of decorative variants available. As long as makers or users remain within the range, which we might expect could and would change over time (for example, by ca. A.D. 300 midwestern cooking jars no longer carried elaborate decorations), their adaptedness, at least relative to this one dimension, is not affected adversely. But pot makers or users who consistently defy the limits of acceptability could have their adaptedness affected. Again, what is important from the standpoint of potential adaptedness is *not* that the pots specifically have birds or chevrons on their exteriors—or that the pots are decorated at all—but that *if* the pots are decorated the makers and users know which elements are acceptable and act accordingly.

It isn't profound to say there are different scales at which features in the archaeological record can be examined and that a healthy dose of common sense is needed to reduce making errors of the first order. For example, without a perspective on the recurrence of cooking-vessel designs across broad regions of the Midwest, our picture of the life histories of ceramic "types" would be heavily biased. We could be left wondering whether there was some reason for a local group to decorate its pots for a while and then to abandon decoration. It is not too much off the point to note that lack of attention to detail at the regional level seriously impeded our understanding of post-ca. A.D. 300 developments in the midwestern United States. For years the received wisdom among archaeologists working in the Midwest was that the "Hopewell Interaction Sphere," characterized at many sites by nicely decorated vessels and the occurrence of exotic materials, came to a sudden halt as a result of groups becoming more isolated in their behavior and the concurrent lack of benefit from participating in the sphere. Braun (1977, 1985a), however, shows conclusively that instead of becoming more isolated, at least in terms of ceramic similarities, post-A.D. 300 groups showed heightened homogeneity. The misconception was a result of analytical interest that for decades had focused solely on decoration instead of on manufacture *and* decoration.

Part of the confusion over style and neutrality undoubtedly stems from the fact that, as we mentioned before, the source of selection is tied to human intent. Anthropologists argue that humans select ceramic styles, dress lengths, and myriad other things based on culturally influenced choice. Thus, the argument runs, style cannot be selectively neutral. This problem is nothing more than the result of the same word having more than one meaning. Selection as an evolutionary process has little to do with cultural selection as often applied colloquially. What is meant in the latter sense is simply "choosing" one thing over another. Humans may be selective agents, but only if they affect the adaptedness either of themselves or of other organisms. For example, animal breeders are active selective agents. And, the seemingly capricious, but in reality patterned, choice by collectors of butterflies of one color or another is as potent an agent of selection as is the choice by any bird. In both cases the butterflies meet unhappy endings, and the gene pool of which they were a part is adjusted accordingly (O'Brien and Holland 1990:57). But this is very different from choosing one design element over another for vessel decoration. Clearly, the more-important analytical problem is understanding the pool of acceptable variation for given points in time and determining how remaining in the pool vs. straying outside it affects adaptedness.

To summarize, functional traits are seen as those that contribute directly to adaptedness and that are under selection. They are equivalent to traits in category 1 and are termed adaptations. Non-functional traits, such as design motifs on ceramic vessels, are not under selective control and do not affect adaptedness. They fall in our category 3. But what about category-2 traits, i.e., those that may affect fitness but are not under selective control? A biological example of such a trait would be a mutation. The corresponding nonbiological feature would be an invention, discovery, or similar product of a moment in time.

Not all such products of the moment affect adaptedness, especially those that arise and go unnoticed. Others very well could affect adaptedness, and many of them will go on to become adaptations. For example, a human who picks up an animal hide, punches a hole in it and puts it on may increase his adaptedness relative to others in his group. At that point, the hide is not an adaptation; it is merely a "mutation" relative to one human's phenotype. A number of sequences could follow. If, after a few generations, the person's offspring were living longer and producing more children than were their conspecifics, then the wearing of skins would become an adaptation. Or, if after a few weeks or months other members in the group noticed that the skin wearer appeared more comfortable than they, then they might start wearing skins. The wearing of skins might then be considered an adaptation. But suppose the skin wearer died the day after he started wearing skins, without telling anyone else how warm he felt? Then we have another example of a mutation that remained a novelty.[3]

Several interesting points come out of this example, perhaps the most important being we do not necessarily have to wait for generations to see if something is going to affect adaptedness or to come under selective control. The wearing of skins could become an adaptation almost over night. But, one might ask, don't we have to wait for succeeding generations to manifest themselves before we can decide whether the features are adaptations? Not if we are interested in *potential* adaptedness instead of in *realized* adaptedness. An engineering study could help us in determining whether an advantage was to be gained by wearing skins (of course, in this instance we can rely on common sense). One also could question whether our experimenting human really knew that by putting on a skin he was raising his body temperature to well above a life-threatening point and whether he could tell this to others in his group. This point really is irrelevant. *If* the trait spread because it was selected for, intentionally or not, and *if* the trait affected the adaptedness of the bearers, then it was an adaptation. No one in the group had to make any connection between body warmth and increased longevity.

In this single example we potentially have the makings of all three categories of traits. The wearing of skins, we can predict, affects adaptedness, regardless of the time we make the examination, i.e., when the feature is a mutation or when it is an adaptation. Thus the trait falls in category 2 and then, if it is acted upon by selection, category 1. But does the *kind* of skin matter? Is bear skin superior to wolf skin, or does each confer an equivalent advantage to the wearer, i.e., are the relative fitnesses equivalent? (Certainly if we were debating the relative merits of bison hide vs. rabbit skin for use as shield coverings, then the answer would be clear.) Notice that the level of examination has shifted here from the trait itself—skin or no skin—to the attributes of the trait, similar to the shift seen in our example of pot decoration. Detailed engineering studies of different types of skins found in our imaginary archaeological record would have to be conducted before this question could be answered.

Concomitant with our engineering study, we might want to track changes through time in the occurrence of skins, both as a whole and of different kinds of skins. We propose that the manner in which frequencies of variants behave over time might be of more-than-passing analytical interest. Dunnell's (1978a:199) view of how such frequencies behave when they are either under or not under selective control is a starting point: "Traits that have discrete selective values over measurable amounts of time should be accountable by natural selection and a set of external conditions. Traits identified as adaptively neutral will display a very different kind of behavior because their frequencies in a population are not directly accountable in terms of selection and external contingencies. Their behavior should be more adequately accommodated by stochastic processes."

Variants under selective control *do* behave differently than do those that are not. Traits or alternative states of traits not under selective control can (a) drift through a population from generation to generation, their frequencies fluctuating randomly—sometimes in one direction, then another, and so on, or (b) come under selective control. Under the latter, mutations are either immediately acted upon by selection and the magnitude function shifts upward, or the feature or state drifts along, perhaps increasing in frequency, and then the magnitude function shifts upward. Under the former, given infinite time without selection, one of two outcomes is possible: Either the state will hit zero and thus be eliminated from the population, or it will become fixed. In reality, we find it difficult to believe that a neutral trait, or state of a trait, could ever reach fixation by chance without a drastic reduction of population numbers, as a result either of disaster or of fragmentation. By far the more likely outcome will be that the trait disappears from the population.

It is not, however, the random zig-zag curve that is of interest here but rather the familiar battleship-shaped curve that characterizes archaeological seriations. If most archaeological seriation curves are based on changes in stylistic frequencies, and if style is neutral and thus not under selective control, then why don't seriation curves exhibit the random zig-zag pattern shown by alleles not under selective control? We elsewhere (O'Brien and Holland 1990:54) claimed a close correlation between ordered seriation curves and the disorderly appearing, random-fluctuation curves. This was an overstatement on our part, we now realize, caused in large part by conflation of randomness on one hand and stochastic processes on the other. Stochastic processes are perfectly capable of producing orderly appearing events, whether they be design changes on pots or computer-generated clades of organisms (e.g., Gould et al. 1977). With clades, the result exemplifies the Markovian side of evolution's nature, where the form of each state depends in large part on the previous state. Archaeological "styles" also are Markovian in nature, i.e., styles are constructed from other styles, building on previous developments. On the other hand, the zig-zag pattern of allele fluctuations is nothing more than a graphic presentation of what in essence is the flip of a coin. Heads the allele frequency increases, tails it decreases. If the coin rests on its edge, the frequency remains unchanged.

As opposed to what happens to a trait not under selective control, a trait or, similarly, an alternative *state* of a trait that is being selected for, will begin at some arbitrary point above zero and increase in frequency at a steadily decelerating rate toward some optimal value. This gives selection its apparent "directional" component. Selection against the trait or state—the result of changes in the selective environment—reverses the trend and sends the curve downward. As selection favors new characteristics that arise, the fall-off in frequency of variants being replaced should be rapid. Given the rapidity with which variation can be generated among groups of humans, successive sigmoid curves with abrupt truncations should be the rule rather than the exception.

The decelerating curve applies equally to a trait or to a single state of a trait—depending on the level of analysis—under selection. States of traits (things) found in the archaeological record are not the equivalent of alleles, in the normal sense of the word, though at one level they can vary in the same way that alleles do. If, for example, we examine the kinds of temper added to cooking vessels through time in a region, we might find that over a 1,000-year span shell, sand, grog, and limestone were the major temper constituents, each with its own particular life history. What we need to track are the life histories of *all* temper kinds through time and to compare the curves. When we examine a fragment of tempered pottery, we will find one of two things: Either the vessel was tempered with a single material or with a combination of materials. Thus a vessel can be unimorphic or polymorphic with respect to temper.[4]

Pottery is an interesting class of materials to examine relative to adaptedness and adaptation, especially from the standpoint of nested units of adaptation (Kirch 1980:132). First, were prehistoric pots adaptations? Clearly it is not difficult to understand advantages that would accrue from having containers for transporting and cooking food. So if nothing else we can state that, from the standpoint of potential fitness, pots at least contribute to relative adaptedness in specific environments. Upon examining the life history of pottery and its meteoric rise in frequency once invented or introduced into various regions of the eastern United States, we would argue pottery was an adaptation. But even though we would argue pottery was an adaptation, we need to examine the life history of pottery in *individual regions* (O'Brien and Holland 1991). It is entirely possible for pottery, or pottery technology, to have been introduced into an area but used, for whatever reasons, only rarely. Thus it would not have been an adaptation for groups in that area.

Second, what technological factors relative to vessel construction might be adaptations? Braun's (1983, 1985b, 1987) work on Woodland-period cooking jars from west-central Illinois is a landmark study of the dynamics of prehistoric-vessel technology, especially of the covariation of technological dimensions. His early work (Braun 1983, 1985b) focused on tracking changes in vessel-wall thickness through time, a classic case of directional selection moving the mean slowly toward thinner walls. Braun argued that thin-walled vessels were being selected for their increased ability to conduct heat and their increased resistance to thermal shock. Further analysis (Braun 1987) showed that despite the neatness of this scenario, the logistic curve created by measuring vessel-wall thickness obscured many components that together created the curve, i.e., components that reflect the myriad decisions and limitations facing Woodland potters as they considered changing demands for performance characteristics in their products (Schiffer and Skibo 1987). An especially important technology—the production of extremely thin-walled bowls (almost always tempered with limestone)—was developed around A.D. 200–300, and though it lasted only a short time may have led to a transfer in technology to the production of cooking vessels with far-thinner walls per unit of vessel size than those manufactured previously. The general trends in vessel-wall thickness tracked by Braun—despite the complexity of underlying logistical components—suggest thin-walled vessels not only contributed to adaptedness but also were adaptations (O'Brien and Holland 1991).

Third, was tempering—another technological dimension—an adaptation? Engineering studies (e.g., Feathers 1989; Grimshaw 1971) suggest the addition of temper greatly enhances a vessel's ability to withstand stresses that occur during firing. This fact, along with the almost-universal presence of aplastic inclusions in prehistoric vessels, suggests tempered vessels were adaptations (O'Brien and Holland 1991).

Fourth, were *individual* tempering agents adaptations? Based on our assessment of published and unpublished data on sherds and associated radiometric dates from one region of the Midwest, we suggest that in the lower Illinois River valley and in select portions of the Central Mississippi River valley vessels tempered with grit (various-size angular to subangular particles) were adaptations that later were replaced by vessels tempered with burned shell. Both appear to have had the requisite histories to qualify them as adaptations (Figure 1). In the case of grit tempering, angular particles were used from the beginning (ca. 500 B.C.) to temper first crudely made, thick-walled jars, and then thinner-walled vessels. Other materials sometimes were used, in most cases in conjunction with grit. By A.D. 600 in some areas shell was used as a minor tempering agent, but by A.D. 1000 it had become the predominant material used throughout the Mississippi River valley and over large portions of the Southeast. In other words, shell tempering began as a mutation that drifted along for several centuries before coming under active selective control.

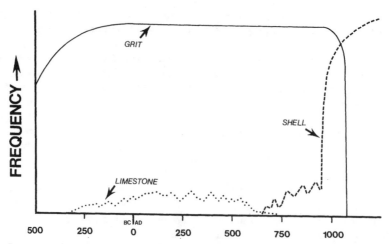

Figure 1. Hypothetical changes in frequency of grit-, shell-, and limestone-tempered vessels. Shell-tempered and grit-tempered vessels were under selective control; limestone-tempered vessels were not.

The case of pottery in the Midwest allows us to view two of the modes of selection mentioned earlier: stabilizing selection and directional selection. It also illustrates the manner in which each kind of selection operates. Although pottery was introduced into the southeastern United States during the third millennium B.C., with few exceptions (Reid 1984) it is recognized in the Midwest only in contexts that date after ca. 500–600 B.C. Pottery either was introduced into the Midwest or began as a mutation. Pottery manufacture in the Midwest accelerated in frequency around 500 B.C. In other words, there was strong directional selection for pottery manufacture. Concomitant with the rise in pottery production was the rise in grit as a tempering agent—again, a product of strong directional selection. After approximately 200 B.C., there was strong directional selection for thinner-walled cooking vessels, though the effects of this selection were ameliorated by another type of selection, stabilizing selection, which tended to eliminate certain variants that would have moved the thinning process along at a faster rate. Under stabilizing selection grit was kept as the predominate tempering agent, though other materials were in use in small amounts (Figure 1). Importantly, prehistoric potters knew about these other materials but rarely used them alone when manufacturing a cooking jar. Under directional selection, ca. A.D. 1000, shell as a temper began its rapid ascent.

We can pose some interesting questions regarding the directional selection and subsequent stabilizing selection of shell-tempered pottery, specifically questions regarding the kinds of advantages that shell tempering offered (Dunnell and Feathers 1991; Feathers 1988). Several studies (e.g., Million 1975; Stimmell et al. 1982) suggest that shell enhances the workability of sticky flood-plain clays, which were the matrix constituents of pre- and post-A.D. 900 ceramics in the Mississippi River valley. Late Woodland pottery was made from the same kinds of sticky clays—illites containing fine quartz, plagioclase feldspar, and traces of titanium dioxide (Feathers 1988)—but before ca. A.D. 900 sand and grog (in different areas) were the preferred tempers.

Feathers (1988) demonstrates that paste plasticity is increased through the addition of shell, apparently through increased flocculation caused by the presence of calcium cations. Increased plasticity eventually led to the production of a wide variety of ceramic forms. His tests also show an increase in the strength of shell-tempered ceramics over those tempered with sand. Also, the somewhat large platelike structures created by crushed shell are a better deterrent to crack propagation than are sand particles, thus causing fewer failed vessels during heating. The key to successful use of shell tempering is controlling firing temperatures below about 700°C—the point at which calcite, upon cooling and hydration, changes to $Ca(OH)_2$ (Dunnell and Feathers 1991; Feathers 1988). Once prehistoric potters attained the skill needed to control firing temperature, shell-tempered pottery spread rapidly across the southeastern United States.

Has our discussion precluded the roles of human intent and choice played in the "evolution" of pottery? Not really. We would not argue that prehistoric potters did not set out to make certain forms, nor that they didn't experiment with tempers (see Rye [1976] for ethnographic examples of temper choice and desired results) and firing temperatures. We *would* argue, however, that it is impossible to know what went on in the minds of prehistoric potters and that regardless, the outcome is still measurable in terms of engineering design and by inference relative fitness. Occasionally one hears disparaging remarks directed toward archaeological studies that attempt to understand technological aspects of pottery manufacture—remarks stemming from a belief that little is to be gained from using high-tech equipment to measure things such as precise temperatures at which pots were fired, since prehistoric potters did not have similar equipment. But is retroactively measuring firing temperature of pots any different from measuring beak length in a group of finches or measuring the height of beaver dams? Such misplaced criticism grows out of a feeling that unless prehistoric peoples were aware of the variation inherent in their products, why would we want to measure it? Prehistoric potters obviously did not use pyrometers, at least as we know them, to measure firing temperatures, but they learned, eventually, to maintain temperatures below 700°C. Again, the point is that selection is blind to the source of variation, regardless of origin. Pottery would be an adaptation whether it was introduced into an area or arose because of independent invention. Human intent neither adds to nor subtracts from increased adaptedness and adaptation. As Rindos (1984:4) notes, "Man may indeed select, but he cannot direct the variation from which he must select." Human selection—choice—because of the extremely imprecise way in which it replicates things, is a tremendous source of variation in its own right, producing new variants at a high rate. Any variant can affect adaptedness, and all are ripe for selection to begin operating on them.

ADAPTATION IN A LARGER PERSPECTIVE

Scientific approaches can be sound, but if no one uses them, either because of tradition or because they are too complicated, what use are they? We have argued here that the ways in which adaptation and adaptedness have been applied in archaeology and anthropology have little in common with the ways in which they have been applied in biology, and we have attempted to show how this noncongruity can be overcome. We do not think the approach is so complex that progress will not be made, though we suspect advances will be slow to come. Whether archaeologists break with tradition is irrelevant at this stage. There are, however, three points that could, and probably will, be leveled against the approach—points that need clarification before some researchers will feel comfortable in changing their views on adaptation.

First, is our focus on adaptations atomistic? Does a long and tedious examination of changes in temper inclusions in midwestern pottery—regardless of whether or not tempered pots are "adaptations"—really tell us anything about people? What about the bigger picture, which anthropology has always claimed as its objective? Our only answer to these questions is that in the end such detailed examinations will tell us considerably more about prehistoric peoples than will reference to vaguely defined terms such as "adaptive plateaus," "preadaptive strategies," and the like. It may sound trite to say that long journeys begin with but single steps, but that is exactly what faces us relative to the study of human adaptation. To understand the intricate process of adaptation and the ever-changing state of adaptedness, we need to establish as many small reference points as possible—reference points that eventually can be used to construct temporal curves for the examination of trajectories taken by various traits and their states.

We have, by necessity, limited discussion to analysis of individual traits and various ways of determining whether traits are the products of selection, but despite our focus on individual traits we emphasize that selection works on whole phenotypes. Nowhere have we suggested that traits or states of traits are fit or not fit; rather, we have argued that traits have *fitness values*. We *have* suggested that a design study of phenotypic features and a close tracking of the life history of the feature can yield significant results concerning adaptation, but at some point we can move beyond asking functional, "how-does-it-work" questions and focus on broader issues, placing our knowledge of discrete functions into an organized synthesis of adaptive behavior.

For example, the changes in ceramic-vessel technology discussed above have been used to track other aspects of human adaptedness in the riverine Midwest during the period 200 B.C.–A.D. 750. Vessel-wall-thickness curves for western Illinois (Braun 1985b, 1987), eastern Missouri (O'Brien and Holland 1991), and southern Illinois (Hargrave 1981) show that around A.D. 50 vessel walls began at least a 700-year-long decline in mean thickness. Braun (1985b, 1987) infers that adjustments in pottery technology track changes that took place among Woodland groups producing the vessels— changes inferred from the archaeological record to be increased sedentariness (Asch 1976; O'Brien 1987), shifts in household composition and size (Braun 1987), population growth (Buikstra et al. 1986; Holland 1989; O'Brien 1987), increased localization of resource procurement (Styles 1981), and increased nutritional dependence on the seeds of starchy and oily annuals (Asch and Asch 1985). In coevolutionary fashion, Woodland pottery technology shifted, coincident with increased use of seed plants, toward production of thinner-walled vessels that could be used to extract nutritional value from the seeds. It has been suggested (Buikstra et al. 1986; O'Brien 1987) that such a technology could have led to an increase in fertility, as babies were shifted to starchy gruels at an earlier age, thereby decreasing the birth interval. The findings of Buikstra et al. (1986) show that increased fertility *did* occur during the Late Woodland period.

Concomitant with increased sedentism, localization of resource procurement, increased use of starchy seeds, and changes in cooking-vessel technology, a dramatic change took place in the treatment of the exteriors of cooking jars. Vessels made before ca. 200 B.C. were undecorated except for cordmarking and/or deep incising over most if not all the vessel exteriors. After that date, and for approximately the next 500 years, exteriors of cooking jars often were incised, stamped, and punctated to produce literally dozens of fancy motifs. Remarkably, the same series of designs was produced at many different locales along the Mississippi River and its major tributaries such as the Illinois and Missouri rivers (Braun 1985a). Braun (1986) and Braun and Plog (1982) view this phenomenon in terms of information exchange—part of a social network that distributed risk and benefits among members, transmitted information about the environment to participants, defined lines of fusion and fission for periodic aggregation and dispersion, and delegated decision-making responsibilities (see O'Brien [1987] for extended summary). Whether Braun and Plog are correct on all counts is immaterial. What is important is that they demonstrate that there *could* have been a distinct adaptive advantage in participating in such a network. And if one of the signifiers of group membership was decorating the exteriors of cooking jars, then decoration was an adaptive feature.

Second, one might question our emphasis on potential fitness rather than on realized fitness. Aren't we interested more in what happened than we are in what *might* have happened? Yes, we are, though here we are faced with some of the same problems facing paleontologists. How does one adequately demonstrate that possession of a certain feature made an organism more fit than its conspecifics without the feature? Obviously one way would be to show an inequality in the number of offspring produced by each organism (and their successors) in succeeding generations. Archaeologically this would require massive burial data, the size of which probably is unattainable. There is reason to suspect, however, that eventually, with enough data points, it will be possible to infer realized fitness from potential fitness. Engineering-design studies produce the kinds of information needed to create the data points and head us in the right direction, as shown in the example from the Illinois River valley cited above. There, the implied linkage among increased use of starchy seeds, thinner-walled vessels, and increased fertility has paved the way for more-intensive examination of the archaeological record relative to increased realized fitness.

Third, one might ask what the difference is between the kind of approach we advocate and the approach that has a venerated place in anthropology, namely functionalism. This is an interesting question and one that was posed by one of the reviewers. If we accept the term functionalism at face value—understanding how things work—then our approach to adaptation can be termed functional. A selectionist approach, to be anything other than a metaphysical exercise, has to be functional. Darwin, despite claims to the contrary, was a functionalist, i.e., he was fascinated in how things work. Adaptation, if it is anything, is a record of how well organisms function *in particular locales at particular times*.

So what are the differences between a Darwinian view of function and what has commonly come to be known in anthropology as functionalism? Functionalists from Malinowski on down have been interested in how cultures operate, and in several significant respects their ideas and approaches live on in the cultural evolutionists/ecologists of the mid- and late-twentieth century who have taken functional analysis to even greater heights. The close ties between the earlier functionalists and the later cultural evolutionists are clear: "The concept of 'stages' remains as valid as that of origins. We would, however, have to make any evolutionary scheme of successive developmental stages either very general or else valid only for certain regions and under certain conditions" (Malinowski 1960:16). Here Malinowski sounds very much like Steward (e.g., 1955). And at the center of functional analyses has been adaptation. But the ways in which the functionalists/cultural ecologists view adaptation have little in common with the Darwinian view of adaptation. And, as we pointed out earlier, it is the non-Darwinian functionalist view that has pervaded anthropology.

Adaptation, to the functionalists/evolutionists, is a preordained conclusion: "no invention, no revolution, no social or intellectual change, ever occurs except when needs are created and thus new devices or techniques, in knowledge, or in belief are fitted into the cultural processes of an institution" (Malinowski 1960:16). This is about as non-Darwinian a statement as one could make. As Rindos (1989:34) points out, "Functionalists extend to culture the dominant mode of evolutionary explanation used by the nineteenth-century biologist—the very model of environmentally induced variation that Darwin utilized before developing the mature theory in the *Origin*." As we discussed earlier, Darwin's immature view held that organisms constantly monitor their environments, adjusting only when the environment instructs them to do so, and then only in precisely described manners.

Nowhere is the functionalist approach more apparent in anthropology than in efforts to understand the origins of agriculture—efforts in large part directed toward understanding how and why agriculture started when and where it did. Or, conversely, efforts are expended to understand why it did *not* begin in a certain area, since plant domestication would seem to have been the "logical" adaptation. Pryor (1986), for example, concludes a study of the origins of agriculture by asking why *all* societies have not adopted agriculture, since he assumes that over the past 10,000 years four conditions have prevailed: (1) groups had the requisite knowledge for practicing agriculture; (2) hunting and gathering presented such risks that groups should have wanted to adopt some agriculture; (3) in many groups cultural and natural conditions that would have precluded agriculture were small; and (4) population growth would have led to diminishing returns without agriculture. In other words, in the face of risk to a group, it *should have*, following the functionalist approach, turned to agriculture as the logical adaptation. Researchers such as Pryor are clearly cut from the Steward mold of cultural ecology: "The most fruitful course of investigation would seem to be the search for laws which formulate the interrelationships of particular phenomena which may recur cross-culturally but are not necessarily universal" (Steward 1955:29).

A Darwinian approach to anthropology in no way precludes cross-cultural comparisons, though it does preclude, we would argue, searching for "laws which formulate the interrelationships of particular phenomena." The only laws that apply under a Darwinian perspective are laws of contingency. This is not to say that there are not *design constraints* placed on behaviors as there are on somatic features. It makes little sense, for example, to wonder why igloos were not in use on the Great Plains. But design constraints are not the same as laws that govern outcomes. Searching for functional laws that *govern* behavior is based on the belief that some nearly perfect ideal exists toward which cultures are pushed. We agree with Rindos (1989:37) that "In calling upon the perfect adaptation of the pre-*Origin* Darwin, [functionalism] cannot help but posit a cultural adaptationism that is motivated by the generation of directed variation to account for all cultural response to stress." The orthogenetic view of history that guides such attempts is distinctly different from the view we advocate here. Under the functionalist view, if the tape of life is rewound and played a hundred times, the outcomes should be, within reason, almost similar. In other words, human groups would show similar adjustments relative to their adaptive behaviors. Under the Darwinian view, as Gould has pointed out ad nauseum (e.g., Gould 1989), the replays should show a spectacular range of outcomes, with each adaptation contingent in part upon what came before (design constraint) but open to countless possibilities.

CONCLUSIONS

Taylor (1948:95) noted over 40 years ago that archaeologists were becoming "as Tolstoy once said of modern historians, like deaf men answering questions which no one has asked them." We have no doubt that much of what we have said in this paper will be perceived in a similar light. But the questions have been asked, even if we have not always heard them so clearly. And at the center of the questions is the concept of adaptation. As Kirch (1980:101) points out, a long-standing aim of anthropology has been to explain "man's myriad adaptations to the environmental challenges of existence." This goal is both valid and worthy of attention, though in practice the role of adaptation too often has been confined to a post-facto "explanation" of the appearance and persistence of a particular trait. We firmly believe that it is not altogether unreasonable to begin with a more-rigorous definition of what adaptation is and, by extension, what it is not.

In defining adaptation, we take our lead from evolutionary biology. To most biologists, an adaptation not only must contribute to an organism's adaptedness, but it must have a pedigree molded by selection. Thus an innovation or invention (or accident) cannot be an adaptation. It is only after an adaptive innovation is replicated (and thus ceases to be an innovation) and is subsequently shaped by selection that an adaptation exists. Use of this more rigorously defined concept of adaptation helps to unravel the archaeological knot composed of conflating style and function. Within the framework offered by this definition, functional traits are those that affect adaptedness, but *only* those with a history shaped by selection are considered adaptations. On the other hand, style is regarded as more than merely the absence of function. A stylistic trait is one that neither affects adaptedness nor is under selective control.

The problem facing archaeologists interested in adaptation (and most profess to be) would appear to be twofold. First, it is necessary to identify which archaeological features contributed to the adaptedness of the human group(s) under study. This procedure is linked directly to an analytical separation of potential adaptedness from realized adaptedness. Second, archaeologists are obliged to chart the evolutionary history of a particular feature in order to decide whether it has been shaped by selection, since then and only then can a trait be considered an adaptation. Determining whether or not a trait was (is) adaptive is not always easy. For example, adaptations may be nested in a number of hierarchical units, and it is necessary first to adjust the level of analysis to the proper unit. It then may be possible to determine the potential adaptedness of a trait (or suite of traits). Engineering studies are a viable means of assessing fitness, and we suggest elsewhere (O'Brien and Holland 1991) that perhaps this is the most-useful role that the field of archaeometry can play.

The archaeological record, composed mainly of fossilized evidence of successful variants (and which has been disturbed by numerous cultural and natural forces), cannot be assumed to hold all the evidence needed to understand completely prehistoric adaptedness and adaptation. Yet, despite methodological problems, archaeology is well poised to make significant contributions to the study of adaptation. Indeed, archaeologists have a unique laboratory in which to explore human adaptation over an expanse of time not available to the biologist. We need not be, as Taylor warned, like deaf men. The past speaks in a loud voice, but it is up to us to use solid theory, sound analysis, and logical inference to hear the words. But neither can we, as Lewontin (1986:235) warns, act like vulgarizers who by crossing over "the narrow line that separates a genuinely fruitful and powerful theory from its sterile caricature . . . seize upon the powerful explanatory element and, by its indiscriminate use, destroy its usefulness." That powerful element is the concept of adaptation.

Acknowledgments.   We thank J. Marks, H. C. Wilson, R. C. Dunnell, R. L. Bettinger, H. Neff, R. Boyd, J. J. Reid, and T. Majewski for numerous helpful insights on the manuscript. The shape of the fall-off curve for traits and states under selection was recognized by W. Durham; Dunnell pointed out differences between randomness and stochastic processes; Wilson proposed the example in Note 3; and Reid suggested the distinction between function and functionalism. Axel E. Nielsen prepared the Spanish abstract.

REFERENCES CITED

Alland, A., Jr.
  1975   Adaptation. *Annual Review of Anthropology* 4:59–73.

Asch, D. L.
  1976   *The Middle Woodland Population of the Lower Illinois Valley: A Study in Paleodemographic Models.* Scientific Papers No. 1. Northwestern University Archeological Program. Evanston, Illinois.
Asch, D. L., and N. B. Asch
  1985   Prehistoric Plant Cultivation in West-Central Illinois. In *The Nature and Status of Ethnobotany*, edited by R. I. Ford, pp. 149–203. Anthropological Papers No. 75. Museum of Anthropology, University of Michigan, Ann Arbor.
Bethell, T.
  1976   Darwin's Mistake. *Harper's* February:70–75.
Bock, W. J.
  1980   The Definition and Recognition of Biological Adaptation. *American Zoologist* 20:217–227.
Braidwood, R.
  1967   *Prehistoric Men.* 7th ed. Scott, Foresman, Glenview, Illinois.
Brandon, R. N.
  1978   Adaptation and Evolutionary Theory. *Studies in History and Philosophy of Science* 9:181–206.
  1990   *Adaptation and Environment.* Princeton University Press, Princeton, New Jersey.
Braun, D. P.
  1977   *Middle Woodland-Early Late Woodland Social Change in the Prehistoric Central Midwestern U.S.* Ph.D. Dissertation, University of Michigan. University Microfilms, Ann Arbor.
  1983   Pots as Tools. In *Archaeological Hammers and Theories*, edited by J. Moore and A. Keene, pp. 107–134. Academic Press, New York.
  1985a   Ceramic Decorative Diversity and Illinois Woodland Regional Integration. In *Decoding Prehistoric Ceramics*, edited by B. A. Nelson, pp. 128–153. Southern Illinois University Press, Carbondale.
  1985b   Absolute Seriation: A Time-Series Approach. In *For Concordance in Archaeological Analysis: Bridging Data Structure, Quantitative Technique, and Theory*, edited by C. Carr, pp. 509–539. Westport, Kansas City, Missouri.
  1986   Midwestern Hopewellian Exchange and Supralocal Interaction. In *Peer-Polity Interaction and Sociopolitical Change*, edited by C. Renfrew and J. Cherry, pp. 117–126. Cambridge University Press, New York.
  1987   Coevolution of Sedentism, Pottery Technology, and Horticulture in the Central Midwest, 200 B.C.–A.D. 600. In *Emergent Horticultural Economies of the Eastern Woodlands*, edited by W. F. Keegan, pp. 153–181. Occasional Paper No. 7. Center for Archaeological Investigations, Southern Illinois University–Carbondale.
  1990   Selection and Evolution in Nonhierarchical Organization. In *The Evolution of Political Systems: Sociopolitics in Small-Scale Sedentary Societies*, edited by S. Upham, pp. 62–86. Cambridge University Press, New York.
Braun, D. P., and S. Plog
  1982   Evolution of "Tribal" Social Networks: Theory and Prehistoric North American Evidence. *American Antiquity* 47:504–525.
Buikstra, J. E., L. Koningsberg, and J. Bullington
  1986   Fertility and the Development of Agriculture in the Prehistoric Midwest. *American Antiquity* 51:528–546.
Burian, R.
  1983   Adaptation. *In Dimensions of Darwinism*, edited by M. Grene, pp. 287–314. Cambridge University Press, New York.
Campbell, B. G.
  1966   *Human Evolution: An Introduction to Man's Adaptation.* Aldine, Chicago.
Darwin, C.
  1859   *On the Origin of Species by Means of Natural Selection, or the Preservation of Favored Races in the Struggle for Life.* Murray, London.
Dobzhansky, T.
  1982   *Genetics and the Origin of Species.* Columbia University Press, New York.
Dobzhansky, T., F. J. Ayala, G. L. Stebbins, and J. W. Valentine
  1977   *Evolution.* Freeman, San Francisco.
Dunnell, R. C.
  1971   *Systematics in Prehistory.* The Free Press, New York.
  1978a   Style and Function: A Fundamental Dichotomy. *American Antiquity* 43:192–202.
  1978b   Archaeological Potential of Anthropological and Scientific Models of Function. In *Archaeological Essays in Honor of Irving B. Rouse*, edited by R. C. Dunnell and E. S. Hall, Jr., pp. 41–73. Mouton, The Hague.
  1980   Evolutionary Theory and Archaeology. In *Advances in Archaeological Method and Theory*, vol. 3, edited by M. B. Schiffer, pp. 35–99. Academic Press, New York.
  1985   Methodological Issues in Contemporary Americanist Archaeology. In *Proceedings of the 1984 Biennial Meeting of the Philosophy of Science Association*, vol. 2, edited by P. D. Asquith and P. Kitcher, pp. 717–744. Philosophy of Science Association, East Lansing, Michigan.
  1988   Archaeology and Evolutionary Theory. Ms. on file, Department of Anthropology, University of Missouri–Columbia.

Dunnell, R. C., and J. K. Feathers
  1991   Late Woodland Manifestations of the Malden Plain, Southeast Missouri. In *Stability, Transformation, and Variation: The Late Woodland Southeast*, edited by M. S. Nassaney and C. R. Cobb, pp. 21–45. Plenum, New York.
Feathers, J. K.
  1988   Explaining the Transition from Sand to Shell Temper in Southeastern Missouri Pottery. Ms. on file, Department of Anthropology, University of Missouri–Columbia.
  1989   Effects of Temper on Strength of Ceramics: Response to Bronitsky and Hamer. *American Antiquity* 54:579–588.
Fisher, D. C.
  1985   Evolutionary Morphology: Beyond the Analogous, the Anecdotal, and the Ad Hoc. *Paleobiology* 11: 120–138.
Futuyma, D. J.
  1979   *Evolutionary Biology.* 1st ed. Sinauer, Sunderland, Massachusetts.
  1986   *Evolutionary Biology.* 2nd ed. Sinauer, Sunderland, Massachusetts.
Ghiselin, M. T.
  1966   On Semantic Pitfalls of Biological Adaptation. *Philosophy of Science* 33:147–153.
  1969   *The Triumph of the Darwinian Method.* University of California Press, Berkeley, California.
Gould, S. J.
  1976   Darwin's Untimely Burial. *Natural History* 85:24–30.
  1989   *Wonderful Life: The Burgess Shale and the Nature of History.* Norton, New York.
Gould, S. J., and R. Lewontin
  1979   The Spandrels of San Marco and the Panglossian Paradigm: A Critique of the Adaptationist Programme. *Proceedings of the Royal Society of London* B205:581–598.
Gould, S. J., and E. Vrba
  1982   Exaptation—A Missing Term in the Science of Form. *Paleobiology* 8:4–15.
Gould, S. J., D. M. Raup, J. J. Sepkoski, Jr., T. J. M. Schopf, and D. S. Simberloff
  1977   The Shape of Evolution: A Comparison of Real and Random Clades. *Paleobiology* 3:23–40.
Grimshaw, R.
  1971   *The Chemistry and Physics of Clays.* Ernest Benn, London.
Hargrave, M. L.
  1981   *Woodland Ceramic Chronometry and Occupational Intensity at the Carrier Mills Archaeological District, Saline County, Illinois.* Unpublished Master's thesis, Department of Anthropology, Southern Illinois University–Carbondale.
Holland, T. D.
  1989   Fertility in the Prehistoric Midwest: A Critique of Unifactorial Models. *American Antiquity* 54:389–426.
Kirch, P. V.
  1980   The Archaeological Study of Adaptation: Theoretical and Methodological Issues. In *Advances in Archaeological Method and Theory*, vol. 3, edited by M. B. Schiffer, pp. 101–156. Academic Press, New York.
Krimbas, C. B.
  1984   On Adaptation, Neo-Darwinian Tautology, and Population Fitness. *Evolutionary Biology* 17:1–57.
Leonard, R. D., and G. T. Jones
  1987   Elements of an Inclusive Evolutionary Model for Archaeology. *Journal of Anthropological Archaeology* 6:199–219.
Lewontin, R. C.
  1978   Adaptation. *Scientific American* 239:156–169.
  1986   Adaptation. Reprinted in *Conceptual Issues in Evolutionary Biology: An Anthology*, edited by E. Sober, pp. 235–251. MIT Press, Cambridge.
Malinowski, B.
  1960   *A Scientific Theory of Culture.* Oxford University Press, New York.
Malthus, T. R.
  1798   *An Essay on the Principle of Population.* Johnson, London.
Marks, J., and E. Staski
  1988   Individuals and the Evolution of Biological and Cultural Systems. *Human Evolution* 3:147–161.
Mayr, E.
  1973   *Populations, Species, and Evolution.* Harvard University Press, Cambridge.
  1982   *The Growth of Biological Thought.* Harvard University Press, Cambridge.
  1988   *Toward a New Philosophy of Biology: Observations of an Evolutionist.* Harvard University Press, Cambridge.
Million, M. G.
  1975   Ceramic Technology of the Nodena Phase People (ca. AD 1400–1700). *Southeast Archaeological Conference Bulletin* 18:201–208.
Mills, S., and J. Beatty
  1979   The Propensity Interpretation of Fitness. *Philosophy of Science* 46:263–286.

194

Neff, H.
  1992   Ceramics and Evolution. In *Archaeological Method and Theory*, vol. 4, edited by M. B. Schiffer. University of Arizona Press, Tucson, in press.
O'Brien, M. J.
  1987   Sedentism, Population Growth, and Resource Selection in the Woodland Midwest: A Review of Coevolutionary Developments. *Current Anthropology* 28:177–197.
O'Brien, M. J., and T. D. Holland
  1990   Variation, Selection, and the Archaeological Record. In *Archaeological Method and Theory*, vol. 2, edited by M. B. Schiffer, pp. 31–79. University of Arizona Press, Tucson.
  1991   Evolutionary Selectionism and the Role of Archaeology. Paper presented at the 56th Annual Meeting of the Society for American Archaeology, New Orleans.
Ospovat, D.
  1981   *The Development of Darwin's Theory*. Cambridge University Press, New York.
Pryor, F. L.
  1986   The Adaptation of Agriculture: Some Theoretical and Empirical Evidence. *American Anthropologist* 88:879–897.
Reid, K.
  1984   Fire and Ice: New Evidence for the Production and Preservation of Late Archaic Fiber-Tempered Pottery in the Mid-Latitude Lowlands. *American Antiquity* 49:55–76.
Reynolds, V.
  1984   The Relationship Between Biological and Cultural Evolution. *Journal of Human Evolution* 13:71–79.
Rindos, D.
  1984   *The Origins of Agriculture: An Evolutionary Perspective*. Academic Press, New York.
  1985   Darwinian Selection, Symbolic Variation, and the Evolution of Culture. *Current Anthropology* 26:65–88.
  1986   The Evolution of the Capacity for Culture: Sociobiology, Structuralism, and Cultural Selection. *Current Anthropology* 27:315–332.
  1989   Undirected Variation and the Darwinian Explanation of Cultural Change. In *Archaeological Method and Theory*, vol. 1, edited by M. B. Schiffer, pp. 1–45. University of Arizona Press, Tucson.
Ruse, M.
  1971   Functional Statements in Biology. *Philosophy of Science* 38:87–95.
Rye, O. S.
  1976   Keeping Your Temper Under Control: Materials and the Manufacture of Papuan Pottery. *Archaeology and Physical Anthropology in Oceania* 11:106–137.
Schiffer, M. B., and J. M. Skibo
  1987   Theory and Experiment in the Study of Technological Change. *Current Anthropology* 28:595–622.
Sober, E.
  1984   *The Nature of Selection: Evolutionary Theory in Philosophical Focus*. MIT Press, Cambridge.
Steward, J. H.
  1955   *Theory of Culture Change*. University of Illinois Press, Urbana.
  1956   Cultural Evolution. *Scientific American* 194(5):69–80.
Stimmell, C., R. B. Heimann, and R. G. V. Hancock
  1982   Indian Pottery from the Mississippi Valley: Coping with Bad Raw Materials. In *Archaeological Ceramics*, edited by J. S. Olin and A. D. Franklin, pp. 219–228. Smithsonian Institution Press, Washington, D.C.
Styles, B. W.
  1981   Early Late Woodland Subsistence in the Lower Illinois Valley. Scientific Papers No. 8. Northwestern University Archeological Program, Evanston, Illinois.
Taylor, W. W., Jr.
  1948   A Study of Archeology. Memoir Series No. 69. American Anthropological Association, Menasha, Wisconsin.
Van Valen, L.
  1973   A New Evolutionary Law. *Evolutionary Theory* 1:1–30.
Williams, M. B.
  1986   The Logical Status of the Theory of Natural Selection and Other Evolutionary Consequences. Reprinted in *Conceptual Issues in Evolutionary Biology: An Anthology*, edited by E. Sober, pp. 83–98. MIT Press, Cambridge.
Wobst, H. M.
  1977   Stylistic Behavior and Information Exchange. In *For the Director: Research Essays in Honor of James B. Griffin*, edited by C. E. Cleland, pp. 317–342. Anthropological Papers No. 61. Museum of Anthropology, University of Michigan, Ann Arbor.

NOTES

[1] "Struggle for existence" is perhaps not the best of terms, but Darwin (1859:62) noted he was using it in a "large and metaphorical sense."

[2] Sober (1984) makes a strong argument for the force concept, which is acceptable as long as one keeps in mind that the "force" rarely is constant. But in so doing one also has to refer to mutation and drift as evolutionary forces.

[3] We recognize another possibility. Suppose, for the sake of argument, that wearing skins diminishes the amount of sunlight needed to synthesize vitamin D and the population dies out. Thus, over time, the "adaptation" becomes maladaptive. This exemplifies organismal response lagging behind the source of selection.

[4] We are not suggesting a cooking pot has a phenotype; in reality it the user of the pot who is polymorphic. Nor are we suggesting that pots really have fitnesses except in terms of replicative success. The important point is that replicative success of pots may affect human adaptedness.

Received March 19, 1991; accepted August 22, 1991

POINT TYPOLOGIES, CULTURAL TRANSMISSION, AND THE SPREAD OF BOW-AND-ARROW TECHNOLOGY IN THE PREHISTORIC GREAT BASIN

Robert L. Bettinger and Jelmer Eerkens

Decrease in projectile point size around 1350 B.P. is commonly regarded as marking the replacement of the atlatl by the bow and arrow across the Great Basin. The point typology most widely employed in the Great Basin before about 1980 (the Berkeley typology) uses weight to distinguish larger dart points from smaller, but similarly shaped, arrow points. The typology commonly used today (the Monitor typology) uses basal width to distinguish wide-based dart points from narrow-based arrow points. The two typologies are in general agreement except in central Nevada, where some dart points are light, hence incorrectly typed by the Berkeley typology, and in eastern California, where some arrow points are wide-based, hence incorrectly typed by the Monitor typology. Scarce raw materials and resharpening may explain why dart points are sometimes light in central Nevada. That arrow point basal width is more variable in eastern California than central Nevada likely reflects differences in the cultural processes attending the spread and subsequent maintenance of bow-and-arrow technology in these two localities.

La disminución en el tamaño de las puntas proyectil hacia 1350 AP se considera generalmente una indicación de la sustitución del atlatl por el arco y flecha en la Gran Cuenca de los Estados Unidos. La tipología común en esta área antes de 1980 (tipología de Berkeley) utilizó el peso para distinguir puntas más grandes de puntas más pequeñas pero de forma parecida. La tipología generalmente empleada hoy (Monitor tipología) utiliza el ancho para distinguir puntas de bases anchas de puntas de bases estrechas. Típicamente, estos dos sistemas de tipología están de acuerdo con la excepción de Nevada central donde algunas puntas proyectil ligeras están clasificadas equivocamente en la tipología de Berkeley. Además, en California oriental algunas puntas de proyectil tienen bases anchas y están clasificadas equivocamente en la tipología Monitor. Probablemente, las puntas de Nevada central son ligeras debido a la falta de materia prima y al proceso de reafilación. Hay más variabilidad en el ancho de las puntas en California oriental que en Nevada central y probablamente refleja diferencias en los procesos culturales relacionados a la propagación y mantenimiento subsiguiente de la tecnología de arco y flecha en estas dos localidades.

Typologies are basic to archaeology. Well-defined artifact types facilitate communication between archaeologists and permit recognition of regional and temporal patterns that would otherwise pass unnoticed. In that sense, it can be argued that typologies themselves are of no intrinsic interest; they are merely intermediary constructions useful in investigating the "real" behaviors and processes we want to study. In this view, typologies should be evaluated mainly in pragmatic terms: "good" ones work—they reveal the patterns in which we are interested; "bad" ones don't. There is much to be said for this view. Nevertheless, it is occasionally worth asking why our "good" typologies work—and more importantly, why and where they don't. As we demonstrate below, such analyses can unexpectedly reveal novel patterns and behaviors as important and interesting as those for which the typologies were originally designed. In particular, we think such

work is likely to be especially revealing of basic evolutionary processes connected with the way individuals acquire, modify, and transmit basic cultural knowledge. This is so because "good" typologies identify consistently recurring combinations of attributes, suggesting the presence of evolutionary forces that caused these combinations to be maintained more or less intact across space and time. Myriad processes can produce such associations, of course, but, as we show here, it is possible to narrow the possibilities by observing the performance level of different typologies within given units of time and space. The first part of our analysis is given to such a comparison, showing how two different projectile point typologies succeed and fail in two regions of the western Great Basin of North America. We demonstrate that these typological successes and failures are due to regional differences in morphology and attribute correlation in generally similar point

Robert L. Bettinger ■ Department of Anthropology, University of California, Davis 95616
Jelmer Eerkens ■ Department of Anthropology, University of California, Santa Barbara 93106

American Antiquity, 64(2), 1999, pp. 231–242
Copyright © 1999 by the Society for American Archaeology

197

types. In the second part of our analysis, we argue these regional differences in morphology and attribute correlation are due to differences in the degree to which dart points were resharpened and to differences in the cultural mechanisms through which a new technology—the bow and arrow—spread and was maintained in different parts of the western Great Basin. The latter argument is informed by use of a version of evolutionary theory, termed *culture transmission theory* (or dual inheritance theory). We close with a brief discussion regarding the relationship of cultural transmission to Darwinian evolution and of the importance of identifying different modes of cultural transmission in the archaeological record.

Typologies in Conflict

The subject of our discussion is an unexpected conflict between two "good" Great Basin projectile point typologies. One is the Berkeley typology developed by Robert Heizer and others in the 1960s at the University of California-Berkeley (Baumhoff and Byrne 1959; Clewlow 1967, 1968; Heizer and Baumhoff 1961; Heizer et al. 1968; Heizer and Clewlow 1968; Lanning 1963). The other is the Monitor Valley typology developed by Thomas (1981). Both of these typologies were developed to identify time-sensitive projectile points that could be used in dating archaeological sites, especially surface sites that resist dating by other means, which are especially common in the Great Basin. The conflict is unexpected because the Monitor typology is a revision of an earlier typology that Thomas (1970) designed specifically to formalize the Berkeley typology and duplicate its results using explicit quantitative criteria.

The Monitor typology has been immensely successful in bringing coherence to Great Basin projectile point studies, and, overall, it reproduces the Berkeley typology (Bettinger 1975:167–189). As we shall show, however, there is systematic disagreement in some parts of the western Great Basin on the identification of two key forms: *Elko Corner-notched*, a large point form held to date between 3150–1350 B.P. (i.e., in the western Great Basin), and Rosegate, a smaller corner-notched point form held to date between 1350–650 B.P. (Figure 1).[1] This size difference is commonly regarded as marking the replacement of the atlatl by the bow and arrow (Fenenga 1953; Lanning 1963:249). The question immediately at hand, however, is one of telling time,

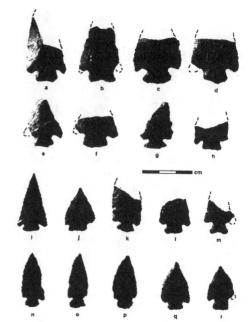

Figure 1. Corner-notched Projectile points from the White Mountains, California. a-h, Elko Corner-notched. i-m, Wide-based Rosegate. n-r, Narrow-based Rosegate.

i.e., distinguishing corner-notched points dating 3150–1350 B.P. (Elko) from corner-notched points dating 1350–650 B.P. (Rosegate). The Berkeley typology uses weight: Rosegate points weigh less than 3 gm; Elko Corner-notched points weigh more

Figure 2. Map locating Eastern California and Central Nevada.

Table 1. Berkeley and Monitor Valley Classification of Rosegate and Elko Corner-notched Points from Eastern California.

			MONITOR	
		Rosegate	Elko Corner-notched	Total
BERKELEY	Rosegate	113	45	158
	Elko Corner-notched		37	37
	Total	113	82	195

Note: Data from Ainsworth and Skinner 1994; Basgall and McGuire 1988; Bettinger 1989; Bouscaren 1985; Burton 1986; Clarke et al. 1991; Delacorte and McGuire 1993: Appendices 1-3; Delacorte et al. 1995: Appendix; Eerkens 1998; and Gilreath 1995: Appendix.

Table 2. Berkeley and Monitor Valley Classification of Rosegate and Elko Corner-notched Points from Central Nevada.

			MONITOR	
		Rosegate	Elko Corner-notched	Total
BERKELEY	Rosegate	152	122	274
	Elko Corner-notched	5	248	253
	Total	157	370	527

Note: Data from Thomas 1983:Table 44, 45, 1988:Tables 5, 6, 20, 21, 46,47, 49, 53, 54, 57, 59, 60, 61, 62.

than that (Clewlow 1967; Heizer and Baumhoff 1961; Lanning 1963; O'Connell 1967). Alternatively, on the premise that resharpening makes weight unstable (by changing original weight), the Monitor typology uses basal width, which is less affected by resharpening.[2] In the Monitor typology, Elko points have basal widths greater than 10 mm; Rosegate points have basal widths less than that (Thomas 1981: 14–15, 19–22).

Because the two typologies use different criteria to distinguish the age of corner-notched points, some disagreement is to be expected. In eastern California (Figure 2, Table 1) and central Nevada (Table 2), however, these disagreements are too large and systematic to be ignored. Specifically, of the points that are Rosegate by the Berkeley typology (weight), 28 percent in eastern California and 45 percent in central Nevada are Elko Corner-notched by the Monitor typology (basal width). In both places, the samples in question include many sites and surface isolates, suggesting this is a regional phenomenon. It is pointless to argue whether weight or basal width is inherently better at distinguishing older (Elko) from younger (Rosegate) corner-notched points, because both methods achieve only local success.[3]

In central Nevada, basal width is superior to weight. At Gatecliff Shelter, for example, the 10 mm basal width cutoff correctly predicts the stratigraphic position of about 97 percent of all corner-notched points relative to the boundary between Horizons 3 and 4, which dates to roughly 1350 B.P. (Thomas 1983: 177). By contrast, weight is a poorer predictor of age at this site, the 3 gm cutoff correctly predicting stratigraphic position of only 72 percent of these points.

In eastern California, on the other hand, weight is superior to basal width. For instance, as Lanning (1963: Table 3) showed, the Berkeley typology correctly predicts the stratigraphic position of Elko and Rosegate points above or below 48 in (122 cm) 94 percent of the time at the Rose Spring Site (CA-Iny-372). This near-complete stratigraphic separation by weight was confirmed by Davis (1963), and again by Yohe (1992: Tables 17, 24). Basal width is much less predictive of age in comparison. Yohe (1992: 180,Tables 14a-d) measured 145 Rosegate points recovered from all contexts (i.e., surface and buried) at the Rose Spring site between 1951 and 1989, including those in the collections of Lanning and Davis. Of these, all 53 complete specimens weigh less than 3 gm, as they should according to the Berkeley typology.[4] By contrast, basal widths greater than 10 mm cause the Monitor typology to classify 26 (27 percent) of those 96 specimens measurable on this dimension as Elko Corner-notched. As a result, the Monitor Valley typology correctly predicts the stratigraphic position of the 98 Elko and Rosegate points found in buried contexts and measurable for basal width only about 67 percent of the time (Yohe 1992: Tables 14a-d, 17).

Similarly, the larger eastern California sample demonstrates that weight is superior to basal width

Tables 3a, b. Weight and Basal Width of Obsidian Hydration-Dated Rosegate and Elko Corner-Notched Points from Eastern California.

Weight

Date	< 3 gm	≥ 3 gm	Total
< 1350 B.P.	16 (94%)	1 (6%)	17
> 1350 B.P.	5 (28%)	13 (72%)	18
Total	21	14	35

Basal Width

Date	≤ 10 mm	>10 mm	Total
< 1350 B.P.	25 (66%)	13 (34%)	38
> 1350 B.P.	9 (31%)	20 (69%)	29
Total	34	33	67

Note: Source specific hydration rates (Hall and Jackson 1989; Basgall and Giambastiani 1995; Delacorte et al. 1995) were used to derive dates B.P. Many more points can be measured for basal width than for weight, hence the unequal total number of observations on the two attributes.

in predicting the age of corner-notched points dated by obsidian hydration relative to the 1350 B.P. Elko/Rosegate boundary (Tables 3a,b). Here, the 3 gm cutoff correctly predicts the age 83 percent of the time, the 10 mm basal width cutoff only 67 percent of the time. These findings concur with a number of reports from all parts of eastern California suggesting that corner-notched points younger than 1350 B.P. are consistently light (3 gm) but frequently wide-based (10mm; e.g. Basgall and Giambastiani 1995: 47, Table B.1; Bettinger 1991a; Delacorte and McGuire 1993: Appendix A). For example, in alpine villages in the White Mountains of eastern California, 180 km north of the Rose Springs site (Bettinger 1991a), 36 percent of the Rosegate points occurring stratigraphically above a tephra layer dating to approximately 1245 B.P. are wide-based and would be classified incorrectly as Elko Corner-notched by the Monitor typology (Table 4; Figure 1 i–m). The larger basal width of eastern California Rosegate

Table 4. Distribution of Narrow- and Wide-based Rosegate Points Relative to Ash Layer in Alpine Villages, White Mountains, California (Bettinger 1991a).

	Narrow-Based ≤ 10 mm	Wide-Based > 10 mm	Total
Above Ash	54 (64%)	31 (36%)	85
In Ash (ca. 1245 B.P.)	19 (70%)	8 (30%)	27
Below Ash	26 (70%)	11 (30%)	37
Total	99 (66%)	50 (34%)	149

points is not a function of their overall size; they are, on average, shorter, narrower, and lighter than Rosegate points from central Nevada (Table 5).

We summarize the situation in Table 6. In eastern California, the Berkeley and Monitor typologies agree on the identification of corner-notched points older than 1350 B.P., which are consistently both heavy and wide-based, but disagree on the identification of points younger than 1350 B.P., which are light (3.0 gm) but often wide-based (10 mm). The Berkeley typology correctly classifies these light, wide-based forms as Rosegate, the Monitor typology misclassifies them as Elko. The situation is just the reverse in central Nevada, where the typologies agree on the identification of corner-notched points younger than 1350 B.P., which are consistently both light and narrow-based, but disagree on the identification of those older than 1350 B.P., which are wide-based but often light. The Monitor typology correctly classifies these light, wide-based forms as Elko; the Berkeley typology misclassifies them as Rosegate.

Explaining Regional Differences in Point Morphology

What do they mean, these regional differences in point morphology? Why do Elko Corner-notched points vary in weight in central Nevada but not eastern California, and why do Rosegate points vary in basal width in eastern California but not central Nevada? One obvious possibility, of course, is that Elko Corner-notched points are not all dart points, as commonly supposed, and that the light Elko Corner-notched points of central Nevada are really arrow points that pre-date 1350 B.P. Similarly, it is possible that not all Rosegate points are arrow points, and that the wide-based Rosegate points of eastern California are really dart points that postdate 1350 B.P. Metrical data provide little support for these suggestions. Shott (1997) examined a sample of 39 hafted, hence relatively unambiguous, dart points and 130 similarly unambiguous hafted arrow points, and used discriminant analysis to derive classification functions to separate darts from arrows. Table 7 summarizes the application of Shott's (1997:94) 2-variable discriminant classification function to the central Nevada Elko Corner-notched point sample and the Rosegate points from the Rose Spring site (CA-Iny-372) in eastern California. These data strongly suggest that the light Elko Corner-notched points in central Nevada are dart points, and that the

Table 5. Summary Metrical Data for Rosegate Points from Monitor Valley (Thomas 1983, 1988), the Rose Spring Site (Cainy-372; Yohe 1992), and Eastern California (See Table 1 for References). See Thomas (1981, 1983) for Description of Measurements.

	Maximum Length mm	Axial Length mm	Maximum Width mm	Basal Width mm	Neck Width mm	Thickness mm	Weight gm
Monitor Valley[a]							
mean	29.68	29.47	16.97	8.19	7.11	3.49	1.64
std	7.30	7.33	3.25	1.22	1.21	0.67	0.68
n	33	33	83	120	120	120	20
Eastern California							
mean	25.54	25.05	15.31	8.79	7.78	3.86	1.12
std	5.30	5.57	2.93	2.30	1.67	0.90	0.44
n	55	57	114	157	182	157	39
Rose Spring Site							
mean	27.66	no data	15.08	9.10	7.87	3.77	1.17
std	4.91	no data	2.11	1.88	1.46	0.63	0.46
n	83	no data	129	96	130	144	53

[a] Reference here is to specimens actually measured and omits estimated values routinely given by Thomas (1983, 1988).

wide-based Rosegate points in eastern California are arrow points.[5] Thus, the replacement of Elko Corner-notched points by Rosegate points about 1350 B.P. in central Nevada and eastern California almost certainly reflects the replacement of the atlatl by the bow and arrow, as long suspected.

Unfortunately, this conclusion still leaves us with our original problem of explaining the weight variability observed in central Nevada Elko points and basal width variability observed in eastern California Rosegate points. Following Thomas (1981:14–15,19–20), we think it likely that excessive resharpening makes dart point weight highly variable in central Nevada, producing the light, wide-based Elko Corner-notched points that the Berkeley typology incorrectly types as Rosegate. Support for this idea is provided by the length-width ratio; i.e., maximum length (maximum width) of light Elko Corner-notched points in the central Nevada sample, which is significantly lower than that for the heavy Elko Corner-notched points in that sample (mean$_{light}$ = 1.62, mean$_{heavy}$ = 1.75, $p < .001$, one-tailed t-test, df =345), suggesting the stubbier, lighter forms were more extensively resharpened. That resharpening does not cause similar problems in eastern California, where Elko Corner-notched points are uniformly heavy and long relative to width (mean$_{length:width}$ =2.02, n =10 complete specimens), may be explained by the abundance of high-quality obsidian sources there, perhaps causing Elko points to be discarded without substantial resharpening (cf. Bettinger 1991b; Delacorte 1994). Resharpening, of course, cannot explain why Rosegate points are more variable in basal width in eastern California than central Nevada. We think this variance can be attributed to differences in how these regions' inhabitants obtained and subsequently modified bow-and-arrow technology.

Cultural Transmission and the Spread of the Bow and Arrow

As noted above, it has long been accepted that the appearance of Rosegate points marks the advent of the bow and arrow (Jennings 1986: 116) as reflected

Table 6. Summary of Formal Variation in Elko Corner-notched and Rosegate Points and Success of Berkeley and Monitor Typologies in Identifying Them in Eastern California and Central Nevada.

	Eastern California Forms	Typology Success	Central Nevada Forms	Typology Success
Elko Corner-notched	Heavy, Wide-based	Both Correct	Heavy, Wide-based	Both Correct
			Light, Wide-based	Berkeley Incorrect
Rosegate	Light, Narrow-based	Both Correct	Light, Narrow-Based	Both Correct
	Light, Wide-based	Monitor Incorrect		

Table 7. Classification of Central Nevada Elko Corner-notched and Eastern California Rosegate Points from the Rose Spring Site (Ca-iny-372) Using the 2 Variable Function of Shott (1997).

	Dart	Arrow	Total
Central Nevada			
Heavy Elko Corner-notched	97%	3%	229
Light Elko Corner-notched	76%	24%	120
All Elko Corner Notched	90%	10%	349
Shott (1997) Sample Darts	85%	15%	39
Eastern California (CA-INY-372)			
Narrow-based Rosegate	5%	95%	66
Wide-based Rosegate	9%	91%	23
All Rosegate	6%	94%	89
Shott (1997) Sample Arrows	11%	89%	130

Table 8: Pearson's R Correlation Coefficients for Basal Width and Weight in Central Nevada and Eastern California Rosegate Points.

	Monitor Typology	Berkeley Typology
Central Nevada	.80	.65
	$p_{r=0} < .0001$	$p_{r=0} = .0005$
Eastern California	.06	.14
	$p_{r=0} = .36$	$p_{r=0} = .20$

Note: Correlations are on actual measurements because basal width and weight estimates for broken points given in Thomas (1983, 1988) are unavailable for eastern California.

by a reduction in point size (Fenenga 1953; Lanning 1963). This size reduction has been recognized across all of the Great Basin, consistently around 1650–1350 B.P. Appearance of the Rosegate series at essentially the same time throughout the Great Basin is usually taken to support the companion assumption (generally unstated) that the spread of bow-and-arrow technology was a unitary phenomenon— that is, it was accomplished by the same mode of cultural transmission across the entire Great Basin, probably from a common source. Under this assumption, the changes in projectile point morphology from Elko to Rosegate that accompanied the introduction of the bow and arrow should be essentially the same throughout the Great Basin. This is not the case. As we have shown, the Elko-Rosegate transition in both central Nevada and eastern California almost certainly represents the introduction of the bow and arrow somewhere around 1350 B.P. However, the characteristics that distinguish Elko from Rosegate points in central Nevada, and thus the transition to the bow and arrow, are not the ones that distinguish them, and thus the transition, in eastern California.

In central Nevada, Rosegate points fit the criteria of both Berkeley and Monitor typologies: a corner-notched point with a narrow base is nearly always light. This suggests that in central Nevada the two variables these typologies use to distinguish Rosegate from Elko—weight and basal width—were linked together in the transmission of bow-and-arrow technology. Weight and basal width, however, are not linked in this way in eastern California. This is clearly illustrated in Table 8, which shows correlation coefficients between weight and basal width in Rosegate age corner-notched points from multiple sites in east-

ern California and central Nevada. Using the Monitor typology, basal width and weight are highly correlated in Rosegate points from central Nevada. Because these points nearly always simultaneously fit the criteria of both typologies, the same high correlation is achieved when they are classified according to the Berkeley typology. On the other hand, no matter which way one classifies them, Rosegate points from eastern California are uncorrelated on these two attributes.[6] This suggests that the circumstances surrounding the spread and maintenance of bow-and-arrow technology during Rosegate times in eastern California were different than those in central Nevada.

Boyd and Richerson (1985: 94–95, 243) have identified two contrasting modes of cultural transmission, *guided variation* and *indirect bias*, that are useful in interpreting these differences in trait correlation and their implications for the spread and maintenance of bow-and-arrow technology in the Great Basin. In *guided variation*, individuals acquire new behaviors by directly copying other social models and subsequently modifying these behaviors to suit their own needs by individual trial-and-error experiments. Complex behaviors are frequently compiled in this fashion, using different individuals as social models for various components of the behavior. The result is a composite behavior that is more or less unique to the individual, i.e., as a consequence of experimentation and the particular set of social models that were chosen. In *indirect bias*, on the other hand, individuals acquire complex behaviors by choosing a single social model on the basis of a trait that is deemed to index general proficiency in the activity to which the desired behavior is related. Highly successful hunters, for example, might be chosen as social models by those trying to learn how to make all sorts of hunting gear. In this case, in con-

Table 9. Pearson's r Correlation Coefficients for Various Point Attributes in Central Nevada and Eastern California Rosegate Points.

		Axial Length	Maximum Width	Basal Width	Neck Width	Thickness	Distal Shoulder Angle	Proximal Shoulder Angle	Weight
Max. Length	C. NV	1.00	.58[a]	.48[a]	.51	.51[a]	-.19	-.34	.86
	E. CA	1.00	.24	.07	.21	.15	-.24	-.24	.76
Axial Length	C. NV		.59[a]	.49[a]	.51[a]	.49[a]	-.18	-.33	.86
	E. CA		.22	.04	.16	.14	-.24	-.27	.74
Maximum Width	C. NV			.44	.72	.12	-.48	-.53[a]	.62
	E. CA			.54	.69	.26	-.47	-.08	.71
Basal Width	C. NV				.71	.21	.11	.26	.80[a]
	E. CA				.78	-.05	-.06	.31	.14
Neck Width	C. NV					.23	-.15	-.15	.61
	E. CA					.11	-.06	.15	.40
Thickness	C. NV						.14	-.02	.70
	E. CA						.03	-.02	.57
Distal Shoulder Angle	C. NV							.53[a]	-.12
	E. CA							.16	-.38
Proximal Shoulder Angle	C. NV								-.21
	E. CA								-.01

Note: Correlations are on actual measurements. See Thomas (1981, 1983) for description of measurements.
[a]Significantly stronger correlation ($\alpha = 0.05$).

trast to guided variation, the result is a complex behavior that matches more or less closely in all details of the behavior of just this one social model. Further, since there tends to be general agreement within local groups about the proficiency of potential social models, the individual generally deemed the most proficient will frequently be chosen as a social model by many individuals trying to learn new, complex behaviors. It is impossible to observe these transmission processes directly in the archaeological record, of course, but their statistical signatures should be clear nonetheless. Variables acquired by guided variation will be much less strongly correlated than variables acquired by indirect bias. Following this logic, we contend that in eastern California, where basal width and weight are poorly correlated, bow-and-arrow technology was maintained, and may have spread initially, by guided variation. Conversely, in central Nevada, where the attributes are strongly correlated, we suggest it was maintained, and may have spread initially, by indirect bias.

In many ways, the situation in eastern California, where basal width and weight are not linked, is the one to be expected. This is so because, beyond the minimal effect basal width has on total weight, these two attributes respond to different design constraints that are capable of varying independently, as they clearly do in eastern California Rosegate points. However, basal width and weight do not vary independently, but are instead correlated in central

Nevada Rosegate points. This correlation suggests that these elements of design were connected—not as a matter of function, but because central Nevada Rosegate point makers acquired the multiple elements of arrow point design as a package using a mode of transmission akin to indirect bias, copying, as it were, the whole point rather than individual attributes piecemeal and independently. On the other hand, that weight and basal width are uncorrelated in eastern California suggests the bow-and-arrow technology may have spread, and was in any case maintained, by a mode of cultural transmission akin to guided variation, in which craftsmen copied, evaluated, and modified the various elements of point design independently. This hypothesis is strongly supported by observed differences in strength of correlation between other major attributes of Rosegate points, which are consistently larger for central Nevada than eastern California (Table 9). In 22 of these 36 paired correlations, the central Nevada value exceeds the eastern California value, far more than the 18 one would expect under the null hypothesis of no difference in magnitude of attribute correlation in the two samples (p =.015). The central Nevada correlation is significantly larger in 10 of these cases (p = 0.05).[7] In short, during Rosegate times in central Nevada, individuals seem to have maintained (and may have acquired) this new weapon system—bow, arrow, and point—as a complete package, while individuals in eastern California maintained (and may have acquired) its attributes individually using a great deal of experimentation.

Discussion

Why the peoples of eastern California might have acquired and maintained bow-and-arrow technology through a different mode of transmission than the peoples of central Nevada is unclear. Following a suggestion of the late M. A. Baumhoff, however, we would tentatively propose that eastern California groups may have acquired the bow and arrow from peoples with whom they interacted only minimally, possibly a different linguistic unit occasionally contacted through trade. Owing to this lack of contact, individuals may have had to perfect a workable bow-and-arrow technology largely by trial and error. Bettinger (1989: 64–65,229–232) previously noted that Rose Springs points from eastern California seem unusually prone to breakage (especially across the neck) and suggested this faulty design might reflect early arrow point-makers experimenting with various combinations of point size, basal width and foreshaft diameter. Perhaps some craftsmen attempted to adapt existing dart foreshaft types fitted to wide-based arrow points, while others tried to develop new, narrower foreshafts fitted to narrow-based arrow points. Alternatively, craftsmen may have initially adopted the bow and arrow as a complex, as in central Nevada, but immediately set about modifying it to suit their own individual preferences, so that, as a result, weight, basal width, and other attributes in the points came to be relatively uncorrelated. On the other hand, the spread and perpetuation of bow-and-arrow technology in central Nevada seems to have relied more heavily on social transmission, perhaps facilitated by closer social contacts than characterized the situation in eastern California. Whether the bow and arrow came to central Nevada from the same source as in eastern California, from an entirely different area, or perhaps even from eastern California itself, is unclear. What seems clear, however, is that point makers in central Nevada adopted the projectile point used with the bow and arrow by faithfully copying all its various attributes in detail, which suggests they experimented very little with this new technology, then or subsequently.

Is It Evolution?

The thrust of our paper is about cultural transmission: how cultural behavior is acquired, modified,

and subsequently transmitted, and how one might go about identifying different kinds of cultural transmission in the archaeological record. Such mechanisms seem to us to be of great potential importance for humans, because so much of our behavior is acquired socially rather than determined by individual learning or genes. Whether this reliance on social transmission so fundamentally separates humans from other biological organisms as to require that we be regarded as unique, and in some sense beyond the reach of forces that shape the rest of the biological world, has been endlessly debated inside and outside anthropology. Certainly, such a disconnection might be implied if cultural transmission had nothing to do with genetic fitness. We only say "might" because Darwinian theory is really not about genes any more than it is just about the differential reproductive fitness of individuals. Genes are the linchpin in how biological evolution works but genes as we now know them are required neither by Darwinian theory nor for it to operate: Darwin got the story basically right without them; the "modern synthesis" occurred without Watson and Crick. Darwinian evolution requires a mechanism of transmission and genes happen to serve this role in biological evolution. It is possible to imagine all sorts of other transmission mechanisms. Genetic reproduction itself is not a unitary phenomenon. Asexual and sexual reproduction, and in sexual reproduction, the transmission of sex-linked and autosomal traits, for example, are quite different and require comparably different quantitative algorithms. One could not possibly understand the individual fitness of a biological organism without also knowing whether it reproduced asexually or sexually and, in the latter case, which traits were sex-linked and whether it was monogamous or polygamous. The "details" of reproduction and mating count. No one model applies universally. Of course, there is more to biological evolution than just individuals—populations and species matter, for example. The genius of Darwin and especially those after him was in tracing through complex evolutionary recursions: Forces act on specific individuals, play out at the population level, affect individuals in return, and so on. The forces need not be strong. Minor differences often have unexpectedly large evolutionary consequences. Here, again, individual fitness is important in this process, but there are myriad other, sometimes more important, forces. Causal relationships are often complex and evolutionary outcomes are frequently counter-intuitive.

It seems clear to us that cultural transmission simply must affect Darwinian fitness—how could it be otherwise? And Darwinian fitness also must bear on cultural transmission. Again, how could that not be true? At minimum, humans must have the biological, hence, genetically transmitted, ability for the cultural transmission of behaviors that certainly affect Darwinian fitness. It is obvious, at the same time, that cultural transmission differs in fundamental ways from any form of genetic transmission. The two are asymmetric. Again, this is what we would expect, since cultural transmission must be doing something that genes cannot do, just as sexual reproduction is doing something that asexual reproduction cannot. It does not follow, however, that this process disconnects cultural transmission from Darwinian fitness. To the contrary, as with sexual reproduction, the human use of cultural transmission is simply the exploiting of an evolutionary opportunity. To deny that would imply that the culturally-mediated evolutionary success of anatomically modern humans is merely serendipitous happenstance.

Do Differences in Cultural Transmission Matter?

There is general tendency for archaeologists to assume that differences in cultural transmission are unimportant (Bettinger et al. 1996). We suppose that reflects a common misperception that Darwinian forces are all obvious, strong, and life-threatening. That, of course, is to misread Darwin, whose uniformitarian gradualism stood in direct opposition to explanations relying on supremely powerful forces and catastrophes capable of instantaneously transforming the world and its species. As we have said, in Darwinian evolution details often matter, and that is the case here.

Our paper contrasts two different modes of cultural transmission, guided variation and indirect bias, that highlight what is perhaps the fundamental contrast in evolutionary potential between genetic and cultural transmission. As Boyd and Richerson (1985:132–171; see also Cavalli-Sforza 1988) observe, where cultural transmission takes the form of guided variation and other modes of transmission involving substantial individual experimentation and learning, human behavior will tend to optimize fitness in accord with the predictions of the genetic model. By contrast, where cultural transmission is by indirect bias and other modes that bypass individual experimentation and learning, there is an opportunity for a much different range of behaviors that are normally precluded when only genes are involved. This situation largely occurs because indirect bias and related forms of social transmission tend to produce behaviorally homogenous local populations. It is precisely under these conditions that the force of selection can fall more heavily on groups than on individuals, i.e., as group selection. That, in turn, makes it easier to understand and explain a host of human characteristics suggesting the presence of selective forces acting at the group level—most notably our ultra-social character and tendency to cooperate despite sometimes extensive personal costs—that have proven difficult to explain with reference to the genetic model.

It has been argued that the hunting behavior of certain hunter-gatherer groups contains built-in restraints that act to prevent resource depletion (e.g., Moore 1965). Such an explanation, however, does not account for individual hunters devising and using alternative behaviors that produce higher short-term returns and thus a benefit from the resource abundance arising from the more restrained practices of their fellow hunters. In that event, restraint quickly gives way to strategies that are more successful in the short term, as in the familiar "tragedy of the commons" (Hardin 1968). In short, individual learning and experimentation prevent the development and maintenance of behaviors that potentially benefit the group. Conversely, because it insulates cultural transmission from both individual learning/experiment and exotic social models, indirect bias produces the conditions under which group-beneficial behaviors can evolve and persist. Accordingly, if, during Rosegate times in eastern California, behaviors connected with hunting (e.g., when, where, and how to hunt, and who to hunt with) were acquired and transmitted by the same means as bow-and-arrow technology, the emphasis on individual learning and experimentation likely would have prevented the development of group-beneficial cooperative behaviors. By contrast, the emphasis on indirectly biased social transmission and imitation suggested by the uniformity of Rosegate projectile point technology in central Nevada implies the presence of the ideal conditions for such group-beneficial, cooperative behaviors to develop and persist. Thus, despite the general similarities in technology, it is quite possible that hunting behaviors and social organization overall differed substantially between the two regions during this interval.

Supporting this argument is evidence which suggests that Numic-speaking groups occupying the Great Basin in ethnographic times spread rapidly out of eastern California sometime after 1000 B.P. (Bettinger and Baumhoff 1982; see also Madsen and Rhode 1994). This rapid occupation, it is argued, succeeded through the competitive advantages of the Numic adaptive strategy over that of pre-Numic peoples, and the latter's failure to readapt to Numic competition through slow culture change partly caused by indirectly biased social transmission (although not specifically labeled as such; Bettinger and Baumhoff 1982: 488–493). The emphasis on indirectly biased social transmission suggested here for central Nevada during Rosegate times is clearly consistent with this hypothesis.

Our hypothesis is just that—an hypothesis. Yet it remains that weight, basal width, and nearly all other attributes are highly correlated in Rosegate points from central Nevada and poorly correlated in Rosegate points from eastern California. The lack of correlation in eastern California establishes that the high correlation in central Nevada is unlikely due to functional constraints. Accordingly, we have chosen to interpret these differences in correlation using the tenets of cultural transmission theory, on the hypothesis that attributes passed on through processes that emphasize social learning over individual learning, such as indirectly biased transmission, should be more highly correlated than those passed on through processes that emphasize individual over social learning, such as guided variation.

It is widely held that evolutionary theory, especially culture transmission theory, has little to offer the archaeologist, partly because evolutionary processes are difficult to detect in the archaeological record. We have shown, with reasonable samples, the possibility for casting standard archaeological data in ways that reveal the basic mechanisms through which cultural evolution operates—in this case, the way in which real individuals acquired and subsequently modified important cultural knowledge. Our main point is that differences in cultural transmission are detectable archaeologically and, in fact, seem to distinguish the maintenance and pos-

sibly introduction of bow-and-arrow technology in different parts of the Great Basin. It is about evolutionary theory, then, to the extent that transmission, in this case cultural transmission, is a critical Darwinian process that requires investigation. The approach is straightforward and applicable in a variety of other archaeological contexts. We hope our application will stimulate further research and debate into the study of evolutionary culture change in the Great Basin and elsewhere.

Acknowledgments. We are indebted to Elizabeth Klarich, who provided the Spanish abstract translation; Robert Yohe, who provided data for points from the Rose Spring site; and Susan Harriss, Cynthia Herhahn, Mike Jochim, Lisa Deitz, Frank Deitz, and Brian Ramos who read and commented on various drafts of this paper and helped out here and there with the manipulation of data. We further wish to thank Lynne Goldstein, editor of *American Antiquity,* and three serious reviewers who commented on the previous version of this paper.

References Cited

Ainsworth, P., and E. Skinner
1994   Appendix 1. In *Archaeological Resources Evaluation at CA-INY-384, CA-INY-3790, CA-INY-4547, CA-INY-4549H, CA-INY-4550, Inyo County California,* edited by B. Wickstrom, R. Jackson, and T. L. Jackson, pp A1–1–89. Report submitted to California Department of Transportation, Environmental Branch, District 9, Bishop, California. Contract 09H077.
Basgall, M. E., and K. R. McGuire
1988   *The Archaeology of CA-INY-30: Prehistoric Culture Change in the Southern Owens Valley, California.* Report submitted to California Department of Transportation, Sacramento. Contract No. 09G519. Far Western Anthropological Research Group, Davis, California.
Basgall, M.E., and M.A. Giambastiani
1995   *Prehistoric Use of a Marginal Environment: Continuity and Change in Occupation of the Volcanic Tablelands, Mono and Inyo Counties, California.* Publication 12. Center for Archaeological Research, Davis, California.
Baumhoff, M.A., and J.S. Byrne
1959   Desert Side-Notched Points as a Time Marker in California. *Archaeological Survey Reports* 48: 32–65. University of California, Berkeley.
Bettinger, R.L.
1975   *The Surface Archaeology of Owens Valley, Eastern California: Prehistoric Man-Land Relationships in the Great Basin.* Unpublished Ph.D. dissertation, Department of Anthropology, University of California, Riverside.
1989   *The Archaeology of Pinyon House, Two Eagles, and Crater Middens: Three Residential Sites in Owens Valley, Eastern California.* Anthropological Papers 67. American Museum of Natural History, New York.
1991a   Aboriginal Occupation at High Altitude: Alpine Villages in the White Mountains of Eastern California. *American Anthropologist* 93: 656–679.
1991b   Native Land Use: Archaeology and Anthropology. In *Natural History of the White-Inyo Range, Eastern California,* edited by C. A. Hall, pp. 463–486. University of California Press, Berkeley.

Bettinger, R. L., and M. A. Baumhoff
 1982 The Numic Spread: Great Basin Cultures in Competi-
    tion. *American Antiquity* 47:485–503.
Bettinger, R. L., P. J. Richerson, and R. Boyd
 1996 Style, Function, and Cultural Evolutionary Processes. In
    Darwinian Archaeologies, edited by D.G. Maschner, pp.
    133–164. Plenum Press, New York.
Bettinger, R.L., and J.W. Eerkens
 1997 Evolutionary Implications of Metrical Variation in Great
    Basin Projectile Points. In *Rediscovering Darwin: Evolu-
    tionary Theory and Archaeological Explanation*, edited by
    C. M. Barton and G. A. Clark, pp. 177–191. Archaeological
    Papers 7. American Anthropological Association, Arling-
    ton, Virginia.
Bouscaren, S.
 1985 *Archaeological Excavations in the Lowlands of North-
    ern Owens Valley: Report on the Sawmill Road Site (CA-
    INY-1386)*. Unpublished Master's thesis. University of
    California, Riverside.
Boyd, R., and Richerson, P. J.
 1985 *Culture and the Evolutionary Process*. University of
    Chicago Press, Chicago.
Burton, J.F.
 1986 *Archaeological Investigations at Bajada Camp (CA-Iny-
    2596), Inyo County California*. Prepared for Baxter Ranch
    by Trans-Sierran Archaeological Research, Columbia, Cal-
    ifornia.
Cavalli-Sforza, L.
 1988 Cultural Transmission and Adaptation. *International
    Social Science Journal* 40:239–253.
Clark, M., T. Jones, T. Fung, and S. Grantham
 1991 *Extended Phase I Investigation of CA-INY-3694, CA-
    INY-3695, CA-INY-3696/H, and CA-INY-3697/H, Near Lone
    Pine, Inyo County, California*. Prepared for California
    Department of Transportation, District 9, Bishop, Califor-
    nia. Contract Number 09-INY-395, P.M 54.6/59.0, 09-
    213000.
Clewlow, C. W. Jr.
 1967 Time and Space Relations of Some Great Basin Projec-
    tile Point Types. *Archaeological Survey Reports* 70: 141–150.
    University of California, Berkeley.
 1968 Surface Archaeology of the Black Rock Desert, Nevada.
    Archaeological Survey Reports 73: 1–94. University of Cal-
    ifornia, Berkeley.
Davis, J. T.
 1963 Test Excavations at Site Iny-372 Conducted in 1961. In
    Archaeology of the Rose Spring Site Iny-372, by E. Lanning,
    Appendix 5, pp. 296–304. Publications in American Archae-
    ology and Ethnology 49(3): 237–336. University of Cali-
    fornia, Berkeley.
Delacorte, M. G.
 1994 The Role of Population in Relation to the Use of Alpine
    Environments in the White Mountains of California and
    Nevada. *Areta Archaeological Carpathia*. Warsaw. In press.
Delacorte, M. G., M. C. Hall, and M. E. Basgall
 1995 *Final Report on the Evaluation of Twelve Archaeologi-
    cal Sites in the Southern Owens Valley, Inyo County, Cali-
    fornia*. Report submitted to California Department of
    Transportation, Sacramento. Contract No. 09HO78. Far West-
    ern Anthropological Research Group, Davis, California.
Delacorte, M. G., and K. R. McGuire
 1993 *Report of Archaeological Test Evaluations at Twenty-
    Three Sites in Owens Valley, California*. Report prepared for
    Contel of California and the Bureau of Land Management,
    California Desert District. Contract No. SC-33-90. Far West-
    ern Anthropological Research Group, Davis, California.

Eerkens, J.W., and R.L. Bettinger
 1994 Variance in Great Basin Projectile Points. Paper pre-
    sented at the 59th Annual Meeting of the Society for Amer-
    ican Archaeology, Anaheim.
Eerkens, J.W.
 1998 Field Notes from Archaeological Survery and Excava-
    tion in Southern Owens Valley, California. Manuscript on
    file, Department of Anthropology, University of California-
    Santa Barbara.
Fenenga, F.
 1953 The Weights of Chipped Stone Points: A Clue to their
    Functions. *Southwest Journal of Anthropology* 9: 309–323.
Gilreath, A. J.
 1995 *Archaeological Evaluation of Thirteen Sites for the Ash
    Creek Project, Inyo County, California*. Report submitted to
    California Department of Transportation, Sacramento. Far
    Western Anthropological Research Group, Davis, Califor-
    nia.
Hardin, R.
 1968 Tragedy of the Commons. *Science* 162:1243–1248.
Hall, M.C., and R.J. Jackson
 1989 Obsidian Hydration Rates in California. In *Current
    Directions in California Obsidian Studies*, edited by R.E.
    Hughes, pp. 31–58. Contributions No. 48. Archaeological
    Research Facility, University of California, Berkeley.
Heizer, R.F., and M.A. Baumhoff
 1961 The Archaeology of Wagon Jack Shelter. In The Archae-
    ology of Two Sites at Eastgate, Churchill County, Nevada.
    Anthropological Records 20(4): 119–138. University of Cal-
    ifornia, Berkeley.
Heizer, R.F., M.A. Baumhoff, and C.W. Clewlow Jr.
 1968 Archaeology of South Fork Shelter (NV-El-11), Elko
    County, Nevada. *Archaeological Survey Reports* 71: 1–58.
    University of California, Berkeley.
Heizer, R.F., and C.W. Clewlow Jr.
 1968 Projectile Points from Site NV-CH-15, Churchill County,
    Nevada. *Archaeological Survey Reports* 71: 59–88. Univer-
    sity of California, Berkeley.
Jennings, J.D.
 1986 Prehistory: Introduction. In *Great Basin*, edited by W.
    L. D'Azevedo, pp. 113–119. Handbook of North American
    Indians, vol. 11, W. C. Sturtevant, general editor. Smithson-
    ian Institution, Washington, D.C.
Lanning, E.P.
 1963 Archaeology of the Rose Spring Site Iny-372. *Publica-
    tions in American Archaeology and Ethnology* 49(3):
    237–336. University of California, Berkeley.
Madsen, D. B., and D. R. Rhode (editors)
 1994 *Across the West: Human Population Movement and the
    Expansion of the Numa*. University of Utah Press, Salt Lake
    City.
Moore, O. K.
 1965 Divination: A New Perspective. *American Anthropolo-
    gist* 59:69–74.
O'Connell, J. F.
 1967 Elko Eared/Elko Corner-notched Projectile Points as
    Time Markers in the Great Basin. *Archaeological Survey
    Reports* 70: 129–140. University of California, Berkeley.
Shott, M. J.
 1997 Stones and Shafts Redux: The Metric Discrimination of
    Chipped Stone Dart and Arrow Points. *American Antiquity*
    62:86–101.
Thomas, D. H.
 1970 Archaeology's Operational Imperative: Great Basin Pro-
    jectile Points as a Test Case. *University of California Archae-
    ological Survey Annual Report* 12: 27–60. Los Angeles.

1981 How to Classify the Projectile Points from Monitor Valley, Nevada. *Journal of California and Great Basin Anthropology* 3: 7–43.

1983 *The Archaeology of Monitor Valley 2. Gatecliff Shelter.* Anthropological Papers 59(1). American Museum of Natural History, New York.

1988 *The Archaeology of Monitor Valley 3. Survey and Additional Excavations.* Anthropological Papers 66(2). American Museum of Natural History, New York.

Yohe, R. M. II

1992 *Reevaluation of Western Great Basin Cultural Chronology and Evidence for the Timing of the Introduction of the Bow and Arrow to Eastern California Based on New Excavations at the Rose Spring Site (CA-INY-372).* Unpublished Ph.D. dissertation, Department of Anthropology, University of California, Riverside.

Notes

[1] The Berkeley and Monitor typologies differ somewhat in terminology. The Berkeley typology recognizes separate Rose Spring series and Eastgate series, each with several distinct types. The Monitor lumps all the *corner-notched* forms of Rose Spring and Eastgate into a single Rosegate series. Because our problem concerns corner-notched point forms, we follow the Monitor convention for the sake of clarity, cautioning the reader that many of the references we cite follow the Berkeley terminology.

[2] In the original version of what became the Monitor typology, Thomas (1970) used weight, as in the Berkeley typology.

[3] Note, however, that Thomas (1981) did not argue for the universal applicability of the Monitor typology.

[4] A *fragmentary* surface specimen identified by Yohe as Rosegate weighed 3.2 gm (1992: 288, Table 14a). However, this piece could as easily be classified as Elko. Note also that Yohe (1992) inadvertently ommitted metrics for the 30 Rosegate points he recovered between 1987–1989, but provided these data (labeled Table 16) at our request.

[5] As one would expect, light Elko Corner-notched points are more frequently classified as arrow points than heavy ones. However, the error-rate for the central Nevada Elko Corner-notched sample as a whole (i.e., including light and heavy forms) is lower than for Shott's (1997) dart sample, and the error-rate for light Elko Corner-notched points does not differ significantly from that obtained in Shott's dart sample. Filtering Shott's dart sample to include only specimens weighing (3 gm would almost certainly increase the relative frequency of incorrect classifications in much the same way that filtering the Elko Corner-notched for weight does in the central Nevada sample.

[6] This is not a function of excessive variation in basal width in Rosegate points from eastern California. We have shown elsewhere (Eerkens and Bettinger 1994; Bettinger and Eerkens 1997) that Rosegate basal width is relatively stable in this region, and more stable than Rosegate basal width in central Nevada. Further, those data demonstrate that the variability in basal width of other point types is essentially the same in eastern California and central Nevada (Bettinger and Eerkens 1997: Table 10.5), suggesting that raw material access (i.e., to stone, wood, etc.) is likely not causing the regional difference in Rosegate basal width. The Rosegate series does subsume two formally distinct types, Rose Spring Corner-notched and Eastgate Split-stem, but in eastern California, the two are virtually identical in basal width. In the White Mountains sample (Bettinger 1991a) illustrates this nicely. Eastgate basal width: mean $= 1.01$ cm, std $= 0.19$, n $= 20$; Rose Spring Corner-notched basal width: mean $= 0.96$, std $= 0.18$, n $= 37$).

[7] Note in contrast here, that while eastern California Elko Corner-notched points tend to be somewhat more highly correlated across major attributes than central Nevada Elko Corner-notched points, the difference between the two is not significant ($p = .37$).

Received December 18, 1997; accepted August 25, 1998; revised October 30, 1998

EVIDENCE AND METAPHOR IN EVOLUTIONARY ARCHAEOLOGY

Douglas B. Bamforth

Evolutionary theory and terminology are widely used in recent archaeological work, and many evolutionary archaeologists have argued that the integration of such theory and terminology is essential to the future of our field. This paper considers evolutionary archaeology from two perspectives. First, it examines substantive claims that archaeology can study the operation of Darwinian evolution, either through a reliance on optimal-foraging theory or by linking the process of natural selection to archaeological data. It concludes that there are serious problems with both of these claims on Darwin: the relation between evolution and foraging theory has never been documented, and midrange arguments linking selection and archaeological data are unsustainable. Second, it argues that archaeologists rely metaphorically on evolutionary terminology to help make sense out of archaeological data. Although the use of evolutionary metaphor can be, and has been, problematic, it also offers a powerful conceptual framework for our research. However, this framework is only of one of a number of comparable frameworks that have been offered to our field, as a comparison of systems archaeology and evolutionary archaeology shows.

La teoría y terminología evolucionarias son usadas ampliamente en el trabajo arqueólogico reciente, y muchos arqueólogos evolucionarios han argumentado que la integración de dicha teoría y terminología es esencial para el futuro de nuestro campo. Este escrito considera la arqueología evolucionaria desde dos perspectivas. Primero, examina pretensiones substantivas de que la arqueología puede estudiar el funcionamiento de la evolución Darwiniana, ya sea a través de la confianza en la teoria del abastecimiento óptimo o enlazando el proceso de la selección natural a los datos arqueológicos. Concluye que hay serios prolemas con estos dos alegatos sobre Darwin: la relación entre evolución y la teoría del abastecimiento nunca ha sido documentada, y los argumentos de mediano alcance enlazando la selección y los datos arqueólogicos son insostenibles. Segundo, a pesar to eso, también los arqueólogos metafóricante confían en la terminologia evolucionaria para mejorar la comprensión de los datos arqueológicos. Aunque el uso de la metáfora evolucionaria puede ser, y ha sido, problemático, igualmente ofrece un marco conceptual poderosos para nuestra investigación. Sin embargo, este armazón ideológico es sólo una de varias estructuras de pensamiento comparables que han sido ofrecidas a nuestro campo, conforme un cotejo entre la arqueología de sistemas y la arqueología evolucionaria nos muestra.

Many archaeologists (and many other social scientists) lately have drawn heavily on theoretical arguments derived from Darwinian research in biology. This is not the first time our field has appealed to Darwin (see, for example, Childe 1951), and explanatory frameworks rooted in Darwinian theory (notably optimal-foraging theory) have been widespread in archaeology since the 1970s (Jochim 1976; Wilmsen 1973). However, many of these recent appeals (i.e., Dunnell 1978, 1980; Lipo et al. 1997; Lyman and O'Brien 1998; O'Brien and Holland 1990; and many others) go beyond past work, often arguing that archaeology's future as a science depends on adopting an explicitly Darwinian perspective. My goal here is to consider some of the very different kinds of claims on evolutionary the-

ory that archaeologists have made recently. As is true in all sciences, every step of archaeological research relies inevitably on theoretical arguments and constructs, and the development and refinement of such arguments and constructs is critical to progress in our field. However, archaeologists, Darwinian or otherwise, include a variety of different kinds of generalizations under the term "theory," and evolutionary archaeology exemplifies this.

Darwinian thought has expanded through the social sciences (including archaeology) in at least two distinct ways. First, social scientists are increasingly trying to identify the ways in which the process of biological evolution by natural selection has shaped and, presumably, continues to shape human ways of life (I discuss some of the anthropological research

Douglas B. Bamforth ■ Anthropology Department, CB 233, University of Colorado, Boulder, CO 80309-0233

American Antiquity, 67(3), 2002, pp. 435–452
Copyright© 2002 by the Society for American Archaeology

209

on this topic in a later section). Work in this area thus attempts to generate general, empirically testable knowledge comparable to that generated in any empirical science. Second, Darwinian thought is increasingly viewed as a useful and even essential framework for thinking about processes of nonbiological change (see Dawkins [1976:203–215] for an early example of this). This kind of expansion of Darwinian thought rests not on empirical documentation that this view of the world is correct, but rather on programmatic statements that have more to do with how we should think about the world than with what the world is like.

Evolutionary archaeology has made both of these kinds of claims on Darwin, and I argue here that it is important to distinguish between them because they depend on very different kinds of support and have very different implications for our practice. If archaeology can claim Darwinian theory in the narrow biological sense, we have the potential to integrate our work with an increasingly important body of work that examines an important topic in many disciplines. However, I argue here that no archaeological claims that have been made on Darwinian process in this sense are sustainable (although much of the research that makes these claims offers important insights into the settings in which evolution occurs). Recognizing this, I turn to consider the more programmatic claims archaeologists have made on Darwin. I argue that this second kind of claim is fundamentally metaphoric and that, although metaphors are powerful and widely used sources of insight in many areas of science, it is important to recognize both their potential and their limits. Finally, I argue that, while evolutionary thought offers important tools for archaeological research, the emphasis on this thought during the 1990s, and especially the more metaphoric aspects of this thought, represent the most recent version of a recurrent process of conceptual development in our field.

I begin by briefly considering Darwinian process in the narrow biological sense. Human evolutionary theory is clearly in a period of rapid development and intense and complex debate (see, for example, Cronk et al. 2000; Rose and Rose 2000). My goal here is not to review or synthesize this debate, although recent developments in evolutionary thought may have important implications for archaeology, and archaeology ought to be important to at least some of these developments. Instead, with this brief discussion as background, I focus specifically on two streams of thought that have been the main source of evolutionary thought in archaeology (cf. Boone and Smith 1998; Broughton and O'Connell 1999; Neff 2000). The first is our field's widespread reliance on optimization models, particularly foraging models, drawn from behavioral ecology, that are often asserted to rely on Darwinian theory. The second is a more uniquely archaeological body of evolutionary thought that is generally referred to as "selectionist" archaeology. As I discuss below, each of these streams of thought makes both substantive and metaphoric claims on Darwin, and recognizing this helps to clarify what they do and do not offer to our field.

Evolution Defined

The theory of Darwinian evolution developed in the specific context of biology as the basis for understanding the processes that created the earth's marvelous diversity of plant and animal species. My starting point is, therefore, the universally understood meaning of "evolution" and associated terms in a modern biological context. In this context, "evolution" refers most fundamentally to changes through time in the relative frequency of genes in a given biological population, and this is the sense in which I use it here. I stress that I do this not because it cannot mean something more general but because using this narrow definition helps to identify important limits on archaeology's access to evolutionary process.

Changes in the genetic makeup of a given population result from a variety of processes. The best known of these processes, and the process that gives its name to the "selectionist" stream of evolutionary thought in archaeology, is natural selection. Theoretical analysis and empirical documentation make it clear that natural selection works primarily through the differential reproductive success of the individual organisms carrying a given set of genes. Some researchers have argued that selection also operates at the level of the individual gene (i.e., Dawkins 1976), although many evolutionary geneticists find this argument unconvincing (i.e., Dover 2000; Jones 1999). In addition, there is an emerging consensus that selection can also operate at the level of the group (Sober and Wilson 1998), although the supporting work acknowledges the simultaneous, and perhaps greater, importance of selection at the individual level. Evolution also works through genetic drift, in which a portion of a population's genetic variation is geographically isolated in a small population, and through adaptively neutral processes that drive evolution at the molecular level of genetic change (Dover 2000; Kimura 1983). History also strongly conditions the evolutionary process, both through unforeseen accidents (for example, some mass extinctions) and because a species' developmental and evolutionary background closes off possibilities for future developments (Gould 2000).

While genetic change measures evolution, simply observing such change is only one step toward understanding the process(es) that caused it. The mechanisms of genetic change are ultimately mediated through the process by which individual organisms reproduce themselves, and the core problem for evolutionary analysis lies in sorting out the many behavioral, environmental, historical, and other forces that affect reproductive success. This success, in turn, depends on surviving to reproductive age and ensuring that one's offspring also survive. Survival and reproduction are thus linked, but it is important to recognize that they are not the same thing—many organisms survive well but reproduce poorly. Recognizing this difference clarifies important issues within the general domain of evolutionary anthropology and archaeology, a point I return to below (also see Merrell 1994:17).

With these issues in mind, for the remainder of this paper I use the terms "fitness" to mean the reproductive success of individual organisms and "selection" to mean the process by which differences among organisms result in different rates of reproduction. Again, this is not the way these terms are often used in evolutionary archaeology (e.g., Lyman and O'Brien 1998:616), but I repeat that one of my points here is to examine how we get from the core meaning of these terms to the ones that are currently in relatively wide use.

The narrow biological definition of evolution highlights two critical problems that anthropology has struggled with. First, because so little of what humans do is genetically determined, the study of evolutionary process in human populations demands an understanding of how non-genetic mechanisms—that is, behavior or, perhaps, "culture"—are related to differences in individual reproductive fitness. Second, because it is not obvious that every non-genetically determined aspect of human behavior/culture

contributes to reproductive fitness, it is necessary to find a way of identifying those aspects of our behavior/culture that do and do not make such contributions. There are many modes of evolutionary research applied to modern humans that address these problems, ranging from direct genetic research to the search for universal biological or behavioral characteristics of modern humans that may reflect our common evolutionary heritage. Furthermore, evolutionary theory and concepts enter into the study of human beings in many different ways. For present purposes, I focus on evolutionary claims in archaeology that rely in one way or another on evidence and evolutionary claims that rely mainly on terminology.

Evidence and Evolution in Archaeology

It is clear that large-scale evolutionary changes in the hominid lineage are manifest in the archaeological record and that archaeology has contributed to the study of these patterns for decades and will continue to do so indefinitely. Traditional paleoanthropological approaches to such changes focus on morphological alterations in past species that are visible in human and proto-human skeletons and that presumably resulted from population-level genetic change. Archaeology provides a crucial means of expanding this kind of research by supplying additional information on ancient human and proto-human behavior that cannot be obtained simply from the study of fossils themselves. However, this work stands in stark contrast to the bulk of recent evolutionary archaeology, which hopes to use changes in artifact assemblages to illuminate the operation of natural selection in anatomically modern human populations. Archaeological approaches to this take several forms.

Foraging Theory and Natural Selection

> The consequences of natural selection of genotypes, for the life history of populations and species, depend in detail on the particular biology of the species and its form of interaction with others. No empirical generalizations seem possible. . . . At the very least, we must say that the price of optimality arguments is eternal vigilance [Lewontin 1979:21].

One set of links to Darwinian process relies on the claimed evolutionary component of optimal-foraging theory. Foraging theory is one part of a rich and diverse research domain referred to as evolutionary or behavioral ecology. Behavioral ecology's view of behavior in terms of a balance of costs and benefits is potentially applicable to essentially any domain of human action, but archaeology has focused largely on optimization studies of diet and foraging behavior, and my discussion here focuses on this work. (Bettinger [1991:83–112], Kaplan and Hill [1992], Kelly [1995], Smith and Winterhalder [1992], and Winterhalder and Smith [1980] summarize optimization theory and its applications in anthropology; see Bamforth and Bleed [1997] and Torrence [1989] for other archaeological applications of optimization perspectives.)

Archaeologists have relied heavily on foraging theory for decades with little or no comment on its Darwinian roots, and we have benefited significantly from its conceptual clarity and rigor. As Bettinger (1991:107–110) notes, the balance of costs and benefits that optimization theory makes explicit underlies virtually all ecological thought in anthropology, including that purporting to reject optimization reasoning. Optimization theory in general, and the empirically well-supported foraging models in particular, clearly illuminate important aspects of human behavior and have greatly enhanced archaeological analyses of human-environment interactions (Bamforth 1988; Broughton 1994; Glassow and Wilcoxen 1988; Jochim 1976, 1998; O'Connell et al. 1982; and many others).

Foraging theory developed in evolutionary biology in response to the difficulty of studying differential reproduction and genetic change in natural populations (Grafen 1984; Lewontin 1979). Recognizing the importance of survival, and especially of obtaining food, to reproductive success, evolutionary biologists argued that foraging success should serve as an adequate proximate measure of fitness: organisms that cannot maintain themselves somatically clearly cannot produce viable offspring, and proper functioning of an organism's reproductive system (and of its other systems) depends very strongly on its nutritional state. Foraging theory's links to Darwin are thus indirect and depend on asserting or assuming that natural selection ought to favor organisms that rely on the kind of economic rationality that underlies optimization models. Just how selection might favor these organisms, or how it might have favored them in the past, has never been a central question that foraging theorists have addressed; instead, research in this area has empha-

sized the ways in which variable environmental conditions are linked to variable phenotypic and behavioral responses.

It is not obvious that foraging theory's benefits derive from its ability to document evolutionary process: somatic and reproductive success are different things, and while foraging theory illuminates the first of these, it does not necessarily tell us anything about the second. As Kacelnik and Krebs (1997:22; also see Lewontin 1979:6–10) argue:

> Although optimality models use an evolutionary logic, they are not constructed to test the hypothesis that evolution has occurred. Nor do individual studies test the principle of making predictions about behavior using the notion of "design by natural selection." . . . The output of [optimization] research is a mechanistic understanding of social dynamics. . . . We do not gain much further knowledge about human evolution, but we learn a lot about what current humans do.

The imprecision of foraging theory's links to evolutionary mechanisms highlights this issue. Foraging theorists particularly do not distinguish between the possibility that selection once favored organisms with the cognitive ability to make something approximating optimal choices and the claim that ongoing selection continues to favor such organisms. In the first case (suggested, for example, by Broughton and O'Connell's [1999:154] assertion that "evolutionary ecology assumes only that natural selection has designed organisms to behave in ways that tend to enhance fitness"), this claim would be something like evolutionary psychology's assertion that selection produced a more-or-less fixed cognitive architecture at some time in the past. Such a claim would essentially assert that some form of economic rationality is a normal part of human cognitive abilities, but it would not necessarily assume any ongoing relation between foraging and fitness. However, other usages, particularly the fundamental assumption that variables like foraging efficiency measure "fitness-correlated pay-offs" (Smith 2000:34), imply just such an ongoing relation.

The assumption that measures of food intake or foraging efficiency can be taken as a proximate measure, or correlate, of fitness is problematic a priori: as noted above, we all know that many individuals survive well, presumably foraging and eating, but do not reproduce. Adequate nutrition is obviously essential to reproductive success, but simply being well-nourished does not guarantee such success. Taking the existence of evidence documenting the beneficial effects of improved nutritional status on reproductive functioning as evidence that, as one reviewer of this paper put it, "the relationship between food and fitness appears to be quite strong" is deeply confused—all that such research indicates is that the link between food and reproductive *capacity* is quite strong. Fitness, and evolutionary process driven by fitness, depends on actual reproduction, and this does not depend only on what we eat or on how we forage for what we eat.

Documenting the links among foraging, food, and fitness would require evidence showing that better foragers and/or better-nourished individuals have greater reproductive success than other individuals, and relying on such evidence in an archaeological context would require a reason to suppose that such a pattern is cross-culturally valid. The concept of "correlates of fitness" presumably implies that the variables analyzed in place of fitness—for example, foraging efficiency and caloric intake—vary predictably with fitness and might even imply that this can be, or has been, documented empirically. It is certainly clear that the kinds of variables that foraging theory examines must be related in some way to successful reproduction, if only because it is necessary to obtain and consume food in order to survive and reproduce. However, foraging theorists have simply made this common-sense observation and then asserted that the variation they document in caloric intake or foraging efficiency predicts comparable variation in reproductive fitness, without ever looking to see if this is actually the case. The (limited) available evidence suggests that it is not.

The *only* aspect of human behavior that has been shown to be a cross-culturally valid predictor of fitness—that is, the only empirically documented correlate of fitness—is individual male status. At least in tribal societies, higher-status men seem universally to have higher reproductive success than lower-status men (Barkow 1977; Chagnon 1979, 1988; Cronk 1989a, 1989b; J. Hill 1984; Hill and Hurtado 1996; Irons 1979; Kaplan and Hill 1985a). Routes to high status are culturally diverse and include hunting success among the Ache of Paraguay, ferocity and political acumen among the Yanömamö of Brazil, and wealth among the Turkmen of Turkmenistan. In these cases, the benefits of high status regularly appear to include increased reproductive success (Barkow

1989; Betzig 1986; Flinn 1997; Perusse 1993).

Furthermore, although there are currently no systematic tests of the assumed relation between fitness and foraging behavior, data derived from research among the Ache are inconsistent with it. Although the Ache illuminate some of the limitations on optimization models, it is clear that, overall, they are impressively optimal foragers (Hawkes et al. 1982; K. Hill 1988; Hill et al. 1984, 1987). However, it is equally clear that the Ache optimize as a group; the data showing that their behavior conforms, for example to the diet-breadth model, were aggregated from the activities of all Ache foragers whose behavior could be observed, as is usual in optimization studies. It is also clear that there is great variation in the foraging behavior of Ache individuals, including differences both between men and women and, most significantly here, among men, who do not all pursue the same resources or pursue them equally effectively. Foraging behavior is linked indirectly to reproductive fitness among the Ache, both because the most productive male hunters have more reproductive opportunities and because the offspring of these hunters have higher survival rates than offspring of other men (Hill and Hurtado 1996; Hill and Kaplan 1988a, 1988b; Hill et al. 1987; Kaplan and Hill 1985a; Wood and Hill 2000).

The link in the Ache data between foraging and reproductive success violates the assumption that explicitly underlies general optimization thought in anthropology, that is, that natural selection should prefer foragers who optimize, with optimization generally conceived as maximizing the efficiency of resource acquisition. Among the Ache, better hunters tend to hunt longer than other men (Hill and Hawkes 1983), thereby disproportionately increasing their contribution to the food supply, and it is this pattern that provides the mechanism driving evolutionary process in this case. Reproductively successful hunters among the Ache do not appear to optimize; instead, it may be more accurate to say that they maximize, and they often do this by ignoring resources that should be in the optimal diet. The full range of resources that should be in the optimal diet is taken by less skilled and less reproductively successful men (Kaplan and Hill 1985a).

The Ache also do not offer much support for the assumption that higher food intake correlates with greater fitness; essentially all the food the Ache bring in, particularly the hunted food that provides 87 percent of the total calories the Ache consume in the forest, is pooled without regard to family relationship. Data on diet prior to settling on a reservation show no detectable interfamilial variation in food intake (Kaplan and Hill 1985b; Kaplan et al. 1984), and the available pre-reservation data for women show no relation between nutrition and fertility (Hill and Hurtado 1996). Despite this, as I note above, there is substantial variation in individual reproductive fitness—better hunters (termed "showoffs" by Hawkes [1991]) have more children and higher survival rates among their children than other men (variation in female fertility is less clearly understood). This pattern also highlights the complexity of the evolutionary process and the great variation of the ways in which selection can operate in different situations: among the Kubo of Papua New Guinea, more successful hunters do *not* have higher reproductive success than less successful hunters (Dwyer and Minnegal 1993).

The assumption that food intake is a reasonable proximate measure of reproductive fitness rests on the unexceptional observation that adequate nutrition is necessary for successful reproduction. However, the association in the Ache case between minimal to nonexistent variation in nutritional status and substantial variation in reproductive success shows that, beyond this simple level of biological necessity, it is not possible to assume a priori that we know how food and fitness are linked in any given case. Furthermore, the Ache's contrast with the Kubo suggests that links between foraging behavior and fitness vary from society to society, mirroring the point that Lewontin (1979:13–21) made regarding optimization theory long ago. Working within an optimization framework derived from behavioral ecology thus has many benefits, but it does not necessarily imply that we have illuminated the operation of Darwinian process in any substantial way.

Mid-Range Theory and Natural Selection

Where foraging theory claims Darwin through the assumed links between optimization models and evolutionary process, other work, including that grounded in optimization thought, focuses more specifically on the problem of recognizing evolutionary process in archaeological data. That is, it attempts to build links between artifacts and evolution at the level of archaeological (or mid-range) theory.

Two aspects of nonarchaeological research into the operation of selection in modern or recent societies are important in this context. First, with fairly direct access to information on reproductive success, many Darwinian ethnographers have been able to study empirically the ongoing process of selection in modern groups in some detail. Second, whatever the role of group selection among humans may be, the studies that are currently available highlight the importance of selection at the level of the individual. In contrast, archaeologists cannot directly observe the actual processes of evolution that operated in the past; instead, we are forced to infer the operation of these (and other) processes from patterns in material culture. Furthermore, archaeological data pertain in virtually every case to the activities of groups of human beings whose social and/or familial relations are unknown, and this is especially true for analyses that aggregate data from sites scattered over large regions and long spans of time.

These points highlight archaeology's similarity to paleontology, whose success in studying evolution is undoubted. Like archaeologists, paleontologists study evolution indirectly by examining its outcomes as they are manifest in the remains of groups of organisms. However, while these broad disciplinary similarities illuminate some aspects of the general character of archaeological inference, in the case of evolutionary research they are superficial and profoundly misleading. The primary data that paleontologists study are observations of the skeletal remains of past organisms. Even evolution that operates entirely through the role of individual-level selection is ultimately manifest in population-level genetic changes, and, although skeletal morphology is not completely determined by such changes, its study clearly informs us concretely about biological and evolutionary process. The problem of linking temporal patterns of change in paleontological data to evolution essentially does not arise because the link is obvious and relatively well-understood. Outside of research on the archaeology of human ancestors, archaeological data consist of observations made on the artifacts and features left behind by a single, largely unchanging species. In contrast to skeletal morphology, the links between material culture and evolutionary process are essentially unknown.

Broadly speaking, our field tends to solve the general problem of building links from things to people in one of two ways. First, we often rely on some form of systematic evidence linking artifacts and behavior, often experimental or ethnoarchaeological evidence. Second, in the many cases where such evidence is not available, we rely on reasoned arguments about what these links ought to be like. This second form of bridging argument essentially proposes plausible but untested hypotheses about the relations between things and people and uses those hypotheses to make sense out of archaeological data. Although such hypotheses are often correct, the recent history of our field offers many cases where evidence, particularly ethnoarchaeological evidence, indicates that they were wrong: ceramic styles do not monitor postmarital residence rules in the ways that some archaeologists once proposed that they ought to; recurrent spatial associations among different classes of tools do not necessarily imply that those tools formed a functionally integrated toolkit; and flaked stone tools are not exclusively men's tools.

The core selectionist claim on Darwin rests on the assertion that we can see "evolution in action" because specific kinds of patterns in the archaeological record either monitor natural selection or show that selection is not operating. However, no study documents this claim empirically, and, in some cases, the patterns claimed as evolutionary in the strict Darwinian sense are clearly incorrect. For example, some studies (i.e., Larson et al. 1996; Leonard and Reed 1993) equate population growth and evolution. However, as Bamforth and Bleed (1997; also see Smith 1991:34) note, this equation is incorrect: populations can grow with or without differential reproduction and selection can operate while population is stable, growing, or shrinking.

There have been no attempts to document the evolutionary significance of archaeological patterns in a well-understood setting. Instead, archaeologists have simply asserted this significance for a given kind of pattern, often basing this assertion on examples of patterns documented for genetic evolution. This is clearest for the body of research that argues that specific patterns of change in archaeological trait frequencies over time reflect the operation of natural selection, in contrast to other patterns (for example, the smooth battleship-shaped curves produced in a successful ceramic seriation), that are said to reflect selectively neutral (or "stylistic") processes (Dunnell 1978, 1980; Lipo et al. 1997; Niemann 1995; O'Brien and Holland 1990, 1992; Shennan and Wilkinson 2001). As Niemann (1995:8) put it, "variation along a dimension is stylistic when the fitness values associated with each variant (the expected reproductive success they confer on their bearers) are effectively the same, rendering the variants selectively neutral. Variation is functional when different variants have effectively different fitness values." This dichotomy is oversimplified—as Shennan and Wilkinson (2001:578) point out, many, and perhaps most, archaeological cases are probably neither purely neutral nor purely selected—but more importantly, the link between particular patterns of archaeological change and particular evolutionary interpretations rests on assertion and, as discussed in a later section, an implicit metaphor, rather than on demonstration.

Selectionist analyses often seem to assume implicitly that selection operates primarily to create permanent, essentially unidirectional changes in the archaeological record. However, as Shennan and Wilkinson (2001:578) observe, fluctuating selection can produce fluctuating evolutionary responses, a point that the best-known example of the operation of natural selection on a biological population illustrates clearly: the gradual patterns of change in the frequency of peppered moths in industrial England from the mid-nineteenth through the late twentieth centuries leave no doubt that selection can produce battleship-shaped curves to rival any archaeological ceramic seriation (i.e., Majerus 1998:97–156). Analogous, archaeologically visible, patterns of fluctuating selection are probably common. For example, construction of fortifications can hardly be explained except as an attempt to protect oneself and one's family from attack. In the Middle Missouri region of the northern Great Plains, horticultural communities dated between A.D. 900–1500 appear to have fortified themselves primarily during episodic periods of sustained drought, and towns built between droughts generally lack defensive structures (Bamforth 2001). That is, there is no sustained pattern in the Middle Missouri prior to Euroamerican contact in which construction of fortifications "begin[s] at some arbitrary point above zero and increase[s] in frequency at a steadily decelerating rate toward some optimal value" (O'Brien and Holland 1992:49), as they should if selectionist arguments linking archaeological and evolutionary change are correct.

Neff (2000) and Nieman (1999) have recently backed away from the argument that the archaeological patterns selectionists have focused on monitor evolutionary process directly. These authors argue that the kinds of archaeological changes that they examine (mainly changes in ceramic design that, as Niemann [1995:18] notes, are a priori very unlikely to have any utilitarian significance) occur too rapidly to attribute to the process of biological evolution. The "selection" involved in archaeological changes is not natural selection but, rather, some form of "cultural" selection. However, this argument fails to distinguish between the rate at which selective conditions change and the rate at which changes in selective conditions generate evolutionary outcomes.

There is no doubt that most population-level genetic changes in long-lived species (like humans) develop gradually over relatively long periods of time. The selective conditions that drive such changes can shift very rapidly, and human behavioral flexibility allows us to respond rapidly to such changes. For example, the correlates of male reproductive fitness among the Ache changed in a single generation, from hunting prowess in the pre-reservation period to wealth on the reservation (Hill and Hurtado 1996). As O'Brien and Holland (1992:38) note, "because of [the human] ability to transmit information intergenerationally, the historical development of adaptations may be short-lived." If rapid changes in lifeways occurred in the past and had material correlates, they would presumably produce just the kinds of rapid archaeological changes to which Neff and Neiman refer. Furthermore, the selectionist argument linking patterns of change to evolutionary process is potentially applicable to longer-term changes in artifact frequencies to which Neff's and Niemann's arguments are not relevant.

Selectionist links between archaeological patterns and Darwinian process are incorrect, not because of the speed of archaeological change but because of the difference between the individual level at which selection is known to operate among human beings and the aggregate, or group, scale at which archaeologists observe past humans. Most patterned, archaeologically visible temporal changes that can be shown to have had practical effects on people's lives have those effects because they enhanced survival. Given the scale at which archaeologists work, we know only that such changes enhanced the lives of what are often very vaguely defined groups of humans. Such changes may reflect the greater reproductive success of a segment of a given population, as selectionists have often argued. However, such

changes may also represent widespread shifts made by many reproductive groups within one or more societies. If archaeologists cannot distinguish these different processes from one another, we cannot link our data to evolutionary process. This, and not the rapidity of some archaeological changes, is the key reason why the selectionist argument is incorrect.

The likelihood that selection sometimes operates at the level of the group as well as at the level of the individual does not necessarily solve this problem. Empirical studies in nonhuman organisms appear to document the effects of group selection (i.e., Goodnight and Stevens 1997), although they also document the simultaneous role of individual selection. However, while the importance of individual-level selection is well established for human beings, evidence for group selection among human beings is rare at present. Soltis et al. (1995) show that group-level benefits can foster the spread of behavioral/cultural adaptations, but these authors are careful to distinguish the processes they consider from the process of evolution by natural selection. Wilson (1998) suggests that food-sharing among hunters and gatherers documents group selection, but his discussion is strongly tied to foraging theory and relies on the same assumed, and problematic, link between food and fitness as does that body of work (also see below). However, regardless of what ongoing research may document about the role of group selection among modern humans, such selection does not eliminate the difficulty of identifying individual selection archaeologically. Recent attention to group selection argues not that individual selection does not occur, but rather that selection operates on both individuals and groups. Integrating group selection into evolutionary archaeology thus complicates rather than eliminates the middle-range issue: if archaeology is to study evolutionary process, we need both to develop more realistic ways of recognizing when archaeological changes are driven by selection rather than by some other process and also of distinguishing between individual and group selection.

Mid-range problems like these are potentially solvable: optimization theorists could focus their attention on the links between foraging and selection, and selectionist archaeologists could do more than simply assert relations between material culture and evolutionary process. All of the claims on Darwin I have considered so far are subject to the same kinds of examination as any scientific claim: we can see whether or not they measure up against the available evidence, and we can work to improve them if they do not. However, evolutionary archaeology also calls on Darwin in another way, largely by extending biological terminology to refer to nonbiological processes. This is a very different use of Darwin, and it helps to situate evolutionary archaeology in the larger history of theoretical development in our field.

Metaphor and Evolution in Archaeology

The concepts on which evolutionary archaeology relies (concepts like fitness, selection, etc.) derive directly from the study of biological evolution, and a second kind of evolutionary thought extends these concepts beyond the specific biological context in which they were first defined. Scholars regularly generalize theories and concepts, including evolutionary theory and concepts, from one domain of inquiry to another, often (although not always) with great success; archaeology has a long and, as Gumerman and Philips (1978) point out, not entirely distinguished history of this. However, it is important to understand how this process of generalization operates and particularly to distinguish between the demonstration that superficially different processes actually *are* examples of the same process and the assertion that truly different processes can be thought of *as if* they are examples of a single process.

In contrast to the process of generalizing a theory by showing empirically that it has a wider scope than was initially thought, evolutionary archaeology often generalizes Darwinian concepts by reconstituting the meanings of terms like "fitness" and "selection"; it relies on argument, not on demonstration. The outcome of this is that evolutionary terms and concepts take on profoundly different meanings in archaeology (and, in practice, in foraging theory; see below) than the meanings they have in evolutionary theory. The use of one word to assert an identity between very different things is the essence of metaphor, and I therefore turn to consider metaphoric arguments in general as a background to several important evolutionary metaphors.

Metaphors

Metaphors are literary devices, and I begin with an example from Shakespeare's *Macbeth* (Act V, Scene III):

My way of life is fallen into the sere, the yellow leaf.

A metaphor like this evokes a kind of intuitive comparison on the part of the reader, and it is possible to find many meanings in this comparison. Macbeth may be telling us that he is an old man with little to look forward to except the end (or, perhaps, the "winter") of his life, or he may be suggesting that his crimes have sucked the life out of him. The metaphor also trivializes Macbeth's life by comparing it to a single leaf, one of tens of thousands on a single tree, each scarcely distinguishable from the others—perhaps it tells us that Macbeth is striving to leave a unique existential mark, no matter how hateful a mark, on the world in the face of such meaninglessness. Or, perhaps Shakespeare had none of these meanings in mind. Regardless of Shakespeare's intent, this example demonstrates several important properties of literary metaphors. In particular, metaphors can be read in a number of different ways, and they operate by deepening the reader's emotional understanding of the metaphor's subject. In this case, metaphors help us to see Macbeth's essential humanity despite the enormity of his crimes.

Academic writing also uses metaphor. Analyses of academic metaphor (often specifically with reference to the uses of Darwinian concepts in the social sciences—Maasen et al. 1995) identify at least three different ways in which metaphors are used. These are "illustrative," "heuristic," and "constitutive":

> Metaphors are illustrative when they are used primarily as a literary device, to increase the power or conviction of an argument, for example. Although the difference between the illustrative and the heuristic function of metaphors is not great, it does exist: metaphors are used for heuristic purposes whenever differences of meaning are employed to open new perspectives and to gain new insights. In the case of "constitutive" metaphors they function to actually replace previous meanings by new ones [Maasen et al. 1995:2].

The distinction between constitutive and other kinds of metaphors is particularly important here. The example from *Macbeth* can be seen as illustrative or, perhaps, heuristic: Shakespeare was using words to illuminate his character by suggesting similarities between very different things. However, whatever Shakespeare's own construction of the meaning of this metaphor might have been, we can be sure that he did not intend this as an example of a constitutive metaphor. He was suggesting that Macbeth was *like* a leaf, not that Macbeth *was* a leaf. We are not intended to conclude that Macbeth's choices were caused by a seasonal deficiency of chlorophyll in his system, or that we need to be familiar with plant physiology in order to make sense out of the play.

Heuristic metaphors are powerful devices for illuminating patterns in the world, for directing our thought in fruitful directions and our attention to possibilities and evidence that we might not otherwise consider. Implicitly or explicitly, they are widely used in anthropology and many other disciplines, and they often provide the basis for influential views of our field that support substantial bodies of research and analysis; the organic analogy that drove much of British social anthropology in the first half of the twentieth century is a good example of this. It is also clear that metaphors have been central to the development of modern evolutionary thought. Ceccarelli (2001:13–60), for example, shows that Dobzhansky's (1937) use of metaphor (particularly the notion of an "adaptive landscape") was central to his ability to frame Darwinian theory in a way that allowed geneticists and naturalists to understand how their differing approaches to biology could be brought together to form the modern synthesis of evolutionary thought. However, while metaphors can play an important role in developing an empirical understanding of the world, they do not substitute for such an understanding, and they are useful only to the extent that that they open profitable avenues for our thought (as in Dobzhansky's case) instead of closing or misdirecting them.

Evolutionary Metaphor in Archaeology

The assertion, implicit or otherwise, of a real identity between two different things—the third, or constitutive, usage of metaphor—is common in Darwinian archaeology and anthropology. While metaphor can be a powerful source of insight, its use carries with it the possibility of transferring theories and concepts from one domain that misrepresents processes in another domain and of distorting the meaning of these theories and concepts to make them fit their new uses. Evolutionary archaeology and anthropology illustrate both the problems and the potential of scientific uses of metaphor.

For example, one of the least-clarifying arguments in recent evolutionary work grows from the claim (Rindos 1985; also see Cohen 1981; Hurt et al. 2001) that nongenetic (that is, behavioral or cultural) variation has to be generated randomly with

respect to adaptive need in order for change based on that variation to qualify as evolutionary. This is a particularly good illustration of the problem of drawing theory developed to account for one kind of phenomena and applying it to account for entirely different phenomena. The requirement of randomness derives, obviously, from the synthetic theory, but in its original context it is not part of an abstract theoretical definition. Rather, it is an inference derived from empirical research into the causes of genetic mutation.

This transformation of evolutionary theory into a nongenetic context illustrates the limitations that the uncritical, and probably unrecognized, use of metaphor can put on our understanding. It is certainly possible that variation in human behavior arises without respect to need, but assuming at the outset that this is so ignores the possibility that we generate inventions in patterned ways (as Dawkins [1982:112], for example, suggests we might), perhaps in response to perceived needs or during periods of time when the costs of experimental failure are low. In fact, we do not know whether or not humans generate innovations randomly with respect to need, systematically in response to need, or in both of these ways. Human beings are clearly the products of genes, but we are not the same as genes, and metaphorically equating us obscures this difference and may blind us to important processes we need to see in order to build a theory about the phenomena we are actually interested in.

Usage of the term "fitness" by foraging theorists also illustrates the constitutive use of metaphor. Formal models of foraging (and other) behavior are abstractions whose heuristic value derives from their rigorous analysis of the relations among some set of mathematically well-defined variables. However, the links between these analytic variables and aspects of the real world are not inherent in any mathematical definition. In the cases where optimization models are subjected to systematic empirical test, their component variables are made meaningful by sets of measurements made on real-world data. In other cases, though, their component variables are given meaning simply by assigning them names. The process of naming variables in optimization models provides a particularly clear example of evolutionary metaphor.

In many cases, the absence of any evidence for a constant relation between food intake and reproductive fitness (discussed above) is at the heart of this problem. In particular, the dependent variable in many recent optimization models is labelled "fitness" in cases where it is not at all clear that the model actually considers anything that resembles fitness. For example, Wilson (1998) uses food-sharing within a group as a way of arguing for the importance of group selection. Despite the specific meaning of fitness in biology, Wilson (1998:75, 77, 79) quite explicitly assumes an equation between meat intake and fitness, and asserts that by sharing meat "hunters increase the fitness of everyone in the group." However, nowhere in Wilson's discussion does he provide any support for this assumption and, as I discuss above, it is problematic at best since interfamilial food (and meat) intake among the forest-era Ache varied hardly at all, but reproductive success varied significantly. The equation of food and fitness in recent theoretical work is so strong that Winterhalder (1997:139) actually seems to treat food as a clear measure of fitness and reproductive success as problematic. He repeatedly refers without comment to the fitness benefits of eating more, but describes as "elusive" the fitness benefits of the mating opportunities obtained by good Ache hunters. This usage is particularly striking because of the well-documented absence of any discernable relation between nutritional intake and fitness among the Ache, discussed above. Optimization models offer important insights into the benefits of behavior patterns like food-sharing, but they do not do this, at least to date, by documenting the effects of these patterns on Darwinian fitness.

Many other metaphors in evolutionary archaeology grow from the use of genetic models to understand archaeological patterns. For example, the term "phenotype" in a biological context refers to the outcome of an interaction between the information included in an organism's genes and the environment that organism occupies. Expanding this term to include artifacts as part of an "extended phenotype" (i.e., Neff 1992:141), perhaps as a result of the influence on some evolutionary thinking of Dawkins's (1976, 1982) notion of a "meme" (Neff 2000; but see Dean 1996:27–28), metaphorically equates the information required to produce an artifact with genetic information. Similarly, Lipo et al. (1997) refer to ceramic "lineages" as part of an analysis that draws its conceptual basis directly from the study of genetic variation (also see Nieman 1995), semanti-

cally equating historically related sequences of changes in artifact design with biologically related families of human beings. None of these equations depends on evidence showing the similarities of genetic and behavioral processes; rather, they assume or assert these similarities and rely on biological terms and models to clarify archaeological data, direct our thought in interesting ways, and justify the transfer of analytic tools and concepts from the study of genetics to the study of archaeological trait frequencies.

In this view, evolutionary theory is "too big a theory to be confined to the narrow context of the gene" (Dawkins 1976:205) or to the study of the biological process by which life on earth has diversified over time. Instead, it is about "the means by which definable entities change from one form into another" (Cohen 1981:201; also see Lyman and O'Brien 1998; Neff 1992). Translated specifically into archaeology, this view asserts that change in material culture is better viewed as the result of the differential persistence of one form of an artifact over another than as the transformation of one way of life into another. That is, humans choose differentially from a range of available behavioral or material options over time in response to changing external conditions, and the result of such differential choices is an archaeologically visible pattern that can be seen as evidence of a kind of evolution. Viewing archaeological change from a selectionist perspective, at least at this general level, fits naturally both with the recognition that we all make choices about our actions based on external circumstance and with the fact that archaeological change is often manifest as changes in the relative frequencies of different classes of artifacts. However, such arguments, implicitly or explicitly, treat archaeological traits as essentially equivalent to genes, and this highlights both the strengths and the potential limitations of scientific metaphor.

Variability is the stuff of which evolution is made, and Darwinian theory offers the best-developed framework for thinking about variability and change known to science. However, drawing analytic tools and concepts from the study of biological, and particularly genetic, evolution and applying them to study archaeological data can both guide our attention to some important issues and make it more difficult to focus on other equally important issues. Recent attention to the concept of "neutral variation" in ceramic design (for example, Lipo et al. 1997; Niemann 1995; Shennan and Wilkinson 2001) illustrates this clearly. This work draws heavily on analyses of the ways in which selectively neutral genetic variation contributes to evolutionary change in biological populations.

In a genetic context, selectively neutral variation (for example, the variation that produces differences in hair or eye color) has no effect on reproductive fitness. The specific question that studies of neutral variation ask is essentially whether or not the choice to decorate a pot using one or another of the range of kinds of decorations in use in a particular time and place had any practical effects on people's lives. This question is a more or less direct translation of the question a geneticist studying neutral variation would ask, and answering it has the potential to inform us about important aspects of social and other processes at work in the past. However, selection affects both the implications of choosing from a range of variation and also the nature of that range (cf. Jones et al. 1995). A geneticist might or might not find it interesting to ask why the range of variation in human hair color does not include, for example, green. However, such a question may be profoundly important in many archaeological contexts. Shennan and Wilkinson (20001:591), for example, note the possibility that the extremely restricted range of decoration on Linearbandkeramik pots during the early stages of agricultural settlement of the Merzbach valley in western Germany represents a deliberate choice—that is, that it represents selection against variation. Their data thus suggest both that it may not have made any difference which of the very limited range of designs a potter chose to use on any given pot, and also that it may have made a big difference if that potter chose a design outside of that range. Such a possibility has important social implications that can be obscured by the direct translation of analytic perspectives from evolutionary genetics.

Archaeology has often tended both implicitly and explicitly to minimize the importance of variability, and evolutionary archaeology's reliance on a Darwinian framework makes such a minimization essentially impossible. Selectionist archaeology's emphasis on the differential persistence of one variant over another offers important correctives for such essentialist arguments as Binford's (1979) equation of overgeneralized technological habits with equally overgeneralized patterns of hunter-gatherer mobility (an equation he made after he himself described

important technological variation). Furthermore, as Neff (2000; also see Ladefoged and Graves 2000) suggests, behavioral ecology's emphasis on evaluating the costs and benefits of such variation almost certainly fills a substantial gap in selectionist thinking, implying that these two domains of research are less distinct than some of their practitioners suggest (i.e., Boone and Smith 1998; Lyman and O'Brien 1998). Evolutionary archaeology's recognition of the importance of historical contingency also corrects a naive focus on highly abstracted generalizations that are thought to apply to all humans. General processes (evolutionary and other) that affect us do so within the frameworks set by our highly variable historical backgrounds, and these backgrounds affect the ways in which those processes operate. Importantly, a metaphorically Darwinian framework for looking at archaeological change holds these benefits regardless of our ability to identify evolution by natural selection in our data.

Note, though, that all of these benefits refer to potential clarifications in general archaeological thought rather than to empirically verified, or verifiable, expansions of archaeology's knowledge of past humans. Archaeology has sought to clarify its thinking in many ways at many times in its history, and recognizing the potential value of Darwinian metaphor for archaeological thought highlights the fact that our field has seen great value in other metaphors in the past. Science-fiction writer Samuel Delany (1977:283) once referred to abstract intellectual concepts as "sharpening stones for the blade with which we strike the face of reality," and evolutionary archaeology's conceptual framework may well offer us a particularly useful sharpening stone. However, similarities between evolutionary archaeology in the 1990s and the systems archaeology in the 1970s helps to situate recent work in a more historical context.

Evolutionary Archaeology and Systems Archaeology

It is this systemic view of culture with its multivariate approach and emphasis on relationships and variability that should be the interpretive framework of scientifically oriented archaeology. . . .

There is already a voluminous body of literature and laws concerning the nature of systems and processes which is available for application to the archaeological record. . . .

The adoption of systems theory as an interpretive and investigatory framework necessitates modifications in the methods of contemporary archaeology. . . . The assumption of systems theorists that culture and processes are complex until proven otherwise requires that the collection and analysis of data that emphasizes the variability in the archaeological record and attempts to sample its range of variation. . . .

Proper use of the systems approach will enable archaeology to deal with problems of increasingly greater interest and relevance to culture process [Watson et al. 1972:65, 67, 84, 87].

If not a theory, what does [systems theory] offer to the archaeologist? Well, some flashy vocabulary for one thing. . . . A new language does sometimes enable us to look at things in a new way. And if it can do that it is not merely jargon. Nor is it jargon if it can clarify our thinking by reducing imprecision. But we should be wary of trying to apply precisely defined terms outside of their restricted limits. . . . Archaeology will not become scientifically respectable by merely adopting systems theory jargon.

The holistic approach of systems theory also has the healthy effect of reducing tendencies to excessive narrowness in research efforts. For this purpose, however, a brief dose is sufficient and will enable one to avoid the unpleasant side effects of prolonged treatment [Salmon 1978:182].

Thirty years ago, systems theory occupied much the same niche in archaeology that evolutionary theory occupies today. Like evolutionary archaeology, systems archaeology was going to finally make us scientists; like evolutionary archaeology, systems archeology was going to enable us to draw directly on a well-developed and explicit body of existing explanatory theory; and, like evolutionary archaeology, systems archaeology was going to lead us toward theoretical integration with other academic disciplines. Systems archaeology was also driven substantially by technical terminology and characterized more by polemics and preliminary illustrative studies than by detailed empirical analysis. Systems archaeology generalized a set of concepts that were asserted, but not demonstrated, to characterize relations among the parts of any organized whole in much the same way that evolutionary archaeology generalizes a set of evolutionary concepts that are asserted, but not demonstrated, to characterize most, if not all, processes of temporal change. In doing this, systems theory metaphorically

glossed over differences among disparate kinds of "systems" just as evolutionary archaeology metaphorically glosses over differences between biology and behavior.

Neither systems archaeology nor evolutionary archaeology offered a testable, scientific basis for claiming that it is better to view cultural change as adjustments among subsystems or as the product of some form of quasi-Darwinian selection. In fact, the notion of "testing" these claims is essentially meaningless. Such frameworks became widely popular because archaeologists found them to be useful stones for sharpening their thoughts, not because the weight of the evidence indicated that they were preferable to some other way of thinking about our data. Changes in their popularity thus must reflect factors other than their demonstrated ability to account for the processes archaeologists study. Addressing these factors in detail is beyond the scope of this paper, but it seems likely that there are at least two that are particularly important.

First, the kinds of questions archaeologists ask change over time, in part because of changes in our knowledge and in part because of changes in the culture/society of which archaeology is a part. The difference between systems archeology's focus on holistic analysis of the ways in which different aspects of human ways of life interact with one another and selectionist archaeology's narrower focus on the differential persistence of variation may perhaps reflects forces like these. The widespread resurgence of Darwinian thought in the social sciences over the past decade is surely linked to sociocultural as well as to scientific factors (it is certainly, in part, a reaction to the wretched antiscientific excesses of much of postmodernism), as well as to improvements in our understanding of evolutionary process. Second, it also is likely that frameworks like systems archaeology fall out of favor as archaeologists become disillusioned with our ability to link them in more than a very general, programmatic way to detailed archaeological data.

In fact, at the same time that Flannery (1973) was spelling archaeology with a capital S, other archaeologists were finding intellectual sharpening stones in ethnoarchaeological and experimental research, in the development of more effective flotation techniques and of bone-chemistry analysis, and in more careful attention to taphonomic process. These sharpening stones are still with us and will clearly continue to be with us. In contrast, systems archaeology is manifest today more in the ways in which it has shaped our thinking than as an explicit body of theory. For example, the ideas of positive and negative feedback underlie more concrete concepts like Flannery's (1968) concepts of seasonality and scheduling and inform many current ideas about how things change and why they sometimes do not change. Some conceptual frameworks that remain influential—for example, Binford's (1980) forager/collector continuum—are explicitly rooted in a systems perspective, and archaeological views of the development and operation of complex societies owe a great debt to systems-based analyses (for example, Redman 1978). Increasingly sophisticated use of systems concepts also continues in the study of complex adaptive systems (i.e., Wills et al. 1994), although, like simpler forms of systems thought (and like much of evolutionary archaeology), this work has yet to be linked in any detail to the archaeological record. If nothing else, the essence of archaeological systems theory—that everything is connected to everything else—implicitly justifies our persistent search for linkages between such diverse areas of human endeavor as flaked-stone technology and gender.

Evolutionary archaeology has many of the hallmarks of a systems archaeology for the 1990s. However, like systems archaeology, its current popularity reflects a core of real value; I have noted the importance of evolutionary ecology's explicit focus on costs and benefits and of selectionist views of change and recognition of the importance of historical context. If we learn nothing else from the recent literature, concepts like these will have clarified our ideas in important ways. However, recognizing these benefits also highlights what evolutionary archaeology does not offer us. Seeing cultural change as the result of the differential "success" of behavioral variants tells us neither how to recognize meaningful variation nor how to measure success, and acknowledging the importance of historical contingency identifies neither important events in human history nor the ways in which they "select" one variant over another. Similarly, systems archaeology's focus on the interconnectedness of the world told us neither how to identify relevant systems or subsystems nor how the connections among them might operate (Salmon 1978). These benefits sharpen our thinking about the world, but they tell us little of substance about the things in the world that we want to think sharply about. Most concretely, they tell us nothing about how to translate these kinds of issues into the peculiar context of archaeological interpretation.

Conclusions

Much of this discussion can be summed up by distinguishing between two very different questions. The first is whether or not archaeology can examine evolution in the same context as biology examines it, and can therefore use terms like "selection" and "fitness" in the same ways in which biologists use them. Understanding how biological evolution has shaped our species and how the process of natural selection continues to affect us and our ways of life is an important domain of research. If archaeology can devise ways of monitoring the process of evolution by natural selection in the past, our ability to examine long periods of time for which few or no nonarchaeological data exist could make a profoundly important contribution to such understanding. However, I have argued here that archaeology's essentially universal reliance on aggregate data sets that represent the activities of human groups whose familial and reproductive relations are unknown currently precludes us from making such a contribution. It may be possible to develop modes of analysis that allow us to surmount this problem, but we have certainly not yet accomplished this.

A second and distinct kind of question has to do not with whether we can study evolutionary process directly but with how the analytic concepts developed in the context of evolutionary research can be generalized to help to make sense out of nonbiological processes. Certainly, the word "evolution" is commonly used to mean many different things, and there is no a priori reason why temporal changes in material culture cannot be one of these things. The basic conceptual tools archaeologists have appropriated from evolutionary biology have the broader potential to describe many processes of change in terms of concrete human decision making, and this can be very valuable. If we do better archaeology by conceiving of artifacts as "replicators" rather than as indicators of "mental templates," then that is what we should do. However, I have argued here that the process by which we extend terms and concepts from one domain of research to another is fundamentally metaphoric, and that recognizing this may help us to avoid using such terms and concepts inappropriately.

The distinction between using archaeological data to study the evolutionary process and using evolutionary concepts to make sense out of archeological data also helps to identify where a more-than-metaphoric evolutionary archaeology might be able to go. We may or may not ever be able to recognize the operation of differential reproduction in ancient human groups; a glance at any recent summary of research in either general or human evolutionary research (i.e., Cronk et al. 2000; Krebs and Davies 1997) will indicate just how far this work is from the kinds of topics archaeology studies effectively. However, archaeological data should have profound implications for other aspects of evolutionary research, particularly such topics as evolutionary psychology's claim that the human mind evolved once and has subsequently changed little, if at all. Research on ancient human cognition (i.e., Gowlett 1997; Mithen 1990, 1996) is important in this context, as is the possible disjuncture between the dates for the appearance of anatomical modernity, indicated by human skeletal material from eastern and southern Africa, and archaeological evidence that may document the much later appearance of behavioral modernity (Klein 1995; but see McBrearty 1999).

Warnings of an impending disciplinary crisis that can be avoided by adopting a particular conceptual framework are not new in archaeology (i.e., Leone 1972; Taylor 1948), and the field has grown past them without universal adherence to any single theoretical perspective. Darwinian theory and ideas drawn from it do not provide the only set of concepts that may illuminate ancient or modern humans, and archaeologists' status as scientists does not depend on our degree of devotion to evolutionary thought. However, understanding the ways in which evolution has shaped our species is likely to have important implications for our work, and archaeology has the potential to offer a uniquely long-term perspective on this issue. However, we will not realize the benefits of understanding evolutionary process or make meaningful contributions to such an understanding by asserting unsubstantiated connections to evolutionary theory or by simply using Darwinian terminology, regardless of the conceptual benefits such terminology may offer us.

The issues I have considered here are important because evolution is important. The premium our discipline puts on theoretical insight often slights the serious difficulty of translating such insight into meaningful archaeological terms. The links between natural selection and cultural behavior are difficult to sort out, and adding the problem of linking cultural behavior to the archaeological record only increases the complexity. We will not overcome this problem by positing plausible but unsupported rules for interpreting patterns in archaeological data, or by assuming rather than demonstrating the relation between evolutionary process and the phenomena (such as food procurement) that we happen to be most able to study. Rigorous technical analysis and careful consideration both of multiple lines of evidence and of multiple potential explanations for patterns in that evidence are what make us competent scientists, not our commitment to any particular theoretical perspective. Systems archaeology foundered in large part because it failed to deal with issues like these, and we are well on our way to seeing whether or not evolutionary archaeology will have the same fate.

Acknowledgments. I presented an early version of this paper in a session at the 1999 Society for American Archaeology meetings entitled "Evolutionary Theory in Archaeology," organized by Doug MacDonald. It has benefited from the comments of many people, some of whom disagree strenuously (to put it mildly) with what I say here. I have particularly profited from the thoughts of Bob Bettinger, Brenda Bowser, Cathy Cameron, Claudio Cioffi, Geoff Clark, Linda Cordell, Mike Jochim, Tim Kohler, Steve Lekson, Hector Neff, John Patton, Payson Sheets, Eric Smith, Alison Wylie, and a remarkable number of anonymous referees. Gustavo Gamez translated the abstract into Spanish.

References Cited

Bamforth, D.
  1988 *Ecology and Human Organization on the Great Plains.* Plenum Press, New York.
  2001 Radiocarbon Calibration, Tree-Rings, Climate, and the Course of War in the Middle Missouri. Paper presented at the 66th Annual Meeting of the Society for American Archaeology, New Orleans.
Bamforth, D., and P. Bleed
  1997 Technology, Flaked Stone Technology, and Risk. In *Rediscovering Darwin,* edited by C. Barton and G. Clark, pp. 109–140. Archaeological Papers of the American Anthropological Association No. 7. Arlington, Virginia.
Barkow, J.
  1977 Conformity to Ethos and Reproductive Success in Two Hausa Communities: An Empirical Evaluation. *Ethos* 5:409–425.
  1989 *Darwin, Sex, and Status.* University of Toronto Press, Toronto.
Bettinger, R.
  1991 *Hunter-Gatherers: Archaeological and Evolutionary Theory.* Plenum Press, New York.

Betzig, N.
1986 *Despotism and Differential Reproduction: A Darwinian View of History.* Aldine de Gruyter, Hawthorne, New Jersey.
Binford, L.
1979 Organization and Formation Processes: Looking at Curated Technologies. *Journal of Anthropological Research* 35:255–273.
1980 Willow Smoke and Dog's Tails: Hunter-Gatherer Settlement Systems and Archaeological Site Formation. *American Antiquity* 45:4–20.
Boone, J., and E. Smith
1998 Is It Evolution Yet?: A Critique of Evolutionary Archaeology. *Current Anthropology* 39:141–173.
Broughton, J.
1994 Declines in Mammalian Foraging Efficiency During the Late Holocene, San Francisco Bay. *Journal of Anthropological Archaeology* 13:371–401.
Broughton, J., and J. O'Connell
1999 On Evolutionary Ecology, Selectionist Archaeology, and Behavioral Archaeology. *American Antiquity* 64:153–165.
Ceccarelli, L.
2001 *Shaping Science with Rhetoric.* University of Chicago Press, Chicago.
Chagnon, N.
1979 Is Reproductive Success Equal in Egalitarian Societies? In *Evolutionary Biology and Human Social Behavior,* edited by N. Chagnon and W. Irons, pp. 374–401. Duxbury Press, N. Scituate, Massachusetts.
1988 Life Histories, Blood Revenge, and Warfare in a Tribal Society. *Science* 239:985– 992.
Childe, V. G.
1951 *Man Makes Himself.* Mentor Books, New York.
Cohen, R.
1981 Evolutionary Epistemology and Values. *Current Anthropology* 22:201–218.
Cronk, L.
1989a From Hunters to Herders: Subsistence Change as a Reproductive Strategy Among the Mukogodo. *Current Anthropology* 30:224–234.
1989b Low Socio-Economic Status and Female-Biased Parental Investment: The Mukogodo Example. *American Anthropologist* 91:414–429.
Cronk, L., N. Chagnon, and W. Irons
2000 *Adaptation and Human Behavior.* Aldine De Gruyter, New York.
Dawkins, R.
1976 *The Selfish Gene.* Oxford University Press, New York.
1982 *The Extended Phenotype.* Freeman, San Francisco.
Dean, J.
1996 Demography, Environment, and Subsistence Stress. In *Evolving Complexity and Environmental Risk in the Prehistoric Southwest,* edited by J. Tainter and B. Tainter, pp. 25–56. Addison-Wesley, New York.
Delany, S.
1977 *The Fall of the Towers.* Bantam Books, New York.
Dobzhansky, T.
1937 *Genetics and the Origin of Species.* Columbia University Press, New York.
Dover, G.
2000 Anti-Dawkins. In *Alas Poor Darwin,* edited by H. Rose and S. Rose, pp. 55–77. Harmony Books, New York.
Dunnell, R.
1978 Style and Function: A Fundamental Dichotomy. *American Antiquity* 43:192–202.

1980 Evolutionary Theory and Archaeology. *Advances in Archaeological Method and Theory* 3:35–99.
Dwyer, P., and M. Minnegal
1993 Are Kubo Hunters 'Show Offs'? *Ethology and Sociobiology* 14:53–70.
Flannery, K.
1968 Archaeological Systems Theory and Early Mesoamerica. In *Anthropological Archaeology in the Americas,* edited by B. Meggars, pp. 67–87. Anthropological Society of Washington, Washington, D.C.
1973 Archaeology With a Capital S. In *Research and Theory in Current Archaeology,* edited by C. Redman, pp. 47–53. Wiley and Sons, New York.
Flinn, M.
1997 Culture and Evolution of Social Learning. *Evolution and Human Behavior* 18:23– 67.
Glassow, M., and L. Wilcoxen
1988 Coastal Adaptations Near Point Conception, California, With Particular Regard to Shellfish Exploitation. *American Antiquity* 53:36–51.
Goodnight, C., and L. Stevens
1997 Experimental Studies of Group Selection: What Do They Tell Us about Group Selection in Nature? *American Naturalist* 150, Supplement: S59–S79.
Gould, S. J.
2000 More Things in Heaven and Earth. In *Alas Poor Darwin,* edited by H. Rose and S. Rose, pp. 101–126. Harmony Books, New York.
Gowlett, J.
1997 Why the Muddle in the Middle Matters: The Language of Comparative and Direct in Human Evolution. In *Rediscovering Darwin,* edited by C. Barton and G. Clark, pp. 49–66. Archaeological Papers of the American Anthropological Association No. 7. Arlington, Virginia.
Grafen, A.
1984 Natural Selection, Kin Selection, and Group Selection. In *Behavioral Ecology: An Evolutionary Approach,* edited by J. Krebs and N. Davies, pp. 62–84. Sinauer Associates, Sunderland, Massachusetts.
Gumerman, G., and D. Phillips
1978 Archaeology Beyond Anthropology. *American Antiquity* 43:184–192.
Hawkes, K.
1991 Showing Off: Tests of an Hypothesis about Men's Foraging Goals. *Ethology and Sociobiology* 12:29–54.
Hawkes, K., K. Hill, and J. O'Connell
1982 Why Hunters Gather: Optimal Foraging and the Ache of Eastern Paraguay. *American Ethnologist* 9:379–398.
Hill, J.
1984 Prestige and Reproductive Success in Man. *Ethology and Sociobiology* 5:77–95.
Hill, K.
1988 Macronutrient Modifications of Optimal Foraging Theory: An Approach Using Indifference Curves Applied to Some Modern Foragers. *Human Ecology* 16:157– 197.
Hill, K., and K. Hawkes
1983 Neotropical Hunting Among the Ache of Eastern Paraguay. In *Adaptive Responses of Native Amazonians,* edited by R. Hames and W. Vickers, pp. 139–188. Academic Press, New York.
Hill, K., and M. Hurtado
1996 *Ache Life History.* Aldine de Gruyter, Hawthorne, New Jersey.
Hill, K., and H. Kaplan
1988a Tradeoffs in Male and Female Reproductive Strategies Among the Ache: Part 1. In *Human Reproductive Behavior,*

edited by L. Betzig, M. Borgerhoff Mulder, and P. Turke, pp. 277–289. Cambridge University Press, New York.

1988b   Tradeoffs in Male and Female Reproductive Strategies Among the Ache: Part 2. In *Human Reproductive Behavior,* edited by L. Betzig, M. Borgerhoff Mulder, and P. Turke, pp. 291–305. Cambridge University Press, New York.

Hill, K., K. Hawkes, A. Hurtado, and H. Kaplan
1984   Seasonal Variance in the Diet of Ache Hunter-Gatherers in Eastern Paraguay. *Human Ecology* 12:145–180.

Hill, K., H. Kaplan, K. Hawkes, and A. Hurtado
1987   Foraging Decisions Among Ache Hunter-Gatherers: New Data and Implications for Optimal Foraging Models. *Ethology and Sociobiology* 8:1–36.

Hurt, T., G. Rakita, and R. Leonard
2001   Models, Definitions, and Stylistic Variation: Comment on Ortmann. *American Antiquity* 66:742–743.

Irons, W.
1979   Cultural and Biological Success. In *Evolutionary Biology and Human Social Behavior,* edited by N. Chagnon and W. Irons, pp. 257–272. Duxbury Press, N. Scituate, Massachusetts.

Jochim, M.
1976   *Hunter-Gatherer Subsistence and Settlement: A Predictive Model.* Academic Press, New York.
1998   *A Hunter-Gatherer Landscape.* Plenum Press, New York.

Jones, G., R. Leonard, and A. Abbott
1995   The Structure of Selectionist Explanations in Archaeology. In *Evolutionary Archaeology: Methodological Issues,* edited by P. Teltser, pp. 13–32. University of Arizona Press, Tucson.

Jones, S.
1999   *Almost Like A Whale: The Origin of Species Updated.* Bantam Books, London.

Kacelnik, A., and J. Krebs
1997   Yanomamo Dreams and Starling Payloads: The Logic of Optimality. In *Human Nature,* edited by L. Betzig, pp. 21–35. Oxford University Press, Oxford.

Kaplan, H., and K. Hill
1985a   Hunting Ability and Reproductive Success Among Male Ache Foragers: Preliminary Results. *Current Anthropology* 26:131–133.
1985b   Food Sharing Among Ache Foragers: Tests of Explanatory Hypotheses. *Current Anthropology* 26:223–246.
1992   The Evolutionary Ecology of Food Acquisition. In *Evolutionary Ecology and Human Behavior,* edited by E. Smith and B. Winterhalder, pp. 167–201. Aldine de Gruyter, Hawthorne, New York.

Kaplan, H., K. Hill, K. Hawkes, and A. Hurtado
1984   Food Sharing Among the Ache Hunter-Gatherers of Eastern Paraguay. *Current Anthropology* 25:113–115.

Kelly, R.
1995   *The Foraging Spectrum.* Smithsonian Institution Press, Washington, D.C.

Kimura, M.
1983   *The Neutral Theory of Molecular Evolution.* Cambridge University Press, New York.

Klein, R.
1995   Anatomy, Behavior, and Modern Human Origins. *Journal of World Prehistory* 9:167–197.

Krebs, J., and N. Davies
1997   *Behavioral Ecology: An Evolutionary Approach.* 4th ed.. Blackwell Scientific Publications, Boston.

Ladefoged, T., and M. Graves
2000   Evolutionary Theory and the Historical Development of Dry-Land Agriculture in North Kohala, Hawai'i. *Ameri-*

can Antiquity 65:423–448.

Larson, D., H. Neff, D. Graybill, J Michaelson, and E. Ambos
1996   Risk, Climatic Variability, and the Study of Southwestern Prehistory: An Evolutionary Perspective. *American Antiquity* 61:217–242.

Leonard, R. and H. Reed
1993   Population Aggregation in the Prehistoric American Southwest: A Selectionist Model. *American Antiquity* 58:648–661.

Leone, M.
1972   Issues in Anthropological Archaeology. In *Contemporary Archaeology,* edited by M. Leone, pp. 14–27. Southern Illinois University Press, Carbondale.

Lewontin, R.
1979   Fitness, Survival, and Optimality. In *Analysis of Ecological Systems,* edited by D. Horn, R. Mitchell, and G. Stairs, pp. 3–21. Ohio University Press, Columbus.

Lipo, C., C. Madsen, R. Dunnell, and T. Hunt
1997   Population Structure, Cultural Transmission, and Frequency Seriation. *Journal of Anthropological Archaeology* 16:301–333.

Lyman, R., and M. O'Brien
1998   The Goals of Evolutionary Archaeology. *Current Anthropology* 39:615–652.

Maasen, S., E. Mendelsohn, and P. Weingart
1995   Metaphors: Is There a Bridge Over Troubled Waters. In *Biology as Society, Society as Biology: Metaphors,* edited by S. Maasen, E. Mendelsohn, and P. Weingart, pp. 1–10. Kluwer Academic Publishers, Boston.

Majerus, M.
1998   *Melanism: Evolution in Action.* Oxford University Press, New York.

McBrearty, S.
1999   Society of Africanist Archaeologists. *Evolutionary Anthropology* 8:1–3.

Merrell, D.
1994   *The Adaptive Seascape: The Mechanism of Evolution.* University of Minnesota Press, Minneapolis.

Mithen, S.
1990   *Thoughtful Foragers.* Cambridge University Press, New York.
1996   *The Prehistory of the Mind.* Thames and Hudson, London.

Neff, H.
1992   Ceramics and Evolution. *Archaeological Method and Theory* 4:141–193.
2000   On Evolutionary Ecology and Evolutionary Archaeology: Some Common Ground? *Current Anthropology* 41:427–429.

Niemann, F.
1995   Stylistic Variation in Evolutionary Perspective: Inferences from Decorative Diversity and Interassemblage Distance in Illinois Woodland Ceramic Assemblages. *American Antiquity* 60:7–36.
1999   Discussion on the Limits of Evolutionary Archaeology. Paper Presented at the 64th Annual Meeting of the Society for American Archaeology, Chicago.

O'Brien, M., and T. Holland
1990   Variation, Selection, and the Archaeological Record. *Archaeological Method and Theory* 2:31–79.
1992   The Role of Adaptation in Archaeological Explanation. *American Antiquity* 57:36–59.

O'Connell, J., K. Jones, and S. Simms
1982   Some Thoughts on Prehistoric Archaeology in the Great Basin. In *Man and Environment in the Great Basin,* edited by D. Madsen and J. O'Connell, pp. 227–240. Society for

American Archaeology Papers No. 2. Washington, D.C.

Perusse, D.
1993 Cultural and Reproductive Success in Industrial Societies: Testing the Hypothesis at the Proximate and Ultimate Levels. *Behavioral and Brain Sciences* 16:267– 322.

Redman, C.
1978 *The Rise of Civilization.* W. H. Freeman, San Francisco.

Rindos, D.
1985 Darwinian Selection, Symbolic Variation, and the Evolution of Culture. *Current Anthropology* 26:65–88.

Rose, H., and S. Rose
2000 *Alas Poor Darwin.* Harmony Books, New York.

Salmon, M.
1978 What Can Systems Theory Do for Archaeology? *American Antiquity* 43:174–183.

Shennan, S., and J. Wilkinson
2001 Ceramic Style Change and Neutral Evolution: A Case Study from Neolithic Europe. *American Antiquity* 66:577–594.

Smith, E. A.
1991 *Inujjuamiut Foraging Strategies: Evolutionary Ecology of an Arctic Hunting Economy.* Aldine de Gruyter, Hawthorne, New York.
2000 Three Styles in the Evolutionary Analysis of Human Behavior. In *Adaptation and Human Behavior,* edited by L. Cronk, N. Chagnon, and W. Irons, pp. 27–47. Aldine de Gruyter, New York.

Smith, E. A., and B. Winterhalder
1992 *Evolutionary Ecology and Human Behavior.* Aldine de Gruyter, Hawthorne, New Jersey.

Sober, E., and D. Wilson
1998 *Unto Others: The Evolution and Psychology of Unselfish Behavior.* Harvard University Press, Cambridge.

Soltis, J., R. Boyd, and P. Richerson
1995 Can Group-Functional Behaviors Evolve by Cultural Group Selection? *Current Anthropology* 36:473–494.

Taylor, R.
1948 *A Study of Archaeology.* American Anthropological Association Memoir 69. Washington, D.C.

Torrence, R.
1989 *Time, Energy, and Stone Tools.* Cambridge University Press, New York.

Watson, P., S. LeBlanc, and C. Redman
1972 *Explanation in Archaeology: An Explicitly Scientific Approach.* Columbia University Press, New York.

Wills, W., P. Crown, J. Dean, and C. Layton
1994 Complex Adaptive Systems and Southwestern Prehistory. In *Understanding Complexity in the Prehistoric Southwest,* edited by G. Gumerman and M. Gell Mann, pp. 297–340. Santa Fe Institute Studies in the Science of Complexity, Proceedings XVI. Addison-Wesley, Reading, Massachusetts.

Wilmsen, E.
1973 Interaction, Spacing Behavior, and the Organization of Hunting Bands. *Journal of Anthropological Research* 29:1–31.

Wilson, D.
1998 Hunting, Sharing, and Multilevel Selection. *Current Anthropology* 39:73–97.

Winterhalder, B.
1997 Gifts Given, Gifts Taken: The Behavioral Ecology of Nonmarket Intergroup Exchange. *Journal of Archaeological Research* 5:121–168.

Winterhalder, B., and E. Smith
1980 *Hunter-Gatherer Foraging Strategies.* University of Chicago Press, Chicago.

Wood, B., and K. Hill
2000 A Test of the "Showing-Off" Hypothesis with Ache Hunters. *Current Anthropology* 41:124–125.

Received August 17, 2001; Revised February 11, 2002; Accepted February 12, 2002.

ARCHAEOLOGICAL CONTEXT AND SYSTEMIC CONTEXT

MICHAEL B. SCHIFFER

ABSTRACT

The cultural aspect of the processes responsible for forming the archaeological record is argued to be an underdeveloped branch of archaeological theory. A flow model is presented by which to view the "life history" or processes of systemic context of any material element. This model accounts for the production of a substantial portion of the archaeological record. The basic processes of this model are: procurement, manufacture, use, maintenance, and discard. Refuse labels the state of an element in archaeological context. The spatial implications of the model suggest a largely untapped source of behavioral information. Differential refuse disposal patterns are examined as they affect artifact location and association. The meaning of element relative frequencies in refuse is discussed.

Department of Anthropology
University of Arizona
May, 1971

Perhaps the most important assumption made by many archaeologists is that the spatial patterning of archaeological remains reflects the spatial patterning of past activities (Binford 1962, 1964; Brose 1970; Clarke 1968; Hill 1970a, 1970b; Longacre 1970; McPherron 1967; Struever 1968; Wilmsen 1970; and many others).

The loss, breakage, and abandonment of implements and facilities at different locations, where groups of variable structure performed different tasks, leaves a "fossil" record of the actual operation of an extinct society [Binford 1964:425].

This statement suggests that the proveniences of artifacts in a site correspond to their actual locations of use in activities. Clearly this is not always the case. But to what extent it may be so and under what conditions, would appear to be a problem worthy of some attention. In the most general terms, what I am asking is, How is the archaeological record formed by behavior in a cultural system?

I would emphasize that I am not asking the equally general and important question of why there is variability in past cultural systems. I am inquiring first, Why is there an archaeological record? Second, How does a cultural system produce archaeological remains? And third, What kinds of inter-cultural and intra-cultural variables determine the structure (as distinct from the form and content) of the archaeological record?

The branch of archaeological theory which treats these and related questions may be defined as the conceptual system that explains how the archaeological record is formed. As such, it has both cultural and non-cultural components. The latter area has received major emphasis to date; regular patterns of post-depositional changes in both artifact inventories and site morphologies have been elucidated (Hole and Heizer 1969). Explanations of variability in this non-cultural domain usually incorporate the laws of other sciences, such as chemistry, physics, and geology.

The cultural aspect of *formation process concepts* has not been appreciably developed. Archaeologists do in fact employ interpretive frameworks that include assumptions about these formation processes. These assumptions are rarely explicit, and therefore do not readily lend themselves to testing and modification. The small body of explicit concepts deals almost exclusively with chronological relationships (Dunnell 1970; Rowe 1961, 1962). While the correct chronological placement of past events is necessary for a successful reconstruction of past cultural systems, especially as they change, it can in no way be considered sufficient.

What is advocated here, and elsewhere (Binford and Binford 1968:1-3), is a concern with explaining how the archaeological record is produced in terms of explicit models, theories, and laws of how cultural systems operate. This paper will be an attempt to suggest, in the regrettable absence of such a corpus of rigorously tested concepts (Fritz and Plog 1970; Aberle 1970), some ways by which we may begin to think about the questions raised so far. Hypotheses will be presented, which, if adequately tested, can contribute to the eventual synthesis and systematization of an archaeological theory having both explanatory and predictive utility. Without this kind of a scrutinizable framework, any use of archaeological data to infer past activities or organization is highly suspect (Binford 1968a) and subject to interminable dispute. Explicit generation and use of formation process concepts, and other branches of archaeological theory, will allow genuinely intersubjective statements to be made about the past.

PRELIMINARY DEFINITIONS

Some preliminary considerations of a general nature are required at the outset. For present purposes, a culture is viewed as a behavioral system of self-regulating and interrelated subsystems which procures and processes matter, energy, and information (Miller 1965a, 1965b; Clarke 1968). A self-regulating or homeostatic system is defined as one in which at least one variable is maintained within specifiable values despite changes in the system's environment (Miller 1965a; Hagen 1961).

The values of subsystem variables are maintained within their ranges by the performance of *activities*. An activity is a transformation of energy, minimally involving an energy source, often human, acting on one or more proximate material elements. An activity may be viewed simply as a patterned energy transformation (White 1959), which serves to maintain the values of system variables. An *activity structure* is defined as the activities performed and their performance frequencies, usually with reference to a site, but not of necessity.

I define *elements* to include foods, fuels, tools, facilities, machines, human beings, and all other materials which one might list in a complete inventory of a cultural system. A provisional division of elements into the categories of *durables* and *consumables* will be made for later use. Durable elements are tools, machines and facilities—in short, transformers and preservers of energy (Wagner 1960). Consumables are foods, fuels, and other similar elements whose consumption results in the liberation of energy. Although numerous other dimensions could be used to delineate categories of elements, that is the task of an investigator attempting to solve more specific problems than those of concern here. It should be mentioned, however, that elements are often compounded into larger, more complex elements, and that complex elements may be further compounded into hierarchies of element combinations.

In order to continue activity performance, and hence maintain the values of subsystem variables, it is necessary to replace elements which become exhausted or otherwise unserviceable. The failure of an element to articulate properly with other elements is a significant bit of information to the system, which initiates the performance of other activities resulting eventually in element replacement, or activity structure change. That it also initiates the processes of discarding the replaced element is a significant bit of information to archaeologists. What it introduces is the life cycle or history of any element—the stages of its "life" within a cultural system—and how these relate to the eventual transition of elements to the archaeological record. *Systemic context* labels the condition of an element which is participating in a behavioral system. *Archaeological context* describes materials which have passed through a cultural system, and which are now the objects of investigation of archaeologists.

THE MODEL

While one may readily visualize the flow of pottery, or food, or even projectile points, through a cultural system, it is the case that all elements enter a system, are modified, broken down, or combined with other elements, used, and eventually discarded. This is so even for those elements, such as houses, which at certain points in time appear to be permanent features. This observation can provide the basis for the construction of a simple flow model with which to view the life history of any element, and account behaviorally for the production of the archaeological record. I acknowledge that the model to be presented here, and the behavioral complexities to which it calls attention, has been anticipated by Lewis R. Binford (1968a:21) and K. C. Chang (1967:106-107); a general debt is acknowledged to Walter Taylor's (1948) seminal work.

For analytical purposes, the activities in which a durable element participates during its life, or systemic context, may be broadly divided into 5 *processes: procurement, manufacture, use, maintenance,* and *discard.* A process consists of one or more *stages,* such as the stages of manufacture of a ceramic vessel. A stage consists of one or more activities, which for some analyses might be further broken down.

The model for consumable elements is parallel to and adapted from the model for durable elements. Such an adaptation is necessary to bring the model into congruence with standard terminology. One would scarcely refer, for example, to the manufacture and use of poached eggs. The terms for each process of the flow model for consumables are: *procurement, preparation, consumption,* and *discard.* Because consumption occurs but once during the systemic context of a consumable, the maintenance process has been deleted. For the sake of convenience, the discussions to follow will exclusively use the terminology of the durable element model.

In addition to the 5 basic processes of systemic context, it will be necessary for some problems to consider *storage* and *transport.* Storage and transport are activities which provide, respectively, a temporal or spatial displacement of an element. Transport and storage may take place singly or in combination between any 2 processes, stages, or activities of one stage.

Not all elements follow a unilinear path through a system. Some are rerouted at strategic points to processes or stages through which they have already passed. Archaeologists encounter items of this sort frequently; this condition is often known as *reuse.* Two varieties of reuse, *recycling* and *lateral cycling* will be defined here.

Recycling labels the routing of an element at the completion of use to the manufacture process of the same or a different element. In our system, precious metals and gems are recycled. Some systems recycle potsherds, bifaces, ground stone, and many other elements, most of which are routed to the manufacturing processes of different elements. Sometimes the use modification or maintenance activities of one element can be viewed as the manufacturing activities of another. Continued retouching of a scraper will result in an implement unsuited for further use. But in this form, the element may be adapted for reuse in some other activity.

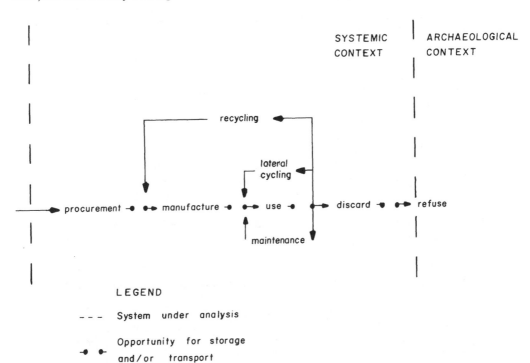

Fig. 1. A flow model for viewing the life cycle of durable elements.

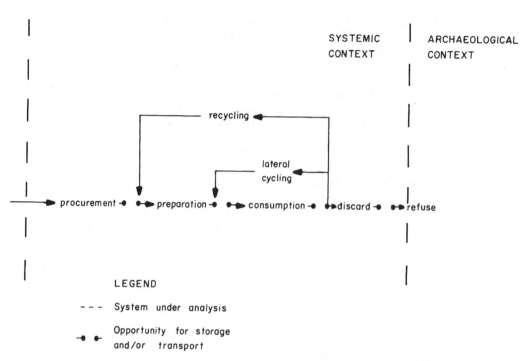

Fig. 2. A flow model for viewing the life cycle of consumable elements.

Lateral cycling describes the termination of an element's use (*use-life*) in one set of activities and its resumption in another, often with only maintenance, storage, and transport intervening. Specifically, reference is made to the movement of clothing, tools, furniture, and other elements, which in simple and complex systems circulate among and between social units, classes, and castes.

Figs. 1 and 2 illustrate the completed basic models for durables and consumables, respectively.

I wish to emphasize that these models are only simplifications of a stubbornly complex reality. They are not likely to fit neatly the sequences of activities in which elements of all cultural systems participate within their systemic contexts. Some regular cases of apparent divergence from the models can be listed. For example, an element need not pass through all processes. *Trade* elements are those which have no manufacture process in the recipient system. Some elements have no manufacture process in any system; unmodified stone used in construction, and some percussion flaking tools are common examples. Some items will be discarded without maintenance ever having been performed on them. Defective items may be discarded directly after manufacture. An element having no use process, such as an unutilized flake, is designated as *waste*; this is not to imply that such items are devoid of information, only that they are an unused by-product of some activity.

At the termination of an element's use-life (assuming no reuse), elements will be discarded. *Refuse* labels the post-discard condition of an element—the condition of no longer participating in a behavioral system. The normal flow of elements through the system in the manner outlined above accounts for most of the materials that become a part of the archaeological record.

Although most refuse material consists of those elements which have broken down or worn out during use, whole, apparently serviceable items are frequently encountered in excavation. These materials present additional problems of explanation. Some may have been accidentally deposited, or their presence may reflect change—an element has become obsolete and discarded. In our own cultural system, undamaged and potentially reusable elements whose recycling costs are higher than replacement costs are discarded. "No deposit no return" bottles are a notorious example. The presence of such items in the archaeological record is still accounted for in terms of the flow model, but their formal properties must be accounted for in terms of economic principles. These various factors are important and worthy of further investigation, yet they do not account for a great deal of the remaining "anomalous" material found in archaeological context.

Elements discarded with the deceased after ceremonial use provide a significant source of intact elements in archaeological context, especially among simple systems. The subject of grave accompaniments and their relationships to other aspects of the system that discarded them, especially social organization, will not be discussed here; although a comprehensive treatment is long overdue.

The principal set of variables responsible for the presence of usable elements in the archaeological record is obviously that having to do with the abandonment of the site. Archaeological context includes all the materials found in a site, whether or not they are in specialized discard locations and whether or not they have been deliberately discarded by the past occupants of a site. It is well known, for example, that elements are found in every stage of manufacture and use. The way in which a site is abandoned—the variables operative at the time the occupants leave the site, or die without replacement—has demonstrable effects on the kinds and quantities of non-discarded elements found in archaeological context. Elements which reach archaeological context without the performance of discard activities will be termed *de facto refuse*.

Robert Ascher's provocative Seri study (1968) suggests a hypothesis, which, when generalized is relevant here: *differential abandonment of a site changes the normal ratios of elements in various processes of their systemic contexts and the normal spatial distribution of elements*. Specifically, reference is being made to activities which result in the removal of raw materials and usable elements from abandoned areas of the site and their reuse in the still-occupied portion. At the time of their abandonment, these elements were still in systemic context. We would expect to find relatively fewer elements in pre-discard processes of systemic context, that is, less de facto refuse, in sites which undergo differential abandonment. On the other hand, sites abandoned rapidly and completely as a result of some catastrophe will have relatively greater numbers of elements in manufacture, use, and maintenance processes. Pompeii comes to mind as an example of this kind of abandonment, in which no change occurred in the provenience of elements or their distributions among the various systemic processes.

More often, abandonment, even if sudden, involves the removal of some elements and their transport to another site or sites. The kinds and quantities of elements so removed should be related systematically to other variables operative at the time of abandonment. Among them might be expected: distance to the next site, season of movement, size of emigrating population, technological development of both donor and recipient sites, means of available transportation, and other variables. More complex models will have to be devised to account for the effects that processes of abandonment have on the formation of the archaeological record.

SPATIAL IMPLICATIONS

Perhaps the most important aspect of the notion of systemic context is that there is a specifiable spatial location, or locations, for each process through which an element passes.

The term "location" is used here in its broadest possible meaning. A location can be a point on a site, or it can be a set of points. It can also be an entire site if, during one process, an element has the same chance of being found at one place on the site as any other. Such a concept of spatial location might be better expressed as a set of probabilities for finding an element or class of like elements at any point on a site surface during a particular process or stage. A site or other unit of spatial analysis is divided into squares of equal area and the probability values for each square are indicated. The smaller the squares, the greater the potential accuracy (see Cole and King 1968 for numerous examples of how one might model distributions). This flexibility in depicting locations allows the frame of reference to be shifted conveniently to any variable of interest to suit the needs of the investigator; the metate of a woman, or the metates of a village. The relationships between the locations of each process or stage for an element are complex but I predict that eventually determinate relationships between these and behavioral variables will be specifiable.

The overlapping of these locations for different elements, and the activities into which they articulate, reflect a behavioral matrix of bewildering complexity, even for simple systems. While this complexity presents problems for some uses of archaeological data, it also provides a hitherto neglected source of information for generating and testing behavioral hypotheses.

Archaeologists are often able to reconstruct the manufacturing activities of elements when they are recovered in various stages of manufacture, often in association with waste materials. That the various stages and processes of an element's systemic context should be reflected spatially as well has been less frequently used as a basis for generating or testing hypotheses. A projectile point found in association with an antler flaker and tiny pressure flakes of the same material in a habitation structure is a different projectile point from one found in a midden, or another found eroding from the wall of an arroyo with no other associated cultural material. In the first case, one would be dealing with the location of some manufacturing activities, the second a location of discard activities, while in the third perhaps the location of use. The cultural inferences possible from a projectile point in each process are different, as are the potential hypotheses against which these morphologically similar elements may be brought to bear as evidence.

In another example of the relationship between systemic context and the spatial differentiation of cultural behavior, one may take the case of the simple subterranean storage pit. Because such pits occupy the same location during all processes, one is permitted to state with certainty that a pit was dug, used, and repaired by the inhabitants of the site at the same provenience where it was found in archaeological context. This is hardly a revelation, yet I suggest that such rigorous justification for a primary behavioral inference is necessary if we are to succeed in formulating and answering the kinds of questions which are now being asked about past cultural systems. The archaeological record will produce sets of information on subjects which we can scarcely contemplate at the present, when, and as, progress is made in building models to relate the production of the archaeological record to cultural behavior in the past—models which include explicit reference to the spatial dimension of cultural behavior.

REFUSE DISPOSAL PATTERNS

If this model of cultural element flow and its spatial aspect are to be of value in enabling us to gain knowledge of the past, they must illuminate some of the questions posed earlier. These questions and others will be examined and rephrased in terms more amenable to treatment by the concepts sketched out here. Additional hypotheses will be introduced as the need for them arises; they are intended, as are all hypotheses, to be suggestive and not definitive.

We shall now return to the question raised originally in the quotation from Binford; that is, to what extent can remains at a site be expected to occur at their use locations as opposed to any other, when found in archaeological context? We aim to know what some of the determinants of variability in patterns of refuse transport and disposal are. I shall distinguish between *primary refuse* and *secondary refuse*. Both refer to elements which have been discarded (compare to de facto refuse) but, in the case of secondary refuse, the location of final discard is not the same as the location of use. Primary refuse is material discarded at its location of use (Fig. 3).

I believe that the general problem of refuse disposal may be seen as the balancing of 2 major sets of variables. The particular solutions arrived at by site occupants for handling the by-products of activity performance will take into consideration the ease of moving the activity or activities versus the ease of moving the refuse.

Let us assume that there is a site at which only one activity is being conducted by a single person during brief periods of the year. In this case one might expect few pressures to favor the development of a separate location for the final discard of elements replaced during activity performance. One would obtain a general correspondence between the location of use and the location of final discard for elements used in that activity. Let us, then, increase the population of the site to a small village, and increase the intensity of occupation to year-round. In this instance, one would expect such factors as the necessity for unrestricted access between principal activity areas, sanitation, and competition for scarce activity space to place a premium upon the transport of at least some of the materials and their discard at another location. Modern cities provide the

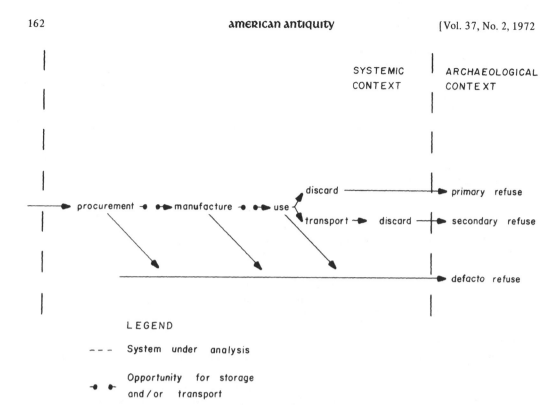

Fig. 3. Simplified flow model for explicating the differences between primary, secondary, and de facto refuse.

extreme example, as we know it today, where almost no elements are discarded at their places of use within the site; consequently, almost all archaeological context material is secondary refuse.

The general principle which these hypothetical cases illustrate is that *with increasing site population (or perhaps site size) and increasing intensity of occupation, there will be a decreasing correspondence between the use and discard locations for all elements used in activities and discarded at a site*. In addition, there will be an increasing development of specialized discard areas, occupations, and transport networks. From this principle, admittedly unpolished and untested, we can predict that limited activity locations (Wilmsen 1970) such as kill and butchering sites, quarry sites, and many seasonally occupied sites, will consist largely of primary refuse. A major characteristic of these sites will be the repeated clusterings of elements in discrete and overlapping locations.

Let it be given that many sites of many systems had at least moderately developed refuse transport and disposal activities and, as a result, elements used in many activities were removed from their locations of use. The question that would appear to be before someone interested in inferring the past activity structure of such a site is, To what extent are elements associated in use also associated as secondary refuse? No definitive answers are presently at hand, though one hypothesis may account for some element associations in secondary refuse.

If storage intervenes between the termination of an element's use-life and its final discard, there is a likelihood that one or more other elements of the same activity would have been replaced and stored along with the first element awaiting final discard. Therefore, *as there is a decrease in the ratio of final discard frequency to replacement frequency of one or more elements of an activity, there is an increasing probability that several elements, especially those with short use-life expectancies, will be discarded at the same time and in the same place within secondary refuse areas*. The optimum conditions for element association as secondary refuse occur in modern industrial societies where many storage and transport steps intervene between element replacement and final discard. Most other activities in most other cultural systems will result in secondary refuse which lies somewhere along this continuum of activity-based element association. Future research in both extant and extinct cultural systems must be undertaken to provide more knowledge on the regularities of dumping behavior.

The relative frequencies of elements, or element fragments, found as primary or secondary refuse, are raw data for many statements made about the past. I think it is fair to question any use of this information until we know the ways in which refuse element frequencies reflect the system of which they were once a part. A general solution to this problem based on previous hypotheses, which will admit of many sources of exceptions, can now be presented.

Assuming that there is no change in the activity structure during the occupation of a site, and that there is only one refuse area, which may be the entire site, the ratios of elements in that area will correspond to their relative replacement frequencies. For example, although only 1 mano is used with 1 metate at any given time, the ratio of discarded manos to discarded metates (assuming no recycling) will correspond to how often one is worn out and replaced with respect to the other, which may be 6 or 8 manos per metate. This model is complicated by elements which have several discard locations, one or more of which are not known or accessible to the investigator. Particularly acute is the problem posed by projectile point disposal patterns. Any statement, whether for chronological control, cultural affiliation, activity reconstruction, or the measurement of a past systemic variable, requires strict consideration of the multiple discard areas for this kind of an element. A potentially fruitful topic for investigation is the conditions under which projectile points, or any similar element, will be discarded at a habitation site. It may turn out that such points are a perfectly representative sample of all points in use; yet at the moment, we really do not know one way or the other.

In offering inferences about past activity structure, reports have sometimes been made that ritual activities were infrequent or absent. A different interpretation is possible. I hypothesize that *durable elements used largely in ritual activities will have on the average a longer use-life expectance than non-ritual durable elements of the same system.* If this is the case, then even if ritual activities were present and frequent, non-ritual elements would be expected to predominate disproportionately as refuse, simply as a result of differential replacement frequencies. Any statement asserting the absence or infrequent performance of any activity should be treated skeptically until the biases introduced by differential replacement frequencies and multiple discard locations have been taken into account.

CONCLUSION

Archaeologists have gone from the one extreme of viewing a site as spatially and behaviorally undifferentiated rubbish to the other extreme of viewing remains as mostly reflecting their locations of use in past activities. At this point, it appears that neither extreme is often the actual case. Clearly, though all remains in a site are refuse when uncovered in archaeological context, when viewed by the model and hypotheses presented here (and used implicitly by many investigators) they are potentially much more. In order to realize this potential, we will have to link archaeological context material to behavioral and organizational hypotheses about elements in systemic context.

I submit that this linking process is the central problem of archaeological inference (see Binford 1968b for similar statements). Once high probability statements about activity structures are possessed, hypotheses regarding the composition of task groups, their means of recruitment, and how they are structured within the total system organization, and especially how these organizations change, will be capable of precise formulation and *archaeological* test. Whether one begins at the level of archaeological context material, or with models of system organization and change, the form of the final inference or tested model will be similar: statements about past organization or other systemic properties are linked by arguments of relevance (Binford 1968b; Fritz 1968; Schiffer 1970) to the activity structure. The activity structure, in turn, is linked to the archaeological context data by formation process concepts.

The construction and use of formation process concepts along the lines sketched out above will allow the rigorous justification of our inferences. Without a base of explicit, logically related credible laws about the formation processes of the archaeological record, debates about the validity of an inference, or any use of the data from the record, can only focus on epiphenomena or ad hominem arguments (Binford 1968a). I would hope that the crude first approximations to explicit formation process concepts presented here will stimulate a round of vigorous criticism aimed at improving the conceptual tools with which we manipulate the remains of past cultural systems. As more sophisticated and comprehensive models are developed, confidence will be gained in the uses to which we put the data of the archaeological record.

Acknowledgments. I am indebted to the following individuals for their patient and instructive criticisms of various versions of this paper: Daniel C. Bowman, David A. Gregory, John A. Hanson, William A. Longacre, Henri A. Luebbermann, Paul S. Martin, David R. Wilcox, and the Editor. I am solely responsible for the misconceptions which persist. In the context of solving a different problem, Michael B. Collins (1971) has independently developed a lithic-specific flow model similar to the general model presented here; I have profited from discussions with him. Sharon Urban kindly prepared the figures. I gratefully acknowledge the support of the Field Museum of Natural History and the National Science Foundation (Grant GY-7225). I am especially indebted to the director of the Field Museum Southwest Expedition, Paul S. Martin, for his constant encouragement and for providing an unmatched climate of intellectual freedom.

Aberle, David F.
   1970   Comments. In *Reconstructing prehistoric pueblo societies*, edited by W. A. Longacre, pp. 214-223. University of New Mexico Press, Albuquerque.
Ascher, Robert
   1968   Time's arrow and the archaeology of a contemporary community. In *Settlement archaeology*, edited by K.C. Chang, pp. 43-52. National Press Books, Palo Alto.
Binford, Lewis R.
   1962   Archaeology as anthropology. *American Antiquity* 28:217-225.
   1964   A consideration of archaeological research design. *American Antiquity* 29:425-441.
   1968a Archeological perspectives. In *New perspectives in archeology*, edited by Sally R. and Lewis R. Binford, pp. 5-32. Aldine, Chicago.
   1968b Some comments on historical versus processual archaeology. *Southwestern Journal of Anthropology* 24:267-275.
Binford, Sally R., and Lewis R. Binford
   1968   Archeological theory and method. In *New perspectives in archeology*, edited by Sally R. and Lewis R. Binford, pp. 1-3. Aldine, Chicago.
Brose, David S.
   1970   The Summer Island site: a study of prehistoric cultural ecology and social organization in the northern Lake Michigan area. *Case Western Reserve University Studies in Anthropology* 1.
Chang, K.C.
   1967   *Rethinking archaeology*. Random House, New York.
Clarke, David
   1968   *Analytical archeology*. Methuen, London.
Cole, John P., and Cuchlaine A.M. King
   1968   *Quantitative geography: techniques and theories in geography*. John Wiley & Sons, New York.
Collins, Michael B.
   1971   The role of lithic analysis in socio-cultural inference. Paper presented at the 1971 meeting of The Society for American Archaeology, Norman.
Dunnell, Robert C.
   1970   Seriation method and its evaluation. *American Antiquity* 35:305-319.
Fritz, John M.
   1968   Archaeological epistemology: two views. Unpublished M.A. thesis. Department of Anthropology, University of Chicago.
Fritz, John M., and Fred T. Plog
   1970   The nature of archaeological explanation. *American Antiquity* 35:405-412.
Hagen, Everett E.
   1961   Analytical models in the study of social systems. *The American Journal of Sociology* 67:144-151.
Hill, James N.
   1970a Prehistoric social organization in the American Southwest: theory and method. In *Reconstructing prehistoric pueblo societies*, edited by W.A. Longacre, pp. 11-58. University of New Mexico Press, Albuquerque.
   1970b Broken K Pueblo: prehistoric social organization in the American Southwest. *University of Arizona, Anthropological Papers* 18.
Hole, Frank, and Robert F. Heizer
   1969   *An introduction to prehistoric archeology*. Holt, Rinehart and Winston, New York.
Longacre, William A.
   1970   Archaeology as anthropology: a case study. *University of Arizona, Anthropological Papers* 17.

McPherron, Alan
   1967   The Juntunen site and the Late Woodland prehistory of the Upper Great Lakes area. *University of Michigan, Museum of Anthropology, Anthropological Papers* 30.
Miller, James G.
   1965a   Living systems: basic concepts. *Behavioral Science* 10:193-237.
   1965b   Living systems: structure and process. *Behavioral Science* 10:337-379.
Rowe, John H.
   1961   Stratigraphy and seriation. *American Antiquity* 26:324-330.
   1962   Worsaae's law and the use of grave lots for archaeological dating. *American Antiquity* 28:129-137.
Schiffer, Michael B.
   1970   Cultural laws and the reconstruction of past lifeways. Paper presented at the 1970 meeting of The Society for American Archaeology, Mexico City.
Struever, Stuart
   1968   Woodland subsistence-settlement systems in the Lower Illinois Valley. In *New perspectives in archeology*, edited by Sally R. and Lewis R. Binford, pp. 285-312. Aldine, Chicago.
Taylor, Walter W.
   1948   A study of archeology. *American Anthropological Association, Memoir* 69.
Wagner, Philip L.
   1960   *The human use of the Earth*. The Free Press, Glencoe.
White, Leslie A.
   1959   *The evolution of culture*. McGraw-Hill, New York.
Wilmsen, Edwin N.
   1970   Lithic analysis and cultural inference: a Paleo-Indian case. *University of Arizona, Anthropological Papers* 16.

SOME RELATIONSHIPS BETWEEN BEHAVIORAL
AND EVOLUTIONARY ARCHAEOLOGIES

Michael Brian Schiffer

Diversity in archaeology's social theories is desirable, but factioning of the discipline into antagonistic, paradigm-based camps undermines the scientific enterprise. In order to promote efforts at building bridges between different theoretical programs, this paper examines relationships between behavioral archaeology and evolutionary (selectionist) archaeology. Potential common ground is brought to light, incompatibilities are critically examined, and possible synergies are explored. It is concluded that there is no fundamental reason why these two programs cannot work in concert to achieve the goal of explaining behavioral (or evolutionary) change in human societies. Whether productive relationships can be established between other programs remains to be determined on a case-by-case basis.

La diversidad de teorías sociales en arqueología es necesaria, pero la partición de la disciplina en facciones antagonísticas basadas en paradigmas sabotea la empresa científica. Para promover esfuerzos destinados a crear puentes entre programas teóricos distintos, este artículo examina las relaciones entre arqueología conductual y arqueología evolucionista (seleccionista). Se resaltan las áreas comunes, se examinan críticamente las incompatibilidades, y se exploran posibles sinergias. Se concluye que no existen razones fundamentales por las que estos programas no puedan trabajar en concierto para alcanzar la meta de explicar cambio conductual (o evolutivo) en sociedades humanas. La posibilidad de que se establezcan relaciones productivas entre otros programas queda por determinarse caso por caso.

Science consists in grouping facts so that general laws or conclusions may be drawn from them

—Charles Darwin, *The Autobiography of Charles Darwin, 1809–1882*, p. 70

Since the early 1970s, processual archaeology's social theory (*sensu* Schiffer 1988) has suffered many indignities at the hands of critics (for useful discussions, see Lamberg-Karlovsky 1989; Preucel 1991; Trigger 1989; Yoffee and Sherratt 1993). Even so, processualism—albeit now in many varieties—remains well entrenched in everyday practice, and it is doubtful that any competing program will be able to dislodge it and achieve a comparable position of dominance. For the foreseeable future, then, a multitude of minority programs, including behavioral, evolutionary, cognitive, and Marxist archae-ologies, will struggle to win followers and alter disciplinary practice (see discussions in Wandsnider 1992). As a result, archaeologists may need to become accustomed to an abundance of seemingly incompatible social theories, contributing to the "thousand archaeologies" I previously welcomed (Schiffer 1988:479). Although diversity in social theory is desirable (Knapp 1996), division of archaeology into antagonistic camps, seemingly incapable of engaging each other in discussions of substantive issues, diminishes the integrity of the discipline as a scientific enterprise.

An alternative pattern of communication can be envisioned. Instead of caricaturing, misrepresenting, or summarily dismissing rival programs, archaeologists might make a diligent effort to understand each other's social theory—maybe even build some intellectual bridges. Perhaps because their positions on significant issues of

Michael Brian Schiffer ■ Department of Anthropology, University of Arizona, Tucson, AZ 85721

American Antiquity, 61(4), 1996, pp. 643–662.
Copyright © by the Society for American Archaeology

237

social theory lie between today's theoretical extremes, some behavioral archaeologists are eager to hold discussions with practitioners of other programs (Walker et al. 1995:8); many papers in *Expanding Archaeology* (Skibo et al. 1995), for example, initiate promising dialogues (e.g., McGuire 1995; Nielsen 1995; O'Brien and Holland 1995b; Orser 1995; Senior 1995; Wylie 1995). Similarly, in the context of historical case studies, I have already exploited common ground between behavioral and postprocessual archaeologies for explaining instances of behavioral change pertaining to portable radios (Schiffer 1991) and early electric automobiles (Schiffer et al. 1994). Surprisingly, both studies also have evolutionary features in that they treat, diachronically, the interplay between variation and selection processes (more on this below). Although handling unconventional subjects, the portable radio and automobile researches nonetheless raise hopes that additional work along these lines might lead eventually to a more integrated discipline (see also Duke 1995).

An explicit experiment in communication, this paper examines some relationships between behavioral and evolutionary archaeologies (both are defined below). That there may be important relationships between these two programs has already been suggested by several evolutionists (O'Brien and Holland 1995a:178–179, 193, 1995b; O'Brien et al. 1994). Needless to say, the structure and content of the following discussions reflect but one behavioral archaeologist's perspective.

The relationships examined between evolutionary and behavioral archaeologies are of three kinds. First, areas of potential common ground are set forth; possible shared tenets turn out to be surprisingly numerous and significant. Second, the paper treats the assumptions of evolutionary archaeology that seem incompatible with behavioral principles. It is suggested that some evolutionary positions are insupportable and, more importantly, are actually peripheral—if not detrimental—to evolutionary archaeology. And third, possible synergies between the two programs are explored. I begin with a brief overview of both programs.

Behavioral Archaeology

An outgrowth of processual archaeology, behav-

ioral archaeology crystallized as an explicit program in the early 1970s at the University of Arizona (for a history, see Schiffer 1995a). Confronted even then by a plethora of competing archaeologies, J. Jefferson Reid, William Rathje, and I offered a framework of four interdependent strategies for reintegrating the discipline (Reid et al. 1975; Schiffer 1976:Chapter 1). The foundation of this framework is a new definition of archaeology as "the study of the relationships between human behavior and material culture in all times and all places" (Reid et al. 1975:864). The discipline, we maintained, had outgrown its traditional boundaries and was reconfiguring as a new science—a *behavioral* archaeology.

Behavioral archaeologists, depending on their interests, ask idiographic (historical) or nomothetic (general) questions about the relationships between people and artifacts (Reid et al. 1975; Schiffer 1975a). Although behavioral theorists tend to privilege nomothetic questions (e.g., Schiffer 1975a, 1976, 1988, 1992), if only to make up for their profound neglect elsewhere in the discipline, much behavioral archaeology has been idiographic. Behavioralists emphatically see no conflict between history and science (Reid 1995; Schiffer 1995b).

During its brief existence, behavioral archaeology's main nomothetic contributions have been to the realms of reconstruction theory and methodological theory (*sensu* Schiffer 1988). This should not be surprising given that processual archaeology had failed to lay a firm foundation for inference; without the tools for creating a behavioral past, the prospects for a behavioral archaeology seemed bleak. In view of the improvement of inference in recent years, however, some behavioralists now assign to the creation of social theory a higher priority (Schiffer 1992, 1995b; Walker et al. 1995). Although progress remains modest, behavioral archaeology nonetheless offers a distinctive conceptual framework that can inform the development of new social theory.

Behavioralists seek to explain variability and change in human behavior by emphasizing the study of relationships between people and their artifacts. By focusing on people-artifact interactions, behavioralists have crafted a framework of concepts, principles, and procedures for investigating human behavior whenever and wherever it occurs. (For an introduction to behavioral archaeology, see Schiffer [1995c]; for a concise codification of fundamental tenets, from which much of this section is adapted, see Schiffer [1995d]; for recent developments, see Longacre and Skibo [1994] and Skibo et al. [1995].) In the following synopsis, I highlight the tenets of behavioral archaeology most relevant for engaging the evolutionary program.

As the name implies, behavioralists lay stress on studying behavior: what people actually did or do (Nielsen 1995; Reid 1995; Walker et al. 1995). The basic units of behavior are activities, defined as the interaction between elements (e.g., human, artifact, animal), at least one of which is an energy source (Rathje and Schiffer 1982:Chapter 3; Schiffer 1992; Schiffer and Skibo 1997). Thus, artifacts are an integral part of human activities, from a marriage ceremony to rebuilding a diesel engine. After all, a white wedding gown is as essential to a traditional church wedding as wrenches are to tearing down an engine; in the absence of either, crucial interactions would be adversely affected.

The artifacts (and even people) taking part in an activity have, by virtue of their material composition and form, specific properties that affect their suitability for interacting in particular ways. These activity-specific capabilities are known as performance characteristics and can pertain to any kind of interaction—mechanical, thermal, visual, etc. (Nielsen 1995; Schiffer and Skibo 1987, 1997).

Activities are usually carried out, often recurrently, by people in behavioral components—a society's units of organization. Behavioral components, such as households and communities, consist of people, places, and artifacts (Rathje and Schiffer 1982:Chapter 2; Schiffer 1992:Chapter 1).

Because each kind of artifact tends toward uniqueness in its set of properties and performance characteristics, there are few true "functionally equivalent" artifact types (Schiffer 1979). Activities, which vary in energy sources, other elements, and interaction patterns, also usually lack exact functional equivalents (Schiffer 1979). Thus, when one kind of artifact replaces another in an activity or when one kind of activity replaces another in a behavioral component, "disjunctions"

are created that can initiate further change processes. As a result, much behavioral change occurs in response to the (often unintended) consequences of previous artifact and activity replacements (Schiffer 1979, 1992:Chapter 7).

Change processes, which involve selection between alternative artifacts or alternative activities, entail compromises among performance characteristics and interactions (McGuire and Schiffer 1983; Schiffer and Skibo 1987); patterns in these compromises are influenced by specific behavioral factors of lifeway and social organization (McGuire and Schiffer 1983; Schiffer 1992; Schiffer and Skibo 1987, 1997). These compromises can be illuminated, in the case of artifact types, by use of performance matrices, which furnish explicit comparisons in relation to activity-specific performance characteristics (Schiffer 1995b; Schiffer and Skibo 1987).

Far from being autonomous, individual activities in a behavioral system (e.g., a society) are connected, directly or indirectly, to all other activities by movements of people and artifacts. The structured relationships between activities establish the causal pathways along which behavioral changes travel (Schiffer 1979; Schiffer and Skibo 1997). Change processes can also restructure relationships between activities.

The life history of artifacts (and of people) is a favored framework for organizing behavioral studies (Rathje and Schiffer 1982:Chapter 4; Schiffer and Skibo 1997; Walker 1995; Walker et al. 1995). Life histories based on groups of related activities or processes (e.g., procurement, manufacture, and use) are known as flow models (Schiffer 1972, 1976), whereas those focused on individual activities are termed behavioral chains (Schiffer 1975b, 1976). Developmental cycles (Goody 1971), another organizing framework, are the definable stages of existence in the life histories of behavioral components (Rathje and Schiffer 1982:Chapter 4; Reid and Shimada 1982; Rock 1974).

Behavioral archaeology's basic concepts and principles establish a basis for formulating researchable questions about variability and change. Above all, this theoretical framework emphasizes that behavioral or societal change is change in activities.

The explanation of behavioral variability and change depends on having available countless new experimental laws and theories; the fashioning of these principles, while an effort still in its infancy (Schiffer 1995b), has enjoyed some success (contra Dunnell 1992a, 1992b). Behavioralists, however, cannot supply off-the-shelf answers to explanatory questions. Rather, we have a framework that, when realized through varied research strategies—e.g., experimental archaeology, ethnoarchaeology, prehistory, historical archaeology, and history—can contribute, principle by principle, to building a new behavioral science (Walker et al. 1995).

Evolutionary Archaeology

Evolutionary archaeology has its proximate roots in the writings of Robert C. Dunnell, especially his 1980 paper in *Advances in Archaeological Method and Theory* (see also Dunnell 1978a, 1982, 1989). Beginning in the mid-1980s, contributions to the literature of evolutionary archaeology have come from many investigators, some of whom, especially in the context of case studies, are elaborating and broadening the program (e.g., the papers in Teltser 1995a). Although the discussions below treat mostly Dunnell's seminal formulation of evolutionary archaeology, recent contributions—some seemingly more behavioral—are also consulted.

The evolutionary program rests on the claim that Darwinian theory has not been properly or widely applied to cultural phenomena (Dunnell 1980). This contention, however, does not sit well with the processual archaeologists who also consider themselves to be evolutionists or regard their work as evolutionary (for examples of the latter, see Johnson and Earle 1987; Sanders et al. 1979; Spencer 1990). Similarly, archaeologists whose research is informed by behavioral ecology or evolutionary ecology also wear the Darwinian mantle (e.g., Bettinger 1991; O'Connell and Hawkes 1981, 1984; Simms 1987). Perhaps appreciating that their program is but one of several maintaining an evolutionary stance, proponents of evolutionary archaeology have taken recently to calling themselves "selectionists" (e.g., Graves and Ladefoged 1995:160; Jones et al. 1995:16; Leonard and Reed 1993:648; Neff 1992:179,

1993:27; O'Brien and Holland 1990:45). The term "selectionist" also identifies the process—natural selection—that these latter archaeologists believe to be most important for explaining evolutionary change. In this paper, selectionist and evolutionist are used interchangeably.

Evolution for the selectionist is the differential persistence of discrete variants (Dunnell 1980:38). Commonly, variants are alternative varieties of an artifact class that are winnowed over time by selection processes. Selectionists stress that artifact variants can affect the biological fitness of human organisms; artifacts having such effects are "functional," whereas artifacts neutral with respect to fitness are "stylistic" (Dunnell 1978a, 1980). However, many selectionist studies focus on the "replicative success" of artifact types rather than on the reproductive success of individuals (Leonard and Jones 1987:214; O'Brien and Holland 1990; but see Neff 1992:156). The concept of extended phenotype (Dawkins 1982), which readily encompasses human activities and artifacts (Jones et al. 1995; Neff 1992; O'Brien and Holland 1995b; O'Brien et al. 1994), permits selectionists to integrate evolutionary concerns with the reality that the archaeological record is mainly artifacts, "the hard parts of the behavioral segment of phenotypes" (Dunnell 1989:44).

Explanation consists in showing how specific factors of the selective environment—usually the natural environment—were responsible for the differential persistence of competing variants (Leonard and Reed 1993:650). The selectionist, then, strives to account for the unique contingency-bound successes and failures of artifact classes (and other traits of the extended human phenotype) in the history of a locality or region (Dunnell 1980:39; Neff 1993:28).

A distinction of signal importance is that between processes of variety-generation and variety-selection (Dunnell 1980:39), evolutionists emphasize the latter, showing little interest in investigating the sources of new variants.

Selectionists take pains to distinguish their program from others in archaeology that are seemingly evolutionary. For example, neoevolutionary stage models, which posit transformations of entire societies from tribe to chiefdom or chiefdom to state, are dismissed as Spencerian or Lamarckian, not Darwinian (e.g., Dunnell 1980:40). Similarly, the adaptive-systems models built by processualists and sometimes by behavioralists are also heavily criticized as being non-Darwinian because they conflate variety-generation and variety-selection processes (e.g., Leonard and Jones 1987:200–201). These "adaptationist" scenarios assume that systems change as a result of people intentionally solving problems, steering their behavior in ways that are "adaptive," such as intensifying subsistence in response to demographic or environmental stress. In recent case studies, however, some ostensibly selectionist models closely resemble adaptationist scenarios (e.g., Graves and Ladefoged 1995; Leonard 1989; Leonard and Reed 1993). When processualists and behavioralists use these latter case studies to obtain a quick peek into the evolutionary program, they are apt to become confused, wondering what is different or distinctive about selectionism.

In Search of Common Ground

Because neither evolutionary archaeology nor behavioral archaeology is a homogeneous program, the search for common ground between them is an exercise fraught with peril. Practitioners of each will doubtless take exception to some statements enumerated in this section. Nonetheless, the identification of widely—if not universally—shared assumptions, tenets, and principles establishes a starting point for further discussions. The following 11 statements represent a first approximation of the common ground.

1. That both programs espouse a scientific epistemology is an uncontroversial claim: we are scientists striving to explain empirical phenomena by explicitly employing well warranted theories and laws. Because scientific activity involves not only the explicit use of theories and laws but also their origination and evaluation, behavioralists have been energetic in establishing new principles; selectionists, however, have been disinclined thus far to ask or answer nomothetic questions (see discussions below).

2. Scientists are also permitted to pose historical questions. Both programs attach importance to these questions and emphasize that scientific methods are appropriate for evaluating our tentative answers—i.e., models and hypotheses.

3. In the *explanation* of variation and change, culture is not treated as a causal agent (Braun 1991:427; O'Brien and Holland 1992:37; Ramenofsky 1995:137; Schiffer 1995a; Walker et al. 1995:2–4). The adjective "cultural" merely means learned, as in cultural transmission; human, as in cultural phenomena; or societal, as in cross-cultural regularity. Selectionists should take no exception to this statement, but some behavioralists might be rather reluctant to jettison anthropology's most sacred cow.

4. The phenomenological world of interest is variation and change in human behavior or societies. Despite Dunnell's (1980:48) occasional acknowledgment that "human behavior" is "the principal subject matter," some selectionists may contest this tenet, which is expressed in systemic-context terms, because they believe that their realm is the archaeological record (Teltser 1995b:3). Operating analytically in the systemic context, however, requires behavioral reconstruction or inference, which in the abstract is anathema to many selectionists (e.g., Dunnell 1978a, 1978b, 1989, 1992a, 1992b). In practice, however, selectionists make behavioral inferences and seek to explain change in systemic-context phenomena (see "On Behavioral Inference" below). As this becomes generally appreciated, selectionists may accept variation and change in human behavior or societies as the focus of inquiry.

5. Evolutionary change is regarded as the differential persistence of discrete variants. Selectionists insist that all change be treated in this way, because any other move forsakes a Darwinian perspective (Dunnell 1980). Doubtless influenced by selectionists, some behavioralists have come to appreciate the value of treating change as the differential persistence of discrete variants (e.g., Schiffer 1991; Schiffer and Skibo 1987, 1997; Schiffer et al. 1994); yet, the possibility is kept open that other kinds of change also occur—perhaps even some that are transformation-like.

6. To explain evolutionary change, the investigator situates the competition between alternative variants within a specific selective environment, showing how the replication (or reproduction) of each kind of variant was favored or disadvantaged by virtue of its properties and performance char-

acteristics (e.g., Maxwell 1995; Neff 1992, 1993; O'Brien et al. 1994). In accounting for differential persistence in these terms, specific historical explanations offered by selectionists and behavioralists converge—at least structurally—to a considerable extent (compare, for example, Braun 1983; O'Brien et al. 1994; Schiffer and Skibo 1987), as can data requirements (O'Brien and Holland 1995b).

7. Behavior and artifacts are part of the human phenotype. So long as behavior is defined as activities (specific matter-energy interactions between people, artifacts, etc.), this statement should be acceptable to most practitioners in both programs (compare O'Brien and Holland 1995 with Walker et al. 1995).

8. Artifacts play diverse roles in activities, involving performance-based interactions of many kinds (Braun 1995; Nielsen 1995; Schiffer and Skibo 1997). This statement is the stock and trade of the behavioralist but should occasion few objections from selectionists.

9. In comparison with genetic transmission of variation, cultural transmission involves different processes and mechanisms, and their understanding may require new laws and theories (Dunnell 1978a:198, 200). To behavioralists, this statement is self-evident, but selectionists have been slow to follow up its implications with appropriate nomothetic research.

10. The life-history framework is useful for sorting out some causes of variation. In behavioral archaeology, studying the life histories of artifacts, people, and behavioral components is fundamental (Rathje and Schiffer 1982; Schiffer 1992), and new applications appear frequently (e.g., Schiffer and Skibo 1997; Walker 1995). Implicitly selectionists employ this framework in their recognition, for example, that lithic blanks, preforms, and bifaces were not competitive variants but stood in ontogenetic (developmental) relations to one another. There is also interest in tracking the life histories of phenotypic features (O'Brien and Holland 1992:52). Whether selectionists are willing to extend the life-history framework to other classes of variants (e.g., behavioral components) remains to be seen.

11. It is important to distinguish between variety-generation and variety-selection processes. This tenet is widely championed by selectionists

(e.g., Dunnell 1989:39; Teltser 1995b:6) and also seems compatible with behavioral archaeology. Behavioralists might add that explanations for variety-generation and variety-selection processes are apt to require different bodies of theory (for further discussion, see "Seeking Synergies" below).

Incompatibilities

Although the common ground between evolutionary and behavioral archaeologies may be appreciable, there are also some formidable incompatibilities. Surprisingly, the selectionist tenets that cannot be assimilated by behavioralists have nothing to do with evolutionary theory per se. Indeed, a case can be made that these selectionist positions are also at odds with modern evolutionary biology. The argument developed in this section is simple: the parts of selectionism that behavioralists find most unpalatable are without foundation, and, moreover, these ideas actually undermine efforts to establish an evolutionary archaeology.

Theory and Model Building in Science

From a behavioral perspective, it appears that selectionists have unusual views about theory and model building. For example, according to Dunnell (1989:36), one grand theory generates all of a field's hypotheses and links all of its explanations (Dunnell 1982:5). Apparently, then, evolutionary theory alone can solve archaeology's myriad explanatory problems. Although a few fields do have grand theories, such as Darwinian evolution in biology and general relativity in physics, these theories are but a tiny part of the nomothetic products of those sciences—the part most visible to people on the outside. On the inside, as textbooks and journal articles demonstrate, are countless other theories and experimental laws (sensu Nagel 1961; see also Salmon 1982), many—if not most—exhibiting independence from the grand theory. Even in biology, explanations for mitosis and DNA replication are not deducible from evolutionary theory, and in physics general relativity cannot explain thermionic emission or the effects of doping on semiconductors. Each of these phenomena is made intelligible by process-specific principles. The actual structure of theory in any science, then, is a multitude of principles—ranging from simple to complex, concrete to abstract, and narrow to broad—that often deal with unrelated phenomena. (On the structure of theory in archaeology, see Schiffer 1988.)

Another curious view is that laws and theories are true by definition. Dunnell (1982:16) argues that

> Laws, or theoretical laws, are rational, ideational constructs that ultimately are deductions . . . from primitive definitions. They are always true by virtue of their construction and are not contingency bound.

The example he provides, d = vt (distance equals velocity times time), does conform to these criteria because, in fact, it is not a scientific law or theory at all, but a mathematical law (on the distinction, see Salmon 1982). The position that theory is immune to empirical falsification (Dunnell 1982:16) manifestly contradicts scientific practice; as Sober (1984:82) notes, "theoretical claims ought to be testable." The most abstract and general theories, of course, may be difficult to test—even today, Einstein's theory of general relativity is still undergoing evaluation—yet they are potentially testable (Nagel 1961). Finally, I note that the concept of "true by definition" is itself problematic (e.g., Sober 1984:62).

In view of the contention that theories are definitionally true, it is surprising that theories are also said to have a substantial empirical content. According to Dunnell (1989:44), a discipline's grand theory must "generate its own data" and the units specified in the theory must be "directly measurable in the phenomenological world" (Dunnell 1982:7, 1994:34). A view more generally held in science is that the entities, mechanisms, or processes postulated by a theory have no immediate empirical content, for they are often unobservable. To operationalize or test a theory, one employs appropriate units and instruments for measuring the variables that it implicates. These instruments (and the rules of correspondence that link them to the theory) involve still other laws and theories. For example, in testing the kinetic theory of gases, which involves invisible entities called molecules, one has to measure a gas's temperature. Temperature can be measured, for example, with a mercury thermometer or infrared thermometry; in either case the instru-

ment's operation is based on principles other than the kinetic theory. In addition, from the kinetic theory one can deduce neither mercury's coefficient of thermal expansion nor a gas's infrared emission spectrum. In short, scientific theories do not articulate immediately with the empirical world (Sober 1984:73); interposed between theories and observations are rules of correspondence, lower-level principles, and measuring instruments that are based on still other theories and laws (Nagel 1961; Tschauner 1996).

Failure to appreciate the complex, principle-rich apparatus that links theories to observations can lead to unhelpful advice on building archaeological theory and models. To wit, Dunnell (1980:88) asserts that a theory's variables "cannot be defined in behavioral terms." Going further he claims, "If archaeologists are going to employ evolutionary theory, they must rewrite it in terms of variables that are empirical in the [archaeological] record" (Dunnell 1980:88). If this recipe were followed literally, then a theory would be precluded from implicating mechanisms and processes, which are decidedly behavioral phenomena unobservable in the static archaeological record. At best, archaeologists would be reduced to crafting relationships between measurements on sherds, chips of stone, and so on—scarcely the stuff of theory (but see O'Brien and Holland 1992); at worst, archaeologists would be operating in the murky world of merged systemic and archaeological contexts (on the necessity of keeping these contexts conceptually and analytically distinct, see Reid 1985, 1995). In the final analysis, evolutionary theory itself cannot be rewritten in archaeological-context terms: sherds were not part of anyone's phenotype (unless reused), yet a cooking pot—a systemic-context entity operationalized through behavioral inference—was.

The selectionist prohibition against framing models and theories in behavioral terms is out of step with practice in modern evolutionary biology. In the latter discipline, theories and models incorporate behavioral variables on a wide range of systemic phenomena, such as predator-prey interactions, mating patterns, foraging behavior, and maintenance of territories, none of which is empirical in the paleontological and paleoenvironmental records. It could not be otherwise; after all, "behavior is at once cause and consequence of evolution" (Plotkin 1988:8).

In accord with evolutionary biologists, and in contrast to the selectionist position, behavioralists maintain that theories, models, and explanations—even those offered by selectionists—must be framed in behavioral terms. Ironically, support for this claim can be found in Dunnell's (1989) own effort to build an evolutionary model. In that paper he seeks to explain the selection for "waste" behavior, specifically the Woodland mortuary cults of the eastern United States that left behind obtrusive burial mounds. The variables and parameters of the model include "mean carrying capacity," "no change or difference in subsistence," "populations in equilibrium at different sizes," "shortfalls in productivity," "intensification" of subsistence, "waste-type behavior," and "mortuary cult" (Dunnell 1989:48). To my knowledge, survey archaeologists never encounter a carrying capacity or a waste-type behavior, nor do excavators uncover a productivity shortfall or a mortuary cult. In every instance, these variables and parameters are more-or-less behavioral (i.e., systemic context), not—as Dunnell (1980:88) prescribes—written in terms "that are empirical in the record." Other selectionist models invoke variables and parameters that are equally systemic (e.g., Graves and Ladefoged 1995; Leonard 1989; Leonard and Reed 1993; O'Brien et al. 1994). Despite rhetoric to the contrary, selectionists build models almost as behavioral as behavioralists.

Because theories and models are formulated in behavioral terms, the investigator is obligated to forge links, through measurement, to empirical units in the archaeological record. This linkage process is called inference, and it brings us to a second incompatibility.

On Behavioral Inference

Many selectionists deny the need for behavioral inference and denigrate as unscientific the activities of archaeologists who reconstruct the past. These efforts are labeled "reconstructionism," which Dunnell (1978a:194) elevates to the status of a paradigm, attributing its full flowering to processual and behavioral archaeologies. According to Dunnell (1978a:195), "behavioral reconstructions . . . cannot be the foundation of an approach that professes to be both scientific and evolutionary." Behavioral reconstruction is not science (Dunnell 1980:78, 1982:20, 1989:43, 1992a:87), but a purveyor of "just-so stories" (Dunnell 1982:20) that should be abandoned (Dunnell 1989:45).

The decisive dismissal of inference contradicts many thoughtful works in archaeological epistemology (e.g., Fritz 1972; Patrik 1985; Salmon 1982; Schiffer 1976; Sullivan 1978; Wylie 1985) and also ignores the countless, well-established inferences that have greatly enhanced the understanding of past societies worldwide. What is more, modern evolutionary biology could not exist without paleoenvironmental and paleoecological reconstruction, not to mention a host of inferences about the behavior of particular taxa.

Because selectionist models are actually expressed in behavioral terms, they do require inference (see also Wylie 1995:207–208). Evidence that supports this latter claim can be found in Dunnell's (1989) own explanatory sketch dealing with "waste" behavior. When treating specifics of the Woodland case, he is forced to operationalize the model by means of behavioral inferences. Dunnell does not himself construct these inferences from archaeological evidence, but relies mainly on reconstructions proffered by other investigators, as in "the nonagricultural status of the Woodland associated with the mortuary cult" (1989:49). Sometimes, without any evidence or argument, he makes assertions about past behavior, such as that the mortuary cult "frequently entails the laborious construction of earthen mounds and the manufacture and disposal of vast quantities of goods, many of which are costly imports" (1989:48). Dunnell's study of waste is indicative: every selectionist model can be shown to rest, implicitly or explicitly, on a network of behavioral inferences (for other examples, see Graves and Ladefoged 1995; Leonard 1989; Leonard and Reed 1993; O'Brien and Holland 1992; O'Brien et al. 1994).

Despite the selectionists' anti-reconstructionist rhetoric, evaluation of their models patently requires behavioral inference, and in this respect evolutionary archaeology does not differ from behavioral, processual, or postprocessual archaeologies (on the latter's dependence on behavioral inference, see Duke [1995], Saitta [1992], and Tschauner [1996])—or evolutionary biology (e.g., Thomason 1995). In view of the contradiction between their pronouncements and practice on inference (Watson et al. 1984:255–256), evolutionary archaeologists cannot credibly maintain any longer that reconstruction is defective and unscientific. Indeed, until selectionists take archaeological inference seriously by treating it explicitly and adopting modern methodology, the goals of their program would appear to be out of reach. Fortunately, in several recent selectionist papers, there is modest movement toward explicitly countenancing behavioral inference (e.g., Jones et al. 1995; O'Brien and Holland 1995b; Teltser 1995b).

Closely related to the claims that theories and models should not be built in behavioral terms and that reconstruction of past behavior is to be avoided is the selectionist position on functional principles and actualistic studies, a third point of incompatibility.

Functional Principles and Actualist Studies

Selectionists downplay the importance of functional principles in specific explanations and disregard the actualistic sources of these principles. Dunnell notes that ecology and evolution are distinct bodies of theory, the former concerned with functional relationships and mechanism, the latter with historical explanations (Dunnell 1980:36; 1982:12). Both bodies of theory, he does grant, "are commonly intermingled in particular explanations" (Dunnell 1980:36, cf. 39). Indeed, specific evolutionary explanations in biology are utterly dependent on functional and behavioral principles supplied by actualistic studies, including experiments and ethology (Endler 1986; Krebs and Davies 1981:28–29). Moreover, without principles produced by functional anatomy, ethology, and behavioral ecology, modern evolutionary biology would be explanatorily impotent. A close examination of selectionist studies also reveals use of many functional and behavioral principles, and some are even explicit (e.g., Graves and Ladefoged 1995). Given that the construction of selectionist explanations requires such principles, it is troublesome that nowhere in the selectionist literature can one find a discussion on the place of the archaeological equivalent of behavioral ecology with its actualistic, nomothetic emphasis. When Dunnell does mention the necessity of func-

tional principles, he is alluding to laws of chemistry and physics, not behavioral laws built by archaeologists (e.g., Dunnell 1992b).

One reason for the reluctance of evolutionists to call attention to functional and behavioral principles may stem from a defective argument they raise against reconstruction. It is asserted that such principles presuppose that "behavior cannot change" (Dunnell 1989:44; cf. Dunnell 1992a:81, 1992b:213; O'Brien and Holland 1995b; Neff 1992). Because behavior is "continuously changing," laws of human behavior "are structurally impossible" (Dunnell 1992b:213). Since behavioralists above all appreciate that behaviors do change, the ability to establish general principles must rest on a basis other than the belief in behavioral stasis.

In their own version of uniformitarianism, behavioralists argue that certain behavioral processes—such as boiling food in a ceramic vessel over an open fire or disposal of secondary refuse in cities—although not universal, exhibit some regularities whenever and wherever they occur (Schiffer 1975c, 1978, 1996; Skibo 1992:25–28; Walker et al. 1995). The identification of a behavioral process enables the investigator to seek or create the "behavioral contexts" (*sensu* Walker et al. 1995:4) where nomothetic research may lead to the recognition of regularities (such as correlates and c-transforms). Boundary conditions of behavioral processes enumerate the identical characteristics among seemingly dissimilar—often culturally diverse—empirical phenomena. For example, the McKellar principle specifies that in frequently maintained activity areas, only small artifacts remain behind as primary refuse (McKellar 1983; Schiffer 1976:188–189, 1987:62–63). The behavioral process of activity-area maintenance is bounded by the term "in frequently maintained activity areas." In these activity areas, and only in these activity areas, does this behavioral regularity hold. It holds, however, despite temporal and spatial differences in artifact types, in kinds of activities, and in the nature of activity areas. (The threshold size of residual primary refuse is expected to vary with situational factors such as the maintenance technology employed, permeability of the substrate, and the nature of the refuse [Schiffer 1976:189, 1987:63].) The concepts of behavioral process and boundary conditions can help us to resolve the apparent paradox between the constancy of behavioral regularities (and the principles that describe them) and the inconstancy of specific behaviors (cf. Hull 1988:463).

It should now be clear why the theories and experimental laws yielded by nomothetic research in actualistic contexts are seldom, if ever, "universal": behavioral processes can have very limited temporal and spatial distributions. Thus, principles describing these processes often exhibit a highly circumscribed generality. But this is no cause for concern since the behavioralist is content to devise and employ principles having quite confining boundary conditions—as long as they are useful for answering research questions.

To achieve anything like the richly textured, historically contingent explanations crafted by evolutionary biologists, selectionists will need to employ countless functional and behavioral principles (see Sober 1984). What is more, to create the new principles that an evolutionary archaeology requires, selectionists will have to ask their own nomothetic questions in making full use of the discipline's actualistic research strategies (e.g., experimental archaeology and ethnoarchaeology—see Schiffer 1978; Schiffer et al. 1994; Skibo 1992).

In the very recent selectionist literature, some investigators have begun to find roles for experimental and ethnoarchaeological findings (e.g., Dunnell 1995:42; Dunnell and Feathers 1991; Dunnell et al. 1994; Maxwell 1995; Neff 1992:150; O'Brien and Holland 1990:60, 1995:184; O'Brien et al. 1994). Moreover, in recognizing that performance characteristics of artifact types affect their replicative success in particular selective environments, a few selectionists themselves are beginning to carry out experiments (e.g., Dunnell and Feathers 1991; O'Brien et al. 1994). Perhaps one day soon selectionist practice will include even ethnoarchaeology.

Discussion

As originally formulated, the evolutionary program contains a number of tenets that contradict important parts of behavioral (and processual) archaeologies. Try as I might, however, I fail to appreciate why any of these ideas is necessary for an evolutionary archaeology. Nothing in Darwinian theory per se nor in modern evolution-

ary biology precludes framing theories and models in behavioral terms, prohibits making inferences about the past, or rules out the conduct of actualistic, nomothetic studies. These views in fact distance selectionism from productive research strategies, practiced by behavioralists and evolutionary biologists alike, that could improve the evolutionary program. Moreover, by maintaining tenets that behavioralists and processualists regard as clearly wrong, selectionists alienate the very archaeologists who ought to be most receptive to their insights on evolution. Selectionists may be well advised to cast off the conceptual baggage that has so burdened the program (see also Wylie 1995).

Seeking Synergies

Building on the common ground between evolutionary and behavioral archaeologies, and exploiting ideas from both programs, I now attempt to indicate, with examples, how the study of behavioral (or evolutionary) change might be enhanced.

Clarifying Selection Processes

In using the term "natural selection," Darwin called attention to a kind of selection different from that practiced, for example, by plant and animal breeders. In natural selection, competing organisms are winnowed by environmental factors, such as predators and temperature extremes. Today the term "cultural selection" is in vogue to designate processes internal to a human population (e.g., Durham 1991:165), whereas natural selection is retained for selective agents in the natural environment. Evolutionary archaeologists have discussed the necessity of a concept like cultural selection, but no consensus has emerged (for various viewpoints, see Braun 1995:132–133; Dunnell 1980:53, 63, 1989:41; Leonard and Jones 1987:211; O'Brien and Holland 1992:45, 48, 1995:178; Rindos 1984, 1989).

In considering cultural selection, Dunnell evinces skepticism while asking,

> Is there a point in human evolutionary history at which selection does become an internal cultural matter independent of environmental constraint and change becomes transformational? I think not, or more precisely, I think it would be premature to assume so [Dunnell 1980:65].

Internal selection is not a process Dunnell is

eager to embrace because it implies to him that change is transformational, no longer the differential persistence of discrete variants. However, Dunnell furnishes no argument showing that internal selection must be transformational; I suggest that it need not be.

In demonstrating that internal selection is compatible with a Darwinian view of change, one first needs appropriate ways to conceptualize both the entities being selected and the selection process. Drawing inspiration from Hull's (1988) expansive view of selection, I define a population as *any collection of potentially competing variants*. The differential persistence of variants is governed by the population's selective environment, which exerts selective pressures. Clearly, if a population is internal to a human society, the selective environment may also be internal. For example, the population of all condoms being offered for sale in the United States today has a selective environment that includes condom-purchasing activities—an environment internal to U.S. society. In contrast, a population's selective environment may consist mainly of external, noncultural processes. An example is a community's population of wild-animal procurement activities, which are subject to selection, for example, by the abundance and accessibility of game. One can even conceive of populations that undergo both internal and external selective pressures, such as a neolithic village's agricultural activities.

None of these processes need be called "cultural" selection or "natural" selection. This distinction perhaps had utility in the nineteenth century, but it is not useful today in the study of cultural phenomena. Of transcendent importance is the identification of populations, consisting of discrete variants, and the specific selective pressures to which such populations are subject. Selection is selection, regardless of the cultural or noncultural character of environmental agents and mechanisms (Hull 1988; O'Brien and Holland 1990). More importantly, evolution remains the differential persistence of discrete variants; there is no theoretical need to embrace transformational change.

In archaeological cases, however, we will encounter instances of transformation-like change. The bulk of these may result from ontogenetic processes, as in lithic reduction sequences (Dibble 1995; Goodyear 1974), "devolutionary

cycles" of structures (David 1971), sequences of ceramic reuse (Deal and Hagstrum 1995), stages of household development (Schiffer et al. 1981), and growth-related alterations in community organization (Wills and Leonard 1994). The possible occurrence of non-ontogenetic transformations of one variant into another is, for now, best left an open question.

Appropriate Units and Scales of Selection

A question following immediately from the previous discussion is, Which populations of variants should be the foci of evolutionary study? In selectionist archaeology, this question is framed as one of scale. Although Dunnell (1980:53) notes that selection goes on "at a variety of different scales," he does not discuss scales other than those of the individual organism and the cultural system as a whole; he also doubts that natural selection can be effective above the individual organism (1980:55) until "the appearance of complex society" (1980:66; see also Wenke 1981). In short, the scale problem remains essentially unresolved (Dunnell 1989:39, 41, 1995). Another rendering of the question is, What are the appropriate units of selection (Dunnell 1995; Teltser 1995b)? This question, too, lacks definitive answers at present, even in evolutionary biology (Hull 1988; Lloyd 1988; Sober 1984; Williams 1992). It is clear, however, that modern evolutionary biologists embrace and study evolutionary change in diverse units at many scales (e.g., Dawkins 1982:113).

As in evolutionary biology, one can find in behavioral archaeology the employment of a bewildering array of units along with analyses conducted at countless scales. This seemingly undisciplined approach reflects the recognition that the evolution of cultural phenomena occurs simultaneously at a great many scales. This comes about because (1) there is a vast diversity in kinds of units, (2) units occur in multiple hierarchies, (3) units are interrelated in complex ways both within and between hierarchies, and (4) there are highly varied selection processes, at many scales, that affect different kinds of units differentially.

Although the units employed by behavioralists were not adopted with evolutionary questions explicitly in mind, they can nonetheless be conceived as general kinds of systemic populations, particular examples of which exhibit discrete variation; thus, they might be useful in evolutionary studies. Provisionally I suggest that the *general* units of behavioral evolution—i.e., the scales at which selection takes place—are artifacts, activities, behavioral processes, and behavioral components. Each of these units, of course, is actually a hierarchy of more specific units; the latter need to be identified in particular research contexts. For present purposes, I focus on the artifact (including its constituent parts and assemblies), activity, and several types of behavioral component.

Parts are the separately fabricated pieces or substances of an artifact; examples include a chert arrow point and a personal computer's (PC) power transformer. The assembly is a set of parts that functions together in an artifact. An arrow and a PC's power supply are examples. Assembly is a very flexible concept that can be used to designate the many levels lying between discrete parts and artifacts (for another approach to subdividing artifacts and linking the latter into systems, see Oswalt 1976). The artifact is the set of integrated assemblies that functions together in an activity; examples are a bow-and-arrow and a PC. Activities are exemplified by hunting with a bow-and-arrow and writing with a PC's word processor.

Behavioral components, the "tangible units of a society's social organization" (Schiffer 1992:4), are entities that carry out recurrent sets of activities in patterned locations (Rathje and Schiffer 1982). There are two main kinds of behavioral components. The first is residentially based, and is defined by ever-larger aggregates of people; from least to most inclusive are households, communities, regional systems, and empires (Rathje and Schiffer 1982; Schiffer 1992:4–6). A second type of behavioral component, which has no residential basis, is the task group. In task groups, such as work parties, religious congregations, and corporations, people come together to perform activities such as hunting or assembling PCs (Schiffer 1992:6); they may or may not have dedicated activity areas and facilities.

At each scale (or for each type of unit), one can define populations of discrete variants. For example, the population of automobiles being used in the United States today contains numerous variants on the basis of manufacturer, body style, engine size, type of transmission, luxury appointments, etc. Similarly, among the population of U.S. households are variants based on wealth, richness of artifact inventory, generational composition, size of dwelling, degree of residential mobility, and so forth. One can also define subpopulations of behavioral components, such as all corporations that manufacture radios, and delineate variants (e.g., radio-making companies differing in size, output, variety of models manufactured).

Having specified provisional scales and units for evolutionary study, I next turn to the problem of identifying the selective environment for any particular unit. Because behavioralists have done much of their work at the scale of artifacts, especially on artifact-activity relations, the following discussion is most applicable at that scale.

The *immediate selective context* can be defined as all activities in the life history of an artifact type; that is, the activities that take place during processes of procurement, manufacture, transport, distribution, storage, use, maintenance, reuse, disposal, etc. These activities exert selective pressures, and the result is the differential persistence of variants (O'Brien et al. 1994; Schiffer and Skibo 1997). The replicative success of a given variant is influenced by its activity-specific—i.e., behaviorally relevant—properties and performance characteristics. Selection pressures in the immediate selective context lead to artifacts that embody design compromises of many kinds, as in trade-offs between performance characteristics pertaining to manufacture, use, and maintenance processes (McGuire and Schiffer 1983; O'Brien and Holland 1990, 1992; O'Brien et al. 1994; Schiffer and Skibo 1987) or even between activities within a given process (Schiffer and Skibo 1997). Compromises are necessitated because, ordinarily, no single design can maximize an artifact's entire set of activity-specific performance characteristics. An understanding of the patterns in design compromises requires one to delve, sometimes deeply, into what can be called the *extended selective context*. Activities, agents, and mechanisms that make up the extended selective context are those coupled, by flows of energy, artifacts, or people, to activities in the immediate selective context (on such connections, see Schiffer 1979, 1992). Examples of immediate and extended selective contexts are furnished below.

Variety-Generating Processes and Stimulated Variation

The literature of selectionist archaeology is largely silent about variety-generating processes, perhaps because Dunnell (1978a:197) in an early paper proclaimed "that the specific origin or invention of new elements becomes a trivial inquiry." Dunnell (1978a:197) also asserted that invention "is analogous to mutation in biological systems;" thus, as a "random phenomenon" (Dunnell 1980:66), new variants would be beyond prediction (Dunnell 1980:62). Construing variety-generating processes in this manner has, I suggest, hampered the study of behavioral evolution.

Like modern evolutionary biologists (e.g., Nitecki 1990), archaeologists should regard variation and its sources as subjects eminently worthy of explanation. Variation in a population at one point in time is a consequence of both prior selection *and* variety-generating processes (e.g., invention and borrowing). Study of the latter is clearly crucial, for the creation of new variants in cultural populations occurs commonly and sometimes at high rates. Because selection operates on variation, the state of variation at one point in time immediately constrains the outcome of selection (cf. Dawkins 1982:42–46; Neff 1992:147). Thus, one cannot explain evolutionary change in specific cases without documenting and accounting for large and rapid changes in the available variation. New variants can arise through an expansion of inventive activities in existing behavioral components, through the proliferation of behavioral components undertaking inventive activities, or both.

An argument can be made that variety-generating processes work in patterned ways. Some processes, for example, cause inventions of a particular kind to cluster markedly in time and space. Indeed, the historical and archaeological records furnish evidence of rather dramatic—and sometimes predictable—increases in the conduct of variety-generating activities (Hughes 1983; Schiffer 1993).

One hypothesis to account for some bursts of variety-generation is that information (as matter or energy) coming from changed conditions in selective contexts can stimulate an increase in inventive activities of behavioral components and can foster the creation of new behavioral compo-nents. This process, which is illustrated in some detail below, can be called *stimulated variation* (compare to Neff's [1992:146] discussion of "directed variation" and Braun's [1991:431] concept of "directed innovation"). Unlike "directed mutation" (Dawkins 1982:112) and "guided variation" (Boyd and Richerson 1985:94–98), which more than flirt with Lamarckian mechanisms of change, the process of stimulated variation in no way obviates selection; after all, every variant produced during an instance of stimulated variation can be selected against. Selection thus retains its Darwinian role, but variety-generation becomes central to evolutionary inquiry, the study of its mechanisms and processes far from trivial.

The process of stimulated variation can help us to reconcile adaptationist and selectionist views of behavioral change. In the adaptationist framework, a changing natural environment or a growing population exerts selective pressures that are perceived as stresses or problems by a cultural system's participants (e.g., Hill 1977). Problem-solving behaviors usually lead to an appropriate response, and the result is a new adaptation. As selectionists have pointed out, however, the adaptationist model presumes that people enjoy a certain omniscience in identifying significant problems and in forecasting the future (e.g., Braun 1991:428, 1995:129; Neff 1992:146; see also Schiffer 1979, 1992:Chapter 7). Essentially transformational, adaptationist explanations conflate processes of variety-generation and variety-selection (e.g., Jones et al. 1995:17–18; Rindos 1989:3).

An appreciation for stimulated variation allows us to assign problem-solving its proper role in evolution, that of producing new variants (Braun 1995:129; Rindos 1989:13–15). Variation created by this process (and certainly there are others—Basalla [1988]) is not directed by future adaptive needs, but is shaped by contemporaneous phenomena in the selective environment, such as an artifact that does not reach behaviorally significant performance levels in an activity or an activity that does not effectively play its role in a behavioral component. If stimulated variation happens to furnish a variant that becomes fixed very rapidly, the entire evolutionary process may be so telescoped that it appears transformational—when in fact it was not. The telescoping of evolutionary processes is exacerbated, of course, by the low resolution of most archaeological chronologies, which makes it diffi-cult to discern rapid expansions and contractions of variation. When not utterly overlooked, such varia-tion is likely to be dismissed as mere noise that complicates typology-construction. Aware of this problem, archaeologists should now diligently seek the fine-grained behavioral variation, predicted by the process of stimulated variation, that our cul-ture-historical units so relentlessly obscure (see also Plog 1974).

At the present time, neither adaptationist nor selectionist explanations furnish adequate accounts of transformation-like changes in behav-ior. In stressing that problem solving creates new adaptations, adaptationist explanations are incomplete and misleading because they gloss over the false starts, partial solutions, unintended consequences, and dead-ends that problem solv-ing also begets. Equally unsatisfactory are selec-tionist explanations that ignore large and rapid increases in the variation available to selection. Perhaps the process of stimulated variation can contribute to building a fully general evolutionary theory that assigns ample weight to both variety-generation and variety-selection.

Some Illustrations

To illustrate the concepts just developed, I mainly exploit my historical research on radios, which provides some well-controlled data sets.

In studies of artifacts in capitalist industrial societies, it is useful to examine variety-genera-tion and variety-selection in relation to three processes that occur in the life history of a prod-uct type: invention, commercialization, and adop-tion (e.g., Schiffer 1991; Schiffer et al. 1994). These processes are examined here in turn.

In the invention process, people create proto-types of parts, assemblies, and artifacts in order to demonstrate their performance characteristics to financiers, entrepreneurs, and manufacturers. A major source of variation, invention is hardly a random process; rather, inventive activities can be highly patterned by stimulated variation. These strong effects are often discernible as a clustering in time and space of similar inventions. For exam-ple, just after the turn of the last century, inven-tions proliferated in the parts and assemblies that went into radio transmitters and receivers (Aitken 1976, 1985). This was an instance of stimulated

variation that derived from the immediate selec-tive context of radios—particularly use activities. Radios at that time were used mainly for ship-to-shore communication, which was unreliable, however, over long distances. In response to the blatant performance deficiencies of transmitters and receivers, various task groups invested resources in the invention of parts and assemblies that could raise the power of transmitters and boost the sensitivity and selectivity of receivers. This quickly expanding population of inventions served as the raw material for selection.

Commercialization involves putting a part, assembly, or artifact into production and bringing it to market. This process has both variation-selecting and variation-generating aspects. On the one hand, commercialization is undertaken by task groups, such as financial and manufacturing corporations, that rigorously winnow inventions, with only some reaching the marketplace. On the other hand, commercialization generates variation in the products available for selection by con-sumer activities.

Stimulated variation can also play a role in commercialization, as another radio example demonstrates (Schiffer 1991). Figure 1 shows changes in the frequency of U.S. companies man-ufacturing vacuum-tube radios for the home mar-ket from 1920 to 1955. (It is assumed that variation in this population is directly related to the frequency of different radios commercial-ized.) The graph indicates two dramatic increases in variation in these behavioral components: (1) in the early 1920s, beginning in 1922, and (2) in the late 1940s, commencing in 1946 after the war-caused hiatus in the manufacture of home radios. Both episodes, I suggest, came about through stimulated variation. The first burst of variation in the population of radio companies resulted from the advent of commercial entertainment broad-casting, in November 1920, which some entrepre-neurs and manufacturers interpreted as a portent of profits for firms that commercialized home radios. The second expansion of variation stemmed from the movement, into radio (and tele-vision) manufacture, of electronics companies seeking new products and new markets after the cessation of wartime production. With pent-up demand for consumer products after the priva-tions of the Great Depression and World War II,

250

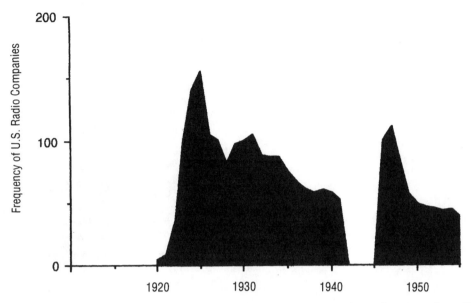

Figure 1. Changes in the frequency of companies in the United States that manufactured vacuum-tube radios for the home market, 1920–1955. Based on data in Grinder (1995), each company's period of radio production was estimated from the time range of annual models listed.

many firms eagerly embraced home-radio manufacture; by 1949, however, the vast majority of newcomers had failed in the radio business.

An even more dramatic instance of stimulated variation during commercialization comes from the history of U.S. portable radios (Schiffer 1991). During the Great Depression, battery-powered sets that were designed to be easily carried around were rare in the marketplace. In 1939 and 1940, however, there was a phenomenal jump in the variety of portable radio models offered to consumers (Figure 2). The cause of this burst of commercialization activity was situated in the extended selective context of radios and radio companies. To wit, with the intensification of warfare activities in Europe, radio makers saw an opportunity to offer a type of product that could allow Americans to hear war news anywhere. It should be noted that this episode of stimulated variation involved the commercialization activities of established radio-making companies; new firms were not founded to produce portable radios (see Figure 1).

During adoption, consumers buy and use commercialized products. Purchasing activities exert selective pressures, and the latter can be swift and sure. In 1953 nearly two million portable radios were sold in the United States (Electronic Industries Association 1970:13)—and every one contained vacuum tubes. Late in 1954 the first transistor portable radio was commercialized, and others were rapidly brought to market. Although for a few years more expensive than their tube counterparts, transistor radios had marvelous battery economy along with the cachet of "modernity." As a result, consumers quickly selected against the tube-based portables and, in less than seven years, only transistor radios remained on the market (Schiffer 1991).

Surprisingly, the adoption process is also an important source of variation, as consumers become inventors, literally playing with their new toys. A new product is tried out in old activities and the possibilities of new activities are explored; the result is an expansion of activity variation, which can contribute to stimulated variation in processes of invention and commercialization. For example, in the early 1920s, people explored the possibilities of home radios, a newly commercialized product, taking them outdoors and using them in diverse activity settings, from motorcycle-police on the beat to hot-air balloon races. These experiments were widely publicized in radio magazines and called attention to possi-

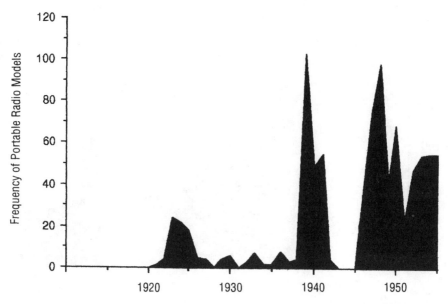

Figure 2. Changes in the frequency of different portable radio models manufactured and sold in the United States, 1920–1955. Based on a ca. 10 percent interval sample of radios listed by Grinder (1995). To be counted as a portable radio, the receiver must use battery or three-way power and be designated as "portable." All portable radios in this database employ vacuum tubes.

bilities for new kinds of radios. Impressed by the opportunities, inventors and entrepreneurs responded with new radio designs for special-purpose communications gear, some of which were commercialized (Schiffer 1991).

Discussion

This framework of processes in the life history of a product type—invention, commercialization, and adoption—allows one to investigate variety-generation and variety-selection in a systematic manner. In histories of the portable radio (and the early electric automobile [Schiffer et al. 1994]), the complex interaction of variety-generation and variety-selection processes has been illuminated.

The intricate connections of variety-generation and variety-selection processes establish relationships between units of evolution at diverse scales. Significantly, in the evolution of cultural phenomena, selection processes at one scale can create variation at others. For example, the selection of inventions for commercialization by financial and manufacturing corporations leads to variation in products available in the wholesale marketplace. Selection of this variation by retailing behavioral components then creates product variation in the retail marketplace. In turn, the selec-

tion processes of consumers influence the variation in household artifact inventories. One can envision that the latter variation will be acted upon by additional selection processes, thereby affecting the differential persistence of households. These cascading effects and complicated relationships of variety-generating and variety-selecting processes ensure that both must be treated in evolutionary explanations.

Conclusion

In an effort to promote constructive dialogue between different theoretical programs, this paper has examined some relationships between evolutionary and behavioral archaeologies, focusing on potential common ground, incompatibilities, and possible synergies.

Various assumptions, tenets, and principles were delineated that have some potential to form common ground between the two programs. The statements summarizing this apparent common ground appear to be of some importance.

Tenets of evolutionary archaeology that cannot be accepted by behavioralists were scrutinized. It was argued that these incompatibilities stem from questionable assumptions that are not, in fact, integral to the selectionist program. Abandonment of these assumptions would make evolutionary archaeology compatible, not just with behavioral archaeology, but also with modern evolutionary biology.

Finally, the possibility that the two programs could enjoy synergies was examined through a treatment of variety-generation and selection processes along with scales and units of selection.

And what of the "thousand archaeologies" I once welcomed (Schiffer 1988:479)? I remain comfortable with a diversity of ideas—even a plethora of social theories. What does concern me, however, is the prospect of archaeology becoming permanently organized into paradigm-based enclaves that exchange only epithets. This is an intellectual luxury that archaeology, a discipline with too few practitioners spread over too much subject matter, cannot afford. Perhaps it is time to dispute the Kuhnian dogma that different paradigms—in this case theoretical programs for explaining variability and change in human behavior and societies—are conceptually incommensurable, and so their practitioners cannot take part in meaningful dialogues. I suggest that the degree of compatibility or complementarity between different programs should be determined on a case-by-case basis. In the case of behavioral and evolutionary archaeologies, there appear to be many opportunities for substantive discussions, and even hints that the two programs working in concert could produce a more integrated and successful science. Perhaps the establishment of a constructive working relationship between evolutionary archaeology and behavioral archaeology could serve as a model for interaction between other, seemingly less reconcilable, theoretical programs.

Acknowledgments. An earlier version of this paper was read at the University of Washington in January 1994. I thank the Department of Anthropology, and especially Julie K. Stein, for the invitation to speak. Annette Schiffer helped to record the data for Figures 1 and 2. I am grateful to the people who furnished perceptive and helpful comments on earlier versions of this paper, including Steven L. Kuhn, Vincent M. LaMotta, R. Lee Lyman, Patrick D. Lyons, Hector Neff, Michael J. Shott, James M. Skibo, Julie K. Stein, Patrice A. Teltser, William H. Walker, LuAnn Wandsnider, and especially Michael J. O'Brien and Stephen L. Zegura. I am indebted to Patrice A. Teltser, visiting scholar in the Laboratory of Traditional Technology, 1992–1995, for leading many stimulating discussions about evolutionary archaeology. I thank María Nieves Zedeño for translating the abstract.

References Cited

Aitken, H.
1976 *Syntony and Spark: The Origins of Radio.* Princeton University Press, Princeton, New Jersey.
1985 *The Continuous Wave: Technology and American Radio, 1900–1932.* Princeton University Press, Princeton, New Jersey.
Basalla, G.
1988 *The Evolution of Technology.* Cambridge University Press, Cambridge.
Bettinger, R. L.
1991 *Hunter-Gatherers: Archaeological and Evolutionary Theory.* Plenum, New York.
Boyd, R., and P. J. Richerson
1985 *Culture and the Evolutionary Process.* University of Chicago Press, Chicago.
Braun, D. P.
1983 Pots as Tools. In *Archaeological Hammers and Theories,* edited by A. Keene and J. Moore, pp. 107–134. Academic Press, New York.
1991 Are There Cross-Cultural Regularities in Tribal Social Practices? In *Between Bands and States,* edited by S. A. Gregg, pp. 423–444. Occasional Paper No. 9. Center for Archaeological Investigations, Southern Illinois University, Carbondale.
1995 Style, Selection, and Historicity. In *Style, Society, and Person: Archaeological and Ethnological Perspectives,* edited by C. Carr and J. E. Neitzel, pp. 123–141. Plenum, New York.
Darwin, C.
1958 *The Autobiography of Charles Darwin, 1809–1882,* edited by N. Barlow. Collins, London.
David, N.
1971 The Fulani Compound and the Archaeologist. *World Archaeology* 3:111–131.
Dawkins, R.
1982 *The Extended Phenotype.* W. H. Freeman, San Francisco.
Deal, M., and M. Hagstrum
1995 Ceramic Reuse Behavior Among the Maya and Wanka: Implications for Archaeology. In *Expanding Archaeology,* edited by J. M. Skibo, W. H. Walker, and A. E. Nielsen, pp. 111–125. University of Utah Press, Salt Lake City.
Dibble, H.
1995 Middle Paleolithic Scraper Reduction: Background, Clarification, and Review of the Evidence to Date. *Journal of Archaeological Method and Theory* 2:299–368.
Duke, P.
1995 Working Through Theoretical Tensions in Contemporary Archaeology: A Practical Attempt from Southwestern Colorado. *Journal of Archaeological Method and Theory* 2:201–229.
Dunnell, R. C.
1978a Style and Function: A Fundamental Dichotomy. *American Antiquity* 43:192–202.
1978b Archaeological Potential of Anthropological and Scientific Models of Function. In *Archaeological Essays in Honor of Irving B. Rouse,* pp. 41–73, edited by R. C. Dunnell and E. S. Hall. Mouton, The Hague.
1980 Evolutionary Theory and Archaeology. *Advances in Archaeological Method and Theory,* vol. 3, edited by M. B. Schiffer, pp. 35–99. Academic Press, New York.
1982 Science, Social Science, and Common Sense: The Agonizing Dilemma of Modern Archaeology. *Journal of Anthropological Research* 38:1–25.

1989 Aspects of the Application of Evolutionary Theory in Archaeology. In *Archaeological Thought in America*, edited by C. C. Lamberg-Karlovsky, pp. 35–49. Cambridge University Press, Cambridge.

1992a Is a Scientific Archaeology Possible? In *Metaarchaeology*, edited by L. Embree, pp. 75–97. Boston Studies in the Philosophy of Science, vol. 147. Kluwer Academic, Dordrecht The Netherlands.

1992b Archaeology and Evolutionary Science. In *Quandaries and Quests: Visions of Archaeology's Future*, edited by L. Wandsnider, pp. 207–222. Occasional Paper No. 20. Center for Archaeological Investigations, Southern Illinois University, Carbondale.

1995 What Is It That Actually Evolves? In *Evolutionary Archaeology: Methodological Issues*, edited by P. A. Teltser, pp. 33–50. University of Arizona Press, Tucson.

Dunnell, R. C., and J. K. Feathers
1991 Late Woodland Manifestations of the Malden Plain, Southeast Missouri. In *Stability, Transformation, and Variation: The Late Woodland Southeast*, edited by M. S. Nassaney and C. R. Cobb, pp. 21–45. Plenum, New York.

Dunnell, R. C., P. T. McCutcheon, M. Ikeya, and S. Toyoda
1994 Heat Treatment of Mill Creek and Dover Cherts on the Malden Plain, Southeast Missouri. *Journal of Archaeological Science* 21:79–89.

Durham, W. H.
1991 *Coevolution: Genes, Culture, and Human Diversity*. Stanford University Press, Palo Alto, California.

Electronic Industries Association
1970 *Electronic Market Data Book, 1970*. Electronic Industries Association, Washington, D.C.

Endler, J. A.
1986 *Natural Selection in the Wild*. Princeton University Press, Princeton, New Jersey.

Fritz, J. M.
1972 Archaeological Systems for Indirect Observation of the Past. In *Contemporary Archaeology*, edited by M. P. Leone, pp. 135–157. Southern Illinois University Press, Carbondale.

Goody, J. (editor)
1971 The Developmental Cycle in Domestic Groups. *Cambridge Papers in Social Anthropology* 1. Cambridge University, Cambridge.

Goodyear, A. C.
1974 *The Brand Site: A Techno-Functional Study of a Dalton Site in Northeast Arkansas*. Research Series No. 7. Arkansas Archeological Survey, Fayetteville.

Graves, M. W., and T. N. Ladefoged
1995 The Evolutionary Significance of Ceremonial Architecture in Polynesia. In *Evolutionary Archaeology: Methodological Issues*, edited by P. A. Teltser, pp. 149–174. University of Arizona Press, Tucson.

Grinder, R. E.
1995 *The Radio Collector's Directory and Price Guide, 1921–1965*. 2nd ed. Sonoran Publishing, Chandler, Arizona.

Hill, J. N. (editor)
1977 *Explanation of Prehistoric Change*. University of New Mexico Press, Albuquerque.

Hughes, T. P.
1983 *Networks of Power: Electrification of Western Society, 1880–1930*. Johns Hopkins University Press, Baltimore.

Hull, D. L.
1988 *Science as a Process: An Evolutionary Account of the Social and Conceptual Development of Science*. University of Chicago Press, Chicago.

Johnson, A. W., and T. Earle

1987 *The Evolution of Human Societies: From Foraging Groups to Agrarian State*. Stanford University Press, Palo Alto, California.

Jones, G. T., R. D. Leonard, and A. L. Abbott
1995 The Structure of Selectionist Explanations in Archaeology. In *Evolutionary Archaeology: Methodological Issues*, edited by P. A. Teltser, pp. 13–32. University of Arizona Press, Tucson.

Knapp, B.
1996 Archaeology Without Gravity? Postmodernism and the Past. *Journal of Archaeological Method and Theory* 3:127–158.

Krebs, J. R., and N. B. Davies
1981 *An Introduction to Behavioral Ecology*. Blackwell, Oxford.

Lamberg-Karlovsky, C. C. (editor)
1989 *Archaeological Thought in America*. Cambridge University Press, Cambridge.

Leonard, R. D.
1989 Resource Specialization, Population Growth, and Agricultural Production in the American Southwest. *American Antiquity* 54:491–503.

Leonard, R. D., and G. T. Jones
1987 Elements of an Inclusive Evolutionary Model for Archaeology. *Journal of Anthropological Archaeology* 6:199–219.

Leonard, R. D., and H. E. Reed
1993 Population Aggregation in the Prehistoric American Southwest: A Selectionist Model. *American Antiquity* 58:648–661.

Lloyd, E.
1988 *The Structure and Confirmation of Evolutionary Theory*. Greenwood Press, New York.

Longacre, W. A., and J. M. Skibo (editors)
1994 *Kalinga Ethnoarchaeology: Expanding Archaeological Method and Theory*. Smithsonian Institution Press, Washington D.C.

McGuire, R. H.
1995 Behavioral Archaeology: Reflections of a Prodigal Son. In *Expanding Archaeology*, edited by J. M. Skibo, W. H. Walker, and A. E. Nielsen, pp. 163–177. University of Utah Press, Salt Lake City.

McGuire, R. H., and M. B. Schiffer
1983 A Theory of Architectural Design. *Journal of Anthropological Archaeology* 2:277–303.

McKellar, J. A.
1983 Correlates and the Explanation of Distributions. *Atlatl, Occasional Papers* No. 4. Anthropology Club, University of Arizona, Tucson.

Maxwell, T. D.
1995 The Use of Comparative and Engineering Analyses in the Study of Prehistoric Agriculture. In *Evolutionary Archaeology: Methodological Issues*, edited by P. A. Teltser, pp. 113–128. University of Arizona Press, Tucson.

Nagel, E.
1961 *The Structure of Science*. Harcourt Brace, and World, New York.

Neff, H.
1992 Ceramics and Evolution. *Archaeological Method and Theory* 4:141–193.

1993 Theory, Sampling, and Technical Studies in Archaeological Ceramic Analysis. *American Antiquity* 58: 23–44.

Nielsen, A. E.
1995 Architectural Performance and the Reproduction of Social Power. In *Expanding Archaeology*, edited by J. M.

Skibo, W. H. Walker, and A. E. Nielsen, pp. 47–66. University of Utah Press, Salt Lake City.

Nitecki, M. H. (editor)
1990 *Evolutionary Innovations*. University of Chicago Press, Chicago.

O'Brien, M. J., and T. D. Holland
1990 Variation, Selection, and the Archaeological Record. *Archaeological Method and Theory* 2:31–79.
1992 The Role of Adaptation in Archaeological Explanation. *American Antiquity* 57:36–59.
1995a The Nature and Premise of a Selection-Based Archaeology. In *Evolutionary Archaeology: Methodological Issues*, edited by P. A. Teltser, pp. 175–200. University of Arizona Press, Tucson.
1995b Behavioral Archaeology and the Extended Phenotype. In *Expanding Archaeology*, edited by J. M. Skibo, W. Walker, and A. Nielsen, pp. 143–161. University of Utah Press, Salt Lake City.

O'Brien, M. J., T. D. Holland, R. J. Hoard, and G. L. Fox
1994 Evolutionary Implications of Design and Performance Characteristics of Prehistoric Pottery. *Journal of Archaeological Method and Theory* 1:259–304.

O'Connell, J. F., and K. Hawkes
1981 Alyawara Plant Use and Optimal Foraging Theory. In *Hunter-Gatherer Foraging Strategies*, edited by B. Winterhalder and E. A. Smith, pp. 99–125. University of Chicago Press, Chicago.
1984 Food Choice and Foraging Sites Among the Alyawara. *Journal of Anthropological Research* 40:504–535.

Orser, C. E., Jr.
1995 Is There a Behavioral Historical Archaeology? In *Expanding Archaeology*, edited by J. M. Skibo, W. H. Walker, and A. E. Nielsen, pp. 187–197. University of Utah Press, Salt Lake City.

Oswalt, W. H.
1976 *An Anthropological Analysis of Food-Getting Technology*. Wiley, New York.

Patrik, L. E.
1985 Is There an Archaeological Record? *Advances in Archaeological Method and Theory* vol. 8, edited by M. B. Schiffer, pp. 27–62. Academic Press, San Diego.

Plog, F.
1974 *The Study of Prehistoric Change*. Academic Press, New York.

Plotkin, H. C.
1988 Behavior and Evolution. In *The Role of Behavior in Evolution*, edited by H. C. Plotkin, pp. 1–17. MIT Press, Cambridge, Massachusetts.

Preucel, R. W. (editor)
1991 *Processual and Postprocessual Archaeologies: Multiple Ways of Knowing the Past*. Occasional Paper No. 10. Center for Archaeological Investigations, Southern Illinois University, Carbondale.

Ramenofsky, A. F.
1995 Evolutionary Theory and Native American Artifact Change in the Postcontact Period. In *Evolutionary Archaeology: Methodological Issues*, edited by P. A. Teltser, pp. 129–147. University of Arizona Press, Tucson.

Rathje, W. L., and M. B. Schiffer
1982 *Archaeology*. Harcourt Brace Jovanovich, New York.

Reid, J. J.
1985 Formation Processes for the Practical Prehistorian. In *Stucture and Process in Southeastern Archaeology*, edited by R. S. Dickens, Jr., and H. T. Ward, pp. 11–33. University of Alabama Press, University, Alabama.

1995 Four Strategies After Twenty Years: A Return to Basics. In *Expanding Archaeology*, edited by J. M. Skibo, W. H. Walker, and A. E. Nielsen, pp. 15–21. University of Utah Press, Salt Lake City.

Reid, J. J., M. B. Schiffer, and W. L. Rathje
1975 Behavioral Archaeology: Four Strategies. *American Anthropologist* 77:864–869.

Reid, J. J., and I. Shimada
1982 Pueblo Growth at Grasshopper: Methods and Models. In *Multidisciplinary Research at Grasshopper Pueblo, Arizona*, edited by W. A. Longacre, S. J. Holbrook, and M. W. Graves, pp. 12–18. Anthropological Papers No. 40. University of Arizona, Tucson.

Rindos, D.
1984 *The Origins of Agriculture: An Evolutionary Perspective*. Academic Press, New York.
1989 Undirected Variation and the Darwinian Explanation of Cultural Change. *Archaeological Method and Theory* 1:1–45.

Rock, J. T.
1974 The Use of Social Models in Archaeological Interpretation. *Kiva* 40:81–91.

Saitta, D. J.
1992 Radical Archaeology and Middle-Range Methodology. *Antiquity* 66:886–897.

Salmon, M.
1982 *Philosophy and Archaeology*. Academic Press, New, York.

Sanders, W., J. Parsons, and R. Santley
1979 *The Basin of Mexico: Ecological Processes in the Evolution of a Civilization*. Academic Press, New York.

Schiffer, M. B.
1972 Archaeological Context and Systemic Context. *American Antiquity* 37:148–157.
1975a Archaeology as Behavioral Science. *American Anthropologist* 77:836–848.
1975b Behavioral Chain Analysis: Activities, Organization, and the Use of Space. In *Chapters in the Prehistory of Eastern Arizona* IV. Fieldiana: Anthropology Vol. 65, pp. 103–119. Field Museum of Natural History, Chicago.
1975c Some Further Comments on Morse's Dalton Settlement Pattern Hypothesis. In *The Cache River Archeological Project: An Experiment in Contract Archeology*, assembled by M. B. Schiffer and J. H. House, pp. 102–112. Research Series No. 8. Arkansas Archeological Survey, Fayetteville.
1976 *Behavioral Archeology*. Academic Press, New York.
1978 Methodological Issues in Ethnoarchaeology. In *Explorations in Ethnoarchaeology*, edited by R. A. Gould, pp. 229–247. University of New Mexico Press, Albuquerque.
1979 A Preliminary Consideration of Behavioral Change. In *Transformations: Mathematical Approaches to Culture Change*, edited by C. Renfrew and K. Cooke, pp. 353–368. Academic Press, New York.
1987 *Formation Processes of the Archaeological Record*. University of New Mexico Press, Albuquerque.
1988 The Structure of Archaeological Theory. *American Antiquity* 53:461–485.
1991 *The Portable Radio in American Life*. University of Arizona Press, Tucson.
1992 *Technological Perspectives on Behavioral Change*. University of Arizona Press, Tucson.
1993 Cultural Imperatives and Product Development: The Case of the Shirt-Pocket Radio. *Technology and Culture* 34:98–113.
1995a A Personal History of Behavioral Archaeology. In

Behavioral Archaeology: First Principles, by M. B. Schiffer, pp. 1–24. University of Utah Press, Salt Lake City.

1995b Social Theory and History in Behavioral Archaeology. In *Expanding Archaeology*, edited by J. M. Skibo, W. H. Walker, and A. E. Nielsen, pp. 22–35. University of Utah Press, Salt Lake City.

1995c *Behavioral Archaeology: First Principles*. University of Utah Press, Salt Lake City.

1995d The Conceptual Structure of Behavioral Archaeology. In *Behavioral Archaeology: First Principles*, by M. B. Schiffer, pp. 251–253. University of Utah Press, Salt Lake City.

1996 Formation Processes of the Historical and Archaeological Records. In *Learning from Things*, edited by W. E. Kingery, pp. 73–80. Smithsonian Institution Press, Washington D.C.

Schiffer, M. B., T. C. Butts, and K. Grimm

1994 *Taking Charge: The Electric Automobile in America*. Smithsonian Institution Press, Washington, D.C.

Schiffer, M. B., T. E. Downing, and M. McCarthy

1981 Waste Not, Want Not: An Ethnoarchaeological Study of Reuse in Tucson, Arizona. In *Modern Material Culture: The Archaeology of Us*, edited by R. A. Gould and M. B. Schiffer, pp. 68–86. Academic Press, New York.

Schiffer, M. B., and J. M. Skibo

1987 Theory and Experiment in the Study of Technological Change. *Current Anthropology* 28:595–622.

1997 The Explanation of Artifact Variability. *American Antiquity* 62:in press.

Schiffer, M. B., J. M. Skibo, T. C. Boelke, M. A. Neupert, and M. Aronson

1994 New Perspectives on Experimental Archaeology: Surface Treatments and Thermal Response of the Clay Cooking Pot. *American Antiquity* 59:197–217.

Senior, L. M.

1995 The Estimation of Prehistoric Values: Cracked Pot Ideas in Archaeology. In *Expanding Archaeology*, edited by J. M. Skibo, W. H. Walker, and A. E. Nielsen, pp. 92–110. University of Utah Press, Salt Lake City.

Simms, S. R.

1987 *Behavioral Ecology and Hunter-Gatherer Foraging: An Example from the Great Basin*. BAR International Series 381. British Archaeological Reports, Oxford.

Skibo, J. M.

1992 *Pottery Function: A Use-Alteration Perspective*. Plenum, New York.

Skibo, J. M., W. Walker, and A. Nielsen (editors)

1995 *Expanding Archaeology*. University of Utah Press, Salt Lake City.

Sober, E.

1984 *The Nature of Selection: Evolutionary Theory in Philosophical Focus*. MIT Press, Cambridge, Massachusetts.

Spencer, C. S.

1990 On the Tempo and Mode of State Formation: Neoevolutionism Reconsidered. *Journal of Anthropological Archaeology* 9:1–30.

Sullivan, A. P.

1978 Inference and Evidence: A Discussion of the Conceptual Problems. In *Advances in Archaeological*

Method and Theory, vol. 1, edited by M. B. Schiffer, pp. 183–222. Academic Press, New York.

Teltser, P. A. (editor)

1995a *Evolutionary Archaeology: Methodological Issues*. University of Arizona Press, Tucson.

1995b The Methodological Challenge of Evolutionary Theory in Archaeology. In *Evolutionary Archaeology: Methodological Issues*, edited by P. A. Teltser, pp. 1–11. University of Arizona Press, Tucson.

Thomason, J. J.

1995 *Functional Morphology in Vertebrate Paleontology*. Cambridge University Press, Cambridge.

Trigger, B. G.

1989 *A History of Archaeological Thought*. Cambridge University Press, Cambridge.

Tschauner, H.

1996 Middle-Range Theory, Behavioral Archaeology, and Post-Empiricist Philosophy of Science in Archaeology. *Journal of Archaeological Method and Theory* 3:1–30

Walker, W. H.

1995 Ceremonial Trash? In *Expanding Archaeology*, edited by J. M. Skibo, W. H. Walker, and A. E. Nielsen, pp. 67–79. University of Utah Press, Salt Lake City.

Walker, W. H., J. M. Skibo, and A. E. Nielsen

1995 Introduction: Expanding Archaeology. In *Expanding Archaeology*, edited by J. M. Skibo, W. H. Walker, and A. E. Nielsen, pp. 1–12. University of Utah Press, Salt Lake City.

Wandsnider, L. (editor)

1992 *Quandaries and Quests: Visions of Archaeology's Future*. Occasional Paper No. 20. Center for Archaeological Investigations, Southern Illinois University, Carbondale.

Watson, P. J., S. A. LeBlanc, and C. L. Redman

1984 *Archaeological Explanation*. Columbia University Press, New York.

Wenke, R. J.

1981 Explaining the Evolution of Cultural Complexity: A Review. In *Advances in Archaeological Method and Theory*, vol. 4, edited by M. B. Schiffer, pp. 79–127. Academic Press, San Diego.

Williams, G. C.

1992 *Natural Selection, Domains, Levels, and Challenges*. Oxford University Press, Oxford.

Wills, W. H., and R. D. Leonard (editors)

1994 *The Ancient Southwestern Community: Models and Methods for the Study of Prehistoric Social Organization*. University of New Mexico Press, Albuquerque.

Wylie, A.

1985 The Reaction Against Analogy. In *Advances in Archaeological Method and Theory*, vol. 8, edited by M. B. Schiffer, pp. 63–111. Academic Press, San Diego.

1995 An Expanded Behavioral Archaeology: Transformation and Redefinition. In *Expanding Archaeology*, edited by J. M. Skibo, W. H. Walker, and A. E. Nielsen, pp. 198–209. University of Utah Press, Salt Lake City.

Yoffee, N., and A. Sherratt (editors)

1993 *Archaeological Theory: Who Sets the Agenda?* Cambridge University Press, Cambridge.

Received September 9, 1995; accepted April 4, 1996.

BASIC INCOMPATIBILITIES BETWEEN EVOLUTIONARY AND BEHAVIORAL ARCHAEOLOGY

Michael J. O'Brien, R. Lee Lyman, and Robert D. Leonard

Schiffer (1996) recently proposed that, despite some incompatibilities, considerable common ground exists between behavioral archaeology and evolutionary, or selectionist, archaeology. He concludes that there is no fundamental reason why the two approaches cannot work in concert to explain human behavioral change. There are, however, several important reasons why the two programs, at least as currently conceived, cannot work together in any thoroughly integrated fashion. Although both programs employ inference, behavioral archaeology conflates the distinct roles of configurational and immanent properties, searches for nomothetic answers to questions about human behavior, overlooks historical contingency when inferring and explaining the nature of past behavior, and in some cases seems to fall back on vitalism as the mechanism of change. Evolutionary archaeology employs immanent properties inferentially, explicitly acknowledges the importance of the historical contingencies of configurational properties, explains human behavior as being time- and spacebound, and calls upon selection and drift (transmission) as the mechanisms of change. Any attempt to integrate the two approaches must begin by addressing these basic differences.

Schiffer (1996) recientemente ha propuesto que, a pesar de algunas incompatibilidades, existen considerables puntos en común entre la arqueología conductual y la arqueología evolucionista, o seleccionista. Concluye que no existen razones fundametales por las que estas dos perspectivas no puedan trabajar en conjunto para explicar los cambios del comportamiento humano. Existen, a pesar de todo, varias razones importantes por lo cual estas dos escuelas, al menos como se les ha concebido hasta ahora, no pueden trabajar juntas bajo ningún planteamiento integrado. Aunque las dos escuelas emplean inferencias, la arqueología conductual conjuga el papel distintivo de las propiedades configuracionales e imanentes, busca respuestas nomotéticas a las preguntas sobre el comportamiento humano, pasa por alto las contingencias históricas al inferir y explicar la naturaleza del comportamiento pasado, y en algunas casos parece recaer en el vitalismo como mecanismo del cambio. La arqueología evolucionista emplea inferencialmente las propiedades inmanentes, reconoce explícitamente la importancia de las contingencias históricas en la configuración de las propiedades, explica el comportamiento humano como único en un tiempo y espacio determinado, y considera a la selección y la transmisión como los mecanismos responsables del cambio. Cualquier intento de integrar estas dos escuelas debe comenzar por resolver estas diferencias básicas.

Recently, Schiffer (1996) pointed out what he saw as specific areas of concordance between evolutionary archaeology and behavioral archaeology, positing that "there is no fundamental reason why these two programs cannot work in concert to achieve the goal of explaining behavioral (or evolutionary) change in human societies" (Schiffer 1996:643). Schiffer is the prime architect of the behavioral archaeology program (Schiffer 1995a) and, together with colleagues and students at the University of Arizona (e.g., Reid et al. 1974, 1975; Skibo et al. 1995), has produced the majority of articles and books that take a behavioral approach to understanding the archaeological record. He also has been more than accommodating in allowing evolutionists to publish in journals and series that he edits; thus he has had to read not only the manuscripts submitted but also the reviews solicited during the editorial process. As a result, he has more than a passing familiarity with evolutionary archaeology, and hence his observations of possible overlap between it and behavioral archaeology are worth considering in detail.

We agree with some of Schiffer's observations and arguments, but disagree with others. The

Michael J. O'Brien and **R. Lee Lyman** ■ Department of Anthropology, University of Missouri, Columbia, MO 65211
Robert D. Leonard ■ Department of Anthropology, University of New Mexico, Albuquerque, NM 87131

American Antiquity, 63(3), 1998, pp. 485–498.
Copyright © by the Society for American Archaeology

points of disagreement underscore deep differences between the two approaches. Both evolutionary and behavioral archaeology seek to explain humankind's past, and in some cases the data requirements are the same (O'Brien and Holland 1995b), but there are significant differences in epistemology, several of which are well discussed in Schiffer's paper. Hence, we address them only in passing and focus primary attention on metaphysical differences between evolutionism and behavioralism—differences that at present cannot be resolved given the contrasting manner in which behavioralists and evolutionists construct their explanations of the past.

History, Evolutionary Archaeology, and Behavioral Archaeology

Schiffer focuses the majority of attention on the work of Dunnell, correctly claiming that evolutionary archaeology "had its proximate roots in [Dunnell's] writings . . . especially his 1980 paper in *Advances in Archaeological Method and Theory*" (Schiffer 1996:646). The 1980 paper to which Schiffer refers (Dunnell 1980) was Dunnell's (1996a:x) "second major foray into evolution and sociobiology," the first having been a conference paper presented in 1978 (Dunnell 1996b). Other papers written late in the 1970s show the growing influence of Darwinism on Dunnell's thinking (e.g., Dunnell 1978; Dunnell and Wenke 1980). There are two points here. First, Dunnell's thinking was not fully developed in the 1970s—the *Advances* paper was written, as Dunnell (1996a:x) put it, by a "neophyte." Second, Dunnell has yet to produce a thorough programmatic statement on how to implement his version of evolutionary archaeology. What Dunnell (1996a:xi) takes as his "best" piece of evolutionary archaeology work is an exploration of artifact variation (Dunnell and Feathers 1991)—an extremely critical factor within evolutionary archaeology that has prompted him to remark on more than one occasion (e.g., Dunnell 1989:46) that archaeology must develop units of measurement and description commensurate with theory.

Most of Dunnell's published statements either are directed to particular issues within the larger context of the evolutionary archaeology program (e.g., Dunnell 1995) or are so general that little critical detail is included (e.g., Dunnell 1989,

1992a, 1992b). One must, therefore, to some degree interpret his writings and fill in apparent gaps. We are aided in this task by our collaborations with him (e.g., Dunnell and Leonard 1998; Lyman et al. 1997; O'Brien and Dunnell 1998), yet our collective view does not precisely mirror Dunnell's. Nor should it necessarily do so. But we agree with Dunnell that "one cannot point to a complete and robust theory [of evolutionary archaeology] at this point in time . . . . [T]here are still important theoretical issues that require resolution" (Dunnell 1989:42). Biological evolutionary theory cannot simply be lifted wholesale from that realm and applied to sherds, post molds, and arrowheads, just as Darwin's theory could not be lifted from *On the Origin of Species* and applied wholesale to the fossil record.

These various facts result in Schiffer committing what we view as errors. His description of Dunnell's (1989) discussion of waste behavior—specifically the Woodland-period mortuary cults of the eastern United States that left behind highly visible burial mounds—as being "almost as behavioral as [a discussion written by] behavioralists" (Schiffer 1996:650) is a case in point. Dunnell (1989:46–49) stated explicitly what the limitations were of what he was doing. Evolutionary archaeology provided only a "gross" understanding of the existence of "waste," and his discussion only served to exemplify the sorts of insights that might result from use of evolutionary theory. The scenario provided was thus of "limited value" and only suggested the "potential" of evolutionary archaeology to help explain the archaeological record; in particular, it indicated which variables were relevant to such scenarios. Schiffer probably would argue that when fleshed out, the scenario would be behavioral, and he would be correct, since human behaviors created the waste. No evolutionary archaeologist ever argued otherwise (O'Brien and Holland 1995b). More importantly, Dunnell (1989) emphasized that (1) if it is granted that artifacts are part of the phenotype, then one must be clear on what makes up an artifact; (2) relevant variables had not yet been described within an evolutionary theory applicable to cultural phenomena such as artifacts; (3) appropriate units for measuring relevant variables in the empirical realm had not been identified and described; and (4) identifying both the variables and the units must be commensurate with theory building. Numerous efforts by many individuals have been made in these directions subsequent to publication of Dunnell's article (see references in O'Brien 1996b), but many issues have not been resolved.

What Is Evolutionary Archaeology?

The premise underlying Darwinian evolutionary archaeology is, as Schiffer (1996:646) points out, that objects occurring in the archaeological record, because they were phenotypic, were shaped by the same evolutionary processes as were the somatic features of their makers and users. This is a shorthand way of saying that the possessors of the objects were acted on by evolutionary processes. Under this perspective, evolution is viewed as the differential persistence of discrete variants (Dunnell 1980:38), regardless of the scale of "variant" being defined. Evolutionary archaeology involves (1) measuring variation—that is, dividing it into discrete sets of empirical units (groups) using ideational units (classes); (2) tracking variants through time and across space to produce a historical narrative about lineages of particular variants; and (3) explaining the differential persistence of individual variants comprising lineages in particular time-space contexts. Selection is a key concept in evolutionary theory, though in modern Darwinian evolutionary theory, selection is only one evolutionary process that works on variation. Few would doubt that selection is the greatest molder of lineages, but it still acts in tandem with other processes such as drift and mutation. Selection is the mechanism that drives much evolutionary change and is external to the system (organisms or cultures) itself. Within Darwinian theory, it serves as a testable explanation of change (Leonard and Reed 1993).

Evolutionary archaeology has many parallels to modern paleobiology (Lyman and O'Brien 1998). It is geared toward providing Darwinian-like explanations of the archaeological record, just as paleobiologists explain the paleontological record. There are two steps: first, build cultural lineages, and second, construct explanations for those lineages being the way they are (O'Hara 1988; Szalay and Bock 1991). Both steps must employ concepts embedded within Darwinian evolutionary theory, such as lineage (a line of development

owing its existence to heritability), natural selection (a mechanism of change), a transmission mechanism (which itself is a source of new variants), invention/innovation (another source of new variants), and heritability (denoting continuity, such that similarity is homologous). The last ensures that we are examining change within a lineage rather than merely convergence, in which case similarity is of the analogous sort.

Within paleobiology, some of the best historical studies were written by Simpson (e.g., 1937a, 1937b, 1937c). Some might question why we refer to such "ancient writings," but what Simpson had to say in the 1930s and 1940s is as relevant today as it was six decades ago (Gould 1980; LaPorte 1983). Some debate has recently arisen as to whether a Simpson-like view is the most appropriate one to adopt in paleobiology (e.g., Gould 1995a, 1995b), and some have, to be sure, adopted (allegedly [see LaPorte 1983]) different views (e.g., Gould and Eldredge 1993), but the important point is that we view these debates as particularly germane to what we see as the central objective of evolutionary archaeology.

We favor definitions of evolution such as "any net directional change or any cumulative change in the characteristics of organisms or populations over many generations—in other words, descent with modification. It explicitly includes the origin as well as the spread of alleles, variants, trait values, or character states. Evolution may occur as a result of natural selection, genetic drift, or both" (Endler 1986:5; see also Richards 1992). Thus, trait variation and inheritance are required for evolutionary change to occur, but fitness differences are not; the last is only required for evolution via natural selection. Such a definition explicitly incorporates both style and function (*sensu* Dunnell 1978) as kinds of variants of archaeological phenomena. Given this definition, we prefer the methods of evolutionary study used by Gingerich (1991), Simpson (1944, 1975), and Szalay and Bock (1991) to understand the paleontological record (Lyman and O'Brien 1998). We do not deny that what is known as punctuated equilibrium (Eldredge and Gould 1972; Gould and Eldredge 1993) is valuable, nor do we deny its potential applicability to archaeology (e.g., Rosenberg 1994). In part, our preference for earlier methods rather than, say, those favored under punctuated equilibrium, resides in the much greater temporal resolution of the archaeological record. This is not to imply that the archaeological record is somehow qualitatively or quantitatively more complete than the paleontological record; the problems with both records are remarkably similar (see overview in Gould 1995a). But both records provide something to which their respective collaborators dealing with living organisms—whether people or fruit flies—do not have access. And that is, simply, time.

As Gould (1995a:4) observed, "the short time scale of *Drosophila* experiments, pigeon breeding, and improvement of crop plants [may provide] direct evidence for the efficacy of selective processes," but these processes may or may not be applicable to "time's vastness." Gould is in part arguing that Darwinian theory must be modified (his and Eldredge's punctuated equilibrium added) to account for the whole of the paleontological record. The important part of Gould's message is that we need not bother studying the fossil record—either paleontological or archaeological—if we can see all evolutionary processes in a petrie dish or among a group of college students. Evolution is historical—it takes place over time— and contingency bound (Beatty 1995), meaning that it is conditioned by what happened at earlier points. Thus, the central objective of paleobiologists and archaeologists is to determine and explain the history—the evolutionary lineages—of the phenomena they study. We believe most behavioral archaeologists would agree with this.

What Is Behavioral Archaeology?

Schiffer and other practitioners of behavioral archaeology claim to provide a richer and more complete picture of the past than evolutionary archaeologists do: "[B]ehavioral theory, immature though it remains, facilitates the fashioning of historical narratives that are both richly contextualized and audience friendly. More significantly, a behavioral narrative is centered on the actual activities of past people" (Schiffer 1995b:34). Certainly behavioral archaeology provides a picture that is more *anthropologically* friendly, given its focus on human activities, than evolutionary archaeology does. But to argue that "the focus of theory building in archaeology is . . . on what people actually do (and did) in specific activities" (Schiffer

1995b:35) seems to us little more than a holdover from Phillips's (1955:246–247) statement that "New World archaeology is anthropology or it is nothing." Why archaeology should be anything other than archaeology is never specified—other than noting that artifacts are the products of humans—by Phillips, Schiffer, or anyone else who aligns with this position.

Schiffer (1995b:24) states that the "behavioralist demands that historical narratives rest . . . on a foundation of well-confirmed behavioral principles." But he also states that constructing behavioral principles or laws "was never viewed by behavioralists as archaeology's final goal. Rather, behavioral inferences provide the basis for generating a view of the past compatible with a particular theoretical stance: the behavioralist premise that the basis of human societies is their complete reliance on complex and intimate relationships between people and artifacts. The study of such relationships, in all times and places, can, behavioralists maintain, lead to the creation of distinctive social theory in archaeology" (Schiffer 1995b:34). We have no dissatisfaction with the "behavioralist premise," but there are two reasons we cannot agree that constructing "behavioral theory to explain variation and change in human behavior, conceived as people-artifact interactions, is archaeology's highest scientific calling" (Schiffer 1995b:35). First, behavioral theory appears to be merely a set of empirical generalizations; second, artifacts, not human behavior, make up the archaeological record.

Behavioral theory is supposed to do two things: (1) improve "behavioral inference" so that it is "sound," thereby making the writing of narratives of behavioral history "rigorous," and (2) answer "with credible theories and laws, the general questions raised in specific [historical] narratives" (Schiffer 1995b:34). The first is accomplished by generating "lawlike statements that, along with other kinds of information, link observations on the archaeological record to behaviors of the past (e.g., Schiffer 1972, 1976)," and by developing a "nomothetic understanding of material culture dynamics" (Schiffer 1995b:22). Such nomothetic principles are "required for reconstructing a behavioral past" (Schiffer 1995b:23) and apparently constitute the basis for building behavioral theory. Historical narratives are "plausible" because they entail "theorylike or lawlike generalizations" in the structure of an often-implicit "nomothetic apparatus" (Schiffer 1995b:28).

An example of an underlying premise of a behavioral theory is that "an artifact's performance characteristics cannot all achieve high values in every use activity" (Schiffer 1995b:29). A Swiss army knife can be used to do lots of things, none of them "in the most effective manner," and thus this artifact represents "compromises in activity performance" (Schiffer 1995b:30). The favored behavioral variable in this case is the transportability of a tool, which is "expectable when there is high user mobility and limited transport capability" (Schiffer 1995b:30). High mobility and limited transport capability are certainly behavioral, but do generalized tools always denote such behaviors? Behavioral theory doesn't tell us, because the mobility-transport capability equation is an empirical generalization founded in common sense and denying any contingencies of particular behavioral contexts. Darwinian evolution provides a theoretical understanding of such a tool by noting that design constraints typically result in things—artifacts or organisms—not attaining all-around optimality (e.g., Gans 1988, 1993; Gould 1989); that is, compromises are always being made. Whether high mobility, limited transport, or some other factor results in the production of such a thing is historically contingent—what we term a historical configuration (see below). Why was such a tool built in a particular time-space position? Evolutionary archaeology seeks an answer in two arenas: selective context and evolutionary history.

Behavioral archaeology comprises the reconstruction of behaviors, arranging them in a historical sequence and then explaining that sequence in behavioral terms. Whether or not the sequence also comprises a lineage in a Darwinian sense is not addressed by behavioral archaeology. Why? Because the critical distinction between homologous and analogous similarities is not mentioned in behavioral archaeology theory; thus, a historical narrative may result, but it need not be an evolutionary narrative. That is, a temporal sequence may be produced under the behavioral archaeology program, but there is no apparent attempt to ensure that it is also an evolutionary lineage or a heritability-dependent sequence (Lyman and O'Brien 1997). Further, given the empirical generalization-

driven approach of behavioral archaeology in conjunction with the general absence of a concept of style, evolutionary archaeology suggests that behavioral archaeology explanations of Swiss army knives will be strictly functional (e.g., Gould 1997; O'Brien and Holland 1992).

Evolutionary archaeologists also wonder how the reconstructions of behavioral archaeology are tested, since they are inductions or inferences. Dunnell (1989:43–44), for example, notes that by allowing such reconstructions, "[r]elations between behavior and material must be invariant if they are to serve as timeless, spaceless rules for reconstruction" (see O'Brien and Holland 1995b). In other words, a particular structure of particular archaeological stuff in a particular context always and everywhere denotes a particular behavior. In short, equifinality is not a problem for behavioral archaeology because, given sufficient actualistic research, a modern analog for every human behavior that has ever occurred in the past can be found.

Common Ground

There are three areas of agreement between behavioral archaeology and evolutionary archaeology. First, both programs recognize the importance of human behavior in the context of archaeology. Behavioral archaeologists and few if any evolutionists would disagree with Mayr's (1973:388) assertion that behavior "is perhaps the strongest selection pressure operating in the animal kingdom." Second, as Schiffer points out, identifying and tracking variation evident in the archaeological record is basic to evolutionary archaeology. But the isolation and measurement of variation is not the purview solely of evolutionists. As one of us has stated repeatedly (e.g., O'Brien and Holland 1995a, 1995b), when Schiffer and his colleagues and students break clay test tiles or carry out myriad other experiments in the Laboratory for Traditional Technology at the University of Arizona (e.g., Schiffer 1990; Schiffer and Skibo 1987; Schiffer et al. 1994; Skibo et al. 1989; Vaz Pinto et al. 1987), they are carrying out the same experiments that evolutionary archaeology requires (e.g., Brandon 1994) in order to understand variation in performance characteristics of objects found in the archaeological record. As O'Brien and Holland (1995b:144) point out, technological and functional analyses of how objects were made and used are important in evolutionary archaeology. Explanations of past behavior "are derived directly from experimental evidence viewed against the archaeological context containing the materials being examined. We contend that this kind of research agenda—one based on experimental evidence [leading to what we here term mechanical inference]—will allow us to begin to understand not only the evolutionary trajectories of the humans responsible for the technological products but also the nature of selective regimes" (O'Brien and Holland 1995b:144).

The third point of agreement concerns how things in the archaeological record are viewed. Basic to evolutionary archaeology is the view that artifacts represent "the hard parts of the behavioral segment of [past] phenotypes" (Dunnell 1989:44; see Leonard and Jones 1987). When artifacts were made and used, they were as much a part of human phenotypes as nests and log dams are parts of bird and beaver phenotypes, respectively (O'Brien and Holland 1995b). Extending the phenotype (Dawkins 1990) to include nonsomatic features is, as Schiffer points out, something that appeals to behavioral archaeology because it emphasizes the behaviors that result in creation of the objects. Yet Schiffer does not follow through on the evolutionary implications of this notion. He argues that "evolutionary theory itself cannot be rewritten in archaeological context terms: sherds were not part of anyone's phenotype (unless reused), yet a cooking pot—a systemic-context entity operationalized through behavioral inference—was" (Schiffer 1996:649). Later, he (Schiffer 1996:653–654) devotes a page and a half to discussing "Appropriate Units and Scales of Selection." The statement on sherds and the later discussion of units and scales are incompatible with each other from our perspective.

If we paraphrase one of Dunnell's (1980:88) statements that Schiffer (1996:649) isolates, paleobiologists have made significant strides in rewriting evolutionary theory "in terms of variables that are empirical in the [fossil] record." Recall that Darwin made minimal reference to the fossil record (see papers in Nitecki and Nitecki 1992). Paleobiologists have had to develop a suite of terms—some borrowed from functional biology such as homolog, synapomorph, autapomorph, and the like—to denote the variables requisite to

applying Darwin's theory to the fossil record. Each variable has a particular significance for determining evolutionary—that is, phylogenetic—history, and each has particular, theoretically founded, empirical manifestations and distributions within the fossil record. Archaeology has only Willey's (1953:363) axiom that "typological similarity [indicates] cultural relatedness." In several respects, this puts the cart before the horse, for as Simpson (1961:69) pointed out when a similar axiom was in use in paleobiology, "individuals do not belong in the same taxon because they are similar, but they are similar because they belong to the same taxon." The significance of this statement is difficult to overemphasize.

Following Schiffer's reasoning, sherds are not part of the phenotype, because a sherd has behavioral relevance only when it is in the systemic context; otherwise it is trash. By the same reasoning, paleobiologists would be surprised to learn that a fossilized fragment of a humerus or a single tooth is not part of an organism's phenotype because the organism is dead. Sherds have attributes—tempering agent, wall thickness, and so forth—any of which, at one time or another, could have been functional. Conversely, any or all could, at one time or another, have been functionally neutral (O'Brien et al. 1994). These attributes are part of a human's phenotype, just as the color of a mammal's hair as represented by a single hair follicle is part of that organism's phenotype, whether or not the hair is attached to the living organism. Schiffer's purely behavioral focus has turned attention away from some of his own most astute observations—namely, those regarding the importance of the scales of units on which evolutionary processes work. There are other differences between evolutionary and behavioral archaeology, and we turn now to some of the most important ones.

Fundamental Differences

Those who have more than a passing familiarity with the literature on evolutionary archaeology will recognize much of the following. However, given that what we discuss seems to be the major stumbling block to understanding this archaeology and how it differs from other approaches, and that critics of evolutionary archaeology (e.g., Boone and Smith 1998; Spencer 1997) fail to grasp the significance of these differences, we believe a few points bear repeating. Rather than parrot what has been said before, we use somewhat different terms for critical concepts in order to make the significance of the message apparent.

Darwinian evolutionary theory deals with history—the explanation of why certain organisms do better than others in a particular environment (Mayr 1961). As a historical science, biological evolution differs ontologically and metaphysically from the ahistorical physical sciences (e.g., Lewontin 1974; Mayr 1987), though the latter offer explanations of how organisms function. If archaeology is taken to be a historical science, the same must hold true for it. The single most fundamental difference between the historical and ahistorical sciences resides in the studied phenomena themselves. As Ereshefsky (1992:91) points out,

> The units of evolutionary theory, taxa, are genealogical sequences of organisms which pass on *historically acquired* information. The units of chemistry and physics, on the other hand, do not consist of such sequences of objects. This difference affords evolutionary theory with a distinctive form of explanation . . . . In evolutionary biology, many (most?) of the similarities among the members of a taxon can be explained by those similarities being homologies. No such explanation is available for the similarities found among the units of physics and chemistry . . . . [Chemical and other similarities between] chunks of gold [do] not depend on the transmission of information from one chunk of gold to another [emphasis added].

Simply put, Darwinian evolution, because it concerns heritability and continuity, comprises a materialist ontology, which means that it views relations between and among phenomena as time- and spacebound (Dunnell 1982; O'Brien 1996a). As such, it contrasts sharply with the essentialist ontology of the physical sciences. In essentialism, the "essential properties" of an object dictate whether it is placed in one pile or another; variation between and among objects is viewed as nothing more than "annoying distraction" (Lewontin 1974:5). Importantly, it is not its focus on human behavior that makes behavioral archaeology essentialistic; rather, it is the belief that human behavior can be explained by inventing nomothetic-like principles. Recalling the "behavioralist premise," such principles allow not only the reconstruction

of past behaviors but also the construction of social-behavioral theory (Schiffer 1995b:34). But where is the explanatory theory?

Problems with Terms and Concepts

Schiffer (1996:648) states that because parts of evolutionary archaeology are variously without foundation, contra modern evolutionary biology, these parts undermine efforts to establish a workable theory. Much of Schiffer's criticism has roots in terminology that has plagued archaeology since the early 1960s. Archaeologists regularly confound the concepts of theory, hypothesis, model, and explanation with each other and with other concepts (Leonard and Reed 1996), and they occasionally provide differing definitions that range from redundant to unique. Evolutionary biologists routinely grapple with such issues (see the journal *Biology and Philosophy*), but archaeologists exacerbate the problem because they often do not define critical terms, assuming we all subconsciously share the same definitional perspective regarding these complex concepts. Schiffer's use of laws, lawlike statements, principles, and generalizations as synonyms, and ideas and theory as synonyms, illustrates this problem.

Schiffer finds it odd that evolutionary archaeology views laws and theories as true by definition— that is, true in terms of specifying logical relationships, not in some cosmological sense. We believe that this is odd only if one confounds the ideational realm with the phenomenological realm. Such is common in archaeology, where theory and hypothesis are often used synonymously. The most fundamental concepts underlying Darwinian evolutionary archaeology—variation, inheritance, natural selection, inclusive phenotype, replicative success, style, function, and so on—are definitionally true and relate to each other in such a way that evolutionary propositions about the past can be constructed. It is these evolutionary propositions— theoretical claims—about the real world that are testable. We call these hypotheses, which are derived from theory—a situation wholly consistent with practice in modern evolutionary biology, contra Schiffer's claims. With this recognition, Schiffer would no longer find it surprising that "theories have a substantial empirical content" (Schiffer 1996:649).

*The Case of Analogy: Immanent and
Configurational Properties*

Earlier we indicated that the reconstruction of cultural behavior, one basis of behavioral archaeology, is founded on what we view as the
inappropriate use of analogy. We emphasize that
we are not saying that analogy is an unacceptable
form of reasoning. But the considerable space in
archaeological literature devoted to discussing the
structure of analogical reasoning and identifying
its strengths and weaknesses (e.g., Simms 1992;
Stahl 1993) suggests that a good many archaeologists do not have a firm comprehension of such
reasoning. Perhaps this should be expected, given
that geologists (e.g., Shea 1982) and paleobiologists (e.g., Gould 1965), too, spend a great deal of
effort describing analogical reasoning within the
context of discussions of uniformitarianism.
Simpson's (1960, 1963, 1970) discussions are
helpful in this respect, largely because he
describes, in different terms, the sorts of linkages
between analogical reasoning and essentialism, as
well as the different sorts of linkages between such
reasoning and materialism.

What is the significance of the ontological distinction between immanence and configuration
when comparing behavioral and evolutionary
archaeology? In Simpson's view, the significance
is clear:

> The unchanging properties of matter and energy
> [chemistry, mechanics, physics] and the like-
> wise unchanging processes and principles aris-
> ing therefrom are immanent in the material
> universe. They are nonhistorical, even though
> they occur and act in the course of history. The
> actual state of the universe or of any part of it at
> a given time, its configuration, is not immanent
> and is constantly changing. It is contingent . . .
> or configurational . . . . History may be defined
> as configurational change through time (Simp-
> son 1963:24–25).

Simpson's "immanent" properties and
processes compose, in our terms, essentialism; his
"configurational" properties are historically contingent and comprise materialism. The dictum that
"the present is the key to the past" holds only with
respect to essentialist, or immanent, properties and
processes: "What we know (or theorize) about the
immanent characteristics of the universe is derived
from observation of the present" (Simpson

1970:81). Were it not for this simple fact, retrodic-
tion and prediction would be impossible, for the
cosmos would be truly random.

Immanent properties and processes are what
allow mechanical inferences to be made. The half-
life of ^{14}C is an immanent property that allows us
to calculate radiocarbon dates; the validity of the
radiocarbon-dating method hinges on the uniformitarianist assumption (analogical reasoning) that
the half-life of ^{14}C is the same, regardless of place
or time. Similarly, the processes that result in biological evolution—genetic transmission, mutation,
drift, differential reproduction and survival, and
selection—involve immanent properties and
processes. The history of an evolutionary lineage
is, however, configurational. Every fossil has "its
particular as well as its general configurational
properties, its significant balance of difference and
resemblance [to other fossils], not only because of
immanent properties of its constituents and immanent processes that had acted on it, but also
because of its history, the configurational sequence
by which these individual things arose" (Simpson
1963:27). Thus, "[h]istorical events, whether in the
history of the earth, the history of life, or recorded
human history, are determined by immanent characteristics of the universe [the source of laws] acting on and within particular configurations, and
never by either the immanent or the configurational alone" (Simpson 1963:29).

It is the task of the evolutionist—whether studying fossils, fruit flies, or sherds—to keep immanent
and configurational characteristics separate (Szalay
and Bock 1991). Note that we are not saying that
evolutionists should ignore immanent properties; in
fact, we have argued just the opposite (Lyman and
O'Brien 1998; O'Brien and Holland 1990, 1995b;
O'Brien et al. 1994). Failure to keep the essentialist ontology and its focus on immanent properties
distinct from configurational, or historically contingent, properties plagues other disciplines such as
paleoecology (e.g., Lawrence 1971)—a discipline
that Schiffer (1996:650) perceives as important to
modern evolutionary biology. But paleoecological
inference is not straightforward when the distinction between immanence and configuration is not
maintained (e.g., Paine 1983; Peterson 1983). Two
examples demonstrate that Schiffer (1996:651)
merges the two.

First, Schiffer (1996:650–651) cites Thomason's

(1995) *Functional Anatomy in Vertebrate Paleontology* as an example of the use of behavioral inference by evolutionary biologists, but if anything, "functional anatomy" is founded on immanent properties. We assume Schiffer realizes this, but his focus on function leads us to suspect that he tends to conflate immanent and configurational properties. Second, Schiffer identifies the McKellar principle—which specifies that in frequently maintained activity areas, only small artifacts remain behind as primary refuse (McKellar 1983)—as a nomothetic principle of human behavior. Simpson provides an excellent argument against such a principle being a behavioral law:

> A certain person's repeatedly picking up and dropping a certain stone may seem to be a recurrent event in all essentials, but there really is no applicable historical law. Abstraction of a law from such repeated events leads to a non-historical law of immanent relationships, perhaps in this case gravity and acceleration or perhaps of neurophysiology, and not to a historical law of which this particular person, picking up a certain stone, at a stated moment, and dropping it a definite number of times would be a determinate instance [Simpson 1963:29–30].

The message here is clear: the present is the key to the past only when immanent properties are involved. Despite the simplicity of what Simpson said, some investigators and commentators (e.g., Watson 1966) have failed to grasp its significance. Precisely the same misunderstanding exists within biological taxonomy (e.g., Mayr 1987, 1996), despite its having been discussed in that context for nearly four decades (e.g., Hull 1965; LaPorte 1997; Mayr 1959; Sober 1980).

Analogy as Behavioral Inference

Schiffer's (1996:656–657) discussion of "stimulated variation" and the notion that "invention is hardly a random process," while intriguing, is particularly conducive to illustrating some of the differences between nomothetic behavioral principles and Darwinian evolution. In short, "stimulated variation" is simply another way of saying that necessity is the mother of invention. Evolutionary archaeology agrees that certain selective environments likely do stimulate more invention than others, and invention is certainly not random except with respect to the operation of selection. But to invoke humankind's unique problem-solving abil-

ities as the cause of culture change is, however, to limit one's analysis substantially. As Steward (1956:72) noted more than 30 years ago: "[A] specific invention is not explained by saying that man is creative." Invoking invention, specifically as it relates to intent, is to view White's (1943:339) "urges, inherent in all living species, to live, to make life more secure, more rich, more full, to insure the perpetuation of the species" as the catalyst for change. Human intent is internal to the cultural system and results in a vitalistic evolutionism that is not testable because the conclusion regarding the mechanism of change is part of the theory.

Appeal to intent as ultimate cause echoes the late nineteenth-century view of Darwinian evolution. Between 1860 and 1900, one of the basic arguments against natural selection, expressed even by some of Darwin's strongest supporters—for example, American botanist Asa Gray—was that it said nothing about the ultimate source of variation. Spencer, for example, believed the problem with natural selection was that "it allowed the individual no freedom to improve itself by its own efforts" (Bowler 1990:171). During the early days of processual archaeology, the role of intent was seriously considered by some processualists. Flannery (1967:122), for example, observed that "individuals do make decisions, but evidence of these individual decisions cannot be recovered by archaeologists."

We do not know how to design a valid empirical test of stimulated variation in the prehistoric past. This, plus the form of evolution that results from invoking such mechanisms as catalysts of change, has prompted us and other evolutionary archaeologists to focus our efforts on areas other than the "variety-generating processes" that behavioral archaeology finds intriguing. Evolutionists have tended to concentrate on what happens to variation after it is generated, instead of looking for laws to explain why it was generated in the first place. It should by now be clear that such laws do not exist. There is, of course, a plethora of mechanisms we might call upon—diffusion, acculturation, invention, and the like—but these are immanent properties of how cultures work. Precisely how and why each of these mechanisms works in particular time-space-cultural contexts is, of course, configurational, or, as some (e.g., Beatty 1995) prefer to label it, historically contingent.

Ignoring for the moment style, or selectively neutral features, selection is the final arbiter of what is transmitted and perpetuated. It is opportunistic and tinkers with the variation available to produce something that works (Jacobs 1977), regardless of the source of variation (O'Brien and Holland 1995b). This point has been missed by other critics of evolutionary archaeology (Boone and Smith 1998; Spencer 1997). If a workable solution cannot be produced by such tinkering, the organism has little option but to buy a tombstone. If Schiffer is looking for first principles, the closest we can get is the principle of contingency—that what happens at point C is conditioned to some extent by what happened at point B, which itself is conditioned by what happened at point A. This gives evolutionary lineages their stochastic appearance.

Transmission

Citing Dunnell (1978), Schiffer (1996:648) states that compared to genetic transmission of variation, "cultural transmission involves different processes and mechanisms, and their understanding may require new laws and theories." He then notes that this statement is self-evident to behavioralists, though "selectionists have been slow to follow up its implications with appropriate nomothetic research" (Schiffer 1996:648). This is true, but not for the reasons Schiffer implies. No one would argue that the study of cultural transmission is unimportant. Researchers such as Boyd and Richerson (1985) and Cavalli-Sforza and Feldman (1981) have made significant strides in understanding the "processes and mechanisms" of cultural transmission. As yet, nothing they have proposed casts doubt on the application of Darwinian evolutionary theory to the archaeological record, though it has been observed that the strides made tend not to explain why transmission occurs the way that it does (Lyman and O'Brien 1998; Sober 1992). The greatest weakness of evolutionary archaeology to date is determining how to measure transmission. Evolutionary biologists know a great deal about the processes and mechanisms of genetic transmission and the appropriate units-genes. Anthropologists are struggling with similar units variously termed "memes," "culturgens," and the like, but how these are to be detected archaeologically is only now being made clear. Applications of transmission models by evo-

lutionary archaeologists suggest this may, for a time, be an empirical matter (e.g., Lipo et al. 1997; Neiman 1995).

We agree with Schiffer (1996:648) that it is important to distinguish between the processes that give rise to variation and those that result in the differential persistence of certain variants as opposed to others. In cultural systems, variation results in part from differences in human perception and intention. In fact, Rindos (1985, 1986) argued that if there is a genetic capacity for culture, it actually is a capacity for intentional behavior. Cultural systems, similar to organisms, tend to be overbuilt. That is, they tend to be plastic, adaptive systems capable of accomplishing much more than they regularly do (Boone and Smith 1998). Lability was, no doubt, built by selection (Gould 1991). Efforts to ascribe a function to every attribute of the archaeological record fail to recognize, for example, that the human organism uses only a fraction of its brain power, just as a computer can do much more than we ask of it. Such spandrels—metaphorically, architectural features resulting from design requirements but with no immediate function (Gould and Lewontin 1979; see also Gans 1988)—serve as a stockpile of variation—in some respects stylistic, or adaptively neutral, because they were not shaped by selection but rather by design requirements—that may, in a fluctuating selective environment, be co-opted for some future function (Gould and Vrba 1982). Herein may reside much of what evolutionary archaeology terms style (Dunnell 1978).

Gould (1991) argues that system lability, with particular reference to our overbuilt brains, is crucial to an evolutionary psychology. Fully in concert with a Darwinian viewpoint (Gans 1988; Mayr 1991), we can propose that self-awareness is a spandrel, an unintended outcome of selection having produced a somatic central-processing unit that, in the last 30 years, has built similar units from plastic, metal, and glass. Add reading, writing, language, and other uniquely human or cultural attributes to the list of human-associated traits, many of which may have begun as spandrels. If the last is true, then "[s]tructural consequences have outstripped original bases" (Gould 1991:59). We suspect that those archaeologists with leanings toward the various postprocessual programs could help us gain significant insights here.

Concluding Remarks

Behavioral archaeology originally sought to replace culture history and cultural reconstruction and to improve on processual archaeology. It is underlain by an essentialist ontology, which holds that human behavior, regardless of time or space, has configurational properties that all members of the species possess. In such a view, the configurational present is the key to the configurational past. The evolutionary program is underlain by a materialist ontology, which holds that things are always in the process of becoming something else. In such a historical view, the configurational present is not and cannot be the key to the configurational past. Temporal and spatial context matter a great deal. Only immanent properties can be keys to the historical particulars of the past (Lyman and O'Brien 1998). Scientists are free to pose whatever kinds of questions they wish, though logic dictates that the kinds of questions they ask be derived naturally from the kind of science being practiced. When that science is Darwinian evolution, the questions must be of the historical (configurational, contingent, materialist) kind. The last is not to say that essentialism and immanent properties do not have a role to play, because they certainly do. And, at the risk of sounding redundant, it is behavioralists such as Schiffer (e.g., Schiffer and Skibo 1987; Schiffer et al. 1994; Skibo et al. 1989; Vaz Pinto et al. 1987) who have made many of the important strides in understanding the nature of immanent properties.

We agree with Dunnell (1989) that one grand theory generates all of a field's hypotheses and links all explanations. Given our interest in studying the evolutionary history of cultures, the most workable theory is Darwinian evolutionism. Schiffer (1996) states, perhaps facetiously, that "[a]pparently, then, evolutionary theory alone can solve archaeology's myriad explanatory problems." To this we answer, No, it cannot. It can, however, solve archaeology's evolutionary problems. To this end, evolutionary archaeology has constructed concepts and principles to make the theory applicable to the archaeological record. Most fundamentally, artifacts, as well as behaviors that created them, are conceived of as being part of the human phenotype. The concepts of replicative success, style, and function are also necessary inclusions. In our view, modern Darwinian evolutionary theory dictates appropriate methods.

This is not to say that behavioral archaeology does not have significant things to contribute to an evolutionary theory, because it does—a point we have made in the past (O'Brien and Holland 1995b). Other programs, in particular evolutionary ecology (see papers in Maschner 1996) and postprocessualism, given the latter's interest in the symbolic, also have important contributions to make. However, before a truly integrative approach to the historical study of humans and their artifacts emerges—that is, one that investigates the evolutionary pathways of humans and the groups in which they live—we must make clear what the points of contention are among the various approaches. This of necessity will dictate that all interested parties, ourselves included, make sure that we understand the underlying premises of the various approaches in detail.

Acknowledgments. We thank E. J. O'Brien, L. Goldstein, L. Wandsnider, and G. Forbes for their many suggestions on how to improve the manuscript. Helpful comments were received from T. Van Pool, G. Raymond, G. Rakita, E. Hill, T. Hurt, L. Lundquist, J. O'Connell, and several anonymous reviewers. Finally, we thank M. B. Schiffer for his comments on the final draft. We appreciate his constructive criticism of it, but more importantly we appreciate the forums he has afforded evolutionary archaeologists over the years in the several journals he has edited.

References Cited

Beatty, J.
  1995 The Evolutionary Contingency Thesis. In *Concepts, Theories, and Rationality in the Biological Sciences*, edited by G. Wolters and J. G. Lennox, pp. 45–81. University of Pittsburgh Press, Pittsburgh.
Boone, J. L., and E. A. Smith
  1998 Is It Evolution Yet? A Critique of Evolutionary Archaeology. *Current Anthropology* 39:S141–S173.
Bowler, P. J.
  1990 *Charles Darwin: The Man and His Influence*. Blackwell, Oxford.
Boyd, R., and P. J. Richerson
  1985 *Culture and the Evolutionary Process*. University of Chicago Press, Chicago.
Brandon, R. N.
  1994 Theory and Experiment in Evolutionary Biology. *Synthese* 99:59–73.
Cavalli-Sforza, L. L., and M. W. Feldman
  1981 *Cultural Transmission and Evolution: A Quantitative Approach*. Princeton University Press, Princeton, New Jersey.
Dawkins, R.
  1990 *The Extended Phenotype: The Long Reach of the Gene*. Oxford University Press, Oxford.
Dunnell, R. C.
  1978 Style and Function: A Fundamental Dichotomy. *American Antiquity* 43:192–202.

1980 Evolutionary Theory and Archaeology. In *Advances in Archaeological Method and Theory*, vol. 3, edited by M. B. Schiffer, pp. 35–99. Academic Press, New York.

1982 Science, Social Science, and Common Sense: The Agonizing Dilemma of Modern Archaeology. *Journal of Anthropological Research* 38:1–25.

1989 Aspects of the Application of Evolutionary Theory in Archaeology. In *Archaeological Thought in America*, edited by C. C. Lamberg-Karlovsky, pp. 35–49. Cambridge University Press, Cambridge.

1992a Archaeology and Evolutionary Science. In *Quandaries and Quests: Visions of Archaeology's Future*, edited by L. Wandsnider, pp. 209–224. Occasional Paper No. 20. Center for Archaeological Investigations, Southern Illinois University, Carbondale.

1992b Is a Scientific Archaeology Possible? In *Metaarchaeology*, edited by L. Embree, pp. 75–97. Boston Studies in the Philosophy of Science, vol. 147. Kluwer, Dortrecht, The Netherlands.

1995 What Is It That Actually Evolves? In *Evolutionary Archaeology: Methodological Issues*, edited by P. A. Teltser, pp. 33–50. University of Arizona Press, Tucson.

1996a Foreword. In *Evolutionary Archaeology: Theory and Application*, edited by M. J. O'Brien, pp. vii–xii. University of Utah Press, Salt Lake City.

1996b Natural Selection, Scale, and Cultural Evolution: Some Preliminary Considerations. In *Evolutionary Archaeology: Theory and Application*, edited by M. J. O'Brien, pp. 24–29. University of Utah Press, Salt Lake City.

Dunnell, R. C., and J. K. Feathers
1991 Later Woodland Manifestations of the Malden Plain, Southeast Missouri. In *Stability, Transformation, and Variation: The Late Woodland Southeast*, edited by M. S. Nassaney and C. R. Cobb, pp. 21–45. Plenum Press, New York.

Dunnell, R. C., and R. D. Leonard (editors)
1998 Explanation of Change: Case Studies in Evolutionary Archaeology. Manuscript on file, Department of Anthropology, University of New Mexico, Albuquerque.

Dunnell, R. C, and R. J. Wenke
1980 Cultural and Scientific Evolution: Some Comments on *The Decline and Rise of Mesopotamian Civilization*, by N. Yoffee. *American Antiquity* 45:605–609.

Eldredge, N., and S. J. Gould
1972 Punctuated Equilibria: An Alternative to Phyletic Gradualism. In *Models in Paleobiology*, edited by T. J. M. Schopf, pp. 82–115. Freeman, Cooper, San Francisco.

Endler, J. A.
1986 *Natural Selection in the Wild*. Princeton University Press, Princeton, New Jersey.

Ereshefsky, M.
1992 The Historical Nature of Evolutionary Theory. In *History and Evolution*, edited by M. H. Nitecki and D. V. Nitecki, pp. 81–99. State University of New York Press, Albany.

Flannery, K. V.
1967 Culture History v. Cultural Process: A Debate in American Archaeology. *Scientific American* 217(2):119–122.

Gans, C.
1988 Adaptation and the Form-Function Relation. *American Zoologist* 28:681–697.

1993 On the Merits of Adequacy. *American Journal of Science* 293A:391–406.

Gingerich, P. D.
1991 Fossils and Evolution. In *Evolution of Life: Fossils,*

Molecules, and Culture, edited by S. Osawa and T. Honjo, pp. 3–20. Springer-Verlag, Tokyo.

Gould, S. J.
1965 Is Uniformitarianism Necessary? *American Journal of Science* 263:223–228.

1980 Paleontology. In *The Evolutionary Synthesis: Perspectives on the Unification of Biology*, edited by E. Mayr and W. B. Provine, pp. 153–172. Harvard University Press, Cambridge, Massachusetts.

1989 A Developmental Constraint in Cerion, with Comments on the Definition and Interpretation of Constraint in Evolution. *Evolution* 43:516–539.

1991 Exaptation: A Crucial Tool for an Evolutionary Psychology. *Journal of Social Issues* 47(3):43–65.

1995a A Task for Paleobiology at the Threshold of Majority. *Paleobiology* 21:1–14.

1995b Tempo and Mode in the Macroevolutionary Reconstruction of Darwinism. In *Tempo and Mode in Evolution*, edited by W. M. Fitch and F. J. Ayala, pp. 125–144. National Academy Press, Washington, D.C.

1997 The Exaptive Excellence of Spandrels as a Term and Prototype. *Proceedings of the National Academy of Sciences* 94:10750–10755.

Gould, S. J., and N. Eldredge
1993 Punctuated Equilibrium Comes of Age. *Nature* 366:223–227.

Gould, S. J., and R. C. Lewontin
1979 The Spandrels of San Marco and the Panglossian Paradigm: A Critique of the Adaptationist Programme. *Proceedings of the Royal Society of London* series B, 205:581–598.

Gould, S. J., and E. S. Vrba
1982 Exaptation—A Missing Term in the Science of Form. *Paleobiology* 8:4–15.

Hull, D. L.
1965 The Effect of Essentialism on Taxonomy—Two Thousand Years of Stasis. *British Journal for the Philosophy of Science* 15:314–326; 16:1–18.

Jacobs, F.
1977 Evolution and Tinkering. *Science* 196:1161–1166.

LaPorte, J.
1997 Essential Membership. *Philosophy of Science* 64:96–112.

LaPorte, L. F.
1983 Simpson's Tempo and Mode in Evolution Revisited. *Proceedings of the American Philosophical Society* 127:365–417.

Lawrence, D. R.
1971 The Nature and Structure of Paleoecology. *Journal of Paleontology* 45:593–607.

Leonard, R. D., and G. T. Jones
1987 Elements of an Inclusive Evolutionary Model for Archaeology. *Journal of Anthropological Archaeology* 6:199–219.

Leonard, R. D., and H. E. Reed
1993 Population Aggregation in the Prehistoric American Southwest: A Selectionist Model. *American Antiquity* 58:648–661.

1996 Theory, Models, Explanation, and the Record: Response to Kohler and Sebastian. *American Antiquity* 61:603–608.

Lewontin, R. C.
1974 *The Genetic Basis of Evolutionary Change*. Columbia University Press, New York.

Lipo, C., M. Madsen, R. C. Dunnell, and T. Hunt
1997 Population Structure, Cultural Transmission, and Frequency Seriation. *Journal of Anthropological Archaeology* 16:301–333.

Lyman, R. L., and M. J. O'Brien
1997 The Concept of Evolution in Early Twentieth-Century Americanist Archaeology. In *Rediscovering Darwin: Evolutionary Theory in Archaeological Explanation,* edited by C. M. Barton and G. A. Clark, pp. 21–48. Archeological Papers No. 7. American Anthropological Association, Arlington, Virginia.
1998 The Goals of Evolutionary Archaeology: History and Explanation. *Current Anthropology* 39, in press.
Lyman, R. L., M. J. O'Brien, and R. C. Dunnell
1997 *The Rise and Fall of Culture History.* Plenum, New York.
McKellar, J. A.
1983 *Correlates and the Explanation of Distributions.* Atlatl, Occasional Papers No. 4. Anthropology Club, University of Arizona, Tucson.
Maschner, H. D. G. (editor)
1996 *Darwinian Archaeologies.* Plenum, New York.
Mayr, E.
1959 Darwin and the Evolutionary Theory in Biology. In *Evolution and Anthropology: A Centennial Appraisal,* edited by B. J. Meggers, pp. 1–10. Anthropological Society of Washington, Washington, D.C.
1961 Cause and Effect in Biology. *Science* 134:1501–1506.
1973 *Populations, Species, and Evolution.* Harvard University Press, Cambridge, Massachusetts.
1987 The Ontological Status of Species: Scientific Progress and Philosophical Terminology. *Biology and Philosophy* 2:145–166.
1991 *One Long Argument: Charles Darwin and the Genesis of Modern Evolutionary Thought.* Harvard University Press, Cambridge, Massachusetts.
1996 What Is a Species, and What Is Not? *Philosophy of Science* 63:262–277.
Neiman, F.
1995 Stylistic Variation in Evolutionary Perspective: Inferences from Decorative Diversity and Inter-assemblage Distance in Illinois Woodland Ceramic Assemblages. *American Antiquity* 60:7–36.
Nitecki, M. H., and D. V. Nitecki (editors)
1992 *History and Evolution.* State University of New York Press, New York.
O'Brien, M. J.
1996a The Historical Development of an Evolutionary Archaeology. In *Darwinian Archaeologies,* edited by H. D. G. Maschner, pp. 17–32. Plenum, New York.
O'Brien, M. J. (editor)
1996b *Evolutionary Archaeology: Theory and Application.* University of Utah Press, Salt Lake City.
O'Brien, M. J., and R. C. Dunnell (editors)
1998 *Changing Perspectives on the Archaeology of the Central Mississippi Valley.* University of Alabama Press, Tuscaloosa.
O'Brien, M. J., and T. D. Holland
1990 Variation, Selection, and the Archaeological Record. In *Archaeological Method and Theory,* vol. 2, edited by M. B. Schiffer, pp. 31–79. University of Arizona Press, Tucson.
1992 The Role of Adaptation in Archaeological Explanation. *American Antiquity* 57:36–59.
1995a The Nature and Premise of a Selection-based Archaeology. In *Evolutionary Archaeology: Methodological Issues,* edited by P. A. Teltser, pp. 175–200. University of Arizona Press, Tucson.
1995b Behavioral Archaeology and the Extended Phenotype. In *Expanding Archaeology,* edited by J. M. Skibo, W. H. Walker, and A. E. Nielsen, pp. 143–161. University of Utah Press, Salt Lake City.

O'Brien, M. J., T. D. Holland, R. J. Hoard, and G. L. Fox
1994 Evolutionary Implications of Design and Performance Characteristics of Prehistoric Pottery. *Journal of Archaeological Method and Theory* 1:259–304.
O'Hara, R. J.
1988 Homage to Clio, or, Toward an Historical Philosophy for Evolutionary Biology. *Systematic Zoology* 37:142–155.
Paine, R. T.
1983 On Paleoecology: An Attempt to Impose Order on Chaos. *Paleobiology* 9:86–90.
Peterson, C. H.
1983 The Pervasive Biological Explanation. *Paleobiology* 9:429–436.
Phillips, P.
1955 American Archaeology and General Anthropological Theory. *Southwestern Journal of Anthropology* 11:246–250.
Reid, J. J., W. L. Rathje, and M. B. Schiffer
1974 Expanding Archaeology. *American Antiquity* 39:125–126.
Reid, J. J., M. B. Schiffer, and W. L. Rathje
1975 Behavioral Archaeology: Four Strategies. *American Anthropologist* 77:864–869.
Richards, R. I.
1992 Evolution. In *Keywords in Evolutionary Biology,* edited by E. F. Keller and E. A. Lloyd, pp. 95–105. Harvard University Press, Cambridge, Massachusetts.
Rindos, D.
1985 Darwinian Selection, Symbolic Variation, and the Evolution of Culture. *Current Anthropology* 26:65–88.
1986 The Evolution of the Capacity for Culture: Sociobiology, Structuralism, and Cultural Selection. *Current Anthropology* 27:315–332.
Rosenberg, M.
1994 Pattern, Process, and Hierarchy in the Evolution of Culture. *Journal of Anthropological Archaeology* 13:307–340.
Schiffer, M. B.
1972 Archaeological Context and Systemic Context. *American Antiquity* 37:156–165.
1976 *Behavioral Archeology.* Academic Press, New York.
1990 The Influence of Surface Treatment on Heating Effectiveness of Ceramic Vessels. *Journal of Archaeological Science* 17:373–381.
1995a *Behavioral Archaeology: First Principles.* University of Utah Press, Salt Lake City.
1995b Social Theory and History in Behavioral Archaeology. In *Expanding Archaeology,* edited by J. M. Skibo, W. H. Walker, and A. E. Nielsen, pp. 22–35. University of Utah Press, Salt Lake City.
1996 Some Relationships between Behavioral and Evolutionary Archaeologies. *American Antiquity* 61:643–662.
Schiffer, M. B., and J. M. Skibo
1987 Theory and Experiment in the Study of Technological Change. *Current Anthropology* 28:595–622.
Schiffer, M. B., J. M. Skibo, T. C. Boelke, M. A. Neupert, and M. Aronson
1994 New Perspectives on Experimental Archaeology: Surface Treatments and Thermal Response of the Clay Cooking Pot. *American Antiquity* 59:197–217.
Shea, J. H.
1982 Twelve Fallacies of Uniformitarianism. *Geology* 10:455–460.
Simms, S. R.
1992 Ethnoarchaeology: Obnoxious Spectator, Trivial

Pursuit, or the Keys to a Time Machine? In *Quandaries and Quests: Visions of Archaeology's Future*, edited by L. Wandsnider, pp. 186–198. Occasional Paper No. 20. Center for Archaeological Investigations, Southern Illinois University, Carbondale.

Simpson, G. G.
1937a *Notes on the Clark Fork, Upper Paleocene, Fauna.* American Museum Novitates No. 954. American Museum of Natural History, New York.
1937b Patterns of Phyletic Evolution. *Geological Society of America Bulletin* 48:303–314.
1937c Super-Specific Variation in Nature and in Classification from the View-Point of Paleontology. *American Naturalist* 71:236–267.
1944 *Tempo and Mode in Evolution.* Columbia University Press, New York.
1960 The History of Life. In *Evolution after Darwin, vol. 1: The Evolution of Life*, edited by S. Tax, pp. 117–180. University of Chicago Press, Chicago.
1961 *Principles of Animal Taxonomy.* Columbia University Press, New York.
1963 Historical Science. In *The Fabric of Geology*, edited by C. C. Albritton, Jr., pp. 24–48. Freeman, Cooper, Stanford, California.
1970 Uniformitarianism: An Inquiry into Principle, Theory, and Method in Geohistory and Biohistory. In *Essays in Evolution and Genetics in Honor of Theodosius Dobzhansky*, edited by M. K. Hecht and W. C. Steere, pp. 43–96. Appleton, New York.
1975 Recent Advances in Methods of Phylogenetic Inference. In *Phylogeny of Primates: A Multidisciplinary Approach*, edited by W. P. Luckett and F. S. Szalay, pp. 3–19. Plenum, New York.

Skibo, J. M., M. B. Schiffer, and K. C. Reid
1989 Organic Tempered Pottery: An Experimental Study. *American Antiquity* 54:122–146.

Skibo, J. M., W. H. Walker, and A. E. Nielsen (editors)
1995 *Expanding Archaeology.* University of Utah Press, Salt Lake City.

Sober, E.
1980 Evolution, Population Thinking, and Essentialism. *Philosophy of Science* 47:350–383.

1992 Models of Cultural Evolution. In *Trees of Life*, edited by P. Griffiths, pp. 17–39. Kluwer, Dordrecht, The Netherlands.

Spencer, C. S.
1997 Evolutionary Approaches in Archaeology. *Journal of Archaeological Research* 5:209–264.

Stahl, A. B.
1993 Concepts of Time and Approaches to Archaeological Reasoning in Historical Perspective. *American Antiquity* 58:235–260.

Steward, J. H.
1956 Cultural Evolution. *Scientific American* 194(5):69–80.

Szalay, F. S., and W. J. Bock
1991 Evolutionary Theory and Systematics: Relationships between Process and Pattern. *Zeitschrift für Zoologische Systematik und Evolutionsforschung* 29:1–39.

Thomason, J. J.
1995 *Functional Morphology in Vertebrate Paleontology.* Cambridge University Press, Cambridge.

Vaz Pinto, I., M. B. Schiffer, S. Smith, and J. M. Skibo
1987 Effects of Temper on Ceramic Abrasion Resistance: A Preliminary Investigation. *Archeomaterials* 1:119–134.

Watson, R. A.
1966 Discussion: Is Geology Different: A Critical Discussion of "The Fabric of Geology." *Philosophy of Science* 33:172–185.

White, L. A.
1943 Energy and the Evolution of Culture. *American Anthropologist* 45:335–356.

Willey, G. R.
1953 Archaeological Theories and Interpretation: New World. In *Anthropology Today*, edited by A. L. Kroeber, pp. 361–385. University of Chicago Press, Chicago.

Received March 10, 1997; revised February 3, 1998; revised February 12, 1998.

THE SCIENTIFIC NATURE OF POSTPROCESSUALISM

Christine S. VanPool and Todd L. VanPool

The compatibility of processual and postprocessual archaeology has been heavily debated. This discussion is frequently phrased in terms of scientific vs. nonscientific/humanistic archaeology. We suggest that the "postprocessual debate" is based on a mischaracterization of science that is pervasive in archaeology, and is largely unnecessary when a more reasonable view of the nature of science is considered. To demonstrate this point, we begin our discussion by identifying several commonalities within most postprocessual approaches to provide a foundation for our discussion. We then consider the two classic criteria used to differentiate science and nonscience, Baconian inductivism and falsification, and demonstrate why these views lead to an incomplete and inaccurate understanding of science. We next examine seven attributes that are commonly accepted as characteristics of science in order to provide a more accurate view of the nature and workings of science. Based on this discussion, we argue that much postprocessual research is in fact scientific, and we ultimately conclude that postprocessual approaches as currently applied can contribute to a scientific understanding of the archaeological record.

La compatibilidad del procesualismo y postprocesualismo se ha discutido extensivamente. Con frecuencia este debate supone una oposición fundamental entre la arqueología científica y la arqueología humanística. Sugeremos que el debate procesual-postprocesual se deriva de un entendimiento falso del método científico, desgraciadamente muy común en la arqueología, y que es posible tomar una perspectiva más balanceada. Para desarrollar nuestras ideas, comenzamos con identificar aspectos comunes de la mayoría de las posiciones teóricas del postprocesualismo. Consideramos los dos criterios típicamente usados para distinguir lo científico de lo no científico, el razonamiento inductivo de Bacon y la falsificación, y demostramos que estas perspectivas nos dan un entendimiento incompleto y distorsionado de la ciencia. Identificamos siete cualidades de la ciencia comunamente aceptadas para mejor entender cómo funciona el método científico. En base a esta discusión, proponemos que muchos estudios postprocesuales merecen llamarse científicos, y que el postprocesualismo puede contribuir al entendimiento científico de los restos arqueológicos.

With the development of postprocessual approaches in the 1980s, the debate over the correct or appropriate form of archaeology has been intense (see Binford 1989; Hodder et al. 1995; Lamberg-Karlovsky 1989; Maschner 1996; Pinsky and Wylie 1989; Preucel, ed. 1991; Preucel and Hodder 1996; Trigger 1989a; Yoffee and Sherratt 1993). Archaeological theory appears to have fragmented into "a thousand archaeologies" (Schiffer 1988:479). A great deal of recent theoretical discussion has focused on the relationships and similarities between these apparently distinct approaches (e.g., Boone and Smith 1998; Patterson 1990; Schiffer 1996; Skibo et al. 1995; Spencer 1997; Trigger 1989a; Wylie 1993), especially the relationships between processual and postprocessual frameworks. This discussion, which has been called "the postprocessual debate" (Hodder 1997:691), has been the focal point for

many of the discourses concerning archaeological theory (e.g., Binford 1989; Clark 1993; Cowgill 1993; Duke 1995; Earle 1991; Earle and Preucel 1987; Hodder 1991a; Kosso 1991; Preucel, ed. 1991, 1995; Renfrew 1989; Saitta 1992; Trigger 1991; Tschauner 1996; Watson 1990, 1991; Watson and Fotiadas 1990; Wylie 1993).

Often, the "postprocessual debate" has been phrase in terms of scientific versus humanistic/nonscientific archaeology (e.g., Bintliff 1991, 1992; Tilley 1992; Watson 1993). For example, many postprocessualists have argued that the positivist, scientific approach of the "New Archaeology" is inadequate (see Clark 1993:224; Duke 1995; Gibbon 1989; Hodder 1986, 1991a; Leone 1991; Shanks and Tilley 1987; Vinsrygg 1988; Wylie 1992a). They suggest that they can provide insightful alternative interpretations by abandoning the requirements of an "explicitly scientific archaeol-

Christine S. VanPool and **Todd L. VanPool** ∎ Department of Anthropology, University of New Mexico, Albuquerque, New Mexico 87131–1086

American Antiquity, 64(1), 1999, pp. 33–53
Copyright © 1999 by the Society for American Archaeology

ogy" (sensu Watson et al. 1984) as outlined by the processualists through the early 1980s, and by adopting a more humanistic approach. While most do not reject science as a whole (e.g., they will still use radiocarbon dates), they do reject the applicability of science in certain aspects of their work (e.g., Bapty 1990; Shanks and Tilley 1992:243; Yates 1990; see Watson 1990:674–679). Others do not reject "science" *per se*, but instead reject scientism (Hodder 1986:xiv; Preucel 1991b; Shanks and Tilley 1992:48) and a view of science that constrains research questions and approaches (Hodder 1991a:37–40; Leone 1986:431–432). In response, though, many processualists have contended that postprocessual approaches are unable to provide useful or rigorous insight into the archaeological record, and therefore the application of these approaches waste important archaeological resources (Binford 1986, 1987, 1989:27–40; Bintliff 1991; O'Shea 1992; Watson and Fotiadis 1990; R. Watson 1990, 1991). Unfortunately, much of this discussion has been argumentative and hostile in its tone[1].

Debate over appropriate archaeological method and theory is an important component of archaeology, because our theoretical structures affect the very nature of archaeology as a discipline. Alternate theoretical perspectives will affect the questions archaeologists ask and the types of data that they collect to answer their questions. If processual and postprocessual approaches are in fact different and incompatible, then archaeology is no longer a coherent discipline. Researchers such as P. Watson (1991) have suggest that this fragmentation could have the effect of causing archaeology to loose its intellectual, scientific, and funding credibility. If such a fission occurs, archaeology would necessarily undergo a split similar to the division between classical archaeology and anthropological archaeology, or between cultural historic archaeology and processual archaeology. Such a fundamental shift in archaeology is unpalatable for many researchers, and several authors have attempted to reconcile processual and postprocessual approaches in various ways (Duke 1995; Preucel, ed. 1991, 1995; Schiffer 1991; Tschauner 1996; Wylie 1992a, 1992b).

Various authors have argued that the differences between postprocessual and processual approaches are very limited and relatively unimportant (Gibbon

1989; Kohl 1993; Kosso 1991; Preucel 1991a, 1995; Schiffer 1995; Trigger 1989a, 1989b). Generally, these arguments are based on the assertion that there are "many types of science," and that processual and postprocessual both are legitimate scientific approaches (e.g., Preucel, ed. 1991, 1995). Unfortunately, there has been little explicate discussion of what it is that makes some postprocessual approaches scientific or what makes postprocessual and processual approaches compatible. As a result, the split and then the subsequent reconciliation remain largely sociological movements.

We agree with Schiffer (1996:643) and Redman (1991) that the division of archaeologists into antagonist camps across which little discussion of substantive issues is possible is both unnecessary and harmful to archaeology as an intellectual endeavor. However, the reconciliation of processual and postprocessual approaches must be based on more than a general commitment to "just get along." Discussions between practioners of alternate theoretical structures must be based on a correct understanding of the underlying points of contention and the relationship between the two approaches.

We suggest that much of the discussion of the relationship between processual and postprocessual archaeology is based on subtle, yet important, misconceptions. Specifically, we argue that much of it is based on an incorrect view of the nature of science, and that many postprocessual archaeologies are in fact scientific. To support this position, we will discuss seven recognized characteristics of science and demonstrate that processualism and postprocessualism both possess most of these characteristics. We therefore suggest that the conflict between the practitioners of processual and postprocessual archaeological approaches is largely unnecessary, not because of the social implications of the conflict, but because of their substantive intellectual similarities.

This paper is organized into two sections. The first section provides a foundation for discussion by presenting commonalities in postprocessual perspectives. Specifically, we discuss how the concepts of meanings, interpretations, social structures, and hermeneutics provide a foundation for postprocessual approaches. Because of the diversity of postprocessual approaches (Hodder 1991a:37), this discussion is necessarily general. We realize that the generalizations we present do not reflect the variation among the individual post-processual approaches and refer readers interested in the nuances of these approaches to any of the excellent overviews available (e.g., Hodder et al. 1995; Preucel 1995; Trigger 1989a; Wylie 1992a). We do suggest, however, that few postprocessualists will find our discussion at odds with the general principles underlying most postprocessual theories.

The second section discusses the nature and demarcations (i.e., identifying characteristics) of science, and illustrates why much of postprocessual archaeology is, in reality, scientific. The suggestion that much of the recent postprocessual research is scientific is not unique to us. For example, Pruecel (1991a:287, 1995) suggests that there are different types of science, which includes types that are compatible with postprocessual and processual research. However, what has been missing from the discussion, and what this article is intended to provide, is an explicit identification of what it is about a portion of postprocessual research that makes it scientific. We will accomplish this task by identifying the requirements for a scholarly pursuit to qualify as science, and then demonstrating that much of the recent postprocessual research meets these requirements.

Specifically, we will address the "classic" demarcation criteria proposed by Hempel (1965) and Popper (1980) and will argue that neither of their criteria are acceptable. Instead, we present seven characteristics typifying science, and argue that many postprocessual approaches process these characteristics. Our ultimate goal is not to change postprocessual research. Instead, we wish to demonstrate that the conflict between the practitioners of the various perspectives is unnecessary, and that postprocessual and processual approaches are compatible and can contribute in conjunction with one another to a rigorous understanding of the archaeological record.

While processual and postprocessual research may entail different intellectual approaches to the archaeological record, the diversity in approaches can be beneficial, in so far that they each force the other to examine their underlying assumptions. Additionally, the diversity in research questions and analytical approaches may produce a more complete understanding of the past. However, these potential benefits of diversity are only possible if the underlying similarities and differences are

properly understood. By considering why much of the recent postprocessual research is science, this paper hopes to demonstrate that postprocessualism can contribute to a scientific, rigorous understanding of the past.

Postprocessual Archaeology

Postprocessual archaeology is a manifestation of the growing influence of postmodern thought in the social sciences (Bintliff 1991; Duke 1995:211; Knapp 1996; Watson 1990:675). Postmodernism shares many elements with critical theory, feminist theory, hermeneutics, neo-Marxism, Western Marxism, and poststructuralism (Rosenau 1992:13). As a general movement, postmodernism is a reaction against modernism, i.e., the Enlightenment. It is largely based on the beliefs that science is not objective, not based on absolute and true laws, and in practice has not improved humanity (Bintliff 1991; Rosenau 1992). In fact, some postmodernists (and postprocessualists) argue that adherence to rigid positivist science has dehumanized disciplines such as archaeology by removed the spiritual nature from the human experience by saying non-empirical entities don't exist (Fields 1995; see Leone 1986:431–432; Shanks 1992; Shanks and Tilley 1987, 1992)[2]. Extreme postmodernism questions epistemological and ontological assumptions, refutes methodology, resists knowledge claims, obscures all versions of truth, challenges beliefs about reality, and discards policy recommendations based on any political, religious, or social knowledge systems (Fields 1995; Rosenau 1992:3).

In comparison to other social sciences such as psychology and sociology, archaeology has been slow to incorporate elements of postmodernist thought (Bintliff 1991:275; Rosenau 1992). In fact, just as the postmodern movement was gaining momentum in philosophy during the 1960s, archaeologists were beginning to apply the framework of logical positivism. It was almost two decades before postmodernism's influence was felt in archaeology through the works of Ian Hodder in the early 1980s (Bintliff 1991; Hodder 1982). This brand of postmodern thought is commonly called postprocessualism because it was viewed as a reaction to perceived weaknesses of the processual school. Preucel (1995) has noted, though, that postprocessualism is no longer just a critique of the processual program, but instead has its own research programs and methodologies.

As with the postmodern movement in philosophy, there is no unified postprocessual school of thought within archaeology (Hodder 1991a:37-38). Discussing postprocessual approaches in a general sense is problematic, because they reject unifying or "static" theory and methodology (Hodder et al.1995; Patterson 1989, 1990; Preucel 1995; Rosenau 1992; Trigger 1989a; although see Hodder 1997). We will not separate the different approaches into distinct schools, but, rather will instead attempt to examine their commonalities (for discussion of the various postprocessual schools see Patterson 1989, 1990; Preucel 1995; Trigger 1989a). As Trigger (1989c, 1991) has argued, though, we feel it is important to differentiate between two "types" of postprocessualists: moderate postprocessualists and the hyperrelativists.[3]

Hyperrelativist research follows the more extreme postmodernists in rejecting all truth and knowledge, and questioning the human ability to perceive any sort of personal or physical reality (Miller and Tilley 1984:151; Rosenau 1992; Shanks and Tilley 1992; Shanks 1992; Trigger 1989c, 1991). These individuals argue that experience is inherently subjective, and that we are unaware of our own biases or underlying motivations (Englestad 1991; Shanks and Tilley 1992). As a result, they contend there is no aspect of the archaeological record, prehistoric peoples, or knowledge about either the present or the past that can be understood through archaeological research. Any analysis of the archaeological record, therefore, is completely subjective; interpretations are created by our own biases. Additionally, our interpretations cannot be communicated to others, since all knowledge is subjective and there is no way to accurately force another individual to think exactly the same thought. Therefore, any interpretation we might try to communicate to others will be mixed with their own biases and will necessarily be different from our own understanding.

Because our interpretations are created by our own biases which are partly a result of our group ideology, the study of the archaeological record is inherently political according to some individuals (Englestad 1991; Fotiadis 1994; Handsman and Leone 1989; Leone 1986; Leone et al. 1987; Leone and Preucel 1992). Thus, hyperrelativists view the study of the archaeological record as a means of accomplishing specific political goals (i.e., empowering disenfranchised groups), not as something worthy of study in-and-of-itself (Fotiadis 1994; Shanks and Tilley 1987; Trigger 1989c:77; Watson 1990). Such individuals act in a manner similar to lawyers; they use the evidence gained from the archaeological record as a means of argumentation and persuasion, but they may not necessarily attempt to develop a systematic body of knowledge about the archaeological past or the archaeologist's present.

In contrast, most moderate postprocessual archaeologists recognize that the archaeological record does exist and that it can be studied. They do not reject all knowledge in an absolute way, but instead tend to concentrate on identifying those assumptions that have been uncritically and often subconsciously accepted (Conkey and Spector 1984; Englestad 1991; Gero 1983; Handsman and Leone 1989; Hodder 1986; Leone et al. 1987; Leone 1991; Rosenau 1992:8; Shanks 1992; Shanks and Tilley 1992). Instead of simply deconstructing others' work, postprocessualists have worked to reconstruct archaeology in a less harsh or modernistic framework by developing "interpretations" without the claim of absolute objectivity.

Most postprocessualists also believe that archaeological research is inherently political (Arnold 1990; Fotiadis 1994; Leone 1986, 1991; Leone et al. 1987; Leone and Preucel 1992). Their interpretations are intended to empower aboriginal and other disenfranchised groups, show inequities or inconsistencies within the current social structures, and challenge the dominant views of archaeological knowledge. However, they argue that the archaeological record places limits on their interpretations. As Hodder (1986:16) states, "the real world does constrain what we can say about it." These postprocessual archaeologists believe that: 1) there is a reality in that objects are empirical and real, although objects may have multiple social meanings (Leone 1986; Leone et al. 1987), 2) their own writings must be logically coherent and non-contradictory (Hodder et al.1995; Hodder 1989; Renfrew 1989; Trigger 1989b), and 3) their conclusions must be plausible given the archaeological data and their own understanding (Shanks and Hodder 1995). Thus, the political nature of postprocessualism is not the driving force behind its interpretations, but is rather a portion of the process for developing them (Leone 1986; Leone et al. 1987; Leone and Preucel 1992; Trigger 1989c, 1991). The following discussion is intended to apply to the vast majority of postprocessualists who reject hyperrelativism.

The Postprocessualist Deconstruction of Processualism

Many scholars in the 1970s were growing increasingly pessimistic with processual archaeology as presented by Binford (1968), Fritz and Plog (1970) and Watson et al. (1971). Their criticisms were threefold. First and foremost, postprocessualists (and many processualists) argued that there are no (or at the least only a very limited number of) universal generalities, laws, or absolute truths of human behavior to be found by archaeologists (Hodder 1986, 1992; Leone 1986; Shanks and Hodder 1995; Shanks and Tilley 1987; Trigger 1993; see also Clarke 1979; Flannery 1986; Renfrew 1989). They further argued that archaeological knowledge is subjective, not objective (Hodder 1986; Shanks and Hodder 1995; Shanks and Tilley 1987, 1992). Postprocessualists discarded the natural science model of archaeology underlying the positivist approach (Hodder 1991a). They also rejected generalizing theory and replaced it with a particularist view of culture; by knowing the specific history of the culture, the postprocessual archaeologists argued they could provide understandings of certain aspects of society (e.g., symbolism and ideology) that could never be obtained using a strict positivistic framework. Thus, postprocessual archaeologists believed that archaeology should be and is a humanistic field of inquiry, rather than a natural science (Bawden 1996; Hodder et al. 1995; Shanks 1992; Shanks and Tilley 1987, 1992; Vinsrygg 1988).

Another philosophical disagreement between the postprocessual and processual approaches is that the postprocessual archaeologists believe that society is not composed of a set of patterns that accurately and absolutely produce behavior. Postprocessual archaeologists criticized the processualists for asking questions that only pertain to the collective group (i.e., Why societies change?, How did societies impact one another?, and so on) (Cowgill 1993; Shanks 1992; Shanks and Tilley 1987; Wylie 1992a). The postprocessualists believed that such an approach causes individuals to be systematically ignored (Vinsrygg 1988). Postprocessual archaeologists also disagree with some processualists' view that environmental or external social forces are the major factors causing cultural change in a society, which are inherent in system theories, functionalism, and ecological approaches (Hodder 1982; Leone 1986; Leone et al. 1987; Preucel 1995; Trigger 1993). Instead, postprocessualists argue that the social negotiation of individuals causes cultural change. Change is thus made by individuals, and the understanding of culture change requires an understanding of the motives and intentions of individuals, not groups, societies, or cultures (Bawden 1996; Thomas 1991,1996; Trigger 1993). Therefore, postprocessual archaeologists argue that we should not look for patterns to define behavior, but should instead focus on the motivations and desires that drive people based on their "culturally constructed" perceptions of the world (Bawden 1996; Vinsrygg 1988).

Finally, postprocessual archaeologists rejected the categorization of societies into cultural evolutionary types such as band, tribes, chiefdoms, and states common in archaeology and anthropology. According to the postprocessualists, these groupings are totally subjective and do not accurately represent any aspect of the archaeological record (Bawden 1989; Hodder et al. 1995). This criticism has been echoed by researchers using different theoretical perspectives (Dunnell 1980; Fried 1967; Leonard and Jones 1987; Yoffee 1992).

Fundamental Concepts in Postprocessual Approaches

In addition to criticizing the processual archaeology program, postprocessual archaeologists have presented a series of general suggestions and goals they believe will lead to a richer understanding of the past. One major method of postprocessualism is *deconstruction* through critical hermeneutics (for discussion, see Bleicher 1980; Leone et al. 1987; Preucel 1991b,1995). Deconstruction in archaeology is partly an outgrowth of Marxist approaches created by the extension of the concept of ideology to archaeological research (Leone et al. 1987: 283–285). Ideology is the naturalization of unequal distribution of power and resources between social classes. Thus, ideology relates to social stratification, wealth holding, and power relations.

Postprocessualists observe that archaeology can serve as ideology by legitimizing current social structures (Leone 1986:427–431). Archaeological interpretations can therefore acquire meanings that are both intended and unintended by the researcher, but that are not inherent in the data themselves.

Deconstruction is accomplished when a researcher analyzes a text, revealing its contradictions, assumptions, and the author's acknowledged or unacknowledged intent. The goal of deconstruction for some postmodernists is not to improve, revise, offer a better version of the text, or to find the truth within the text, but to simply illuminate the logical and cultural weaknesses and biases within the work (Rosenau 1992). If carried to its logical extreme, deconstructionists would reject all empirical, political, social, and religious knowledge as biased (Yates 1990).

However, hermeneutics and deconstruction also can be used for knowledge construction and the evaluation of interpretations. Many postprocessualists use hermeneutics as a method (e.g., poststructuralist's hermeneutics, feminist's hermeneutics, Marxist's hermeneutics, or the hermeneutic spiral; for a discussion, see Hodder 1986; Mueller-Vollmer 1994; Preucel 1995). It is a way of evaluating interpretations of the past to determine if they are congruent with the theoretical concepts of the present, and then reexamining the theoretical concepts of the present to determine if they are congruent with the interpretations of the past. Likewise, deconstruction can help identify hidden biases allowing them to be directly evaluated, and potentially resulting in knowledge about the past that is less culturally contingent. The methods of deconstruction and hermeneutics can therefore help to establish the validity of archaeological interpretations, and help archaeologists modify their theoretical approaches so that they fit the "realities of archaeological data" (Leone et al. 1987:285).

Just as functional explanation is the heart of processual archaeology, social interpretations are the heart of postprocessual archaeology. Postprocessualists argue that there are no ultimate or correct interpretations. Instead, they argue that there may be many plausible interpretations consistent with the archaeological record. Therefore, postprocessualists expect a plurality of archaeological interpretations suited to different needs and desires

(Shanks and Hodder 1995). Although there may be infinite interpretations, postprocessualists do not believe all interpretations are valid (Hodder 1985; Preucel 1995). Most postprocessual archaeologists have several criteria for evaluating interpretations: 1) interpretations must be consistent with the data (Hodder 1992; Saitta 1992; Wylie 1993), 2) interpretations must take into account group needs, especially aboriginal or disenfranchised groups (Handsman and Leone 1989; Saitta 1992; Shanks and Tilley 1987), and 3) interpretations must be logically coherent (Hodder et al. 1995; Preucel 1995:161–162; Saitta 1992; Trigger 1993). Any interpretation that meets these criteria is plausible, and therefore an appropriate interpretation.

To meet these criteria, postprocessual archaeologists have developed several loose methodologies based on several general concepts. The core of their methodology is the use of some form of hermeneutics and/or contextualism to derive and evaluate interpretations from archaeological data (Bleicher 1980; Hodder 1986, 1991b, 1997; Hodder et al.1995; Mueller- Vollmer 1994; Preucel 1991b, 1995; Saitta 1992; Thomas 1996). Other important concepts including the use of meanings, interpretations, symbols, and social structures are discussed below.

Meanings, Interpretations, and Symbols

Postprocessual archaeologists are concerned with individuals, specifically how the social negotiations of individuals affect social structures represented by the archaeological record. Basic to their research, then, are the concepts of meaning, symbols, and interpretation. All three of these concepts are difficult to separate, but for the purpose of our argument, we think it is necessary to do so.

Social meaning can be given to material objects, people, societies, and places through interpretation. Interpretation and meaning are dictated by the ideology, the politics, and the religion of both past individuals and the archaeologist (Bapty and Yates 1990; Bawden 1996; Hodder 1992; Hodder et al. 1995; Leone 1991; Leone et al. 1987; Thomas 1991, 1996). As a result, postprocessual archaeologists are concerned with meanings, including both past and modern meanings, assigned to artifacts and features in the archaeological record. Many postprocessualists have argued that interpretations developed by archaeologists are related to each archaeologist's personal practices, methods, and cultural biases (Arnold 1990; Engelstad 1991; Gero 1991; Leone 1991; Leone et al. 1987). Therefore, archaeological interpretation is the extension of the "here and now" of the archaeologists into the past.

Meaning reflected in material symbols informs us of the meanings that were formed by and created in the political, ideological, and cultural structure of a society (Bawden 1995:268). Symbolism is the communication of important cultural information (i.e., cultural interpretation) through material means (e.g., objects, gestures, writing) (Hodder 1986; Hodder et al. 1995). Symbols are the center of the human existence, according to many postprocessualists. They are an integrated part of daily life and are the means through which people are socialized and controlled (Bawden 1996; Hodder 1986; Thomas 1996; Trigger 1993).

Leone (1986:417) argues that material objects can have a hierarchy of meanings stretching from ecological, technological, and demographic meanings, to vaguely defined ideological or religious meanings. The meanings of objects can be different at each level, and can be potentially contradictory. For example, the crown of a king can have the utilitarian meaning of a hat, a social meaning as a sign of authority, and an ideological meaning of a god or godliness. Each of these meanings represent different scales of meaning and none is more correct than the others.

Meanings are abstract—that is, they are separate from the artifact itself. Abstract meanings are completely subjective, and no longer share a link with the "objective world." Our common sense tells us that the artifact or object is real in-and-of-itself, but bringing meaning to the object involves abstractions (Shanks 1992:43). The specific meanings of objects or a set of objects will vary with the context of their use (Hodder 1992:109). Many postprocessual archaeologists view material culture in the context of human activity as a part of language and structure as seen through their use of hermeneutics. They suggest it is comparable with spoken or written language in its ability to order human life (Bawden 1996; Hodder 1986; Leone 1986; Thomas 1996). The ordering of objects through action can be used to communicate meanings in the same way that words, which also are symbols with a multitude of meanings, can. Additionally, the meaning of objects is tied to language because it

can only be expressed through language (Shanks and Tilley 1987).

The Concept of Social Structure

As with many of the concepts in postprocessual approaches, there is not a single unified concept of structure. What we consider important to this discussion is that many postprocessual archaeologists use sociological concepts of "structure" derived from various poststructuralists including Bourdieu (1977), Foucault (1970), Giddens (1984), and Heidegger (see Macquarrie and Robinson 1962) (for examples, see Bawden 1996; Hodder 1986; Thomas 1996). When used, these different approaches allow the researcher to:

1. interpret structures of past social actors (agencies),

2. find some of the shared knowledge that is constructed by the rules and institutions of a group of people through time and space through the discourses of Foucault (1970) or the continuity of Giddens (1984), or

3. determine how symbols, artifacts, meanings, interpretations, and structures can be explored (Preucel 1995).

Postprocessual and Scientific Approaches

We argue that the incompatibility between the recent processual and postprocessual programmes in archaeology is largely illusory; postprocessual approaches are more scientific than many practitioners of either group are willing to admit. Clearly, many postprocessual archaeologists believe that they use methods and theories that are incompatible with science to answer questions that science cannot address (Tilley 1992), a view that is accepted by many processualists (Binford 1989; Watson 1990; Yoffee 1992). This view has been succinctly summarized by Fotiadas (Watson and Fotiadas 1990:622) when he observed, "Watson's challenge to a 'Hodderian' approach to the prehistoric past follows forcefully: to claim that the study of the mental processes of prehistoric men and women are within the reach of science is to claim that we can communicate with the nonexistent." Many processualists and postprocessualists alike feel that postprocessual research falls outside of "science" and therefore postprocessualists are not scientists. This may be true for the hyperrelativists, but this is not the case for most postprocessualists.

We argue, along with others (e.g., Hodder 1989; Preucel 1991b, 1995; Renfrew 1989; Trigger 1989a,1989b), that most postprocessual and processual archaeologists have a very narrow and inaccurate view (i.e., "the legendary view") of science based on the logical positivist model, and that much of postprocessual archaeology is compatible with science and *is* scientific when a more realistic view of science is considered.

Demarcations of Science

No one has developed an universally accepted definition of science. However, in our common usage, science has a special meaning that distinguishes it from philosophy, religion, theoretical ethics, law, and art/aesthetics. It is not just a belief system, but is a method of inquiry in which knowledge is subject to revision. A commonly held view of science, especially among positivists, is illustrated by the idea of the "legendary scientist" (Kitcher 1992:3–10). The legendary view of science states that scientists are completely rational, objective observers who meticulously record data; propose logical hypotheses; evaluate every scientific perspective without the influence of greed, personality conflicts, or dogmatism; and will readily drop any aspect of their pet theories anytime that contradictory evidence suggests a better perspective. While this view is widely accepted, it is fictional, as many scientists have observed (see Woodward and Goodstein 1996 for a more complete discussion). Far from being supermen, scientists are humans that are driven by the same desires and weakness, e.g., greed, ambition, pride, cultural bias, as everyone else. Therefore, the demarcation (i.e., difference) between science and nonscience is based on the structure of the knowledge system, not the behavior of its practitioners.

Two demarcation criteria[4] have been presented and have at one time or another received considerable support. The first criterion, and the basis of the legendary science myth, was originally proposed by Francis Bacon. Baconian inductivists suggest that science is a uniquely structured reasoning system based on inductive logic. To separate science from nonscience, they use the demarcation that scientific investigation begins with scientists carefully recording aspects of the empirical world free from the bias of culture, religion, or theory. As observations are synthesized, patterns in the natural world

will become evident. Scientists then extrapolate from the patterns to propose hypotheses which they believe characterize the world, creating universal laws (Hempel 1965). Through this process, the Baconian inductivists argue that our descriptions of the world will become more accurate until they are perfect and true. According to the inductivist demarcation, then, science is different from other types of knowledge systems because of the presence of inductive logical and systematic observation leading to universal laws.

The Baconian inductivist view has been severely criticized. Popper (1980:34–37) argues that inductivist logic is inappropriate for scientific study. He refers to Hume's problem of induction in which the logical structure of inductive conclusions cannot be substantiated. The objection is simple; past experience cannot be used as a logically secure means of predicting future events. For example, we have all heard that the sun will come up tomorrow. An inductivist argument derived from this statement would be:

1. Every day of my life, the sun has come up every morning.
2. In the lives of all individuals who have lived in the past that I am aware of, the sun has risen every morning, therefore
3. The sun will come up tomorrow.

While past experience does suggest this is true, it is in no way logically valid to derive the conclusion (Statement 3) from the premises in Statements 1 and 2. The sun could blow up, or some supernatural force could stop the spinning of the world. However unlikely these events, they are logically consistent with, or at least not precluded by, Statements 1 and 2.

Popper (1980:34) also launches a more practical and potentially more damaging attack on the use of inductivist logic as a demarcation criterion. He observes that many commonly accepted nonscientific or pseudoscientific knowledge systems including religion, Freudian psychology, astrology, and water witching can all claim to be science based on inductivist logic and systematic observation. Therefore, this demarcation is practically insufficient since it will allow nonsciences to be classed as science.

An additional objection has been raised by Feyerabend (1975), Thagard (1978), and Woodward and Goodstein (1996). These authors observe that science simply cannot be done in accordance with the inductivist view, and that science would in fact be hurt if it tried to do so. They argue that scientists cannot record everything, and that scientists cannot be free from theoretical bias. These authors point out that an infinite number of possible observations can be made of any empirical phenomenon. It is only with a theoretical system that a problem can be addressed so that the important observations can be identified. They also argue that every observation is theory laden, since we must use language to conceptualize and describe our observation (see Hanson 1958:4–11). Language is based on previous experience and on our conceptual system. It is impossible, then, to have theory-free observations since observers interpret any event or observation on the basis of their language. All of these authors with the exception of Feyerabend (1975) also argue that if scientists tried to use an inductivist approach, the progress of science would be greatly impeded. According to these authors, scientists would waste resources gathering uninformative data, waste their time trying to be theory free, and, by rejecting the role of theory in science, reject the very basis of what makes science a progressive system for understanding the world.

In connection with his critique of Baconian inductivism, Popper (1980:78–92, 1963) argues that falsification is the best demarcation criterion. According to Popper, scientists should directly test hypotheses derived through theory against empirically derived data. They should organize their experiments to be able to provide information that could lead to the rejection of the hypotheses, and by association, the theory.[5] In this way, scientists will weed out poor theories that are in contradiction with nature and develop stronger theories. Bad science or nonscience will be characterized by not announcing in advance what types of evidence would lead to the falsification of a theory, ignoring or discarding contradictory evidence of a pet theory, introducing ad hoc hypotheses to protect a theory from falsification, or decreasing the scope of one's theory so that it does not apply to situations that might lead to its falsification.

Falsification, according to Popper, escapes the problem of induction by requiring the use of deductive logic. A scientific theory can come from any source including dreams, generalized patterns from previously observed data, or hunches (Popper

1980:31–32). However, expectations are derived from theory and must be compared to data. In contradiction to the inductive view presented above that relies on justification or verification (Watson et al. 1971, 1984), Popper's falsification criterion stipulates that justification is unimportant. As Popper observes, it is easy to find supporting evidence for nearly any theory. The difficulty is reconciling theory with contradictory or negative data. Therefore, for an individual to be a scientist, he or she must formulate theories with empirical consequences, derive empirical expectations, and test them against the empirical world. If the theory survives the test (i.e., is in agreement with the data), the scientist must design a more comprehensive test that can potentially provide contradictory evidence and lead to the falsification of the theory. This testing program should continue until the theories are falsified. While Popper does not ever suggest this approach will lead to the "Truth," he does believe that it will cause science to progress while at the same time delineating science from nonscience.

Just as with inductivism, Popper's falsification has been greatly criticized. The most damaging objection is that it is impossible to logically falsify a theory (Duhem 1962; Quine 1961; Woodward and Goodstein 1996:484). Popper himself understood the validity of this objection (Popper 1980:41–42), although he thought it was a fairly minor point and simply a result of the humanness of science. In practice, though, the problem of the unfalsifiability of theory, often called the Duhem-Quine objection, can be severe. Theories as defined by Popper are not empirical themselves, but have empirical consequences only when provided with auxiliary conditions. If the data do not agree with one's expectations, it is entirely possible that one of the auxiliary conditions is wrong, not the theory itself. Poor experimental design, experimental error, or a simple misunderstanding of the conditions of the experiment can cause expectations to be violated. The logical strength of the deductive falsification argument is therefore impinged and no more certain than the inductivist approach.

The flip side of the Duhem-Quine objection discussed in the previous paragraph has also been suggested. Thagard (1978) argues that many pseudo-sciences and nonsciences can derive propositions that are at least potentially falsifiable. He contends that according to Popper's criterion, astrology or virtually any other nonscience or pseudo-science can be made to appear as a science. An example that Thagard uses is astrology, which makes predictions of human behavior. Characteristics of individuals could be predicted using astrology and then compared to the individuals to evaluate the reliability of the predictions. If the predictions are wrong, then astrology could be falsified. Therefore, Thagard (1978) concludes that falsification is not acceptable as a demarcation criterion.

Other authors have argued that applying a falsification criterion would prevent young and fragile theories from ever being developed, and would therefore impede scientific progress (Bartley 1968; Feyerabend 1975; Kuhn 1957; Lauden 1977; Woodward and Goldstein 1996). They observe that young theories, such as Copernicus' sun-centered view of the universe and Newton's initial formulation of terrestrial physics, were full of misunderstandings and contradictions that were only solved after scientists continued to develop the theories, in spite of contradictory evidence. If Popper's falsification criterion was followed by scientists involved in these scientific revolutions, these theories would have been rejected and a great amount of scientific knowledge would have been lost. Therefore, these authors conclude that falsification is not an acceptable criterion for demarcating science and nonscience, because it is not a criterion that should be widely applied in science itself.

The criticisms of both the Baconian inductivist's justification and Popper's falsification demarcation criteria are powerful, and illustrate their basic weaknesses. We believe that there is simply no clear distinction between science and nonscience. Science can take many forms that may not share a single underlying characteristic (Feyerabend 1975). As Popper states, the distinction between science and metaphysics or other types of knowledge is a convention (Popper 1980:53–56). What is at one time accepted as science may very well not be accepted under other circumstances. We suggest, though, that we can often identify what is science more easily by considering a number of traits, instead of developing a single rule to differentiate science and nonscience. While the demarcation criterion is a subject of heavy debate, most authors agree that a science must have certain characteristics. By identifying what these characteristics are,

we can evaluate the level of compatibility of postprocessual archaeology with science.

Characteristics of Science and the Scientific Nature of Postprocessual Research

We have identified seven characteristics of science that most scientists and philosophers of science agree are important. While none of these seven criteria are considered sufficient demarcation criteria by themselves, most scientists and philosophers of science would agree that they include the characteristics that make a research program scientific. We suggest that given these criteria, much of the archaeological research we call postprocessual or post-positivist archaeology is scientific. It is certainly as "scientific" as processual archaeology and other recognized sciences, such as physics.

The first criterion is that science, including the social sciences, must study empirical (i.e., physically observable) subjects (Popper 1980:93–111; Kitcher 1982). Scientific knowledge must deal with some aspect of the physical world, although empirical subjects can include non-tangibles such as behavior as in psychology or social systems as in sociology. This characteristic of science explains why ethics, law, and religion may have aspects that appear scientific, but as a whole are not; their fundamental research subject is not empirical. It is important to note, though, that the theoretical structure does not have to be empirical itself (Lakatos 1970; Tuggle et al. 1972; see also Schiffer 1988). It is only necessary that the expectations derived from the theory be empirical.

Most postprocessual interpretations meet the requirement of empiricism, in our opinion (also see Saitta 1992:890–891). Postprocessual archaeologists do study empirical phenomena: artifacts created within past social structures. While they might vehemently deny that these social structures are empirical, and would certainly deny that variables such as meaning and ideology are empirical, their variables and the social structures that they study are every bit as empirical as the subject matter and variables used in other accepted sciences.

The flaw in the postprocessual archaeologists argument is that most postprocessual archaeologists have mistakenly equated empirical with "real," tangible objects that one can touch and observe using one of the five senses (Saitta 1992; Hodder et al. 1995; Shanks 1992; Shanks and Tilley 1987;

Trigger 1993). Even though this view of empirical is common, it is certainly wrong (Stace 1967). For example, social structures are at least as empirical as the plethora of quantum particles postulated in quantum mechanics. No physicist has ever seen any particle of matter smaller than an electron. The ontological status of these items is in question, yet they are still empirical subjects of scientific study (Maxwell 1964). An additional example from physics is the force of gravity. It is an unseen *force* that cannot be directly observed and is not tangible. Even Einstein's time-space circles are not "empirical" according to the common postprocessualist (and processualist) definition of empirical. However, gravity has been and is the subject of empirical scientific study. While these examples come from physics—an undisputed science—any number of similar examples directly dealing with social systems could be gleaned from the sciences of sociology, psychology, and economics.

Why, then, are the unseen phenomena such as gravity and social systems empirical? Part of the reason is that they both have observable consequences that are intersubjectively identifiable. Gravity causes material objects on the Earth's surface to fall towards the Earth's center. While we cannot directly observe gravity, we can observe its consequences. Therefore, gravity can be empirically studied. Likewise, social systems have empirical consequences (Bawden 1996; Vinsrygg 1988). For example, the Indian caste system causes the artifacts and features created by human behavior to be organized in certain ways. While the caste system itself is not empirical, just like gravity, it has empirical consequences.

The argument for the empiricalness of gravity is logically identical to the argument presented by postprocessual archaeologists for connecting the archaeological record to past social and ideological systems. Most postprocessualists (Bawden 1995; Handsman and Leone 1989; Hodder 1986; Thomas 1991, 1996) argue that the rules, social structures, and ideologies are reflected in symbols (i.e., artifacts and features) recovered from the archaeological record. Postprocessual archaeologists are interested in the social world of individuals. By their own admission, they believe it has reality. Social structures can be reproduced, modified, negotiated, and resisted. While social systems themselves cannot be directly quantified or observed, they are reflected in artifacts and features, according to the majority of postprocessual archaeologists. Therefore, by their own argument, it can be demonstrated that the subject matter of most postprocessual archaeologists is as empirical as much as the subject matter of physics. Furthermore, logically similar arguments are advanced to justify the empiricalness of the subjects of other social sciences such as sociology, psychology, and economics.

The second criterion is that scientific knowledge is based on theoretical structures. It must be more than isolated facts gathered by people who call themselves scientists. Scientific knowledge is a systematic body of knowledge based on a body of theory organizing all of the facts and variables into a coherent system. Non-empirical or abstract ideas are not necessarily theoretical, and a theoretical structure is much more than the agglomeration of miscellaneous hypotheses, propositions, or ideas created using analogy or experience (Kuhn 1970; Lakatos 1970; Lauden 1977). As Kuhn (1970) observes, theoretical structures are coherent bodies of thought that link important variables together in specific ways such that their interaction can be understood. Thus, the statement, "water freezes at 0 degrees Centigrade at sea level under normal atmospheric pressure," is not a theoretical statement, but an understanding of molecular theory, which explains why water freezes, is theoretical.

A related criterion is that a scientific theory must, or at least ideally should, be non-contradictory. While the view of the world presented by a scientific theory need not be *True* in an absolute sense, it must at least be possible. Scientific theories are not always held to this ideal, but extreme contradictions will make a theory nonscientific according to most authors (e.g., Lauden 1977; Popper 1980:39; Thagard 1978).

While Marxist archaeologists contend that they do have a coherent theoretical structure (e.g., Saitta 1992), other postprocessual archaeologists might argue that they do not have a coherent or systematic body of theory, and therefore are not scientific. According to such arguments, postprocessual archaeological interpretations are based on whatever the particular archaeologists wishes it to be. Such a scattered theoretical structure would appear to contradict the noncontradictory theory criterion of science, as well as deny the presence of a theoretical structure at all. However, it does not for two reasons.

First, most postprocessual archaeologists share certain theoretical premises (as discussed previously). For example, many of them including Bawden (1995), Gibbon (1989), Hodder (1986), McGuire and Paynter (1991), and Thomas (1991, 1996) accept some variation of poststructural theory. These views include a large number of theoretical propositions previously discussed that may comprise a noncontradictory theoretical system, especially when compared to the theoretical fragmentation of processualism. Any number of processualists will hold contradictory theoretical positions on any issues you wish to suggest. The chronic debate over the use of the theoretical terms of function and style illustrates this point (Conkey 1990; Dunnell 1978; Hegmon 1992; Sackett 1982, 1985; Weissner 1983, 1985). The lack of a coherent universal body of theory does not make postprocessual archaeology any less scientific than processual archaeology. In fact, some of the theoretical statements held by postprocessualists (e.g., humans have agency, ideology is used to legitimate social structures and social inequities) are more widely accepted within their research program than virtually any theoretical premise in processual archaeology. In our opinion, based on this criterion alone, the postprocessualists might even be more scientific!

More importantly, though, it is in no way necessary that all or even any postprocessual archaeologists share a body of non-contradictory theory as a whole. What is important is that individual postprocessual archaeologists do not use internally contradictory theoretical premises within a single piece of research. And even this requirement is loose. As Lauden (1977) observes, scientists often have competing views of the way the world is structured, even during periods of Kuhnian normal science. If they didn't, scientific revolutions would never occur and a large amount of scientific research designed to evaluate competing ideas would never be completed. Scientists thus often hold completely contradictory theoretical positions between each other. Additionally, individual scientists can even hold contradictory theoretical statements in their own theoretical system under certain circumstances. For example, physicists have alternately treated light as a wave and a particle even though this is in explicit contradiction with their theoretical system of Newtonian physics. Given that postprocessual archaeologists do evaluate the logical cohesiveness of their research and interpretations, the criterion of noncontradiction appears to be met.

In addition, postprocessual archaeologists often argue that they do not develop their hypotheses and theories in the same way that scientists do. They observe that they draw their theoretical propositions from virtually any source that they wish. Often, these propositions can be taken from other fields of study such as sociology, or they can be taken from good, old-fashioned common sense. This is in fact exactly how scientists develop their theoretical positions. Scientists do use inductive observation to develop commonsensical theoretical propositions. They do use ideas from other bodies of knowledge. Scientists may form their theoretical propositions from any source they choose. As Popper (1980:31–32) observes, there is no scientific logic to the process of proposing a new hypothesis or theoretical premise. Scientists make "bold, unsubstantiated conjectures" which they then evaluate. Thus, the process of hypothesis and theory formation is identical between postprocessual archaeology and science.

The fourth criterion is that science must be objective. When used to refer to science, the term objective does not mean impartial, absolute, or true as many postprocessual and processual archaeologists (Binford 1972, 1982, 1989; Hodder et al. 1995:240) assume.[6] Instead, it means intersubjectively testable and verifiable. As Popper (1980:44) states, "the *objectivity* of scientific statements lies in the fact that they can be *inter-subjectively tested*" (italics in original).

For example, the statement, "I am cold," is a subjective statement. It is a statement of internal belief that cannot be evaluated by others. In contrast, the statement, "the temperature in this room is 10 degrees Centigrade," is objective. We could each pull out a thermometer and evaluate whether the statement is accurate or not. Obviously, the statement is not free from bias, nor is it absolutely True, even if it is 10 degrees Centigrade in the room. Our statement implies a theoretical system (explaining temperature through the movement of molecules), a scale of measurement (the Centigrade scale), and an instrument or series of acceptable instruments of measurement (e.g., thermometers). Any of these attributes of the statement can be modified. Perhaps molecular theory is incorrect. Maybe a particular thermometer does not accurately measure temperature. Perhaps we will decide to use the Fahrenheit or Kelvin scale of temperature instead. Regardless, we can all evaluate the accuracy of the statement independently, thereby making it objective.

Postprocessual archaeologists have spent a great deal of time and ink asserting that they are openly and explicitly subjective in contrast to the supposed objectivity of scientists, in particular the processualists (Hodder et al. 1995; Fotaidis 1994; Little 1994; Shanks and Tilley 1992; Tilley 1992). In making this claim, though, they define objectivity as free from bias or "true" in an absolute sense, a definition of objectivity that few scientists or philosophers of science would accept (Popper 1980:44; Kitcher 1992; Wylie 1992b:19). While their definition is in line with the work of Hempel and the other logical positivists, it is a view that was abandoned by many if not most scientists and philosophers of science by the early 1950s (Trigger 1989a). As a result, many of the postprocessualists have created a strawman (see Hodder 1989:15, 1991b:10).

Many postprocessual archaeologists do in fact require that their interpretations be intersubjectively testable and therefore objective, even though this requirement is often implicit (Preucel 1995:161–162). Their evaluation of the plausibility of interpretations must necessarily make reference to some form of objectivity. As Hodder (1991b:10) states, "a guarded objectivity of the past needs to be retained." Plausibility as they use it is more than mere opinion. It is agreement with aspects of the archaeological record such that interpretations are logically compatible with the record (Preucel 1995). This form of evaluation is indistinguishable from scientific objectivity.

Postprocessualists might also counter that their explicit pursuit of political goals conflicts with scientific objectivity (Shanks and Tilley 1987, 1992). However, Hodder (1991b:10–13) and others (e.g., Preucel 1995; Wylie 1992b) explicitly and persuasively argue that political goals and the form of objectivity discussed here are compatible. As Wylie (1992b:30) states, "politically engaged science is often much more rigorous, self-critical, and responsive to the facts than allegedly neutral science." Their argument is simple; while interpretations are "constrained" by the data, the goals and the inspiration of

the research questions asked are not. This position is completely compatible with Popper's (1980:31–32) observation that scientists gain the inspiration for their research from any source available (including politics). Thus, while many postprocessual archaeologists correctly observe that their interpretations are culturally and intellectually biased, they are incorrect when they argue that their subjectivity is incompatible with scientific objectivity.

Postprocessualists might also argue that the similarities between the objectivity of sciences such as physics, sociology, psychology, and economics and their view of objectivity and plausibility are superficial, and that the difference between them is that physicists and the other scientists believe their phenomena are Real and seek Truth while postprocessualists do not. Once again, this argument is based on a misunderstanding of scientific practice. As discussed previously, postprocessualists do accept that the past is real and that they can know something about it (Conkey and Spector 1984; Englestad 1991; Gero 1983; Handsman and Leone 1989; Hodder 1986; Leone et al. 1987; Leone 1991). Likewise, scientists believe that the world is real, and that they can know something about it. While a few scientists might suggest they ideally seek the Truth, most scientists would never suggest they have it. The influence of Popper's (1980) falsification criterion and Kuhn's (1970) view of scientific revolutions illustrates this point. Good scientists assume they are wrong! Scientists seek to produce better and better descriptions and explanations of the world. This often means working within an established theoretical structure. However, most do not believe their conclusions, explanations, or theories are "true." Eventually, they believe their work will be replaced by others who develop better explanatory systems and possess a greater understanding of the phenomenon of study (Mayr 1982, 1997). As a group, most scientists do not believe they have truth any more than most postprocessual archaeologists do. Scientists may not even believe that the non-observable entities that they posit are potentially true (see Maxwell 1964 and Toulmin 1988 for a more complete discussion). Therefore, the objectivity of postprocessual archaeologists is indistinguishable from the objectivity of other physical and social sciences.

Fifth, scientific study must in some way be based on experience and include some component of evaluation. As Popper (1980:39) observes, "Science could even be called the method of experience." This does not mean that science must be inductive. It merely means that scientists must compare the expectations derived from their theory to the empirical world.

Postprocessualist archaeologists do have a limited form of falsification. The idea of plausibility and critique used by most postprocessual archaeologists necessitates comparing the ideas of the archaeologist to the archaeological record to see if the proposed interpretations are reasonable and possible, given the data (Hodder 1986, 1992:191; Preucel 1995:161; Shanks and Hodder 1995; Shanks and Tilley 1987:104; Thomas 1996; Wylie 1993). This is in fact the role of hermeneutics (Preucel 1991b, 1995:158), and it is exactly the same process that scientists undergo when comparing their explanations or descriptions to their data (Kosso 1991; see Thomas 1989: 80 for a discussion of the "scientific cycle"). The logical positivists called it justification, Popper called it falsification, and postprocessualists call it plausibility or critique.

Postprocessual archaeologists might object to our equating plausibility with the justification or falsification of scientific statements. He or she might suggest that postprocessual archaeologists simply evaluate whether their interpretations are reasonable, but that they do not hold their theoretical statements available for testing (Hodder et al. 1995). If their interpretations are not reasonable given the available archaeological data, a postprocessual archaeologist is not compelled to reject the underlying theoretical propositions as false, as Popperian (1980) science would suggest. Instead, postprocessual archaeologists will seek to apply their theory in any way they can. They will interpret their data in such a way that their theory will work and will produce a plausible interpretation.

Once again, postprocessual archaeologists are not as different from scientists as many of processualists and postprocessualists would like to believe. Many scientists and philosophers of science have observed that scientists do not really test *theories*. They instead test *expectations*. This fact is the heart of the Duhem-Quine objection to Popper's falsification mentioned previously (Duhem 1962; Quine 1961). Scientists simply cannot logically falsify theoretical statements. Lakatos (1970) and others have gone even further and sug-

gested that scientists hold certain core ideas or aspects of their theories above falsification. These ideas define their theoretical structure. For example, an evolutionary biologist will not reject the idea of natural selection as false because of the problems produced by altruistic or communal behavior (Sober 1993). They will instead work diligently to develop an interpretation based on their theoretical structure that will account for the observed data. Only in the face of long-term and significant problems that elude solution and in the presence of another theoretical structure that solves the problems will scientists abandon their core theoretical concepts (Kuhn 1970; Lauden 1977). In reality, this is no different than what most postprocessual archaeologists purport to do. Once again, postprocessual practice is indistinguishable from science.

The final two characteristics are more heavily debated than the preceding criteria. The sixth criterion, proposed by the positivists including Hempel (1965:231–244), Nagel (1979:52–55), and Popper (1961, 1980) argues that science must necessarily use universal and strict laws of nature. This position has been heavily criticized and effectively challenged in the practical application of biology (see Hull 1988 and Mayr 1997), the philosophy of science (W. Salmon 1984), and even within the Processual archaeological program (Dunnell 1982; Flannery 1986; Morgan 1973, 1974; Renfrew 1973, 1989), itself.

In the philosophy of science, Feyerabend (1975), W. Salmon (1984), M. Salmon (1982a, 1982b), Willer and Willer (1973) and others have argued that universal laws are unnecessary for science. Feyerabend (1975) contends that scientific reasoning may take any form that scientists feel is appropriate for a given situation. In fact, he suggests the concentration on universal laws may impede scientific progress. Wesley and Merrilee Salmon (M. Salmon 1982 a, 1982b; W. Salmon 1984) do not totally reject the role of laws as Feyerabend does. Instead, they suggest that science does not require *universal* laws. They argue that social science should employ probabilistic laws instead. General biology has rejected the logical positivist view of laws in science (Hull 1988; Mayr 1997; Sober 1993). Instead of using universal laws, biology uses a theoretical system with clearly defined variables, but is devoid of "*laws*" in the sense that the positivists discussed them (see Hull 1988:78–81 for a more complete discussion and Nagel 1979 and Popper 1961 for the positivist response).

Although the processualists initially believed that a scientific archaeology required universal laws (Binford 1968; Watson et al. 1971, 1984), they quickly retreated from this position. Within the new archaeology, the use of laws came under almost immediate attack (Clarke 1979; Dunnell 1978; Flannery 1973; Morgan 1973, 1974; Renfrew 1973; Salmon 1982a, 1982b; Tuggle et al. 1972). When they failed to find laws, they retreated to "law-like generalizations" (Watson et al. 1984). Now they only mention laws in passing.[7] At best, modern processualists only use "laws" as heuristic devices or probabilistic statements (e.g., laws based on ethnographic analogy such as "women work in the domestic sphere"). More recently, the requirement of laws for a scientific archaeology has been challenged by evolutionary archaeologists (e.g., Dunnell 1989; Leonard and Jones 1987).

Dunnell (1982) has argued that there are in fact two types of science: time-like sciences and space-like sciences (see also Flannery 1986; Kroeber 1952:66–78; Mayr 1982:36–76; Simpson 1963, 1970; Sober 1980, 1988 for related discussions). Examples of space-like sciences are physics and chemistry. These sciences deal with phenomena that demonstrate consistent patterns across time. The "natural laws" identified by these sciences do not change. Space-like sciences can use laws. In contrast, Dunnell argues that archaeology is a time-like science, similar in structure to biology. Time-like sciences are historical in the sense that previous conditions affect future manifestations. These sciences cannot use laws in the same way as space-like sciences because their subject matter is constantly changing. For example, biological evolution cannot be made to follow the logical structure of Newtonian physics. They cannot develop natural laws like "eyes will always evolve on mammals" because the situation affecting what will evolve changes as the circumstance of evolution changes. As we discussed previously, *"laws"* (as defined by the logical positivists) are simply impossible within time-like sciences (Hull 1988; Mayr 1982, 1997). We, therefore, argue that while universal laws and generalities may be useful in space-like sciences, they are not a necessary characteristic of science.

Postprocessualist archaeologists have argued strenuously and at length that they are different from science because they do not develop, wish to develop, nor do they believe in the existence of universal laws for human behavior. Their rejection of universal laws of human behavior is insufficient to make the postprocessual perspective nonscientific. As previously mentioned, many sciences and many scientists do not search for, develop, or believe in universal laws. If this criterion were enough to conclude that all postprocessual archaeology is nonscientific, we would also be forced to conclude that evolutionary biology is also nonscientific. While postprocessual archaeologists are correct that the rejection of universal laws does differentiate them from the earliest formations of processual archaeology, and even some more recent formulations of processual (Watson et al. 1984; Kelley and Hanen 1988) and behavioral archaeology (e.g., Schiffer 1995), it does not make their research program nonscientific. However, many processualists have abandoned the search for laws as previously discussed.

Finally, the seventh characteristic frequently used to differentiate scientific and nonscientific research programs is the concept of progress (Lauden 1977; Thagard 1978). These authors define progress as the development of more complex and complete theoretical systems that encompass more facts and possess fewer unanswered questions/problems. Scientific programs increase knowledge and therefore are progressive while nonscientific programs fail to increase knowledge or in fact impede progress. While the authors do not contend this is a sufficient demarcation criteria, they do suggest it is necessary for the research program to be progressive to be scientific.

To illustrate this view, we return to the astrology example provided by Thagard (1978) previously mentioned. Thagard argues that at one time, astrology was scientific. When Ptolomy initially developed it, it was an empirically based system with a theoretical framework. Over time, it became a pseudoscience, though, when it ceased to progress and deal with significant problems. It is now nonscience because its theoretical structure has been destroyed by modern astronomy and physics. Based on this example, Thagard (1978:49) argues that a research program becomes a pseudoscience or a nonscience if and only if:

1) it has been less progressive than alternative theories over a long period of time, and it faces many unsolved problems; but

2) the community of practitioners make little attempt to develop the theory towards solutions of the problems, shows no concern for attempts to evaluate theory in relationship to others, and is selective in considering confirmation or disconfirmation.

While many authors such as Lauden (1977) have observed that the progress of a research program can only be evaluated after the fact, postprocessual research demonstrates all of the characteristics indicating it is a progressive program. Postprocessual archaeologists deal with logical, theoretical, and empirical problems in their interpretations. They bring new perspectives and ideas to bear on both new and old theoretical and empirical problems. They also develop new theoretical statements that can at least potentially advance our understanding of past social systems. While it is unclear how much the postprocessual program in archaeology will contribute to a knowledge of past social systems, the researchers appear to be involved in a growing, progressive research program.

Conclusion

A realistic view of the nature of science is necessary for any discipline that wishes to employ scientific approaches. We suggest that science is more inclusive than most archaeologists believe. Most discussions of science in archaeology have been, and continue to be, based on the "Legendary View of Science" (Kitcher 1992), a view that has been discredited. We have attempted to provide a more complete discussion of the nature of science, and have demonstrated why much of the postprocessual research is scientific, in spite of claims to the contrary.

Clearly, hyperrelativists and extreme positivistic scientists do not share compatible worldviews. Some scientists, particularly those influenced by the writings of Hempel, will only accept the "legendary" view of science. They will never accede to postprocessual study as science. For these individuals, postprocessual archaeology, psychology, history, economics, and even evolutionary biology are inherently nonscientific, because their subject matter cannot be addressed using a nomological approach. Likewise, hyperrelativists who argue that there is not a "real" world beyond the mind will never meet the accepted criteria of science.

Ultimately, however, based on *any reasonable criteria or characteristics of science one wishes to use,* much of postprocessual archaeology qualifies as science. In fact, postprocessual research may more fully meet several of these criteria than does processual archaeology.

By concluding that much of postprocessual archaeology is scientific, we do not suggest that postprocessualists should adopt a new name indicating their scientific status, or change their behavior or research to ensure that they remain scientific. We wish instead to observe that the ongoing antagonism between "scientific" archaeologists and postprocessual archaeologists is unnecessary. Regardless of their other differences, the distinction between postprocessualism and processualism does not lie at the level of science versus nonscience. They can both contribute to a rigorous and "objective" understanding of the archaeological record, an understanding that is the ultimate goal of both groups of archaeologists. Ultimately, then, we suggest that an intellectual synergy between processual and postprocessual approaches is possible, a synergy in which the two programs working together can create a rich and robust understanding of the archaeological record by prompting archaeologists to ask a broader range of questions and to employ a greater number of analytic strategies.

Acknowledgments. We sincerely thank Ian Hodder, Lynne Goldstein, Robert Pruecel, Lynne Sebastian, and three anonymous reviewers for *American Antiquity* for their thoughtful comments and helpful editorial advice. We would also like to thank Elizabeth Bagwell, Jonathan Driver, Marcel Harmon, Bruce Huckell, Teresa Hurt, Anne Ogle-Leonard, Lance Lundquist, Gerry Raymond, Marcos Rosas, Dean Saitta, Brian Shaffer, Donald Smith, Sandra Smith, David Vaughn, and Alison Wylie for their insightful suggestions improving early drafts of this paper. In addition, James Boone, Erica Hill, Mark Leone, David Phillips, Gordon Rakita, and Bruce Trigger deserve special recognition for their patience, encouragement, and extremely beneficial comments. They have contributed tremendously to this manuscript. Finally, we owe a great debt to Garth Bawden, Barbara Hannan, and Robert Leonard. Without their help, this work would have been impossible.

References Cited

Arnold, B.
   1990 The Past as Propaganda: Totalitarian Archaeology in Nazi Germany. *Antiquity* 64:464–478.
Bapty, I.
   1990 Nietzche, Derrida, and Foucault: Re-excavating the

Meaning of Archaeology. In *Archaeology After Structuralism: Post-Structuralism and the Practice of Archaeology*, edited by I. Bapty and T. Yates, pp. 240–276. Routledge, London.

Bapty, I. and T. Yates
1990 *Archaeology After Structuralism: Post-Structuralism and the Practice of Archaeology*. Routledge, London.

Bartley, W.W. III
1968 Theories of the Demarcation Between Science and Metaphysics. In *Problems in the Philosophy of Science*, edited by I. Lakatos and A. Musgrave, pp. 40–119. North-Holland Publishing, Amsterdam.

Bawden, G.
1989 The Andean State as a State of Mind. *Journal of Anthropological Research* 45:327–333.
1995 The Structural Paradox Moche Culture as Political Ideology. *Latin American Antiquity* 6: 255–273.
1996 *The Moche*. Blackwell Publishers, London.

Binford, L. R.
1968 Archaeology Perspectives. In *New Perspectives in Archaeology*, edited by S. R. Binford and L. R. Binford, pp. 5–32. Aldine Press, Chicago.
1972 *An Archaeological Perspective*. Seminar Press, New York.
1982 Objectivity-Explanation-Archaeology 1981. In *Theory and Explanation in Archaeology*, edited by C. Renfrew, M. J. Rowlands, and B. A. Segraves, pp. 125–138. Academic Press, New York.
1986 In Pursuit of the Future. In *American Archaeology Past and Future*, edited by D. J. Meltzer, D. D. Fowler, and J. A. Sabloff, pp. 459–479. Smithsonian Institution Press, Washington, D.C.
1987 Data, Relativism, and Archaeological Science. *Man* 22:391–404.
1989 *Debating Archaeology*. Academic Press, San Diego.

Bintliff, J.
1991 Postmodernism, Rhetoric and Scholasticism at TAG: The Current State of British Archaeology. *Antiquity* 65:274–278.
1992 Response to Comments by J. Thomas and C. Tilley. *Antiquity* 66:111–114.

Bleicher, J.
1980 *Contemporary Hermeneutics: Hermeneutics as Method, Philosophy and Critique*. Routledge, New York.

Boone, J. L., and E. A. Smith
1998 Is It Evolution Yet? A Critique of Evolutionary Archaeology. *Current Anthropology, Supplement* 39:S141–S157.

Bourdieu, P.
1977 *Outline of a Theory of Practice*. Cambridge University Press, Cambridge.

Clark, G.A.
1993 Paradigms in Science and Archaeology. *Journal of Archaeological Research* 1:203–234.

Clarke, D.L.
1979 *Analytical Archaeologist*. Academic Press, New York.

Conkey, M.
1990 Experimenting with Style in Archaeology. In *The Uses of Style in Archaeology*, edited by M. Conkey and C. Hastorf, pp. 5–18. Cambridge University Press, Cambridge.

Conkey, M. and J. Spector
1984 Archaeology and the Study of Gender. *Advances in Archaeological Method and Theory* 7:1–38.

Cowgill, G.
1993 Beyond Criticizing New Archaeology. *American Anthropologist* 95:551–573.

Duhem, P.
1962 *The Aim and Structure of Physical Theory*. Atheneum, New York.

Duke, P.
1995 Working through Theoretical Tension in Contemporary Archaeology: A Practical Attempt from Southwestern Colorado. *Journal of Archaeological Method and Theory* 2:201–229.

Dunnell, R. C.
1978 Style and Function: A Fundamental Dichotomy. *American Antiquity* 43:192–202.
1980 Evolutionary Theory and Archaeology. In *Advances in Archaeological Method and Theory*, vol. 3, edited by M. B. Schiffer, pp. 35–99. Academic Press, New York.
1982 Science, Social Science and Common Sense: The Agonizing Dilemma of Modern Archaeology. *Journal of Anthropological Research* 38:1–25.
1989 Aspects of the Application of Evolutionary Theory in Archaeology. In *Archaeological Thought in America*, edited by C. C. Lamberg-Karlovsky, pp. 35–49. Cambridge University Press, Cambridge.

Earle, T.K.
1991 Toward a Behavioral Archaeology. In *Processual and Postprocessual Archaeologies: Multiple Ways of Knowing the Past*, edited by R.W. Preucel, pp. 17–29. Occasional Paper No. 10. Center for Archaeological Investigations, Southern Illinois University, Carbondale.

Earle, T., and R. Preucel
1987 Processual Archaeology and the Radical Critique. *Current Anthropology* 28:501–527.

Engelstad, E.
1991 Images of Power and Contradiction: Feminist Theory and Post-processual Archaeology. *Antiquity* 65:502–514.

Feyerabend, P.
1975 *Against Method: Outline of an Anarchistic Theory of Knowledge*. New Left Books, London.

Fields, D.M.
1995 Postmodernism. *Premise* 2(8):5–14.

Flannery, K.V.
1973 Archeology with a Capital S. In *Research and Theory in Current Archaeology*, edited by C.L. Redman, pp. 47–58. John Wiley and Sons, New York.
1986 *Guilá Naquitz: Archaic Foraging and Early Agriculture in Oaxaca, Mexico*. Academic Press, Orlando.

Flax, J.
1990 *Thinking Fragments: Psychoanalysis, Feminism, and Postmoderneism in the Contemporary West*. University of California Press, Berkeley.

Fotiadis, M.
1994 What is Archaeology's "Mitigated Objectivism" Mitigated By? Comments on Wylie. *American Antiquity* 59:545–555.

Foucault, M.
1970 *The Order of Things: An Anthology of the Human Sciences*. Vintage Books, New York.

Fried, M.
1967 *Evolution of Political Society*. Random House, New York.

Fritz, J.M. and F.T. Plog
1970 The Nature of Archaeological Explanation. *American Antiquity* 35:405–412.

Gero, J. M.
1983 Gender Bias in Archaeology: A Cross-Cultural Perspective. In *Analyzing Gender*, edited by J. M. Gero, D. Lacy, and M. L. Blakey, pp. 51–57. University of Massachusetts, Amherst.
1991 Gender Divisions of Labor in the Construction of

Archaeological Knowledge. In *The Archaeology of Gender*, edited by D. Walde and N. D. Willows. Proceedings of the 22nd Annual Chacmool Conference. Archaeological Association of Calgary.

Gibbon, G.
1989 *Explanation in Archaeology*. Basil Blackwell, New York.

Giddens, A.
1984 *The Constitution of Society: Outline of the Theory of Structuration*. University of California Press, California.

Handsman, R. F., and M.P. Leone
1989 Living History and Critical Archaeology in the Reconstruction of the Past. In *Critical Traditions in Contemporary Archaeology*, edited by V. Pinsky and A. Wylie, pp. 117–135. Cambridge University Press, Cambridge.

Hanson, N. R.
1958 *Patterns of Discovery*. Cambridge University Press, New York.

Hempel, C. G.
1965 *Aspects of Scientific Explanations*. Free Press, New York.

Hegmon, M.
1992 Archeological Research on Style. *Annual Review of Anthropology* 21:517–36.

Hodder, I.
1982 *Symbolic and Structural Archaeology*. Cambridge University Press, Cambridge.
1985 Post-Processual Archaeology. In *Advances in Archaeological Method and Theory* vol. 8, pp. 1–26. Academic Press, New York.
1986 *Reading the Past: Current Approaches and Interpretations in Archaeology*. Cambridge University Press, Cambridge.
1989 Comments on Archaeology into the 1990s. *Norwegian Archaeological Review* 22: 15–18.
1991a Processual Archaeology and the Current Debate. In *Processual and Postprocessual Archaeologies: Multiple Ways of Knowing the Past*, edited by R. W. Preucel, pp. 30–41. Occasional Paper No. 10. Center for Archaeological Investigations, Southern Illinois University, Carbondale.
1991b Interpretive Archaeology and Its Role. *American Antiquity* 56:7–18.
1992 *Theory and Practice in Archaeology*. Routledge, London and New York.
1997 "Always Momentary, Fluid and Flexible": Towards a Reflexive Excavation Methodology. *Antiquity* 71:691–700.

Hodder, I., M, Shanks, A. Alexandri, A. Buchli, J. Carman, J. Last, and G. Lucas (eds.)
1995 *Interpreting Archaeology: Finding Meaning in the Past*. Routledge, New York.

Hull, D. L.
1988 *Science as a Process: An Evolutionary Account of the Social and Conceptual Development of Science*. University of Chicago Press, Chicago.

Kelley, J. H. and M. P. Hanen
1988 *Archaeology and the Methodology of Science*. University of New Mexico Press, Albuquerque.

Kitcher, P.
1982 *Abusing Science: The Case Against Creationism*. MIT Press, Cambridge.
1992 *The Advancement of Science: Science without Legend, Objectivity without Illusions*. Oxford University Press, New York.

Knapp, A.B.
1996 Archaeology without Gravity: Postmodernism and the Past. *Journal of Archaeological Method and Theory* 3:127–158.

Kohl, P.
1993 Limits to a Post Processual Archaeology. In *Archaeological Theory: Who Sets the Agenda?* edited by N. Yoffee and A. Sheratt, pp. 13–20.

Kosso, P.
1991 Method in Archaeology: Middle-Range Theory as Hermeneutics. *American Antiquity* 56:621–627.

Kroeber, A. L.
1952 *The Nature of Culture*. University of Chicago Press, Chicago.

Kuhn, T.
1970 The Structure of Scientific Revolutions. University of Chicago Press, Chicago.
1957 *The Copernican Revolution: Planetary Astronomy in the Development of Western Thought*. Harvard University Press, Cambridge.

Lakatos, I.
1970 Falsification and the Methodology of Scientific Research Programmes. In *Criticism and the Growth of Knowledge*, edited by I. Lakatos and A. Musgrave. Cambridge University Press, Cambridge.

Lamberg-Karlovsky, C. C. (editor)
1989 *Archaeological Thought in America*. Cambridge University Press, Cambridge.

Lauden, L.
1977 *Progress and its Problems: Towards a Theory of Scientific Growth*. University of California Press, Berkeley.

Leonard, R. D., and G. T. Jones
1987 Elements of an Inclusive Evolutionary Model for Archaeology. *Journal of Anthropological Archaeology* 54:491–503.

Leone, M. P.
1986 Symbolic, Structural, and Critical Archaeology. In *American Archaeology. Past and Future*, edited by D.J. Meltzer, D.D. Fowler, and J.A. Sabloff, pp. 415–438. Smithsonian Institution Press, Washington, D.C.
1991 Material Theory and the Formation of Questions in Archaeology. In *Processual and Postprocessual Archaeologies: Multiple Ways of Knowing the Past*, edited by R.W. Preucel. Occasional Papers No. 10:235–241. Center for Archaeological Investigations, Southern Illinois University, Carbondale.

Leone, M. P., P. B. Potter Jr., and P. A. Shackel
1987 Toward a Critical Archaeology. *Current Anthropology* 28:283–302.

Leone, M. P., and R. W. Preucel
1992 Archaeology in a Democratic Society: A Critical Theory Perspective. In *Quandaries and Quests: Vision of Archaeology's Future*, edited by LuAnn Wandsnider, pp. 115–135. Occasional Paper No. 20, Center for Archaeological Investigations, Southern Illinois University, Carbondale.

Little, B. J.
1994 Consider the Hermaphroditic Mind: Comments on "The Interplay of Evidential Constraints and Political Interests: Recent Archaeological Research on Gender." *American Antiquity* 59:539–544.

Macquairrie, J., and E. Robinson.
1962 Translation of Heidegger, M. *Being and Time*. Blackwell, Oxford.

Maschner, H. D. G. (editor)
1996 *Darwinian Archaeologies*. Plenum Press, New York.

Maxwell, G.
 1964 The Ontological Status of Theoretical Entities. In *Minnesota Studies in the Philosophy of Science,* Vol. III, edited by H. Feigl and G. Maxwell, pp. 3–14. University of Minnesota Press, Minneapolis.
Mayr, E.
 1982 *The Growth of Biological Thought: Diversity, Evolution, and Inheritance.* Harvard University Press, Cambridge.
 1997 *This is Biology: The Science of the Living World.* Harvard University Press, Cambridge.
McGuire, R. H., and R. Paynter (eds.)
 1991 *The Archaeology of Inequality.* Basil Blackwell, Oxford.
Miller, D., and C. Tilley (eds.)
 1984 *Ideology, Power, and Prehistory.* Cambridge University Press, Cambridge.
Morgan, C.
 1973 Archaeology and Explanation. *World Archaeology* 4:259–276.
 1974 Explanation and Scientific Archaeology. *World Archaeology* 6:135–137.
Mueller-Vollmer, K.
 1994 *The Hermeneutics Reader.* Continuum, New York.
Nagel, E.
 1979 *The Structure of Science: Problems in the Logic of Scientific Explanation.* Hackett Publishing Company, Indianapolis.
O'Shea, J.
 1992 Review of Ian Hodder's *The Domestication of Europe. American Anthropologist* 94:752–753.
Patterson, T.C.
 1989 History and Postprocessual Archaeology. *Man* 24:555–566.
 1990 Some Theoretical Tensions Within and Between the Processual and Postprocessual Archaeologies. *Journal of Anthropological Archaeology* 9:189–200.
Pinsky, V., and A. Wylie (editors)
 1989 *Critical Traditions in Contemporary Archaeology: Essays in the Philosophy, History and Socio-Politics of Archaeology.* University of New Mexico Press, Albuquerque.
Popper, K. R.
 1961 *The Poverty of Historicism.* Routledge, New York.
 1962 *Conjectures and Refutations.* Harper and Row, New York.
 1980 *The Logic of Scientific Discovery.* Routledge, New York.
Preucel, R.W.
 1991a Comments to Richard Watson's *What the New Archaeology Has Accomplished. Current Anthropology* 32:287–288.
 1991b The Philosophy of Archaeology. In *Processual and Postprocessual Archaeologies: Multiple Ways of Knowing the Past,* edited by R.W. Preucel. Occasional Papers No. 10:17–29. Center for Archaeological Investigations, Southern Illinois University, Carbondale.
 1995 The Postprocessual Condition. *Journal of Archaeological Research* 3:147–175.
Preucel, R. W. (editor)
 1991 *Processual and Postprocessual Archaeologies: Multiple Ways of Knowing the Past.* Occasional Paper No. 10. Center for Archaeological Investigations, Southern Illinois University, Carbondale.
Preucel, R. W., and I. Hodder (editors)
 1996 *Contemporary Archaeology in Theory: A Reader.* Blackwell Publishers, Cambridge, Massachusetts.

Quine, W.V.O.
 1961 *From a Logical Point of View.* Harper and Row, New York.
Redman, C. L.
 1991 Distinguished Lecture in Archaeology: In Defense of the Seventies—The Adolescence of the New Archaeology. *American Anthropologist* 93:295–307.
Renfrew, C.
 1989 Comments on Archaeology into the 1990s. *Norwegian Archaeological Review* 22: 33–41.
 1973 *The Explanation of Cultural Change: Models in Prehistory.* Duckworth, London.
Rosenau, P. M.
 1992 *Postmodernism and the Social Sciences: Insights, Inroads, and Intrusions.* Princeton University Press, Princeton.
Sackett, J. R.
 1982 Approaches to Style in Lithic Archaeology. *Journal of Anthropological Archaeology* 1:59–112.
 1985 Style and Ethnicity in the Kalahari: A Reply to Weissner. *American Antiquity* 50:154–159.
Saitta, D.J.
 1992 Radical Archaeology and Middle-Range Theory Methodology. *Antiquity* 66:886–897.
Salmon, M. H.
 1982a *Philosophy and Archaeology.* Academic Press, New York.
 1982b Models of Explanation: Two Views. In *Theories and Explanation in Archaeology: The Southampton Conference,* edited by C. Renfrew, pp. 35–44. Academic Press, New York.
Salmon, W.
 1984 *Scientific Explanation and the Causal Structure of the World.* Princeton University Press, Princeton.
Schiffer, M.B.
 1988 The Structure of Archaeological Theory. *American Antiquity* 53:461–485.
 1991 *The Portable Radio in American Life.* University of Arizona Press, Tucson.
 1995 *Behavioral Archaeology, First Principles.* University of Utah Press, Salt Lake City.
 1996 Some Relationships between Behavioral and Evolutionary Archaeologies. *American Antiquity* 61:643–662.
Shanks, M.
 1992 *Experiencing The Past: On the Character of Archaeology.* Routledge, New York.
Shanks, M. and I. Hodder
 1995 Processual, Postprocessual and Interpretive Archaeologies. In *Interpreting Archaeology: Finding Meaning in the Past,* edited by I. Hodder et al., Routledge, New York.
Shanks M. and C. Tilley
 1987 *Social Theory and Archaeology.* University of New Mexico Press, Albuquerque.
 1992 *Re-constructing Archaeology: Theory and Practice.* Routledge, New York.
Simpson, G.G.
 1963 Historical Science. In *The Fabric of Geology,* edited by C.C. Albritton Jr., pp. 24–48. Freeman & Couper, Stanford.
 1970 Uniformitariansim: An Inquiry into Principle, Theory, and Method in Geohistory and Biohistory. In *Essays in Evolution and Genetics in Honor of Theodosius Dobzhansky,* edited by M.K. Hecht and W.C. Steeve, pp. 43–96. Appleton, New York.

Skibo, J., and M. Schiffer
  1995 The Clay Cooking Pot: An Exploration of Women's Technology. In *Expanding Archaeology*, edited by J. Skibo, W. Walker, and A. Nielson, pp. 80–91. University of Utah Press, Salt Lake City.

Skibo, J. M., W. Walker, and A. Nielsen (editors)
  1995 *Expanding Archaeology*. University of Utah Press, Salt Lake City.

Sober, E.
  1980 Evolution, Population Thinking and Essentialism. *Philosophy of Science* 47:350-383.
  1988 *Reconstructing the Past: Parsimony, Evolution, and Inference*. MIT Press, Cambridge.
  1993 *Philosophy of Biology*. Westview Press, Boulder.

Spencer, C. S.
  1997 Evolutionary Approaches in Archaeology. *Journal of Archaeological Research* 5: 209–264.

Stace, W.T.
  1967 *Man Against Darkness*. University of Pittsburgh Press, Pittsburgh.

Thagard, P. R.
  1978 Why is Astrology a Psuedoscience? *Proceedings of Philosophy of Science Association* 1:223–224.

Thomas, D. H.
  1989 *Archaeology*. 2nd ed. Holt, Rinehart, and Winston, Fort Worth, Texas.

Thomas, J.
  1991 *Rethinking the Neolithic*. Cambridge University Press, Cambridge.
  1996 *Time, Culture and Identity*. Routledge, New York.

Tilley, C.
  1992 Book Review of *Debating Archaeology*. *American Antiquity* 57:164–166.

Toulmin, S.
  1988 Do Sub-Microscopic Entities Exist? In *Philosophy of Science*, edited by E.D. Klemke, R. Hollinger, and A. D. Kline, pp. 202–206. Prometheus Books, Buffalo, New York.

Trigger, B.
  1989a *A History of Archaeological Thought*. Cambridge University Press, Cambridge.
  1989b Comments on Archaeology into the 1990s. *Norwegian Archaeological Review* 22:28–31.
  1989c Hyperrelativism, Responsibility, and the Social Sciences. *Canadian Review of Sociology and Anthropology* 26:776–797.
  1991 Post-Processual Developments in Anglo-American Archaeology. *Norwegian Archaeological Review* 24:65–76.
  1993 Marxism in Contemporary Western Archaeology. In *Archaeological Method and Theory*, Vol. 5, edited by M.B. Schiffer, pp. 159–200. University of Arizona Press, Tucson.

Tschauner, H.
  1996 Middle-Range Theory, Behavioral Archaeology, and Postempiricist Philosophy of Science in Archaeology. *Journal of Archaeological Method and Theory* 3:1–20.

Tuggle, H. D., A. H. Townsend, and T. J. Riley
  1972 Laws, Systems, and Research Designs: A Discussion of Explanation in Archaeology. *American Antiquity* 37:3–12.

Vinsrygg, S.
  1988 Archaeology—As If People Mattered. A Discussion of Humanistic Archaeology. *Norwegian Archaeological Review* 21:1–20.

Watson, P. J.
  1991 A Parochial Primer: The New Dissonance As Seen from the Midcontinental United States. In *Processual and Postprocessual Archaeologies: Multiple Ways of Knowing the Past*, edited by R. W. Preucel, pp. 265–275. Occasional Paper No. 10. Center for Archaeological Investigations, Southern Illinois University, Carbondale.
  1993 Archaeology and Science. In *Archaeology: Discovering our Past*, edited by R.J. Sharer and W. Ashmore, pp. 38–40. Mayfield Publishing, Mountain View, California.

Watson, P. J., and M. Fotiadas
  1990 The Razor's Edge: Symbolic-Structuralist Archaeology and the Expansion of Archaeological Inference. *American Anthropologist* 92:613–629.

Watson, P.J., S. LeBlanc, and R. Redman
  1971 *Explanation in Archaeology: An Explicitly Scientific Approach*. Columbia University Press, New York.
  1984 *Archaeological Explanation: The Scientific Method in Archaeology*. Columbia University Press, New York.

Watson, R.
  1990 Ozymandias, King of Kings: Postprocessual Radical Archaeology as Critique. *American Antiquity* 92:673–89.
  1991 What the New Archaeology Has Accomplished. *Current Anthropology* 32:275–291.

Wiessner, P.
  1983 Style and Information on Kalahari San Projectile Points. *American Antiquity* 48: 253–275.
  1985 Style or Isochrestic Variation? A Reply to Sackett. *American Antiquity* 50:154–159.

Willer, D., and J. Willer
  1973 *Systematic Empiricism: Critique of a Pseudoscience*. Prentice-Hall, Englewood Cliffs.

Woodward, J., and D. Goodstein
  1996 Conduct, Misconduct, and the Structure of Science. *American Scientist* 84:479–490.

Wylie, A.
  1992a Feminist Theories of Social Power: Some Implications for a Processual Archaeology. *Norwegian Archaeological Review* 25:51–68.
  1992b The Interplay of Evidential Constraints and Political Interests: Recent Archaeological Research on Gender. *American Antiquity* 57:15–35.
  1993 A Proliferation of New Archaeologies: "Beyond Objectivism and Relativism." In *Archaeological Theory: Who Sets the Agenda?*, edited by N. Yoffee and A. Sherratt, pp. 20–26. Cambridge University Press, Cambridge.

Yates, T.
  1990 Archaeology through the Looking-Glass. In *Archaeology After Structuralism: Post- Structuralism and the Practice of Archaeology*, edited by I. Bapty and T. Yates, pp. 153–204. Routledge, London.

Yoffee, N.
  1992 Too Many Chiefs? In *Archaeological Theory: Who Sets the Agenda?*, edited by N. Yoffee and A. Sherratt, pp.60–78. Cambridge University Press, Cambridge.

Yoffee, N., and A. Sherratt (editors)
  1993 *Archaeological Theory: Who Sets the Agenda?* Cambridge University Press, Cambridge.

Notes

[1] The antagonism between the adherents of the two perspectives is generally more subtle, but the hostility is particularly noticeable in statements such as "well, fellow archaeologists, if you do feel tempted to respond to the frantic signals of [postmodernism's] local practioners, the Postprocessualists—be advised that, in the words of that poignant poem

by Stevie Smith, they are 'Not waving, but drowning' (Bintliff 1991:278)", and "Binford's 'science' reduces the study of archaeology to the banal (Tilley 1992:165)".

[2] It is important to note that extreme postmodernists are not humanitistic (Flax 1990).

[3] Of course, the distinction between moderate postprocessualists and hyperrelativists should not be over- stated. An individual's research approach changes according to his or her research interests and intellectual growth. Thus, moderate postprocessualists and hyperrelativists (Trigger 1989c) are not necessarily different people, nor can a given researcher be labeled as a moderate postprocessualist or hyperrelativist. Instead, it is the characteristic of specific works, often written at different times in an archaeologist's development, that make their research either moderate or extreme.

[4] The "Problem of Demarcation" refers to the difficulty of defining a "demarcation criterion" that will allow the empirical sciences to be distinguished from mathematics, logic, and "metaphysical" systems (see Popper 1980:34–39 for a brief overview).

[5] Popper (1980:59–60) defines theory as universal statements with the characteristics of laws such as, "for every thread of the structure S (determined by its material, thickness, etc.) there is a characteristic weight w, such that the thread will break if any weight exceeding w is suspended from it."

[6] Wylie (1992b:19) refers to this definition as "naive objectivism."

[7] With the notable exception of M. Schiffer and his fellow behavioral archaeologists (e.g., Schiffer 1996; Skibo and Schiffer 1995).

Received September 27, 1997; accepted June 3, 1998; revised July 30, 1998.